Introduction to 3D Game Programming with DirectX® 9.0c: A Shader Approach

Frank D. Luna

Wordware Publishing, Inc.

Library of Congress Cataloging-in-Publication Data

Luna, Frank D.
    Introduction to 3D game programming with DirectX 9.0c : a shader approach
    / by Frank D. Luna.
        p. cm.
    Includes index.
    ISBN-13: 978-1-59822-016-2
    ISBN-10: 1-59822-016-0 (pbk.)
    1. Computer games--Programming.   2. DirectX.   I. Title.
    QA76.76.C672L833 2006
    794.8'1526--dc22   2006006448

2320 Los Rios Boulevard
Plano, Texas 75074

ISBN-13: 978-1-59822-016-2
ISBN-10: 1-59822-016-0

10 9 8 7 6 5 4 3 2
0605

All inquiries for volume purchases of this book should be addressed to Wordware Publishing,
Inc., at the above address. Telephone inquiries may be made by calling:

(972) 423-0090

To my parents, Frank and Kathryn

Contents

Part I — Mathematical Prerequisites

Part II — Direct3D Foundations

Acknowledgments

I would like to thank Rod Lopez, Jim Leiterman, Hanley Leung, Rick Falck, Tybon Wu, Tuomas Sandroos, and Eric Sandegren for putting in the time to review this book for both accuracy and improvements. I also want to thank Dale E. La Force, Adam Hault, Gary Simmons, James Lambers, and William Chin for their assistance. Lastly, I want to thank the staff at Wordware Publishing, in particular, Wes Beckwith, Beth Kohler, Martha McCuller, Denise McEvoy, and Alan McCuller.

Introduction

This book presents an introduction to programming interactive computer graphics, with an emphasis on game development, using real-time shaders with DirectX 9.0c. It teaches the fundamentals of Direct3D and shader programming, after which the reader will be prepared to go on and learn more advanced techniques. The book is divided into three main parts. Part I explains the mathematical tools that will be used throughout this book. Part II shows how to implement elementary 3D techniques, such as defining 3D geometry, lighting, texturing, alpha blending, and stenciling, using shaders and the HLSL. Part III is largely about applying Direct3D to implement a variety of interesting techniques and special effects, such as working with meshes, character animation, terrain rendering, picking, particle systems, environment mapping, normal mapping, and rendering to textures.

For the beginner, this book is best read front to back. The chapters have been organized so that the difficulty increases progressively with each chapter. In this way, there are no sudden jumps in complexity that leave the reader lost. In general, for a particular chapter, we will use the techniques and concepts previously developed. Therefore, it is important that you have mastered the material of a chapter before continuing. Readers who are experienced Direct3D users can pick the chapters of interest.

Finally, you may be wondering what kinds of games you can develop after reading this book. The answer to that question is best obtained by skimming through the book and seeing the types of applications that are developed. From that you should be able to visualize the types of games that can be developed based on the techniques taught in this book and some of your own ingenuity.

Changes from an Earlier Version

This update to the author's *Introduction to 3D Game Programming with DirectX 9.0* has been rewritten almost from scratch. This book largely abandons the fixed pipeline used in the earlier version to give a complete programmable, or shader, approach. From Chapter 8 onward, we are transforming, lighting, and coloring vertices and pixels in vertex and pixel shaders. This significant revision in approach reflects the fact that the fixed pipeline will not exist in DirectX 10.

Another key feature is the inclusion of end of chapter exercises. The exercises serve three purposes: first, to test the reader's understanding of each chapter's contents; second, to provide the reader with Direct3D programming experience; and third, to extend the chapter's topics by asking the reader to investigate new ideas on his or her own. In many cases, the exercises are not of the "plug and chug" type, but require the reader to determine how to apply the chapter's topics to the particular assignment. Readers are encouraged to complete chapter exercises before moving on to the next chapter.

Intended Audience

This book was designed with the following three audiences in mind:

- Intermediate level C++ programmers who would like an introduction to 3D programming using the latest iteration of Direct3D — Direct3D 9.0.
- 3D programmers experienced with an API other than DirectX (e.g., OpenGL) who would like an introduction to Direct3D 9.0.
- Experienced fixed-function Direct3D programmers who would like to take a shader approach.

Prerequisites

It should be emphasized that this is an introduction to Direct3D, shader, and game programming; it is *not* an introduction to general computer programming. The reader should satisfy the following prerequisites:

- General knowledge of high school mathematics: algebra, trigonometry, and (mathematical) functions, for example.
- Competent with Visual Studio: should know how to create projects, add files, and specify external libraries to link, for example.
- Intermediate C++ and data structure skills: comfortable with pointers, arrays, operator overloading, linked lists, inheritance and polymorphism, for example. We also use a small subset of the STL, in particular, std::string, std::vector, and std::list.
- Familiarity with Windows programming with the Win32 API is helpful but not required; we provide a Win32 primer in Appendix A.

Required Development Tools and Recommended Hardware

Officially, Microsoft's DirectX 9.0 now only supports versions of Visual Studio 7.0 (i.e., Visual Studio .NET 2002) or higher.

In addition, to program DirectX 9.0 applications, you will need the DirectX 9.0 SDK; the latest version can be downloaded from http://msdn.microsoft.com/directx/sdk/. Once downloaded, follow the instructions given by the installation wizard.

This book's demo programs require DirectX 9.0-capable hardware that supports vertex and pixel shader versions 2.0. At the time of this book's publication, low-end video cards supporting these requirements are available for about $50 (e.g., Radeon 9600, Geforce FX 5500).

Online: Step-by-step instructions for setting up a DirectX project in Visual Studio .NET 2002 and Visual Studio .NET 2005 are provided on this book's website (www.moon-labs.com) and the publisher's website (www.wordware.com/files/dx9c).

Use of the D3DX Library

Since version 7.0, DirectX has shipped with the D3DX (Direct3D Extension) library. This library provides a set of functions, classes, and interfaces that simplify common 3D graphics-related operations, such as math operations, texture and image operations, mesh operations, and shader operations (e.g., compiling and assembling). That is to say, D3DX contains many features that would be a chore to implement on your own.

We use the D3DX library throughout this book because it allows us to focus on more interesting material. For instance, we would rather not spend pages explaining how to load various image formats (such as .bmps and .jpegs) into a Direct3D texture interface when we can do it in a single call to the D3DX function D3DXCreateTextureFromFile. In other words, D3DX makes us more productive and lets us focus more on actual content rather than spending time reinventing the wheel.

Other reasons to use D3DX:

- D3DX is general and can be used with a wide range of different types of 3D applications.

- D3DX is fast, at least as fast as general functionality can be.

- Other developers use D3DX; therefore, you will most likely encounter code that uses D3DX. Consequently, whether you choose to use D3DX or not, you should become familiar with it so that you can read code that uses it.

- D3DX already exists and has been thoroughly tested. Furthermore, it becomes more improved and feature rich with each iteration of DirectX.

Using the DirectX SDK Documentation and SDK Samples

Direct3D is a huge API and we cannot hope to cover all of its details in this one book. Therefore, to obtain extended information it is imperative that you learn how to use the DirectX SDK documentation. You can launch the C++ DirectX online documentation by executing the *DirectX9_c* file in the *\DirectX SDK\Documentation\DirectX9* directory, where *DirectX SDK* is the directory to which you installed DirectX.

The DirectX documentation covers just about every part of the DirectX API; therefore, it is very useful as a reference, but because the documentation doesn't go into much depth and assumes some previous knowledge, it isn't the best learning tool. However, it does get better and better with every new DirectX version released.

As said, the documentation is primarily useful as a reference. Suppose you come across a DirectX-related type or function that you would like more information on (e.g., D3DXMatrixInverse). You simply do a search in the documentation index and you get a description of the object type or, in this case, function, as shown in Figure 1.

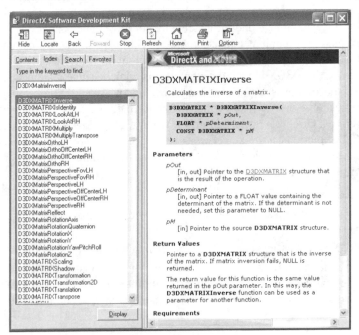

Figure 1: The C++ SDK documentation viewer.

Note   In this book we may direct you to the documentation for further details from time to time.

The SDK documentation also contains some introductory tutorials at the URL *\directx9_c.chm::/dx9_graphics_tutorials_and_samples.htm*. These tutorials correspond to some of the topics in the first part of this book. We recommend that you study these tutorials at the same time you read through Part I so that you can get alternative explanations and examples.

We would also like to point out the available Direct3D sample programs that ship with the DirectX SDK. The C++ Direct3D samples are located in the *DirectX SDK \C++\Direct3D* directory. Each sample illustrates how to implement a particular effect in Direct3D. These samples are fairly advanced for a beginning graphics programmer, but by the end of this book you should be ready to study them. Examination of the samples is a good "next step" after finishing this book.

Clarity

We want to emphasis that the program samples for this book were written with clarity in mind and not performance. Thus, many of the samples may be implemented inefficiently. Keep this in mind if you are using any of the sample code in your own projects, as you may wish to rework it for better efficiency.

Sample Programs and Online Supplements

The website for this book (www.moon-labs.com) plays an integral part in getting the most out of this book. On the website you will find the complete source code and project files for every sample in this book. In many cases, DirectX programs are too large to fully embed in a textbook; therefore, we only embed relevant code fragments based on the ideas being shown. It is highly recommended that the reader study the corresponding demo code to see the program in its entirety. (We have aimed to make the demos small and focused for easy study.) As a general rule, the reader should be able to implement a chapter's demo(s) on his or her own after reading the chapter and spending some time studying the demo code. In fact, a good exercise is trying to implement the samples on your own using the book and sample code as a reference.

In addition to sample programs, the website also contains a message board. We encourage readers to communicate with each other and post questions on topics they do not understand or need clarification on. In many cases, getting alternative perspectives and explanations on a concept shortens the time it takes to comprehend it.

And lastly, the website will contain additional program samples and tutorials on topics that we could not fit into this book for one reason or another.

The companion files can also be downloaded from www.wordware.com/files/dx9c.

Part I

Mathematical Prerequisites

Video games attempt to simulate a virtual world; however, computers, by their very nature, crunch numbers. Thus the problem of how to convey a world to a computer arises. The answer is to describe our worlds, and the interactions therein, completely mathematically. Consequently, mathematics plays a fundamental role in video game development.

In this prerequisites part, we introduce the mathematical tools that will be used throughout this book. The emphasis is on vectors, coordinate systems, matrices, and transformations, as these tools are used in just about every sample program of this book. In addition to the mathematical explanations, a survey and demonstration of the relevant classes and functions from the D3DX math library are provided.

Note that the topics covered here are only those essential to understanding the rest of this book; it is by no means a comprehensive treatment of video game mathematics, as entire books are devoted to this topic. For readers desiring a more complete reference to video game mathematics, we recommend [Verth04] and [Lengyel02].

Chapter 1, "Vector Algebra"

Vectors are, perhaps, the most fundamental mathematical objects used in computer games. We use vectors to represent positions, displacements, directions, velocities, and forces, for example. In this chapter, we study vectors and the operations used to manipulate them.

Chapter 2, "Matrix Algebra"

Matrices provide an efficient and compact way of representing transformations. In this chapter, we become familiar with matrices and the operations defined on them.

Chapter 3, "Transformations and Planes"

This chapter examines three fundamental geometric transformations: scaling, rotation, and translation. We use these transformations to manipulate 3D objects in space. In addition, a brief primer on 3D planes is provided; planes are useful for dividing and sorting 3D space.

Chapter 1

Vector Algebra

Vectors play a crucial role in computer graphics, collision detection, and physical simulation, all of which are common components in contemporary video games. Our approach here is informal and practical; for a more theoretical development, see [Schneider03]. We emphasize the importance of vectors by noting that they are used in just about every demo program in this book.

Objectives:

- To develop an understanding of vectors, their geometry, and the operations defined on them.
- To learn how we can convert the coordinates of points and vectors from one coordinate system to another.
- To find out how vectors can be used to analytically describe other geometric objects such as rays, lines, and line segments.
- To become familiar with a subset of classes and functions provided by the D3DX library that are used for vector mathematics.

1.1 Vectors

A *vector* refers to a quantity that possesses both magnitude and direction. Quantities that possess both magnitude and direction are called *vector-valued quantities*. Examples of vector-valued quantities are forces (a force is applied in a particular direction with a certain strength — magnitude), displacements (the net direction and distance a particle moved), and velocities (speed and direction). Thus, vectors are used to represent forces, displacements, and velocities. In addition, we also use vectors to specify pure directions, such as the direction the player is looking in a 3D game, the direction a polygon is facing, the direction in which a ray of light travels, or the direction in which a ray of light reflects off a surface.

A first step in characterizing a vector mathematically is geometrically: We graphically specify a vector by a directed line segment (see Figure 1.1), where the length denotes the magnitude of the vector and the aim denotes the direction of the vector. We note that the location in which we draw a vector is immaterial because changing the location does not change the magnitude or direction. Consequently, two vectors are equal if and only if they have the same length and point in the same direction. Thus, the vectors $\vec{u}$ and $\vec{v}$ shown in Figure 1.1 are actually equal, that is $\vec{u}=\vec{v}$, because they have the same length and point in the same direction. In fact, because location is unimportant for vectors, we can always translate a vector without changing its meaning (since a translation changes neither length nor direction). Observe that we could translate $\vec{u}$ such that it completely overlaps with $\vec{v}$ (and conversely), thereby making them indistinguishable — hence their equality.

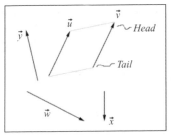

Figure 1.1: Vectors drawn on a 2D plane. Note $\vec{u}=\vec{v}$; since they point in the same direction and have the same length, they are translations of each other.

1.1.1 Vectors and Coordinate Systems

We could now define useful geometric operations on vectors, which can then be used to solve problems involving vector-valued quantities. However, since the computer cannot work with vectors geometrically, we need to find a way of specifying vectors numerically instead. So what we do is introduce a 3D coordinate system in space, and translate all the vectors so that their tails coincide with the origin (Figure 1.2). Then we can identify a vector by specifying the coordinates of its head, and write $\vec{v}=(x,y,z)$ as shown in Figure 1.3. Now we can represent a vector with three floats in a computer program.

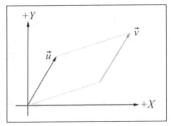

Figure 1.2: Because $\vec{u}$ and $\vec{v}$ have the same length and point in the same direction (they are parallel), we say $\vec{u}=\vec{v}$, and observe that we can translate $\vec{v}$ such that it completely coincides with $\vec{u}$. When a vector's tail coincides with the origin, we say that it is in *standard position*.

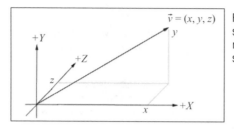

Figure 1.3: A vector specified by coordinates relative to a coordinate system.

Consider Figure 1.4, which shows a vector and two frames in space. (Note that we use the terms *frame, frame of reference, space,* and *coordinate system* to all mean the same thing in this book.) We can translate $\vec{v}$ so that it is in standard position in either of the two frames. Observe, however, that the coordinates of the vector differ based on the frame relative to which the vector is described. In other words, the same vector $\vec{v}$ has a different coordinate representation for distinct frames.

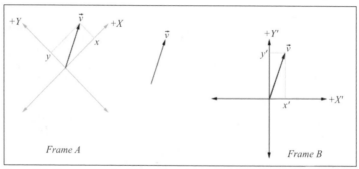

Figure 1.4: The same vector $\vec{v}$ has different coordinates when described relative to different frames.

The idea is analogous to, say, temperature. Water boils at Celsius or Fahrenheit. The physical temperature of boiling water is the same no matter the scale (i.e., we can't lower the boiling point by picking a different scale), but we assign a different scalar number to the temperature based on the scale we use. Similarly, for a vector, its direction and magnitude, which are embedded in the directed line segment, do not change, only the coordinates of it change based on the frame of reference we use to describe it. For example, wind blows in a particular direction and at some speed. We can measure the wind speed and direction relative to different frames of reference. For each distinct frame, we record different measurements. Nevertheless, the measurements are describing the same vector; that is, the frame of reference we pick cannot physically change the direction in which the wind blows nor does it change the magnitude of the wind. This is important because it means whenever we identify a vector by coordinates, those coordinates are relative to some frame of reference. Often, we will utilize more than one frame of reference and, therefore, will need to keep track of which frame the coordinates of a vector are described relative to; additionally, we will need to know how to convert vector coordinates from one frame to another (§1.5 shows how this conversion is done).

Note: We see that both vectors and points can be described by coordinates (x, y, z) relative to a frame. However, they are not the same; a point represents a location in 3-space, whereas a vector represents a magnitude and direction.

1.1.2 Left-Handed Versus Right-Handed Coordinate Systems

Direct3D uses a so-called left-handed coordinate system. If you take your left hand and aim your fingers down the positive x-axis, and then curl your fingers toward the positive y-axis, your thumb points roughly in the direction of the positive z-axis. Figure 1.5 illustrates the differences between left-handed and right-handed coordinate systems.

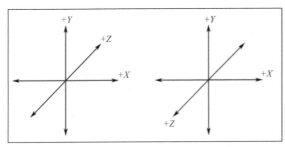

Figure 1.5: On the left we have a left-handed coordinate system. Observe that the positive z-axis goes into the page. On the right we have a right-handed coordinate system. Observe that the positive z-axis comes out of the page.

Observe that for the right-handed coordinate system, if you take your right hand and aim your fingers down the positive x-axis, and then curl your fingers toward the positive y-axis, your thumb points roughly in the direction of the positive z-axis.

1.1.3 Basic Vector Operations

We now define equality, addition, scalar multiplication, and subtraction on vectors using the coordinate representation.

- Two vectors are equal if and only if their corresponding components are equal. Let $\bar{u} = (u_x, u_y, u_z)$ and $\bar{v} = (v_x, v_y, v_z)$. Then $\bar{u} = \bar{v}$ if and only if $u_x = v_x$, $u_y = v_y$, and $u_z = v_z$.
- We add vectors component wise; as such, it only makes sense to add vectors of the same dimension. Let $\bar{u} = (u_x, u_y, u_z)$ and $\bar{v} = (v_x, v_y, v_z)$. Then $\bar{u} + \bar{v} = (u_x + v_x, u_y + v_y, u_z + v_z)$.
- We can multiply a scalar (i.e., a real number) and a vector, and the result is a vector. Let k be a scalar, and let $\bar{u} = (u_x, u_y, u_z)$, then $k\bar{u} = (ku_x, ku_y, ku_z)$. This is called scalar multiplication.

- We define subtraction in terms of vector addition and scalar multiplication. That is, $\vec{u} - \vec{v} = \vec{u} + (-1 \cdot \vec{v}) = \vec{u} + (-\vec{v})$.

Example 1.1

Let $\vec{u} = (1,2,3)$, $\vec{v} = (1,2,3)$, $\vec{w} = (3,0,-2)$, and $k = 2$. Then,

- $\vec{u} + \vec{w} = (1,2,3) + (3,0,-2) = (4,2,1)$;
- Clearly, $\vec{u} = \vec{v}$;
- $\vec{u} - \vec{v} = u + (-v) = (1,2,3) + (-1,-2,-3) = (0,0,0) = \vec{0}$;
- $k\vec{w} = 2(3,0,-2) = (6,0,-4)$.

The difference in the third line illustrates a special vector, called the *zero-vector*, which has zeros for all of its components and is denoted by $\vec{0}$.

Note: When comparing floating-point numbers, care must be taken due to floating-point imprecision. Two floating-point numbers that we expect to be equal may differ slightly, and therefore we test to see if they are approximately equal. We do this by defining an EPSILON constant, which is a very small value we use as a "buffer." We say two values are approximately equal if their distance is less than EPSILON. In other words, EPSILON gives us some tolerance for floating-point imprecision. The following function illustrates how EPSILON can be used to test if two floating-point values are equal:

```
const float EPSILON = 0.001f;
bool Equals(float lhs, float rhs)
{
    // if lhs == rhs their difference should be zero
    return fabs(lhs - rhs) < EPSILON ? true : false;
}
```

Example 1.2

We'll illustrate this example with 2D vectors to make the drawings simpler. The ideas are the same as in 3D; we just work with one less component in 2D.

- Let $\vec{v} = (2,1)$. How do $\vec{v}$ and $-1/2\vec{v}$ compare geometrically? We note $-1/2\vec{v} = (-1,-1/2)$. Graphing both $\vec{v}$ and $-1/2\vec{v}$ (Figure 1.6a), we notice that $-1/2\vec{v}$ is in the direction directly opposite of $\vec{v}$ and its length is 1/2 that of $\vec{v}$. Thus, geometrically, negating a vector can be thought of as "flipping" its direction, and scalar multiplication can be thought of as scaling the length of the vector.
- Let $\vec{u} = (2,1/2)$ and $\vec{v} = (1,2)$. Then $\vec{u} + \vec{v} = (3,5/2)$. Figure 1.6b shows what vector addition means geometrically: We parallel translate $\vec{u}$ so that its *tail* coincides with the *head* of $\vec{v}$. Then, the sum is the vector originating at the tail of $\vec{v}$ and ending at the head of $\vec{u}$. (Note that we could have just as well translated $\vec{v}$ so that its tail coincided with the head of $\vec{u}$, then $\vec{u} + \vec{v}$ would be the vector originating at the tail of $\vec{u}$ and

$\vec{v}$.) Observe also that our rules of vector addition agree with what we would intuitively expect to happen physically when we add forces together to produce a net force: If we add two forces (vectors) in the same direction, we get another stronger force (longer vector) in that direction. If we add two forces (vectors) in opposition to each other, then we get a weaker net force (shorter vector).

■ Let $\vec{u}=(2,1/2)$ and $\vec{v}=(1,2)$. Then $\vec{u}-\vec{v}=(1,-3/2)$. Figure 1.6c shows what vector subtraction means geometrically. Essentially, the difference $\vec{u}-\vec{v}$ gives us a vector aimed from the head of $\vec{v}$ to the head of $\vec{u}$. If we instead interpret $\vec{u}$ and $\vec{v}$ as points, then $\vec{u}-\vec{v}$ gives us a vector aimed from the point $\vec{v}$ to the point $\vec{u}$; this interpretation is important as we will often want the vector aimed from one point to another. Observe also that the length of $\vec{u}-\vec{v}$ is the distance from $\vec{u}$ to $\vec{v}$.

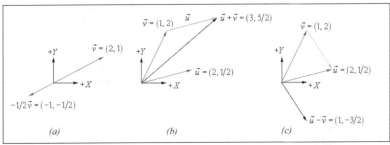

Figure 1.6: (a) The geometric interpretation of scalar multiplication. (b) The geometric interpretation of vector addition. (c) The geometric interpretation of vector subtraction.

1.2 **Length and Unit Vectors**

Geometrically, the magnitude of a vector is the length of the directed line segment. We denote the magnitude of a vector by double vertical bars (e.g., $\|\vec{u}\|$ denotes the magnitude of $\vec{u}$). Now, given a vector $\vec{u}=(x,y,z)$, we wish to compute its magnitude algebraically. The magnitude of a 3D vector can be computed by applying the Pythagorean theorem twice; see Figure 1.7.

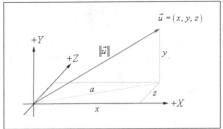

Figure 1.7: The 3D length of a vector can be computed by applying the Pythagorean theorem twice.

First, we look at the triangle in the xz-plane with sides x, z, and hypotenuse a. From the Pythagorean theorem, we have $a=\sqrt{x^2+z^2}$. Now look at the triangle with sides a, y, and hypotenuse $\|\vec{u}\|$. From the Pythagorean theorem again, we arrive at the following magnitude formula:

$$\|\vec{u}\|=\sqrt{y^2+a^2}=\sqrt{y^2+\left(\sqrt{x^2+z^2}\right)^2}=\sqrt{x^2+y^2+z^2} \qquad (1.1)$$

For some applications, we do not care about the length of the vector because we want to use a vector to represent a pure direction. For such direction-only vectors, we want the length of the vector to be exactly one. When we make a vector unit length, we say that we are _normalizing_ the vector. We can normalize a vector by dividing each of its components by its magnitude:

$$\frac{\vec{u}}{\|\vec{u}\|}=\left(\frac{x}{\|\vec{u}\|},\frac{y}{\|\vec{u}\|},\frac{z}{\|\vec{u}\|}\right) \qquad (1.2)$$

Example 1.3

Normalize the vector $\vec{v}=(-1,3,4)$. We have $\|\vec{v}\|=\sqrt{(-1)^2+3^2+4^2}=\sqrt{26}$. Thus,

$$\frac{\vec{v}}{\|\vec{v}\|}=\left(\frac{-1}{\sqrt{26}},\frac{3}{\sqrt{26}},\frac{4}{\sqrt{26}}\right)$$

To verify that $\vec{v}/\|\vec{v}\|$ is indeed a unit vector, we compute its length:

$$\left\|\frac{\vec{v}}{\|\vec{v}\|}\right\|=\sqrt{\left(\frac{-1}{\sqrt{26}}\right)^2+\left(\frac{3}{\sqrt{26}}\right)^2+\left(\frac{4}{\sqrt{26}}\right)^2}=\sqrt{\frac{1}{26}+\frac{9}{26}+\frac{16}{26}}=\sqrt{1}=1$$

1.3 **The Dot Product**

The dot product is a form of vector multiplication that results in a scalar value; for this reason, it is sometimes referred to as the scalar product. Let $\vec{u}=(u_x,u_y,u_z)$ and $\vec{v}=(v_x,v_y,v_z)$; then the dot product is defined as follows:

$$\vec{u}\cdot\vec{v}=u_xv_x+u_yv_y+u_zv_z \qquad (1.3)$$

In words, the dot product is the sum of the products of the individual components.

The dot product definition does not present an obvious geometric meaning. Using the law of cosines, we can find the relationship

$$\vec{u} \cdot \vec{v} = \|\vec{u}\| \|\vec{v}\| \cos\theta \tag{1.4}$$

Equation 1.4 says that the dot product between two vectors is the cosine of the angle between them scaled by the vectors' magnitudes. Thus, if both $\vec{u}$ and $\vec{v}$ are unit vectors, then $\vec{u} \cdot \vec{v}$ is the cosine of the angle between them (i.e., $\vec{u} \cdot \vec{v} = \cos\theta$).

Equation 1.4 provides us with some useful geometric properties of the dot product:

- If $\vec{u} \cdot \vec{v} = 0$, then $\vec{u} \perp \vec{v}$ (i.e., the vectors are orthogonal).
- If $\vec{u} \cdot \vec{v} = 1$, then $\vec{u} \| \vec{v}$ (i.e., the vectors are parallel) and both $\vec{u}$ and $\vec{v}$ point in the same direction.
- If $\vec{u} \cdot \vec{v} = -1$, then $\vec{u} \| \vec{v}$ (i.e., the vectors are parallel) and $\vec{u}$ and $\vec{v}$ point in opposite directions.
- If $\vec{u} \cdot \vec{v} > 0$, then the angle θ between the two vectors is less than 90 degrees (i.e., the vectors make an acute angle).
- If $\vec{u} \cdot \vec{v} < 0$, then the angle θ between the two vectors is greater than 90 degrees (i.e., the vectors make an obtuse angle).

Note: The term "orthogonal" can be used as a synonym for "perpendicular."

Example 1.4

Let $\vec{u} = (1, 2, 3)$ and $\vec{v} = (-4, 0, -1)$. Find the angle between $\vec{u}$ and $\vec{v}$. First observe that

$$\vec{u} \cdot \vec{v} = (1, 2, 3) \cdot (-4, 0, -1) = -4 + 0 - 3 = -7$$

$$\|\vec{u}\| = \sqrt{1 + 2^2 + 3^2} = \sqrt{14}$$

$$\|\vec{v}\| = \sqrt{(-4)^2 + 0^2 + (-1)^2} = \sqrt{17}$$

Applying Equation 1.4 tells us that

$$\frac{\vec{u} \cdot \vec{v}}{\|\vec{u}\| \|\vec{v}\|} = \frac{-7}{\sqrt{14}\sqrt{17}} = \cos\theta$$

We can solve for theta using the trig arccosine function:

$$\theta = \cos^{-1}\left(\frac{-7}{\sqrt{14}\sqrt{17}}\right) \approx 117°$$

Example 1.5

Consider Figure 1.8. Given $\vec{u}$ and the *unit* vector $\vec{n}$, find a formula for $\vec{p}$ using the dot product.

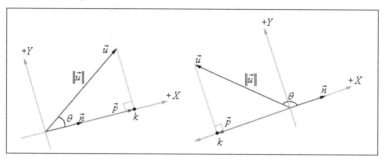

Figure 1.8: The orthogonal projection of $\vec{u}$ on $\vec{n}$.

First, observe from the figure that since $\vec{n}$ is a unit vector, we have $\vec{p} = k\vec{n}$. Thus we must determine k. Using trigonometry, we know that $k = \|\vec{u}\| \cos\theta$; therefore, $\vec{p} = (\|\vec{u}\| \cos\theta)\vec{n}$. However, because $\vec{n}$ is a unit vector, we can say this in another way:

$$\vec{p} = (\|\vec{u}\|\cos\theta)\vec{n} = (\|\vec{u}\|\cdot 1\cos\theta)\vec{n} = (\|\vec{u}\|\|\vec{n}\|\cos\theta)\vec{n} = (\vec{u}\cdot\vec{n})\vec{n}$$

We call $\vec{p}$ the *orthogonal projection* of $\vec{u}$ on $\vec{n}$. If we interpret $\vec{u}$ as a force, $\vec{p}$ can be thought of as the portion of the force $\vec{u}$ that acts in the direction $\vec{n}$.

If $\vec{n}$ is not of unit length, we can always normalize it first to make it unit length.

1.4 **The Cross Product**

The second form of multiplication vector math defines is the cross product. Unlike the dot product, which evaluates to a scalar, the cross product evaluates to another vector. Taking the cross product of two 3D vectors, $\vec{u}$ and $\vec{v}$, yields another vector, $\vec{w}$, that is mutually orthogonal to $\vec{u}$ and $\vec{v}$. By that we mean $\vec{w}$ is orthogonal to $\vec{u}$, and $\vec{w}$ is orthogonal to $\vec{v}$; see Figure 1.9. If $\vec{u} = (u_x, u_y, u_z)$ and $\vec{v} = (v_x, v_y, v_z)$, then the cross product is computed like so:

$$\vec{w} = \vec{u}\times\vec{v} = \left((u_y v_z - u_z v_y), (u_z v_x - u_x v_z), (u_x v_y - u_y v_x)\right) \tag{1.5}$$

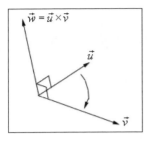

Figure 1.9: The cross product of two 3D vectors, $\vec{u}$ and $\vec{v}$, yields another vector, $\vec{w}$, that is mutually orthogonal to $\vec{u}$ and $\vec{v}$. If you take your left hand and aim the fingers in the direction of the first vector $\vec{u}$, and then curl your fingers toward $\vec{v}$ along an angle $0 \leq \theta \leq \pi$, then your thumb roughly points in the direction of $\vec{w} = \vec{u} \times \vec{v}$; this is called the *left-hand-thumb rule*.

Example 1.6

Let $\vec{u} = (2,1,3)$ and $\vec{v} = (2,0,0)$. Compute $\vec{w} = \vec{u} \times \vec{v}$ and $\vec{y} = \vec{v} \times \vec{u}$, and then verify that $\vec{w}$ is orthogonal to $\vec{u}$ and that $\vec{w}$ is orthogonal to $\vec{v}$. Applying formula 1.5 we have,

$$\vec{w} = \vec{u} \times \vec{v} = (2,1,3) \times (2,0,0) = (1 \cdot 0 - 3 \cdot 0, 3 \cdot 2 - 2 \cdot 0, 2 \cdot 0 - 1 \cdot 2) = (0, 6, -2)$$

and

$$\vec{y} = \vec{v} \times \vec{u} = (2,0,0) \times (2,1,3) = (0 \cdot 3 - 0 \cdot 1, 0 \cdot 2 - 2 \cdot 3, 2 \cdot 1 - 0 \cdot 2) = (0, -6, 2)$$

This result makes one thing clear, generally speaking: $\vec{u} \times \vec{v} \neq \vec{v} \times \vec{u}$. Therefore, we say that the cross product is *anti-commutative*. In fact, it can be shown that $\vec{u} \times \vec{v} = -\vec{v} \times \vec{u}$. You can determine the vector returned by the cross product by the *left-hand-thumb rule*. If you curve the fingers of your left hand from the direction of the first vector toward the second vector (always take the path with the smallest angle), your thumb points in the direction of the returned vector, as shown in Figure 1.9.

To show that $\vec{w}$ is orthogonal to $\vec{u}$ and that $\vec{w}$ is orthogonal to $\vec{v}$, we recall from §1.3 that if $\vec{u} \cdot \vec{v} = 0$, then $\vec{u} \perp \vec{v}$ (i.e., the vectors are orthogonal). Because

$$\vec{w} \cdot \vec{u} = (0, 6, -2) \cdot (2,1,3) = 0 \cdot 2 + 6 \cdot 1 - 2 \cdot 3 = 0$$

and

$$\vec{w} \cdot \vec{v} = (0, 6, -2) \cdot (2, 0, 0) = 0 \cdot 2 + 6 \cdot 0 - 2 \cdot 0 = 0$$

we conclude that $\vec{w}$ is orthogonal to $\vec{u}$ and that $\vec{w}$ is orthogonal to $\vec{v}$.

1.5 Change of Frame

Suppose that the scalar 100° C represents the temperature of boiling water relative to the Celsius scale. How do we describe the *same* temperature of boiling water relative to the Fahrenheit scale? In other words, what is the scalar, relative to the Fahrenheit scale, that represents the temperature of boiling water? To make this conversion (or change of frame), we need to know how the Celsius and Fahrenheit scales relate. They are related as follows: $T_F = \frac{9}{5}T_C + 32°$. Therefore, $T_F = \frac{9}{5}(100°) + 32° = 212°$. That is, the temperature of boiling water is 212° Fahrenheit.

This simple example illustrates that we can convert a scalar k that describes some quantity relative to a frame A into a new scalar k' that describes the *same* quantity relative to a different frame B, provided that we know how frame A and B are related.

In this section, we look at a similar problem, but instead of scalars, we are interested in how to convert vector coordinates from one frame to another.

1.5.1 Vectors

Consider Figure 1.10 in which we have two frames, A and B, and a vector, $\vec{p}$. To avoid ambiguity, let us write $\vec{p} = \vec{p}_A = (x, y)$ when we are specifying $\vec{p}$ by coordinates relative to frame A, and let us write $\vec{p} = \vec{p}_B = (x', y')$ when we are specifying $\vec{p}$ by coordinates relative to frame B. Now, suppose we are given $\vec{p}_A = (x, y)$. How do we find $\vec{p}_B = (x', y')$? In other words, given the coordinates identifying a vector relative to one frame, how do we find the coordinates that identify the same vector relative to a different frame?

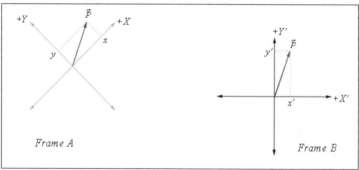

Figure 1.10: Two frames, A and B, and a vector, $\vec{p}$. The same vector $\vec{p}$ has different coordinates relative to the two frames.

First, because we are talking about vectors in which location does not matter, we translate the coordinate systems so that their origins coincide as shown in Figure 1.11. Now let $\vec{u} = (u_x, u_y)$ and $\vec{v} = (v_x, v_y)$ be unit vectors *relative to frame B*, which aim, respectively, along the x- and y-axes of frame A. Then from Figure 1.11, we see that

$$\vec{p}_B = (x', y') = x\vec{u} + y\vec{v}$$

Note the relationship between the two frames that allowed us to do this conversion: The relationship was that we described the axes of frame A

relative to frame B with the vectors $\vec{u}$ and $\vec{v}$. Thus, if we are given $\vec{p}_A=(x,y)$ and we know the vectors $\vec{u}$ and $\vec{v}$, then we can always find $\vec{p}_B=(x',y')$.

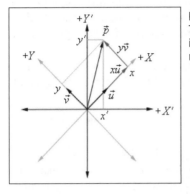

Figure 1.11:
The geometry of
identifying $\vec{p}$
relative to frame B.

Generalizing to 3D, if $\vec{p}_A=(x,y,z)$, then $\vec{p}_B=(x',y',z')=x\vec{u}+y\vec{v}+z\vec{w}$, where $\vec{u}$, $\vec{v}$, and $\vec{w}$ describe the x-, y-, and z-axes of frame A relative to frame B.

We call the process of converting the coordinates that describe a vector relative to a frame A into new coordinates that describe the same vector relative to frame B a *change of frame* or *change of coordinates transformation*.

Note: The vectors $\vec{u}$, $\vec{v}$, and $\vec{w}$ actually do not need to be unit vectors. If they are not, it means that the two coordinate systems also differ in scale (in addition to orientation and position). For example, if frame A used meters and frame B used centimeters, then $\vec{u}$, $\vec{v}$, and $\vec{w}$ would have magnitudes of 100 centimeters since there are 100 centimeters per meter.

Note: The coordinate system chosen is somewhat arbitrary; however, picking a convenient coordinate system can sometimes make a problem easier. In other words, the geometry might have simpler coordinates in one coordinate system and more complex coordinates in another. Moreover, it is sometimes useful to use multiple coordinate systems. For example, we may want an answer in coordinate system A, but the problem is solved more easily in coordinate system B. In this case, we convert from A to B, solve the problem in B, and then convert back to A to give the answer.

1.5.2 **Points**

We can also use a vector to represent a 3D location in space; we call this a *position vector* or *point*. In this case, the location of the tip of the vector (when the vector is in standard position; see §1.1.1) is the characteristic of interest, not the direction and magnitude. Since location is important for points, we cannot just translate the coordinate systems like we did in the previous section; this makes the change of frame transformation for points slightly different.

If $\vec{p}_A=(x,y)$ represents a point $\vec{p}$ relative to frame A, how do we describe the same point relative to frame B? In other words, what is $\vec{p}_B=(x',y')$? From Figure 1.12, we see that

$$\vec{p}_B=(x',y')=\vec{O}+x\vec{u}+y\vec{v}$$

where $\vec{O}=(O_x,O_y)$ describes the origin of frame A relative to frame B, and $\vec{u}=(u_x,u_y)$ and $\vec{v}=(v_x,v_y)$ describe the x- and y-axes of frame A relative to frame B. In 3D, if $\vec{p}_A=(x,y,z)$, then $\vec{p}_B=(x',y',z')=\vec{O}+x\vec{u}+y\vec{v}+z\vec{w}$.

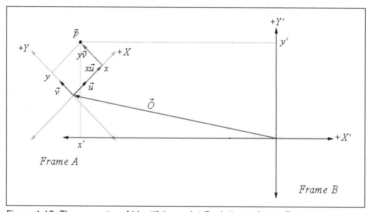

Figure 1.12: The geometry of identifying point $\vec{p}$ relative to frame B.

1.6 **Rays, Lines, and Segments**

Suppose a player in a game we are working on fires his gun at an enemy. How would we determine whether the bullet starting from a particular position and aimed in a direction hit the target? One approach would be to model the bullet with a ray and model the enemy with a bounding sphere. (A *bounding sphere* is simply a sphere that tightly surrounds an object, thus roughly approximating its volume.) Then mathematically we can determine whether the ray hit the sphere and where. In this section we learn how to model rays mathematically.

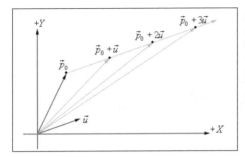

Figure 1.13: A ray described by an origin $\vec{p}_0$ and direction $\vec{u}$. We can generate points on the ray by plugging in scalars for t that are greater than or equal to zero.

A ray can be described with an origin and a direction, as shown in Figure 1.13. The parametric equation of a ray is:

$$\vec{p}(t) = \vec{p}_0 + t\vec{u}$$

where $\vec{p}_0$ is the origin of the ray, $\vec{u}$ is a vector specifying the direction of the ray (not necessarily of unit length), and t is the parameter. By plugging in different values for t we obtain different points on the ray. The parameter t must be in the interval $[0, \infty)$ to describe a ray. Values less than zero will generate points behind the ray (i.e., on the line that coincides with the ray). In fact, if we let $t \in (-\infty, \infty)$, then we have a line in 3-space.

   Now suppose we wish to define a line segment by the points $\vec{p}_0$ and $\vec{p}_1$. We first construct a vector $\vec{u} = \vec{p}_1 - \vec{p}_0$ from $\vec{p}_0$ to $\vec{p}_1$, as shown in Figure 1.14. Then, for $t \in [0, 1]$, the graph of the equation $\vec{p}(t) = \vec{p}_0 + t\vec{u}$ is the line segment defined by $\vec{p}_0$ and $\vec{p}_1$. Note that if you go outside the range $t \in [0, 1]$, then you get a point on the line that coincides with the segment but which is not on the segment.

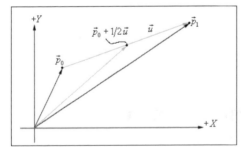

Figure 1.14: We generate points on the line segment by plugging in different values for t in [0, 1]. For example, the midpoint of the line segment is given at $t = \frac{1}{2}$. Also note that if $t = 0$, we get $\vec{p}_0$, and if $t = 1$, we get $\vec{p}_1$.

1.7 **D3DX Vectors**

In this section, we spend some time becoming familiar with the D3DXVECTOR3 class, which is the class we often use to store the coordinates of both points and vectors in code relative to some coordinate system. Its class definition is:

```
typedef struct D3DXVECTOR3 : public D3DVECTOR
{
public:
    D3DXVECTOR3() {};
    D3DXVECTOR3( CONST FLOAT * );
    D3DXVECTOR3( CONST D3DVECTOR& );
    D3DXVECTOR3( CONST D3DXFLOAT16 * );
    D3DXVECTOR3( FLOAT x, FLOAT y, FLOAT z );

    // casting
    operator FLOAT* ();
    operator CONST FLOAT* () const;

    // assignment operators
    D3DXVECTOR3& operator += ( CONST D3DXVECTOR3& );
    D3DXVECTOR3& operator -= ( CONST D3DXVECTOR3& );
    D3DXVECTOR3& operator *= ( FLOAT );
    D3DXVECTOR3& operator /= ( FLOAT );

    // unary operators
    D3DXVECTOR3 operator + () const;
    D3DXVECTOR3 operator - () const;

    // binary operators
    D3DXVECTOR3 operator + ( CONST D3DXVECTOR3& ) const;
    D3DXVECTOR3 operator - ( CONST D3DXVECTOR3& ) const;
    D3DXVECTOR3 operator * ( FLOAT ) const;
    D3DXVECTOR3 operator / ( FLOAT ) const;

    friend D3DXVECTOR3 operator * (FLOAT, CONST struct
                                         D3DXVECTOR3& );

    BOOL operator == ( CONST D3DXVECTOR3& ) const;
    BOOL operator != ( CONST D3DXVECTOR3& ) const;

} D3DXVECTOR3, *LPD3DXVECTOR3;
```

Note that D3DXVECTOR3 inherits its coordinate data from D3DVECTOR, which is defined as:

```
typedef struct _D3DVECTOR {
    float x;
    float y;
    float z;
} D3DVECTOR;
```

In addition to the above class, the D3DX library includes the following useful functions for computing the length of a vector, normalizing a vector, computing the dot product of two vectors, and computing the cross product of two vectors.

■   FLOAT D3DXVec3Length(// Returns $\|\vec{v}\|$
    CONST D3DXVECTOR3 *pV);   // Input $\vec{v}$

■   D3DXVECTOR3* D3DXVec3Normalize(
        D3DXVECTOR3 *pOut,   // Outputs $\vec{v}/\|\vec{v}\|$
        CONST D3DXVECTOR3 *pV);   // Input $\vec{v}$

■   FLOAT D3DXVec3Dot(// Outputs $\vec{v}_1 \cdot \vec{v}_2$
        CONST D3DXVECTOR3 *pV1,   // Input $\vec{v}_1$
        CONST D3DXVECTOR3 *pV2); // Input $\vec{v}_2$

■   D3DXVECTOR3 *D3DXVec3Cross(
        D3DXVECTOR3 *pOut,   // Outputs $\vec{v}_1 \times \vec{v}_2$
        CONST D3DXVECTOR3 *pV1,   // Input $\vec{v}_1$
        CONST D3DXVECTOR3 *pV2); // Input $\vec{v}_2$

Note: Remember to link the d3dx9.lib library file with your application to use any D3DX code; moreover, you will also need to #include <d3dx9.h>.

The following short code provides some examples on how to use the D3DXVECTOR3 class and the four functions mentioned above.

```cpp
#include <d3dx9.h>
#include <iostream>
using namespace std;

// Overload the "<<" operators so that we can use cout to
// output D3DXVECTOR3 objects.

ostream& operator<<(ostream& os, D3DXVECTOR3& v)
{
    os << "(" << v.x << ", " << v.y << ", " << v.z << ")";
    return os;
}

int main()
{
    // Using constructor, D3DXVECTOR3(FLOAT x,FLOAT y,FLOAT z);
    D3DXVECTOR3 u(1.0f, 2.0f, 3.0f);

    // Using constructor, D3DXVECTOR3(CONST FLOAT *);
    float x[3] = {-2.0f, 1.0f, -3.0f};
    D3DXVECTOR3 v(x);

    // Using constructor, D3DXVECTOR3() {};
    D3DXVECTOR3 a, b, c, d, e;

    // Vector addition: D3DXVECTOR3 operator +
    a = u + v;
```

```
            // Vector subtraction: D3DXVECTOR3 operator -
            b = u - v;

            // Scalar multiplication: D3DXVECTOR3 operator *
            c = u * 10;

            // ||u||
            float length = D3DXVec3Length(&u);

            // d = u / ||u||
            D3DXVec3Normalize(&d, &u);

            // s = u dot v
            float s = D3DXVec3Dot(&u, &v);

            // e = u x v
            D3DXVec3Cross(&e, &u, &v);

            cout << "u       = " << u << endl;
            cout << "v       = " << v << endl;
            cout << "a       = " << a << endl;
            cout << "b       = " << b << endl;
            cout << "c       = " << c << endl;
            cout << "d       = " << d << endl;
            cout << "e       = " << e << endl;
            cout << "||u||   = " << length << endl;
            cout << "u dot v = " << s << endl;

            return 0;
        }
```

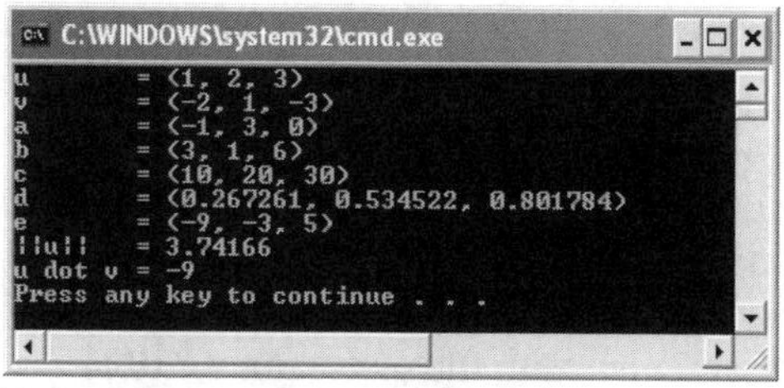

Figure 1.15: Output for the above program.

Note: The D3DX library also provides the D3DXVECTOR2 and D3DXVECTOR4 classes for working with 2D and 4D vectors. Later in this book we use 2D vectors to describe 2D points on texture maps. The purpose of 4D vectors will make more sense after you read Chapter 2, "Matrix Algebra."

1.8 **Summary**

- Vectors are used to model physical quantities that possess both magnitude and direction. Geometrically, we represent a vector with a directed line segment. A vector is in standard position when it is translated parallel to itself so that its tail coincides with the origin of the coordinate system. A vector in standard position can be described analytically by specifying the coordinates of its head relative to a coordinate system.

- If $\vec{u} = (u_x, u_y, u_z)$ and $\vec{v} = (v_x, v_y, v_z)$, then we have the following vector operations:

  Addition: $\vec{u} + \vec{v} = (u_x + v_x, u_y + v_y, u_z + v_z)$

  Subtraction: $\vec{u} - \vec{v} = (u_x - v_x, u_y - v_y, u_z - v_z)$

  Scalar multiplication: $k\vec{u} = (ku_x, ku_y, ku_z)$

  Length: $\|\vec{u}\| = \sqrt{u_x^2 + u_y^2 + u_z^2}$

  Normalization: $\vec{u}/\|\vec{u}\| = \left(u_x/\|\vec{u}\|, u_y/\|\vec{u}\|, u_z/\|\vec{u}\|\right)$

  Dot product: $\vec{u} \cdot \vec{v} = \|\vec{u}\|\|\vec{v}\|\cos\theta = u_x v_x + u_y v_y + u_z v_z$

  Cross product: $\vec{u} \times \vec{v} = (u_y v_z - u_z v_y, u_z v_x - u_x v_z, u_x v_y - u_y v_x)$

- Let $\vec{O}$, $\vec{u}$, $\vec{v}$, and $\vec{w}$ describe the origin and x-, y-, and z-axes of frame A relative to frame B. If $\vec{p}_A = (x, y, z)$ identifies a vector relative to frame A, then the same vector relative to frame B is identified by:

  $\vec{p}_B = (x', y', z') = x\vec{u} + y\vec{v} + z\vec{w}$ For vectors (direction and magnitude)

  $\vec{p}_B = (x', y', z') = \vec{O} + x\vec{u} + y\vec{v} + z\vec{w}$ For position vectors (points)

- Rays are described parametrically with an origin and direction vector: $\vec{p}(t) = \vec{p}_0 + t\vec{u}$ for $t \in [0, \infty)$. By relaxing our restriction on t, we can easily make the same ray equation represent a line; that is, $\vec{p}(t) = \vec{p}_0 + t\vec{u}$ for $t \in [-\infty, \infty)$ represents a line. To define a line segment by the points $\vec{p}_0$ and $\vec{p}_1$, we construct a vector $\vec{u} = \vec{p}_1 - \vec{p}_0$, and then use the ray equation, $\vec{p}(t) = \vec{p}_0 + t\vec{u}$, again but with the restriction $t \in [0, 1]$.

1.9 **Exercises**

1. Let $\vec{u} = (1, 2, 0)$ and $\vec{v} = (3, -4, 0)$. Compute $\vec{u} + \vec{v}$, $\vec{u} - \vec{v}$, $2\vec{u} + 1/2\vec{v}$, and $-2\vec{u} + \vec{v}$, and draw the vectors relative to a coordinate system.

2. Let $\vec{u} = (-2, 1, 4)$ and $\vec{v} = (3, -4, 1)$. Normalize $\vec{u}$ and $\vec{v}$.

3. Show $\vec{u}/\|\vec{u}\|$ has a length of one unit. (Hint: Compute the length of $\vec{u}/\|\vec{u}\|$.)

4. Is the angle between $\vec{u}$ and $\vec{v}$ orthogonal, acute, or obtuse?

   a. $\vec{u} = (1, 1, 1), \vec{v} = (2, 2, 2)$

    b. $\vec{u}=(1,1,0), \vec{v}=(-2,2,0)$

    c. $\vec{u}=(-1,-1,-1), \vec{v}=(3,1,0)$

5.   Let $\vec{u}=(-2,1,4)$ and $\vec{v}=(3,-4,1)$. Find the angle θ between $\vec{u}$ and $\vec{v}$.

6.   Let $\vec{u}=(u_x, u_y, u_z)$ and $\vec{v}=(v_x, v_y, v_z)$. Show that the following properties are true for $\mathbb{R}^3$:

    a. $\vec{u}\cdot\vec{v}=\vec{v}\cdot\vec{u}$

    b. $\vec{u}\cdot(\vec{v}+\vec{w})=\vec{u}\cdot\vec{v}+\vec{u}\cdot\vec{w}$

    c. $k(\vec{u}\cdot\vec{v})=(k\vec{u})\cdot\vec{v}=\vec{u}\cdot(k\vec{v})$

    d. $\vec{v}\cdot\vec{v}=\|\vec{v}\|^2$

    e. $\vec{0}\cdot\vec{v}=0$

    (Hint: Just use the definition, for example,

$$\vec{v}\cdot\vec{v}=v_x v_x + v_y v_y + v_z v_z = v_x^2 + v_y^2 + v_z^2 = \left(\sqrt{v_x^2 + v_y^2 + v_z^2}\right)^2 = \left(\|\vec{v}\|\right)^2.)$$

7.   Use the law of cosines ($c^2 = a^2 + b^2 = 2ab\cos\theta$, where a, b, and c are the lengths of the sides of a triangle and θ is the angle between sides a and b) to show $u_x v_x + u_y v_y + u_z v_z = \|\vec{u}\|\|\vec{v}\|\cos\theta$.

    (Hint: Draw a picture and set $c^2 = \|\vec{u}-\vec{v}\|^2$, $a^2 = \|\vec{u}\|^2$, and $b^2 = \|\vec{v}\|$, and use the dot product properties from the previous exercise.)

8.   Let $\vec{v}=(4,3,0)$ and $\vec{n}=\left(2/\sqrt{5}, 1/\sqrt{5}, 0\right)$. Show that $\vec{n}$ is a unit vector and find the orthogonal projection, $\vec{p}$, of $\vec{v}$ on $\vec{n}$. Then find a vector $\vec{w}$ orthogonal to $\vec{n}$ such that $\vec{v}=\vec{p}+\vec{w}$.

    (Hint: Draw the vectors for insight; what does $\vec{v}-\vec{p}$ look like?)

9.   Let $\vec{u}=(-2,1,4)$ and $\vec{v}=(3,-4,1)$. Find $\vec{w}=\vec{u}\times\vec{v}$, and show $\vec{w}\cdot\vec{u}=0$ and $\vec{w}\cdot\vec{v}=0$.

10. Let the following points define a triangle relative to some coordinate system: $\vec{A}=(0,0,0)$, $\vec{B}=(0,1,3)$, and $\vec{C}=(5,1,0)$. Find a vector orthogonal to this triangle.

    (Hint: Find two vectors on two of the triangle's edges and use the cross product.)

11. Suppose that we have frames A and B. Let $\vec{p}_A = (1,-2,0)$ and $\vec{q}_A = (1,2,0)$ represent a point and force, respectively, relative to frame A. Moreover, let $\vec{O}=(-6,2,0)$, $\vec{u}=\left(1/\sqrt{2}, 1/\sqrt{2}, 0\right)$, $\vec{v}=\left(-1/\sqrt{2}, 1/\sqrt{2}, 0\right)$, and $\vec{w}=(0,0,1)$ describe frame A relative to frame B. Find $\vec{p}_B = (x, y, z)$ and $\vec{q}_B = (x, y, z)$ that describe the point and force relative to frame B.

12. Let $\vec{p}(t)=(1,1)+t(2,1)$ be a ray relative to some coordinate system. Plot the points on the ray at $t = 0.0, 0.5, 1.0, 2.0,$ and 5.0.

13. Let $\vec{p}_0$ and $\vec{p}_1$ define the endpoints of a line segment. Show that the equation for a line segment can also be written as $\vec{p}(t)=(1-t)\vec{p}_0+t\vec{p}_1$ for $t\in[0,1]$.

14. Rewrite the program in §1.7 twice, first using 2D vectors (D3DXVECTOR2) and then using 4D vectors (D3DXVECTOR4).

    (Hint: Search the index for these keywords in the DirectX SDK documentation: D3DXVECTOR2, D3DXVECTOR4, D3DXVec2, and D3DXVec4.)

Chapter 2

Matrix Algebra

In 3D computer graphics, we use matrices to compactly describe geometric transformations such as scaling, rotation, and translation, and also to change the coordinates of a point or vector from one frame to another. This chapter explores the mathematics of matrices.

Objectives:

- To obtain an understanding of matrices and the operations defined on them.

- To discover how a vector-matrix multiplication can be viewed as a linear combination, and how a vector-matrix multiplication can be used to convert the coordinates of points and vectors from one coordinate system to another.

- To learn how we can use matrix-matrix multiplication to combine several transformations into one matrix.

- To learn what the identity matrix is, and what the transpose and inverse of a matrix are.

- To become familiar with a subset of classes and functions provided by the D3DX library that are used for matrix mathematics.

2.1 Definition

An *m × n matrix M* is a rectangular array of real numbers with m rows and n columns. The product of the number of rows and columns gives the dimensions of the matrix. The numbers in a matrix are called *elements* or *entries*. We identify a matrix element by specifying the row and column of the element using a double subscript notation m_{ij}, where the first subscript identifies the row and the second subscript identifies the column.

Example 2.1

Consider the following matrices:

$$A = \begin{bmatrix} 3.5 & 0 & 0 & 0 \\ 0 & 1 & 0 & 0 \\ 0 & 0 & 0.5 & 0 \\ 2 & -5 & 3 & 1 \end{bmatrix} \quad B = \begin{bmatrix} b_{11} & b_{12} \\ b_{21} & b_{22} \\ b_{31} & b_{32} \end{bmatrix} \quad \vec{u} = [u_1, u_2, u_3, u_4] \quad \vec{v} = \begin{bmatrix} 1 \\ 2 \\ 3 \end{bmatrix}$$

■ Matrix A is a 4×4 matrix; matrix B is a 3×2 matrix; matrix $\vec{u}$ is a 1×4 matrix; and matrix $\vec{v}$ is a 3×1 matrix.

■ We identify the element in the fourth row and second column of matrix A by $a_{42} = -5$. We identify the element in the second row and first column of matrix B by b_{21}.

■ Matrices $\vec{u}$ and $\vec{v}$ are special matrices in the sense that they contain a single row or column, respectively. We sometimes call these kinds of matrices *row vectors* or *column vectors* because they are used to represent a vector in matrix form (e.g., we can freely interchange the vector notations (x, y, z) and $[x, y, z]$). For this reason, we often keep the arrowhead notation when denoting a row vector or column vector matrix. Observe that for row and column vectors, it is unnecessary to use a double subscript to denote the elements of the matrix — we only need one subscript.

Occasionally we like to think of the rows of a matrix as vectors. For example, we might write:

$$\begin{bmatrix} v_{11} & v_{12} & v_{13} \\ v_{21} & v_{22} & v_{23} \\ v_{31} & v_{32} & v_{33} \end{bmatrix} = \begin{bmatrix} \vec{v}_{row1} \\ \vec{v}_{row2} \\ \vec{v}_{row3} \end{bmatrix}$$

where $\vec{v}_{row1} = [v_{11}, v_{12}, v_{13}]$, $\vec{v}_{row2} = [v_{21}, v_{22}, v_{23}]$, and $\vec{v}_{row3} = [v_{31}, v_{32}, v_{33}]$. We use the notation "row" in the subscript so that we know the vector refers to a row in a matrix. Likewise, we do the same for the columns:

$$\begin{bmatrix} v_{11} & v_{12} & v_{13} \\ v_{21} & v_{22} & v_{23} \\ v_{31} & v_{32} & v_{33} \end{bmatrix} = [\vec{v}_{col1} \quad \vec{v}_{col2} \quad \vec{v}_{col3}]$$

where

$$\vec{v}_{col1} = \begin{bmatrix} v_{11} \\ v_{21} \\ v_{31} \end{bmatrix}, \quad \vec{v}_{col2} = \begin{bmatrix} v_{12} \\ v_{22} \\ v_{32} \end{bmatrix}, \text{ and } \vec{v}_{col3} = \begin{bmatrix} v_{13} \\ v_{23} \\ v_{33} \end{bmatrix}$$

We use the notation "col" in the subscript so that we know the vector refers to a column in a matrix.

We now define equality, addition, scalar multiplication, and subtraction on matrices:

- Two matrices are equal if and only if their corresponding components are equal; as such, two matrices must be of the same dimension in order to be compared.
- We add two matrices by adding their corresponding elements; as such, it only makes sense to add matrices of the same dimension.
- We multiply a scalar and a matrix by multiplying the scalar with every element in the matrix.
- We define subtraction in terms of matrix addition and scalar multiplication. That is, $A-B=A+(-1\cdot B)=A+(-B)$.

Example 2.2

Let

$$A=\begin{bmatrix} 1 & 5 \\ -2 & 3 \end{bmatrix}, B=\begin{bmatrix} 6 & 2 \\ 5 & -8 \end{bmatrix}, C=\begin{bmatrix} 1 & 5 \\ -2 & 3 \end{bmatrix}, \text{ and } D=\begin{bmatrix} 2 & 1 & -3 \\ -6 & 3 & 0 \end{bmatrix}$$

Then,

$$A+B=\begin{bmatrix} 1 & 5 \\ -2 & 3 \end{bmatrix}+\begin{bmatrix} 6 & 2 \\ 5 & -8 \end{bmatrix}=\begin{bmatrix} 1+6 & 5+2 \\ -2+5 & 3-8 \end{bmatrix}=\begin{bmatrix} 7 & 7 \\ 3 & -5 \end{bmatrix}$$

Clearly, $A=C$

$$3D=3\begin{bmatrix} 2 & 1 & -3 \\ -6 & 3 & 0 \end{bmatrix}=\begin{bmatrix} 3(2) & 3(1) & 3(-3) \\ 3(-6) & 3(3) & 3(0) \end{bmatrix}=\begin{bmatrix} 6 & 3 & -9 \\ -18 & 9 & 0 \end{bmatrix}$$

$$A-B=\begin{bmatrix} 1 & 5 \\ -2 & 3 \end{bmatrix}-\begin{bmatrix} 6 & 2 \\ 5 & -8 \end{bmatrix}=\begin{bmatrix} 1-6 & 5-2 \\ -2-5 & 3-(-8) \end{bmatrix}=\begin{bmatrix} -5 & 3 \\ -7 & 11 \end{bmatrix}$$

2.2 **Matrix Multiplication**

The next paragraph defines how to multiply two matrices together. Then in the subsequent subsections, we will make some important observations about matrix multiplication and relate it to the change of coordinates transformation we performed in Chapter 1. Furthermore, we will show how matrix-matrix multiplication can be used to combine change of coordinate transformations, which has some efficiency implications.

If A is an $m \times n$ matrix and B is an $n \times p$ matrix, then the product AB is defined and is an $m \times p$ matrix C, where the ij^{th} entry of the product C is given by taking the dot product of the ith row vector in A with the jth column vector in B, that is,

$$c_{ij} = \vec{u}_{row\,i} \cdot \vec{v}_{col\,j} \tag{2.1}$$

Example 2.3

Let $A = \begin{bmatrix} -5 & 5 & -4 \\ 3 & 2 & 1 \end{bmatrix}$ and $B = \begin{bmatrix} 2 & 1 & 0 \\ 0 & -2 & 1 \\ -1 & 2 & 3 \end{bmatrix}$

We first point out that the product AB is defined (and is a 2×3 matrix) because the number of columns of A equals the number of rows of B (i.e., if A is an $m \times n$ matrix and B is an $n \times p$ matrix, then the product AB is defined and is an $m \times p$ matrix). Applying Equation 2.1 yields:

$$AB = \begin{bmatrix} -1 & 5 & -4 \\ 3 & 2 & 1 \end{bmatrix} \begin{bmatrix} 2 & 1 & 0 \\ 0 & -2 & 1 \\ -1 & 2 & 3 \end{bmatrix}$$

$$= \begin{bmatrix} (-1,5,-4)\cdot(2,0,-1) & (-1,5,-4)\cdot(1,-2,2) & (-1,5,-4)\cdot(0,1,3) \\ (3,2,1)\cdot(2,0,-1) & (3,2,1)\cdot(1,-2,2) & (3,2,1)\cdot(0,1,3) \end{bmatrix} = \begin{bmatrix} 2 & -19 & -7 \\ 5 & 1 & 5 \end{bmatrix}$$

Observe that BA is not defined because the number of columns in B does *not* equal the number of rows in A. This demonstrates that, in general, matrix multiplication is not commutative; that is, $AB \neq BA$.

2.2.1 Vector-Matrix Multiplication

Consider the following vector-matrix multiplication:

$$\vec{u}B = [x, y, z] \begin{bmatrix} v_{11} & v_{12} & v_{13} \\ v_{21} & v_{22} & v_{23} \\ v_{31} & v_{32} & v_{33} \end{bmatrix}$$

Observe that $\vec{u}B$ evaluates to a 1×3 row vector in this case. Now, applying Equation 2.1 gives:

$$\vec{u}B = [\vec{u} \cdot \vec{v}_{col1}, \quad \vec{u} \cdot \vec{v}_{col2}, \quad \vec{u} \cdot \vec{v}_{col3}]$$
$$= [(x,y,z)\cdot(v_{11}, v_{21}, v_{31}), \quad (x,y,z)\cdot(v_{12}, v_{22}, v_{32}), \quad (x,y,z)\cdot(v_{13}, v_{23}, v_{33})]$$
$$= [xv_{11} + yv_{21} + zv_{31}, \quad xv_{12} + yv_{22} + zv_{32}, \quad xv_{13} + yv_{23} + zv_{33}]$$
$$= [xv_{11}, \quad xv_{12}, \quad xv_{13}] + [yv_{21}, \quad yv_{22}, \quad yv_{23}] + [zv_{31}, \quad zv_{32}, \quad zv_{33}]$$
$$= x[v_{11}, \quad v_{12}, \quad v_{13}] + y[v_{21}, \quad v_{22}, \quad v_{23}] + z[v_{31}, \quad v_{32}, \quad v_{33}]$$
$$= x\vec{v}_{row1} + y\vec{v}_{row2} + z\vec{v}_{row3}$$

Thus,

$$\vec{u}B = x\vec{v}_{row1} + y\vec{v}_{row2} + z\vec{v}_{row3} \tag{2.2}$$

Equation 2.2 is an example of a *linear combination*, and it says that the vector-matrix product $\vec{u}B$ is equivalent to a linear combination of the row vectors of the matrix B with scalar coefficients x, y, and z given by the vector $\vec{u}$. Note that, although we show this for a 1×3 row vector and a 3×3 matrix, the result is true in general.

In particular, observe that:

$$\vec{p}C = [x, y, z, 1]\begin{bmatrix} u_x & u_y & u_z & 0 \\ v_x & v_y & v_z & 0 \\ w_x & w_y & w_z & 0 \\ O_x & O_y & O_z & 1 \end{bmatrix} = x\vec{u} + y\vec{v} + z\vec{w} + 1\vec{O} = [x', y', z', 1]$$

and

$$\vec{p}C = [x, y, z, 0]\begin{bmatrix} u_x & u_y & u_z & 0 \\ v_x & v_y & v_z & 0 \\ w_x & w_y & w_z & 0 \\ O_x & O_y & O_z & 1 \end{bmatrix} = x\vec{u} + y\vec{v} + z\vec{w} = [x', y', z', 0]$$

This should look familiar, as it resembles our change of frame transformation from §1.5. Thus, if we augment the coordinates of our vectors $\vec{r} = (x, y, z)$ to 4D *homogeneous* coordinates $\vec{r} = (x, y, z, w)$ with the notation that $w = 1$ when $\vec{r}$ is a position vector (i.e., point) and $w = 0$ when $\vec{r}$ is a vector (i.e., magnitude and direction), then we can use the following matrix equation to perform the change of frame transformation:

$$\vec{p}_A C = [x, y, z, w]\begin{bmatrix} u_x & u_y & u_z & 0 \\ v_x & v_y & v_z & 0 \\ w_x & w_y & w_z & 0 \\ O_x & O_y & O_z & 1 \end{bmatrix} = x\vec{u} + y\vec{v} + z\vec{w} + w\vec{O} = \vec{p}_B = [x', y', z', w] \tag{2.3}$$

where the vectors $\vec{O} = (O_x, O_y, O_z, 1)$, $\vec{u} = (u_x, u_y, u_z, 0)$, $\vec{v} = (v_x, v_y, v_z, 0)$, and $\vec{w} = (w_x, w_y, w_z, 0)$ describe the origin, x-axis, y-axis, and z-axis, respectively, of frame A relative to frame B, in homogeneous coordinates.

Observe that Equation 2.3 gives us a very mechanical way of dealing with change of frame transformations. If given the vectors $\vec{O}$, $\vec{u}$, $\vec{v}$, and $\vec{w}$ that describe frame A relative to B, then we just plug these vectors into the rows of a matrix to build the matrix C. (We call C the *change of frame matrix from A to B* or *change of coordinates matrix from A to B*.) Then, given the vector/point $\vec{p}_A = (x, y, z, w)$ that specifies a vector/point relative to frame A, we obtain the same vector/point, identified by $\vec{p}_B=(x',y',z',w)$ relative to frame B, by performing the vector-matrix multiplication: $\vec{p}_B=\vec{p}_A C$.

2.2.2 Matrix-Matrix Multiplication and Associativity

Suppose now that we have three frames: F, G, and H. Moreover, let A be the change of frame matrix from F to G, and let B be the change of frame matrix from G to H. Suppose we have the vector $\vec{p}_F$ and we want to describe the same vector relative to frame H, that is, $\vec{p}_H$. One way to do this is step-by-step:

$$(\vec{p}_F A)B=\vec{p}_H$$
$$(\vec{p}_G)B=\vec{p}_H$$

However, because matrix multiplication is associative (a fact given in any linear algebra text), we can write this as:

$$\vec{p}_F(AB)=\vec{p}_H$$

In this sense, the matrix $C = AB$ can be thought of as the change of frame matrix from F directly to H; it combines the effects of A and B into a net matrix.

This has performance implications. To see this, assume that a 3D object is composed of 20,000 points and that we want to apply two successive change of frame transformations to the object. Using the step-by-step approach, we would require $20{,}000 \times 2$ vector-matrix multiplications. On the other hand, using the combined matrix approach requires 20,000 vector-matrix multiplications and one matrix-matrix multiplication. Clearly, one extra matrix-matrix multiplication is a cheap price to pay for the large savings in vector-matrix multiplications. (The vector-matrix multiplication savings improves even more if we require more than two successive change of frame transformations.)

Note: Again, matrix multiplication is not commutative, so, for A and B being distinct change of frame matrices, we expect that AB and BA do *not* represent the same composite change of frame matrix. More specifically, the order in which you multiply the matrices is the order in which the transformations are applied, and in general, it is not a commutative process.

2.3 The Transpose of a Matrix

The *transpose* of a matrix is found by interchanging the rows and columns of the matrix. Thus the transpose of an $m \times n$ matrix is an $n \times m$ matrix. We denote the transpose of a matrix M as M^T.

Example 2.4

Find the transpose for the following three matrices:

$$A = \begin{bmatrix} 2 & -1 & 8 \\ 3 & 6 & -4 \end{bmatrix} \quad B = \begin{bmatrix} a & b & c \\ d & e & f \\ g & h & i \end{bmatrix} \quad C = \begin{bmatrix} 1 \\ 2 \\ 3 \\ 4 \end{bmatrix}$$

The transposes are found by interchanging the rows and columns, thus

$$A^T = \begin{bmatrix} 2 & 3 \\ -1 & 6 \\ 8 & -4 \end{bmatrix} \quad B^T = \begin{bmatrix} a & d & g \\ b & e & h \\ c & f & i \end{bmatrix} \quad C^T = \begin{bmatrix} 1 & 2 & 3 & 4 \end{bmatrix}$$

2.4 The Identity Matrix

There is a special matrix called the *identity matrix*. The identity matrix is a square matrix that has zeros for all elements except along the main diagonal, and moreover, the elements along the main diagonal are all ones.

For example, below are 2×2, 3×3, and 4×4 identity matrices.

$$\begin{bmatrix} 1 & 0 \\ 0 & 1 \end{bmatrix} \quad \begin{bmatrix} 1 & 0 & 0 \\ 0 & 1 & 0 \\ 0 & 0 & 1 \end{bmatrix} \quad \begin{bmatrix} 1 & 0 & 0 & 0 \\ 0 & 1 & 0 & 0 \\ 0 & 0 & 1 & 0 \\ 0 & 0 & 0 & 1 \end{bmatrix}$$

The identity matrix acts as a multiplicative identity; that is,

$$MI = IM = M$$

In other words, multiplying a matrix by the identity matrix does not change the matrix. Further, multiplying with the identity matrix is a particular case when matrix multiplication is commutative. The identity matrix can be thought of as the number 1 for matrices.

Example 2.5

Let $M = \begin{bmatrix} 1 & 2 \\ 0 & 4 \end{bmatrix}$ and let $I = \begin{bmatrix} 1 & 0 \\ 0 & 1 \end{bmatrix}$. Verify that $MI = IM = M$.

Applying Equation 2.1 yields:

$$MI = \begin{bmatrix} 1 & 2 \\ 0 & 4 \end{bmatrix}\begin{bmatrix} 1 & 0 \\ 0 & 1 \end{bmatrix} = \begin{bmatrix} (1,2)\cdot(1,0) & (1,2)\cdot(0,1) \\ (0,4)\cdot(1,0) & (0,4)\cdot(0,1) \end{bmatrix} = \begin{bmatrix} 1 & 2 \\ 0 & 4 \end{bmatrix}$$

and

$$IM = \begin{bmatrix} 1 & 0 \\ 0 & 1 \end{bmatrix} \begin{bmatrix} 1 & 2 \\ 0 & 4 \end{bmatrix} = \begin{bmatrix} (1,0)\cdot(1,0) & (1,0)\cdot(2,4) \\ (0,1)\cdot(1,0) & (0,1)\cdot(2,4) \end{bmatrix} = \begin{bmatrix} 1 & 2 \\ 0 & 4 \end{bmatrix}$$

Thus it is true that $MI = IM = M$.

2.5 The Inverse of a Matrix

Matrix algebra does not define a division operation, but it does define a multiplicative inverse operation. The following list summarizes the important information about inverses:

■ Only square matrices have inverses; therefore, when we speak of matrix inverses we assume we are dealing with a square matrix.

■ The inverse of an $n \times n$ matrix M is an $n \times n$ matrix denoted as M^{-1}.

■ The inverse is unique.

■ Not every square matrix has an inverse. A matrix that does have an inverse is said to be *invertible*, and a matrix that does not have an inverse is said to be *singular*.

■ Multiplying a matrix with its inverse results in the identity matrix: $MM^{-1} = M^{-1}M = I$. Note that multiplying a matrix with its inverse is a case when matrix multiplication is commutative.

Matrix inverses are useful for solving for other matrices in a matrix equation. For example, suppose that we are given $\vec{p}_B$ and we are given the change of frame matrix, M, from frame A to frame B; that is, $\vec{p}_B = \vec{p}_A M$. We want to solve for $\vec{p}_A$. In other words, instead of mapping from A to B, we want the matrix that maps us from B to A. Then given $\vec{p}_B$ we can find $\vec{p}_A$. To find this matrix, suppose that M is invertible (i.e., M^{-1} exists). We can solve for $\vec{p}_A$ like so:

$$\vec{p}_B = \vec{p}_A M$$
$$\vec{p}_B M^{-1} = \vec{p}_A M M^{-1} \qquad \text{Multiply both sides of the equation by } M^{-1}.$$
$$\vec{p}_B M^{-1} = \vec{p}_A I \qquad \qquad MM^{-1} = I, \text{ by definition of inverse.}$$
$$\vec{p}_B M^{-1} = \vec{p}_A \qquad \qquad \vec{p}_A I = \vec{p}_A, \text{ by definition of the identity matrix.}$$

Thus the matrix M^{-1} is the change of frame matrix from B to A.

Figure 2.1 illustrates the relationship between a change of frame matrix and its inverse. Also note that all of the change of frame mappings that we do in this book will be invertible, so we won't have to worry about whether or not the inverse exists.

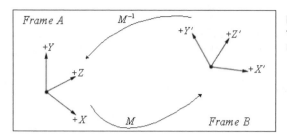

Figure 2.1: *M* maps from *A* to *B* and *M*⁻¹ maps from *B* to *A*.

Techniques for finding inverses are beyond the scope of this book, but they are described in any linear algebra textbook (it is not difficult; it is just not worth digressing into the procedure here). In §2.6 we will learn about a D3DX function that will find the inverse of a matrix for us, and in the next chapter we will simply give the inverses of the important types of matrices that we will work with in this book.

To conclude this section on inverses we present the following useful property for the inverse of a product: $(GH)^{-1} = H^{-1} G^{-1}$. This property assumes both G and H are invertible and that they are both square matrices of the same dimension. This property is easy to see if we view the matrices G and H as change of frame matrices, as shown in Figure 2.2.

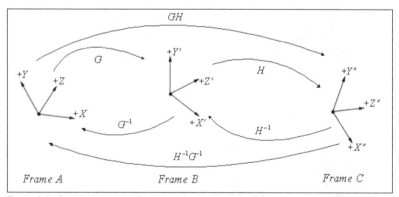

Figure 2.2: *G* maps from *A* to *B*, *H* maps from *B* to *C*, and *GH* maps from *A* directly to *C*. *H*⁻¹ maps from *C* to *B*, *G*⁻¹ maps from *B* to *A*, and *H*⁻¹*G*⁻¹ maps from *C* directly to *A*.

2.6 **D3DX Matrices**

As equation 2.3 illustrated, we can use 1×4 and 4×4 matrices to map a vector from one frame to another. In the next chapter, we will find that 1×4 and 4×4 matrices can be used to geometrically transform vectors as well. However, it is important to note that in this book, we generally use 3D vectors up until the time we are ready to multiply them by a matrix; then, right before we do the multiplication, we augment the 3D vector to a 4D vector and place a 0 or 1 in the fourth component based on whether the vector represents a point or a magnitude and direction quantity.

To represent matrices in D3DX, we use the D3DXMATRIX class, which is defined as follows:

```
typedef struct D3DXMATRIX : public D3DMATRIX
{
public:
D3DXMATRIX() {};
D3DXMATRIX( CONST FLOAT * );
D3DXMATRIX( CONST D3DMATRIX& );
D3DXMATRIX( CONST D3DXFLOAT16 * );
D3DXMATRIX(FLOAT _11, FLOAT _12, FLOAT _13, FLOAT _14,
           FLOAT _21, FLOAT _22, FLOAT _23, FLOAT _24,
           FLOAT _31, FLOAT _32, FLOAT _33, FLOAT _34,
           FLOAT _41, FLOAT _42, FLOAT _43, FLOAT _44);

// access grants
FLOAT& operator () ( UINT Row, UINT Col );
FLOAT  operator () ( UINT Row, UINT Col ) const;

// casting operators
operator FLOAT* ();
operator CONST FLOAT* () const;

// assignment operators
D3DXMATRIX& operator *= ( CONST D3DXMATRIX& );
D3DXMATRIX& operator += ( CONST D3DXMATRIX& );
D3DXMATRIX& operator -= ( CONST D3DXMATRIX& );
D3DXMATRIX& operator *= ( FLOAT );
D3DXMATRIX& operator /= ( FLOAT );

// unary operators
D3DXMATRIX operator + () const;
D3DXMATRIX operator - () const;

// binary operators
D3DXMATRIX operator * ( CONST D3DXMATRIX& ) const;
D3DXMATRIX operator + ( CONST D3DXMATRIX& ) const;
D3DXMATRIX operator - ( CONST D3DXMATRIX& ) const;
D3DXMATRIX operator * ( FLOAT ) const;
D3DXMATRIX operator / ( FLOAT ) const;

friend D3DXMATRIX operator*(FLOAT,
                            CONST D3DXMATRIX& );

BOOL operator == ( CONST D3DXMATRIX& ) const;
BOOL operator != ( CONST D3DXMATRIX& ) const;

} D3DXMATRIX, *LPD3DXMATRIX;
```

Observe that D3DXMATRIX inherits its data members from D3DMATRIX, which is defined as:

```
typedef struct _D3DMATRIX {
    union {
        struct {
            float     _11, _12, _13, _14;
            float     _21, _22, _23, _24;
            float     _31, _32, _33, _34;
            float     _41, _42, _43, _44;
        };
        float m[4][4];
    };
} D3DMATRIX;
```

The D3DXMATRIX class has a myriad of useful operators, such as testing for equality, adding, subtracting, and multiplying matrices. In addition, the over-loaded parenthesis operator provides a convenient syntax for accessing the elements in a matrix.

In addition to the above class, the D3DX library includes the following four useful functions for obtaining the 4×4 identity matrix, computing the transpose of a matrix, computing the inverse of a matrix, and multiplying a 1×4 vector and a 4×4 matrix.

■ D3DXMATRIX *D3DXMatrixIdentity(
        D3DXMATRIX *pOut);   // Makes input the identity matrix.

■ D3DXMATRIX *WINAPI D3DXMatrixTranspose(
        D3DXMATRIX *pOut,   // Output M^T
        CONST D3DXMATRIX *pM);   // Input M

■ D3DXMATRIX *WINAPI D3DXMatrixInverse(
        D3DXMATRIX *pOut,   // Output M^{-1}
        FLOAT *pDeterminant,   // Not needed, specify zero
        CONST D3DXMATRIX *pM);   // Input M

■ D3DXVECTOR4 *WINAPI D3DXVec4Transform(
        D3DXVECTOR4 *pOut,   // Output $\bar{v}M$
        CONST D3DXVECTOR4 *pV,   // Input $\bar{v}$
        CONST D3DXMATRIX *pM);   // Input M

Note: Remember to link the d3dx9.lib library file with your applica-tion to use any D3DX code; moreover, you will also need to #include <d3dx9.h>.

The following code provides some examples on how to use the D3DXMATRIX class and the four functions listed above.

```
#include <d3dx9.h>
#include <iostream>
using namespace std;

// Overload the "<<" operators so that we can use cout to
// output D3DXVECTOR4 and D3DXMATRIX objects.

ostream& operator<<(ostream& os, D3DXVECTOR4& v)
{
    os << "(" << v.x << ", " << v.y << ", "
        << v.z << ", " << v.w << ")";
    return os;
}

ostream& operator<<(ostream& os, D3DXMATRIX& m)
{
    for(int i = 0; i < 4; ++i)
    {
        for(int j = 0; j < 4; ++j)
            os << m(i, j) << "  ";
        os << endl;
    }
    return os;
}

int main()
{
    D3DXMATRIX A(1.0f, 0.0f, 0.0f, 0.0f,
                 0.0f, 2.0f, 0.0f, 0.0f,
                 0.0f, 0.0f, 4.0f, 0.0f,
                 1.0f, 2.0f, 3.0f, 1.0f);

    D3DXMATRIX B;
    D3DXMatrixIdentity(&B);

    // matrix-matrix multiplication
    D3DXMATRIX C = A*B;

    D3DXMATRIX D, E, F;

    D3DXMatrixTranspose(&D, &A);

    D3DXMatrixInverse(&E, 0, &A);

    F = A * E;

    D3DXVECTOR4 P(2.0f, 2.0f, 2.0f, 1.0f);
    D3DXVECTOR4 Q;
    D3DXVec4Transform(&Q, &P, &A);
```

```
        cout << "A = "              << endl << A << endl;
        cout << "B = "              << endl << B << endl;
        cout << "C = A*B = "        << endl << C << endl;
        cout << "D = transpose(A)= " << endl << D << endl;
        cout << "E = inverse(A) = "  << endl << E << endl;
        cout << "F = A*E = "        << endl << F << endl;
        cout << "P = "              << P << endl;
        cout << "Q = P*A = "        << Q << endl;


        return 0;
}
```

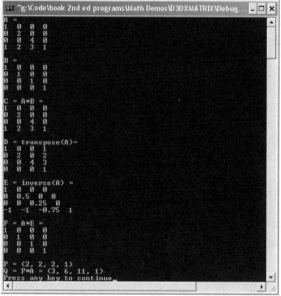

Figure 2.3: Output of the above program.

2.7 **Summary**

- An $m \times n$ matrix M is a rectangular array of real numbers with m rows and n columns. Two matrices of the same dimensions are equal if and only if their corresponding components are equal. We add two matrices of the same dimension by adding their corresponding elements. We multiply a scalar and a matrix by multiplying the scalar with every element in the matrix.

- If A is an $m \times n$ matrix and B is an $n \times p$ matrix, then the product AB is defined and is an $m \times p$ matrix C, where the ij^{th} entry of the product C is given by taking the dot product of the ith row vector in A with the jth column vector in B; that is, $c_{ij} = \vec{u}_{row\,i} \cdot \vec{v}_{col\,j}$.

■ Given $\vec{p}_A = (x, y, z, w)$ that specifies a vector (if $w = 0$) or point (if $w = 1$) relative to frame A, we obtain the same vector/point identified by $\vec{p}_B = (x', y', z', w)$ relative to frame B by performing the vector-matrix multiplication:

$$\vec{p}_A C = \begin{bmatrix} x, & y, & z, & w \end{bmatrix} \begin{bmatrix} u_x & u_y & u_z & 0 \\ v_x & v_y & v_z & 0 \\ w_x & w_y & w_z & 0 \\ O_x & O_y & O_z & 1 \end{bmatrix} = x\vec{u} + y\vec{v} + z\vec{w} + w\vec{O} = \vec{p}_B$$

where the vectors $\vec{O}$, $\vec{u}$, $\vec{v}$, and $\vec{w}$ describe the origin, x-axis, y-axis, and z-axis, respectively, of frame A relative to frame B.

■ Suppose we have three frames, F, G, and H, and let A be the change of frame matrix from F to G, and let B be the change of frame matrix from G to H. Using matrix-matrix multiplication, the matrix $C = AB$ can be thought of as the change of frame matrix from F directly to H; that is, matrix-matrix multiplication combines the effects of A and B into one net matrix, and so we can write: $\vec{p}_F (AB) = \vec{p}_H$.

■ The *transpose* of a matrix is found by interchanging the rows and columns of the matrix. Thus the transpose of an $m \times n$ matrix is an $n \times m$ matrix. We denote the transpose of a matrix M as M^T.

■ The identity matrix is a square matrix that has zeros for all elements except along the main diagonal, and moreover, the elements along the main diagonal are all ones.

■ Multiplying a matrix with its inverse results in the identity matrix: $MM^{-1} = M^{-1}M = I$. The inverse of a matrix, if it exists, is unique. Only square matrices have inverses and even then, a square matrix may not be invertible.

2.8 Exercises

1. Let

$$S = \begin{bmatrix} 3 & 0 & 0 & 0 \\ 0 & -2 & 0 & 0 \\ 0 & 0 & 4 & 0 \\ 0 & 0 & 0 & 1 \end{bmatrix}, T = \begin{bmatrix} 1 & 0 & 0 & 0 \\ 0 & 1 & 0 & 0 \\ 0 & 0 & 1 & 0 \\ 2 & -5 & -1 & 1 \end{bmatrix}, \text{ and } \vec{u} = \begin{bmatrix} 2 & -1 & 1 & 1 \end{bmatrix}$$

Compute the following matrix products: ST, TS, $\vec{u}S$, $\vec{u}T$, and $\vec{u}(ST)$. Does $ST = TS$?

2. Show that

$$\vec{u}\vec{v} = \begin{bmatrix} u_x, & u_y, & u_z \end{bmatrix} \begin{bmatrix} v_x \\ v_y \\ v_z \end{bmatrix} = \vec{u} \cdot \vec{v}$$

3. Using S and T from exercise 1, compute S^T, T^T, and $(ST)^T$. What is $(S^T)^T$ and $(T^T)^T$? Does $(ST)^T = T^T S^T$?

4. Using S and T from exercise 1, verify that $(ST)^{-1} = T^{-1} S^{-1}$. (Use D3DXMatrixInverse to do the calculations.)

5. Write the following linear combination as a vector-matrix multiplication: $\vec{v} = 2(1,2,3) + -4(-5,0,-1) + 3(2,-2,-3)$

6. Redo exercise 11 from Chapter 1 using Equation 2.3.

7. Show that

$$AB = \begin{bmatrix} u_{11} & u_{12} & u_{13} \\ u_{21} & u_{22} & u_{23} \\ u_{31} & u_{32} & u_{33} \end{bmatrix} \begin{bmatrix} v_{11} & v_{12} & v_{13} \\ v_{21} & v_{22} & v_{23} \\ v_{31} & v_{32} & v_{33} \end{bmatrix} = \begin{bmatrix} \vec{u}_{row1} \\ \vec{u}_{row2} \\ \vec{u}_{row3} \end{bmatrix} \begin{bmatrix} \vec{v}_{col1} & \vec{v}_{col2} & \vec{v}_{col3} \end{bmatrix} = \begin{bmatrix} \vec{u}_{row1}B \\ \vec{u}_{row2}B \\ \vec{u}_{row3}B \end{bmatrix}$$

Chapter 3

Transformations and Planes

We describe objects in our 3D worlds geometrically; that is, as a collection of triangles that approximate the exterior surfaces of the objects. It would certainly be a dull world if our objects remained motionless. Thus, we are interested in methods for transforming geometry; examples of geometric transformations are translation, rotation, and scaling. In this chapter, we develop matrix equations, which can be used to transform points and vectors in 3D space. In addition, we provide a brief primer on planes in 3-space.

Objectives:

- To understand how linear and affine transformations can be represented by matrices.
- To derive fundamental 3D affine transformation matrices used to scale, rotate, and translate objects.
- To learn how several transformation matrices can be combined into one net transformation matrix through matrix-matrix multiplication.
- To become familiar with a subset of functions provided by the D3DX library that are used for constructing transformation matrices.
- To learn why planes are useful and how we can represent them mathematically.
- To become familiar with a subset of the D3DX library used for working with planes.

3.1 **Linear Transformations**

3.1.1 **Definition**

We give a more specific definition than that found in linear algebra texts because we do not need such generality here. Let $T: \mathbb{R}^3 \to \mathbb{R}^3$ denote a (mathematical) function T that inputs 3D vectors and outputs 3D vectors. A function $T: \mathbb{R}^3 \to \mathbb{R}^3$ is a *linear transformation* if and only if, for vectors $\vec{u}=(u_x, u_y, u_z)$ and $\vec{v}=(v_x, v_y, v_z)$ and scalars α and β, we can write:

$$T(\alpha\vec{u}+\beta\vec{v})=\alpha T(\vec{u})+\beta T(\vec{v})=(x',y',z') \tag{3.1}$$

Note: All of the linear transformations in this chapter will be $T: \mathbb{R}^3 \to \mathbb{R}^3$; therefore, we will omit the "$\mathbb{R}^3 \to \mathbb{R}^3$" qualifier.

3.1.2 **Matrix Representation**

Let $\vec{u}=(x, y, z)$. Observe that we can always write this as:

$$\vec{u}=(x,y,z)=x\vec{i}+y\vec{j}+z\vec{k}=x(1,0,0)+y(0,1,0)+z(0,0,1)$$

The vectors $\vec{i}=(1,0,0)$, $\vec{j}=(0,1,0)$, and $\vec{k}=(0,0,1)$, which are unit vectors that aim along the coordinate axes, respectively, are called the *standard basis vectors* for $\mathbb{R}^3$. Now let T be a linear transformation; by linearity (i.e., Equation 3.1), we have:

$$T(\vec{u})=T(x\vec{i}+y\vec{j}+z\vec{k})=xT(\vec{i})+yT(\vec{j})+zT(\vec{k}) \tag{3.2}$$

Observe that this is nothing more than a linear combination, which, as we learned in the previous chapter, can be written by a vector-matrix multiplication. By Equation 2.2 we rewrite Equation 3.2 as:

$$T(\vec{u})=\vec{u}A=\begin{bmatrix} x, & y, & z \end{bmatrix}\begin{bmatrix} T(\vec{i}) \\ T(\vec{j}) \\ T(\vec{k}) \end{bmatrix}=\begin{bmatrix} x, & y, & z \end{bmatrix}\begin{bmatrix} a_{11} & a_{12} & a_{13} \\ a_{21} & a_{22} & a_{23} \\ a_{31} & a_{32} & a_{33} \end{bmatrix} \tag{3.3}$$

where $T(\vec{i})=(a_{11}, a_{12}, a_{13})$, $T(\vec{j})=(a_{21}, a_{22}, a_{23})$, and $T(\vec{k})=(a_{31}, a_{32}, a_{33})$.

We call the matrix A the matrix representation of the linear transformation T.

3.1.3 **Scaling**

Scaling refers to changing the size of an object as shown in Figure 3.1.

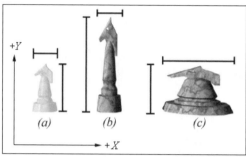

Figure 3.1: (a) Original horse. (b) The original horse scaled by 2 units on the y-axis. (c) The original horse scaled by 3 units on the x-axis. Scaling alters the size of objects — it can increase their size by scaling by a factor $x > 1$, or it can diminish their size by scaling by a factor $0 < x < 1$. In 3D graphics, a 3D object is typically composed of triangles, which in turn are defined by vertices (i.e., points); to scale a 3D object we apply a scaling transform to each of the object's vertices. This strategy applies to other transformations as well.

Let $\vec{u} = (x, y, z)$. We define the scaling transformation by:

$$S(\vec{u}) = (s_x x, s_y y, s_z z) \tag{3.4}$$

Observe that S scales the vector by s_x units on the x-axis, s_y units on the y-axis, and s_z units on the z-axis.

We now show that S is indeed a linear transformation. Consider,

$$S(\alpha\vec{u} + \beta\vec{v}) = \left(s_x(\alpha u_x + \beta v_x), s_y(\alpha u_y + \beta v_y), s_z(\alpha u_z + \beta v_z)\right)$$
$$= \left(s_x \alpha u_x, s_y \alpha u_y, s_z \alpha u_z\right) + \left(s_x \beta v_x, s_y \beta v_y, s_z \beta v_z\right)$$
$$= \alpha\left(s_x u_x, s_y u_y, s_z u_z\right) + \beta\left(s_x v_x, s_y v_y, s_z v_z\right)$$
$$= \alpha S(\vec{u}) + \beta S(\vec{v})$$

So it is linear, and thus there exists a matrix representation. To find the matrix representation, we just apply S to each of the standard basis vectors, as in Equation 3.2, and then stick the resulting vectors into the rows of the matrix (as in Equation 3.3):

$$S(\vec{i}) = (s_x \cdot 1, s_y \cdot 0, s_z \cdot 0) = (s_x, 0, 0)$$
$$S(\vec{j}) = (s_x \cdot 0, s_y \cdot 1, s_z \cdot 0) = (0, s_y, 0)$$
$$S(\vec{k}) = (s_x \cdot 0, s_y \cdot 0, s_z \cdot 1) = (0, 0, s_z)$$

Thus, the matrix representation of S is:

$$S = \begin{bmatrix} s_x & 0 & 0 \\ 0 & s_y & 0 \\ 0 & 0 & s_z \end{bmatrix}$$

We call this matrix the *scaling matrix*.

The inverse of the scaling matrix is given by:

$$S^{-1} = \begin{bmatrix} 1/s_x & 0 & 0 \\ 0 & 1/s_y & 0 \\ 0 & 0 & 1/s_z \end{bmatrix}$$

Example 3.1

Suppose we have a square defined by a minimum point $(-4, -4, 0)$ and a maximum point $(4, 4, 0)$. Suppose now that we wish to scale the square 0.5 units on the x-axis, 2.0 units on the y-axis, and leave the z-axis unchanged. The corresponding scaling matrix is:

$$S = \begin{bmatrix} 0.5 & 0 & 0 \\ 0 & 2 & 0 \\ 0 & 0 & 1 \end{bmatrix}$$

Now to actually scale (transform) the square, we multiply both the minimum point and maximum point by this matrix:

$$[-4,-4,0] \begin{bmatrix} 0.5 & 0 & 0 \\ 0 & 2 & 0 \\ 0 & 0 & 1 \end{bmatrix} = [-2,-8,0] \qquad [4,4,0] \begin{bmatrix} 0.5 & 0 & 0 \\ 0 & 2 & 0 \\ 0 & 0 & 1 \end{bmatrix} = [2,8,0]$$

The result is shown in Figure 3.2.

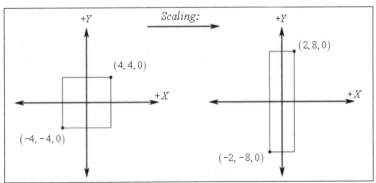

Figure 3.2: Scaling by one-half units on the *x*-axis and two units on the *y*-axis. Note that when looking down the negative *z*-axis, the geometry is basically 2D since $z = 0$.

3.1.4 **Rotation about the Coordinate Axes**

In this section, we show how to rotate about one of the coordinate axes. Figure 3.3 shows an example of a rotation.

Figure 3.3:
Clockwise rotation of an object by an angle θ.

Consider Figure 3.4, where we are looking directly down the positive x-axis to see the yz-plane. We have the vector $\vec{u}=(x,y,z)$ and, if we rotate it clockwise by an angle θ around the x-axis, we get the new rotated vector $\vec{u}'=(x',y',z')$. Our goal is to find a relationship that expresses the coordinates of $\vec{u}'$ in terms of the coordinates of $\vec{u}$ and the angle θ; in this way, we will have a formula for rotating a vector by an angle θ.

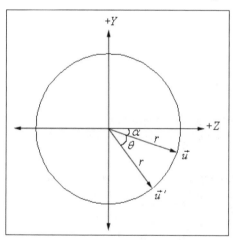

Figure 3.4: We rotate a vector $\vec{u}$ by an angle θ to get a new vector $\vec{u}'$. Note that rotation preserves length; thus, both $\vec{u}$ and $\vec{u}'$ have length r.

First note that because we are rotating about the x-axis, the x-coordinates for $\vec{u}$ and $\vec{u}'$ are the same; that is, $x'=x$. Now observe that we can express the y and z coordinates of $\vec{u}$ using polar coordinates, as follows:

$$y=-r\sin\alpha \qquad (3.5)$$
$$z=r\cos\alpha \qquad (3.6)$$

(The negative sign comes from the fact that we measure positive angles clockwise.) Similarly, we express the y and z coordinates of $\vec{u}'$ using polar coordinates, then apply the sum of angles trigonometric identity, and then use Equations 3.5 and 3.6:

$$y' = -r\sin(\alpha+\theta) = -r\sin\alpha\cos\theta - r\cos\alpha\sin\theta = y\cos\theta - z\sin\theta$$
$$z' = -r\cos(\alpha+\theta) = -r\cos\alpha\cos\theta - r\sin\alpha\sin\theta = z\cos\theta - y\sin\theta$$

Hence, we define the x-axis rotation transform R_x by:

$$R_x(\vec{u}) = \left(x, y\cos\theta - z\sin\theta, y\sin\theta + z\cos\theta\right) \tag{3.7}$$

We leave it as an exercise to show that this transformation is linear. To find the matrix representation, we just apply R_x to each of the standard basis vectors, as in Equation 3.2, and then stick the resulting vectors into the rows of the matrix (as in Equation 3.3):

$$R_x\left(\vec{i}\right) = \left(1, 0\cdot\cos\theta - 0\cdot\sin\theta, 0\cdot\sin\theta + 0\cdot\cos\theta\right) = \left(1, 0, 0\right)$$
$$R_x\left(\vec{j}\right) = \left(0, 1\cdot\cos\theta - 0\cdot\sin\theta, 1\cdot\sin\theta + 0\cdot\cos\theta\right) = \left(0, \cos\theta, \sin\theta\right)$$
$$R_x\left(\vec{k}\right) = \left(0, 0\cdot\cos\theta - 1\cdot\sin\theta, 0\cdot\sin\theta + 1\cdot\cos\theta\right) = \left(0, -\sin\theta, \cos\theta\right)$$

Thus, the matrix representation of R_x is:

$$R_x = \begin{bmatrix} 1 & 0 & 0 \\ 0 & \cos\theta & \sin\theta \\ 0 & -\sin\theta & \cos\theta \end{bmatrix}$$

We call this matrix the *x-axis rotation matrix*.

Note: In a left-handed coordinate system, positive angles go clockwise when looking down the positive axis of rotation toward the origin.

In an analogous way, we can construct the y- and z-axis rotation matrices:

$$R_y = \begin{bmatrix} \cos\theta & 0 & -\sin\theta \\ 0 & 1 & 0 \\ \sin\theta & 0 & \cos\theta \end{bmatrix} \text{ and } R_z = \begin{bmatrix} \cos\theta & \sin\theta & 0 \\ -\sin\theta & \cos\theta & 0 \\ 0 & 0 & 1 \end{bmatrix}$$

The rotation matrices have an interesting property. Each row vector is unit length (verify) and the row vectors are mutually orthogonal (verify). Thus the row vectors are *orthonormal* (i.e., mutually orthogonal and unit length). A matrix whose rows are orthonormal is said to be an *orthogonal matrix*. An orthogonal matrix has the attractive property that its inverse is actually equal to its transpose. For example:

$$R_x^{-1} = R_x^T = \begin{bmatrix} 1 & 0 & 0 \\ 0 & \cos\theta & -\sin\theta \\ 0 & \sin\theta & \cos\theta \end{bmatrix}$$

In general, orthogonal matrices are desirable to work with since their inverses are easy (and efficient) to compute.

Example 3.2

Suppose we have a square defined by a minimum point (–1, 0, –1) and a maximum point (1, 0, 1). Suppose now that we wish to rotate the square –30° clockwise about the y-axis (i.e., 30° counterclockwise). The corresponding rotating matrix is:

$$R_y = \begin{bmatrix} \cos\theta & 0 & -\sin\theta \\ 0 & 1 & 0 \\ \sin\theta & 0 & \cos\theta \end{bmatrix} = \begin{bmatrix} \cos(-30°) & 0 & -\sin(-30°) \\ 0 & 1 & 0 \\ \sin(-30°) & 0 & \cos(-30°) \end{bmatrix} = \begin{bmatrix} \frac{\sqrt{3}}{2} & 0 & \frac{1}{2} \\ 0 & 1 & 0 \\ -\frac{1}{2} & 0 & \frac{\sqrt{3}}{2} \end{bmatrix}$$

Now to actually rotate (transform) the square, we multiply both the minimum point and maximum point by this matrix:

$$[-1,0,-1]\begin{bmatrix} \frac{\sqrt{3}}{2} & 0 & \frac{1}{2} \\ 0 & 1 & 0 \\ -\frac{1}{2} & 0 & \frac{\sqrt{3}}{2} \end{bmatrix} \approx [-0.36, 0, -1.36]$$

$$[1,0,1]\begin{bmatrix} \frac{\sqrt{3}}{2} & 0 & \frac{1}{2} \\ 0 & 1 & 0 \\ -\frac{1}{2} & 0 & \frac{\sqrt{3}}{2} \end{bmatrix} \approx [0.36, 0, 1.36]$$

The result is shown in Figure 3.5.

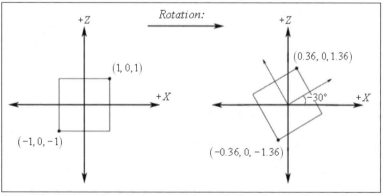

Figure 3.5: Rotating –30° clockwise around the y-axis. Note that when looking down the positive y-axis, the geometry is basically 2D since $y = 0$.

3.1.5 **Rotation about an Arbitrary Axis**

If you have a pivot joint and attached rod, as shown in Figure 3.6, you will observe that you can, in fact, aim the rod "axis" in any direction and rotate about that axis. Such pivot and rod models appear in real life; for example, you can point your arm in some arbitrary direction and rotate it (albeit, your range of motion is restricted). Thus, having an arbitrary axis rotation matrix is desirable.

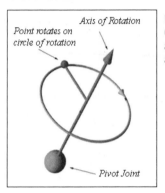

Figure 3.6: Clockwise rotation about an arbitrary axis.

The arbitrary axis rotation matrix is given by:

$$R_q = \begin{bmatrix} c+x^2(1-c) & xy(1-c)+zs & xz(1-c)-ys \\ xy(1-c)-zs & c+y^2(1-c) & yz(1-c)+xs \\ xz(1-c)+ys & yz(1-c)-xs & c+z^2(1-c) \end{bmatrix}$$

where $c=\cos\theta$, $s=\sin\theta$, and $\vec{q}=(x,y,z)$ is the vector (axis) we want to rotate θ radians around. For a derivation of this matrix, see [Schneider03] or [Möller02]; each text offers a different perspective/explanation. As with the other rotation matrices, this matrix is orthogonal and hence the inverse is equal to its transpose.

3.2 **Affine Transformations**

3.2.1 **Definition and Matrix Representation**

A linear transformation cannot describe all the transformations we wish to do; therefore, we augment to a larger class of functions called affine transformations. An *affine transformation* is a linear transformation plus a translation vector $\vec{b}$; that is:

$$T(\vec{u})=\vec{u}A+\vec{b}=\begin{bmatrix} x, & y, & z \end{bmatrix}\begin{bmatrix} a_{11} & a_{12} & a_{13} \\ a_{21} & a_{22} & a_{23} \\ a_{31} & a_{32} & a_{33} \end{bmatrix}+\begin{bmatrix} b_x, & b_y, & b_z \end{bmatrix}=\begin{bmatrix} x', & y', & z' \end{bmatrix}$$

where A is the matrix representation of a linear transformation. If we augment to homogeneous coordinates with $w = 1$, then we can write this more compactly as:

$$\begin{bmatrix} x, & y, & z & 1 \end{bmatrix} \begin{bmatrix} a_{11} & a_{12} & a_{13} & 0 \\ a_{21} & a_{22} & a_{23} & 0 \\ a_{31} & a_{32} & a_{32} & 0 \\ b_x & b_y & b_z & 1 \end{bmatrix} = \begin{bmatrix} x', & y', & z', & 1 \end{bmatrix} \qquad (3.8)$$

Observe that the addition by $\vec{b}$ is essentially a translation (i.e., change in position). We do not want to apply this to vectors because vectors have no position. However, we still want to apply the linear part of the affine transformation to vectors. If we set $w = 0$ in the fourth component for vectors, then the translation by $\vec{b}$ is *not* applied (verify by doing the matrix multiplication). If we set $w = 1$ in the fourth component for points, then the translation by $\vec{b}$ is applied (verify by doing the matrix multiplication). Thus, once again we augment to homogeneous coordinates and use the notation that $w = 0$ for vectors and $w = 1$ for points, as we did in Equation 2.3.

3.2.2 **Translation**

The *identity transformation* is a linear transformation that just returns its argument; that is, $I(\vec{u}) = \vec{u}$. It can be shown that the matrix representation of this linear transformation is the identity matrix.

Now, we define the translation transformation to be the affine transformation whose linear transformation is the identity transformation; that is,

$$T(\vec{u}) = \vec{u} \begin{bmatrix} 1 & 0 & 0 \\ 0 & 1 & 0 \\ 0 & 0 & 1 \end{bmatrix} + \vec{b} = \vec{u} + \vec{b}$$

As you can see, this affine transformation simply translates (or displaces) $\vec{u}$ by $\vec{b}$, as shown in Figure 3.7.

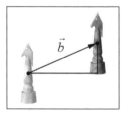

Figure 3.7: Displacing the horse by some displacement vector $\vec{b}$.

By Equation 3.8, the affine matrix representation of this is:

$$T = \begin{bmatrix} 1 & 0 & 0 & 0 \\ 0 & 1 & 0 & 0 \\ 0 & 0 & 1 & 0 \\ b_x & b_y & b_z & 1 \end{bmatrix}$$

We call this the *translation matrix*.

The inverse of the translation matrix is given by:

$$T^{-1} = \begin{bmatrix} 1 & 0 & 0 & 0 \\ 0 & 1 & 0 & 0 \\ 0 & 0 & 1 & 0 \\ -b_x & -b_y & -b_z & 1 \end{bmatrix}$$

Example 3.3

Suppose we have a square defined by a minimum point (–8, 2, 0) and a maximum point (–2, 8, 0). Suppose now that we wish to translate the square 12 units on the x-axis, –10 units on the y-axis, and leave the z-axis unchanged. The corresponding translation matrix is:

$$T = \begin{bmatrix} 1 & 0 & 0 & 0 \\ 0 & 1 & 0 & 0 \\ 0 & 0 & 1 & 0 \\ 12 & -10 & 0 & 1 \end{bmatrix}$$

Now to actually translate (transform) the square, we multiply both the minimum point and maximum point by this matrix:

$$[-8,2,0,1] \begin{bmatrix} 1 & 0 & 0 & 0 \\ 0 & 1 & 0 & 0 \\ 0 & 0 & 1 & 0 \\ 12 & -10 & 0 & 1 \end{bmatrix} = [4,-8,0,1]$$

$$[-2,8,0,1] \begin{bmatrix} 1 & 0 & 0 & 0 \\ 0 & 1 & 0 & 0 \\ 0 & 0 & 1 & 0 \\ 12 & -10 & 0 & 1 \end{bmatrix} = [10,-2,0,1]$$

The result is shown in Figure 3.8.

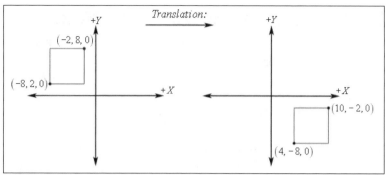

Figure 3.8: Translating 12 units on the *x*-axis and −10 units on the *y*-axis. Note that when looking down the negative *z*-axis, the geometry is basically 2D since $z = 0$.

3.2.3 Affine Matrices for Scaling and Rotation

Observe that if $\vec{b}=\vec{0}$, the affine transformation reduces to a linear transformation. Thus, we can express any linear transformation as an affine transformation with $\vec{b}=\vec{0}$. This, in turn, means we can represent any linear transformation by an affine matrix. The scaling and rotation matrices written using 4×4 affine matrices are as follows:

$$S=\begin{bmatrix} s_x & 0 & 0 & 0 \\ 0 & s_y & 0 & 0 \\ 0 & 0 & s_z & 0 \\ 0 & 0 & 0 & 1 \end{bmatrix} \quad S^{-1}=\begin{bmatrix} 1/s_x & 0 & 0 & 0 \\ 0 & 1/s_y & 0 & 0 \\ 0 & 0 & 1/s_z & 0 \\ 0 & 0 & 0 & 1 \end{bmatrix} \quad R_x=\begin{bmatrix} 1 & 0 & 0 & 0 \\ 0 & \cos\theta & \sin\theta & 0 \\ 0 & -\sin\theta & \cos\theta & 0 \\ 0 & 0 & 0 & 1 \end{bmatrix}$$

$$R_y=\begin{bmatrix} \cos\theta & 0 & -\sin\theta & 0 \\ 0 & 1 & 0 & 0 \\ \sin\theta & 0 & \cos\theta & 0 \\ 0 & 0 & 0 & 1 \end{bmatrix} \quad R_z=\begin{bmatrix} \cos\theta & \sin\theta & 0 & 0 \\ -\sin\theta & \cos\theta & 0 & 0 \\ 0 & 0 & 1 & 0 \\ 0 & 0 & 0 & 1 \end{bmatrix}$$

$$R_q=\begin{bmatrix} c+x^2(1-c) & xy(1-c)+zs & xz(1-c)-ys & 0 \\ xy(1-c)-zs & c+y^2(1-c) & yz(1-c)+xs & 0 \\ xz(1-c)+ys & yz(1-c)-xs & c+z^2(1-c) & 0 \\ 0 & 0 & 0 & 1 \end{bmatrix}$$

In this way, we can express all of our transformation consistently using 4×4 matrices.

Note: The inverses of the rotation matrices are still equal to the transpose of the 4×4 matrix.

3.3 **D3DX Transformation Functions**

In this section we summarize the D3DX-related functions for building the various transformation matrices for reference.

```
// Constructs a scaling matrix:
D3DXMATRIX *WINAPI D3DXMatrixScaling(
    D3DXMATRIX *pOut,               // Returns S
    FLOAT sx, FLOAT sy, FLOAT sz);  // Scaling factors


// Constructs an x-axis rotation matrix:
D3DXMATRIX *WINAPI D3DXMatrixRotationX(
    D3DXMATRIX *pOut,               // Returns Rx
    FLOAT Angle);                   // Angle θ to rotate


// Constructs a y-axis rotation matrix:
D3DXMATRIX *WINAPI D3DXMatrixRotationY(
    D3DXMATRIX *pOut,               // Returns Rv
    FLOAT Angle);                   // Angle θ to rotate


// Constructs a z-axis rotation matrix:
D3DXMATRIX *WINAPI D3DXMatrixRotationZ(
    D3DXMATRIX *pOut,               // Returns Rz
    FLOAT Angle);                   // Angle θ to rotate


// Constructs an arbitrary axis rotation matrix:
D3DXMATRIX *WINAPI D3DXMatrixRotationAxis(
    D3DXMATRIX *pOut,               // Returns Rñ
    CONST D3DXVECTOR3 *pV,          // Axis q̄ to rotate about
    FLOAT Angle);                   // Angle θ to rotate


// Constructs a translation matrix:
D3DXMATRIX *WINAPI D3DXMatrixTranslation(
    D3DXMATRIX *pOut,               // Returns T
    FLOAT x, FLOAT y, FLOAT z);     // Translation factors
```

Note: For the rotation matrices, the angles are given in radians. Observe that the above D3DX functions return pointers to `D3DXMATRIX*` objects; these pointers point to the same object as `pOut`, thereby allowing us to pass the functions as parameters to other functions (other D3DX functions do this also, which you may have noticed from Chapters 1 and 2). For example,

```
D3DXMATRIX M, T;
D3DXMatrixTranspose(&T, D3DXMatrixRotationX(&M));
```

3.4 **Composition of Affine Transformations**

Suppose S is a scaling matrix, R_y is a y-axis rotation matrix, and T is a translation matrix. We have a cube made up of eight vertices, $\vec{v}_i$ for $i = 0, 1, \dots, 7$, and we wish to apply these three transformations to each vertex successively. The obvious way to do this is step-by-step:

$$\big((\vec{v}_i S) R_y \big) T = \big(\vec{v}_i' R_y \big) T = \vec{v}_i'' T = \vec{v}_i''' \text{ for } i = 0, 1, \dots, 7$$

However, because matrix multiplication is associative, we can instead write this equivalently as:

$$\vec{v}_i \big(S R_y T \big) = \vec{v}_i''' \text{ for } i = 0, 1, \dots, 7$$

We can think of the matrix $C = S R_y T$ as a matrix that encapsulates all three transformations into one net affine transformation matrix. In other words, matrix-matrix multiplication allows us to concatenate transforms.

This has performance implications. To see this, assume that a 3D object is composed of 20,000 points and that we want to apply these three successive geometric transformations to the object. Using the step-by-step approach, we would require 20,000×3 vector-matrix multiplications. On the other hand, using the combined matrix approach requires 20,000 vector-matrix multiplications and two matrix-matrix multiplications. Clearly, two extra matrix-matrix multiplications is a cheap price to pay for the large savings in vector-matrix multiplications.

Note: Again, we point out that matrix multiplication is not commutative. This is even seen geometrically. For example, a rotation followed by a translation, which we can describe by the matrix product R_yT, does not result in the same transformation as the same translation followed by the same rotation, that is, TR_y. Figure 3.9 demonstrates this.

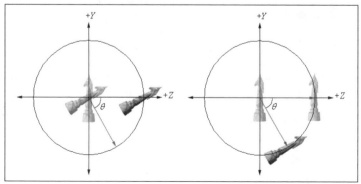

Figure 3.9: On the left, we rotate first and then translate. On the right, we translate first and then rotate.

3.5 **Planes**

We now switch gears and focus on planes for the rest of this chapter. A plane, commonly denoted by the symbol π, can be viewed as an infinitely thin, wide, and long sheet of paper. A plane can be specified with a vector $\vec{n}$ and a point on the plane $\vec{p}_0$. The vector $\vec{n}$, not necessarily unit length, is called the plane's *normal vector* and is perpendicular to the plane, as shown in Figure 3.10. A plane divides space into a positive half-space and a negative half-space. The *positive half-space* is the space in front of the plane, where the *front* of the plane is the side from which the normal vector emanates. The *negative half-space* is the space behind the plane.

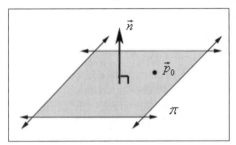

Figure 3.10: A plane defined by a normal vector $\vec{n}$ and a point on the plane $\vec{p}_0$.

By Figure 3.11, we see that the graph of a plane is all the points $\vec{p}$ that satisfy the equation:

$$\vec{n} \cdot \left(\vec{p} - \vec{p}_0 \right) = 0 \tag{3.9}$$

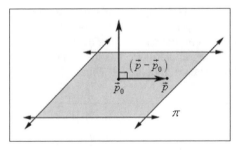

Figure 3.11: If $\vec{p}_0$ is a point on the plane, then the point $\vec{p}$ is also on the plane if the vector formed from $\left(\vec{p} - \vec{p}_0 \right)$ is orthogonal to the plane's normal vector.

When describing a particular plane, the normal $\vec{n}$ and a known point on the plane $\vec{p}_0$ are fixed, so it is typical to rewrite Equation 3.9 as:

$$\vec{n} \cdot \left(\vec{p} - \vec{p}_0 \right) = \vec{n} \cdot \vec{p} - \vec{n} \cdot \vec{p}_0 = \vec{n} \cdot \vec{p} + d = 0 \tag{3.10}$$

where $d = -\vec{n} \cdot \vec{p}_0$

Note: If the plane's normal vector $\vec{n}$ is of unit length, then $d=-\vec{n}\cdot\vec{p}_0$ gives the shortest signed distance from the origin to the plane (see Figure 3.12).

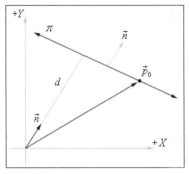

Figure 3.12: $|d|=|-\vec{n}\cdot\vec{p}_0|$ gives the length of the projection of $\vec{p}_0$ on $\vec{n}$. If we omit the absolute values, we get a signed length/distance (i.e., it may be negative).

Note: To make the illustrations simpler, we draw our figures in 2D and use a line to represent a plane. A line with a perpendicular normal can be thought of as a 2D plane since the line divides the 2D space into a positive half-space and negative half-space.

3.5.1 **D3DXPLANE**

When representing a plane in code, it suffices to store only the normal vector $\vec{n}$ and the constant d. It is useful to think of this as a 4D vector, which we denote as $(\vec{n},d)=(n_x,n_y,n_z,d)$. The D3DX library uses the following structure for a plane:

```
typedef struct D3DXPLANE
{
#ifdef __cplusplus
public:
    D3DXPLANE() {}
    D3DXPLANE( CONST FLOAT* );
    D3DXPLANE( CONST D3DXFLOAT16* );
    D3DXPLANE( FLOAT a, FLOAT b, FLOAT c, FLOAT d );

    // casting
    operator FLOAT* ();
    operator CONST FLOAT* () const;

    // assignment operators
    D3DXPLANE& operator *= ( FLOAT );
    D3DXPLANE& operator /= ( FLOAT );

    // unary operators
    D3DXPLANE operator + () const;
    D3DXPLANE operator - () const;

    // binary operators
    D3DXPLANE operator * ( FLOAT ) const;
```

```
   D3DXPLANE operator / ( FLOAT ) const;

   friend D3DXPLANE operator*( FLOAT, CONST D3DXPLANE& );

   BOOL operator == ( CONST D3DXPLANE& ) const;
   BOOL operator != ( CONST D3DXPLANE& ) const;

#endif //__cplusplus
   FLOAT a, b, c, d;
} D3DXPLANE, *LPD3DXPLANE;
```

where a, b, and c form the components of the plane's normal vector $\vec{n}$ and d is the constant d from Equation 3.10.

3.5.2 Point and Plane Spatial Relation

Equation 3.10 is primarily useful for testing the spatial location of points relative to a plane. Let $\pi = (\vec{n}, d)$ specify a plane and let $\vec{p}$ be a point, then:

If $\vec{n} \cdot \vec{p} + d = 0$, then $\vec{p}$ is coplanar with the plane.

If $\vec{n} \cdot \vec{p} + d > 0$, then $\vec{p}$ is in front of the plane and in the plane's positive half-space.

If $\vec{n} \cdot \vec{p} + d < 0$, then $\vec{p}$ is in back of the plane and in the plane's negative half-space.

For example, consider Figure 3.13a. Let $k = \vec{n} \cdot \vec{p}$ and $k_0 = \vec{n} \cdot \vec{p}_0$, and observe that in the case of the figure, $k > 0$, $k_0 > 0$, and $k > k_0$. Because $k - k_0 = \vec{n} \cdot \vec{p} - \vec{n} \cdot \vec{p}_0 = \vec{n} \cdot \vec{p} + d > 0$, we conclude the point $\vec{p}$ is in front of the plane, which agrees with the figure. As another example, suppose that we invert the plane normal as in Figure 3.13b. Then $k < 0$, $k_0 < 0$, and $k < k_0$. Because $k - k_0 = \vec{n} \cdot \vec{p} - \vec{n} \cdot \vec{p}_0 = \vec{n} \cdot \vec{p} + d < 0$, we conclude the point $\vec{p}$ is in back of the plane, which agrees with the figure. In the case that $\vec{p}$ is on the plane, then $k = k_0 \Rightarrow k - k_0 = \vec{n} \cdot \vec{p} - \vec{n} \cdot \vec{p}_0 = \vec{n} \cdot \vec{p} + d = 0$.

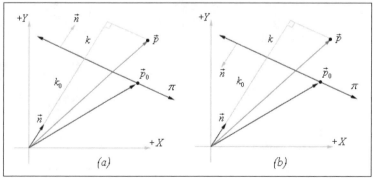

Figure 3.13: Point/plane spatial relation.

Note: If the plane's normal vector $\vec{n}$ is of unit length, then $\vec{n} \cdot \vec{p} + d$ gives the shortest signed distance from the plane to the point $\vec{p}$. This also comes from Figure 3.13; the shortest signed distance from $\vec{p}$ to the plane is $k - k_0 = \vec{n} \cdot \vec{p} + d$.

This next D3DX function evaluates $\vec{n} \cdot \vec{p} + d$ for a particular plane and point:

```
FLOAT D3DXPlaneDotCoord(
    CONST D3DXPLANE *pP,          // plane.
    CONST D3DXVECTOR3 *pV         // point.
);

// Test the locality of a point relative to a plane.
D3DXPLANE p(0.0f, 1.0f, 0.0f, 0.0f);

D3DXVECTOR3 v(3.0f, 5.0f, 2.0f);

float x = D3DXPlaneDotCoord( &p, &v );

if( x approximately equals 0.0f )  // v is coplanar to the plane.
if( x > 0 )                        // v is in positive half-space.
if( x < 0 )                        // v is in negative half-space.
```

Note: We say "approximately equals" due to floating-point imprecision.

Note: Methods similar to D3DXPlaneDotCoord are D3DXPlaneDot and D3DXPlaneDotNormal. See the DirectX documentation for details.

3.5.3 Construction

Besides directly specifying the normal and signed distance of a plane, we can calculate these two components in two other ways. Given the normal $\vec{n}$ and a known point on the plane $\vec{p}_0$, we can solve for the d component:

$$\vec{n} \cdot \vec{p}_0 + d = 0 \Rightarrow -d = \vec{n} \cdot \vec{p}_0 \Rightarrow d = -\vec{n} \cdot \vec{p}_0$$

The D3DX library provides the following function to perform this calculation:

```
D3DXPLANE *D3DXPlaneFromPointNormal(
    D3DXPLANE* pOut,              // Result.
    CONST D3DXVECTOR3* pPoint,    // Point on the plane.
    CONST D3DXVECTOR3* pNormal    // The normal of the plane.
);
```

The second way we can construct a plane is by specifying three distinct points on the plane.

Given the points $\vec{p}_0$, $\vec{p}_1$, $\vec{p}_2$, we can form two vectors on the plane:

$$\vec{u} = \vec{p}_1 - \vec{p}_0$$
$$\vec{v} = \vec{p}_2 - \vec{p}_0$$

From that we can compute the normal of the plane by taking the cross product of the two vectors on the plane. (Remember the left-hand-thumb rule.)

$$\vec{n} = \vec{u} \times \vec{v}$$

Then, we compute the signed distance as before; that is, $-(\vec{n} \cdot \vec{p}_0) = d$.

The D3DX library provides the following function to compute a plane given three points on the plane:

```
D3DXPLANE *D3DXPlaneFromPoints(
    D3DXPLANE* pOut,            // Result.
    CONST D3DXVECTOR3* pV1,     // Point 1 on the plane.
    CONST D3DXVECTOR3* pV2,     // Point 2 on the plane.
    CONST D3DXVECTOR3* pV3      // Point 3 on the plane.
);
```

3.5.4 Normalizing a Plane

Sometimes we might have a plane and would like to normalize the normal vector. At first thought, it would seem that we could just normalize the normal vector as we would any other vector. But recall $d = -\vec{n} \cdot \vec{p}_0$ in $\vec{n} \cdot \vec{p} + d = 0$. We see that the length of the normal vector influences the constant d. Therefore, if we normalize the normal vector, we must also recalculate d. We note that $\dfrac{d}{\|\vec{n}\|} = -\dfrac{\vec{n}}{\|\vec{n}\|} \cdot \vec{p}_0$.

Thus, we have the following formula to normalize the normal vector of the plane $\pi = (\vec{n}, d)$:

$$\frac{1}{\|\vec{n}\|}(\vec{n}, d) = \left(\frac{\vec{n}}{\|\vec{n}\|}, \frac{d}{\|\vec{n}\|}\right)$$

We can use the following D3DX function to normalize a plane's normal vector:

```
D3DXPLANE *D3DXPlaneNormalize(
    D3DXPLANE *pOut,          // Resulting normalized plane.
    CONST D3DXPLANE *pP       // Input plane.
);
```

3.5.5 **Transforming a Plane**

[Lengyel02] shows that we can transform a plane $\pi = (\vec{n}, d)$ by treating it as a 4D vector and multiplying it by the inverse-transpose of the desired transformation matrix. Note that the plane's normal vector must be normalized first.

We use the following D3DX function to do this:

```
D3DXPLANE *D3DXPlaneTransform(
    D3DXPLANE *pOut,         // Result
    CONST D3DXPLANE *pP,     // Input plane.
    CONST D3DXMATRIX *pM     // Transformation matrix.
);
```

Sample code:

```
D3DXMATRIX T(...);              // Initialize T to a desired transformation.
D3DXMATRIX inverseOfT;
D3DXMATRIX inverseTransposeOfT;


D3DXMatrixInverse( &inverseOfT, 0, &T );
D3DXMatrixTranspose( &inverseTransposeOfT, &inverseOfT );


D3DXPLANE p(...);              // Initialize plane.
D3DXPlaneNormalize( &p, &p ); // Make sure normal is normalized.


D3DXPlaneTransform( &p, &p, &inverseTransposeOfT );
```

3.5.6 **Nearest Point on a Plane to a Particular Point**

Suppose we have a point $\vec{p}$ in space and we would like to find the point $\vec{q}$ on the plane, $\pi = (\vec{n}, d)$, that is closest to $\vec{p}$. We note the plane's normal vector is assumed to be of unit length, which simplifies the problem a bit.

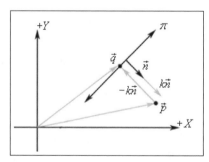

Figure 3.14: The point $\vec{q}$ on the plane $(\vec{n}, d)$ nearest to $\vec{p}$. Observe that the shortest signed distance k from $\vec{p}$ to the plane is positive since $\vec{p}$ is in the positive half-space of $(\vec{n}, d)$. If $\vec{p}$ were behind the plane, then $k < 0$.

By Figure 3.14 we can see that $\vec{q} = \vec{p} + (-k\vec{n})$, where k is the shortest signed distance from $\vec{p}$ to the plane, which is also the shortest signed distance between the points $\vec{p}$ and $\vec{q}$. Recall that if the plane's normal vector $\vec{n}$ is of unit length, then $\vec{n} \cdot \vec{p} + d$ gives the shortest signed distance from the plane to the point $\vec{p}$, that is, $k = \vec{n} \cdot \vec{p} + d$, and therefore, $\vec{q} = \vec{p} - (\vec{n} \cdot \vec{p} + d)\vec{n}$.

3.5.7 **Ray/Plane Intersection**

Given a ray $\vec{p}(t) = \vec{p}_0 + t\vec{u}$ and a plane $\vec{n} \cdot \vec{p} + d = 0$, we would like to know if the ray intersects the plane and also the point of intersection. To do this, we plug the ray into the plane equation and solve for the parameter t that satisfies the plane equation, thereby giving us the parameter that yields the intersection point:

$$\vec{n} \cdot \vec{p}(t) + d = 0 \qquad \text{Plug ray into plane equation}$$

$$\vec{n} \cdot \left(\vec{p}_0 + t\vec{u}\right) + d = 0 \qquad \text{Substitute}$$

$$\vec{n} \cdot \vec{p}_0 + \vec{n} \cdot t\vec{u} + d = 0 \qquad \text{Distributive property}$$

$$\vec{n} \cdot t\vec{u} = -d - \left(\vec{n} \cdot \vec{p}_0\right) \qquad \text{Add } -d - \left(\vec{n} \cdot \vec{p}_0\right) \text{ to both sides of the equation}$$

$$t\left(\vec{n} \cdot \vec{u}\right) = -d - \left(\vec{n} \cdot \vec{p}_0\right) \qquad \text{Associative property}$$

$$t = \frac{-d - \left(\vec{n} \cdot \vec{p}_0\right)}{\left(\vec{n} \cdot \vec{u}\right)} \qquad \text{Solve for } t$$

If t is not in the interval $[0, \infty)$, the ray does not intersect the plane, but the line coincident with the ray does. If t is in the interval $[0, \infty)$, then the ray does intersect the plane and the intersection point is found by plugging the parameter that satisfies the plane equation into the ray equation:

$$\vec{p}\left(\frac{-d - \left(\vec{n} \cdot \vec{p}_0\right)}{\left(\vec{n} \cdot \vec{u}\right)}\right) = \vec{p}_0 + \frac{-d - \left(\vec{n} \cdot \vec{p}_0\right)}{\left(\vec{n} \cdot \vec{u}\right)}\vec{u}$$

3.6 **Summary**

■   The fundamental affine transformation matrices — scaling, rotation, and translation — are given by:

$$S = \begin{bmatrix} s_x & 0 & 0 & 0 \\ 0 & s_y & 0 & 0 \\ 0 & 0 & s_z & 0 \\ 0 & 0 & 0 & 1 \end{bmatrix} \quad T = \begin{bmatrix} 1 & 0 & 0 & 0 \\ 0 & 1 & 0 & 0 \\ 0 & 0 & 1 & 0 \\ b_x & b_y & b_z & 1 \end{bmatrix}$$

$$R_x = \begin{bmatrix} 1 & 0 & 0 & 0 \\ 0 & \cos\theta & \sin\theta & 0 \\ 0 & -\sin\theta & \cos\theta & 0 \\ 0 & 0 & 0 & 1 \end{bmatrix} \quad R_y = \begin{bmatrix} \cos\theta & 0 & -\sin\theta & 0 \\ 0 & 1 & 0 & 0 \\ \sin\theta & 0 & \cos\theta & 0 \\ 0 & 0 & 0 & 1 \end{bmatrix}$$

$$R_z = \begin{bmatrix} \cos\theta & \sin\theta & 0 & 0 \\ -\sin\theta & \cos\theta & 0 & 0 \\ 0 & 0 & 1 & 0 \\ 0 & 0 & 0 & 1 \end{bmatrix}$$

■ We use 4×4 matrices to represent transformations and 1×4 homogeneous vectors to describe points and vectors, where we denote a point by setting the fourth component to $w=1$ and a vector by setting $w=0$. In this way, translations are applied to points but not to vectors.

■ A matrix is orthogonal if all of its row vectors are of unit length and mutually orthogonal. An orthogonal matrix has the special property that its inverse is equal to its transpose, thereby making the inverse computation very efficient. All the rotation matrices are orthogonal.

■ From the associative property of matrix multiplication, we can combine several transformation matrices into one net transformation matrix, which represents all of the individual transformations combined. In other words, matrix-matrix multiplication allows us to concatenate transforms.

■ Planes divide 3D space into two parts: a positive half-space, which is the space in front of the plane, and a negative half-space, which is the space behind the plane. Planes are useful for testing the locality of points relative to them (i.e., in what half-space a point exists relative to a particular plane). The plane equation is given by $\vec{n} \cdot \vec{p} + d = 0$, and its graph is the set of all points $\vec{p}$ that satisfy this equation.

3.7 Exercises

1. Show that the x-axis rotation transformation given by Equation 3.7 is a linear transformation.

2. Show that the identity function, defined by $I(\vec{u})=\vec{u}$, is a linear transformation, and show that its matrix representation is the identity matrix.

3. Show that the row vectors in the y-axis rotation matrix R_y are orthonormal.

4. Let R_y be the y-axis rotation matrix. Show that the transpose of this matrix is its inverse; that is, show $R_y R_y^T = R_y^T R_y = 1$.

5. In §3.1.4, we showed how the x-axis, y-axis, and z-axis rotation matrices could be derived directly. Another perspective is to think of these rotation matrices as special cases of the arbitrary axis rotation matrix. Show that the arbitrary axis rotation matrix reduces to the x-axis, y-axis, and z-axis rotation matrices when $\vec{q}$ equals $\vec{i}$, $\vec{j}$, and $\vec{k}$ (i.e., the standard basis vectors), respectively.

6. Show that the translation matrix affects points but not vectors. That is, by directly doing the matrix multiplication, show that:

$$\begin{bmatrix} x,y,z,1 \end{bmatrix} \begin{bmatrix} 1 & 0 & 0 & 0 \\ 0 & 1 & 0 & 0 \\ 0 & 0 & 1 & 0 \\ b_x & b_y & b_z & 1 \end{bmatrix} = \begin{bmatrix} x+b_x, y+b_y, z+b_z, 1 \end{bmatrix}$$

and

$$\begin{bmatrix} x,y,z,0 \end{bmatrix} \begin{bmatrix} 1 & 0 & 0 & 0 \\ 0 & 1 & 0 & 0 \\ 0 & 0 & 1 & 0 \\ b_x & b_y & b_z & 1 \end{bmatrix} = \begin{bmatrix} x,y,z,0 \end{bmatrix}$$

7. Verify that the given scaling matrix inverse is indeed the inverse of the scaling matrix; that is, show that by directly doing the matrix multiplication, $SS^{-1}=S^{-1}S=I$. Similarly, verify that the given translation matrix inverse is indeed the inverse of the translation matrix; that is, show that by directly doing the matrix multiplication, $TT^{-1}=T^{-1}T=I$.

8. Let $\vec{p}_0=(0,1,0)$, $\vec{p}_1=(-1,3,6)$, and $\vec{p}_2=(8,5,3)$ be three points. Find the plane these points define.

9. Let $\pi=\left(\frac{1}{\sqrt{3}},\frac{1}{\sqrt{3}},\frac{1}{\sqrt{3}},-5\right)$ be a plane. Define the locality of the following points relative to the plane: $\left(3\sqrt{3},5\sqrt{3},0\right)$, $\left(2\sqrt{3},\sqrt{3},2\sqrt{3}\right)$, and $\left(\sqrt{3},-\sqrt{3},0\right)$.

10. Let $\pi=\left(\frac{1}{\sqrt{3}},\frac{1}{\sqrt{3}},\frac{1}{\sqrt{3}},-5\right)$ be a plane, and let $\vec{r}(t)=(-1,1,-1)+t(1,0,0)$ be a ray. Find the point at which the ray intersects the plane. Then write a short program using the D3DXPlaneIntersectLine function (see the SDK documentation for the prototype) to verify your answer.

Part II

Direct3D Foundations

In this part, we study fundamental Direct3D concepts and techniques that are used throughout the rest of this book. With these fundamentals mastered, we can move on to writing more interesting applications. A brief description of the chapters in this part follows.

Chapter 4, "Direct3D Initialization"

In this chapter, we learn what Direct3D is and how to initialize it in preparation for 3D drawing. Basic Direct3D topics are also introduced, such as surfaces, pixel formats, double buffering, and multisampling. In addition, we show how to output 2D text and give some tips on debugging Direct3D applications. We develop and use our own application framework — not the SDK's framework.

Chapter 5, "Timing, Direct Input, Animation, and Sprites"

This chapter is a warmup before diving into 3D programming. We learn how to measure time with the performance counter, which we use to compute the frames rendered per second. In addition, we learn how to initialize and use Direct Input for keyboard and mouse input. Finally, we provide an introduction to 2D graphics programming with the ID3DXSprite interface to give a taste of graphics programming.

Chapter 6, "The Rendering Pipeline"

The first theme of this chapter is to learn, mathematically, how to describe a 3D world and represent a virtual camera that describes the volume of space the camera "sees." The second theme is to learn the steps necessary to take a 2D "picture" that corresponds to the 3D space the camera sees; these steps as a whole are referred to as the rendering pipeline.

Chapter 7, "Drawing in Direct3D — Part A"

In this chapter, we show how to draw 3D geometry in Direct3D. We learn how to store geometric data in a form usable by Direct3D, and we learn the Direct3D drawing commands. We also show how to configure the way in which Direct3D draws geometry using render states.

Chapter 8, "Drawing in Direct3D — Part B"

In this chapter, we write our first simple vertex and pixel shaders using the HLSL (high-level shading language) and effects framework (i.e., the ID3DXEffect interface). We conclude by examining the D3DX functions used to create simple geometric meshes like cylinders, spheres, boxes, and teapots.

Chapter 9, "Color"

In this chapter, we learn how color is represented in Direct3D and how to apply color to solid 3D geometric primitives. We also show how we can animate the position and color of vertices completely in a vertex shader. Finally, we describe two render states that control how colors, specified per vertex, can be shaded across a primitive.

Chapter 10, "Lighting"

This chapter shows how to create light sources and define the interaction between light and surfaces via materials. In particular, we show how to implement directional lights, point lights, and spotlights with vertex and pixel shaders, which mimic the traditional fixed-function pipeline lighting model. We also show how to do per-pixel lighting with interpolated per-pixel normal vectors (i.e., Phong shading).

Chapter 11, "Texturing"

This chapter describes texture mapping, which is a technique used to increase the realism of the scene by mapping 2D image data onto a 3D primitive. For example, using texture mapping, we can model a brick wall by applying a 2D brick wall image onto a 3D rectangle. Other key texturing topics covered include multi-texturing, and animated texture transformations. As always, all of our work is done in the programmable pipeline with vertex and pixel shaders.

Chapter 12, "Blending"

In this chapter, we look at a technique called blending, which allows us to implement a number of special effects like transparency. In addition, we discuss the alpha test, which enables us to mask out certain parts of an image; this can be used to implement fences and gates, for example. An exercise gets you started on implementing y-axis aligned billboards, which, when combined with the alpha test, enable us to simulate trees.

Chapter 13, "Stenciling"

This chapter describes the stencil buffer, which, like a stencil, allows us to block pixels from being drawn. To illustrate the ideas of this chapter, we include a thorough discussion on implementing reflections and planar shadows using the stencil buffer. An exercise describes an algorithm for using the stencil buffer to render the depth complexity of a scene and asks you to implement the algorithm.

Chapter 4

Direct3D Initialization

Initialization of Direct3D has historically been a tedious chore. Fortunately, version 8.0 adopted a simplified initialization model, which Direct3D 9.0x also follows. However, the initialization process still assumes the programmer is familiar with basic graphics concepts and is familiar with some fundamental Direct3D types. The first few sections of this chapter address these requirements. With these prerequisites met, the second part of the chapter explains the initialization process.

Objectives:

- To learn how Direct3D interacts with graphics hardware.
- To understand the role COM plays with Direct3D.
- To learn fundamental graphics concepts, such as how 2D images are stored, page flipping, and depth buffering.
- To find out how to initialize and draw text with Direct3D.
- To become familiar with the general structure of the application framework that the demos of this book employ.
- To discover how to debug your Direct3D applications.

4.1 **Direct3D Overview**

Direct3D is a low-level graphics API (application programming interface) that enables us to render 3D worlds using 3D hardware acceleration. Direct3D can be thought of as a mediator between the application and the graphics device (3D hardware). For example, to instruct the graphics device to clear the screen, the application would call the Direct3D method IDirect3DDevice9::Clear. Figure 4.1 shows the relationship between the application, Direct3D, and the hardware.

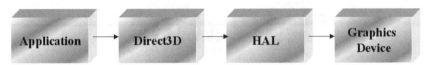

Figure 4.1: The relationship between the application, Direct3D, and the hardware.

The "Direct3D" part of Figure 4.1 is the defined set of interfaces and functions Direct3D exposes to the application/programmer. These interfaces and functions represent the entire features set that the current version of Direct3D supports. Note that just because Direct3D exposes a feature, it doesn't imply available graphics hardware supports it.

As Figure 4.1 shows, there is an intermediate step between Direct3D and the graphics device — the HAL (hardware abstraction layer). Direct3D cannot interact directly with graphics devices because there are a variety of different cards on the market, and each card has different capabilities and ways of implementing things. For instance, two different graphics cards may implement the clear screen operation differently. Therefore, Direct3D requires device manufacturers to implement a HAL. The HAL is the set of device-specific code that instructs the device to perform an operation. In this way, Direct3D avoids having to know the specific details of a device, and its specification can be made independent of hardware devices.

Device manufacturers implement all the features their device supports into the HAL. Features exposed by Direct3D but not supported by the device are not implemented into the HAL. Calling a Direct3D function that is not implemented by the HAL results in failure. Therefore, when using the latest features that are only supported by a minority of graphics devices on the market, be sure to verify that the device supports the feature. (Device capabilities are explained in §4.2.9.)

Note: The DirectX SDK ships with a utility program called DirectX Caps Viewer, which should be located, relative to your root DirectX SDK folder, in *DirectX SDK\Utilities\Bin\x86*. With the DirectX Caps Viewer you can see the capabilities your primary graphics device supports. Figure 4.2 shows a screenshot of the application.

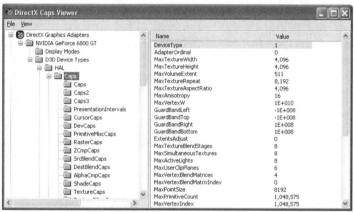

Figure 4.2: The DirectX Caps Viewer utility application that ships with the DirectX SDK.

4.1.1 Devices

At the beginning of this section we referenced the Direct3D method IDirect3DDevice9::Clear. You can think of the IDirect3DDevice9 interface as our software controller of the *physical* graphics device hardware; that is, through this interface we can interact with the hardware and instruct it to do things (such as clearing a surface and drawing 3D geometry).

There are three kinds of devices we can create: a hardware device (HAL), a software device (SW), and a reference device (REF). For modern 3D games, the HAL device is always used because we want to take advantage of 3D hardware acceleration. The software device implements Direct3D operations in software. The advantage of this is that you can then use features that are not available in hardware; the disadvantage is that a software implementation will be slower than a hardware implementation. For advanced effects, especially pixel processing effects, a software implementation will actually be too slow for practical use; consequently, a SW device seldom implements all Direct3D operations.

It is worth noting that Direct3D does not ship with a "ready to use" software device (see the note at the end of this section); consequently, to use a software device, you must either implement a so-called *pluggable software device* yourself or acquire a third-party Direct3D pluggable software device; then you must register it with the IDirect3D9::Register-

`SoftwareDevice` method. In this book, we do not concern ourselves with software devices, and therefore will make no further mention of them.

The REF device is a bit interesting and deserves some discussion. You may wish to write programs that use functionality that Direct3D exposes but are not implemented on your device (or any currently available device — hardware usually lags behind software development). For this purpose, Direct3D provides a reference rasterizer (known as a REF device), which is a device that emulates the entire Direct3D API in software. This allows you to write and test code that uses Direct3D features that are not available on your device. For example, suppose that you want to write some code using vertex and pixel shader model 3.0. If your graphics card does not support these shader models, you can still test the sample code with the REF device. It is important to understand that the REF device is for development only. It ships only with the DirectX SDK and cannot be distributed to end users. In addition, the REF is slow enough that it's not practical to use for anything but testing. Finally, the REF device is also useful for checking for potential driver bugs. For example, if code that should run on your hardware devices works on the REF device but not with the hardware device, then there may be a driver bug.

To identify these three types of devices, Direct3D introduces the `D3DDEVTYPE` enumerated type. A HAL device is specified by `D3DDEVTYPE_HAL`, a SW device is specified by `D3DDEVTYPE_SW`, and a reference device is specified by `D3DDEVTYPE_REF`.

Note: Although Direct3D does not ship with a full software device, Direct3D can emulate vertex processing operations (operations that act on 3D geometry rather than pixels) in software. Thus, if the hardware does not support a vertex processing function in hardware, you can fall back to a slower software emulation. However, this is true only for vertex processing operations (i.e., you cannot emulate pixel processing operations).

4.1.2 **COM**

Component Object Model (COM) is the technology that allows DirectX to be programming language independent and have backward compatibility. We usually refer to a COM object as an interface, which for our purposes can be thought of and used as a C++ class. Most of the details of COM are transparent to us when programming DirectX with C++. The only thing that we must know is that we obtain pointers to COM interfaces through special functions or by the methods of another COM interface — we do not create a COM interface with the C++ `new` keyword. In addition, when we are done with an interface we call its `Release` method (all COM interfaces inherit functionality from the `IUnknown` COM interface, which provides the `Release` method) rather than `delete` it — COM objects perform their own memory management.

There is, of course, much more to COM, but more detail is not necessary for using DirectX effectively.

Note: COM interfaces are prefixed with a capital I. For example, the COM interface that represents a surface is called `IDirect3DSurface9`.

4.2 **Some Preliminaries**

The initialization process of Direct3D requires us to be familiar with some basic graphics concepts and Direct3D types. We introduce these ideas and types in this section, making the next section that discusses Direct3D initialization more focused.

Note: A lot of terminology, Direct3D structures, and Direct3D functions will be introduced in the following subsections. At this point, attention should be paid to the general ideas; the details will be filled in as we progress through this book. Moreover, you can always come back and look up the Direct3D structure names and functions later on.

4.2.1 **Surfaces**

A *surface* is a matrix of pixels that Direct3D uses primarily to store 2D image data. Figure 4.3 identifies some components of a surface. Note that while we visualize the surface data as a matrix, the pixel data is actually stored in a linear array.

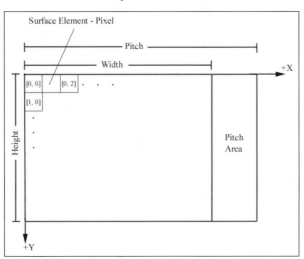

Figure 4.3: A surface is a matrix of data elements called pixels.

The width and height of a surface are measured in pixels. The pitch is measured in bytes. Furthermore, the pitch may be wider than the width, depending on the underlying hardware implementation, so you *cannot* assume that *pitch = width · sizeof(pixelFormat)*.

In code, we describe surfaces with the IDirect3DSurface9 interface. This interface provides several methods for reading and writing data directly to a surface, as well as a method to retrieve information about the surface. The most important methods of IDirect3DSurface9 are:

- LockRect: This method allows us to obtain a pointer to the surface memory (i.e., a pointer to the pixel data array). Then, with some pointer arithmetic, we can read and write to each pixel in the surface.

- UnlockRect: After you have called LockRect and are done accessing the surface's memory, you must unlock the surface by calling this method.

- GetDesc: This method retrieves a description of the surface by filling out a D3DSURFACE_DESC structure.

Locking a surface and writing to each pixel can be somewhat confusing at first, considering the surface pitch, so we have provided the following code block that locks a surface and colors each pixel red.

```
// Assume surface is a pointer to an IDirect3DSurface9 interface.
// Assumes a 32-bit pixel format for each pixel.

// Get the surface description.
D3DSURFACE_DESC surfaceDesc;
surface->GetDesc(&surfaceDesc);

// Get a pointer to the surface pixel data.
D3DLOCKED_RECT lockedRect;
surface->LockRect(
    &lockedRect,  // pointer to receive locked data
    0,            // lock entire surface
    0);           // no lock flags specified

// Iterate through each pixel in the surface and set it to red.
DWORD* imageData = (DWORD*)lockedRect.pBits;
for(int i = 0; i < surfaceDesc.Height; i++)
{
  for(int j = 0; j < surfaceDesc.Width; j++)
  {
    // Index into texture, note we use the pitch and divide by
    // four since the pitch is given in bytes and there are
    // 4 bytes per DWORD.
    int index = i * lockedRect.Pitch / 4 + j;

    imageData[index] = 0xffff0000; // red
  }
}
surface->UnlockRect();
```

The D3DLOCKED_RECT structure is defined as:

```
typedef struct _D3DLOCKED_RECT {
    INT Pitch;   // the surface pitch
    void *pBits; // pointer to the start of the
                 // surface memory
} D3DLOCKED_RECT;
```

A few comments about the surface lock code: The 32-bit pixel format assumption is important since we cast the bits to DWORDs, which are 32 bits. This lets us treat every DWORD as representing a pixel in the surface. (Don't worry about understanding how 0xffff0000 represents red, as colors are covered in Chapter 9.)

4.2.2 The Swap Chain and Page Flipping

Direct3D maintains a collection of surfaces, usually two or three, called a *swap chain* that is represented by the IDirect3DSwapChain9 interface. We will not go into the specifics of this interface since Direct3D manages it and we rarely need to manipulate it. Instead, we will simply outline its purpose.

Swap chains, and more specifically the technique of *page flipping* (or *double buffering*), are used to provide smooth, flicker-free animation between frames. Figure 4.4 shows a swap chain graphically with two surfaces.

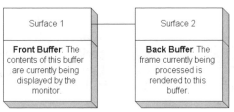

Figure 4.4: A swap chain with two surfaces: a front buffer and a back buffer.

From Figure 4.4, the surface in the *front buffer* slot is the surface that corresponds to the image presently being displayed on the monitor. The monitor does not display the image represented by the front buffer instantaneously; it takes one-sixtieth of a second on a monitor with a refresh rate of 60 Hertz, for instance. The application's frame rate is often out of sync with the monitor's refresh rate; for example, the application may be able to render frames faster than the monitor can display them. We do not want to update the contents of the front buffer with the next frame of animation until the monitor has finished drawing the current frame, but we do not want to halt our rendering while waiting for the monitor to finish displaying the contents of the front buffer either. Therefore, we render to an off-screen surface (*back buffer*); then when the monitor is done displaying the surface in the front buffer, we move it to the end of the swap chain and the next back buffer in the swap chain is promoted to be the front buffer. This process is called *presenting*. Figure 4.5 shows the swap chain before and after a presentation.

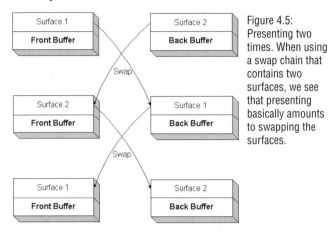

Figure 4.5: Presenting two times. When using a swap chain that contains two surfaces, we see that presenting basically amounts to swapping the surfaces.

Thus, the structure of our rendering code is:

1. Render to back buffer.
2. Present the back buffer.
3. Goto (1).

4.2.3 **Pixel Formats**

When we create surfaces in Direct3D, we need to specify the pixel format. That is to say, how many bits we allocate for the red, green, blue, and, perhaps, alpha components and how the bits are organized in memory.

Note: Computer color is talked about more in depth in Chapter 9; however, we assume a basic knowledge about how colors are represented in computers and paint programs — namely as an additive mixing of various intensities of red, green, and blue. Users of 2D computer graphics programs may recognize the alpha component as a means of controlling how two pixels are combined together; alpha blending is discussed in Chapter 12.

The format of a pixel is defined by specifying a member of the D3DFORMAT enumerated type. Some common pixel formats are:

■   D3DFMT_X1R5G5B5: Specifies a 16-bit pixel format where, starting from the leftmost bit, 1 bit is not used, 5 bits are allocated for red, 5 bits are allocated for green, and 5 bits are allocated for blue.

■   D3DFMT_R5G6B5: Specifies a 16-bit pixel format where, starting from the leftmost bit, 5 bits are allocated for red, 6 bits are allocated for green, and 5 bits are allocated for blue.

■ D3DFMT_R8G8B8: Specifies a 24-bit pixel format where, starting from the leftmost bit, 8 bits are allocated for red, 8 bits are allocated for green, and 8 bits are allocated for blue.

■ D3DFMT_X8R8G8B8: Specifies a 32-bit pixel format where, starting from the leftmost bit, 8 bits are not used, 8 bits are allocated for red, 8 bits are allocated for green, and 8 bits are allocated for blue.

■ D3DFMT_A8R8G8B8: Specifies a 32-bit pixel format where, starting from the leftmost bit, 8 bits are allocated for alpha, 8 bits are allocated for red, 8 bits are allocated for green, and 8 bits are allocated for blue.

■ D3DFMT_A8: Specifies an 8-bit alpha-only pixel format.

■ D3DFMT_R16F: Specifies a 16-bit red floating-point pixel format.

■ D3DFMT_A16B16G16R16F: Specifies a 64-bit floating-point pixel format. Starting from the leftmost bit, 16 bits are allocated for alpha, 16 bits are allocated for blue, 16 bits are allocated for green, and 16 bits are allocated for red.

■ D3DFMT_R32F: Specifies a 32-bit red floating-point pixel format.

■ D3DFMT_A32B32G32R32F: Specifies a 128-bit floating-point pixel format. Starting from the leftmost bit, 32 bits are allocated for alpha, 32 bits are allocated for blue, 32 bits are allocated for green, and 32 bits are allocated for red.

In general, 32-bit pixel formats are used for the display and back buffer surfaces. For a complete list of supported pixel formats, look up D3DFORMAT in the DirectX SDK documentation.

Most graphics cards should support the first six formats (D3DFMT_X1R5G5B5, D3DFMT_R5G6B5, D3DFMT_R8G8B8, D3DFMT_X8R8G8B8, D3DFMT_A8R8G8B8, D3DFMT_A8) in some way without a problem. The floating-point pixel formats are still relatively new and are not yet as widely supported. In general, you should always check to see if the hardware supports a particular format before using it.

You may wonder why formats like D3DFMT_A8, D3DFMT_R16F, and D3DFMT_R32F are even useful — why would you want a format that only has one channel? The reason for these formats is because we often want to use surfaces to store information other than colors; that is, we generalize the idea of surfaces to be more general purpose in order to achieve some special effects, such as normal mapping and displacement mapping. Hence, these kinds of formats are useful for just storing single numbers in a surface. As another note, we can even generalize data to the multi-component surface formats like D3DFMT_X8R8G8B8. With D3DFMT_X8R8G8B8, we could encode a point or vector (x, y, z) in the color components (red, green, blue) of the surface. Using surfaces to store general data is important for special effects, which will be discussed toward the end of this book.

4.2.4 **Display Adapters**

A display adapter refers to a physical graphics card, although a graphics card with a dual-head display has more than one adapter. Because a system may have more than one adapter (via multiple video cards or dual-head displays), a commercial Direct3D program should enumerate all available adapters and pick the best one for the application. To facilitate this enumeration process, Direct3D provides the IDirect3D9 interface.

The IDirect3D9 object is used as a stepping-stone to creating the IDirect3DDevice9 object. Via this interface, we can find information about all the adapters on the system, such as the number of adapters on the system (IDirect3D9::GetAdapterCount) and which display modes each adapter supports (IDirect3D9::EnumAdapterModes). The following code snippet shows how you might enumerate over each adapter and each of its display modes.

```
D3DDISPLAYMODE mode;
for(int i = 0; i < d3dObject->GetAdapterCount(); ++i)
{
    UINT modeCnt = d3dObject->GetAdapterModeCount(
        i, D3DFMT_X8R8G8B8);

    for(int j = 0; j < modeCnt; ++j)
    {
        d3dObject->EnumAdapterModes(i,
            D3DFMT_X8R8G8B8, j, &mode);

        outFile << "Width = "  << mode.Width << "  ";
        outFile << "Height = " << mode.Height << "  ";
        outFile << "Format = " << mode.Format << "  ";
        outFile << "Refresh = " << mode.RefreshRate << endl;
    }
}
```

Here, outFile is of type std::ofstream, which is just used to dump the data to a file. Figure 4.6 shows the contents of the file on the author's system. The key methods used in the above snippet are:

- IDirect3D9::GetAdapterCount: Returns the number of adapters on the system.

- IDirect3D9::GetAdapterModeCount: Returns the number of display modes supported by the specified adapter (parameter one) in the specified format (parameter two). In the above snippet we specify the ith adapter and the format D3DFMT_X8R8G8B8.

- IDirect3D9::EnumAdapterModes: Returns (via the fourth "output" parameter by filling out a D3DDISPLAYMODE structure) information about the jth display mode (parameter three) of the specified format (parameter two) of the specified adapter (parameter one). In other words, for a given adapter and surface format, there are $j = 0, 1, \ldots,$

GetAdapterModeCount()-1 many display modes. To get information about the *j*th display mode, we just specify *j* for the third parameter.

The D3DDISPLAYMODE structure is defined like this:

```
typedef struct _D3DDISPLAYMODE {
    UINT Width;          // Screen width, measured in pixels.
    UINT Height;         // Screen height, measured in pixels.
    UINT RefreshRate;    // Refresh rate.
    D3DFORMAT Format;    // Display mode surface format.
} D3DDISPLAYMODE;
```

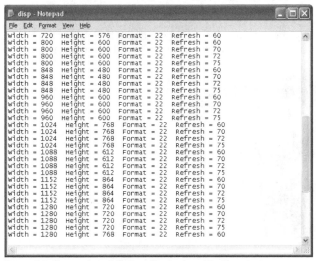

```
🖺 disp - Notepad
File  Edit  Format  View  Help
width = 720   Height = 576   Format = 22   Refresh = 60
width = 800   Height = 600   Format = 22   Refresh = 60
width = 800   Height = 600   Format = 22   Refresh = 70
width = 800   Height = 600   Format = 22   Refresh = 72
width = 800   Height = 600   Format = 22   Refresh = 75
width = 848   Height = 480   Format = 22   Refresh = 60
width = 848   Height = 480   Format = 22   Refresh = 70
width = 848   Height = 480   Format = 22   Refresh = 72
width = 848   Height = 480   Format = 22   Refresh = 75
width = 960   Height = 600   Format = 22   Refresh = 60
width = 960   Height = 600   Format = 22   Refresh = 70
width = 960   Height = 600   Format = 22   Refresh = 72
width = 960   Height = 600   Format = 22   Refresh = 75
width = 1024  Height = 768   Format = 22   Refresh = 60
width = 1024  Height = 768   Format = 22   Refresh = 70
width = 1024  Height = 768   Format = 22   Refresh = 72
width = 1024  Height = 768   Format = 22   Refresh = 75
width = 1088  Height = 612   Format = 22   Refresh = 60
width = 1088  Height = 612   Format = 22   Refresh = 70
width = 1088  Height = 612   Format = 22   Refresh = 72
width = 1088  Height = 612   Format = 22   Refresh = 75
width = 1152  Height = 864   Format = 22   Refresh = 60
width = 1152  Height = 864   Format = 22   Refresh = 70
width = 1152  Height = 864   Format = 22   Refresh = 72
width = 1152  Height = 864   Format = 22   Refresh = 75
width = 1280  Height = 720   Format = 22   Refresh = 60
width = 1280  Height = 720   Format = 22   Refresh = 70
width = 1280  Height = 720   Format = 22   Refresh = 72
width = 1280  Height = 720   Format = 22   Refresh = 75
width = 1280  Height = 768   Format = 22   Refresh = 60
```

Figure 4.6: Screenshot of the text file produced by the adapter enumeration code snippet on the author's system. Format 22 is just the integer D3DFMT_X8R8G8B8 is defined as.

In addition to obtaining the adapter display modes, the IDirect3D9 object is also used for determining various hardware support of the adapters, such as which kind of surface formats they support and in which combinations, which surface formats the hardware can convert between, and multisampling support. Some of these additional methods will be discussed, as needed, throughout the book.

Direct3D refers to the *primary display adapter* (i.e., the one displaying the Windows desktop) with the identifier D3DADAPTER_DEFAULT. For the demo programs in this book, we will make it easy and select the primary adapter, and use the current display mode for windowed mode and the commonly supported format D3DFMT_X8R8G8B8 for full-screen mode, thereby bypassing the chore of enumerating adapters and display modes. This is sufficient for the book's demo applications. That said, the first problem in the Exercises section asks you to explore adapter enumeration in further detail.

4.2.5 **Depth Buffers**

The *depth buffer* is a surface that does not contain image data but rather depth information about a particular pixel. The possible depth values range from 0.0 to 1.0, where 0.0 denotes the closest an object can be to the viewer and 1.0 denotes the farthest an object can be from the viewer. There is an entry in the depth buffer that corresponds to each pixel in the back buffer (i.e., the *ij*th element in the back buffer corresponds to the *ij*th element in the depth buffer). So if the back buffer had a resolution of 1280×1024, there would be 1280×1024 depth entries.

Note: Actually, the requirement is that the depth buffer dimensions be greater than or equal to the render target (back buffer).

Figure 4.7: A group of objects that partially obscure each other.

Figure 4.7 shows a simple scene where some objects partially obscure the objects behind them. In order for Direct3D to determine which pixels of an object are in front of another, it uses a technique called *depth buffering* or *z-buffering*. Let us emphasize that with depth buffering, the order in which we draw the objects does not matter.

Remark: To handle the depth problem, one might suggest drawing the objects in the scene in the order of farthest to nearest. In this way, near objects will be painted over far objects, and the correct results should be rendered. This is how a painter would draw a scene. However, this method has its own problems — sorting a large data set and intersecting geometry. Besides, the graphics hardware gives us depth buffering for free.

To illustrate how depth buffering works, let's look at an example. Consider Figure 4.8, which shows the volume the viewer sees (a) and a 2D side view of that volume (b). From the figure, we observe that three different pixels can be rendered to the arbitrary pixel P (of course, we know the closest pixel should be rendered to P since it obscures the ones behind it, but the computer does not). First, before any rendering takes place, the back buffer is cleared to a default color (like black or white), and the depth buffer is cleared to a default value — usually 1.0 (the farthest depth value a pixel can have). Now, suppose that the objects are rendered in the order of cylinder, sphere, and cone. As the cylinder is drawn, a depth test occurs for each of its pixels. In particular for P_3, since $d_3 < 1.0$, the pixel P_3 overwrites the pixel P on the back buffer, and d_3 overwrites the default depth buffer entry corresponding to P. Next, when we render the sphere, a depth test again takes place for each of its pixels. In particular for P_1, since $d_1 < d_3$, P_1 overwrites the pixel $P = P_3$ on the back buffer, and d_1 overwrites the depth buffer entry corresponding to P (namely d_3). Finally, when we render the cone, a depth test takes place again for each of its pixels. In particular for P_2, since $d_1 < d_2$, we have that P_2 does *not* overwrite $P = P_1$ and d_2 does *not* overwrite the corresponding element d_1 in the depth buffer. Thus, after all is said and done, the pixel that is closest to the viewer will be rendered — P_1. (You can try switching the drawing order around and working through this example again if you are still not convinced.)

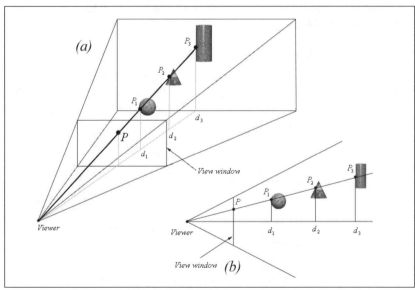

Figure 4.8: (a) The 3D volume the viewer sees; (b) a 2D side view of the volume the viewer sees. The view window corresponds to the 2D image (back buffer) we generate of the 3D space. We see that three different pixels can be projected to the pixel P. Intuition tells us that P_1 should be written to P since it is closer to the viewer and blocks the other two pixels. The depth buffer algorithm provides a mechanical procedure for determining this on a computer. Note that we show the depth values relative to the 3D scene being viewed, but they are actually normalized to the range [0.0, 1.0] when stored in the depth buffer.

To summarize, depth buffering works by computing a depth value for each pixel and performing a depth test. The *depth test* basically compares the depths of pixels competing to be written to a particular pixel location on the back buffer. The pixel with the depth value closest to the viewer wins, and that is the pixel that gets written to the back buffer. This makes sense because the pixel closest to the viewer obscures the pixels behind it.

The format of the depth buffer determines the accuracy of the depth test. That is, a 24-bit depth buffer is more accurate than a 16-bit depth buffer. In general, most applications work fine with a 24-bit depth buffer, although Direct3D also exposes a 32-bit depth buffer.

- D3DFMT_D32: Specifies a 32-bit depth buffer.
- D3DFMT_D24S8: Specifies a 24-bit depth buffer with 8 bits reserved as the stencil buffer.
- D3DFMT_D24X8: Specifies a 24-bit depth buffer only.
- D3DFMT_D24X4S4: Specifies a 24-bit buffer, with 4 bits reserved for the stencil buffer.
- D3DFMT_D16: Specifies a 16-bit depth buffer only.

Note: The stencil buffer is a more advanced topic and will be explained in Chapter 13.

4.2.6 **Multisampling**

Because the pixels on a monitor are not infinitely small, an arbitrary line cannot be represented perfectly on the computer monitor. Figure 4.9 illustrates a "stairstep" (*aliasing*), which can occur when approximating a line by a matrix of pixels.

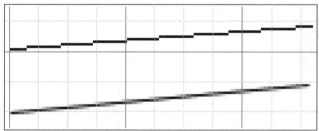

Figure 4.9: On the top we witness aliasing (the stairstep effect when trying to represent a line with a matrix of pixels). On the bottom, we see an antialiased line, which generates the final color of a pixel by sampling its neighboring pixels; this results in a smoother image and dilutes the stairstep effect.

Shrinking the pixel sizes by increasing the monitor resolution can alleviate the problem significantly to where the stairstep effect goes largely unnoticed.

When increasing the monitor resolution is not possible or not enough, we can apply antialiasing techniques. Direct3D supports an antialiasing technique called *multisampling*, which works by taking the neighboring pixels into consideration when computing the final color of a pixel. Thus, the technique is called multisampling because it uses multiple pixel samples to compute the final color of a pixel. For an example of how the Geforce3 GPU implements multisampling, consult the paper *HRAA: High-Resolution Antialiasing through Multisampling*, available for download at http://www.nvidia.com/object/feature_hraa.html.

The D3DMULTISAMPLE_TYPE enumerated type consists of values that allow us to specify the number of samples to use in multisampling:

- D3DMULTISAMPLE_NONE: Specifies no multisampling.

- D3DMULTISAMPLE_2_SAMPLES, ..., D3DMULTISAMPLE_16_SAMPLES: Specifies to use 2, ..., 16 samples.

There is also a quality level associated with the multisampling type; this is described as a DWORD. We actually specify the multisampling type and quality level for the back buffer during device creation (see §4.3.4).

Before using a particular multisampling type (other than D3DMULTISAMPLE_NONE), we need to check whether the hardware supports it. We do this with the IDirect3D9::CheckDeviceMultiSampleType method:

```
HRESULT IDirect3D9::CheckDeviceMultiSampleType(
    UINT Adapter,
    D3DDEVTYPE DeviceType,
    D3DFORMAT SurfaceFormat,
    BOOL Windowed,
    D3DMULTISAMPLE_TYPE MultiSampleType,
    DWORD* pQualityLevels);
```

The first parameter identifies the adapter we are querying for multi-sampling support; the second parameter is the device type we are using (usually D3DDEVTYPE_HAL); the third parameter is the pixel format of the surface we want multisampled (usually the back buffer or depth buffer format); the fourth parameter indicates whether or not we are in windowed mode (true if windowed, false if full screen); the fifth parameter is a member of the D3DMULTISAMPLE_TYPE enumerated type and specifies the type of multisampling we want to see if the adapter supports; and finally, the last parameter returns the number of quality levels for the specified multi-sample type (ranges from 0 to $n - 1$, where n is the value returned by the pQualityLevels parameter). The function returns D3D_OK if the hardware supports the multisampling type, and D3DERR_NOTAVAILABLE if the hardware does not support the multisampling type. The following code snippet shows how this function is used:

```
// gd3dPP is a D3DPRESENT_PARAMETERS instance (§4.3.4).
// gd3dObject is an IDirect3D9 object.
D3DMULTISAMPLE_TYPE mst = D3DMULTISAMPLE_2_SAMPLES;
DWORD quality = 0;
// Is it supported for the back buffer format?
```

```
if(SUCCEEDED(gd3dObject->CheckDeviceMultiSampleType(
    D3DADAPTER_DEFAULT, D3DEVTYPE_HAL, D3DFMT_X8R8G8B8,
    true, mst, &quality)))
{
    // Is it supported for the depth format?
    if(SUCCEEDED(gd3dObject->CheckDeviceMultiSampleType(
        D3DADAPTER_DEFAULT, D3DEVTYPE_HAL, D3DFMT_D24S8,
        true, mst, &quality)))
    {
        // Okay to use:
        gd3dPP.MultiSampleType    = mst;
        gd3dPP.MultiSampleQuality = quality-1;
    }
}
```

In the above snippet, we test for hardware multisampling support using both a back buffer format and a depth buffer format. We have to test both since both the back buffer and depth buffer need to be multisampled if they are to work simultaneously.

Note: To use multisampling, the swap effect (§4.3.4) must be D3DSWAPEFFECT_DISCARD.

4.2.7 Memory Pools

A Direct3D resource, such as a surface, can exist in system memory (RAM), video memory (VRAM), or AGP memory. Device accessible memory refers to either VRAM or AGP memory since the graphics device can directly access memory of these types; the device cannot access system memory. The *Direct3D memory pool* determines the memory type in which a resource is placed. A memory pool is specified by one of the members of the D3DPOOL enumerated type. The three main members of this type are:

■ D3DPOOL_MANAGED: Resources placed in the managed pool are backed up in system memory, and are automatically moved between system memory and device accessible memory as needed, based on the Direct3D Runtime's own management system. When resources in this pool are accessed and changed by the application, they work with the system memory backup copy, and then Direct3D automatically updates them to device accessible memory as needed. Managed resources do not need to be destroyed prior to an IDirect3DDevice9::Reset call, and do not need to be reinitialized after the reset call.

■ D3DPOOL_DEFAULT: The default memory pool instructs Direct3D to place the resource in the memory that is best suited for the resource type and usage — usually VRAM or AGP memory. Resources in the default pool are not backed up in system memory by Direct3D, and must be destroyed (released) prior to an IDirect3DDevice9::Reset call and reinitialized after the reset call.

■ D3DPOOL_SYSTEMMEM: Specifies that the resource be placed in system memory. Note that the graphics device cannot use a resource placed in this pool. This pool is usually used when the application needs to do some work on the resource before copying it into device accessible memory, or when the application just wants its own local backup copy of a resource. System resources do not need to be destroyed prior to an IDirect3DDevice9::Reset call, and do not need to be reinitialized after the reset call.

Note: IDirect3DDevice9::Reset is covered in §4.4.

4.2.8 Vertex Processing and Pure Devices

Vertices are the building blocks for 3D geometry and they can be processed in two different ways: in software (*software vertex processing*) or in hardware (*hardware vertex processing*). Software vertex processing is always supported and can always be used. Hardware vertex processing can only be used if the graphics card supports vertex processing in hardware.

Hardware vertex processing is always preferred since dedicated hardware is faster than software. Furthermore, performing vertex processing in hardware unloads calculations from the CPU, which implies the CPU is free to perform other calculations.

The IDirect3DDevice9 provides many Get style methods, which return information about the device. A *pure device* refers to a device in which some of these Get methods (e.g., render state, transform state, lights, and texture Get methods) are disabled; moreover, a pure device can only be specified with hardware vertex processing. The benefit, however, for using a pure device is that it may lead to a speed increase.

Note: There is also a mixed vertex processing mode, which allows you to mix both software and hardware vertex processing. For example, you may want to do some vertex processing in software and some in hardware. The typical reason for doing this is if the hardware doesn't support a certain vertex processing feature (e.g., some vertex shader), then you emulate that particular feature by using software vertex processing, and use hardware vertex processing wherever you can.

Another way of saying a graphics card supports hardware vertex processing in hardware is to say that the graphics card supports transformation and lighting calculations in hardware.

4.2.9 **Device Capabilities**

Every feature Direct3D exposes has a corresponding data member or bit in the D3DCAPS9 structure. The idea is to initialize the members of a D3DCAPS9 object based on the capabilities of a particular hardware device. In our application, we can check whether a device supports a feature by checking the corresponding data member or bit in a D3DCAPS9 instance.

The following example illustrates this feature checking. Suppose we wish to check if a hardware device is capable of doing vertex processing in hardware, and is capable of being a pure device. By looking up the D3DCAPS9 structure in the SDK documentation, we find that the bit D3DDEVCAPS_ HWTRANSFORMANDLIGHT in the data member D3DCAPS9::DevCaps indicates whether the device supports hardware vertex processing. Similarly, we find that the bit D3DDEVCAPS_PUREDEVICE in the data member D3DCAPS9::DevCaps indicates whether the device can be a pure device. Our test then, assuming caps is a D3DCAPS9 instance and has already been initialized, is:

```
bool hardwareVP = false;
bool pure       = false;
if( caps.DevCaps & D3DDEVCAPS_HWTRANSFORMANDLIGHT )
    // The bit is on, so hardware vertex processing supported.
    hardwareVP = true;

if( caps.DevCaps & D3DDEVCAPS_PUREDEVICE )
    // The bit is on, so pure device supported.
    pure = true;
```

4.3 **Initializing Direct3D**

The following subsections show how to initialize Direct3D. Our process of initializing Direct3D can be broken down into the following steps:

1. Acquire a pointer to an IDirect3D9 interface. Recall that this interface is used for finding information about the physical hardware devices on a system and for creating the IDirect3DDevice9 interface, which is our C++ object that represents the physical hardware device we use for displaying 3D graphics.

2. Verify hardware support for using the current display mode format as a display format and back buffer format in windowed mode, and for using the format D3DFMT_X8R8G8B8 as a display format and back buffer format in full-screen mode.

3. Check the device capabilities (D3DCAPS9) to see if the primary display adapter (primary graphics card) supports hardware vertex processing and a pure device. We will need to know if it can when we create the IDirect3DDevice9 interface.

4. Initialize an instance of the D3DPRESENT_PARAMETERS structure. This struc-
    ture consists of a number of data members that allow us to specify the
    characteristics of the IDirect3DDevice9 interface we are going to create.

5. Create the IDirect3DDevice9 object based on an initialized
    D3DPRESENT_PARAMETERS structure. As said, the IDirect3DDevice9 object is
    our C++ object that represents the physical hardware device we use
    for displaying 3D graphics.

Note: Remember that for the demo programs in this book, we will
make it easy by selecting the primary adapter, and using the current
display mode for windowed mode and the commonly supported format D3DFMT_X8R8G8B8 for full-screen mode, thereby bypassing the
chore of enumerating adapters and display modes.

4.3.1 **Acquiring an IDirect3D9 Interface**

Initialization of Direct3D begins by acquiring a pointer to an IDirect3D9
interface. This is easily done using a special Direct3D function, as the following lines of code show:

```
IDirect3D9* md3dObject;
md3dObject = Direct3DCreate9(D3D_SDK_VERSION);
```

The single parameter to Direct3DCreate9 should always be D3D_SDK_VERSION,
which guarantees that the application is built against the correct header
files. If this function fails, it will return a null pointer.

4.3.2 **Verifying HAL Support**

After we have created the IDirect3D9 object, we should verify that the pixel
format combination that we are using for the display and back buffer are
supported by the hardware. To do this, we use the IDirect3D9::Check-
DeviceType method:

```
HRESULT IDirect3D9::CheckDeviceType(
    UINT Adapter,
    D3DDEVTYPE DeviceType,
    D3DFORMAT DisplayFormat,
    D3DFORMAT BackBufferFormat,
    BOOL Windowed);
```

The first parameter identifies the display adapter for which we are testing
support; the second parameter identifies the device type (usually
D3DDEVTYPE_HAL since we want to test for hardware acceleration support); the
third and fourth parameters specify the display and back buffer formats,
respectively, of which we are testing if the display adapter supports hardware acceleration; and finally, the fifth parameter specifies whether we will
be using these formats in windowed mode — specify true if windowed or
false if full screen. The reason for this last parameter is that a certain

display and back buffer format configuration may work in windowed mode but not full-screen mode, or conversely. This function will return an error code if the formats are not supported by the specified adapter in the specified settings.

Note: For windowed applications, the back buffer format need not match the display format. However, you should call IDirect3D9:: CheckDeviceFormatConversion to see if the hardware supports a conversion between the two formats you want to use.

In our sample framework, for windowed mode rendering, we are going to use the current display mode pixel format; this can be obtained by making a call to IDirect3D9::GetAdapterDisplayMode, which returns (via the second parameter) the current display mode of the specified adapter (first parameter); then the pixel format of the current display mode is just given by mode.Format. For full-screen mode, we are going to use the commonly supported format D3DFMT_X8R8G8B8 as both the display format and back buffer format. The following code snippet illustrates our HAL verification code:

```
D3DDISPLAYMODE mode;
md3dObject->GetAdapterDisplayMode(D3DADAPTER_DEFAULT, &mode);
HR(md3dObject->CheckDeviceType(D3DADAPTER_DEFAULT,
        D3DDEVTYPE_HAL, mode.Format, mode.Format, true));
HR(md3dObject->CheckDeviceType(D3DADAPTER_DEFAULT,
        D3DDEVTYPE_HAL, D3DFMT_X8R8G8B8, D3DFMT_X8R8G8B8, false));
```

Note: HR is a macro that handles the return codes returned by the Direct3D functions; it is discussed in §4.7.

4.3.3 Checking for Hardware Vertex Processing

When we create an IDirect3DDevice9 object to represent the primary display adapter, we must specify the type of vertex processing to use with it. We want to use hardware vertex processing if we can (and also a pure device), but because not all cards support hardware vertex processing and pure devices, we must first check whether the card supports it. (We also only take a pure device if using hardware vertex processing.)

To do this, we must first initialize a D3DCAPS9 instance based on the capabilities of the primary display adapter. We use the following method:

```
HRESULT IDirect3D9::GetDeviceCaps(UINT Adapter,
        D3DDEVTYPE DeviceType, D3DCAPS9 *pCaps);
```

The first parameter specifies the physical display adapter for which we are going to get the capabilities; the second parameter specifies the device type to use (e.g. hardware device (D3DDEVTYPE_HAL) or reference device (D3DDEVTYPE_REF)); and the last parameter returns the initialized capabilities structure.

Then, we can check the capabilities as we did in §4.2.9. The following code snippet illustrates:

```
D3DCAPS9 caps;
HR(md3dObject->GetDeviceCaps(D3DADAPTER_DEFAULT, mDevType, &caps));

DWORD devBehaviorFlags = 0;
if( caps.DevCaps & D3DDEVCAPS_HWTRANSFORMANDLIGHT )
    devBehaviorFlags |= mRequestedVP;
else
    devBehaviorFlags |= D3DCREATE_SOFTWARE_VERTEXPROCESSING;

// If pure device and HW T&L supported
if( caps.DevCaps & D3DDEVCAPS_PUREDEVICE &&
    devBehaviorFlags & D3DCREATE_HARDWARE_VERTEXPROCESSING)
        devBehaviorFlags |= D3DCREATE_PUREDEVICE;
```

Note that `mRequestedVP` is a variable that stores the requested vertex processing mode (it will be specified at application initialization time), which is either hardware, mixed, or software vertex processing. Thus, if hardware vertex processing is available, we can always satisfy the requested vertex processing mode (hardware, mixed, or software). If hardware vertex processing is not supported, then we cannot use a hardware or mixed vertex processing mode, and we default to software vertex processing.

The identifiers `D3DCREATE_HARDWARE_VERTEXPROCESSING`, `D3DCREATE_SOFTWARE_VERTEXPROCESSING`, and `D3DCREATE_PUREDEVICE` are predefined "creation flag" values that denote hardware vertex processing, software vertex processing, and pure device, respectively. A combination (combined using bitwise OR) of these creation flags is specified when we create the `IDirect3DDevice9` object. Therefore, we save the creation flags we are going to use in the variable `devBehaviorFlags` for later use. (The creation flag for mixed vertex processing is `D3DCREATE_MIXED_VERTEXPROCESSING`.)

4.3.4 **D3DPRESENT_PARAMETERS**

The next step in the initialization process is to fill out an instance of the `D3DPRESENT_PARAMETERS` structure. This structure is used to specify some of the characteristics of the `IDirect3DDevice9` object we are going to create, and is defined as:

```
typedef struct _D3DPRESENT_PARAMETERS_ {
    UINT        BackBufferWidth;
    UINT        BackBufferHeight;
    D3DFORMAT   BackBufferFormat;
    UINT        BackBufferCount;
    D3DMULTISAMPLE_TYPE MultiSampleType;
    DWORD       MultiSampleQuality;
    D3DSWAPEFFECT SwapEffect;
    HWND        hDeviceWindow;
    BOOL        Windowed;
    BOOL        EnableAutoDepthStencil;
```

```
    D3DFORMAT AutoDepthStencilFormat;
    DWORD     Flags;
    UINT      FullScreen_RefreshRateInHz;
    UINT      PresentationInterval;
} D3DPRESENT_PARAMETERS;
```

Note: In the following data member descriptions for the `D3DPRESENT_PARAMETERS` structure we only cover the flags and options we feel are most important to a beginner at this point. For a description of further flags, options, and configurations, refer to the SDK documentation.

- `BackBufferWidth`: Width of the back buffer surface in pixels. For windowed mode, we can specify 0 and it will use the client area width.

- `BackBufferHeight`: Height of the back buffer surface in pixels. For windowed mode, we can specify 0 and it will use the client area height.

- `BackBufferFormat`: Pixel format of the back buffer (e.g., 32-bit pixel format: `D3DFMT_X8R8G8B8`). For windowed mode, you can also specify the format `D3DFMT_UNKNOWN` for this member, which means that Direct3D should use the current display mode's pixel format.

- `BackBufferCount`: The number of back buffers to use. Usually we specify 1 to indicate we want only one back buffer.

- `MultiSampleType`: The type of multisampling to use with the back buffer and also with the depth-stencil buffer (provided `EnableAutoDepthStencil` is set to `true`); see §4.2.6 for further details on multisampling. Note that to use multisampling, both the render target (back buffer) and depth-stencil buffer must use the same multisampling type.

- `MultiSampleQuality`: The quality level of multisampling; see §4.2.6.

- `SwapEffect`: A member of the `D3DSWAPEFFECT` enumerated type that specifies how the buffers in the flipping chain will be swapped. Specifying `D3DSWAPEFFECT_DISCARD` is the most efficient; see the SDK documentation for other swap methods. Also note that multisampling can only be used with `D3DSWAPEFFECT_DISCARD`.

- `hDeviceWindow`: The window handle associated with the device. Specify the application window into which you want to draw.

- `Windowed`: Specify `true` to run in windowed mode or `false` for full-screen mode.

- `EnableAutoDepthStencil`: Set to `true` to have Direct3D create and maintain the depth/stencil buffer automatically; set to `false` otherwise. Note that if you do not specify `true`, your application will either not have a depth buffer corresponding to the back buffer, or you will have to attach a depth buffer manually; see `IDirect3DDevice9::CreateDepthStencilSurface` and `IDirect3DDevice9::SetDepthStencilSurface` in the SDK documentation.

- AutoDepthStencilFormat: The format of the depth/stencil buffer (e.g., 24-bit depth with 8 bits reserved for the stencil buffer: D3DFMT_D24S8).
- Flags: Some additional characteristics. Specify zero (no flags) or a member of the D3DPRESENTFLAG set. See the documentation for a complete list of valid flags. Two common flags are:

  D3DPRESENTFLAG_LOCKABLE_BACKBUFFER: Specifies that the back buffer can be locked. Note that using a lockable back buffer can degrade performance.

  D3DPRESENTFLAG_DISCARD_DEPTHSTENCIL: Specifies that the depth/stencil buffer contents will be discarded (invalid) after the next back buffer is presented. This can improve performance.

- FullScreen_RefreshRateInHz: Refresh rate. Use the default refresh rate by specifying D3DPRESENT_RATE_DEFAULT.
- PresentationInterval: A member of the D3DPRESENT set. See the documentation for a complete list of valid intervals. Two common intervals are:

  D3DPRESENT_INTERVAL_IMMEDIATE: Presents immediately.

  D3DPRESENT_INTERVAL_DEFAULT: Direct3D will choose the present rate. Usually this is equal to the refresh rate.

Note: The back buffer dimensions should always match the client area dimensions for a crisp image. If they do not match, Direct3D will do a rectangle stretch to make it fit, but this stretch degrades the visual quality.

An example of filling this structure out is:

```
D3DPRESENT_PARAMETERS d3dpp;
d3dpp.BackBufferWidth            = 800;
d3dpp.BackBufferHeight           = 600;
d3dpp.BackBufferFormat           = D3DFMT_X8R8G8B8;
d3dpp.BackBufferCount            = 1;
d3dpp.MultiSampleType            = D3DMULTISAMPLE_NONE;
d3dpp.MultiSampleQuality         = 0;
d3dpp.SwapEffect                 = D3DSWAPEFFECT_DISCARD;
d3dpp.hDeviceWindow              = hwnd;
d3dpp.Windowed                   = true;
d3dpp.EnableAutoDepthStencil     = true;
d3dpp.AutoDepthStencilFormat     = D3DFMT_D24S8;
d3dpp.Flags                      = 0;
d3dpp.FullScreen_RefreshRateInHz = D3DPRESENT_RATE_DEFAULT;
d3dpp.PresentationInterval       = D3DPRESENT_INTERVAL_IMMEDIATE;
```

4.3.5 **Creating the IDirect3DDevice9 Interface**

With the D3DPRESENT_PARAMETERS filled out, we can finally create the
IDirect3DDevice9 object with the following method:

```
HRESULT IDirect3D9::CreateDevice(
    UINT Adapter,
    D3DDEVTYPE DeviceType,
    HWND hFocusWindow,
    DWORD BehaviorFlags,
    D3DPRESENT_PARAMETERS *pPresentationParameters,
    IDirect3DDevice9** ppReturnedDeviceInterface);
```

- Adapter: Specifies the physical display adapter we want the created
  IDirect3DDevice9 object to represent.

- DeviceType: Specifies the device type to use (e.g., hardware device
  [D3DDEVTYPE_HAL] or reference device [D3DDEVTYPE_REF]).

- hFocusWindow: Handle to the window the device will be associated with.
  This is typically the window into which the device will draw, and for our
  purposes it will be the same handle we specified for the data member
  d3dpp.hDeviceWindow of the D3DPRESENT_PARAMETERS structure.

- BehaviorFlags: Here we specify the creation flags we checked for in
  §4.3.3; that is, we specify either: D3DCREATE_HARDWARE_VERTEXPROCESSING,
  D3DCREATE_HARDWARE_VERTEXPROCESSING | D3DCREATE_PUREDEVICE, D3DCREATE_
  SOFTWARE_VERTEXPROCESSING, or D3DCREATE_MIXED_VERTEXPROCESSING.

  There are other additional flags; see D3DCREATE in the SDK documentation for details.

- pPresentationParameters: Specify an initialized D3DPRESENT_PARAMETERS
  instance that defines some of the characteristics of the device to create.

- ppReturnedDeviceInterface: Returns the created device.

Note: If hardware vertex processing is supported, you can actually use D3DCREATE_MIXED_VERTEXPROCESSING, which allows you to
switch between hardware vertex processing and software vertex processing at run time. To switch, you use the following method:

```
HRESULT SetSoftwareVertexProcessing(BOOL bSoftware);
```

Example call:

```
IDirect3DDevice9* gd3dDevice = 0;
HR(md3dObject->CreateDevice(
    D3DADAPTER_DEFAULT,   // primary adapter
    D3DDEVTYPE_HAL,       // device type
    mhMainWnd,            // window associated with device
    devBehaviorFlags,     // vertex processing / pure device
    &md3dPP,              // present parameters
    &gd3dDevice));        // return created device
```

Note: Only one IDirect3DDevice9 object should be created per application. Consequently, since there is only one IDirect3DDevice9 object, it is typical to provide access to this object at the global scope.

4.4 **Lost Devices**

The device object can become lost due to various reasons. The standard example of an event that causes the device to be lost is using Alt+Tab from full-screen mode. When a device is lost, only two device methods work:

- IDirect3DDevice9::TestCooperativeLevel
- IDirect3DDevice9::Reset

The IDirect3DDevice9::TestCooperativeLevel method returns the current state of the device and is one of the following:

- D3DERR_DEVICELOST: The device is lost and cannot be reset yet.
- D3DERR_DRIVERINTERNALERROR: An internal driver error has occurred; in this case, the application should terminate.
- D3DERR_DEVICENOTRESET: The device is lost but can be restored by calling IDirect3DDevice9::Reset.
- D3D_OK: The device is running in a normal operational state.

Our demo application framework, which we discuss in the next section, handles lost devices with the following method:

```
bool D3DApp::isDeviceLost()
{
    // Returns true if lost, false otherwise.

// Get the state of the graphics device.
    HRESULT hr = gd3dDevice->TestCooperativeLevel();

    // If the device is lost and cannot be reset yet, then
    // sleep for a bit and we'll try again on the next
    // message loop cycle.
    if( hr == D3DERR_DEVICELOST )
    {
        Sleep(20);
        return true;
    }
    // Driver error, exit.
    else if( hr == D3DERR_DRIVERINTERNALERROR )
    {
        MessageBox(0, "Internal Driver Error...Exiting", 0, 0);
        PostQuitMessage(0);
        return true;
    }
    // The device is lost but we can reset and restore it.
    else if( hr == D3DERR_DEVICENOTRESET )
```

```
    {
        onLostDevice();
        HR(gd3dDevice->Reset(&md3dPP));
        onResetDevice();
        // Not lost anymore.
        return false;
    }
    else
        // Not lost anymore.
        return false;
}
```

This function is called every cycle of the application message loop.

IDirect3DDevice9::Reset takes a single parameter to a filled-out D3DPRESENT_PARAMETERS instance; for this reason, the D3DPRESENT_PARAMETERS instance used to create the device should be saved so that it can be used for subsequent Reset calls.

Observe the two methods, onLostDevice and onResetDevice, that surround the Reset call. These methods are part of our application framework. Recall that resources in the D3DPOOL_DEFAULT memory pool need to be released prior to invoking the Reset method, and need to be restored after invoking the Reset method. For resources in D3DPOOL_DEFAULT, we put the resource release code in onLostDevice and the resource restoration code in onResetDevice.

4.5 **The Demo Application Framework**

The demos in this book use code from the *d3dUtil.h*, *d3dApp.h*, and *d3dApp.cpp* files, which can be downloaded from the book's website. The *d3dUtil.h* file contains useful utility code, and the *d3dApp.h* and *d3dApp.cpp* files contain the core Direct3D application class code that is used to encapsulate a Direct3D application. Be aware that the *d3dUtil.h* file will be appended throughout this book as we learn about new functionality; *d3dApp.cpp* will also be modified slightly in the next chapter.

4.5.1 **D3DApp**

The D3DApp class is the base Direct3D application class, which provides functions for creating the main application window, running the application message loop, handling window messages, initializing Direct3D, handling lost devices, and enabling full-screen mode. Moreover, the class defines the framework functions for the demo applications. Clients are to derive from D3DApp, override the virtual framework methods, and instantiate only a single instance of the derived D3DApp class. Since there is only going to be one application instance, it is useful to keep a pointer to the derived application instance at the global scope; the client code should set the global application pointer gd3dApp (declared in *d3dUtil.h*) to point to the application instance during instantiation. For example, gd3dApp = new DerivedApp(...)).

D3DApp is defined as follows:

```
class D3DApp
{
public:
        D3DApp(HINSTANCE hInstance, std::string winCaption,
                D3DDEVTYPE devType, DWORD requestedVP);
        virtual ~D3DApp();

        HINSTANCE getAppInst();
        HWND      getMainWnd();

        virtual bool checkDeviceCaps()    { return true; }
        virtual void onLostDevice()       {}
        virtual void onResetDevice()      {}
        virtual void updateScene(float dt) {}
        virtual void drawScene()          {}

        virtual void initMainWindow();
        virtual void initDirect3D();
        virtual int run();
        virtual LRESULT msgProc(UINT msg, WPARAM wParam, LPARAM lParam);

        void enableFullScreenMode(bool enable);
        bool isDeviceLost();

protected:
        std::string mMainWndCaption;
        D3DDEVTYPE  mDevType;
        DWORD       mRequestedVP;

        HINSTANCE            mhAppInst;
        HWND                 mhMainWnd;
        IDirect3D9*          md3dObject;
        bool                 mAppPaused;
        D3DPRESENT_PARAMETERS md3dPP;
};
```

We discuss the data members here; the methods are discussed in the subsequent sections.

- mMainWndCaption: This data member is to be initialized in the constructor of the class that derives from D3DApp; set it to the string value you want to appear in the main window's title bar.

- mDevType: This data member is set by the third parameter of the D3DApp constructor, which specifies the device type (D3DDEVTYPE_HAL or D3DDEVTYPE_REF) you want to use for the demo application.

- mRequestedVP: This data member is set by the fourth parameter of the D3DApp constructor, which specifies the vertex processing type you want to use for the demo application (D3DCREATE_HARDWARE_VERTEXPROCESSING, D3DCREATE_MIXED_VERTEXPROCESSING, or D3DCREATE_SOFTWARE_VERTEXPROCESSING).

- `mhAppInst`: Stores a copy of the application instance handle.
- `mhMainWnd`: Stores a copy of the main application window handle.
- `md3dObject`: Stores a pointer to an `IDirect3D9` object.
- `mAppPaused`: `True` if the application is paused; `false` otherwise.
- `md3dPP`: Stores a copy of the presentation parameters used to create the device; this is useful to have when we need to reset the device.

Note: The *d3dUtil.h* file declares the following global variables:

```
extern D3DApp* gd3dApp;
extern IDirect3DDevice9* gd3dDevice;
```

4.5.2 Non-Framework Methods

- `D3DApp`: The constructor internally calls `initMainWindow` and `initDirect3D`; thus, by the time execution reaches the constructor of the derived class, we can assume the main application window and Direct3D have already been initialized. The parameters to the constructor are simply passed on to the corresponding data members (e.g., the parameter `hInstance` gets assigned to `mhAppInst`).

- `~D3DApp`: The destructor releases the COM interfaces `md3dObject` and `gd3dDevice`.

- `getAppInst`: Trivial access function returns a copy of the application instance handle.

- `getMainWnd`: Trivial access function returns a copy of the main window handle.

- `initMainWindow`: Initializes the main application window; we assume the reader is familiar with basic Win32 window initialization.

- `initDirect3D`: Initializes Direct3D by implementing the five steps discussed in §4.3 to create the Direct3D device.

- `enableFullScreenMode`: Provides the ability to switch to full-screen mode and back to windowed mode at run time; this method is discussed in §4.5.5.

- `isDeviceLost`: Checks the state of the device (lost or not) and reacts accordingly; we discussed this method in §4.4.

- `msgProc`: This method implements the window procedure function for the main application window; we study it in more detail in §4.5.4.

- `run`: This method wraps the application message loop. It uses the Win32 `PeekMessage` function so that it can process our game logic when no messages are present, and it is implemented as follows:

```
int D3DApp::run()
{
    MSG msg;
    msg.message = WM_NULL;
    while(msg.message != WM_QUIT)
    {
        // If there are Window messages then process them.
        if(PeekMessage( &msg, 0, 0, 0, PM_REMOVE ))
        {
            TranslateMessage( &msg );
            DispatchMessage( &msg );
        }
        // Otherwise, do animation/game stuff.
        else
        {
            // If the application is paused then free some CPU
            // cycles to other applications and then continue on
            // to the next frame.
            if( mAppPaused )
            {
                Sleep(20);
                continue;
            }

            if( !isDeviceLost() )
            {
                updateScene(0.0f);
                drawScene();
            }
        }
    }
    return (int)msg.wParam;
}
```

Note: Although some of these non-framework functions are made virtual, they typically never need to be overridden. In fact, we never override them once in the entire book. However, they are made virtual to give you the option of overriding them if their default behavior is not satisfactory.

Note: Right now, we simply pass in 0.0 to the updateScene method. In Chapter 5, however, we discuss timing and we will pass in a time differential value to updateScene.

4.5.3 Framework Methods

For each sample application in this book, we consistently override five virtual functions of D3DApp. These five functions are used to implement the code specific to the particular sample. The benefit of this setup is that all the initialization, message handling, etc., is implemented in the non-framework methods of D3DApp; thus, for each sample, we only need to concentrate on these five framework functions, which contain the code specific to the particular sample application we are working on. Here is a description of the framework methods:

- checkDeviceCaps: For this method, we implement device checking to verify that the hardware supports any special features our demo application requires. Note that we only check new features, and assume most older features are supported. This function is to return true if the device meets the required capabilities, and false if it does not.

- onLostDevice: This method is called by D3DApp before a device is to be reset, and so it should execute code that needs to be invoked prior to a device reset, such as releasing resources in D3DPOOL_DEFAULT.

- onResetDevice: This method is called by D3DApp after a device has been reset, and so it should execute code that needs to be invoked after a device reset, such as restoring resources in D3DPOOL_DEFAULT and restoring device states.

- updateScene: This method is called every frame and should be used to update the 3D application over time (e.g., perform animation and collision detection, check for user input, calculate the frames per second, etc.).

- drawScene: This method is invoked every frame and is used to draw the current frame of our 3D scene.

Note: Device states are covered in Chapter 7, but they too are lost when the device is reset, and therefore must be restored after.

4.5.4 The Message Handler: msgProc

The window procedure we implement for our application framework does the bare minimum. In general, we won't be working very much with Win32 messages anyway. In fact, the core of our application code gets executed during idle processing (i.e., when no window message is present). Still, there are some important messages we do need to process. Because of the length of the window procedure, we do not embed all the code here; rather, we just explain the motivation behind each message we handle. We encourage the reader to download the source code files and spend some time becoming familiar with the application framework code (it has been generously commented), as it is the foundation of every sample for this book.

The first message we handle is the WM_ACTIVATE message. This message is sent when an application becomes activated or deactivated. When our application becomes deactivated, we set the data member mAppPaused to true, and when our application becomes active, we set the data member mAppPaused to false. If we look back at the implementation of D3DApp::run, we find that if our application is paused, then we do not execute our application code, but instead free some CPU cycles back to the OS and continue on to the next loop cycle. In this way, our application does not hog CPU cycles when it is inactive.

The next message we handle is the WM_SIZE message. Recall that this message is called when the window is resized. The reason for handling this message is that we want the back buffer dimensions to match the dimensions of the client area rectangle (so no stretching occurs). Thus, every time the window is resized, we want to resize the back buffer dimensions. To do this, we simply execute some code like this:

```
md3dPP.BackBufferWidth  = LOWORD(lParam);
md3dPP.BackBufferHeight = HIWORD(lParam);
onLostDevice();
HR(gd3dDevice->Reset(&md3dPP));
onResetDevice();
```

Now, if the user is dragging the resize bars, we must be careful because dragging the resize bars sends continuous WM_SIZE messages, and we do not want to continuously reset the Direct3D device. Therefore, if we determine that the user is resizing by dragging, we actually do nothing.

Still, we do want to reset the device with the correct back buffer dimensions when the user is done dragging the resize bars. We can do this by handling the WM_EXITSIZEMOVE message. This message is sent when the user releases the resize bars:

```
case WM_EXITSIZEMOVE:
     GetClientRect(mhMainWnd, &clientRect);
     md3dPP.BackBufferWidth  = clientRect.right;
     md3dPP.BackBufferHeight = clientRect.bottom;
     onLostDevice();
     HR(gd3dDevice->Reset(&md3dPP));
     onResetDevice();
     return 0;
```

Finally, the last three messages we handle are trivially implemented and so we just show the code:

```
// WM_CLOSE is sent when the user presses the 'X' button in the
// caption bar menu.
case WM_CLOSE:
     DestroyWindow(mhMainWnd);
     return 0;

// WM_DESTROY is sent when the window is being destroyed.
case WM_DESTROY:
     PostQuitMessage(0);
     return 0;

case WM_KEYDOWN:
     if( wParam == VK_ESCAPE )
          enableFullScreenMode(false);
```

```
        else if( wParam == 'F' )
                enableFullScreenMode(true);
        return 0;


    }
    return DefWindowProc(mhMainWnd, msg, wParam, lParam);
```

Observe that the application can be switched to full-screen mode by pressing the "F" key and can be switched back to windowed mode by pressing
the Escape key.

4.5.5 Switching to Full-Screen Mode and Back

An unnecessary but nice-to-have feature of the application framework is the
ability to switch back and forth between full-screen mode and windowed
mode at run time. To implement this functionality, we have added an
enableFullScreenMode function to the D3DApp class; specify true for the single
parameter to switch to full-screen mode and false for the single parameter
to switch back to windowed mode.

```
void D3DApp::enableFullScreenMode(bool enable)
{
    // Switch to full screen mode.
    if( enable )
    {
        // Are we already in full screen mode?
        if( !md3dPP.Windowed )
            return;

        // Get the current screen resolution.
        int width  = GetSystemMetrics(SM_CXSCREEN);
        int height = GetSystemMetrics(SM_CYSCREEN);

        md3dPP.BackBufferFormat = D3DFMT_X8R8G8B8;
        md3dPP.BackBufferWidth  = width;
        md3dPP.BackBufferHeight = height;
        md3dPP.Windowed         = false;

        // Change the window style to a more full screen
        // friendly style.
        SetWindowLongPtr(mhMainWnd, GWL_STYLE, WS_POPUP);

        // If we call SetWindowLongPtr, MSDN states that we need
        // to call SetWindowPos for the change to take effect.
        // In addition, we need to call this function anyway
        // to update the window dimensions.
        SetWindowPos(mhMainWnd, HWND_TOP, 0, 0,
                width, height, SWP_NOZORDER | SWP_SHOWWINDOW);
    }
    // Switch to windowed mode.
    else
```

```
{
    // Are we already in windowed mode?
    if( md3dPP.Windowed )
        return;

    // Default to a client rectangle of 800x600.
    RECT R = {0, 0, 800, 600};
    AdjustWindowRect(&R, WS_OVERLAPPEDWINDOW, false);
    md3dPP.BackBufferFormat = D3DFMT_UNKNOWN;
    md3dPP.BackBufferWidth  = 800;
    md3dPP.BackBufferHeight = 600;
    md3dPP.Windowed         = true;

    // Change the window style to a more windowed
    // friendly style.
    SetWindowLongPtr(mhMainWnd,GWL_STYLE,WS_OVERLAPPEDWINDOW);

    // If we call SetWindowLongPtr, MSDN states that we
    // need to call SetWindowPos for the change to take effect.
    // In addition, we need to call this function anyway to
    // update the window dimensions.
    SetWindowPos(mhMainWnd, HWND_TOP, 100, 100,
        R.right, R.bottom, SWP_NOZORDER | SWP_SHOWWINDOW);
}

// Reset the device with the changes.
onLostDevice();
HR(gd3dDevice->Reset(&md3dPP));
onResetDevice();
}
```

A few remarks about `enableFullScreenMode`:

- The function uses the current screen resolution when switching to full screen; it does not support changing the resolution.

- When switching to full-screen mode, we switch to a simpler window style that is better suited for a full-screen window — no border, caption, system menu, min/max buttons, etc.

- Recall that the window size is larger than the client area size. Thus, to have a client area rectangle of dimensions 800×600, we need to make the window rectangle slightly larger. The `AdjustWindowRect` function calculates precisely how much larger it needs to be given the desired client rectangle size (800×600) and window style (`WS_OVERLAPPEDWINDOW`).

- Observe that we have changed the back buffer dimensions, and thus need to reset the device in order for the changes to take place.

4.6 **Demo Application: Hello Direct3D**

Finally, we can put everything we have learned thus far together and write our first Direct3D program. In this demo application, we initialize Direct3D and output text to the client area using Direct3D. To make the demo less boring, we draw the text using a new random color each frame. Figure 4.10 shows a screenshot of the demo:

Figure 4.10: A screenshot of the demo application we create in this chapter.

When beginning a new application, we derive a new class from D3DApp and override the framework functions:

```cpp
class HelloD3DApp : public D3DApp
{
public:
    HelloD3DApp(HINSTANCE hInstance,
                std::string winCaption,
                D3DDEVTYPE devType, DWORD requestedVP);
    ~HelloD3DApp();

    bool checkDeviceCaps();
    void onLostDevice();
    void onResetDevice();
    void updateScene(float dt);
    void drawScene();

private:

    ID3DXFont* mFont;
};
```

This child class has one data member, an ID3DXFont interface from which text output in Direct3D is done.

To get the application rolling, we instantiate an instance of our child class and enter the message loop:

```
int WINAPI WinMain(HINSTANCE hInstance, HINSTANCE prevInstance,
                   PSTR cmdLine, int showCmd)
{
    // Enable run-time memory check for debug builds.
    #if defined(DEBUG) | defined(_DEBUG)
        _CrtSetDbgFlag( _CRTDBG_ALLOC_MEM_DF |
            _CRTDBG_LEAK_CHECK_DF );
    #endif


    HelloD3DApp app(hInstance);
    gd3dApp = &app;


    return gd3dApp->run();
}
```

Note that the first few lines of WinMain are used for debugging and are discussed in the next section, so just ignore them for now. Also recall that gd3dApp is a global D3DApp pointer declared in *d3dUtil.h*; in this way, we have access to the Direct3D application instance at the global scope.

Now, let's examine the implementation of the constructor, destructor, and framework methods.

```
HelloD3DApp::HelloD3DApp(HINSTANCE hInstance,
                         std::string winCaption,
                         D3DDEVTYPE devType, DWORD requestedVP)
: D3DApp(hInstance, winCaption, devType, requestedVP)
{
    srand(time_t(0));

    if(!checkDeviceCaps())
    {
        MessageBox(0, "checkDeviceCaps() Failed", 0, 0);
        PostQuitMessage(0);
    }


    D3DXFONT_DESC fontDesc;
    fontDesc.Height         = 80;
    fontDesc.Width          = 40;
    fontDesc.Weight         = FW_BOLD;
    fontDesc.MipLevels      = 0;
    fontDesc.Italic         = true;
    fontDesc.CharSet        = DEFAULT_CHARSET;
    fontDesc.OutputPrecision = OUT_DEFAULT_PRECIS;
    fontDesc.Quality        = DEFAULT_QUALITY;
    fontDesc.PitchAndFamily = DEFAULT_PITCH | FF_DONTCARE;
    _tcscpy(fontDesc.FaceName, _T("Times New Roman"));


    HR(D3DXCreateFontIndirect(gd3dDevice, &fontDesc, &mFont));
}
```

The constructor first constructs its parent part in the initialization list. Then it seeds the random number generator. Next it checks the device capabilities with `checkDeviceCaps`. It then fills out a `D3DXFONT_DESC` structure, which describes the attributes of the font we use for text drawing. Finally, it invokes the `D3DXCreateFontIndirect` function, which returns a pointer to an `ID3DXFont` interface (via the third parameter) based on the specified font description (parameter two). Note that the function also requires that we pass in a copy of a valid Direct3D device pointer (parameter one), since the font will need the device for drawing the text (all drawing is done through the Direct3D device).

Because the constructor created an `ID3DXFont` object, the destructor must destroy it:

```
HelloD3DApp::~HelloD3DApp()
{
    ReleaseCOM(mFont);
}
```

The `ReleaseCOM` macro is defined in *d3dUtil.h* and simply calls the `Release` method and sets the pointer to null:

```
#define ReleaseCOM(x) { if(x){ x->Release();x = 0; } }
```

For this simple demo, there are no device capabilities to check; thus our `checkDeviceCaps` implementation simply returns `true`:

```
bool HelloD3DApp::checkDeviceCaps()
{
    // Nothing to check.
    return true;
}
```

Similarly, there is nothing to update in this demo, so our `updateScene` function does nothing:

```
void HelloD3DApp::updateScene(float dt)
{
}
```

Recall that certain resources need to be released before resetting the device, and certain resources and device states need to be restored after resetting the device. To handle these situations, our framework provides the `onLostDevice` and `onResetDevice` methods, which are called before and after a device is reset, respectively. The `mFont` object contains Direct3D resources internally and needs to do some work before a reset and after; thus we have:

```
void HelloD3DApp::onLostDevice()
{
    HR(mFont->OnLostDevice());
}
void HelloD3DApp::onResetDevice()
```

```
{
    HR(mFont->OnResetDevice());
}
```

Here `mFont->OnLostDevice` invokes whatever code `ID3DXFont` needs to execute before a reset, and `mFont->OnResetDevice` invokes whatever code `ID3DXFont` needs to execute after a reset. (We don't know what that code is since we didn't implement `ID3DXFont`, but the documentation says to use these functions like this, so we do it.)

Finally, we implement the `drawScene` method and output the text:

```
void HelloD3DApp::drawScene()
{
    HR(gd3dDevice->Clear(0, 0, D3DCLEAR_TARGET | D3DCLEAR_ZBUFFER,
        D3DCOLOR_XRGB(255, 255, 255), 1.0f, 0));

    RECT formatRect;
    GetClientRect(mhMainWnd, &formatRect);

    HR(gd3dDevice->BeginScene());

    mFont->DrawText(0, _T("Hello Direct3D"), -1,
        &formatRect, DT_CENTER | DT_VCENTER,
        D3DCOLOR_XRGB(rand() % 256, rand() % 256, rand() % 256));

    HR(gd3dDevice->EndScene());
    HR(gd3dDevice->Present(0, 0, 0, 0));
}
```

Observe first that we call the `IDirect3DDevice9::Clear` method, which clears the back buffer (target) and depth buffer to `D3DCOLOR_XRGB(255, 255, 255)` (white) and 1.0, respectively. The declaration of `IDirect3DDevice9::Clear` is:

```
HRESULT IDirect3DDevice9::Clear(
    DWORD Count,
    const D3DRECT* pRects,
    DWORD Flags,
    D3DCOLOR Color,
    float Z,
    DWORD Stencil);
```

- `Count`: Number of rectangles in the `pRects` array.

- `pRects`: An array of screen rectangles to clear. This allows us to only clear parts of a surface.

- `Flags`: Specifies which surfaces to clear. We can clear one or more (combined by a bitwise OR) of the following surfaces:

    `D3DCLEAR_TARGET`: The render target surface, usually the back buffer.

    `D3DCLEAR_ZBUFFER`: The depth buffer.

    `D3DCLEAR_STENCIL`: The stencil buffer.

- `Color`: The color to which we wish to clear the render target.

- `Z`: The value to which we wish to set the depth buffer (z-buffer).

■ Stencil: The value to which we wish to set the stencil buffer.

After we have cleared the back buffer and depth buffer, we get the dimensions of the client area rectangle, which will be used to format the text in the window.

Now observe that the text drawing method ID3DXFont::DrawText is between IDirect3DDevice9::BeginScene and IDirect3DDevice9::EndScene calls; this is important, as all drawing by the Direct3D device must always take place between these two functions. The ID3DXFont::DrawText function takes six parameters:

```
INT ID3DXFont::DrawText(
    LPD3DXSPRITE pSprite,
    LPCTSTR pString,
    INT Count,
    LPRECT pRect,
    DWORD Format,
    D3DCOLOR Color);
```

■ pSprite: Pointer to an ID3DXSprite interface. Set this to null for now; we talk about the ID3DXSprite interface in Chapter 5.

■ pString: Pointer to the string to draw.

■ Count: Number of characters in the string. We can specify –1 if the string is null terminating.

■ pRect: Pointer to a RECT structure that defines the area on the screen to which the text is to be drawn and formatted.

■ Format: Optional flags that specify how the text should be formatted in the RECT specified by pRect. In drawScene, we use the combination DT_CENTER | DT_VCENTER, which means to center the text horizontally and vertically relative to the formatting rectangle.

■ Color: The text color. To obtain a D3DCOLOR type, we use the D3DCOLOR_ XRGB macro, which returns a D3DCOLOR based on the combination of red (first parameter), green (second parameter), and blue (third parameter) intensity; note that color component intensities range from 0 (no intensity) to 255 (full intensity). In drawScene, we use a random color each frame and thus specify: D3DCOLOR_XRGB(rand() % 256, rand() % 256, rand() % 256).

Finally, after drawing is done, we present the back buffer (§4.2.2) by calling the IDirect3DDevice9::Present method; problem 3 of the Exercises asks you to investigate the parameters of this method, but for now we just want to present the back buffer and can specify null for the four parameters.

Note: Before continuing, or at least before moving on to the next chapter, you should compile this first demo application and familiar- ize yourself with the code. It is important to have a good handle on the basics before moving on to more difficult topics.

> **Note:** Remember to link the following DirectX library files into your project: *d3d9.lib*, *d3dx9.lib*, *dxguid.lib*, *DxErr9.lib*, and *dinput8.lib*.

4.7 **Debugging Direct3D Applications**

In this section, we provide some basic tips for debugging Direct3D applications. The first thing you need to do is enable Direct3D debugging; this can be done by going to the Control Panel and double-clicking the DirectX icon (see Figure 4.11).

Figure 4.11: Double-click the DirectX icon from the Control Panel to launch the DirectX Properties dialog box.

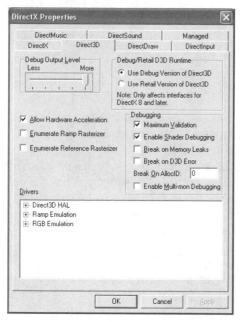

Figure 4.12: The DirectX Properties dialog box. Select the Direct3D tab, turn up the Debug Output Level setting, select the debug version of the Direct3D Runtime, and check any additional debugging options you want.

A dialog box should appear (Figure 4.12). Select the Direct3D tab and set the Debug Output Level slide bar to the maximum value. Then select the Use Debug Version of Direct3D radio button. Finally, check the debug options you want: Maximum Validation, Enable Shader Debugging, etc. Press Apply and then OK. Note that using the Direct3D debugger will significantly decrease performance speed, so you will probably want to turn it on and off frequently during development.

By turning on Direct3D debugging, Direct3D should output information in the debug spew of Visual C++, as shown in Figure 4.13.

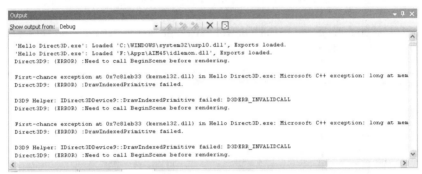

Figure 4.13: By enabling debugging, Direct3D will output error information to the debug spew window in Visual C++. The figure here shows the errors that can occur if we attempt to draw outside a `BeginScene` and `EndScene` block.

You can enable extra Direct3D debugging by defining the following symbol (note that this symbol must be defined before you include the Direct3D header files):

```
#if defined(DEBUG) | defined(_DEBUG)
#ifndef D3D_DEBUG_INFO
#define D3D_DEBUG_INFO
#endif
#endif
```

By construction, this symbol will only be defined in debug mode and not release mode, which is exactly what you want. Our demo framework defines this symbol in *d3dUtil.h*.

Another important thing to do for debugging is to link *d3dx9d.lib* (for debug builds) instead of *d3dx9.lib*. With the "d" suffix, you link the debug version of the D3DX library. For release versions, just link *d3dx9.lib*.

For general-purpose (non-Direct3D) memory leak detection, we can call the following function in debug builds:

```
// Enable run-time memory check for debug builds.
#if defined(DEBUG) | defined(_DEBUG)
_CrtSetDbgFlag( _CRTDBG_ALLOC_MEM_DF | _CRTDBG_LEAK_CHECK_DF );
#endif
```

This function turns on memory leak checking at application exit, and will provide an error report in the debug spew of Visual C++ if there were memory leaks. We write the above code as the first thing in `WinMain` of every demo application.

We have seen the use of an HR macro when we use Direct3D methods; for example, HR(gd3dDevice->Present(0, 0, 0, 0)). Each Direct3D method returns a return value of type HRESULT, which is just a return code. To test whether the function failed or succeeded, we pass the returned HRESULT to the Win32 FAILED macro, which returns true if the HRESULT is an error code and false if there is no error (usually D3D_OK). For further details about an error code, we can use the DXTrace function, which is prototyped as follows:

```
HRESULT DXTrace(CHAR *strFile, DWORD dwline,
    HRESULT hr, CHAR *strMsg, BOOL bPopMsgBox);
```

The first parameter is the string of the source code file in which the function was called (you can get this with the predefined __FILE__ macro, which returns the filename in which the macro is placed); the second parameter is the source code line number on which the function was called (you can get this with the predefined __LINE__ macro, which returns the source code line number where the macro is placed); the third parameter is the failing HRESULT code; the fourth parameter is a string message to display; and the fifth parameter is true if you want an error dialog box to pop up (which asks the user to break into the debugger — see Figure 4.14), and false otherwise.

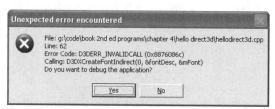

Figure 4.14: The message box displayed by the DXTrace function if a Direct3D function returns an error. It tells us the file, the line number, and a description of the error, and asks if we want to break into the debugger.

Note: To use DXTrace, link *dxerr9.lib* and include *dxerr9.h*.

In our code, we do not call DXTrace explicitly. Instead, we wrap it in another macro that fills in the parameters for us:

```
#if defined(DEBUG) | defined(_DEBUG)
    #ifndef HR
    #define HR(x)                                                \
    {                                                            \
        HRESULT hr = x;                                          \
        if(FAILED(hr))                                           \
        {                                                        \
            DXTrace(__FILE__, __LINE__, hr, #x, TRUE); \
        }                                                        \
    }
    #endif
```

```
#else
    #ifndef HR
    #define HR(x) x;
    #endif
#endif
```

In this way, we can handle errors with very little additional code. For example:

```
HR(D3DXCreateFontIndirect(gd3dDevice, &fontDesc, &mFont));
```

■ Observe that we pass #x into the fourth parameter; this turns the HR macro's argument token into a string. In this way, we can output the function call that caused the error; see Figure 4.14 (in particular, the "Calling: D3DXCreateFontIndirect...," which corresponds to this fourth parameter of DXTrace).

■ By construction, the HR macro only does anything in debug mode. This is fine, because by the time we are shipping an application, all the Direct3D bugs should be worked out.

■ HR needs to be a macro and not a function, because if it were a function, _FILE_ and _LINE_ would refer to the file and line of the function implementation, and not the file and line where the function HR was called. So we need a macro so that the code is actually *substituted* into the place where we write HR.

4.8 **Summary**

■ Direct3D can be thought of as a mediator between the programmer and the graphics hardware. The programmer calls a Direct3D function, which in turn instructs the physical hardware to perform the operation by interfacing with the device's HAL (hardware abstraction layer). Direct3D is an immediate mode API, and the hardware will execute commands as immediately as possible.

■ The REF device allows developers to test features Direct3D exposes but that are not implemented by available hardware.

■ Component Object Model (COM) is the technology that allows DirectX to be language independent and have backward compatibility. Direct3D programmers don't need to know the details of COM and how it works; they need only to know how to acquire COM interfaces and how to release them.

■ Surfaces are special Direct3D interfaces used to store 2D images. A member of the D3DFORMAT enumerated type specifies the pixel format of a surface. Surfaces and other Direct3D resources can be stored in several different memory pools as specified by a member of the D3DPOOL enumerated type. In addition, some surfaces can be multisampled if the hardware supports it, which creates a smoother image by using antialiasing.

■ The IDirect3D9 interface is used to find information about the system's graphics devices. For example, through this interface we can enumerate adapter display modes, obtain the capabilities of a device, check for multisampling support, and verify whether the hardware supports rendering to certain surface formats and in different combinations. It is also used to create the IDirect3DDevice9 interface.

■ The IDirect3DDevice9 interface can be thought of as our software interface for controlling the graphics device. For instance, calling the IDirect3DDevice9::Clear method will command the graphics device to clear the specified surface.

■ The sample framework is used to provide a consistent interface that all demo applications in this book follow. The code provided in the _d3dUtil.h, d3dApp.h_, and _d3dApp.cpp_ files wrap standard initialization code that every application must implement. By wrapping this code up, we hide it, which allows the samples to be more focused on demonstrating the current topic.

■ To debug Direct3D applications, the debug runtime must be selected in the Direct3D tab of the DirectX Properties dialog box (accessed from the Control Panel). For additional Direct3D debugging help, the application should define D3D_DEBUG_INFO before it includes the Direct3D header files. For D3DX debugging, link the debug D3DX library, _d3dx9d.lib_ (for debug builds), instead of _d3dx9.lib_. For general-purpose memory leak detection, use the Win32 API function _CrtSetDbgFlag.

4.9 **Exercises**

1. For each adapter on your system, enumerate the display modes for the formats D3DFMT_X8R8G8B8 and D3DFMT_R5G6B5. Save your results to a text file; your output should look similar to that of Figure 4.6. Check your results by comparing it to the results given in the DirectX Caps Viewer.

2. For the primary display adapter, check to see which of the following multisample types the adapter supports in both windowed mode and full-screen mode: D3DMULTISAMPLE_2_SAMPLES, ..., D3DMULTISAMPLE_16_ SAMPLES. Use a HAL device, and try it with formats D3DFMT_X8R8G8B8 and D3DFMT_R5G6B5. Save your results to a text file in a readable descriptive format. Check your results by comparing it to the results given in the DirectX Caps Viewer.

3. Look up the following methods in the SDK and write a summary, in your own words, on how to use them.

   a. IDirect3D9::CheckDepthStencilMatch

   b. IDirect3D9::CheckDeviceFormat

   c. IDirect3DSurface9::GetDC

   d. IDirect3DSwapChain9::GetBackBuffer

   e. IDirect3DDevice9::Present

4. Modify the Hello Direct3D demo program so that it does not resize the back buffer when the window is resized. Explain your results.

5. Write a program that checks if your primary adapter supports the following device capabilities:

   a. D3DPRESENT_INTERVAL_IMMEDIATE

   b. D3DPTADDRESSCAPS_CLAMP

   c. D3DFVFCAPS_PSIZE

   d. D3DCAPS2_CANAUTOGENMIPMAP

   e. D3DPRASTERCAPS_DITHER

   Moreover, determine the MaxPointSize, MaxPrimitiveCount, MaxActiveLights, MaxUserClipPlanes, MaxVertexIndex, and MaxVertexShaderConst of the primary display adapter. (Hint: All this information can be found by looking at the D3DCAPS9 structure — you will need to look up "D3DCAPS9" in the SDK documentation for help on this exercise.)

6. Look up ID3DXLine in the SDK documentation and see if you can figure out how to draw some lines to the window. (Hint: Particularly concern yourself with the function D3DXCreateLine and the methods ID3DXLine::Begin, ID3DXLine::End, ID3DXLine::OnLostDevice, ID3DXLine::OnResetDevice, and ID3DXLine::Draw. Once you have basic line drawing working, you can experiment with the other methods that allow you to change the attributes of the line, such as its width and pattern.)

Chapter 5

Timing, Direct Input, and Animation and Sprites

This chapter covers several small topics. We show how to use the performance counter for computing the frames per second and for updating game objects based on time (animation); we also show how to initialize Direct Input for immediate mode keyboard and mouse input; and in addition, we show how to draw 2D sprites using the ID3DXSprite interface. It is also the last chapter before we dive into 3D graphics programming.

Objectives:

- To learn how to use the Win32 performance counter functions for obtaining high-resolution timer readings.
- To find out how to compute the time that elapses between frames, how to compute the frames being rendered per second, and how to compute the time spent processing a frame.
- To become familiar with basic Direct Input concepts, and how to use immediate mode Direct Input to obtain input from the mouse and keyboard.
- To discover how to draw 2D images with the ID3DXSprite interface, and how to animate these images over time.

5.1 **The Performance Timer**

For accurate time measurements, we use the performance timer (or performance counter). To use the Win32 functions for querying the performance timer, we must #include<windows.h>.

The performance timer measures time in units called *counts*. We obtain the current time value (measured in counts) of the performance timer with the QueryPerformanceCounter function like so:

```
__int64 prevTimeStamp = 0;
QueryPerformanceCounter((LARGE_INTEGER*)&prevTimeStamp);
```

Observe that this function returns the current time value through its parameter, which is a 64-bit integer value.

Note: The values returned by the QueryPerformanceCounter function are not particularly interesting in and of themselves. What we do is get the current time value using QueryPerformanceCounter, and then get the current time value a little later using QueryPerformanceCounter again. Then the time (in counts) that elapsed between those two time calls is just the difference. The following better illustrates the idea:

```
__int64 A = 0;
QueryPerformanceCounter((LARGE_INTEGER*)&A);

/* Do work */

__int64 B = 0;
QueryPerformanceCounter((LARGE_INTEGER*)&B);
```

How much time did it take to "do work"? In units of counts, it took B – A counts.

Now this "counts" unit is not particularly meaningful to us; we would like to convert it to something that makes more sense to us, such as seconds. Fortunately, there is another API function, QueryPerformanceFrequency, which returns the performance timer's frequency (counts per second) so that we can convert time readings from units of counts to units of seconds. The function is invoked as follows:

```
__int64 cntsPerSec = 0;
QueryPerformanceFrequency((LARGE_INTEGER*)&cntsPerSec);
```

Then the number of seconds per count is just the reciprocal of the counts per second:

```
float secsPerCnt = 1.0f / (float)cntsPerSec;
```

Thus, to convert a counts time reading `valueInCounts` to seconds, we just multiply it by the conversion factor `secsPerCnt` (which tells us how many seconds [or fraction of a second] there are in one count):

```
valueInSecs = valueInCounts * secsPerCnt;
```

Note: The function `QueryPerformanceFrequency` returns a `BOOL` type; specifically, `true` is returned if the performance timer exists and `false` otherwise. Pentiums and above have the performance timer, so it can be assumed to exist. Still, if you do not want to make that assumption, you can fall back to the Win32 multimedia timer function `timeGetTime`.

5.1.1 Time Differential between Frames

Computing the time differential between frames (i.e., the elapsed time between frames) is easy. Let t be the time returned by the performance counter during the ith frame and let t_{i-1} be the time returned by the performance counter during the previous frame. Then the time that elapsed between the t_{i-1} reading and the t_i reading is just: $\Delta t = t_i - t_{i-1}$. For real-time rendering, we typically require at least 30 frames per second (and we usually have much higher rates); thus, $\Delta t = t_i - t_{i-1}$ tends to be a relatively small number.

In our application framework, we compute the time differential, $\Delta t = t_i - t_{i-1}$, every frame and pass this value into our `updateScene` method. In this way, our application can update the game state with respect to time. Our application framework's modified `run` method now looks like this (new code lines bolded):

```
int D3DApp::run()
{
  MSG  msg;
  msg.message = WM_NULL;

  __int64 cntsPerSec = 0;
  QueryPerformanceFrequency((LARGE_INTEGER*)&cntsPerSec);
  float secsPerCnt = 1.0f / (float)cntsPerSec;

  __int64 prevTimeStamp = 0;
  QueryPerformanceCounter((LARGE_INTEGER*)&prevTimeStamp);

  while(msg.message != WM_QUIT)
  {
    // If there are Window messages then process them.
    if(PeekMessage( &msg, 0, 0, 0, PM_REMOVE ))
    {
      TranslateMessage( &msg );
      DispatchMessage( &msg );
    }
    // Otherwise, do animation/game stuff.
```

```
        else
        {
            if( mAppPaused )
            {
                Sleep(20);
                continue;
            }
            if( !isDeviceLost() )
            {
                __int64 currTimeStamp = 0;
                QueryPerformanceCounter((LARGE_INTEGER*)&currTimeStamp);
                float dt = (currTimeStamp - prevTimeStamp)*secsPerCnt;

                updateScene(dt);
                drawScene();

                // Prepare for next iteration: The current time
                // stamp becomes the previous time stamp for the
                // next iteration.
                prevTimeStamp = currTimeStamp;
            }
        }
    }
    return (int)msg.wParam;
}
```

5.1.2 Frames Per Second Calculation

It is common for games and graphics applications to measure the number of frames being rendered per second (FPS). To do this, we simply count the number of frames processed (and store it in a variable n) over some specified time period t. Then, the average FPS over the time period t is $fps_{avg} = n/t$. If we set $t=1$, then $fps_{avg} = n/1 = n$. In our code, we use $t=1$ since it avoids a division, and moreover, one second gives a pretty good average — it is not too long and not too short. The code to compute the FPS is provided as a method of the GfxStats class (which we discuss in the next subsection) as follows:

```
void GfxStats::update(float dt)
{
    // Make static so that their values persist across
    // function calls.
    static float numFrames  = 0.0f;
    static float timeElapsed = 0.0f;

    // Increment the frame count.
    numFrames += 1.0f;

    // Accumulate how much time has passed.
    timeElapsed += dt;

    // Has one second passed?--we compute the frame statistics once
```

```
        // per second.  Note that the time between frames can vary, so
        // these stats are averages over a second.
        if( timeElapsed >= 1.0f )
        {
                // Frames Per Second = numFrames / timeElapsed,
                // but timeElapsed approx. equals 1.0, so
                // frames per second = numFrames.

                mFPS = numFrames;

                // Average time, in milliseconds, it took to render a
                // single frame.
                mMilliSecPerFrame = 1000.0f / mFPS;

                // Reset time counter and frame count to prepare
                // for computing the average stats over the next second.
                timeElapsed = 0.0f;
                numFrames   = 0.0f;
        }
}
```

This method would be called every frame to count the frame.

In addition to computing the FPS, the above code also computes the number of milliseconds it takes, on average, to process a frame:

```
    mMilliSecPerFrame = 1000.0f / mFPS;
```

Note: The seconds per frame is just the reciprocal of the FPS, but we multiply by 1000 ms / 1 s to convert from seconds to milliseconds (recall that there are 1000 ms per second).

The idea behind this line is to compute the time, in milliseconds, it takes to render a frame; this is a different quantity than FPS (but observe this value can be derived from the FPS). In actuality, the time it takes to render a frame is more useful than the FPS, as we may directly see the increase/decrease in time it takes to render a frame as we modify our scene. On the other hand, the FPS does not immediately tell us the increase/decrease in time as we modify our scene. Moreover, as Robert Dunlop [Dunlop03] points out in his article "FPS Versus Frame Time," due to the non-linearity of the FPS curve, using the FPS can give misleading results. For example, consider situation (1): Suppose our application is running at 1000 FPS, taking 1 ms (millisecond) to render a frame. If the frame rate drops to 250 FPS, then it takes 4 ms to render a frame. Now consider situation (2): Suppose that our application is running at 100 FPS, taking 10 ms to render a frame. If the frame rate drops to about 76.9 FPS, then it takes about 13 ms to render a frame. In both situations, the rendering per frame increased by 3 ms, and thus both represent the same increase in time it takes to render a frame. Reading the FPS is not as straightforward. The drop from 1000 FPS to 250 FPS seems much more drastic than the drop from 100 FPS to 76.9

FPS; however, as we have just shown, they actually represent the same increase in time it takes to render a frame.

5.1.3 Graphics Stats Demo

To facilitate calculating and drawing the FPS and milliseconds per frame, we define and implement a graphics stats class called GfxStats:

```
class GfxStats
{
public:
        GfxStats();
        ~GfxStats();

        void onLostDevice();
        void onResetDevice();

        void addVertices(DWORD n);
        void subVertices(DWORD n);
        void addTriangles(DWORD n);
        void subTriangles(DWORD n);

        void setTriCount(DWORD n);
        void setVertexCount(DWORD n);

        void update(float dt);
        void display();

private:
        // Prevent copying
        GfxStats(const GfxStats& rhs);
        GfxStats& operator=(const GfxStats& rhs);

private:
        ID3DXFont* mFont;
        float mFPS;
        float mMilliSecPerFrame;
        DWORD mNumTris;
        DWORD mNumVertices;
};
```

Observe that the class contains an ID3DXFont object for displaying the statistics data, and it has members for storing the FPS and milliseconds per frame. A pointer to an ID3DXFont interface is obtained in the constructor just like it was in the Hello Direct3D demo from the previous chapter. We saw how the update method was implemented in the preceding subsection. The display method simply wraps the ID3DXFont::DrawText method to output the information:

```
void GfxStats::display()
{
    // Make static so memory is not allocated every frame.
    static char buffer[256];

    sprintf(buffer, "Frames Per Second = %.2f\n"
        "Milliseconds Per Frame = %.4f\n"
        "Triangle Count = %d\n"
        "Vertex Count = %d", mFPS, mMilliSecPerFrame,
                mNumTris, mNumVertices);

    RECT R = {5, 5, 0, 0};
    HR(mFont->DrawText(0, buffer, -1, &R, DT_NOCLIP,
        D3DCOLOR_XRGB(0,0,0)));
}
```

Note that the DT_NOCLIP flag means that the text will not be clipped by the formatting rectangle (i.e., the text can go outside the rectangle bounds and not be chopped off). Thus, the dimensions of the formatting rectangle are not needed — we really only need to specify the upper-left corner of the formatting rectangle to specify the position of the text in screen space.

To make the class more useful, it also keeps track of the overall scene triangle and vertex count; as we will learn in Chapter 6, our 3D worlds are composed of triangles and vertices. The triangle count and vertex count can be modified with the following methods:

```
void GfxStats::addVertices(DWORD n)    { mNumVertices += n;}
void GfxStats::subVertices(DWORD n)    { mNumVertices -= n;}
void GfxStats::addTriangles(DWORD n)   { mNumTris += n;    }
void GfxStats::subTriangles(DWORD n)   { mNumTris -= n;    }
void GfxStats::setTriCount(DWORD n)    { mNumTris = n;     }
void GfxStats::setVertexCount(DWORD n) { mNumVertices = n; }
```

Figure 5.1 shows a screenshot of the demo application illustrating the GfxStats class. It is rather trivial, and very similar to the Hello Direct3D demo, except that it computes the FPS and milliseconds per frame. Consequently, it also illustrates the performance timer functions. Be sure to familiarize yourself with the source code of the demo before moving on to the next chapter.

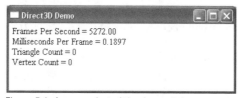

Figure 5.1: A screenshot of the demo stats screen.

5.2 **Direct Input Primer**

We know that via the Win32 API message system, we can obtain mouse and keyboard input. However, wouldn't it be faster to bypass the message system and work directly with the input drivers? This is exactly what Direct Input allows us to do. For the purposes of this book, we only use the keyboard and mouse, but Direct Input can work with joysticks, game controllers (including force feedback ones), and other game input devices; see the DirectX SDK documentation for details.

As we work through our discussion of Direct Input, we implement a DirectInput class at the same time. For reference, the class is defined as follows:

```
class DirectInput
{
public:
    DirectInput(DWORD keyboardCoopFlags, DWORD mouseCoopFlags);
    ~DirectInput();

    void poll();
    bool keyDown(char key);
    bool mouseButtonDown(int button);
    float mouseDX();
    float mouseDY();
    float mouseDZ();

private:
    // Make private to prevent copying of members of this class.
    DirectInput(const DirectInput& rhs);
    DirectInput& operator=(const DirectInput& rhs);

private:
    IDirectInput8*      mDInput;

    IDirectInputDevice8* mKeyboard;
    char                mKeyboardState[256];

    IDirectInputDevice8* mMouse;
    DIMOUSESTATE2       mMouseState;
};
```

The methods and data members will become evident as you work through this section.

Note that this class is designed to be instantiated only once. For convenient access, we declare the following global variable in *DirectInput.h*:

```
extern DirectInput* gDInput;
```

This variable should be made to point to the one and only instantiation of DirectInput; in this book's demos, we do this in WinMain:

```
int WINAPI WinMain(HINSTANCE hInstance, HINSTANCE prevInstance,
                   PSTR cmdLine, int showCmd)
{
    // Sprite demo discussed later
    SpriteDemo app(hInstance, "Sprite Demo", D3DDEVTYPE_HAL,
                   D3DCREATE_HARDWARE_VERTEXPROCESSING);
    gd3dApp = &app;

    DirectInput di(DISCL_NONEXCLUSIVE |
                   DISCL_FOREGROUND,
                   DISCL_NONEXCLUSIVE |
                   DISCL_FOREGROUND);
    gDInput = &di;

    return gd3dApp->run();
}
```

Note: The DirectInput class is defined and implemented in *DirectInput.h/.cpp*. To employ Direct Input, we need to #include <dinput.h> and link *dinput8.lib*.

In this book, we use immediate mode Direct Input, which looks at a snapshot of the input devices frequently. Another technique is buffered input, which records the state of the input devices over a period of time in a data buffer.

5.2.1 Interfaces

We concern ourselves with two Direct Input interfaces:

■   IDirectInputDevice8: This interface is Direct Input's analog to the IDirect3DDevice9 interface; that is, this interface is our software representation of a physical input device (mouse, keyboard, joystick) and it allows us to communicate with that input device. For example, through this interface we find out which keys are currently down or how the mouse position is changing.

■   IDirectInput8: This interface is Direct Input's analog to the IDirect3D9 interface; through it we can enumerate input devices on the system, and it is used for obtaining pointers to IDirectInputDevice8 objects. Since we restrict ourselves to only the mouse and keyboard, we do not concern ourselves with input device enumeration (you would use enumeration to look for joysticks, game controllers, etc.). Moreover, we assume every computer that runs our applications has at least a mouse and keyboard.

A pointer to an IDirectInput8 object can be obtained with the DirectInput8Create function, which is invoked like so:

```
HR(DirectInput8Create(
    gd3dApp->getAppInst(),  // Application instance
    DIRECTINPUT_VERSION,    // Version number
    IID_IDirectInput8,      // Unique interface ID
    (void**)&mDInput,       // Return pointer
    0));                    // Not used, specify null
```

The first parameter is a handle to the application instance, which we can get from the D3DApp::getAppInst method (recall we keep a global pointer, gd3dApp, to the one and only application instance). The second parameter specifies the Direct Input version number. Before including *<dinput.h>*, you should define the symbol DIRECTINPUT_VERSION by:

```
#define DIRECTINPUT_VERSION 0x0800,
```

which indicates to use version 8.0. For parameter three, we specify a unique interface ID of the Direct Input interface we want to create — this will always be IID_IDirectInput8. Via the fourth parameter, the function returns a pointer to the newly created IDirectInput8 object (provided the function returned successfully). Finally, we don't need the last parameter and can specify null.

Note: The latest version of the Direct Input interfaces is 8.0 — the Direct Input interfaces were never augmented to version 9.0.

5.2.2 Initializing the Keyboard and Mouse

There are four basic steps to initializing the keyboard and mouse with Direct Input:

1. Create the device.
2. Set the data format.
3. Set the cooperative level.
4. Acquire the device.

Step 1: Create the Device

Recall that an IDirectInputDevice8 object represents an input device (e.g., mouse, keyboard, or joystick). IDirectInputDevice8 objects can be created with the IDirectInput8::CreateDevice method. For example, to create IDirectInputDevice8 objects representing the keyboard and mouse, we write:

```
HR(mDInput->CreateDevice(GUID_SysKeyboard, &mKeyboard, 0));
HR(mDInput->CreateDevice(GUID_SysMouse, &mMouse, 0));
```

Here, mKeyboard and mMouse are pointers of type IDirectInputDevice8, which are to point to the newly created device instances. The GUID GUID_SysKeyboard identifies the default system keyboard, and the GUID

GUID_SysMouse identifies the default system mouse (via the first parameter we identify the input device we want to create). Because we do not use the last parameter, we specify null for it.

Step 2: Set the Data Format

After the input devices representing the keyboard and mouse have been created, we need to specify the type of data they will work with. Fortunately, for the standard keyboard and mouse, Direct Input provides some default data formats. We set the formats with the following code:

```
HR(mKeyboard->SetDataFormat(&c_dfDIKeyboard));
HR(mMouse->SetDataFormat(&c_dfDIMouse2));
```

Here c_dfDIKeyboard and c_dfDIMouse2 are Direct Input global variables that indicate the data format of the keyboard and mouse, respectively.

The data structure c_dfDIKeyboard corresponds with is a 256-byte array, where each element represents the state of a key on the keyboard. The data structure c_dfDIMouse2 corresponds with is a DIMOUSESTATE2 structure, which is defined as follows:

```
typedef struct DIMOUSESTATE2 {
    LONG lX;
    LONG lY;
    LONG lZ;
    BYTE rgbButtons[8];
} DIMOUSESTATE2, *LPDIMOUSESTATE2;
```

Here lX, lY, and lZ specify the *change* in the mouse position along the x-, y-, and z-axes (mouse wheel), and the rgbButtons array specifies the state of the mouse buttons (this format supports an eight-button mouse). We show how these data structures are filled out with the current state of the input device in §5.2.4.

Step 3: Set the Cooperative Level

For the next step in the initialization process, we specify the cooperation level, which indicates how the input device associated with a particular window cooperates with the rest of the system. The following cooperation level flag combinations are valid:

- DISCL_FOREGROUND | DISCL_EXCLUSIVE
- DISCL_FOREGROUND | DISCL_NONEXCLUSIVE
- DISCL_BACKGROUND | DISCL_EXCLUSIVE
- DISCL_BACKGROUND | DISCL_NONEXCLUSIVE

DISCL_FOREGROUND means that the input device is unacquired and cannot be acquired when its associated window is no longer in the foreground. DISCL_BACKGROUND means that the input device can be acquired even if its associated window moves into the background. DISCL_NONEXCLUSIVE means that the application doesn't have exclusive access to the input device and other applications may access it. On the other hand, DISCL_EXCLUSIVE means that the application does have exclusive access to the input device and other applications cannot access the input device exclusively (but they still can non-exclusively). For the most part, you will not want your application to receive input while in the background, and therefore you will use DISCL_FOREGROUND, and you should probably not specify exclusive access unless you are running in full-screen mode, so that you do not interfere with other applications that may require exclusive access.

The following code sets the cooperative level for the keyboard and mouse. Observe that for the first parameter, we specify the window handle with which to associate the input device. For the second parameter, we specify the cooperative level flags:

```
HR(mKeyboard->SetCooperativeLevel(gd3dApp->getMainWnd(),
    DISCL_FOREGROUND | DISCL_NONEXCLUSIVE));
HR(mMouse->SetCooperativeLevel(gd3dApp->getMainWnd(),
    DISCL_FOREGROUND | DISCL_NONEXCLUSIVE));
```

Step 4: Acquire the Device

Lastly, before we can use an input device, we must acquire it. This is done with the IDirectInputDevice8::Acquire method. The following code performs all four steps for initializing the mouse and keyboard (including acquiring the device).

```
DirectInput::DirectInput(DWORD keyboardCoopFlags, DWORD mouseCoopFlags)
{
    ZeroMemory(mKeyboardState, sizeof(mKeyboardState));
    ZeroMemory(&mMouseState, sizeof(mMouseState));

    HR(DirectInput8Create(gd3dApp->getAppInst(), DIRECTINPUT_VERSION,
        IID_IDirectInput8, (void**)&mDInput, 0));

    HR(mDInput->CreateDevice(GUID_SysKeyboard, &mKeyboard, 0));
    HR(mKeyboard->SetDataFormat(&c_dfDIKeyboard));
    HR(mKeyboard->SetCooperativeLevel(gd3dApp->getMainWnd(),
                                      keyboardCoopFlags));
    HR(mKeyboard->Acquire());

    HR(mDInput->CreateDevice(GUID_SysMouse, &mMouse, 0));
    HR(mMouse->SetDataFormat(&c_dfDIMouse2));
    HR(mMouse->SetCooperativeLevel(gd3dApp->getMainWnd(),
                                   mouseCoopFlags));
    HR(mMouse->Acquire());
}
```

5.2.3 **Cleanup**

To clean up Direct Input, we simply unacquire the devices and release the COM interfaces.

```
DirectInput::~DirectInput()
{
    ReleaseCOM(mDInput);
    mKeyboard->Unacquire();
    mMouse->Unacquire();
    ReleaseCOM(mKeyboard);
    ReleaseCOM(mMouse);
}
```

5.2.4 **Polling the Keyboard and Mouse**

We use the phrase *polling the keyboard and mouse* to refer to the process of getting the current state of these devices; that is, to find out which keys are pressed, how the mouse position has changed since the last time we checked, and which mouse buttons are down. To obtain the current state of an input device, we use the IDirectInputDevice8::GetDeviceState method, as the following code shows.

```
void DirectInput::poll()
{
    // Poll keyboard.
    HRESULT hr = mKeyboard->GetDeviceState(sizeof(mKeyboardState),
                                  (void**)&mKeyboardState);
    if( FAILED(hr) )
    {
        // Keyboard lost, zero out keyboard data structure.
        ZeroMemory(mKeyboardState, sizeof(mKeyboardState));

        // Try to acquire for next time we poll.
        hr = mKeyboard->Acquire();
    }

    // Poll mouse.
    hr = mMouse->GetDeviceState(sizeof(DIMOUSESTATE2),
                            (void**)&mMouseState);
    if( FAILED(hr) )
    {
        // Mouse lost, zero out mouse data structure.
        ZeroMemory(&mMouseState, sizeof(mMouseState));

        // Try to acquire for next time we poll.
        hr = mMouse->Acquire();
    }
}
```

Here, `mKeyboardState` and `mMouseState` are declared as:

```
char                mKeyboardState[256];
DIMOUSESTATE2       mMouseState;
```

Note that these data structures correctly correspond to the data formats we set in Step 2 of §5.2.2. For the keyboard, `GetDeviceState` fills the byte array `mKeyboardState` with a snapshot of the current state of the keyboard. Each element in the byte array refers to a key. We can then check if a key is pressed with the following code:

```
bool DirectInput::keyDown(char key)
{
    return (mKeyboardState[key] & 0x80) != 0;
}
```

The parameter `key` is a symbol predefined by Direct Input; it indexes the element in `mKeyboardState` that corresponds to a particular key. For example, `DIK_ESCAPE` provides the index into `mKeyboardState` that refers to the Escape key. Other examples include: `DIK_N`, `DIK_SPACE`, `DIK_TAB`, and `DIK_7` ("N" key, Spacebar key, Tab key, number 7 key); for a complete list of key symbols, examine the Direct Input header file *<dinput.h>*. A key is defined to be down if the bits `0x80` are set in the element of `mKeyboardState` that corresponds to the particular key we are checking. For example, the Escape key is down if the following is true:

```
(mKeyboardState[DIK_ESCAPE] & 0x80) != 0;
```

On the other hand, for the mouse, `GetDeviceState` fills out `mMouseState` with a snapshot of the current state of the mouse. Recall that the `DIMOUSESTATE2` structure looks like this:

```
typedef struct DIMOUSESTATE2 {
    LONG lX;
    LONG lY;
    LONG lZ;
    BYTE rgbButtons[8];
} DIMOUSESTATE2, *LPDIMOUSESTATE2;
```

The mouse state differentials `mMouseState.lX`, `mMouseState.lY`, and `mMouseState.lZ` measure the instantaneous change in position of the mouse along the axes at the time it was polled, and these units are measured in device units, which means that they will likely need to be scaled to make sense in the application. A mouse button is defined to be down if the bits `0x80` are set in the element of `mMouseState.rgbButtons` that corresponds to the particular mouse button we are checking. For example, the second mouse button is down if the following is true:

```
(mMouseState.rgbButtons[1] & 0x80) != 0;
```

Note: With a three-button mouse, you will only be concerned with the first three elements of `mMouseState.rgbButtons`.

With our `DirectInput` class, we can obtain the current mouse differentials, and check if a mouse button is currently down with the following methods:

```
bool DirectInput::mouseButtonDown(int button)
{
    return (mMouseState.rgbButtons[button] & 0x80) != 0;
}

float DirectInput::mouseDX()
{
    return (float)mMouseState.lX;
}

float DirectInput::mouseDY()
{
    return (float)mMouseState.lY;
}

float DirectInput::mouseDZ()
{
    return (float)mMouseState.lZ;
}
```

Note: Our Direct Input class will be demonstrated in the sample application of the next section.

5.3 **Sprites and Animation**

In computer graphics, a *sprite* refers to a small 2D image (see Figure 5.2). In this section, we show how to create, animate, and draw sprites using the `ID3DXSprite` interface. Note that this section does not present a comprehensive discussion of sprites, as 2D graphics is not our primary aim. We include this discussion for the following reasons:

- To provide a test driver for our Direct Input class.
- To show how to update graphical objects with respect to time; updating 2D objects is similar to updating 3D objects.
- To present a "taste" of Direct3D and interactive computer graphics in an easier 2D setting.
- We utilize some techniques that won't be discussed until later chapters. In this way, we hope to provoke questions, and thus motivate you to begin the examination of Direct3D.

Figure 5.2: (Left) This 2D sprite is used to represent the background of the demo we make; it may be tiled, which means we can repeat the image along its edges without creating a seam. (Middle) This 2D sprite is used to represent our ship in the demo. (Right) This 2D sprite represents a bullet fired by the ship.

5.3.1 **ID3DXSprite**

D3DX represents a sprite with the ID3DXSprite interface; a pointer to an object of this type may be obtained with the D3DXCreateSprite function:

```
HRESULT WINAPI D3DXCreateSprite(
    LPDIRECT3DDEVICE9 pDevice,
    LPD3DXSPRITE *ppSprite);
```

- pDevice: Pointer to the rendering device.

- ppSprite: Outputs a pointer to an ID3DXSprite instance.

After we have created a pointer to an ID3DXSprite object, we can draw it. Five methods are required for successfully drawing an ID3DXSprite object:

- ID3DXSprite::SetTransform: Sets a transformation matrix, which will be applied to the sprite during drawing to transform it (e.g., translate, rotate, scale).

- ID3DXSprite::Begin: Prepares the sprite for drawing. This function takes a single parameter, which allows us to specify a combination of flags that determine how the sprite should be drawn. The flags we use are:

  D3DXSPRITE_OBJECTSPACE: This means the sprite's coordinates are relative to its own local coordinate system. Omitting this flag means the sprite's coordinates are specified in screen space (i.e., in units of pixels with the positive *y*-axis going down and the positive *x*-axis going to the right).

  D3DXSPRITE_DONOTMODIFY_RENDERSTATE: This flag means the ID3DXSprite should not change any render states. Render states affect how objects are drawn by the rendering device. In our example, we manually control the render states ourselves, and thus apply this flag.

- `ID3DXSprite::Draw`: Unintuitively, this method does not draw the sprite. Instead, it adds the sprite to a list of sprites to be drawn. This is done for efficiency reasons — it is not efficient to draw the sprites one by one. Instead, they should be batched together and drawn all at once.

- `ID3DXSprite::Flush`: Draws all of the batched sprites.

- `ID3DXSprite::End`: This method flushes the sprite list storing the sprites to be drawn and executes the drawing commands (i.e., it does what `Flush` does). In addition, it may restore the graphics render states (if it changed any) to their prior settings (i.e., settings before calling `ID3DXSprite::Begin`).

The `ID3DXSprite::Draw` method is prototyped like this:

```
HRESULT ID3DXSprite::Draw(
    LPDIRECT3DTEXTURE9 pTexture,
    CONST RECT *pSrcRect,
    CONST D3DXVECTOR3 *pCenter,
    CONST D3DXVECTOR3 *pPosition,
    D3DCOLOR Color);
```

- `pTexture`: A pointer to the texture image we want to map over the sprite surface.

- `pSrcRect`: A pointer to a `RECT` object that specifies a subset of the texture image to map over the sprite. Specify null if you want to map the entire texture over the sprite.

- `pCenter`: A `D3DXVECTOR3` pointer that identifies the center of the sprite in image coordinates.

- `pPosition`: Specifies the position of the sprite. We can specify null for this and change the sprite position with a translation transformation matrix.

- `Color`: A `D3DCOLOR` value that specifies a color that is to be blended in with the image texture; for example, you can add a hint of blue to the overall texture image by specifying a blue color for this parameter, or specify white (`D3DCOLOR_XRGB(255, 255, 255)`) to keep the original texture image unmodified.

Because `ID3DXSprite` objects are COM objects, they should be released when done:

```
ReleaseCOM(mShip);
```

Note that we only need one `ID3DXSprite` interface to draw all the different kinds of sprites we have. The following code snippet illustrates the general drawing structure:

```
HR(mSprite->Begin(D3DXSPRITE_OBJECTSPACE |
                  D3DXSPRITE_DONOTMODIFY_RENDERSTATE));

// [Set Sprite A Type Render States...]
```

```
// Suppose there are m type A sprites.
for(j = 0; j < m; ++j)
{
        HR(mSprite->SetTransform(&spriteATransform[j]));
        HR(mSprite->Draw(spriteATex[j], 0, &spriteACenter[j], 0,
                          D3DCOLOR_XRGB(255, 255, 255)));
}
// Now draw all of Type A sprites.
HR(mSprite->Flush());

// [Set Sprite B Type Render States...]

// Suppose there are n type B sprites.
for(k = 0; k < n; ++k)
{
        HR(mSprite->SetTransform(&spriteBTransform[k]));
        HR(mSprite->Draw(spriteBTex[k], 0, &spriteBCenter[k], 0,
                          D3DCOLOR_XRGB(255, 255, 255)));
}
// Now draw all of Type B sprites.
HR(mSprite->Flush();

[...and so on for other sprite types...]

// Done drawing.
HR(mSprite->End());
```

Note: By *sprite types*, we simply mean a collection of sprites that can be drawn together; that is, they are drawn with the same render states. For example, in the next demo, we draw several bullet sprites at one time in different positions. Since all the bullets are drawn using the same render states, they form a type and we can batch them together and then draw them all at once.

5.3.2 The Sprite Demo

Figure 5.3 shows a screenshot of the demo developed in this section. Sprite objects represent the background, the ship, and the bullets. In addition, the user can move the ship and rotate it; the DirectInput class handles the input. Updating the game objects (i.e., animating) is also done with respect to time.

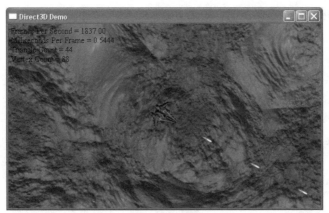

Figure 5.3: Screenshot of the Sprite demo.

Warning: This demo uses Direct3D code and concepts that won't be explained until later chapters (such as texturing and alpha blending). At this point, do not worry about the details on how it works, but just try to understand why it is useful.

5.3.2.1 *Bullet Structure*

Before we examine the Sprite demo application class, let's introduce a small auxiliary structure:

```
struct BulletInfo
{
    D3DXVECTOR3 pos;
    float rotation;
    float life;
};
```

The `BulletInfo` structure contains the properties of a bullet — its position, rotation angle (which indicates the direction the bullet is traveling), and life (i.e., the amount of time the bullet has existed). A bullet is "born" when it is fired and the bullet "dies" after a prescribed amount of time has elapsed, in which case we know the bullet is now far away and cannot be seen anymore on the screen. More technically, when a bullet is born, it is added to a list that maintains all the bullets that are currently fired and moving along their trajectory; when a bullet dies, it is removed from the list. Thus, we need to keep track of how long the bullet has existed so that we know when we can remove it from the list.

5.3.2.2 *Demo Application Class Data Members*

Below is the definition of the Sprite demo application class:

```
class SpriteDemo : public D3DApp
{
public:
    SpriteDemo(HINSTANCE hInstance);
    ~SpriteDemo();

    bool checkDeviceCaps();
    void onLostDevice();
    void onResetDevice();
    void updateScene(float dt);
    void drawScene();

    // Helper functions.
    void updateShip(float dt);
    void updateBullets(float dt);
    void drawBkgd();
    void drawShip();
    void drawBullets();
private:
    GfxStats* mGfxStats;

    ID3DXSprite* mSprite;

    IDirect3DTexture9* mBkgdTex;
    D3DXVECTOR3 mBkgdCenter;

    IDirect3DTexture9* mShipTex;
    D3DXVECTOR3 mShipCenter;
    D3DXVECTOR3 mShipPos;
    float       mShipSpeed;
    float       mShipRotation;

    IDirect3DTexture9* mBulletTex;
    D3DXVECTOR3 mBulletCenter;
    std::list<BulletInfo> mBulletList;

    const float BULLET_SPEED;
    const float MAX_SHIP_SPEED;
    const float SHIP_ACCEL;
    const float SHIP_DRAG;
};
```

- ■ mSprite: The one and only sprite interface through which we do all of our sprite drawing.

- ■ mBkgdTex: Texture containing the background image. In case you are not familiar with textures from general computer game experience, they are essentially 2D image data that gets mapped onto polygons; here it will be the 2D image data mapped onto a sprite.

- `mBkgdCenter`: The center of the background measured in image coordinates. For example, if the texture dimensions are 512×512, then the center is (256, 256). Note that in image coordinates, the positive y-axis goes down and the positive x-axis goes to the right, and the units are in pixels.

- `mShipTex`: Texture containing the ship image.

- `mShipCenter`: The center of the ship measured in image coordinates.

- `mShipPos`: The position of the ship in world space.

- `mShipSpeed`: The speed of the ship.

- `mShipRotation`: An angle, in radians, storing the current rotation of the ship measured from the positive y-axis, where positive angles go counterclockwise when looking down the negative z-axis (i.e., clockwise when looking down the positive z-axis).

- `mBulletTex`: Texture containing the bullet image.

- `mBulletCenter`: The center of the ship measured in image coordinates.

- `mBulletList`: A list container storing the bullets the player has fired and that need to be updated and drawn; that is, as the player fires a bullet, we add a bullet to the list. After a short amount of time, when we know the bullet is far away and off the screen, we remove it from the list. Although we use a list here, a fixed size array could also work, where you cap the maximum number of bullets allowed at once. This would be more efficient and prevent frequent memory allocations and deallocations. However, for a demo, the list implementation is fine.

- `BULLET_SPEED`: A constant that specifies the speed of the bullet.

- `MAX_SHIP_SPEED`: A ceiling that specifies the maximum speed of the ship.

- `SHIP_ACCEL`: A constant that specifies how the ship accelerates based on user input.

- `SHIP_DRAG`: A constant in the range [0, 1] that specifies a drag force to decelerate the ship. The drag force is proportional to the velocity of the ship; that is, the faster the ship is going, the higher the drag force. Mathematically, the drag force is given by $-bv$. Here b is the drag constant `SHIP_DRAG`, and v denotes the speed of the ship. The negative sign indicates the drag force always opposes (goes in opposite direction of) the ship's direction.

Note: We do not claim that our physics properties are completely realistic. For instance, we do not take mass into consideration. We just experiment with the numbers until we get a satisfactory result.

What follows is an explanation of each method's implementation.

5.3.2.3 *SpriteDemo*

In the constructor, we create our sprites and textures, and perform general variable initialization.

```
SpriteDemo::SpriteDemo(HINSTANCE hInstance)
: D3DApp(hInstance), BULLET_SPEED(2500.0f), MAX_SHIP_SPEED(1500.0f),
    SHIP_ACCEL(1000.0f), SHIP_DRAG(0.85f)
{
    if(!checkDeviceCaps())
    {
        MessageBox(0, "checkDeviceCaps() Failed", 0, 0);
        PostQuitMessage(0);
    }

    mGfxStats = new GfxStats();

    HR(D3DXCreateSprite(gd3dDevice, &mSprite));

    HR(D3DXCreateTextureFromFile(
        gd3dDevice, "bkgd1.bmp", &mBkgdTex));
    HR(D3DXCreateTextureFromFile(
        gd3dDevice, "alienship.bmp", &mShipTex));
    HR(D3DXCreateTextureFromFile(
        gd3dDevice, "bullet.bmp", &mBulletTex));

    mBkgdCenter = D3DXVECTOR3(256.0f, 256.0f, 0.0f);
    mShipCenter = D3DXVECTOR3(64.0f, 64.0f, 0.0f);
    mBulletCenter = D3DXVECTOR3(32.0f, 32.0f, 0.0f);

    mShipPos    = D3DXVECTOR3(0.0f, 0.0f, 0.0f);
    mShipSpeed  = 0.0f;
    mShipRotation = 0.0f;

    onResetDevice();
}
```

The implementation is rather straightforward. We obtain a pointer to an ID3DXSprite interface with D3DXCreateSprite, create the textures with D3DXCreateTextureFromFile, and initialize some of the data members to default values, as well as set the application constants. Finally, we call onResetDevice, which sets some device states. We have to call this method because we want these device states to be set during construction in addition to when the device is reset.

We have not talked about D3DXCreateTextureFromFile. This function loads the image data from a file (supported image formats include BMP, DDS, DIB, JPG, PNG, and TGA), and then uses the data to create an IDirect3DTexture9 object (i.e., a texture that can be mapped onto a surface — a sprite in this case). The first parameter is a pointer to the rendering device, the second parameter is the filename of the image, and the third parameter returns a pointer to the created texture.

5.3.2.4 ~*SpriteDemo*

In the destructor, we delete any dynamic memory and release all COM interfaces. The implementation is self-explanatory.

```
SpriteDemo::~SpriteDemo()
{
    delete mGfxStats;
    ReleaseCOM(mSprite);
    ReleaseCOM(mBkgdTex);
    ReleaseCOM(mShipTex);
    ReleaseCOM(mBulletTex);
}
```

5.3.2.5 *checkDeviceCaps*

For this demo, we do not use any fancy features and so there are no capabilities to check.

```
bool SpriteDemo::checkDeviceCaps()
{
    // Nothing to check.
    return true;
}
```

5.3.2.6 *onLostDevice*

Recall that in the onLostDevice method, we place any code that needs to be executed before the rendering device is reset.

```
void SpriteDemo::onLostDevice()
{
    mGfxStats->onLostDevice();
    HR(mSprite->OnLostDevice());
}
```

As shown, each of the sprite objects needs to execute some code prior to a device reset, and so does the GfxStats object.

5.3.2.7 *onResetDevice*

Recall that in the onResetDevice method, we place any code that needs to be executed after the rendering device is reset. For this demo, we need to set a variety of device states (and in particular, render states), which control how the rendering device draws the graphics. Device states are lost when the device is reset; therefore, we set the device states in this function so that they are automatically restored after the device is reset. Note that these states will be elaborated on in later chapters of the book; so for now, we just present an intuitive explanation of what the states do (see the comments).

```
void SpriteDemo::onResetDevice()
{
    // Call the onResetDevice of other objects.
    mGfxStats->onResetDevice();
    HR(mSprite->OnResetDevice());

    // Sets up the camera 1000 units back looking at the origin.
    D3DXMATRIX V;
    D3DXVECTOR3 pos(0.0f, 0.0f, -1000.0f);
    D3DXVECTOR3 up(0.0f, 1.0f, 0.0f);
    D3DXVECTOR3 target(0.0f, 0.0f, 0.0f);
    D3DXMatrixLookAtLH(&V, &pos, &target, &up);
    HR(gd3dDevice->SetTransform(D3DTS_VIEW, &V));

    // The following code defines the volume of space the
    // camera sees.
    D3DXMATRIX P;
    RECT R;
    GetClientRect(mhMainWnd, &R);
    float width  = (float)R.right;
    float height = (float)R.bottom;
    D3DXMatrixPerspectiveFovLH(&P, D3DX_PI*0.25f,
        width/height, 1.0f, 5000.0f);
    HR(gd3dDevice->SetTransform(D3DTS_PROJECTION, &P));

    // This code sets texture filters, which helps to smooth
    // out distortions when you scale a texture.
    HR(gd3dDevice->SetSamplerState(
        0, D3DSAMP_MAGFILTER, D3DTEXF_LINEAR));
    HR(gd3dDevice->SetSamplerState(
        0, D3DSAMP_MINFILTER, D3DTEXF_LINEAR));
    HR(gd3dDevice->SetSamplerState(
        0, D3DSAMP_MIPFILTER, D3DTEXF_LINEAR));

    // This line of code disables Direct3D lighting.
    HR(gd3dDevice->SetRenderState(D3DRS_LIGHTING, false));

    // The following code specifies an alpha test and
    // reference value.
    HR(gd3dDevice->SetRenderState(D3DRS_ALPHAREF, 10));
    HR(gd3dDevice->SetRenderState(D3DRS_ALPHAFUNC, D3DCMP_GREATER));

    // The following code is used to set up alpha blending.
    HR(gd3dDevice->SetTextureStageState(
        0, D3DTSS_ALPHAARG1, D3DTA_TEXTURE));
    HR(gd3dDevice->SetTextureStageState(
        0, D3DTSS_ALPHAOP, D3DTOP_SELECTARG1));
    HR(gd3dDevice->SetRenderState(
        D3DRS_SRCBLEND, D3DBLEND_SRCALPHA));
    HR(gd3dDevice->SetRenderState(
        D3DRS_DESTBLEND, D3DBLEND_INVSRCALPHA));
```

```
    // Indicates that we are using 2D texture coordinates.
    HR(gd3dDevice->SetTextureStageState(
        0, D3DTSS_TEXTURETRANSFORMFLAGS, D3DTTFF_COUNT2));
}
```

Although we explain these function calls in much more depth in later chapters, the idea behind the alpha test and alpha blending does deserve further discussion here.

Recall what our ship image looks like (see Figure 5.2). If we render the ship without alpha testing, the black background of the ship is also drawn, as shown in Figure 5.4. To remedy this, we insert a fourth channel into the image called an alpha channel. Many 2D paint programs provide a way to do this; Figure 5.5 shows how it is done in Adobe Photoshop 7.0. Note that an 8-bit alpha channel will typically be inserted, which is represented graphically as a grayscale map, and each pixel value can take on a value from 0 to 255, which represents shades of gray from black to white, respectively.

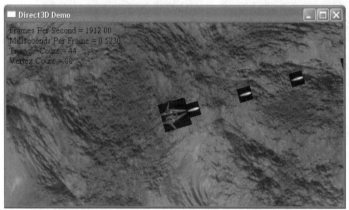

Figure 5.4: By drawing the sprites without any extra work, the black background is drawn, which is not what we want!

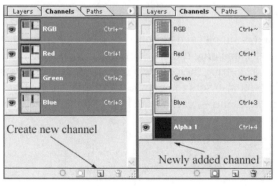

Figure 5.5: Creating an alpha channel in Adobe Photoshop 7.0. You must also save the file to a format that supports an alpha channel, such as a 32-bit BMP file.

Now each color pixel has a corresponding alpha pixel in the alpha channel. In the alpha channel, we manually mark (with a paint program) the pixels corresponding to the main color image we want to be displayed with white (255) and the pixels we do not want to show up with black (0) (see Figure 5.6). Then, the alpha test D3DCMP_GREATER does the following: For each color pixel being processed by Direct3D, it looks at the corresponding alpha value for the pixel, then it asks if the alpha value is *greater* than the reference value specified by the render state D3DRS_ALPHAREF (in our code, we specified 10 for the reference value). If it is greater, then the alpha test succeeds and the pixel is drawn; else, the alpha test fails and the pixel is not drawn. Thus, with this setup, the pixels we marked black in the alpha channel will not be drawn, since $0 \le 10$; i.e., the alpha test will fail for those pixels. The pixels in the alpha channel we marked white (255) will be drawn, since $255 > 10$, which is the exact result we want.

Figure 5.6: Here we show the sprites and their corresponding alpha channels. In the alpha channel, the white pixels mark the pixels we want to draw and the black pixels indicate the pixels we want blocked (not drawn). We actually draw the bullet with alpha blending, which makes the bullet semi-transparent.

Alpha blending is somewhat like alpha testing, except that instead of blocking the pixel completely, the alpha channel specifies how the image should be blended together with the background pixels on which the sprite is being drawn, thus making the object somewhat transparent.

5.3.2.8 *updateScene*

The updateScene method is simple, and merely calls other functions that do the real work; specifically, updating the graphics statistics, polling the mouse and keyboard (i.e., getting their current states), updating the ship, and updating the bullets. It also sets the number of triangles and vertices currently rendered in the scene — each sprite is built from a quad (four vertices) of two triangles.

```
void SpriteDemo::updateScene(float dt)
{
    // Two triangles for each sprite--two for background,
    // two for ship, and two for each bullet. Similarly,
    // four vertices for each sprite.
```

```
        mGfxStats->setTriCount(4 + mBulletList.size()*2);
        mGfxStats->setVertexCount(8 + mBulletList.size()*4);
        mGfxStats->update(dt);

        // Get snapshot of input devices.
        gDInput->poll();

        // Update game objects.
        updateShip(dt);
        updateBullets(dt);
}
```

5.3.2.9 *updateShip*

```
void SpriteDemo::updateShip(float dt)
{
        // Check input.
        if( gDInput->keyDown(DIK_A) ) mShipRotation += 4.0f * dt;
        if( gDInput->keyDown(DIK_D) ) mShipRotation -= 4.0f * dt;
        if( gDInput->keyDown(DIK_W) ) mShipSpeed    += SHIP_ACCEL * dt;
        if( gDInput->keyDown(DIK_S) ) mShipSpeed    -= SHIP_ACCEL * dt;

        // Clamp top speed.
        if( mShipSpeed > MAX_SHIP_SPEED )
           mShipSpeed =  MAX_SHIP_SPEED;
        if( mShipSpeed < -MAX_SHIP_SPEED )
           mShipSpeed = -MAX_SHIP_SPEED;

        // Rotate counterclockwise when looking down -z axis,
        // rotate clockwise when looking down the +z axis.
        D3DXVECTOR3 shipDir(-sinf(mShipRotation),
                            cosf(mShipRotation), 0.0f);

        // Update position and speed based on time.
        mShipPos   += shipDir * mShipSpeed * dt;
        mShipSpeed -= SHIP_DRAG * mShipSpeed * dt;
}
```

The first four conditional statements check Direct Input to see if the "A", "D", "W", or "S" keys are pressed. The "A" and "D" keys rotate the ship counterclockwise and clockwise, respectively, when looking down the –z-axis. The "W" and "S" keys accelerate and decelerate the ship along its current direction, respectively.

Note:　Average acceleration is defined to be the change in velocity over time, i.e., $a = \Delta v / \Delta t$. This implies that the velocity changes by $\Delta v = a \cdot \Delta t$ over the time period Δt. Thus, to update the ship's velocity, we just add/subtract $a \cdot \Delta t$ to it (in our code, a = SHIP_ACCEL and Δt=dt). Note that acceleration and velocity are usually vector-valued quantities, but because we only accelerate along the direction line of the ship, we can omit the arrowheads and treat them as 1D vectors.

The next two conditional statements ensure that the ship never goes faster than the prescribed MAX_SHIP_SPEED value.

Given the ship's rotation angle, measured from the positive y-axis, we can infer the ship's direction using trigonometry, as shown in Figure 5.7.

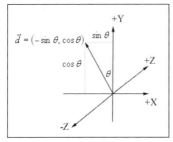

Figure 5.7: Computing the direction vector given the rotation angle measured from the positive y-axis in the counterclockwise direction while looking down the $-z$-axis (i.e., clockwise while looking down the $+z$-axis).

Once we have the ship's direction, we can move along that direction given the ship's speed.

Note: Average velocity is defined to be the change in position (displacement) over time, i.e., $v = \Delta x / \Delta t$. This implies that the position changes by $\Delta x = v \cdot \Delta t$ over the time period Δt. Thus, to update the ship's position, we just add/subtract $v \cdot \Delta t$ to it (in our code, $v =$ mShipSpeed and Δt=dt). Note that velocity and displacement are usually vector-valued quantities, but because we only move along the direction line of the ship, we can omit the arrowheads and treat them as 1D vectors.

Finally, the speed is modified by a drag force, which always opposes the motion of the ship (hence the subtraction). The drag force works like friction to slow the ship down when the user is not accelerating.

5.3.2.10 *updateBullets*

Each time a bullet is fired, we add a bullet to a list that maintains the position and velocity of all the bullets currently active. Based on the bullets' velocities, we then update the position of the bullets with respect to time (in the same way we updated the ship's position with respect to time based on its velocity). After a specified amount of time, when we know the bullet is far away and off the screen, we can remove it from the list.

```
void SpriteDemo::updateBullets(float dt)
{
    // Make static so that its value persists across function calls.
    static float fireDelay = 0.0f;

    // Accumulate time.
    fireDelay += dt;
```

```
// Did the user press the Spacebar key and has 0.1 seconds
// passed? We can only fire one bullet every 0.1 seconds.
// If we do not put this delay in, the ship will fire
// bullets way too fast.
if( gDInput->keyDown(DIK_SPACE) && fireDelay > 0.1f )
{
        BulletInfo bullet;

        // Remember, the ship is always drawn at the center of
        // the window--the origin. Therefore, bullets originate
        // from the origin (i.e., from the ship).
        bullet.pos      = D3DXVECTOR3(0.0f, 0.0f, 0.0f);

        // The bullet's rotation should match the ship's rotating
        // at the instant it is fired.
        bullet.rotation = mShipRotation;

        // Bullet just born.
        bullet.life     = 0.0f;

        // Add the bullet to the list.
        mBulletList.push_back(bullet);

        // A bullet was just fired, so reset the fire delay.
        fireDelay = 0.0f;
}
// Now loop through each bullet, and update its position.
std::list<BulletInfo>::iterator i = mBulletList.begin();
while( i != mBulletList.end() )
{
        // Accumulate the time the bullet has lived.
        i->life += dt;

        // If the bullet has lived for two seconds, kill it.
        // By now the bullet should have flown off the
        // screen and cannot be seen.
        if(i->life >= 2.0f)
            i = mBulletList.erase(i);

        // Otherwise, update its position by moving along
        // its directional path.  Code similar to how we move
        // the ship--but no drag.
        else
        {
            D3DXVECTOR3 dir(
                -sinf(i->rotation),
                cosf(i->rotation),
                0.0f);
            i->pos += dir * BULLET_SPEED * dt;
            ++i;
        }
}
}
```

5.3.2.11 *drawScene*

This method is self-explanatory; the hard work is done by other helper methods.

```
void SpriteDemo::drawScene()
{
    // Clear the back buffer and depth buffer.
    HR(gd3dDevice->Clear(0, 0, D3DCLEAR_TARGET | D3DCLEAR_ZBUFFER,
                         0xffffffff, 1.0f, 0));

    HR(gd3dDevice->BeginScene());
    HR(mSprite->Begin(D3DXSPRITE_OBJECTSPACE|
                      D3DXSPRITE_DONOTMODIFY_RENDERSTATE));
    drawBkgd();
    drawShip();
    drawBullets();
    mGfxStats->display();
    HR(mSprite->End());
    HR(gd3dDevice->EndScene());

    // Present the back buffer.
    HR(gd3dDevice->Present(0, 0, 0, 0));
}
```

5.3.2.12 *drawBkgd*

This method draws the background sprite.

```
void SpriteDemo::drawBkgd()
{
    // Set a texture coordinate scaling transform. Here we scale
    // the texture coordinates by 10 in each dimension. This
    // tiles the texture ten times over the sprite surface.
    D3DXMATRIX texScaling;
    D3DXMatrixScaling(&texScaling, 10.0f, 10.0f, 0.0f);
    HR(gd3dDevice->SetTransform(D3DTS_TEXTURE0, &texScaling));

    // Position and size the background sprite--remember that
    // we always draw the ship in the center of the client area
    // rectangle. To give the illusion that the ship is moving,
    // we translate the background in the opposite direction.
    D3DXMATRIX T, S;
    D3DXMatrixTranslation(&T, -mShipPos.x, -mShipPos.y, -mShipPos.z);
    D3DXMatrixScaling(&S, 20.0f, 20.0f, 0.0f);
    HR(mSprite->SetTransform(&(S*T)));

    // Draw the background sprite.
    HR(mSprite->Draw(mBkgdTex, 0, &mBkgdCenter, 0,
                     D3DCOLOR_XRGB(255, 255, 255)));
    HR(mSprite->Flush());

    // Restore default texture coordinate scaling transform. Mirror
    // texture coordinates with respect to y-axis so the texture is
```

```
// mapped correctly onto the sprite.
D3DXMatrixScaling(&texScaling, 1.0f, -1.0f, 0.0f);
HR(gd3dDevice->SetTransform(D3DTS_TEXTURE0, &texScaling));
}
```

The first few lines set a texture coordinate scaling transform. (Right now you probably don't even know what _texture coordinates_ are, but loosely, they specify how a texture is mapped over a surface.) Scaling the texture coordinates by 10 in both the x- and y-directions has the effect of tiling the texture in both directions 10 times. Figure 5.8 illustrates tiling.

Figure 5.8: The background texture tiled twice in both the x- and y-directions. If you look at the image carefully, you will see that the image is repeated in each of the four quadrants. By repeating the texture (tiling), we get "extra" resolution without adding additional memory; of course, the disadvantage is that the texture does repeat, which breaks the realism.

The reason we tile is because we are going to be stretching a texture over a large sprite. To cover the entire sprite surface, the texture will need to be stretched much larger than its actual dimensions. This stretching will cause distortions; you are probably familiar with the loss of detail that occurs when you enlarge an image in a paint program, and the same thing happens here. By having Direct3D tile the texture 10 times, we essentially make the texture have 10 times the resolution, and thus the details are preserved over the background sprite. To do this, note that the texture must tile nicely; otherwise discontinuities will be observed on the edges where the images are tiled. To help you understand this, we recommend that you experiment with different texture scaling sizes; for example, try 1, 2, 5, 10, and 20.

The next key idea with the above code is the translation transformation. Recall that we always keep the ship in the center of the client area rectangle. Thus, we do not translate the ship itself as it moves, but instead translate the background sprite in the opposite direction; visually, this has the same effect as translating the ship directly and keeping the background stationary.

In addition to translating the background, we also apply a scaling transformation (represented by a scaling matrix). This simply makes the background bigger — the background represents the terrain over which the ship will be flying, so it ought to be big. In this code, we scale it by 20 times.

The next bit of code draws the background; see §5.3.1 for a description of the parameters for ID3DXSprite::Draw.

Finally, the code finishes up by restoring the default texture coordinate scaling transformation back to 1 (i.e., no scaling).

5.3.2.13 *drawShip*

The following code draws the ship sprite:

```
void SpriteDemo::drawShip()
{
    // Turn on the alpha test.
    HR(gd3dDevice->SetRenderState(D3DRS_ALPHATESTENABLE, true));

    // Set ship's orientation.
    D3DXMATRIX R;
    D3DXMatrixRotationZ(&R, mShipRotation);
    HR(mSprite->SetTransform(&R));

    // Draw the ship.
    HR(mSprite->Draw(mShipTex, 0, &mShipCenter, 0,
                 D3DCOLOR_XRGB(255, 255, 255)));
    HR(mSprite->Flush());

    // Turn off the alpha test.
    HR(gd3dDevice->SetRenderState(D3DRS_ALPHATESTENABLE, false));
}
```

Recall that in §5.3.2.7, we set some alpha test render states, and also gave an explanation of what the alpha test does for us. Although we set some properties of the alpha test previously, we did not actually enable it. So the very first thing we do before we draw the ship sprite is enable the alpha test.

Although we do not explicitly translate the ship (we translate the background in the opposite direction instead), we do explicitly rotate the ship. This is accomplished by applying a rotation transformation based on the current angle the sprite makes with the y-axis.

Finally, we draw the ship sprite and then disable the alpha test because we are done with it.

5.3.2.14 *drawBullets*

The process of drawing the bullet sprites is similar to drawing the ship sprite:

```
void SpriteDemo::drawBullets()
{
    // Turn on alpha blending.
    HR(gd3dDevice->SetRenderState(D3DRS_ALPHABLENDENABLE, true));

    // For each bullet...
    std::list<BulletInfo>::iterator i = mBulletList.begin();
    while( i != mBulletList.end() )
```

```
    {
            // Set its position and orientation.
            D3DXMATRIX T, R;
            D3DXMatrixRotationZ(&R, i->rotation);
            D3DXMatrixTranslation(&T, i->pos.x, i->pos.y, i->pos.z);
            HR(mSprite->SetTransform(&(R*T)));

            // Add it to the batch.
            HR(mSprite->Draw(mBulletTex, 0, &mBulletCenter, 0,
                            D3DCOLOR_XRGB(255, 255, 255)));
            ++i;
    }
    // Draw all the bullets at once.
    HR(mSprite->Flush());

    // Turn off alpha blending.
    HR(gd3dDevice->SetRenderState(D3DRS_ALPHABLENDENABLE, false));
}
```

The first thing to note is that we do not use alpha testing with the bullets; instead, we use alpha blending. Both techniques require an alpha channel, but unlike the alpha test, which simply accepts or rejects pixels, alpha blending blends the texture image pixels with the back buffer pixels on which the textured sprite is drawn. This is useful for effects (such as gunfire, laser beams, and smoke) that are not completely opaque.

In alpha blending, the alpha channel pixels can be thought of as weights that specify how much color to use from the texture image (source color) and from the back buffer pixels (destination color) when generating the new back buffer pixel color. Alpha pixels close to white weight the source pixels more heavily, and alpha pixels close to black weight the destination pixels more heavily. For example, pure white uses 100% source color, and pure black uses 100% destination color. Thus, if you do not want to overwrite parts of the back buffer, then specify black in the alpha channel for those pixels (sort of like alpha testing).

Now, once alpha blending is enabled, to draw the bullets we simply loop through each one in the list, set its rotation and translation matrix to orient and position it, and then draw it. Lastly, before exiting the method, we disable alpha blending.

5.3.3 Page Flipping Animation

In the previous section, we animated the graphics by changing their positions slightly every frame. By changing an object's position by small increments over time, a continuous motion is observed. Another way we can carry out animation is by using a *page flipping* technique. The idea is to have an artist generate the animation as a sequence of images (or frames of animation). Then, by displaying the frames (which differ only slightly) in rapid succession, the still frames are brought to life to produce an animation. For games, this animation technique is particularly useful for effects like explosions or fire, as shown in Figure 5.9.

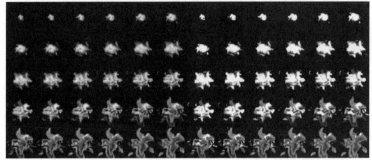

Figure 5.9: Each frame of animation is stored in the texture (including alpha info). After a small amount of time has passed, we increment to the next frame in the animation.

Note: We call a texture that contains several sub-textures, like Figure 5.9, a *texture atlas*.

As far as implementing this technique goes, the basic idea is to store all the frames representing the animation in one texture file. We start by using the first frame, then after a (small) defined time period elapses, we increment to the next frame. For example, if we wanted the animation to play at 20 frames per second, we'd increment to the next texture every time 0.05 seconds elapsed, until the animation is completed.

Recall that the second parameter, pSrcRect, of ID3DXSprite::Draw, allows us to specify a rectangular subset of a texture to use for the sprite. Previously, we always wanted to use the whole texture, and so specified null. However, in our present situation, we have a whole bunch of frame images on one texture, so we will want to use this parameter and specify the rectangle of the particular frame we want to use at a given time. In Figure 5.9, suppose that each frame has dimensions of 64×64 pixels. Since there are five rows and six columns, the entire texture has dimensions of 384×320 pixels. The rectangle corresponding to the frame at position row i and column j is given by:

$$R_{ij} = \{(j) \cdot 64, (i) \cdot 64, (j+1) \cdot 64, (i+1) \cdot 64\}$$

where i and j are zero-based indices; where we are using screen coordinates (i.e., +y-axis goes down); and the rectangle components are given in the format $R_{ij} = \{left, top, right, bottom\}$. The following code illustrates the animation process (it is based on animating Figure 5.9):

Initialization:

```
// Keep internal data member to keep track of current
// animation frame.
mCurrFrame = 0;
```

For each game loop cycle, update as follows:

```
// Keep track of how much time has accumulated.
static float timeAccum = 0.0f;
timeAccum += dt;


// Play animation at 30 frames per second.
if( timeAccum >= 1.0f / 30.0f )
{
    // Move on to the next frame.
    ++mCurrFrame;
    timeAccum = 0.0f;

    // This animation has 30 frames indexed from
    // 0, 1, ..., 29, so start back at the beginning if
    // we go over or STOP the animation.
    if(mCurrFrame > 29)
        mCurrFrame = 0;
}
```

For each game loop cycle, render as follows:

```
// Compute rectangle on texture atlas of the current frame
// we want to use.
int i = mCurrFrame / 6;   // Row
int j = mCurrFrame % 6;   // Column
RECT R = {j*64, i*64, (j+1)*64, (i+1)*64};


// Turn on alpha blending.
HR(gd3dDevice->SetRenderState(D3DRS_ALPHABLENDENABLE, true));

// Don't move explosion--set identity matrix.
D3DXMATRIX M;
D3DXMatrixIdentity(&M);
HR(mSprite->SetTransform(&M));
HR(mSprite->Draw(mFrames, &R, &mSpriteCenter, 0,
            D3DCOLOR_XRGB(255, 255, 255)));
HR(mSprite->End());


// Turn off alpha blending.
HR(gd3dDevice->SetRenderState(D3DRS_ALPHABLENDENABLE, false));
```

Warning: Your sprite texture dimensions should be powers of 2; that is, 2^n for some *n*. Otherwise, the sprites will be scaled to powers of 2 by the D3DXCreateTextureFromFile function, which can mess up some assumptions. Therefore, in the implementation of animating Figure 5.9, even though we only need a 384×320 texture, we augment the texture to 512×512 and waste space. In practice, you would not want to waste this space, but for a demo it is not anything to worry about. Even so, we can prevent D3DX from scaling our texture if we use the D3DXCreateTextureFromFileEx function and specify the D3DX_DEFAULT_NONPOW2 flag. Nonetheless, this extended function is too complicated to get into at this point, and therefore, we stick to our current plan of augmenting the texture to 512×512 and wasting space.

Sometimes, it is useful to *loop* the animation; that is, once it reaches the last texture, it loops back to the beginning. This can be used for continuously animating things that roughly repeat themselves after some short time period — like waves or fire. Note that the animation must be designed for looping so that the last frame coincides with the first frame; otherwise, a discontinuity in the animation will occur.

One thing to watch out for with this technique is memory requirements. Just 30 256×256 24-bit uncompressed images require close to 6 megabytes of memory (a significant amount of memory for a small effect). Moreover, a 30-frame animation only can be made to last around a second, as you need to change the frames at around 24 to 30 frames per second for the animation illusion to occur. Therefore, this technique is best used with small images, such as 64×64 bitmaps, and for short animations like explosions that last less than a second or with short animations that can be lengthened by looping. It is worth noting, however, that Direct3D supports a compressed texture format, which can save a lot of memory. This compressed texture format will be covered in Chapter 11.

For brevity, we do not embed the code here, but we have heavily annotated a demo called PageFlipDemo, which implements the page flipping animation technique. A screenshot is provided in Figure 5.10.

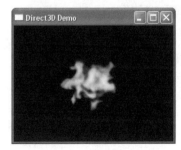

Figure 5.10: A screenshot of the Page Flip demo. The demo may appear grainy since we blow the texture up (i.e., magnify it) for this demo. Ideally, for best quality, the texture pixel dimensions should match the screen pixel dimensions onto which the texture gets mapped so that distortion is minimized.

5.4 **Summary**

- The performance counter is a high-resolution timer that provides accurate timing measurements needed for measuring small time differentials, such as the time elapsed between frames. The performance timer works in time units called _counts_. The QueryPerformanceFrequency outputs the counts per second of the performance timer, which can then be used to convert from units of counts to seconds. The current time value of the performance timer (measured in counts) is obtained with the QueryPerformanceCounter function.

- To compute the frames per second (FPS), we count the number of frames processed over some time interval Δt. Let n be the number of frames counted over time Δt, then the average frames per second over that time interval is $fps_{avg} = n/\Delta t$. The frame rate can give misleading conclusions about performance; the time it takes to process a frame is more informative. The amount of time, in seconds, spent processing a frame is the reciprocal of the frame rate, i.e., $1/fps_{avg}$. We can convert that time value from seconds to milliseconds by multiplying it by 1000.

- Direct Input allows us to bypass the message system and work directly with the input drivers, thereby making it more efficient. To use Direct Input, you need to #include <dinput.h> and link _dinput8.lib_. IDirectInput8 is used to enumerate input devices on the system and for obtaining pointers to IDirectInputDevice8 objects. The IDirectInput-Device8 interface is our software representation of a physical input device (e.g., mouse, keyboard, joystick) and allows us to communicate with that input device. We use the term _polling_ to refer to the process of taking a snapshot of the current state of the input device (e.g., is a key/button pressed, how far has the mouse moved since the last time we polled).

- A _sprite_ refers to a small 2D image. D3DX represents a sprite with the ID3DXSprite interface; a pointer to an object of this type may be obtained with the D3DXCreateSprite function.

- We can animate our game objects by changing their position, orientation, and size in small increments over time; this provides the illusion of smooth continuous motion. Another technique is to rapidly display the frames of a pre-made animation in rapid succession, as an animator would do with a flipbook.

5.5 **Exercises**

1. You can modify the *z*-component of the sprites to change their depth, thus making them smaller or bigger. Recall the following code, from onResetDevice, that sets up the camera:

```
D3DXMATRIX V;
D3DXVECTOR3 pos(0.0f, 0.0f, -1000.0f);
D3DXVECTOR3 up(0.0f, 1.0f, 0.0f);
D3DXVECTOR3 target(0.0f, 0.0f, 0.0f);
D3DXMatrixLookAtLH(&V, &pos, &target, &up);
HR(gd3dDevice->SetTransform(D3DTS_VIEW, &V));
```

Here pos positions the camera –1000 units on the *z*-axis. Thus, to make a sprite bigger (closer to the camera), you would move its depth value toward –1000. Experiment by changing the depth of the ship's position. Also experiment by changing the *z*-coordinate of pos to zoom the camera in and out.

2. The Sprite demo used our Direct Input class for keyboard input only. Write a program that changes the *z*-coordinate of the camera (see exercise 1) based on mouse movement along the *y*-axis.

3. Create or find some free images of alien spaceships. Modify these images by inserting an alpha channel and marking the pixels that are to be displayed. Then modify the Sprite demo by using these modified images to include enemy ship sprites.

4. Modify the Sprite demo again by defining a motion path for the enemy ships. You might have them move along a line back and forth, follow the player-controlled ship, or something else of your own choosing.

5. With the techniques described in this chapter, you can implement many old classic 2D arcade games, such as Pong, Asteroids, Space Invaders, and many others. Try to design and implement a Pong and Asteroids clone.

Chapter 6

The Rendering Pipeline

The primary theme of this chapter is the rendering pipeline. The rendering pipeline is responsible for creating a 2D image given a geometric description of the 3D world and a virtual camera that specifies the volume of the world that is seen.

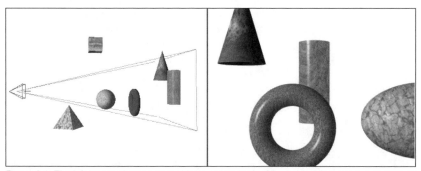

Figure 6.1: The left image shows some objects set up in the 3D world with a camera positioned and aimed. The "pyramid" volume specifies the volume of space that the viewer can see; objects (and parts of objects) outside this volume are not seen. The image on the right shows the 2D image created based on what the camera "sees."

Objectives:

- To discover several key signals used to convey a realistic sense of volume and spatial depth in a 2D image.
- To find out how we represent 3D objects in Direct3D.
- To learn how we model the virtual camera.
- To understand the rendering pipeline — the process of taking a geometric description of a 3D scene and generating a 2D image from it.

147

6.1 **The 3D Illusion**

Before we embark on our journey of 3D computer graphics, a simple question remains outstanding: How do we display a 3D world with depth and volume on a flat 2D monitor screen? Fortunately for us, this problem has been well studied, as artists have been painting 3D scenes on 2D canvases for centuries. In this section, we outline several key techniques that make an image look 3D, even though it is actually drawn on a 2D plane. These techniques are simply based on phenomenon we observe in our physical world.

Suppose that you have encountered a railroad track that doesn't curve, but goes along a straight line for a long distance. The railroad rails always remain parallel to each other, but if you stand on the railroad and look down its path, you will observe that the two rails get closer and closer together as their distance from you increases, and eventually they converge at an infinite distance. This is one observation that characterizes our human viewing system: parallel lines of vision converge to a *vanishing point*, as shown in Figure 6.2.

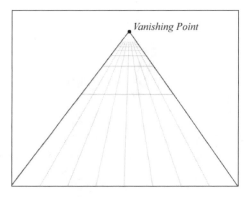

Figure 6.2: Parallel lines converge to a vanishing point. Artists sometimes call this *linear perspective*.

Another simple observation of how humans see things is that the size of an object appears to diminish with depth; that is, objects near us look bigger than objects far away. For example, a house far away on a hill will look very small, while a tree near us will look very large in comparison. Figure 6.3 shows a simple scene where parallel rows of columns are placed behind each other, one after another. The columns are actually all the same size, but as their distance from the viewer increases, they get smaller and smaller. Also notice how the columns are converging to the vanishing point at the horizon.

Figure 6.3: Here, all the columns are of the same size, but a viewer observes a diminishing in size with respect to depth phenomenon.

Object overlap is another reality we experience. Object overlap refers to the fact that opaque objects obscure parts (or all) of the objects behind them. This is important, as it tells us the depth ordering relationship of the objects in the scene. We already discussed (in Chapter 4) how Direct3D uses a depth buffer to figure out which pixels are being obscured and thus should not be drawn. However, for completeness, we show the situation again in Figure 6.4.

Figure 6.4: A group of objects that partially obscure each other because they overlap.

Consider Figure 6.5. On the left we have an unlit sphere, and on the right we have a lit sphere. As you can see, the sphere on the left looks rather flat — maybe it is not even a sphere at all, but just a textured 2D circle! Thus, lighting and shading play a very important role in depicting the solid form and volume of 3D objects.

Figure 6.5: (a) An unlit sphere that looks 2D. (b) A lit sphere that looks 3D.

_(a)_ _(b)_

Finally, Figure 6.6 shows a spaceship and its shadow. The shadow serves two key purposes. First, it tells us the origin of the light source in the scene. And secondly, it provides us with a rough idea of how high off the ground the spaceship is.

Figure 6.6: A spaceship and its shadow. The shadow implies the location of the light source in the scene and also gives an idea of the spaceship's height off the ground.

The observations just discussed, no doubt, are intuitively obvious from our day-to-day experiences. Nonetheless, it is helpful to explicitly write down what we know and to keep these observations in mind as we study and work on 3D computer graphics.

6.2 **Model Representation**

An *object* is represented as a *triangle mesh* approximation, and consequently, triangles form the basic building blocks of the objects we model. We use the following terms interchangeably to refer to the triangles of a mesh: polygons, primitives, and mesh geometry. As Figure 6.7 implies, we can approximate any real-world 3D object by a triangle mesh. Generally speaking, the greater the triangle density of the mesh, the better the approximation. Of course, the more triangles we use, the more processing power is required, so a balance must be made based on the hardware power of the application's target audience.

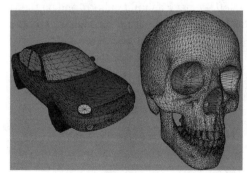

Figure 6.7: (Left) A car approximated by a low-density triangle mesh. (Right) A skull approximated by a high-density triangle mesh.

The point where two edges on a polygon meet is called a *vertex*. To describe a triangle, we specify the three point locations that correspond to the three vertices of the triangle, as shown in Figure 6.8. Then to describe an object, we list the triangles that define it.

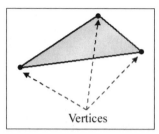

Figure 6.8: A triangle defined by its three vertices.

Vertices

The large number of triangles used in Figure 6.7 makes one thing clear: It would be extremely cumbersome to manually list the triangles of a 3D model. For all but the simplest models, special 3D applications called *3D modelers* are used to generate and manipulate 3D objects. These modelers allow the user to build complex and realistic meshes in a visual and interactive environment with a rich tool set, thereby making the entire modeling process much easier. Examples of popular modelers used for game development are 3D Studio MAX (www.discreet.com), LightWave 3D (www.newtek.com), Maya (www.aliaswavefront.com), and Softimage|XSI (www.softimage.com).

Nevertheless, in Part II of this book, we will generate our 3D models manually by hand or via a mathematical formula (the triangle list for cylinders and spheres, for example, can easily be generated with parametric formulas). In Part III of this book, we show how to load and display 3D models exported to the Direct3D file format (.X).

6.2.1 Vertex Declarations

The previous definition of a vertex is correct mathematically, but it is an incomplete definition when used in the context of Direct3D. This is because a vertex in Direct3D can consist of additional properties besides a spatial location. For instance, a vertex can have a color property as well as a normal property (colors and normals are discussed in Chapters 9 and 10, respectively). Direct3D gives us the flexibility to construct our own vertex formats; in other words, it allows us to define the components (attributes) of a vertex.

To create a custom vertex format we first create a structure that holds the vertex data we choose. For instance, the following illustrates two different kinds of vertex formats; one consists of position and color, and the second consists of position, normal, and texture coordinates (see Chapter 11, "Texturing").

```
struct ColorVertex
{
    D3DXVECTOR3 position;
    D3DCOLOR color;
};

struct NormalTexVertex
{
    D3DXVECTOR3 position;
    D3DXVECTOR3 normal;
    D3DXVECTOR3 texCoords;
};
```

Once we have the vertex structure completed, we need to provide Direct3D with a description of our vertex structure so that it knows what to do with each component. This description is provided to Direct3D in the form of a *vertex declaration*.

Note: The DirectX documentation recommends a 32-byte vertex format for optimal performance (*directx/graphics/programmingguide/ gettingstarted/direct3dresources/vertexbuffers/fvfvertexbuffers.htm*).

We describe a vertex declaration by an array of D3DVERTEXELEMENT9 elements. Each element in the D3DVERTEXELEMENT9 array describes one component of the vertex. So if the vertex structure has three components (e.g., position, normal, color), then the corresponding vertex declaration will be described by an array of three D3DVERTEXELEMENT9 elements. The D3DVERTEXELEMENT9 structure is defined as:

```
typedef struct _D3DVERTEXELEMENT9 {
    BYTE Stream;
    BYTE Offset;
    BYTE Type;
    BYTE Method;
    BYTE Usage;
    BYTE UsageIndex;
} D3DVERTEXELEMENT9;
```

- Stream: Specifies the stream with which the vertex component is associated. In this book, we just use one vertex stream — stream 0.
- Offset: The offset, in bytes, from the start of the vertex structure to the start of the vertex component. This tells Direct3D where the vertex component is in the vertex structure. For example, if the vertex structure is:

```
struct Vertex
{
    D3DXVECTOR3 pos;
    D3DXVECTOR3 normal;
    D3DXVECTOR2 texCoords;
};
```

The offset of the component pos is 0 since it is the first component. The offset of the component normal is 12 because sizeof(pos) == 12 (i.e., the component normal is 12 bytes from the beginning of Vertex). The offset of the component texCoords is 24 because sizeof(pos) + sizeof(normal) == 24 (i.e., the component texCoords is 24 bytes from the beginning of Vertex).

■ Type: Specifies the data type of the vertex element. This can be any member of the D3DDECLTYPE enumerated type — see the documentation for a complete list. Some commonly used types are:

D3DDECLTYPE_FLOAT1: A floating-point scalar.

D3DDECLTYPE_FLOAT2: A 2D floating-point vector.

D3DDECLTYPE_FLOAT3: A 3D floating-point vector.

D3DDECLTYPE_FLOAT4: A 4D floating-point vector.

D3DDECLTYPE_D3DCOLOR: A D3DCOLOR type that is expanded to a 4D floating-point color vector , where each component is normalized to the interval [0, 1].

Returning to the above Vertex structure, the type of pos and normal would be D3DDECLTYPE_FLOAT3 since they are 3D vectors, and the type of texCoords would be D3DDECLTYPE_FLOAT2 since it is a 2D vector.

■ Method: Specifies the tessellation method. We consider this parameter advanced and thus use the default method, which is specified by the identifier D3DDECLMETHOD_DEFAULT.

■ Usage: This member tells Direct3D what the component is going to be used for — does the 3D vector represent a spatial location, a normal, or something else? Valid usage identifiers are of the D3DDECLUSAGE enumerated type. Some common usages are:

D3DDECLUSAGE_POSITION: Vertex component used to store position.

D3DDECLUSAGE_NORMAL: Vertex component used to store a normal.

D3DDECLUSAGE_TEXCOORD: Vertex component used to store a texture coordinate.

D3DDECLUSAGE_COLOR: Vertex component used to store color information.

■ UsageIndex: Used to identify multiple vertex components of the same usage. The usage index is an integer in the interval [0, 15]. For example, suppose we have three vertex components of usage D3DDECLUSAGE_NORMAL. We would specify a usage index of 0 for the first, a usage index of 1 for the second, and a usage index of 2 for the third. In this way we can identify each particular normal by its usage index. For example, the following vertex declaration describes a vertex structure with a position component and three normals:

```
D3DVERTEXELEMENT9 decl[] =
{
{0,  0, D3DDECLTYPE_FLOAT3, D3DDECLMETHOD_DEFAULT, D3DDECLUSAGE_POSITION, 0},
{0, 12, D3DDECLTYPE_FLOAT3, D3DDECLMETHOD_DEFAULT, D3DDECLUSAGE_NORMAL,   0},
{0, 24, D3DDECLTYPE_FLOAT3, D3DDECLMETHOD_DEFAULT, D3DDECLUSAGE_NORMAL,   1},
{0, 36, D3DDECLTYPE_FLOAT3, D3DDECLMETHOD_DEFAULT, D3DDECLUSAGE_NORMAL,   2},
D3DDECL_END()
};
```

The D3DDECL_END macro is used to mark the end of a D3DVERTEXELEMENT9 array. The vertex structure that decl describes looks like this:

```
struct Vertex
{
    D3DXVECTOR3 pos;
    D3DXVECTOR3 normal0;
    D3DXVECTOR3 normal1;
    D3DXVECTOR3 normal2;
};
```

Once we have described a vertex declaration by a D3DVERTEXELEMENT9 array, we can obtain a pointer to an IDirect3DVertexDeclaration9 interface, which represents a vertex declaration using the method:

```
HRESULT IDirect3DDevice9::CreateVertexDeclaration(
    CONST D3DVERTEXELEMENT9* pVertexElements,
    IDirect3DVertexDeclaration9** ppDecl);
```

■ pVertexElements: Array of D3DVERTEXELEMENT9 elements describing the vertex declaration we want created.

■ ppDecl: Used to return a pointer to the created IDirect3DVertexDeclaration9 interface.

For example, suppose that decl is a D3DVERTEXELEMENT9 array; then we create an IDirect3DVertexDeclaration9 like so:

```
IDirect3DVertexDeclaration9* d3dVertexDecl = 0;
HR(gd3dDevice->CreateVertexDeclaration(decl, &d3dVertexDecl));
```

Note: Do not get bogged down in the details of vertex declarations at this point. You will see plenty of easy examples over the next few chapters of this book, and some more advanced examples in the last part of this book.

Note: For a large program, we typically work with numerous vertex structures. It is convenient to define all of these vertex structures in a single location. As we progress through this book, we add all of our vertex structure definitions to the source code files *Vertex.h* and *Vertex.cpp*.

6.2.2 **Triangles**

Triangles are the basic building blocks of 3D objects. To construct an object, we create a triangle list that describes its shape and contours. A triangle list contains the data for each individual triangle we wish to draw. For example, to construct a quad we break it into two triangles, as shown in Figure 6.9a, and specify the vertices of each triangle. Likewise, to construct a rough circle approximation (octagon), we break it up into triangles again and list the vertices of each triangle, as shown in Figure 6.9b. For example, to define the quad we define the vertex list as follows:

```
Vertex quad[6] = {
    v0, v1, v2,   // Triangle 0
    v0, v2, v3    // Triangle 1
};
```

And we can do the same thing for the circle approximation:

```
Vertex circle[24] = {
    v0, v1, v2,   // Triangle 0
    v0, v2, v3,   // Triangle 1
    v0, v3, v4,   // Triangle 2
    v0, v4, v5,   // Triangle 3
    v0, v5, v6,   // Triangle 4
    v0, v6, v7,   // Triangle 5
    v0, v7, v8,   // Triangle 6
    v0, v8, v1    // Triangle 7
};
```

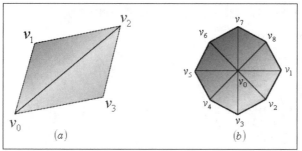

Figure 6.9: (a) A quad built from two triangles. (b) A rough circle approximation built from several triangles.

Note: The order in which you specify the vertices of a triangle is important and is called the *winding order*. See §6.4.5 for details.

6.2.3 **Indices**

As Figure 6.9 illustrates, the triangles that form a 3D object share many of the same vertices. More specifically, each triangle of the quad in Figure 6.9a shares the vertices v_0 and v_2. While duplicating two vertices is not too bad, the duplication is worse in the circle example (Figure 6.9b), as every triangle duplicates the center vertex v_0, and each vertex on the exterior of the

circle is shared by two triangles. In general, the number of duplicate vertices increases as the detail and complexity of the model increases.

There are two reasons why we do not want to duplicate vertices:

1. Increased memory requirements. (Why store the same vertex data
    more than once?)

2. Increased processing by the graphics hardware. (Why process the same
    vertex data more than once?)

To solve this problem, we introduce the concept of indices. It works like
this: We create a vertex list and an index list. The vertex list consists of all
the unique vertices and the index list contains values that index into the
vertex list to define how the vertices are to be put together to form triangles. Returning to the shapes in Figure 6.9, the vertex list of the quad
would be constructed as follows:

```
Vertex v[4] = {v0, v1, v2, v3};
```

Then the index list needs to define how the vertices in the vertex list are to
be put together to form the two triangles.

```
WORD indexList[6] = {0, 1, 2,  // Triangle 0
                     0, 2, 3}; // Triangle 1
```

In the index list, every three elements define a triangle. So the above index
list says, "form triangle 0 by using the vertices v[0], v[1], and v[2], and
form triangle 1 by using the vertices v[0], v[2], and v[3]."

Similarly, the vertex list for the circle would be constructed as follows:

```
Vertex v [9] = {v0, v1, v2, v3, v4, v5, v6, v7, v8};
```

...and the index list would be:

```
WORD indexList[24] = {
      0, 1, 2,  // Triangle 0
      0, 2, 3,  // Triangle 1
      0, 3, 4,  // Triangle 2
      0, 4, 5,  // Triangle 3
      0, 5, 6,  // Triangle 4
      0, 6, 7,  // Triangle 5
      0, 7, 8,  // Triangle 6
      0, 8, 1   // Triangle 7
};
```

After the unique vertices in the vertex list are processed, the graphics card
can use the index list to put the vertices together to form the triangles.
Observe that we have moved the "duplication" over to the index list, but
this is not bad since:

■   Indices are simply integers and do not take up as much memory as a
    full vertex structure (and vertex structures can get big as we add more
    components to them).

- With good vertex cache ordering (see §14.5), the graphics hardware won't have to process duplicate vertices (too often).

6.3 The Virtual Camera

6.3.1 The Frustum

The camera specifies what part of the world the viewer can see and thus what part of the world we need to generate a 2D image of. The camera is positioned and oriented in the world and defines the volume of space that is visible. Figure 6.10 shows a diagram of our camera model.

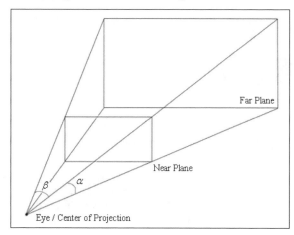

Figure 6.10: A _frustum_, the space enclosed between the near and far planes (i.e., truncated pyramid), defines the volume of space that the camera "sees." The frustum's vertical and horizontal field of view angles are given by α and β, respectively.

The volume of space is a _frustum_ (i.e., a pyramid with its tip chopped off) and is defined by the field of view angles and the near and far planes. The reasons for using a frustum should be made clear when you consider that your monitor screen is rectangular. Objects (or parts of objects) that are not inside this volume cannot be seen and thus should be discarded from further process. The process of discarding such data is called _clipping_. The near plane specifies how close an object can be to the viewer before it is clipped; geometry in front of the near plane is clipped. The far plane specifies the maximum distance 3D geometry can be from the camera and still be visible; geometry behind the far plane is clipped. Typically, only the vertical field of view (FOV) angle is specified, and the horizontal field of view angle is some scalar multiple of the vertical field of view angle, where the scalar multiple compensates for the fact that the width of the back buffer is greater than its height.

Note: Common synonyms used interchangeably for the virtual camera are "the viewer" and "the eye."

6.3.2 **Perspective Projection**

Consider Figure 6.11. Let us call the line from a vertex to the eye point the *vertex's line of projection*. Then, we define the *perspective projection transformation* as the transformation that transforms a 3D vertex v to the point v' where its line of projection intersects the 2D projection plane, and say that v' is the *projection* of v. Moreover, the *projection of a 3D object* refers to the projection of all the vertices that make up the object.

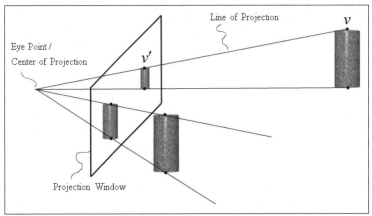

Figure 6.11: Both cylinders in 3D space are the same size but are placed at different depths. The projection of the closer cylinder is bigger than the projection of the farther cylinder. The projection window is a rectangle on the projection plane; vertices whose projections fall inside the projection window are seen by the eye.

Observe that as the 3D depth of an object increases, the size of its projection diminishes, and the projected points converge to the center of the projection window; recall from §6.1 that these two effects are two of the ingredients of the 3D illusion! We derive the mathematics of perspective projection in §6.4.4.

6.4 **The Rendering Pipeline**

Given a geometric description of a 3D scene, and a positioned and aimed virtual camera in that scene, the *rendering pipeline* refers to the entire sequence of steps necessary to generate a 2D image that can be displayed on a monitor screen based on what the virtual camera sees. Figure 6.12 provides an abridged version of the Direct3D pipeline, and the following subsections explain each stage.

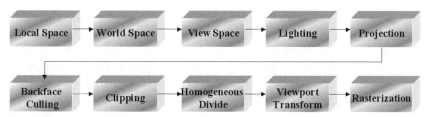

Figure 6.12: An abridged Direct3D rendering pipeline.

Note: The first couple of subsections that follow deal with moving from one coordinate system to another. You may wish to review Part I (in particular, the sections on changing coordinate systems) of this book before continuing.

6.4.1 **Local Space and World Space**

Suppose for a moment that you are working on a film and your team has to construct a miniature version of a train scene for some special effect shots. In particular, suppose that you are tasked with making a small bridge. Now, you would not construct the bridge in the middle of the scene, where you would likely have to work from a difficult angle and be careful not to mess up the other miniatures that compose the scene. Instead, you would work on the bridge at your workbench away from the scene. Then when it is all done, you would place the bridge at its correct position and angle in the scene.

3D artists do something similar when constructing 3D objects. Instead of building an object's geometry with coordinates relative to a global scene coordinate system (*world space*), they specify them relative to a local coordinate system (*local space*), where the object is the center of the coordinate system (see Figure 6.13).

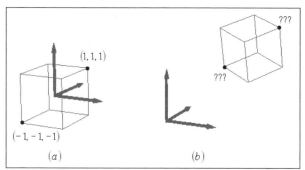

Figure 6.13: (a) The vertices of a unit cube are easily specified when the cube is constructed about its own local coordinate system. (b) It is harder to define vertices at an arbitrary position and orientation in the world space.

Then once the 3D model is finished in local space, it is placed in the global scene; this is done by us specifying where we want the origin and axes of the local space coordinate system relative to the global scene coordinate system, and executing a change of coordinates transformation (see Figure 6.14). The process of changing coordinates relative to a local coordinate system into the global scene coordinate system is called the *world transform*.

Building models in local space and then transforming them to world space allows artists to construct models without regard to their position, size, or orientation in relation to other objects in the world (these scene-dependent relations are handled by the world transform). Note that each object has its own world transformation, as each object will be positioned/oriented differently in the world.

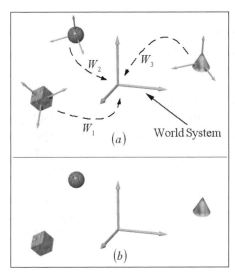

Figure 6.14: (a) The vertices of each object are defined relative to their own local coordinate system; in addition, we specify the position and orientation of each local coordinate system relative to the world space coordinate system based on where we want the object in the scene. Then, we execute a change of coordinates transformation to make all coordinates relative to the world space coordinate system. (b) After the world transform, the objects' vertices are all relative to the same world system.

Recall from Chapter 2, that if we know the origin, $\vec{p}$, and axis vectors, $\vec{r}$, $\vec{u}$, and $\vec{f}$, of the local coordinate system relative to the global coordinate system, then we can change a vertex from the local coordinate system to the global coordinate system by multiplying the vertex point by the following matrix:

$$W = \begin{bmatrix} r_x & r_y & r_z & 0 \\ u_x & u_y & u_z & 0 \\ f_x & f_y & f_z & 0 \\ p_x & p_y & p_z & 1 \end{bmatrix} \tag{6.1}$$

We call the above matrix the *world matrix* or *world transformation matrix*.

Note: If you want to specify a model's vertices directly in world space, then just specify the identity matrix for the world matrix.

6.4.2 View Space

We can think of the camera as an object in the world as well, and we can choose to make the camera the frame of reference in which we describe vertices relative to instead of the world coordinate system. Let the camera be centered about its own local coordinate system (called *view space* or the *camera coordinate system*) looking down the positive z-axis. Moreover, let $\vec{p}$ be the origin and let $\vec{r}$, $\vec{u}$, and $\vec{f}$ be the basis vectors of the camera's local system relative to the world system. Then the world transformation matrix (Equation 6.1) transforms the camera from its local coordinate system to the world space. However, this is not what we want, as projection and other operations are difficult or less efficient when the camera is at an arbitrary position and orientation in the world. To make things easier, we actually want the camera to be the center of the scene (i.e., we describe the objects' vertices relative to the camera coordinate system). Thus, we actually want the reverse transformation; that is, we want to transform all of the objects in world space to view space. But recall from Chapter 2 that the reverse transformation is just given by the inverse. Thus, W^{-1} transforms from world space to view space.

Now observe that a change of frame matrix really does a rotation and translation transformation on the vertices. Thus, we can write $W = RT$, where R is purely a rotation matrix and T is purely a translation matrix. From facts covered in Chapter 2 and 3 (inverse of products and inverse of rotation matrix), we have:

$$V = W^{-1} = (RT)^{-1} = T^{-1}R^{-1} = T^{-1}R^T$$

$$= \begin{bmatrix} 1 & 0 & 0 & 0 \\ 0 & 1 & 0 & 0 \\ 0 & 0 & 1 & 0 \\ -p_x & -p_y & -p_z & 1 \end{bmatrix} \begin{bmatrix} r_x & u_x & f_x & 0 \\ r_y & u_y & f_y & 0 \\ r_z & u_z & f_z & 0 \\ 0 & 0 & 0 & 1 \end{bmatrix} = \begin{bmatrix} r_x & u_x & f_x & 0 \\ r_y & u_y & f_y & 0 \\ r_z & u_z & f_z & 0 \\ -\vec{p}\cdot\vec{r} & -\vec{p}\cdot\vec{u} & -\vec{p}\cdot\vec{f} & 1 \end{bmatrix} \tag{6.2}$$

We call V the *view matrix* or *view transformation matrix*, and it maps vertices from world space to view space (see Figure 6.15).

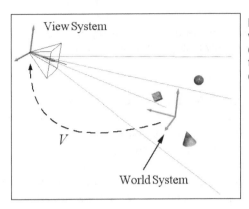

Figure 6.15: Transform
vertices relative to the world
coordinate system and make
them relative to the camera
coordinate system.

As shown, we can compute the view matrix directly ourselves, and we will.
However, D3DX also provides a useful function for generating a view
matrix for us:

```
D3DXMATRIX *D3DXMatrixLookAtLH(
    D3DXMATRIX* pOut,        // pointer to receive resulting view matrix
    CONST D3DXVECTOR3* pEye, // position of camera in world
    CONST D3DXVECTOR3* pAt,  // point camera is looking at in world
    CONST D3DXVECTOR3* pUp   // the world's up vector - (0, 1, 0)
);
```

The pEye parameter specifies the position of the camera in the world. The
pAt parameter specifies the point in the world at which you want to aim the
camera. The pUp parameter is the vector that indicates which direction is
"up" in the 3D world; this is usually always the vector coincident with the
y-axis – (0, 1, 0), but if for some reason you want an upside-down camera,
you can specify (0, –1, 0) instead.

As an example, suppose we want to position the camera at the point
(5, 3, –10) and have the camera look at the center of the world (0, 0, 0). We
can then build the view transformation matrix by writing:

```
D3DXVECTOR3 position(5.0f, 3.0f, -10.0f);
D3DXVECTOR3 targetPoint(0.0f, 0.0f, 0.0f);
D3DXVECTOR3 worldUp(0.0f, 1.0f, 0.0f);

D3DXMATRIX V;
D3DXMatrixLookAtLH(&V, &position, &targetPoint, &worldUp);
```

The function D3DXMatrixLookAtLH does not do anything special to construct
the view matrix. Given the position of the camera in world space, its target
point in world space, and the world up vector, we have the origin of the
camera and can derive its axis vectors relative to the world space. Figure
6.16 illustrates this. Once we have the origin and axis vectors described relative to the world space, we just pop the coordinates into Equation 6.2 to
build the view matrix.

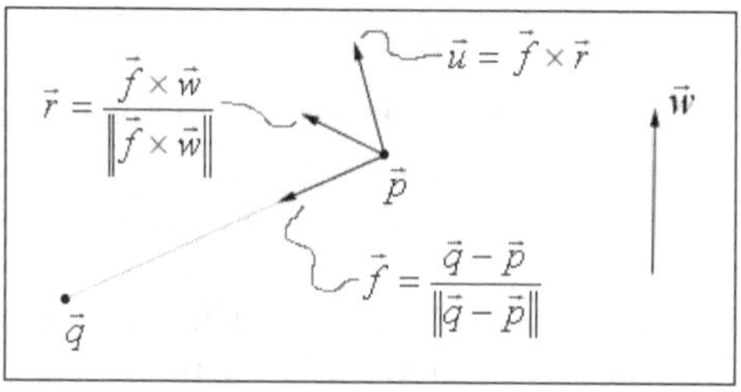

Figure 6.16: The forward vector $\vec{f}$ is given by normalizing the vector from $\vec{p}$ to $\vec{q}$, that is, $\vec{q}-\vec{p}$. A right vector $\vec{r}$ orthogonal to $\vec{f}$ can be found by normalizing the vector returned from $\vec{f}\times\vec{w}$, where $\vec{w}$ is the world "up" vector. Finally, the "up" vector of the camera is given by $\vec{u}=\vec{f}\times\vec{r}$. Normalizing the last vector is unnecessary since the cross product of two orthogonal unit vectors is a unit vector.

6.4.3 **Lighting**

We can place lights in the scene as well. Typically, lights are specified directly in world space relative to the overall scene. However, we can always transform lights into local space or view space, and carry out the lighting calculation in whichever coordinate system is most convenient. Reexamine Figure 6.5 to see how lighting helps depict the solid form and volume of 3D objects.

In addition to the realistic consequences of lighting, lights can be utilized for cinematic effects, such as emphasizing (or hiding) certain parts of a scene, and creating drama.

6.4.4 **Projection Transformation**

Once all the vertices of the scene are in view space and lighting has been completed, a projection transformation is applied. After projection, Direct3D expects the coordinates of the vertices inside the frustum to be in so-called *normalized device coordinates*, where the x- and y-coordinates are in the range [–1, 1], and the z-coordinates are in the range [0, 1]. Projected vertices with coordinates outside these ranges correspond to unprojected vertices outside the frustum. Note, then, that the projection transform maps the frustum into a box (sometimes called the *canonical view volume*). This may seem counterintuitive because isn't the projection transformation supposed to generate 2D projected points? Indeed it actually does: The transformed x- and y-coordinates represent the 2D projected vertices, and the normalized z-coordinate is just used for depth buffering. (Remember that we still need to keep attached the relative depth information for each vertex for the depth buffering algorithm.)

6.4.4.1 *Defining a Frustum and Aspect Ratio*

To define a frustum centered at the origin of view space and looking down the positive z-axis, we specify a near plane n, a far plane f, a vertical field of view angle α, and the so-called *aspect ratio*. What about the horizontal field of view angle? As we will now show, the aspect ratio allows us to determine the horizontal field of view angle β. The *aspect ratio* R is defined by the ratio $R = w/h$, where w is the width of the view window and h is the height of the view window (units in view space). For consistency, we like the *ratio* of the projection window dimensions to be the same as the ratio of the back buffer dimensions; therefore, the ratio of the back buffer dimensions is typically specified as the aspect ratio (it's a ratio so it has no units). For example, if the back buffer dimensions are 800×600, then we specify $R = 800/600 = 4/3 \approx 1.33333$.

To see how R helps us find β, consider Figure 6.17.

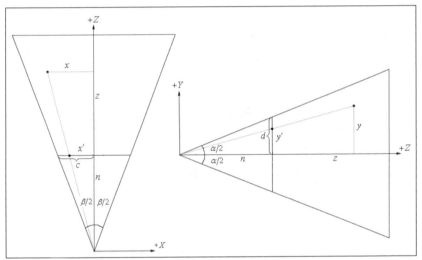

Figure 6.17: Right triangle relations on the *xz*- and *yz*-planes.

Using some trigonometry, we have $(\alpha/2) = d/n$, and $(\beta/2) = c/n$. (Note that $h = 2d$ and $w = 2c$.) However, we also have the aspect ratio relationship: $R = w/h \Rightarrow w = Rh \Rightarrow w/2 = R\,h/2$. Therefore, we can write:

$$\tan(\beta/2) = \frac{w/2}{n} = \frac{Rh/2}{n} = R\frac{d}{n} = R\tan(\alpha/2) \qquad (6.3)$$

So given the vertical field of view angle α *and* the aspect ratio R, we can always get the horizontal field of view angle β.

6.4.4.2 *Projecting Vertices*

We first handle the x- and y-coordinates. Consider Figure 6.17 again, and recall that we define the *perspective projection transformation* as the transformation that transforms a 3D vertex v to the point v' where its line of projection intersects the 2D projection plane (here the projection plane is the near plane). By considering the x- and y-coordinates separately and using trigonometry (similar triangles, specifically), we find:

$$\frac{x'}{n} = \frac{x}{z} \Rightarrow x' = \frac{xn}{z} \quad \text{and} \quad \frac{y'}{n} = \frac{y}{z} \Rightarrow y' = \frac{yn}{z}$$

So now we have the 2D projected point (x', y') on the near plane.

Observe from Figure 6.17 that projected points correspond to unprojected points *inside* the frustum if and only if both $-c \leq x' \leq c$ and $-d \leq y' \leq d$. Projected points outside these ranges correspond to unprojected points *outside* the frustum.

6.4.4.3 *Normalizing the Coordinates*

Recall, however, that Direct3D wants the x- and y-coordinates of the projected points that are *in the frustum* to be in the normalized range $[-1, 1]$, and projected points that are *outside the frustum* to be outside the normalized range $[-1, 1]$. Observe that if we divide x' and y' by c and d, respectively, then we get exactly what we want:

$$-c \leq x' \leq c \Rightarrow -1 \leq x'/c \leq 1$$

$$-d \leq y' \leq d \Rightarrow -1 \leq y'/d \leq 1$$

Thus we have the projected and normalized x- and y-coordinates:

$$\tilde{x} = \frac{x'}{c} = \frac{xn}{z}\bigg/c = \frac{xn}{z}\bigg/n\tan(\beta/2) = \frac{x}{z\tan(\beta/2)} = \frac{x}{zR\tan(\alpha/2)} \tag{6.4}$$

$$\tilde{y} = \frac{y'}{d} = \frac{yn}{z}\bigg/d = \frac{yn}{z}\bigg/n\tan(\alpha/2) = \frac{y}{z\tan(\alpha/2)} \tag{6.5}$$

Here we used Equation 6.3 and the trigonometric facts that $c = n\tan(\beta/2)$ and $d = n\tan(\alpha/2)$.

6.4.4.4 *Transforming the z-coordinate*

Equations 6.4 and 6.5 give the formulas for computing the projected and normalized x- and y-coordinates. So as far as projection in the geometric sense is concerned, we are done. However, recall that Direct3D also wants the z-coordinates of points *inside the frustum* mapped to the normalized interval $[0, 1]$, and points *outside the frustum* mapped outside $[0, 1]$. In other words, we want to map the interval $[n, f]$ to $[0, 1]$.

As we will explain in the next section, whatever transformation result we get here, we will multiply by z. After this multiplication by z, we want the transformation to have the form $z\tilde{z} = zg(z) = uz + v$ so that we can write it in a matrix equation. Therefore, to transform $[n, f]$ to $[0, 1]$, we guess that a transformation of the form $\tilde{z} = g(z) = u + v/z$ does the job. This equation has two unknown variables, u and v, but we also have two conditions that characterize the transformation we want:

Condition 1: $g(n) = u + v/n = 0$ (the near plane gets mapped to zero)
Condition 2: $g(f) = u + v/f = 1$ (the far plane gets mapped to one)

Solving condition 1 for v yields: $v = -un$. Substituting this into condition 2 and solving for u gives:

$$u + (-un)/f = 1$$
$$uf - un = f$$
$$u = f/(f - n)$$

Then $v = -un = -fn/(f - n)$. Therefore,

$$\tilde{z} = g(z) = \frac{f}{f - n} - \frac{fn}{z(f - n)} \tag{6.6}$$

Graphing $g(z)$, as shown in Figure 6.18, we see that it does what we want: It maps only the points in $[n, f]$ to $[0, 1]$.

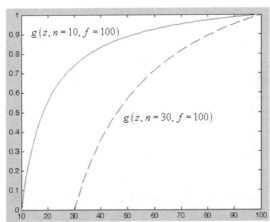

Figure 6.18: Note how $[n, f]$ gets mapped to $[0, 1]$. Also notice for $g(z, n = 10, f = 100)$ how an unfairly large portion of $[0, 1]$ is devoted to depth values in close proximity to the near plane, whereas depth values close to the far plane get mapped to a very small portion of $[0, 1]$ (i.e., the transformed depth values of objects close to the far plane only differ slightly from each other); this can lead to depth buffer precision problems (especially with 16-bit depth buffers, but not so much with 24- or 32-bit depth buffers) because the computer can no longer distinguish between slightly different transformed depth values due to the finite numerical representation. Observe that the problem is less drastic with $g(z, n = 30, f = 100)$, as we bring the near plane closer to the far plane.

6.4.4.5 *Writing the Projection Equations with a Matrix*

We now wish to write Equations 6.4, 6.5, and 6.6 as a matrix equation. However, this gets a bit tricky with the divide by z, which occurs in each
equation. So what we do is first multiply each equation by z to get rid of the
divisions by z so that we can write the equations with a matrix equation.
Then, after the matrix multiplication, in a post-step, we divide by z to invert
the multiplication by z we initially did. The following *perspective projection
matrix* contains Equations 6.4, 6.5, and 6.6 multiplied by z:

$$[x, y, z, 1] \begin{bmatrix} \dfrac{1}{R\tan(\alpha/2)} & 0 & 0 & 0 \\ 0 & \dfrac{1}{\tan(\alpha/2)} & 0 & 0 \\ 0 & 0 & \dfrac{f}{f-n} & 1 \\ 0 & 0 & \dfrac{-fn}{f-n} & 0 \end{bmatrix}$$

$$= \left[\frac{x}{R\tan(\alpha/2)}, \frac{y}{\tan(\alpha/2)}, \frac{zf}{f-n} - \frac{fn}{f-n}, z \right] = [\tilde{zx}, \tilde{zy}, \tilde{zz}, z]$$

Note also how we copy the z-coordinate of the input vector to the w-coordi-
nate of the output vector (this is done by setting entry [2][3] = 1 and entry
[3][3] = 0). We do this so that we have the original z-coordinate available
for the divide by z step (i.e., instead of storing the original z-coordinate in a
new temporary variable, we just store it in the w-coordinate). We can now
complete the projection with a post-step by dividing every coordinate in the
output vector of the above matrix multiplication by the homogeneous coordinate $w = z$:

$$\frac{1}{w}[w\tilde{x}, w\tilde{y}, w\tilde{z}, w] = \left[\frac{x}{zR\tan(\alpha/2)}, \frac{y}{z\tan(\alpha/2)}, \frac{f}{f-n} - \frac{fn}{z(f-n)}, 1 \right] \qquad (6.7)$$

This is commonly called the *perspective divide* or *homogeneous divide*; after
this divide, the coordinates are said to be *normalized device coordinates* or
just *normalized space*. Observe that the x-, y-, and z-coordinates of Equation
6.7 match Equations 6.4, 6.5, and 6.6, respectively.

Note: In the rendering pipeline, the perspective divide does not take place immediately after the projection matrix multiplication. After the projection matrix takes place, we say vertices are in *projection space* or *homogeneous clip space*. In this space, some operations like backface culling and clipping can be done in a simplified manner. These two operations remove geometry, as §6.4.5 and §6.4.6 will show. Thus it is advantageous to do these operations in homogeneous clip space before the perspective divide so that we have fewer vertices on which to perform the perspective divide.

6.4.4.6 *D3DXMatrixPerspectiveFovLH*

A perspective projection matrix can be built with the following D3DX function:

```
D3DXMATRIX *D3DXMatrixPerspectiveFovLH(
    D3DXMATRIX* pOut,  // returns projection matrix
    FLOAT fovY,        // vertical field of view angle in radians
    FLOAT Aspect,      // aspect ratio = width / height
    FLOAT zn,          // distance to near plane
    FLOAT zf           // distance to far plane
);
```

The following code snippet illustrates how to use `D3DXMatrixPerspective-FovLH`. Here, we specify a 45° vertical field of view, a near plane at $z = 1$, and a far plane at $z = 1000$ (these dimensions are in view space).

```
D3DXMATRIX proj;
D3DXMatrixPerspectiveFovLH(
    &proj, D3DX_PI * 0.25f,
    (float)width / (float)height, 1.0, 1000.0f);
```

6.4.5 Backface Culling

A polygon has two sides, and we label one side as the front side and the other as the back side. A polygon whose front side faces the camera is called a *front facing* polygon, and a polygon whose front side faces away from the camera is called a *back facing* polygon; see Figure 6.19a.

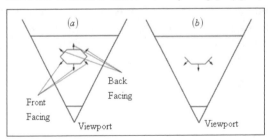

Figure 6.19: (a) A solid object with front facing and back facing triangles. (b) The scene after culling the back facing triangles.

For solid enclosed volumes (e.g., boxes, cylinders, tanks, characters, etc.) that are also opaque, the back sides of polygons are never seen because, as

Figure 6.19a shows, the front facing polygons obscure the back facing polygons that are behind them. Direct3D takes advantage of this by culling (discarding from further processing) the back facing polygons; this is called *backface culling*. Figure 6.19b shows the same object after the back faces have been culled. From the camera's viewpoint, the same scene will be drawn, because the back faces were obscured anyway and would never have been seen. Note that you can guesstimate that about half of the triangles in a scene are back facing, and thus, backface culling can quickly discard about half of the scene's dataset from further processing — an excellent speedup.

For backface culling to work correctly, the camera must never be allowed to enter the solid volume of space inside the object. Because, if it did enter, the viewer would not see the back side of the object since those faces are culled via backface culling — remember, backface culling relies upon the front faces obscuring the back faces, but if the camera is allowed inside a solid object, those front faces no longer obscure the back faces. A corollary to this is that objects must also be opaque, because if an object were to be semi-transparent, then we would be able to see the back sides, but the back sides are culled due to backface culling.

Of course, in order for this to work, Direct3D needs to know which polygons are front facing and which are back facing. By default, Direct3D treats triangles with vertices specified in a clockwise winding order (in view space; 2D triangles in screen space will have the same wind order as 3D triangles in view space) as front facing. Triangles with vertices specified in a counterclockwise winding order (in view space) are considered back facing.

Note: Notice that we said "in view space." This is because when a triangle is rotated 180°, its winding order is flipped. Thus, a triangle that had a clockwise winding order when it was defined in its local space might not have a clockwise winding order when it's transformed to view space due to possible rotations.

If for some reason we are not happy with the default culling behavior (e.g., we need to disable it because we want to render transparent objects), we can change it by changing the D3DRS_CULLMODE render state.

```
gd3dDevice->SetRenderState(D3DRS_CULLMODE, Value);
```

Where Value can be one of the following:

- D3DCULL_NONE: Disables backface culling entirely.
- D3DCULL_CW: Triangles with a clockwise wind are culled.
- D3DCULL_CCW: Triangles with a counterclockwise wind are culled. This is the default state.

6.4.6 **Clipping**

At this point, we need to cull the geometry that is outside the viewing volume; this process is called *clipping*. There are three possible locations of a triangle with regard to the frustum.

■ Completely inside: If the triangle is completely inside the frustum it is kept and will move on to the next stage.

■ Completely outside: If the triangle is completely outside the frustum it is culled.

■ Partially inside (partially outside): If the triangle is partially inside and partially outside the frustum, then the triangle is split into two parts. The part inside the frustum is kept, while the part outside is culled.

Reconsider Figure 6.1. Observe that the cube and pyramid do not make it into the final 2D image — they are outside the view frustum and thus the triangles that make them up are completely culled. On the other hand, only parts of the cone, torus, and sphere are outside the frustum. The triangles forming these objects that are completely inside the frustum are kept, the triangles completely outside the frustum are discarded, and the triangles that are partially inside and partially outside the frustum are split — the part inside the frustum is kept, while the part outside is culled.

Note that clipping is done in homogeneous clip space. Let $(x/w, y/w, z/w, 1)$ be a vertex inside the frustum after the homogeneous divide. Then the coordinates of this point are bounded as follows:

$$-1 \le x/w \le 1$$
$$-1 \le y/w \le 1 \qquad\qquad (6.8)$$
$$0 \le z/w \le 1$$

Multiplying each inequality by w gives the logically equivalent statements:

$$-w \le x \le w$$
$$-w \le y \le w \qquad\qquad (6.9)$$
$$0 \le z \le w$$

Thus, a vertex is inside the frustum if and only if the inequalities of Equation 6.9 are satisfied. Hence, Equation 6.9 gives us an equivalent clipping criterion in homogeneous clip space.

6.4.7 **Viewport Transform**

The viewport transform is responsible for transforming normalized device coordinates to a rectangle on the back buffer called the *viewport*. For games, the viewport is usually the entire back buffer rectangle; however, it can be a subset of the back buffer. This is actually useful if you need to render multiple views at once; for example, you may divide the screen into four quadrants (viewports) and render a separate view of the scene into each viewport. The viewport rectangle is described relative to the back buffer (image coordinates). Figure 6.20 shows an example of using multiple viewports to render to different sections of the back buffer.

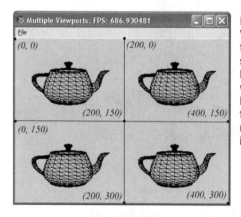

Figure 6.20: Viewports allow us to render to subsections of the back buffer; here we partition the back buffer into four quadrants and render separately into each.

In Direct3D a viewport is represented by the D3DVIEWPORT9 structure. It is defined as:

```
typedef struct _D3DVIEWPORT9 {
    DWORD   X;
    DWORD   Y;
    DWORD   Width;
    DWORD   Height;
    DWORD   MinZ;
    DWORD   MaxZ;
} D3DVIEWPORT9;
```

The first four data members define the viewport rectangle relative to the window in which it resides. The MinZ member specifies the minimum depth buffer value and MaxZ specifies the maximum depth buffer value. Direct3D uses a depth buffer range of 0 to 1, so MinZ and MaxZ should be set to those values respectively unless a special effect is desired.

Once we have filled out the D3DVIEWPORT9 structure, we set the viewport with Direct3D like so:

```
D3DVIEWPORT9 vp = { 0, 0, 800, 600, 0, 1 };
Device->SetViewport(&vp);
```

Note: By default, the viewport is the entire back buffer — so you don't need to set it unless you want to change it.

To illustrate, let's outline the general process of rendering into four viewports, as shown in Figure 6.20. Let w and h be the back buffer width and height, respectively. Then, the four viewports subdividing the back buffer into four quadrants are given by:

```
D3DVIEWPORT9 q1 = {w/2, 0, w/2, h/2, 0.0f, 1.0f};
D3DVIEWPORT9 q2 = {0, 0, w/2, h/2, 0.0f, 1.0f};
D3DVIEWPORT9 q3 = {0, h/2, w/2, h/2, 0.0f, 1.0f};
D3DVIEWPORT9 q4 = {w/2, h/2, w/2, h/2, 0.0f, 1.0f};
D3DVIEWPORT9 vps[4] = {q1, q2, q3, q4};
```

Then, we just loop through each viewport and render what we want into it:

```
gd3dDevice->BeginScene();
for(int i = 0; i < 4; ++i)
{
        // The Clear function clears the currently set viewport.
        gd3dDevice->SetViewport(&vps[i]);
        gd3dDevice->Clear(0L, 0, D3DCLEAR_TARGET |
                D3DCLEAR_ZBUFFER, 0xffcccccc, 1.0f, 0L);
        mTeapot->DrawSubset(0);

}
gd3dDevice->EndScene();
```

Direct3D handles the viewport transformation for us automatically, but for reference, the viewport transformation is described with the following matrix. The variables are the same as those described for the D3DVIEWPORT9 structure.

$$
\begin{bmatrix}
\dfrac{Width}{2} & 0 & 0 & 0 \\
0 & -\dfrac{Height}{2} & 0 & 0 \\
0 & 0 & MaxZ-MinZ & 0 \\
X+\dfrac{Width}{2} & Y+\dfrac{Height}{2} & MinZ & 1
\end{bmatrix}
$$

6.4.8 Rasterization

After the vertices are transformed to the back buffer, we have a list of 2D triangles in image space to be processed one by one. The rasterization stage is responsible for computing the colors of the individual pixels that make up the interiors and boundaries of these triangles. Pixel operations like texturing, pixel shaders, depth buffering, and alpha blending occur in the rasterization stage.

The previous rendering pipeline stages have worked exclusively with the spatial location of the vertices. But what about the other components we can couple with a vertex, such as color, texture coordinates, and the depth value? Well, these components are still coupled to our 2D vertices, but now the task is to compute pixel values. So how do we transfer these vertex attributes to the pixels? We do it with *interpolation*. Interpolation is best explained with a picture, so take a look at Figure 6.21.

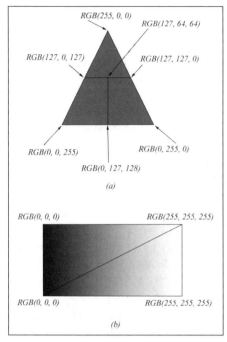

Figure 6.21: (a) A 2D triangle in image space. The triangle has three vertices; one vertex is coupled with a pure red color, a second vertex is coupled with a pure green color, and a third vertex is coupled with a pure blue color. These colors are then interpolated across the face of the triangle line-by-line, thereby filling in the interior and boundary pixel colors. (b) A 2D rectangle, where black and white colors are interpolated.

Figure 6.21 shows color interpolation; the color values coupled to each vertex are interpolated across the face of the triangle in order to color the other pixels that are part of the triangle face. However, other vertex components can be interpolated just as well. Recall that we have a depth component associated with each vertex; these depth values are interpolated across the face of the triangle as well — thus each *pixel* now has its own depth value (and the depth buffering algorithm can be used). Texture coordinates are also interpolated across the 2D triangle. We can even interpolate vertex normals, and do lighting calculations at the pixel level instead of the vertex level for better accuracy (vertex normals are used in lighting calculations). To summarize, interpolation is a way of transferring information at a vertex level to the pixel level.

6.5 **Summary**

- We can simulate 3D scenes on 2D planes by employing several techniques based on the way we see things in real life. We observe parallel lines converge to vanishing points, the size of objects diminish with depth, objects obscure the objects behind them, lighting and shading depict the solid form and volume of 3D objects, and shadows imply the location of light sources and indicate the position of objects relative to other objects in the scene.

■ The point where two edges on a polygon meet is a *vertex*. A vertex in Direct3D includes a 3D spatial location, but we can also couple other data components to the vertex, such as color, normals, and texture coordinates. In Direct3D we may define our own custom vertex structure. In order for Direct3D to know what to do with our vertex data, we must define a vertex declaration, which provides Direct3D with a description of our vertex structure. A vertex declaration is described by an array of `D3DVERTEXELEMENT9` elements.

■ We approximate objects with a triangle mesh. We can define each triangle by specifying its three vertices. In many meshes, vertices are shared among triangles; indexed lists can be used to avoid vertex duplication.

■ The virtual camera is modeled as a frustum. The volume of space inside the frustum is what the camera "sees."

■ Given a geometric description of a 3D scene and a positioned and aimed virtual camera in that scene, the *rendering pipeline* refers to the entire sequence of steps necessary to generate a 2D image that can be displayed on a monitor screen based on what the virtual camera sees.

■ The vertices of each 3D object are defined relative to the object's local coordinate system. Next, the associated world transform of each object changes the object's vertex coordinates so that they are relative to the world coordinate system. After this, all the vertices in the scene are relative to the same coordinate system and should be positioned, oriented, and scaled correctly in relation to each other. We can think of the camera as an object in the world as well, and we can choose to make the camera our frame of reference instead of the world coordinate system. The view transformation changes all the geometry relative to the world coordinate system so that it is relative to the camera coordinate system (so-called view space). Subsequently, the projection matrix modifies each vertex. After the projection matrix modification, back facing triangles are culled, and geometry outside the frustum is discarded or clipped. Next, the homogeneous divide occurs, which finishes the projection process and transforms vertices to normalized device coordinates. At this point, the normalized device coordinates are mapped to a portion of the back buffer (or the entire back buffer) as defined by the viewport transformation. Finally, rasterization takes place.

■ The rasterization stage is responsible for computing the colors of the individual pixels that make up the interiors and boundaries of 2D triangles in image coordinates. Pixel operations like texturing, pixel shaders, depth buffering, and alpha blending occur in the rasterization stage. Data coupled with the vertices of these 2D triangles are interpolated across the face of the triangle. Hence, data at the vertex level is fed to the pixel level, where it can be used in determining the final color of a pixel.

6.6 Exercises

1. Write down the vertex declaration description (i.e., array of D3DVERTEXELEMENT9 elements) that describes the following vertex structure:

```
struct Vertex
{
    D3DXVECTOR3 position;
    D3DXVECTOR3 normal;
    D3DXVECTOR2 texCoord0;
    D3DXVECTOR2 texCoord1;
    D3DCOLOR    color;
};
```

2. Construct the vertex and index list for the following tetrahedron:

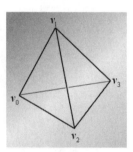

Figure 6.22

3. Construct the vertex and index list for the following box:

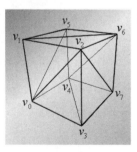

Figure 6.23

4. Relative to the world coordinate system, suppose that the camera is positioned at $(-20, 35, -50)$ and aimed at the point $(10, 0, 30)$. Compute the view matrix, assuming $(0, 1, 0)$ is "up."

5. Let the aspect ratio be 640/480, the vertical field of view angle be $\alpha = 45°$, the near plane be $z = 1$, and the far plane be $z = 100$. Compute the perspective projection matrix and transform the points (50, 60, 30), (–30, 20, 120), (0, 0, 0), and (–25, –10, 70) by it. Use Equation 6.9 to determine which points are inside the frustum. Now perform the perspective divide on each point and use Equation 6.8 to determine which points are inside the frustum.

6. Define the viewport by:

   ```
   D3DVIEWPORT9 vp = {200, 300, 800, 600, 0.0f, 1.0f};
   ```

   Now, apply the viewport transform to each of the *visible* projected vertices from exercise 5.

Chapter 7

Drawing in Direct3D — Part I

In the preceding chapter, we learned the theory behind creating and rendering a 3D scene. In this chapter, we find out how to create and render a scene in Direct3D. Note that the Direct3D interfaces and methods covered in this chapter are of some importance, for they are used throughout the rest of this book.

Objectives:

- To find out how vertex and index data is stored in Direct3D so that the graphics hardware can draw it.
- To discover how to change the way geometry is rendered using render states.
- To draw your first 3D objects.

7.1 Vertex/Index Buffers

Vertex and index buffers are similar interfaces and share similar methods; therefore we cover them together. Loosely, a *vertex buffer* is simply a chunk of contiguous memory that contains vertex data. Similarly, an *index buffer* is a chunk of contiguous memory that contains index data. Simply put then, vertex and index buffers are the Direct3D resources for storing geometry data, which can be placed in video memory. In code, a vertex buffer is represented by the IDirect3DVertexBuffer9 interface and an index buffer is represented by the IDirect3DIndexBuffer9 interface.

7.1.1 **Creating a Vertex and Index Buffer**

We can create a vertex and index buffer with the following two methods.

```
HRESULT IDirect3DDevice9::CreateVertexBuffer(
    UINT Length,
    DWORD Usage,
    DWORD FVF,
    D3DPOOL Pool
    IDirect3DVertexBuffer9** ppVertexBuffer,
    HANDLE* pSharedHandle);

HRESULT IDirect3DDevice9::CreateIndexBuffer(
    UINT Length,
    DWORD Usage,
    D3DFORMAT Format,
    D3DPOOL Pool,
    IDirect3DIndexBuffer9** ppIndexBuffer,
    HANDLE* pSharedHandle);
```

The majority of the parameters are identical for both methods, so we will cover the parameters of both methods together.

■ Length: The number of bytes to allocate for the buffer. If we wanted a vertex buffer to have enough memory to store eight vertices, we would set this parameter to 8 * sizeof(Vertex), where Vertex is our vertex structure.

■ Usage: Specifies some additional properties about how the buffer will be used. This value can be zero, indicating no additional properties, or a combination of one or more of the following flags:

D3DUSAGE_DYNAMIC: Setting this flag makes the buffer dynamic; see the information on static and dynamic buffers following this list.

D3DUSAGE_POINTS: This flag specifies that the buffer will hold point primitives.

D3DUSAGE_SOFTWAREPROCESSING: Vertex processing is done in software.

D3DUSAGE_WRITEONLY: Specifies that the application will only write to the buffer. This allows the driver to place the buffer in the best memory location for write operations. Note that reading from a buffer created with this flag will result in an error.

■ FVF: Not needed — specify zero (the exception to this is if you are going to use the IDirect3DDevice9::ProcessVertices method, but we do not use this method in this book).

■ Pool: The memory pool in which the buffer will be placed (i.e., member of D3DPOOL enumerated type; see §4.2.7). In general, specify D3DPOOL_DEFAULT for dynamic buffers and D3DPOOL_MANAGED for static buffers.

■ ppVertexBuffer: Pointer to receive the created vertex buffer.

■ pSharedHandle: Not used; set to zero.

- **Format**: Specifies the size of the indices; use `D3DFMT_INDEX16` for 16-bit indices or `D3DFMT_INDEX32` for 32-bit indices. Note that not all devices support 32-bit indices — check the device capabilities (`D3DCAPS9::MaxVertexIndex`) — and realize that 32-bit indices may be more expensive on some hardware.

- **ppIndexBuffer**: Pointer to receive the created index buffer.

A buffer created without the `D3DUSAGE_DYNAMIC` flag is called a *static buffer*. Static buffers are generally placed in video memory where their contents can be processed most efficiently. However, once in video memory we cannot efficiently access the data; that is to say, accessing video memory is very slow. For this reason we use static buffers to hold static data (data that will not need to be changed (accessed) very frequently). Terrains and city buildings are examples of good candidates for static buffers because the terrain and building geometry usually does not change during the course of the application. Static buffers should be filled once with geometry at application initialization time and never at run time.

A buffer created with the `D3DUSAGE_DYNAMIC` flag is called a *dynamic buffer*. Dynamic buffers are generally placed in AGP memory where their memory can be transferred over to the graphics card quickly. Dynamic buffers are not processed as quickly as static buffers because the data must be transferred to video memory before rendering, but the benefit of dynamic buffers is that they can be updated reasonably fast (fast CPU writes). Therefore, if you need to update the contents of a buffer frequently, it should be made dynamic. Particle systems are good candidates for dynamic buffers because they are animated, and thus their geometry is usually updated every frame.

Note: Reading video memory and, to a lesser extent, AGP memory from your application is very slow. Therefore, if you need to read your geometry at run time (e.g., for collision detection), it is best to keep a local system memory copy, and then read from that.

For NVIDIA cards, the NVIDIA FAQ (http://developer.nvidia.com/object/General_FAQ.html) states that static vertex buffers are always placed in video memory. Furthermore, the `D3DUSAGE_WRITEONLY` flag only applies to dynamic vertex buffers. Dynamic vertex buffers with the `D3DUSAGE_WRITEONLY` flag are placed in video memory, and dynamic vertex buffers without the `D3DUSAGE_WRITEONLY` flag are placed in AGP memory.

The following example creates a static vertex buffer that has enough memory to hold eight vertices of type `Vertex`.

```
IDirect3DVertexBuffer9* vb;
gd3dDevice->CreateVertexBuffer( 8 * sizeof( Vertex ), 0, 0,
    D3DPOOL_MANAGED, &vb, 0);
```

This next code example shows how to create a dynamic index buffer that has enough memory to hold 36 16-bit indices.

```
IDirect3DIndexBuffer9* ib;
gd3dDevice->CreateIndexBuffer(36 * sizeof( WORD ),
    D3DUSAGE_DYNAMIC | D3DUSAGE_WRITEONLY, D3DFMT_INDEX16,
    D3DPOOL_DEFAULT, &ib, 0);
```

7.1.2 Accessing a Buffer's Memory

To access the memory of a vertex/index buffer, we need to get a pointer to its internal memory contents. We obtain a pointer to its contents by using the Lock method. It is important to unlock the buffer when we are done accessing it. Once we have a pointer to the memory we can read and write information to it.

Note If the vertex/index buffer was created with the usage flag D3DUSAGE_WRITEONLY, then you must not read from the buffer. Doing so will result in a failed read.

```
HRESULT IDirect3DVertexBuffer9::Lock(
    UINT OffsetToLock,
    UINT SizeToLock,
    BYTE** ppbData,
    DWORD Flags);

HRESULT IDirect3DIndexBuffer9::Lock(
    UINT OffsetToLock,
    UINT SizeToLock,
    BYTE** ppbData,
    DWORD Flags);
```

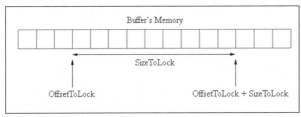

Figure 7.1: The OffsetToLock and SizeToLock parameters specify a subset of the buffer to lock.

The parameters for both methods are exactly the same.

■ OffsetToLock: Offset, in bytes, from the start of the buffer to the location to begin the lock (see Figure 7.1).

■ SizeToLock: Number of bytes to lock.

■ ppbData: Returns a pointer to the start of the locked memory.

- Flags: Flags describing how the lock is done. Some commonly specified flags are:

  0 (zero): Normal lock — no special instructions.

  D3DLOCK_DISCARD: This flag is used only for dynamic buffers. It instructs the hardware to discard the buffer and return a pointer to a newly allocated buffer. This prevents the hardware from stalling by allowing the hardware to continue rendering from the discarded buffer while we access the newly allocated buffer.

  D3DLOCK_NOOVERWRITE: This flag is used only for dynamic buffers. It tells the hardware that we are only going to append data to a buffer. Consequently, it also prevents the hardware from stalling by allowing the hardware to continue rendering previously written geometry at the same time we append new geometry.

  D3DLOCK_READONLY: This flag states that you are locking the buffer only to read data and that you won't be writing to it. This allows for some internal optimizations. Note that you cannot read from a buffer if you specified the D3DUSAGE_WRITEONLY creation flag!

The flags D3DLOCK_DISCARD and D3DLOCK_NOOVERWRITE address the fact that a portion of the buffer's memory could be in use (being rendered) at the time of a lock call. If these flags are not specified, then the graphics card must finish rendering the data before we can access the memory, thereby creating a delay. By specifying these flags, we are able to write to memory that is not currently being used by the hardware (either by accessing a newly allocated buffer [D3DLOCK_DISCARD] or by accessing a section of the buffer we have not written to before [D3DLOCK_NOOVERWRITE]), thereby preventing a stall.

Note: Specifying zero for both OffsetToLock and SizeToLock is a shortcut to lock the entire buffer.

The following example shows how the Lock method is commonly used. Note how we call the Unlock method when we are done.

```
Vertex* vertices;
vb->Lock(0, 0, (void**)&vertices, 0);    // lock the entire buffer

vertices[0] = Vertex(-1.0f, 0.0f, 2.0f); // write vertices to
vertices[1] = Vertex( 0.0f, 1.0f, 2.0f); // the buffer
vertices[2] = Vertex( 1.0f, 0.0f, 2.0f);

vb->Unlock(); // unlock when you're done accessing the buffer
```

7.1.3 **Vertex and Index Buffer Info**

Sometimes we need to get information about a vertex/index buffer. The following example demonstrates the methods used to obtain such info:

```
D3DVERTEXBUFFER_DESC vbDesc;
vertexBuffer->GetDesc(&vbDesc); // get vb info

D3DINDEXBUFFER_DESC ibDesc;
indexBuffer->GetDesc(&ibDesc); // get ib info
```

The D3DVERTEXBUFFER_DESC and D3DINDEXBUFFER_DESC structures are defined as follows:

```
typedef struct _D3DVERTEXBUFFER_DESC {
    D3DFORMAT Format;
    D3DRESOURCETYPE Type;
    DWORD Usage;
    D3DPOOL Pool;
    UINT Size;
    DWORD FVF;
} D3DVERTEXBUFFER_DESC;

typedef struct _D3DINDEXBUFFER_DESC {
    D3DFORMAT Format;
    D3DRESOURCETYPE Type;
    DWORD Usage;
    D3DPOOL Pool;
    UINT Size;
} D3DINDEXBUFFER_DESC;
```

7.2 **Drawing Methods**

The drawing methods instruct the hardware to draw geometry. Essentially, the drawing methods dump geometry into the rendering pipeline for processing.

7.2.1 **DrawPrimitive**

This method is used to draw primitives that do not use index info.

```
HRESULT IDirect3DDevice9::DrawPrimitive(
    D3DPRIMITIVETYPE PrimitiveType,
    UINT StartVertex,
    UINT PrimitiveCount);
```

■ PrimitiveType: The type of primitive we are drawing. For instance, Direct3D supports point, line, and triangle primitives. In this book, we are primarily concerned with drawing solid objects composed of lists of triangles; thus, we always specify D3DPT_TRIANGLELIST for this parameter (unless otherwise noted). The exercises ask you to explore other primitive types.

- StartVertex: Index to an element in the vertex buffer that marks the starting point from which to begin reading vertices. This parameter gives us the flexibility to only draw certain portions of a vertex buffer.

- PrimitiveCount: The number of primitives to draw.

Here is an example call:

```
// Draw 4 triangles.
gd3dDevice->DrawPrimitive( D3DPT_TRIANGLELIST, 0, 4);
```

7.2.2 DrawIndexedPrimitive

This method is used to draw primitives using index info.

```
HRESULT IDirect3DDevice9::DrawIndexedPrimitive(
    D3DPRIMITIVETYPE Type,
    INT BaseVertexIndex,
    UINT MinIndex,
    UINT NumVertices,
    UINT StartIndex,
    UINT PrimitiveCount);
```

- Type: The type of primitive we are drawing. For instance, Direct3D supports point, line, and triangle primitives. In this book, we are primarily concerned with drawing solid objects composed of lists of triangles; thus, we always specify D3DPT_TRIANGLELIST for this parameter (unless otherwise noted). The exercises ask you to explore other primitive types.

- BaseVertexIndex: A base number to be added to the indices used in this call; see the following note.

- MinIndex: The minimum index value that will be referenced in this call.

- NumVertices: The number of vertices that will be referenced in this call.

- StartIndex: Index to an element in the index buffer that marks the starting point from which to begin reading indices.

- PrimitiveCount: The number of primitives to draw.

Here is an example call:

```
// Draw geometry consisting of 12 triangles and 8 vertices.
gd3dDevice->DrawIndexedPrimitive(D3DPT_TRIANGLELIST, 0, 0, 8, 0, 12);
```

Note: The BaseVertexIndex parameter deserves some explanation. Refer to Figure 7.2 during this explanation.

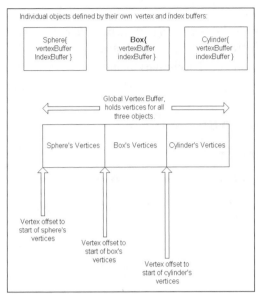

Figure 7.2: Separately defined vertex buffers merged into one global vertex buffer.

The local index buffers reference vertices relative to their corresponding local vertex buffer. However, suppose that we want to combine the vertices of the sphere, box, and cylinder into one global vertex buffer. For each object, we would have to recompute the indices to index correctly into the global vertex buffer; observe that the new indices are computed by adding the position of the object's first vertex, relative to the global vertex buffer, to each index. Thus, given the first vertex position of the object relative to the global vertex buffer (i.e., the base vertex index), Direct3D can recompute the indices for us internally.

Drawing methods must always be called inside an IDirect3DDevice9:: BeginScene and IDirect3DDevice9::EndScene pair. For example, we would write:

```
gd3dDevice->BeginScene();
    gd3dDevice->DrawPrimitive(...);
gd3dDevice->EndScene();
```

7.3 **Drawing Preparations**

Before we can invoke a drawing method, we need to do some preparation work. Specifically, we need to tell Direct3D where to get the vertex and index data that contains the geometry we want to draw, and the format of the vertices we want to draw.

7.3.1 **Vertex Streams**

The Direct3D drawing methods get vertex data from vertex streams (a *vertex stream* is essentially an array of vertex component data). For instance, it is possible to assemble vertices from several vertex streams, where each stream consists of a component of the vertex (e.g., one stream contains position info, another contains color info, and another stream contains texture coordinate info, etc.). That said, in this book we only use one vertex stream — namely, stream 0 — where our vertices are already fully assembled (i.e., we do not split our vertex component data across multiple streams). Now, recall that we store our vertices in vertex buffers; therefore, in order to draw the vertices in a vertex buffer, we need to hook the vertex buffer up to a vertex stream. This is done with the following method:

```
HRESULT IDirect3DDevice9::SetStreamSource(
    UINT StreamNumber,
    IDirect3DVertexBuffer9* pStreamData,
    UINT OffsetInBytes,
    UINT Stride);
```

■ `StreamNumber`: Identifies the stream source to which we are hooking the vertex buffer. In this book we do not use multiple streams, and thus we always use stream 0.

■ `pStreamData`: A pointer to the vertex buffer we want to hook up to the stream.

■ `OffsetInBytes`: An offset from the start of the stream, measured in bytes, that specifies the start of the vertex data to be fed into the rendering pipeline. To set this parameter to something other than zero, see if your device supports it by checking the `D3DDEVCAPS2_STREAMOFFSET` flag in the `D3DCAPS9` structure.

■ `Stride`: Size, in bytes, of each element in the vertex buffer we are attaching to the stream.

For example, suppose `vb` is a pointer to a vertex buffer that has been filled with vertices of type `Vertex`. Then we set the stream source like so:

```
HR(gd3dDevice->SetStreamSource(0, vb, 0, sizeof(Vertex)));
```

7.3.2 **Setting Indices**

In addition to hooking up a vertex buffer to a stream, if we are using an index buffer, then we need to tell Direct3D which index buffer to use for subsequent drawing calls. This is done with the `IDirect3DDevice9::SetIndices` method:

```
// indexBuffer is a pointer to an IDirect3DIndexBuffer9 type.
HR(gd3dDevice->SetIndices(indexBuffer));
```

7.3.3 **Setting the Vertex Declaration**

Recall from §6.2.1 that we need to create a vertex declaration to describe the format of the vertex we are using. After the vertex declaration is created, we need to register it with Direct3D so that it knows how to interpret the vertex data. (In Chapter 8, we will actually learn that the vertex declaration specifies how to map the vertex data members to the vertex shader input registers.) Here is an example of setting the vertex declaration:

```
// decl is a pointer to an IDirect3DVertexDeclaration9 type
gd3dDevice->SetVertexDeclaration(decl);
```

Note: The vertex buffer currently attached to a stream, the currently set index buffer, and the currently specified vertex declaration stay in effect until changed or the device is reset. Probably, however, distinct objects in the scene will have different vertex buffers, index buffers, and vertex declarations. Thus the rendering code is structured as the following pseudocode illustrates:

```
// Object 1 uses its own vertex buffer, index buffer, and
// vertex declaration
gd3dDevice->SetStreamSource( 0, vb1, 0, sizeof( Vertex1 ) );
gd3dDevice->SetIndices(indexBuffer1);
gd3dDevice->SetVertexDeclaration(decl1);

// DRAW OBJECT 1 HERE
gd3dDevice->DrawPrimitive(...);

// Object 2 uses its own vertex buffer, index buffer, and
// vertex declaration
gd3dDevice->SetStreamSource( 0, vb2, 0, sizeof( Vertex2 ) );
gd3dDevice->SetIndices(indexBuffer2);
gd3dDevice->SetVertexDeclaration(decl2);

// DRAW OBJECT 2 HERE
gd3dDevice->DrawPrimitive(...);

// Object 3 uses its own vertex buffer, index buffer, and
// vertex declaration
gd3dDevice->SetStreamSource( 0, vb3, 0, sizeof( Vertex3 ) );
gd3dDevice->SetIndices(indexBuffer3);
gd3dDevice->SetVertexDeclaration(decl3);

// DRAW OBJECT 3 HERE
gd3dDevice->DrawPrimitive(...);
```

7.4 **Cube Demo**

The demo we make in this chapter renders a 3D wireframe cube; we can rotate and zoom the camera with the mouse and adjust the camera height with the "W" and "S" keys. Figure 7.3 shows a screenshot of the demo.

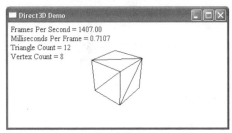

Figure 7.3: A screenshot of the Cube demo.

Before we get into the implementation details of the demo, let's recapitulate, at a high level, what needs to be done to draw something in Direct3D.

- **Define the vertex structure:** The vertex structure defines the data components of a vertex. A corresponding vertex declaration needs to be created that provides Direct3D with a description of the vertex structure so that Direct3D knows what to do with each component. Recall from Chapter 6 that a vertex declaration is created from a D3DVERTEXELEMENT9 array that describes each component in the vertex structure.

- **Create the geometry:** To draw anything, we must define the 3D geometry of the objects we wish to draw. Thus, we need to define our vertex list (and possibly index list if we want to use indices). In order for the hardware to access the vertex list and index list, we need to store these lists in vertex and index buffers, respectively.

- **Build world, view, and projection matrices:** Recall from Chapter 6 that in the rendering pipeline, our geometry undergoes several coordinate transformations as defined by the world, view, and projection transformations. Thus we need to define the world, view, and projection matrices to facilitate these change-of-coordinates transformations.

- **Prep work:** Before we can invoke a drawing method, we need to tell Direct3D where to get the vertex and index data that contains the geometry we want to draw, we need to tell Direct3D the format of the vertices we want to draw, and we need to set up the effect that tells Direct3D how to render the geometry we are drawing.

- **Set render states:** Direct3D encapsulates a variety of rendering states that affect how geometry is rendered. Render states have default values, so you only need to change this if your application requires something other than the default. A render state stays in effect until you change the particular state again (or the device is lost and reset).

To set a render state we use the following method:

```
HRESULT IDirect3DDevice9::SetRenderState(
    D3DRENDERSTATETYPE State, // the state to change
    DWORD Value               // value of the new state
);
```

For example, in this chapter's samples we are going to render our objects in wireframe mode. Therefore we set the following render state:

```
gd3dDevice->SetRenderState(D3DRS_FILLMODE, D3DFILL_WIREFRAME);
```

To switch back to solid fill mode, we would write:

```
gd3dDevice->SetRenderState(D3DRS_FILLMODE, D3DFILL_SOLID);
```

Note: Look up D3DRENDERSTATETYPE in the DirectX SDK to see all the possible render states.

■ **Draw the geometry:** Finally, we can draw the geometry with the DrawPrimitive* functions.

7.4.1 Vertex Structure

Because we are rendering in wireframe mode, the vertex structure we employ is very simple — all we need is position data:

```
struct VertexPos
{
    VertexPos():pos(0.0f, 0.0f, 0.0f){}
    VertexPos(float x, float y, float z):pos(x,y,z){}
    VertexPos(const D3DXVECTOR3& v):pos(v){}

    D3DXVECTOR3 pos;
    static IDirect3DVertexDeclaration9* Decl;
};
```

The structure has some convenience constructors, and note also that we include a static vertex declaration. We only need one vertex declaration per structure, so it is nice to couple it to the vertex structure as a static data member.

The vertex declaration is described and created with the following code:

```
void InitAllVertexDeclarations()
{
    D3DVERTEXELEMENT9 VertexPosElements[] =
    {
        {0, 0, D3DDECLTYPE_FLOAT3, D3DDECLMETHOD_DEFAULT,
                                   D3DDECLUSAGE_POSITION, 0},
```

```
            D3DDECL_END()
    };
    HR(gd3dDevice->CreateVertexDeclaration(VertexPosElements,
                                           &VertexPos::Decl));
}
```

Refer back to §6.2.1 if you require a refresher on the details of vertex declarations.

Recall that as we progress through this book, we add all of our vertex structure definitions to the source code file *Vertex.h*. The global function InitAllVertexDeclarations provides a global function from which we create all of our vertex declarations in one localized place. As we add new vertex structures to *Vertex.h*, we also update this function to create its corresponding vertex declaration.

Similarly, we have a global function that destroys all vertex declarations in one localized place:

```
void DestroyAllVertexDeclarations()
{
    ReleaseCOM(VertexPos::Decl);
}
```

Again, as we add new vertex structures, we also update this function to destroy the corresponding vertex declaration.

InitAllVertexDeclarations should be called in the derived application class's constructor, after the device has been initialized, and DestroyAllVertexDeclarations should be called in the derived application class's destructor. Both of these functions are prototyped and implemented in *Vertex.h* and *Vertex.cpp*, respectively.

7.4.2 CubeDemo Class Data Members

In this section, we outline the data members of our CubeDemo class.

- mVB: Pointer to an IDirect3DVertexBuffer9 interface and is used to store the cube vertices.

- mIB: Pointer to an IDirect3DIndexBuffer9 interface and is used to store the index information defining the triangles of the cube.

- mCameraRotationY: A float that represents the angle of rotation of the camera along the *y*-axis.

- mCameraRadius: A float that represents the camera's distance from the origin (the camera will orbit the origin in a circular fashion).

- mCameraHeight: A float that represents the elevation of the camera from the ground plane (i.e., *xz*-plane).

- mView: A D3DXMATRIX that stores the view matrix.

- mProj: A D3DXMATRIX that stores the projection matrix.

7.4.3 **Construction**

The constructor is implemented below:

```
CubeDemo::CubeDemo(HINSTANCE hInstance)
: D3DApp(hInstance)
{
    mGfxStats = new GfxStats();

    // 10 units from origin.
    mCameraRadius    = 10.0f;
    // Somewhere in the 3rd quadrant of xz-plane.
    mCameraRotationY = 1.2 * D3DX_PI;
    // 5 units off the ground.
    mCameraHeight    = 5.0f;

    buildVertexBuffer();
    buildIndexBuffer();

    onResetDevice();

    InitAllVertexDeclarations();
}
```

The code is rather straightforward since all the hard work is done in helper functions. Let's go through the helper functions one by one.

The buildVertexBuffer method creates a vertex buffer that can store eight VertexPos elements; the reason for eight simply follows from a cube having eight vertices. We are only going to write the vertex data to the buffer, and never need to read from the vertex buffer; therefore, we specify the D3DUSAGE_WRITEONLY flag. Our buffer is not dynamic, so we put it in the D3DPOOL_MANAGED memory pool (It's not dynamic because once we specify the cube vertices we never need to change them again, unless we wanted to later deform the cube by altering the vertices, which we don't here.) In the lock call, we specify 0 for the first two parameters, thereby locking the entire vertex buffer. Figure 7.4 illustrates how the vertices are defined.

```
void CubeDemo::buildVertexBuffer()
{
    // Obtain a pointer to a new vertex buffer.
    HR(gd3dDevice->CreateVertexBuffer(8 * sizeof(VertexPos),
        D3DUSAGE_WRITEONLY, 0, D3DPOOL_MANAGED, &mVB, 0));

    // Now lock it to obtain a pointer to its internal data,
    // and write the cube's vertex data.

    VertexPos* v = 0;
    HR(mVB->Lock(0, 0, (void**)&v, 0));

    v[0] = VertexPos(-1.0f, -1.0f, -1.0f);
    v[1] = VertexPos(-1.0f,  1.0f, -1.0f);
    v[2] = VertexPos( 1.0f,  1.0f, -1.0f);
```

```
v[3] = VertexPos( 1.0f, -1.0f, -1.0f);
v[4] = VertexPos(-1.0f, -1.0f,  1.0f);
v[5] = VertexPos(-1.0f,  1.0f,  1.0f);
v[6] = VertexPos( 1.0f,  1.0f,  1.0f);
v[7] = VertexPos( 1.0f, -1.0f,  1.0f);


HR(mVB->Unlock());
}
```

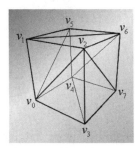

Figure 7.4: Vertices of a cube.

Similarly, buildIndexBuffer creates an index buffer to store 36 16-bit indices (three indices per triangle; a cube has six faces, with two triangles per face; therefore, 3 * 6 * 2 = 36 indices). Figuring out how to compute the indices takes practice — it is simple in 2D, but more challenging in 3D until you've had a lot of practice to build your 3D intuition. The only advice we can give is to study Figure 7.4 methodically until you can see how the indices given below define the triangles of the cube.

```
void CubeDemo::buildIndexBuffer()
{
    // Obtain a pointer to a new index buffer.
    HR(gd3dDevice->CreateIndexBuffer(36 * sizeof(WORD),
        D3DUSAGE_WRITEONLY, D3DFMT_INDEX16, D3DPOOL_MANAGED, &mIB, 0));

    // Now lock it to obtain a pointer to its internal data,
    // and write the cube's index data.

    WORD* k = 0;

    HR(mIB->Lock(0, 0, (void**)&k, 0));

    // Front face.
    k[0] = 0; k[1] = 1; k[2] = 2;
    k[3] = 0; k[4] = 2; k[5] = 3;

    // Back face.
    k[6] = 4; k[7]  = 6; k[8]  = 5;
    k[9] = 4; k[10] = 7; k[11] = 6;

    // Left face.
    k[12] = 4; k[13] = 5; k[14] = 1;
    k[15] = 4; k[16] = 1; k[17] = 0;
```

```
// Right face.
k[18] = 3; k[19] = 2; k[20] = 6;
k[21] = 3; k[22] = 6; k[23] = 7;

// Top face.
k[24] = 1; k[25] = 5; k[26] = 6;
k[27] = 1; k[28] = 6; k[29] = 2;

// Bottom face.
k[30] = 4; k[31] = 0; k[32] = 3;
k[33] = 4; k[34] = 3; k[35] = 7;

    HR(mIB->Unlock());
}
```

7.4.4 Destruction

The destructor is straightforward; delete any dynamic memory and release COM interfaces.

```
CubeDemo::~CubeDemo()
{
    delete mGfxStats;
    ReleaseCOM(mVB);
    ReleaseCOM(mIB);

    DestroyAllVertexDeclarations();
}
```

7.4.5 onLostDevice/onResetDevice

Here we execute any code that needs to be called before the device is reset and after the device is reset. Only the graphics stats object needs to do work here; the vertex buffer and index buffer do not need to be released and restored since they were created in the managed memory pool.

```
void CubeDemo::onLostDevice()
{
    mGfxStats->onLostDevice();
}

void CubeDemo::onResetDevice()
{
    mGfxStats->onResetDevice();

    buildProjMtx();
}
```

One thing to note is that the aspect ratio depends on the back buffer dimensions, which can possibly change after a reset (if the user resized the window, for instance). Therefore, we need to rebuild the projection matrix since the projection matrix depends on the aspect ratio. The `buildProjMtx` method is implemented as follows:

```
void CubeDemo::buildProjMtx()
{
    float w = (float)md3dPP.BackBufferWidth;
    float h = (float)md3dPP.BackBufferHeight;
    D3DXMatrixPerspectiveFovLH(&mProj, D3DX_PI * 0.25f, w/h,
                               1.0f, 5000.0f);
}
```

7.4.6 updateScene

The `updateScene` method updates the graphics statistics, but primarily it handles user input, which is used to animate the camera (i.e., by changing the camera's position/orientation by a small amount each frame, animation is observed). Pressing the "W" or "S" keys alters the elevation of the camera, moving the mouse left or right (*x*-axis) rotates the camera about the origin of the world (orbits), and moving the mouse forward or back (*y*-axis) alters the camera's radius from the origin, thereby zooming the camera in or out.

```
void CubeDemo::updateScene(float dt)
{
    // One cube has 8 vertices and 12 triangles.
    mGfxStats->setVertexCount(8);
    mGfxStats->setTriCount(12);
    mGfxStats->update(dt);

    // Get snapshot of input devices.
    gDInput->poll();

    // Check input.
    if( gDInput->keyDown(DIK_W) )
        mCameraHeight   += 25.0f * dt;
    if( gDInput->keyDown(DIK_S) )
        mCameraHeight   -= 25.0f * dt;

    // Divide by 50 to make mouse less sensitive.
    mCameraRotationY += gDInput->mouseDX() / 50.0f;
    mCameraRadius    += gDInput->mouseDY() / 50.0f;

    // If we rotate over 360 degrees, just roll back to 0
    if( fabsf(mCameraRotationY) >= 2.0f * D3DX_PI )
        mCameraRotationY = 0.0f;

    // Don't let radius get too small.
    if( mCameraRadius < 5.0f )
        mCameraRadius = 5.0f;

    buildViewMtx();
}
```

Because the camera position/orientation relative to the world coordinate system can change every frame based on input, we need to rebuild the view matrix every frame with the latest changes. The `buildViewMtx` method is implemented as follows:

```
void CubeDemo::buildViewMtx()
{
    float x = mCameraRadius * cosf(mCameraRotationY);
    float z = mCameraRadius * sinf(mCameraRotationY);
    D3DXVECTOR3 pos(x, mCameraHeight, z);
    D3DXVECTOR3 target(0.0f, 0.0f, 0.0f);
    D3DXVECTOR3 up(0.0f, 1.0f, 0.0f);
    D3DXMatrixLookAtLH(&mView, &pos, &target, &up);
}
```

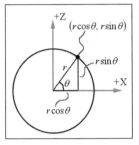

Figure 7.5: Rectangular coordinates computed from polar coordinates (radius and angle).

Figure 7.5 outlines the trigonometry used to compute the x- and z-coordinates of the camera's position.

7.4.7 drawScene

The `drawScene` method draws the cube. As you can see, all the drawing code is between a pair of `BeginScene` and `EndScene` calls, as required. Observe how we do our preliminary drawing work of hooking the vertex buffer up to a stream, setting the index buffer, and setting the vertex declaration. Next, we set the combined world, view, and projection matrix to the device with the `SetTransform` method. (Notice that the world matrix is the identity matrix, which essentially means the local coordinate system of the cube is the same as the world coordinate system; that is, we are actually specifying the vertices directly into world space.) After setting the transformation matrices to the device, we change the fill mode render state so that the cube will be drawn in wireframe mode. Finally, we draw the cube with the `DrawIndexedPrimitive` function.

```
void CubeDemo::drawScene()
{
    // Clear the back buffer and depth buffer.
    HR(gd3dDevice->Clear(0, 0,
        D3DCLEAR_TARGET | D3DCLEAR_ZBUFFER, 0xffffffff, 1.0f, 0));
    HR(gd3dDevice->BeginScene());
```

```
// Let Direct3D know the vertex buffer, index buffer, and vertex
// declaration we are using.
HR(gd3dDevice->SetStreamSource(0, mVB, 0, sizeof(VertexPos)));
HR(gd3dDevice->SetIndices(mIB));
HR(gd3dDevice->SetVertexDeclaration(VertexPos::Decl));

// World matrix is identity.
D3DXMATRIX W;
D3DXMatrixIdentity(&W);
HR(gd3dDevice->SetTransform(D3DTS_WORLD, &W));
HR(gd3dDevice->SetTransform(D3DTS_VIEW, &mView));
HR(gd3dDevice->SetTransform(D3DTS_PROJECTION, &mProj));
HR(gd3dDevice->SetRenderState(D3DRS_FILLMODE, D3DFILL_WIREFRAME));
HR(gd3dDevice->DrawIndexedPrimitive(
            D3DPT_TRIANGLELIST, 0, 0, 8, 0, 12));

mGfxStats->display();
HR(gd3dDevice->EndScene());

// Present the back buffer.
HR(gd3dDevice->Present(0, 0, 0, 0));
}
```

This concludes the explanation of the Cube demo sample; before continuing, you should open the source code, compile and run the program, and then spend some time familiarizing yourself with the code. It is one thing to see the code broken up in a book, but it is helpful to see all of it together in the source code files.

7.5 Summary

- Vertex data is stored in the IDirect3DVertexBuffer9 interface. Similarly, index data is stored in the IDirect3DIndexBuffer9 interface. The reason for using vertex/index buffers is so that the data can be stored in video memory.

- Geometry that is static, that is, does not need to be updated every frame, should be stored in a static vertex/index buffer. On the other hand, geometry that is dynamic, that is, does need to get updated every frame, should be stored in a dynamic vertex/index buffer.

- Render states are states the device maintains that affect how geometry is rendered. Render states remain in effect until changed, and the current values are applied to the geometry of any subsequent drawing operations. All render states have initial default values.

- To draw the contents of a vertex buffer and an index buffer you must:

   1. Call IDirect3DDevice9::SetStreamSource and hook the vertex buffer you wish to draw from to a stream.

   2. Call IDirect3DDevice9::SetVertexDeclaration to set the vertex declaration of the vertices to render.

3. If you are using an index buffer, call IDirect3DDevice9::SetIndices to set the index buffer.

4. Set the world, view, and projection transformation matrices to the device, and change render states as needed.

5. Call either IDirect3DDevice9::DrawPrimitive or IDirect3DDevice9::DrawIndexedPrimitive in between an IDirect3DDevice9::BeginScene and IDirect3DDevice9::EndScene pair.

7.6 **Exercises**

1. Recall that the first argument we pass to both IDirect3DDevice9::Draw-Primitive and IDirect3DDevice9::DrawIndexedPrimitive is a member of the D3DPRIMITIVETYPE enumerated type. We said that in this book we primarily concern ourselves with drawing triangle lists, and thus always specify D3DPT_TRIANGLELIST for this member. In this exercise, you investigate some of the other primitive types. To start, look up D3DPRIMITIVETYPE in the DirectX SDK documentation, and read about each member, and also follow the Triangle Strips and Triangle Fans links in the "remarks" section. Now draw (wireframe only — no shading) Figure 7.6a using the D3DPT_LINESTRIP type and draw (wireframe only — no shading) Figure 7.6b using the D3DPT_TRIANGLEFAN type.

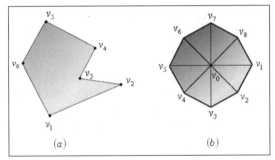

Figure 7.6: Draw (*a*) using the D3DPT_LINESTRIP primitive type and draw (*b*) using the D3DPT_TRIANGLEFAN primitive type.

2. Recall that exercise 2 of Chapter 6 asked you to construct the vertices and indices for the mesh in Figure 6.22. Now write those vertices and indices into vertex and index buffers and render the triangle mesh.

3. Modify the Cube demo by turning off backface culling (see §6.4.5). Describe your results. What happens if you change the cull mode winding order to cull clockwise triangles (i.e., setting D3DCULL_CW)? (Hint: You can turn off backface culling by changing the D3DRS_CULLMODE render state; see D3DRENDERSTATETYPE and D3DCULL in the DirectX SDK documentation.)

4. Describe how you can control the depth buffer test with the D3DRS_ZFUNC render state; also see D3DCMPFUNC.

Chapter 8

Drawing in Direct3D — Part II

In this chapter, we introduce shaders and the effects framework. In addition, we show how to draw some slightly more complicated geometry. Although most of what we learned in Chapter 7 still applies, there are a few differences that stem from the fact that we will now be using shaders (i.e., the programmable pipeline) and the effects framework to draw our geometry instead of using the fixed-function pipeline.

Basically, the *fixed-function pipeline* is where you set different device states to control how geometry and pixels are processed. In the *programmable pipeline* we write short programs, which are executed on the GPU, that control how geometry and pixels are processed. The fixed pipeline is so-called because there are only a fixed number of device states to control, which makes it inflexible. The programmable pipeline is much more flexible since you can program how geometry and pixels are processed, thereby having the potential to create new custom effects. A more detailed comparison between the fixed and programmable pipeline won't be seen in this book since henceforth we will primarily be using the programmable pipeline exclusively. Because the programmable pipeline is much more powerful than the fixed pipeline, the fixed pipeline is being abandoned and won't appear in DirectX 10.

Objectives:

- To become familiar with using the Direct3D effects framework for customizing how the GPU (graphics processing unit) draws geometry.
- To learn how to write simple vertex and pixel shaders.
- To discover how to create more complex 3D shapes using the D3DXCreate* functions.

8.1 Checking for Shader Support

Before we get started, let's first show how to verify that the graphics card running the demo supports the vertex and pixel shader version we use, which, for this book, is vertex and pixel shader versions 2.0. The following code is from the TriGrid demo, which is discussed in §8.4. It checks the device caps to see if the user's graphics card supports shader versions 2.0.

```
bool TriGridDemo::checkDeviceCaps()
{
    D3DCAPS9 caps;
    HR(gd3dDevice->GetDeviceCaps(&caps));

    // Check for vertex shader version 2.0 support.
    if( caps.VertexShaderVersion < D3DVS_VERSION(2, 0) )
        return false;

    // Check for pixel shader version 2.0 support.
    if( caps.PixelShaderVersion < D3DPS_VERSION(2, 0) )
        return false;

    return true;
}
```

The supported vertex shader version of the device is given by the `caps.VertexShaderVersion` data member, and likewise, the pixel shader version of the device is given by the `caps.PixelShaderVersion` data member. So our code asks if the device's vertex shader and pixel shader versions are less than 2.0 with `D3DVS_VERSION(2, 0)` and `D3DPS_VERSION(2, 0)`. If it is, then we return false for the `checkDeviceCaps` function because our demos require support for at least version 2.0.

To test for vertex and pixel shader versions 3.0, for example, we write:

```
if( caps.VertexShaderVersion < D3DVS_VERSION(3, 0) )
    return false;
if( caps.PixelShaderVersion < D3DPS_VERSION(3, 0) )
    return false;
```

8.2 Shaders and the FX Framework

A *vertex shader* is a program executed on the graphics card's GPU (graphics processing unit) that operates on vertices. The responsibilities of a vertex shader include the world, view, and projection transformations; vertex lighting; and any other calculations that need to be done at the vertex level. Vertex shaders can output data, which can then be used as input for pixel shaders; this is done by interpolating the vertex data of a triangle across the face of the triangle during rasterization; see §6.4.8.

Note: Actually, vertex shaders may also be executed in software if `D3DCREATE_SOFTWARE_VERTEXPROCESSING` was specified.

Analogously, a *pixel shader* is a program executed on the graphics card's GPU that operates on *pixel fragments* (candidates that can become screen pixels if they pass various operations that can prevent a pixel from being written, such as the alpha test, stencil test, and depth buffer test). The primary responsibility of a pixel shader is to generate a color based on interpolated vertex data as input.

Note: Because vertex and pixel shaders are programs we implement, there is plenty of room for creativity in devising unique graphical effects — and we'll get plenty of practice writing different kinds of shaders throughout the course of this book.

A Direct3D *effect* encapsulates the code that describes how to render 3D geometry in a particular way. For example, water looks much different from a car, so a water effect would encapsulate the vertex shader, pixel shader, and device states needed to render geometry that looks like water, and a separate car effect would encapsulate the vertex shader, pixel shader, and device states needed to render a car. More specifically, an effect consists of one or more *techniques*, which consist of one or more *passes*. Each pass contains a vertex shader, a pixel shader, and device state settings, which describe how to render the geometry for that particular pass. The reason for multiple passes is that some effects are implemented with multiple layers; that is, each pass renders the geometry differently and creates a layer, but then we can combine all the layers of the passes to form the net result of the rendering technique. (If you do any Photoshop work, you are probably familiar with the idea of working with several image layers and then combining them to form a net image.)

It is often desirable to have a fallback mechanism for rendering effects on different grades of graphics hardware. In other words, we want to have several versions of an effect available that implement the same effect (or attempt to implement the same effect as closely as possible) using the capabilities of different grades of hardware. This fallback mechanism is facilitated in the Direct3D effects framework by the availability of *multiple techniques in an effect file*; that is, each technique implements the effect by targeting different level hardware features. Then based on the game player's system specs, we select the technique for an effect that is most appropriate. For example, consider the water effect again: If we detect that the player's system has the top-of-the-line graphics card, then we would enable a very realistic, but computationally demanding, water technique. On the other hand, if we detect that the player's system has medium-level graphics hardware, we fall back to a simpler water technique. Finally, upon detecting low-grade graphics hardware, we fall back to a more crude water technique.

In addition to the fallback scheme, an effect may contain multiple techniques because the effect is complicated and requires several different techniques combined to complete the final effect. For example, we may have a technique to generate a displacement map, and then another technique that uses the displacement map to produce the final result. So this effect requires two distinct techniques used for one final result; therefore, for encapsulation purposes, you may wish to include both techniques in the same effect file.

Note: Because we are writing demos and not commercial applications in this book, our effects only contain one technique; that is, we do not worry about implementing multiple techniques to support wide ranges of hardware. Furthermore, all of the effects in this book can be implemented in one pass.

Vertex and pixel shaders are programmed in a special language called the *high-level shading language* (HLSL). This language is very similar to C, and thus easy to learn. Our approach for teaching the HLSL and programming shaders will be example based. That is, as we progress through the book, we will introduce any new HLSL concepts that we need in order to implement the demo at hand.

We describe an effect in an .fx file, which is just a text file (like a .cpp) where we write our effects code and program our vertex and pixel shaders. Because the .fx file is an external file, it can be modified without recompiling the main application source code; thus a game developer could update a game to take advantage of new graphics hardware by only releasing updated effect files.

8.2.1 A Simple Vertex Shader

Below is the simple vertex shader TransformVS, which we use for this chapter's demos.

```
uniform extern float4x4 gWVP;

struct OutputVS
{
    float4 posH : POSITION0;
};

OutputVS TransformVS(float3 posL : POSITION0)
{
    // Zero out our output.
    OutputVS outVS = (OutputVS)0;
```

```
// Transform to homogeneous clip space.
outVS.posH = mul(float4(posL, 1.0f), gWVP);

// Done--return the output.
return outVS;
}
```

Before discussing the vertex shader, observe the structure definition before it. As you can see, HLSL structures are defined in a similar C programming language style. This structure defines the data our vertex shader outputs. In this case, we only output a single 4D vector (float4) that describes our vertex after it has been transformed into homogeneous clip space. The semantic notation, ": POSITION0" tells the GPU that the data returned in posH is a vertex position. We will see more examples of using semantics as we progress through the book and program more interesting shaders.

Now observe that the actual vertex shader is essentially a function. It contains parameters (vertex input) and returns vertex output. Conceptually, we can think of a vertex shader as a function that will be executed for each vertex we draw:

```
for(int i = 0; i < numVertices; ++i)
    modifiedVertex[i] = vertexshader( v[i] );
```

So we can see that a vertex shader gives us a chance to execute some per-vertex code to do something. Note again that vertex shaders are executed on the GPU; we could always execute per-vertex operations on the CPU, but the idea is to move all graphics operations over to the graphically specialized and optimized GPU, thereby freeing the CPU for other tasks. Also note that the GPU does expect vertices, at the very least, to be transformed to homogeneous clip space; therefore, we always do the world, view, and projection transformations.

Parameters to the vertex shader correspond to data members in our custom vertex structure (i.e., the input data). The parameter semantic ": POSITION0" tells the graphics card that this parameter corresponds to the data member in the custom vertex structure with usage D3DDECLUSAGE_POSITION and index 0, as specified by the vertex declaration. So remember, in our vertex element description, we indicate for what each data member in the vertex structure is used. Then in the vertex shader, we attach a semantic to each parameter indicating a usage and index. Consequently, we now have a map that specifies how vertex structure elements get mapped to the input parameters of the vertex shader (see Figure 8.1).

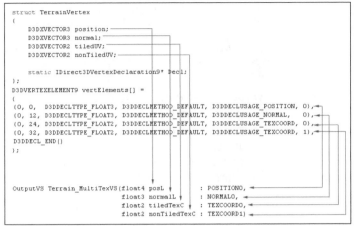

```
struct TerrainVertex
{
    D3DXVECTOR3 position;
    D3DXVECTOR3 normal;
    D3DXVECTOR2 tiledUV;
    D3DXVECTOR2 nonTiledUV;

    static IDirect3DVertexDeclaration9* Decl;
};
D3DVERTEXELEMENT9 vertElements[] =
{
    {0,  0,  D3DDECLTYPE_FLOAT3, D3DDECLMETHOD_DEFAULT, D3DDECLUSAGE_POSITION, 0},
    {0, 12,  D3DDECLTYPE_FLOAT3, D3DDECLMETHOD_DEFAULT, D3DDECLUSAGE_NORMAL,   0},
    {0, 24,  D3DDECLTYPE_FLOAT2, D3DDECLMETHOD_DEFAULT, D3DDECLUSAGE_TEXCOORD, 0},
    {0, 32,  D3DDECLTYPE_FLOAT2, D3DDECLMETHOD_DEFAULT, D3DDECLUSAGE_TEXCOORD, 1},
    D3DDECL_END()
};


OutputVS Terrain_MultiTexVS(float4 posL       : POSITION0,
                            float3 normalL    : NORMAL0,
                            float2 tiledTexC  : TEXCOORD0,
                            float2 nonTiledTexC : TEXCOORD1)
```

Figure 8.1: A vertex structure and its associated vertex element array describing its components, and a vertex shader input parameter listing. The vertex declaration combined with the input parameter semantics define an association between the vertex structure elements and the vertex shader input parameters; in other words, it specifies how vertex shader input parameters map to the vertex structure data members.

Note: From a low-level perspective, the semantic syntax associates a variable in the shader with a hardware register. That is, the input variables are associated with input registers, and the output variables are associated with the output registers. For example, posL : POSITION0 is connected to the vertex input position register. Similarly, outVS.posH : POSITION0 is connected to the vertex output position register.

The first line of code in our vertex shader, OutputVS outVS = (OutputVS)0;, instantiates an OutputVS instance, and zeros out all of its members by casting 0 to OutputVS. The next line of code performs the matrix transformation with the intrinsic HLSL mul function:

```
outVS.posH = mul(float4(posL, 1.0f), gWVP);
```

The left-hand-side argument is a 4D vector and the right-hand-side argument is a 4×4 matrix. (Observe how we augmented to homogeneous coordinates.) The function mul returns the result of the vector-matrix multiplication. Note that mul can also be used to multiply two 4×4 matrices together — mul is overloaded.

Note: The code float4(posL, 1.0f) constructs a 4D vector in the following way: float4(posL.x, posL.y, posL.z, 1.0f). (Observe that posL is a 3D vector — float3.) Since we know the position of vertices are points and not vectors, we place a 1 in the fourth component ($w = 1$).

The variable gWVP is called an *effect parameter,* and it represents the combined world, view, and projection matrix. It is declared as:

```
uniform extern float4x4 gWVP;
```

The uniform keyword means that the variable does not change per vertex — it is constant for all vertices until we change it at the C++ application level. The extern keyword means that the C++ application can see the variable (i.e., the variable can be accessed outside the effect file by the C++ application code). The type float4x4 is a 4×4 matrix.

Note: An effect parameter is not the same as a vertex shader parameter:

```
uniform extern float4x4 gWVP; // <--Effect parameter

OutputVS TransformVS(
    float3 posL : POSITION0)  // <--Vertex shader parameter
```

Effect parameters are important, as they provide a means for the C++ application code to communicate with the effect. For example, the vertex shader needs to know the combined world, view, and projection matrix so that it can transform the vertices into homogeneous clip space. However, the combined matrix may change every frame (as the camera moves around the scene, for instance); thus, the C++ application code must update the effect parameter, gWVP, every frame with the current combined matrix.

After we have saved the transformed vertex into the outVS.posH data member, we are done and can return our output vertex:

```
    return outVS;
```

8.2.2 A Simple Pixel Shader

Below is the simple pixel shader we use for this chapter's demos.

```
float4 TransformPS() : COLOR
{
    return float4(0.0f, 0.0f, 0.0f, 1.0f);
}
```

Essentially a pixel shader computes the color of a pixel fragment based on input parameters for the pixel fragment, such as interpolated vertex colors, normals, and texture coordinates. From where do pixel fragments get their input? Recall that in rasterization, certain vertex data components (colors and texture coordinates) are interpolated across the face of a triangle, thereby passing vertex data down to the pixel fragment level (i.e., the input to a pixel fragment is the interpolated vertex data for that particular pixel fragment).

Note that even though we say colors and texture coordinates, it is really more flexible than that because we can just set an arbitrary 3D vector into a 3D texture coordinate slot; likewise, we can pass general scalar information down to 1D texture coordinates. Figure 8.2 illustrates the idea.

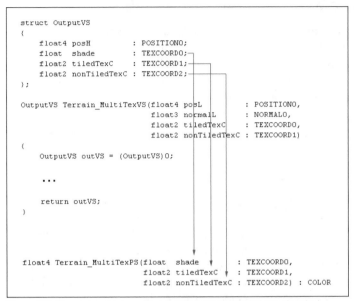

```
struct OutputVS
{
    float4 posH        : POSITION0;
    float  shade       : TEXCOORD0;
    float2 tiledTexC   : TEXCOORD1;
    float2 nonTiledTexC : TEXCOORD2;
};

OutputVS Terrain_MultiTexVS(float4 posL    : POSITION0,
                            float3 normalL  : NORMAL0,
                            float2 tiledTexC : TEXCOORD0,
                            float2 nonTiledTexC : TEXCOORD1)
{
    OutputVS outVS = (OutputVS)0;

    ...

    return outVS;
}


float4 Terrain_MultiTexPS(float  shade      : TEXCOORD0,
                          float2 tiledTexC   : TEXCOORD1,
                          float2 nonTiledTexC : TEXCOORD2) : COLOR
```

Figure 8.2: The vertex shader output is interpolated and fed into the pixel shader as input. Note only the texture coordinate components are passed in (COLOR components are also), but the POSITION type is not; only colors and texture coordinates are fed into the pixel shader, but as said, this is more flexible than it seems because we can disguise arbitrary data as texture coordinates. For instance, in this example we pass an arbitrary scalar as a texture coordinate that won't actually be used as a texture coordinate.

A pixel shader always returns a 4D color value in the form (r, g, b, a), where r, g, b, and a are in the range [0, 1]. Consequently, a pixel shader always has a color semantic (: COLOR) following the parameter list. (We are brief here because color is the topic of the next chapter.)

Turning our attention back to the implementation of TransformPS, observe that we have no inputs into the pixel shader (empty parameter list). This just follows from the fact that the vertex shader defined in §8.2.1 does not output any color or texture coordinate data. This will change in later chapters, but for now, we are stuck computing a color for each pixel fragment based on zero input. In other words, we can just pick any color we want. For this chapter's demos, we use black for every pixel fragment so that when we draw our wireframe lines, they will be black.

As with vertex shaders, conceptually we can think of a pixel shader as a function that will be executed for each pixel fragment:

```
for(int i = 0; i < numPixelFragments; ++i)
    modifiedPixelFragment[i] = pixelshader( p[i] );
```

So we can see that a pixel shader gives a chance to execute some per-pixel code to shade the pixel fragment.

8.2.3 **A Simple FX File**

Now that we have studied the vertex and pixel shaders for this chapter, we can look at the entire .fx file that describes the effect — namely rendering our geometry in wireframe mode.

```
//=====================================================================
// transform.fx by Frank Luna (C) 2004 All Rights Reserved.
//
// Basic FX that simply transforms geometry from local space to
// homogeneous clip space, and draws the geometry in wireframe mode.
//=====================================================================

// FX parameter (global variable to the shader).
uniform extern float4x4 gWVP;

// Structure
struct OutputVS
{
    float4 posH : POSITION0;
};

// Vertex shader
OutputVS TransformVS(float3 posL : POSITION0)
{
    // Zero out our output.
    OutputVS outVS = (OutputVS)0;

    // Transform to homogeneous clip space.
    outVS.posH = mul(float4(posL, 1.0f), gWVP);

    // Done--return the output.
    return outVS;
}

// Pixel shader
float4 TransformPS() : COLOR
{
    return float4(0.0f, 0.0f, 0.0f, 1.0f);
}

technique TransformTech
{
    pass P0
    {
        // Specify the vertex and pixel shader associated
        // with this pass.
        vertexShader = compile vs_2_0 TransformVS();
        pixelShader  = compile ps_2_0 TransformPS();
```

```
        // Specify the render/device states associated with
        // this pass.
        FillMode = Wireframe;
    }
}
```

A technique is defined by the `technique` keyword followed by the name of the technique:

```
technique identifier {...}
```

A technique contains one or more passes (defined with the `pass` keyword), and each pass is given a name — we typically use the identifiers `P0`, `P1`, `P2`, and so on, to denote the first pass, second pass, third pass, and so on, respectively.

```
technique tech-identifier
{
    pass pass1-identifier {...}
    pass pass2-identifier {...}
    pass pass3-identifier {...}
    ...
}
```

Observe that a pass specifies a vertex shader, pixel shader, and any device states that need to be specified. The device state setting

```
FillMode = Wireframe;
```

sets the fill mode to wireframe mode (essentially it instructs the effect to call `gd3dDevice->SetRenderState(D3DRS_FILLMODE, D3DFILL_WIREFRAME)` prior to geometry being rendered for the pass). To specify the solid fill mode, we would write:

```
FillMode = Solid;
```

There are numerous device states that can be set to modify how geometry is rendered in an effect (you already saw some of them in the Sprite demo), and we will introduce them on a need-to-know basis in this book. However, if you are curious, you can look up the complete list in the SDK documentation (from the Contents tab of the documentation, see *directx/graphics/reference/d3d/enums/d3drenderstatetype.htm* and *directx/graphics/reference/effectfilereference/effectfileformat/states.htm*).

The modifiers `vs_2_0` and `ps_2_0` indicate the vertex and pixel shader version, respectively, in which to compile the shader code; here, we use vertex and pixel shader versions 2.0. To specify version 3.0, for example, we would specify `vs_3_0` and `ps_3_0`. Table 8.1 summarizes some differences between the major version numbers to give you an idea of their relative differences. (Additionally, there are quite a few other significant technical differences which we won't get into here, but see *directx/graphics/reference/assemblylanguageshaders/vertexshaders/vertexshaderdifferences.htm* and

directx/graphics/reference/assemblylanguageshaders/pixelshaders/
pixelshaderdifferences.htm in the SDK documentation.)

Table 8.1

Property	Version 1.1	Version 2.0	Version 3.0
Vertex shader constant register count	At least 96	At least 256	At least 256
Vertex shader instruction slots	At least 128	At least 256	At least 512
Pixel shader sampler count	4	16	16
Pixel shader instruction slots	4 texture/8 arithmetic	32 texture/64 arithmetic	At least 512 (no texture instruction limit)

Note: So anytime we want to draw geometry with black wireframe lines, we just use this effect. By the end of this book, we will have a nice collection of different effects that allow us to render geometry in different ways.

8.2.4 Creating an Effect

In code, an effect is represented by the ID3DXEffect interface, which we create with the following D3DX function:

```
HRESULT D3DXCreateEffectFromFile(
    LPDIRECT3DDEVICE9 pDevice,
    LPCSTR pSrcFile,
    CONST D3DXMACRO* pDefines,
    LPD3DXINCLUDE pInclude,
    DWORD Flags,
    LPD3DXEFFECTPOOL pPool,
    LPD3DXEFFECT* ppEffect,
    LPD3DXBUFFER *ppCompilationErrors
);
```

■ pDevice: The device to be associated with the created ID3DXEffect object.

■ pSrcFile: Name of the .fx file that contains the effect source code we want to compile.

■ pDefines: This parameter is optional and we will specify null for it in this book.

■ pInclude: This parameter is optional and we will specify null for it in this book.

■ Flags: Optional flags for compiling the shaders in the effect file; specify zero for no flags. Some common options are:

D3DXSHADER_DEBUG: Instructs the compiler to write debug information.

D3DXSHADER_SKIPVALIDATION: Instructs the compiler not to do any code validation. This should only be used when you are using a shader that is known to work.

D3DXSHADER_SKIPOPTIMIZATION: Instructs the compiler not to perform any code optimization. In practice this would only be used in debugging, where you would not want the compiler to alter the code in any way.

D3DXSHADER_NO_PRESHADER: Instructs the compiler not to use preshaders — preshaders precompute constant expressions in a shader (i.e., expressions that do not change per vertex or per pixel). For example, suppose that you were multiplying two uniform matrices together in a shader. Since the matrices do not change per vertex or per pixel, there is no need to do the matrix multiplication for each vertex or for each pixel. So we can pull the computation "out of the loop" and do it once outside the shader. Preshaders do this optimization for us automatically.

D3DXSHADER_PARTIALPRECISION: Instructs the compiler to use partial precision for computations, which can improve performance on some hardware.

- pPool: Optional pointer to an ID3DXEffectPool interface that is used to define how effect parameters are shared across other effect instances. In this book we will specify null for this parameter, indicating that we will not share parameters between effect files.

- ppEffect: Returns a pointer to an ID3DXEffect interface representing the created effect.

- ppCompilationErrors: Returns a pointer to an ID3DXBuffer that contains a string of error codes and messages.

Here is an example call of D3DXCreateEffectFromFile:

```
ID3DXEffect* mFX = 0;
ID3DXBuffer* errors = 0;
HR(D3DXCreateEffectFromFile(gd3dDevice, "transform.fx",
    0, 0, D3DXSHADER_DEBUG, 0, &mFX, &errors));
if( errors )
    MessageBox(0, (char*)errors->GetBufferPointer(), 0, 0);
```

Note: The ID3DXBuffer interface is a generic data structure that D3DX uses to store data in a contiguous block of memory. It has only two methods:

- LPVOID GetBufferPointer(): Returns a pointer to the start of the data.

- DWORD GetBufferSize(): Returns the size of the buffer in bytes.

To keep the structure generic it uses a void pointer. This means that it is up to us to realize the type of data being stored. For example, with `D3DXCreateEffectFromFile`, it is understood that the `ID3DXBuffer` returned from `ppCompilationErrors` is a Cstring. In general, the documentation of the D3DX function that returns an `ID3DXBuffer` will indicate the type of data being returned so that you know what to cast the data as.

We can create an empty `ID3DXBuffer` using the following function:

```
HRESULT D3DXCreateBuffer(
    DWORD NumBytes,        // Size of the buffer, in bytes.
    LPD3DXBUFFER *ppBuffer // Returns the created buffer.
);
```

The following example creates a buffer that can hold four integers:

```
ID3DXBuffer* buffer = 0;
D3DXCreateBuffer( 4 * sizeof(int), &buffer );
```

8.2.5 Setting Effect Parameters

The `ID3DXEffect` interface provides methods for setting parameters of various types. Here is an abridged list; see the documentation for a complete list.

■ HRESULT ID3DXEffect::SetFloat(
        D3DXHANDLE hParameter,
        FLOAT f);

Sets a floating-point parameter in the effect file identified by `hParameter` to the value `f`.

■ HRESULT ID3DXEffect::SetMatrix(
        D3DXHANDLE hParameter,
        CONST D3DXMATRIX* pMatrix);

Sets a matrix parameter in the effect file identified by `hParameter` to the value pointed to by `pMatrix`.

■ HRESULT ID3DXEffect::SetTexture(
        D3DXHANDLE hParameter,
        LPDIRECT3DBASETEXTURE9 pTexture);

Sets a texture parameter in the effect file identified by `hParameter` to the value pointed to by `pTexture`.

■ HRESULT ID3DXEffect::SetVector(
        D3DXHANDLE hParameter,
        CONST D3DXVECTOR4* pVector);

Sets a vector parameter in the effect file identified by `hParameter` to the value pointed to by `pVector`.

■ HRESULT ID3DXEffect::SetValue(
        D3DXHANDLE hParameter,
        LPCVOID pData,
        UINT Bytes);

Sets an arbitrary data structure parameter of size `Bytes` in the effect file identified by `hParameter` to the value pointed to by `pData`.

A `D3DXHANDLE` is just a way of identifying an internal object in an effect file (e.g., a parameter, a technique, a pass) for access; the idea is similar to using an `HWND` to interact with a window object in Win32 programming. We obtain handles to effect parameters using the following method:

```
D3DXHANDLE ID3DXEffect::GetParameterByName(
    D3DXHANDLE hParent, // scope of variable - parent structure
    LPCSTR pName        // name of variable
);
```

The first parameter is a `D3DXHANDLE` that identifies the parent structure of which the variable we want is a member. For example, if we wanted to get a handle to a single data member of a structure instance, we would pass in the handle to the structure instance here. If we are obtaining a handle to a top-level variable, we can pass 0 for this parameter. The second parameter is the name of the variable as it appears in the effect file.

Here is an example of setting effect parameters:

```
// Data
D3DXMATRIX M;
D3DXMatrixRotationY(&M, D3DX_PI);
D3DXVECTOR4 V(x, y, z, 1.0f);

// Obtain handles (assume "mtx" and "vec" are parameters
// declared in .fx file).
D3DXHANDLE hMatrix = mFX->GetParameterByName(0, "mtx");
D3DXHANDLE hVec = mFX->GetParameterByName(0, "vec");

// Set Parameters
mFX->SetMatrix(hMatrix, &M);
mFX->SetVector(hVec, &V);
```

Figure 8.3 shows an example that illustrates the idea of what we are doing more clearly.

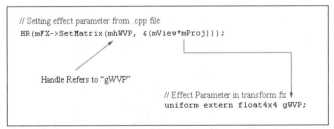

Figure 8.3: The `D3DXHANDLE` refers to an .fx parameter. Then via `ID3DXEffect::Set*` methods, we can set effect parameters in the .fx file from the .cpp file.

Note: There are corresponding `ID3DXEffect::Get*` methods for each `ID3DXEffect::Set*` method that can be used to retrieve the value of a variable in the effect file (see the DirectX SDK documentation). For example, to get a variable that is a matrix type, we would use this function:

```
HRESULT ID3DXEffect::GetMatrix(
    D3DXHANDLE hParameter,
    D3DXMATRIX* pMatrix);
```

8.3 Applying the Effect

In this section we show how to apply an effect once it has been created. The following steps summarize the overall process:

1. Obtain a handle to the technique in the effect file you wish to use.

2. Activate the desired technique and set any effect parameters.

3. Begin the currently active technique.

4. For each rendering pass in the active technique, render the desired geometry. Recall that techniques may consist of several rendering passes and we must render the geometry once for each pass.

5. End the currently active technique.

8.3.1 Obtaining a Handle to an Effect

The first step to using a technique is to obtain a `D3DXHANDLE` to that technique. A handle to a technique can be obtained using the `ID3DXEffect::GetTechniqueByName` method. For example, if "TransformTech" is the name of a technique in the .fx file, then we can obtain a handle to that technique like so:

```
D3DXHANDLE mhTech = mFX->GetTechniqueByName("TransformTech");
```

8.3.2 Activating an Effect and Setting Effect Parameters

Once the handle to the desired technique has been obtained, we must activate that technique. This is done with the `ID3DXEffect::SetTechnique` method:

```
HR(mFX->SetTechnique(mhTech));
```

In addition, any effect parameters that need to be updated should be set. For example, to set the combined world, view, and projection matrix:

```
HR(mFX->SetMatrix(mhWVP, &(mWorld*mView*mProj)));
```

Note that you do not necessarily need to set effect parameters at this point, but effect parameters should always be set prior to calling `ID3DXEffect::Begin`.

8.3.3 **Beginning an Effect**

To render geometry using an effect, we must surround the drawing function calls with ID3DXEffect::Begin and ID3DXEffect::End calls. These functions essentially enable and disable the effect, respectively.

```
HRESULT ID3DXEffect::Begin(UINT* pPasses, DWORD Flags);
```

■ pPasses: Returns the number of passes in the currently active technique.

■ Flags: One of the following flags:

Zero (0): Instructs the effect to save the current device states, and then to restore them after the effect is finished (when ID3DXEffect::End is called). This is useful because the effect can change the device states and it may be desirable to restore the states prior to beginning the effect.

D3DXFX_DONOTSAVESTATE: Instructs the effect to not save and to not restore any device states.

D3DXFX_DONOTSAVESHADERSTATE: Instructs the effect to not save and to not restore shader device states.

D3DXFX_DONOTSAVESAMPLERSTATE: Instructs the effect to not save and to not restore sampler device states.

Here is an example invocation:

```
UINT numPasses = 0;
HR(mFX->Begin(&numPasses, 0));
```

8.3.4 **Setting the Current Rendering Pass**

Before we can render any geometry using an effect, we must specify the rendering pass to use. Recall that a technique consists of one or more rendering passes, where each pass contains the device states and shaders that are to be used for that pass. The rendering passes for a technique are labeled from 0 to $n-1$ for n passes. Thus we can iterate through each pass using a simple for-loop and render the geometry for that pass. We begin a pass with the ID3DXEffect::BeginPass method, which takes an integer parameter from 0, ..., $n-1$ identifying the pass, and we end a pass with ID3DXEffect::EndPass. The following code snippet illustrates this:

```
for(int i = 0; i < numPasses; ++i)
{
    HR(mFX->BeginPass(i));
    HR(gd3dDevice->DrawIndexedPrimitive(D3DPT_TRIANGLELIST,
                                        0, 0, 8, 0, 12));
    HR(mFX->EndPass());
}
```

8.3.5 **Ending an Effect**

Finally, after we have rendered the geometry for each pass, we disable or end the effect with `ID3DXEffect::End`:

```
HR(mFX->End());
```

8.3.6 **Example Code**

The following example code summarizes all the steps needed to draw some geometry with an effect:

```
HR(gd3dDevice->BeginScene());
// Let Direct3D know the vertex buffer, index buffer, and vertex
// declaration we are using.
HR(gd3dDevice->SetStreamSource(0, mVB, 0, sizeof(VertexPos)));
HR(gd3dDevice->SetIndices(mIB));
HR(gd3dDevice->SetVertexDeclaration(VertexPos::Decl));

// Set up the rendering technique
HR(mFX->SetTechnique(mhTech));

// Set effect parameters.
HR(mFX->SetMatrix(mhWVP, &(mView*mProj)));

// Begin passes.
UINT numPasses = 0;
HR(mFX->Begin(&numPasses, 0));
for(int i = 0; i < numPasses; ++i)
{
    HR(mFX->BeginPass(i));

    // Execute drawing commands here. Geometry drawn here
    // will be rendered with this pass's shaders and device
    // states applied.
    HR(gd3dDevice->DrawIndexedPrimitive(D3DPT_TRIANGLELIST,
                                        0, 0, 8, 0, 12));

    HR(mFX->EndPass());
}
HR(mFX->End());
HR(gd3dDevice->EndScene());
```

Note: If you need to change parameters (via `ID3DXEffect::Set*` methods) in the middle of a rendering pass, then you need to call `ID3DXEffect::CommitChanges` for the change to take effect. For example:

```
HR(mFX->BeginPass(i));

HR(mFX->SetMatrix(hWVP, &M1));
HR(mFX->CommitChanges());
HR(gd3dDevice->DrawIndexedPrimitive(D3DPT_TRIANGLELIST,
```

```
                                        0, 0, 8, 0, 12));
    HR(mFX->SetMatrix(hWVP, &M2));
    HR(mFX->CommitChanges());
    HR(gd3dDevice->DrawIndexedPrimitive(D3DPT_TRIANGLELIST,
                                        0, 0, 8, 0, 12));

    HR(mFX->EndPass());
```

8.4 **Triangle Grid Demo**

This section shows how to render a triangle grid, as illustrated in Figure 8.4. This grid geometry is useful in its own right, as it can suffice as a "ground" plane for the time being. In addition, it serves several other useful purposes throughout this book — in particular, a triangle grid is the underlying geometry for both our terrain and water simulations. Incidentally, we do not embed the entire Triangle Grid demo source code here; instead, we highlight the key implementation details of constructing the grid geometry, and then leave it to the reader to investigate the driver source code (most of it is unchanged from the Cube demo — we merely draw a grid instead of a cube).

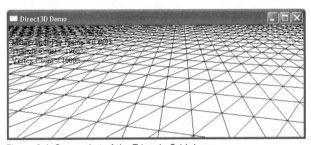

Figure 8.4: Screenshot of the Triangle Grid demo.

To generate the grid geometry we create a GenTriGrid function, which generates the vertex points and triangle indices of the grid. Once the GenTriGrid function generates the geometry, we need to write it into vertex and index buffers for rendering. The prototype of GenTriGrid is as follows:

```
void GenTriGrid(int numVertRows, int numVertCols,
                float dx, float dz,
                const D3DXVECTOR3& center,
                std::vector<D3DXVECTOR3>& verts,
                std::vector<DWORD>& indices)
```

- numVertRows: The number of vertex rows.
- numVertCols: The number of vertex columns.
- dx: The space between grid vertices in the x-direction.
- dz: The space between grid vertices in the z-direction.

- **center**: By default, this function generates a grid about the origin of a coordinate system. This parameter is a translation vector that specifies how to offset the grid from the origin; this enables us to construct a grid at a point other than the origin.
- **verts**: Fills a std::vector with the vertices of the grid.
- **indices**: Fills a std::vector with the indices of the grid.

Figure 8.5 outlines what these parameters mean, and also shows some other properties we can derive from these initial inputs. Also observe that if there are m vertex rows and n vertex columns, then

- There are $m - 1$ cell rows.
- There are $n - 1$ cell columns.
- There are $(m - 1) \times (n - 1)$ cells in all.
- There are $(m - 1) \times (n - 1) \times 2$ triangles (two triangles per cell).
- There are $m \times n$ vertices in all.

And, if the x-direction cell spacing is dx and the z-direction cell spacing is dz, then the width of the grid is $dx \times (n - 1)$ (i.e., cell width times the number of cell columns) and the depth of the grid is $dz \times (m - 1)$ (i.e., cell depth times the number of cell rows).

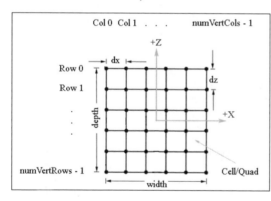

Figure 8.5: The properties of the triangle grid are labeled. The dots along the lines are vertices. Observe the rows go from top to bottom down from row 0 to mNumVertRows-1, and the columns go from left to right from column 0 to mNumVertCols-1.

8.4.1 Vertex Generation

As Figure 8.5 implies, we generate the vertices row by row in a top-down fashion (skipping over the specified step sizes to leave spaces between the vertices). Observe that this format corresponds to the layout of a matrix, where the rows of a matrix "go down" and the columns "go to the right." In particular, this format corresponds to the format of a surface (i.e., matrix of pixels). This correspondence is useful because later on we "lay" an image onto the grid, and we want the top pixel row of the image to correspond with the top vertex row of the grid, the second (row below the top row) pixel row of the image to correspond with the second (row below the top row) vertex row of the grid, and so on.

We generate the vertices in quadrant four starting at the origin. Once that is done, we translate the vertices so that the grid is centered about the origin of some local coordinate system; see Figure 8.6. After that, we translate the vertices one more time by the center parameter in order to construct the grid about a center point other than the origin.

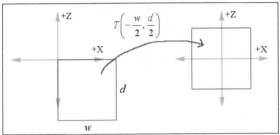

Figure 8.6: We generate the vertices in quadrant four starting from the origin and going row by row, then we translate so that the grid is centered about the coordinate system. Here *w* is the width of the grid and *d* is the depth of the grid.

Note that we do not have to do this as two steps. We can do the translation at the same time we generate a vertex so that we only have to loop through each vertex once. The function GenTriGrid that generates the vertices is given below.

```
void GenTriGrid(int numVertRows, int numVertCols,
                float dx, float dz,
                const D3DXVECTOR3& center,
                std::vector<D3DXVECTOR3>& verts,
                std::vector<DWORD>& indices)
{
    int numVertices = numVertRows*numVertCols;
    int numCellRows = numVertRows-1;
    int numCellCols = numVertCols-1;

    int numTris = numCellRows*numCellCols*2;

    float width = (float)numCellCols * dx;
    float depth = (float)numCellRows * dz;

    //=========================================
    // Build vertices.

    // We first build the grid geometry centered about the origin
    // and on the xz-plane, row by row and in a top-down fashion.
    // We then translate the grid vertices so that they are
    // centered about the specified parameter 'center'.

    verts.resize( numVertices );
```

```
// Offsets to translate grid from quadrant 4 to center of
// coordinate system.
float xOffset = -width * 0.5f;
float zOffset =  depth * 0.5f;

int k = 0;
for(float i = 0; i < numVertRows; ++i)
{
        for(float j = 0; j < numVertCols; ++j)
        {
                // Negate the depth coordinate to put in
                // quadrant four.  Then offset to center about
                // coordinate system.
                verts[k].x =  j * dx + xOffset;
                verts[k].z = -i * dz + zOffset;
                verts[k].y =  0.0f;

                // Translate so that the center of the grid is at the
                // specified 'center' parameter.
                D3DXMATRIX T;
                D3DXMatrixTranslation(&T,
                center.x,
                center.y,
                center.z);
                D3DXVec3TransformCoord(&verts[k], &verts[k], &T);

                ++k; // Next vertex
        }
}
```

8.4.2 Index Generation

To see how to generate the indices of the triangles, let's consider an arbitrary quad of the grid (Figure 8.7).

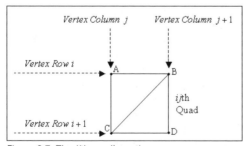

Figure 8.7: The *ij*th quad's vertices.

Then the indices describing the triangles of the *ij*th quad are:

$$\Delta ABC = \{i \cdot m + j, \quad i \cdot m + j + 1, \quad (i+1) \cdot m + j\}$$

$$\Delta CBD = \{(i+1) \cdot m + j, \quad i \cdot m + j + 1, \quad (i+1) \cdot m + j + 1\}$$

where m = numVertCols. Note that we multiply by m because we are storing a matrix (grid) in a linear array (the grid vertices are kept in a linear vertex buffer; thus, we need to multiply by m to "move to the next row" by skipping m vertices in the array per row).

Now we just loop through each quad and apply the above formula to generate the indices for the two triangles of that quad:

```
//===============================================
    // Build indices.

    indices.resize(numTris * 3);

    // Generate indices for each quad.
    k = 0;
    for(DWORD i = 0; i < (DWORD)numCellRows; ++i)
    {
        for(DWORD j = 0; j < (DWORD)numCellCols; ++j)
        {
            indices[k]     =  i    * numVertCols + j;
            indices[k + 1] =  i    * numVertCols + j + 1;
            indices[k + 2] = (i+1) * numVertCols + j;

            indices[k + 3] = (i+1) * numVertCols + j;
            indices[k + 4] =  i    * numVertCols + j + 1;
            indices[k + 5] = (i+1) * numVertCols + j + 1;

            // next quad
            k += 6;
        }
    }
}
```

Note: It is easy to create a large grid where the number of vertices goes outside the range a 16-bit integer can store. For example, consider a 300×300 grid, which means there are 90,000 vertices with indices ranging from 0 to 89,999. How do you index the 70,000th vertex? Unsigned 16-bit integers only go up to 65536. You can try using 32-bit indices if your hardware supports them — test the D3DCAPS9 for the MaxVertexIndex member to see the highest vertex index your hardware supports. Moreover, there is a limit on the maximum number of triangles you can draw with one DrawPrimitive call; see the MaxPrimitiveCount member of the D3DCAPS9 structure. A solution to these problems is to split up the grid into parts and draw the parts one at a time; we do this later on in the book.

8.4.3 **Extracting the Grid Geometry**

Finally, we can generate the grid and then fill the vertex and index buffers with the grid geometry as follows:

```
std::vector<D3DXVECTOR3> verts;
std::vector<DWORD> indices;

GenTriGrid(100, 100, 1.0f, 1.0f,
    D3DXVECTOR3(0.0f, 0.0f, 0.0f), verts, indices);

mNumVertices = 100*100;
mNumTriangles = 99*99*2;


HR(gd3dDevice->CreateVertexBuffer(mNumVertices * sizeof(VertexPos),
    D3DUSAGE_WRITEONLY, 0, D3DPOOL_MANAGED, &mVB, 0));

// Write the vertex data to the vertex buffer.
VertexPos* v = 0;
HR(mVB->Lock(0, 0, (void**)&v, 0));

for(DWORD i = 0; i < mNumVertices; ++i)
    v[i] = verts[i];

HR(mVB->Unlock());


HR(gd3dDevice->CreateIndexBuffer(mNumTriangles*3*sizeof(WORD),
    D3DUSAGE_WRITEONLY, D3DFMT_INDEX16, D3DPOOL_MANAGED, &mIB, 0));

// Write the index data to the index buffer.
WORD* k = 0;
HR(mIB->Lock(0, 0, (void**)&k, 0));

for(DWORD i = 0; i < mNumTriangles*3; ++i)
    k[i] = (WORD)indices[i];

HR(mIB->Unlock());
```

8.5 **D3DX Geometric Objects**

Simple objects like cubes are easy to construct by hand. A grid can be easily computed procedurally (i.e., by a step-by-step procedure that tells the computer how to generate the geometry). Other geometric objects can also be computed procedurally, such as cylinders, spheres, and toruses, for which the D3DX library conveniently provides methods. Specifically, the D3DX library provides the following six mesh creation functions:

■   D3DXCreateBox

■   D3DXCreateSphere

■   D3DXCreateCylinder

- D3DXCreateTorus
- D3DXCreateTeapot
- D3DXCreatePolygon

All six of these functions are similar and utilize the ID3DXMesh interface, which we discuss in a later chapter. For now, we treat the interface as a *black box* (i.e., we use it without knowing how it works "under the hood"). For example, the D3DXCreateCylinder function is prototyped as follows:

```
HRESULT WINAPI D3DXCreateCylinder(LPDIRECT3DDEVICE9 pDevice,
    FLOAT Radius1, FLOAT Radius2, FLOAT Length, UINT Slices,
    UINT Stacks, LPD3DXMESH *ppMesh, LPD3DXBUFFER *ppAdjacency);
```

The first parameter is a pointer to the rendering device. Figure 8.8 describes parameters two through five.

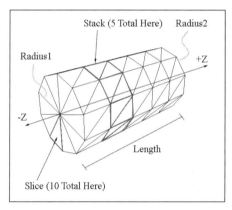

Figure 8.8: D3DXCreateCylinder parameters two through five.

Observe that the cylinder is built along the *z*-axis. The sixth parameter returns a pointer to an ID3DXMesh interface, which stores the cylinder geometry. We ignore the seventh parameter for now and specify null; adjacency info is discussed in a later chapter. Here is an example call:

```
ID3DXMesh* mCylinder;
HR(D3DXCreateCylinder(gd3dDevice, 1.0f, 1.0f,
    6.0f, 20, 20, &mCylinder, 0));
```

Remark: By setting one of the radii to zero, you can make a cone with this function.

To draw the cylinder, we write:

```
HR(mCylinder->DrawSubset(0));
```

Because ID3DXMesh objects are COM interfaces, we must release them when done:

```
ReleaseCOM(mCylinder);
```

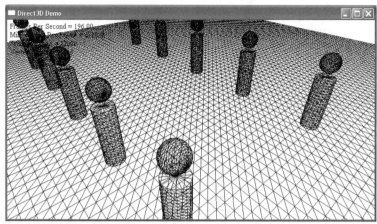

Figure 8.9: Screenshot of the Mesh demo.

Figure 8.9 shows a screenshot of the demo we are making, illustrating the
D3DXCreateCylinder and D3DXCreateSphere functions. The key code of this
demo (called MeshDemo) is contained in the methods MeshDemo::draw-
Cylinders and MeshDemo::drawSpheres. We'll explain MeshDemo::drawCylinders
here; MeshDemo::drawSpheres is essentially analogous.

```
void MeshDemo::drawCylinders()
{
      D3DXMATRIX T, R;

      D3DXMatrixRotationX(&R, D3DX_PI*0.5f);

      for(int z = -30; z <= 30; z+= 10)
      {
            D3DXMatrixTranslation(&T, -10.0f, 3.0f, (float)z);
            HR(mFX->SetMatrix(mhWVP, &(R*T*mView*mProj)));
            HR(mFX->CommitChanges());
            HR(mCylinder->DrawSubset(0));

            D3DXMatrixTranslation(&T, 10.0f, 3.0f, (float)z);
            HR(mFX->SetMatrix(mhWVP, &(R*T*mView*mProj)));
            HR(mFX->CommitChanges());
            HR(mCylinder->DrawSubset(0));
      }
}
```

The first thing we do is instantiate two matrices — a translation and a rotation matrix. We need a rotation matrix because the cylinders are built along
the z-axis in local space, and we want them to be aligned with the world
space's y-axis; therefore, we need to rotate the cylinders 90° about the
x-axis. Then we loop from $z = -30$ to $+30$ by increments of 10. For each
iteration, we draw a cylinder twice at position $(-10, 3, z)$ and $(+10, 3, z)$.
The cylinder is positioned to these locations by a translation matrix.

Observe that every time we change the matrix effect parameter (so the geometry is drawn with the correct matrix applied), we must call ID3DXEffect::CommitChanges, which updates the effect parameters based on ID3DXEffect::Set* calls.

8.6 **Summary**

- A *vertex shader* is a program executed on the graphics card's GPU (graphics processing unit) that operates on vertices. The responsibilities of a vertex shader include the world, view, and projection transformations; vertex lighting; and any other calculations that need to be done at the vertex level. Data computed at the vertex level can be interpolated and input into data at the pixel level.

- A *pixel shader* is a program executed on the graphics card's GPU that operates on pixel fragments (candidates that can become screen pixels if they pass various operations that can prevent a pixel from being written, such as the alpha test, stencil test, and depth buffer test). The primary responsibility of a pixel shader includes generating a fragment color based on interpolated vertex colors, texture data, pixel lighting, fog, and any other calculations that need to be done at the pixel level.

- A Direct3D *effect* encapsulates the code that describes how to render 3D geometry in a particular way. An effect consists of a *technique*, which consists of one or more *passes*. An effect may implement several techniques that all implement the same effect but in different ways. Each implementation will utilize the capabilities of a specific generation of hardware. Thus, the application can choose the technique that is most appropriate for the target hardware. Note that because an effect is typically written in an external file, it can be modified without having to recompile the application source code.

- A *technique* consists of one or more rendering passes. A *rendering pass* consists of the device states and shaders used to render the geometry for that particular pass. Multiple rendering passes are necessary because some effects require the same geometry to be rendered several times, each time with different device states and/or shaders, and then the result of each pass is combined to form the net technique. On a performance note, you should try to avoid multi-pass techniques if possible, as rendering the same geometry multiple times is obviously more expensive.

- Using the D3DXCreate* functions, we can create the geometry of more complex 3D objects such as spheres, cylinders, and teapots.

8.7 **Exercises**

1. Rewrite the Cube demo from Chapter 7 using the programmable pipe-line with *transform.fx*.

2. As you learn in the next chapter, we can represent the color red by the 4D color vector (1, 0, 0, 1). Modify the Triangle Grid demo so that the wireframe lines are drawn with red instead of black.

3. Use D3DXCreateCylinder to draw a cone; see Figure 8.10a.

4. Use D3DXCreateTeapot to draw a teapot; see Figure 8.10b. The prototype of this function is given by:

```
HRESULT WINAPI D3DXCreateTeapot(
    LPDIRECT3DDEVICE9 pDevice,
    LPD3DXMESH *ppMesh,
    LPD3DXBUFFER *ppAdjacency);
```

5. Use D3DXCreateTorus to draw a torus; see Figure 8.10c. The prototype of this function is given by:

```
HRESULT WINAPI D3DXCreateTorus(
    LPDIRECT3DDEVICE9 pDevice,
    FLOAT InnerRadius,
    FLOAT OuterRadius,
    UINT Sides,
    UINT Rings,
    LPD3DXMESH *ppMesh,
    LPD3DXBUFFER *ppAdjacency);
```

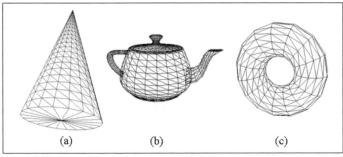

Figure 8.10: Output for exercises 3, 4, and 5.

Chapter 9

Color

In the last chapter, we rendered the objects in the scene using lines to form wireframe meshes. In this chapter, we learn how to render solid objects with color.

Objectives:

- To discover how colors are described in Direct3D.
- To find out what changes need to be made to our vertex and pixel shaders to support color.
- To continue to strengthen our understanding of how vertex and pixel shaders work.
- To learn how to animate and color geometry in a vertex shader.

9.1 Color Representation

Figure 9.1 shows a common color dialog box you can make with the Win32 API function ChooseColor. As you can see, one way to specify a color is by specifying its red, green, and blue color components (RGB triplet); the additive mixing of these three components determines the final color. Each of these components can be in a range 0 to 255 (the range an 8-bit byte can store), and thus, with this setup, $256 \times 256 \times 256 = 16,777,216$ distinct colors can be represented. We can think of the colors red, green, and blue as our "basis" colors from which we can express all other colors as a linear combination.

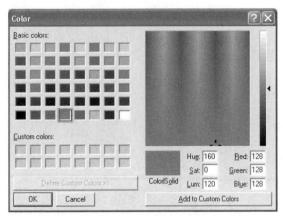

Figure 9.1: Typical color chooser dialog box.

Tip: If you are not experienced with describing colors as RGB values, then you might want to spend some time in your favorite 2D computer paint program experimenting with a dialog like Figure 9.1 to build an intuition of the colors formed by different RGB values.

9.1.1 **D3DCOLOR**

We use two different types of structures to hold the RGB data. The first is the D3DCOLOR type, which is actually typedefed as a DWORD and is 32 bits. The bits in the D3DCOLOR type are divided into four 8-bit sections, where each section stores the intensity of a color component. Figure 9.2 shows the distribution.

Figure 9.2: A 32-bit color, where a byte is allocated for each color component red, green, and blue. A fourth byte is allocated for the alpha component.

Because each ARGB ("A" is included now since there is also an alpha) color component gets a byte of memory, the intensity of the color can range from 0 to 255. For an arbitrary integer n in the range 0 to 255, we have $x = n/255 \cdot 100\%$ in the range from 0% to 100%. Thus, n implies a percentage of intensity of the color component from 0% (black) to 100% (maximum brightness of the color component). For example, suppose n represents the red color component; a value of $n = 64$, $n = 128$, and $n = 191$ means roughly 25%, 50%, and 75% intensity of red, respectively.

Note: Do not worry about the alpha component now; it is used for alpha blending, which is the topic of Chapter 12. For now just set it to 255 (0xff).

Specifying each component and then inserting it into the proper position in the D3DCOLOR type will require some bit operations or familiarity with hex (e.g., pure green can be specified by 0xff00ff00). Direct3D provides a macro called D3DCOLOR_ARGB, which provides a simpler interface for setting a color. There is one parameter for each color component and the alpha component. Each parameter must be in the range 0 to 255 and is used like so:

```
D3DCOLOR brightRed = D3DCOLOR_ARGB(255, 255, 0, 0);
D3DCOLOR someColor = D3DCOLOR_ARGB(255, 144, 87, 201);
```

Alternatively, we can use the D3DCOLOR_XRGB macro, which is similar but does not take the alpha parameter; instead it sets the alpha to 0xff (255) automatically:

```
#define D3DCOLOR_XRGB(r,g,b) D3DCOLOR_ARGB(0xff,r,g,b)
```

9.1.2 **D3DCOLORVALUE**

Another way to store a color in Direct3D is with the D3DCOLORVALUE structure. With this structure, we use a floating-point value to measure the intensity of each component. The range measures from 0 to 1 — 0 being no intensity and 1 being full intensity. Essentially, we are specifying the color component intensity percent directly; that is, $[0, 1] \cdot 100\% = [0\%, 100\%]$. For example, suppose x represents the red color component; a value of $x = 0.25$, $x = 0.5$, and $x = 0.75$ means 25%, 50%, and 75% intensity of red, respectively.

Also note that with this color representation, we can store more colors since we are no longer limited to 256 step sizes per color component. Of course, the D3DCOLORVALUE structure uses 128 bits versus the D3DCOLOR value's 32 bits.

```
typedef struct _D3DCOLORVALUE {
    float r; // the red component, range 0.0-1.0
    float g; // the green component, range 0.0-1.0
    float b; // the blue component, range 0.0-1.0
    float a; // the alpha component, range 0.0-1.0
} D3DCOLORVALUE;
```

9.1.3 **D3DXCOLOR**

Alternatively, we can use the D3DXCOLOR structure, which contains the same data members as D3DCOLORVALUE but provides useful constructors and overloaded operators, making color manipulations easy. In addition, because they contain the same data members, we can cast back and forth between the two. D3DXCOLOR is defined as:

```
typedef struct D3DXCOLOR
{
#ifdef __cplusplus
public:
    D3DXCOLOR() {}
    D3DXCOLOR( DWORD argb );
    D3DXCOLOR( CONST FLOAT * );
    D3DXCOLOR( CONST D3DXFLOAT16 * );
    D3DXCOLOR( CONST D3DCOLORVALUE& );
    D3DXCOLOR( FLOAT r, FLOAT g, FLOAT b, FLOAT a );

    // casting
    operator DWORD () const;

    operator FLOAT* ();
    operator CONST FLOAT* () const;

    operator D3DCOLORVALUE* ();
    operator CONST D3DCOLORVALUE* () const;

    operator D3DCOLORVALUE& ();
    operator CONST D3DCOLORVALUE& () const;

    // assignment operators
    D3DXCOLOR& operator += ( CONST D3DXCOLOR& );
    D3DXCOLOR& operator -= ( CONST D3DXCOLOR& );
    D3DXCOLOR& operator *= ( FLOAT );
    D3DXCOLOR& operator /= ( FLOAT );

    // unary operators
    D3DXCOLOR operator + () const;
    D3DXCOLOR operator - () const;

    // binary operators
    D3DXCOLOR operator + ( CONST D3DXCOLOR& ) const;
    D3DXCOLOR operator - ( CONST D3DXCOLOR& ) const;
    D3DXCOLOR operator * ( FLOAT ) const;
    D3DXCOLOR operator / ( FLOAT ) const;

    friend D3DXCOLOR operator * (FLOAT, CONST D3DXCOLOR& );

    BOOL operator == ( CONST D3DXCOLOR& ) const;
    BOOL operator != ( CONST D3DXCOLOR& ) const;

#endif //__cplusplus
    FLOAT r, g, b, a;
} D3DXCOLOR, *LPD3DXCOLOR;
```

Observe that both the D3DCOLORVALUE and the D3DXCOLOR structures have four floating-point components. This leads to the common notation of treating a color as a 4D vector (r, g, b, a). Color vectors are added, subtracted, and scaled just like regular vectors. On the other hand, dot and cross products do *not* make sense for color vectors, but component-wise multiplication does make sense for colors. The D3DX library provides the D3DXColorModulate function for performing component-wise multiplication, which is prototyped as:

```
D3DXCOLOR* D3DXColorModulate(
        D3DXCOLOR* pOut,       // Returns (c₁,c₂,c₃,c₄)⊗(k₁,k₂,k₃,k₄)
        CONST D3DXCOLOR* pC1,  // (c₁,c₂,c₃,c₄)
        CONST D3DXCOLOR* pC2); // (k₁,k₂,k₃,k₄)
```

The symbol $\otimes$ denotes component-wise multiplication and it is defined as: $(c_1, c_2, c_3, c_4) \otimes (k_1, k_2, k_3, k_4) = (c_1 k_1, c_2 k_2, c_3 k_3, c_4 k_4)$.

9.2 Vertex Colors

Recall that our vertex structures are flexible and we can include additional data; in particular, we can couple a color to each vertex. Then, in the rasterization stage of the rendering pipeline, these vertex colors are interpolated across the face of the triangle to generate pixel colors for the interior and boundary of the triangle. Thus, to add color, all we need to do is modify our vertex structure and the vertex and pixel shader slightly.

Our new vertex structure, and its corresponding vertex declaration, looks like this:

```
struct VertexCol
{
    VertexCol():pos(0.0f, 0.0f, 0.0f),col(0x00000000){}
    VertexCol(float x, float y, float z, D3DCOLOR c)
            :pos(x,y,z), col(c){}
    VertexCol(const D3DXVECTOR3& v, D3DCOLOR c):pos(v),col(c){}

    D3DXVECTOR3 pos;
    D3DCOLOR    col;
    static IDirect3DVertexDeclaration9* Decl;
};

D3DVERTEXELEMENT9 VertexColElements[] =
{
{0, 0, D3DDECLTYPE_FLOAT3, D3DDECLMETHOD_DEFAULT,
                    D3DDECLUSAGE_POSITION, 0},
{0, 12, D3DDECLTYPE_D3DCOLOR, D3DDECLMETHOD_DEFAULT,
                    D3DDECLUSAGE_COLOR, 0},
D3DDECL_END()
};
HR(gd3dDevice->CreateVertexDeclaration(VertexColElements,
                        &VertexCol::Decl));
```

The new properties are in bold, and we have also updated *Vertex.h/.cpp*.

Now our vertices have an extra color component; therefore, our vertex shader has an extra input parameter:

```
uniform extern float4x4 gWVP;
```

```
struct OutputVS
{
    float4 posH  : POSITION0;
    float4 color : COLOR0;
};
OutputVS ColorVS(float3 posL : POSITION0, float4 c : COLOR0)
{
    // Zero out our output.
    OutputVS outVS = (OutputVS)0;

    // Transform to homogeneous clip space.
    outVS.posH = mul(float4(posL, 1.0f), gWVP);

    // Just pass the vertex color into the pixel shader.
    outVS.color = c;

    // Done--return the output.
    return outVS;
}
```

Note that even though we use a D3DCOLOR value in our vertex structure, it is automatically converted to a D3DXCOLOR type format (i.e., a float4 4D color vector) for the vertex shader. Furthermore, observe that the vertex shader does not do anything with the color — it merely passes it on to an output color register, where it will be used for interpolation during rasterization (§6.4.8).

The new pixel shader is trivial — we set the color of the pixel fragment to be the interpolated input color, so no real work needs to be done.

```
float4 ColorPS(float4 c : COLOR0) : COLOR
{
    return c;
}
```

Finally, the technique looks like this:

```
technique ColorTech
{
    pass P0
    {
        // Specify the vertex and pixel shader associated
        // with this pass.
        vertexShader = compile vs_2_0 ColorVS();
        pixelShader  = compile ps_2_0 ColorPS();
    }
}
```

Note: The .fx file all this is in is called *color.fx*.

9.3 **Color Cube Demo**

Figure 9.3 shows a screenshot for this demo, which is a colored cube. The source code for this demo is almost the same as the Cube demo from Chapter 7, except we use *color.fx* and the color vertex structure.

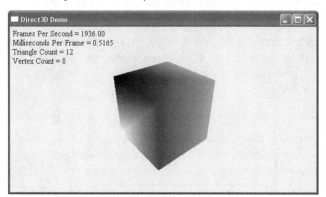

Figure 9.3: Screenshot of the Color Cube demo.

First we define the following constants:

```
const D3DCOLOR WHITE   = D3DCOLOR_XRGB(255, 255, 255); // 0xffffffff
const D3DCOLOR BLACK   = D3DCOLOR_XRGB(0, 0, 0);       // 0xff000000
const D3DCOLOR RED     = D3DCOLOR_XRGB(255, 0, 0);     // 0xffff0000
const D3DCOLOR GREEN   = D3DCOLOR_XRGB(0, 255, 0);     // 0xff00ff00
const D3DCOLOR BLUE    = D3DCOLOR_XRGB(0, 0, 255);     // 0xff0000ff
const D3DCOLOR YELLOW  = D3DCOLOR_XRGB(255, 255, 0);   // 0xffffff00
const D3DCOLOR CYAN    = D3DCOLOR_XRGB(0, 255, 255);   // 0xff00ffff
const D3DCOLOR MAGENTA = D3DCOLOR_XRGB(255, 0, 255);   // 0xffff00ff
```

Observe that we have commented the hexadecimal representation of the D3DCOLORs above; if you are not already, it is a good idea to become comfortable with the hexadecimal and binary number systems.

When we construct the cube's vertices, we just pass in one of the above colors as the color component for each vertex:

```
VertexCol* v = 0;
HR(mVB->Lock(0, 0, (void**)&v, 0));

v[0] = VertexCol(-1.0f, -1.0f, -1.0f, WHITE);
v[1] = VertexCol(-1.0f,  1.0f, -1.0f, BLACK);
v[2] = VertexCol( 1.0f,  1.0f, -1.0f, RED);
v[3] = VertexCol( 1.0f, -1.0f, -1.0f, GREEN);
v[4] = VertexCol(-1.0f, -1.0f,  1.0f, BLUE);
v[5] = VertexCol(-1.0f,  1.0f,  1.0f, YELLOW);
v[6] = VertexCol( 1.0f,  1.0f,  1.0f, CYAN);
v[7] = VertexCol( 1.0f, -1.0f,  1.0f, MAGENTA);

HR(mVB->Unlock());
```

Then, other than small changes, like passing a different .fx filename and specifying a different technique name, the code is the same as the Cube demo from Chapter 7.

9.4 **Digression: Traveling Sine Waves**

The next demo utilizes sine waves and so we go over the basics of them here. (We'll keep it simple here and refer you to any introductory physics textbook for a more detailed look at traveling waves; see, for example, [Halliday01].) A general sine wave may be described by the following function (see Figure 9.4):

$$y = a \cdot \sin(kx)$$

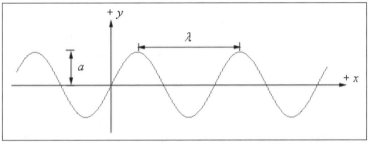

Figure 9.4: The amplitude *a* is the maximum displacement of the wave from the origin on the positive *y*-axis. The wavelength *λ* is the distance from peak to peak of the wave.

The constant *a* is called the *amplitude* of the wave and it essentially scales the sine function. (Recall that $\sin(x)$ evaluates to a real number in the range $[-1, 1]$; thus, $a \cdot \sin(x)$ evaluates to a real number in the range $[-a, a]$, and we have scaled the range of the sine function.)

The constant *k* is called the *angular wave number* and it implies the wavelength *λ* of the wave. Recall that $\sin(x)$ repeats every multiple of 2π radians; thus, by default, it has a wavelength of 2π. We like to control the wavelength, just as we like to control the amplitude to customize our sine wave. To do this, we introduce the angular wave number *k*, which can be thought of as a scaling factor for *x*. That is, for $0 \le k < 1$, *k* scales *x* down, and thus it takes a larger *x* for *kx* to reach a multiple of 2π and repeat, hence lengthening the wavelength (i.e., it takes a longer distance of *x* for the wave to repeat itself — we have lengthened the wavelength). On the other hand, for $1 < k$, *k* scales *x* up, and thus it takes a smaller *x* for *kx* to reach a multiple of 2π and repeat, hence shortening the wavelength (i.e., it takes a shorter distance of *x* for the wave to repeat itself — we have shortened the wavelength). Figure 9.5 illustrates these results.

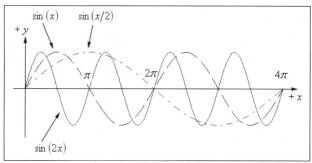

Figure 9.5: For sin(2x), $k = 2$ and the wavelength is π; for sin(x), $k = 1$ and the wavelength is 2π; for sin(x/2), $k = 1/2$ and the wavelength is 4π.

So far, we can control the amplitude and wavelength of our wave, but it just sits there as a static wave. What we want to do is oscillate the points on the wave up and down with respect to time to give a traveling waveform motion. To do this, we introduce a new time variable t: $y = a \cdot \sin(kx - t)$. (The negative sign makes the waveform move in the direction of the $+x$-axis, whereas a plus sign would make the waveform move in the direction of the $-x$-axis.) Note that t does not stand still — it represents the time elapsed, so it is increasing over time. For a *fixed* x_0, the point $(x_0, y) = (x_0, a \cdot \sin(kx_0 - t))$ moves up and down, and makes a complete oscillation every 2π seconds. As with the wavelength, we want to control how long it takes for a point on the wave to move through a complete oscillation. To do this, we introduce the *angular frequency* ω:

$$y = a \cdot \sin(kx - \omega t)$$

The angular frequency (ω) works the same way as the angular wave number (k), but it controls how fast/slow it takes an arbitrary point on the wave to make one oscillation.

Finally, at $t = 0$ the waveform looks like $y = a \cdot \sin(kx)$. We might not always want the initial waveform to look like this; specifically, we may want the wave to be initially shifted. Thus, we add a phase shift parameter ϕ so that we can control the initial waveform:

$$y = a \cdot \sin\left(kx - \omega t + \phi\right)$$

Thus, at $t = 0$ the waveform looks like $y = a \cdot \sin(kx + \phi)$.

9.4.1 **Summing Waves**

Suppose that you want to use sine waves to loosely model the motion of water waves. If you observe water waves, you will notice large, broad waves that move up and down slowly compared to small, sharp choppy waves that move up and down quickly. So how do we capture both the broad waves and the choppy waves? Well, we can make several sine waves, some to model broad waves and some to model choppy waves, and then we can sum the waves to produce a net wave; see Figure 9.6.

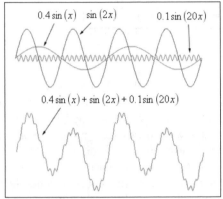

Figure 9.6: Combining different waves together to produce a net wave.

9.4.2 **Circular Waves**

Suppose that we want waves to generate circular waves originating from a source point $\vec{s}$. That is, all points on the circle centered about $\vec{s}$ with radius r have the same y-coordinate, as shown in Figure 9.7. For an arbitrary point $\vec{p}=(p_x, 0, p_z)$ on the xz-plane, the radius of the circle on which $\vec{p}$ lies is given by $r=\|\vec{s}-\vec{p}\|$ (or just $r=\sqrt{p_x^2+p_z^2}$ if $\vec{s}$ is the origin). Now, the vertical displacement of all points on the circle centered about $\vec{s}$ with radius r is given by $y = a \cdot \sin(kr - \omega t + \phi)$.

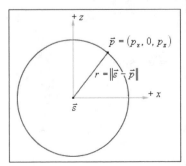

Figure 9.7: To form circular waves, we need all points on a circle with center point $\vec{s}$ and radius r to have the same height value. Thus, we compute the height of a point as a function of the radius of the circle on which the point lies; that is, $y=a\cdot\sin(kr-\omega t+\phi)$. Consequently, because all points on the circle have the same radius, they also have the same height, which is what we want.

9.4.3 **Directional Waves**

Suppose that we want waves to move in the direction of a unit vector $\vec{u}=(u_x,0,u_z)$ on the xz-plane. In other words, we want *wavefronts* to move in the $\vec{u}$ direction, where, in this particular case, a wavefront is a line orthogonal to $\vec{u}$ such that all the points on the line have the same y-coordinate (see Figure 9.8). To describe this mathematically, observe that all points on a wavefront have the same projection onto $\vec{u}$. Thus, the vertical displacement of a point can be given by $y = a \cdot \sin(kx - \omega t + \phi)$, where $x=\vec{u}\cdot\vec{p}$. In this way, all points on the same wavefront will have the same y-coordinate because they will have the same projection $x=\vec{u}\cdot\vec{p}$.

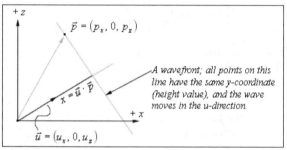

Figure 9.8: Wavefronts; projecting points onto $\vec{u}$.

9.5 **Colored Waves Demo**

We now examine a demo that employs a less trivial vertex shader. The program generates circular waves by summing sine waves together, and it generates a color for each vertex based on the vertical displacement of the vertex (i.e., distance of the y-coordinate from 0). Figure 9.9 shows a screenshot of the animation.

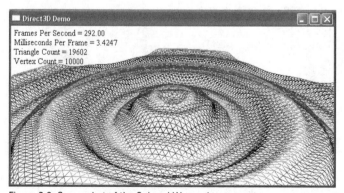

Figure 9.9: Screenshot of the Colored Waves demo.

The vertex shader is given below:

```
OutputVS ColorVS(float3 posL : POSITION0)
{
    // Zero out our output.
    OutputVS outVS = (OutputVS)0;

    // Get the height of the vertex--the height is given by
    // summing sine waves.
    posL.y = SumOfRadialSineWaves(posL.x, posL.z);

    // Generate the vertex color based on its height.
    outVS.color = GetColorFromHeight(posL.y);

    // Transform to homogeneous clip space.
    outVS.posH = mul(float4(posL, 1.0f), gWVP);

    // Done--return the output.
    return outVS;
}
```

We have a couple of quick comments before analyzing this vertex shader. First, this shader expects the input vertices to be on a grid on the *xz*-plane, as it overwrites the input *y*-coordinate based on the position of the vertex and current time. Overwriting the *y*-coordinate in this way for an arbitrary mesh would probably not make sense. Second, observe that the shader does not input a color component; we input only a vertex position and the vertex shader will generate a color based on the vertical displacement of the vertex.

As said, this vertex shader does two things: It animates the vertices based on moving circular waves and it generates a color for each vertex based on the vertical displacement of the vertex. These two tasks are encapsulated in the SumOfRadialSineWaves and GetColorFromHeight functions, respectively. (Observe then that we can write our own functions in an effect file that can be invoked in a vertex/pixel shader.) The SumOfRadialSineWaves function is implemented as follows:

```
// Amplitudes
static float a[2] = {0.8f, 0.2f};

// Angular wave numbers.
static float k[2] = {1.0, 8.0f};

// Angular frequency.
static float w[2] = {1.0f, 8.0f};

// Phase shifts.
static float p[2] = {0.0f, 1.0f};

float SumOfRadialSineWaves(float x, float z)
```

```
{
    // Distance of vertex from source of waves (which we set
    // as the origin of the local space).
    float d = sqrt(x*x + z*z);

    // Sum the waves.
    float sum = 0.0f;
    for(int i = 0; i < 2; ++i)
        sum += a[i]*sin(k[i]*d - gTime*w[i] + p[i]);

    return sum;
}
```

Essentially, all this code does is sum two different kinds of waves in order to get a general broad wave motion along with some choppy chaotic wave motion (§9.4). You can experiment with the amplitude, angular wave number, angular frequency, and phase shifts to see the different results. (The static variables just mean the variables are local to the effect and not external; we put them outside the function because they do not need to be instantiated per-vertex.) The variable gTime is an effect parameter declared like so:

```
uniform extern float gTime;
```

In the application, we update this variable every frame based on the time that has elapsed:

```
mTime += dt;
HR(mFX->SetFloat(mhTime, mTime));
```

In the application constructor, the variable mTime is set to zero. In this way, it stores the time elapsed, in units of seconds, since the start of the program. Note that we do not really need to worry about time elapsing such that mTime accumulates to a value it cannot store; we can represent days in units of seconds with a float without any problem.

Now a few comments on the HLSL code. Observe that for-loops in the HLSL have the same syntax as in C++. Also observe that array syntax is the same as in C++. To compute the sine of an angle in radians, we use the HLSL intrinsic sin function, and to compute the square root of a number in the HLSL we use the intrinsic sqrt function.

The GetColorFromHeight function is defined below:

```
float4 GetColorFromHeight(float y)
{
    if( abs(y) <= 0.2f )        // black
        return float4(0.0f, 0.0f, 0.0f, 1.0f);
    else if(abs(y) <= 0.4f )       // blue
        return float4(0.0f, 0.0f, 1.0f, 1.0f);
    else if(abs(y) <= 0.6f )       // green
        return float4(0.0f, 1.0f, 0.0f, 1.0f);
    else if(abs(y) <= 0.8f )       // red
        return float4(1.0f, 0.0f, 0.0f, 1.0f);
```

```
        else                        // yellow
            return float4(1.0f, 1.0f, 0.0f, 1.0f);
    }
```

This function checks the displacement of the y-coordinate from 0, and returns a color based on the range in which that height lies. In this way, we procedurally generate a color for the vertex in the vertex shader program — the color was not an input into the vertex shader! Also observe that conditional statements (i.e., if/else statements) in the HLSL are just like the conditional statements in C++, and to compute the absolute value, we use the HLSL intrinsic abs function.

9.6 Summary

- Colors are described by specifying an intensity of red, green, and blue. The additive mixing of these three colors at different intensities allows us to describe millions of colors. In Direct3D, we can use the D3DCOLOR, D3DCOLORVALUE, or D3DXCOLOR type to describe a color in code.
- We sometimes treat a color as a 4D vector (r, g, b, a). Color vectors are added, subtracted, and scaled just like regular vectors. On the other hand, dot and cross products do *not* make sense for color vectors, but component-wise multiplication does make sense for colors. The symbol $\otimes$ denotes component-wise multiplication and it is defined as:
  $(c_1, c_2, c_3, c_4) \otimes (k_1, k_2, k_3, k_4) = (c_1 k_1, c_2 k_2, c_3 k_3, c_4 k_4).$
- We specify a color for each vertex and then Direct3D. During the rasterization process, vertex colors are interpolated across the face of a primitive. These interpolated color values serve as input for the pixel shader.

9.7 Exercises

1. Let $\vec{w} = (0.5, 0.5, 0.5, 1)$, $\vec{u} = (0.0, 0.8, 0.3, 1)$, and $\vec{v} = (0.3, 0.3, 0.7, 1)$ be color vectors. Compute the following color operations and clamp any component to the [0, 1] range if it goes outside that range. Convert the answer to a D3DCOLOR value, then use a paint program to see the color of the result of the operation.

    a. $2\vec{w}, \frac{1}{2}\vec{w}, \frac{3}{2}\vec{w}$

    b. $0\vec{u}, \frac{1}{2}\vec{u}, 1\vec{u}$

    c. $0\vec{v}, \frac{1}{2}\vec{v}, 1\vec{v}$

    d. $\vec{u} \otimes \vec{w}, \vec{v} \otimes \vec{w}, \vec{u} \otimes 2\vec{w}, \vec{v} \otimes 2\vec{w}$

    e. $\vec{u} + \vec{v}, \vec{v} + \vec{w}$

    f. $\vec{u} - \vec{v}, \vec{v} - \vec{w}$

2. Modify the Color Cube demo by enabling the render state ShadeMode = Flat in the .fx file. Explain your results. Note that you can also change the shade mode render state in the C++ application by setting the D3DRS_SHADEMODE render state:

    gd3dDevice->SetRenderState(D3DRS_SHADEMODE, D3DSHADE_FLAT);

    The default shade mode is called Gouraud shading; it can be explicitly set by ShadeMode = Gouraud in the .fx file, or by:

    gd3dDevice->SetRenderState(D3DRS_SHADEMODE, D3DSHADE_GOURAUD);

3. Redo exercises 3 and 4 from Chapter 7, but this time add color to the vertices as we did in the Color Cube demo.

4. Instead of using circular waves, rewrite the Color Wave demo using directional waves; your output should look like Figure 9.10.

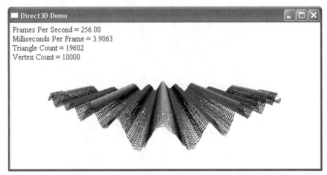

Figure 9.10: Output for exercise 4.

Chapter 10

Lighting

We begin this chapter by reminding you of a figure we saw earlier, which we reproduce here in Figure 10.1.

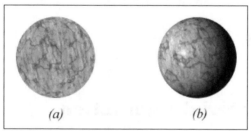

(a)   *(b)*

Figure 10.1: (a) An unlit sphere looks 2D. (b) A lit sphere looks 3D.

On the left, we have an unlit sphere, and on the right, we have a lit sphere. As you can see, the sphere on the left looks rather flat — maybe it is not even a sphere at all but just a textured 2D circle! On the other hand, the sphere on the right does look 3D — the lighting and shading aid in our perception of the solid form and volume of the object. In fact, our visual perception of the world depends on light and its interaction with materials, and consequently, much of the problem of generating photorealistic scenes has to do with physically accurate lighting models.

Of course, in general, the more accurate the model, the more computationally expensive it is; thus a balance must be reached between realism and speed. For example, 3D special FX scenes for films can be much more complex and utilize more realistic lighting models than games because the frames for a film are pre-rendered; that is, because the frames are pre-rendered and not computed at run time, hours or days can be allocated to processing a frame. Games, on the other hand, are real-time applications, and therefore, the frames need to be drawn at a rate of at least 30 frames per second.

Note that the lighting model explained and implemented in this book is largely based on the one described in [Möller02]. Note that that is a good reference for additional theoretical info.

Objectives:

■   To gain a basic understanding of the interactions between lights and materials.

■   To understand the differences between local illumination and global illumination.

■   To find out how we can mathematically describe the direction a point on a surface is "facing" so that we can determine the angle at which incoming light strikes the surface.

■   To learn how to correctly transform normal vectors.

■   To be able to distinguish between ambient, diffuse, and specular light.

■   To learn how to implement directional lights, point lights, and spotlights.

■   To understand how to vary light intensity as a function of depth by controlling attenuation parameters.

■   To learn how to implement per-pixel lighting in a pixel shader.

10.1 **Light and Material Interaction**

When using lighting, we no longer specify vertex colors ourselves; rather, we specify materials and lights, and then apply a lighting equation, which computes the vertex colors for us based on light/material interaction. (Colors generated by lighting tend to be more realistic than those that are manually specified by vertex colors.)

Materials can be thought of as the properties that determine how light interacts with an object. For example, the colors of light an object reflects and absorbs, and also the reflectivity, transparency, and shininess are all parameters that make up the material of the object. In this chapter, however, we only concern ourselves with the colors of light the object reflects and absorbs, and the object's shininess.

We model lights by an additive mixture of red, green, and blue light (RGB); in this way, we can simulate many light colors. When light travels outward from a source and collides with an object, some of that light may be absorbed and some may be reflected (for transparent objects, such as glass, some of the light passes through the medium, but we do not consider transparency here). The reflected light now travels along its new path and may strike other objects where some light is again absorbed and reflected. A light ray may strike many objects before it is fully absorbed. Presumably, some light rays eventually travel into the eye (see Figure 10.2) and strike the light receptor cells (named cones and rods) on the retina.

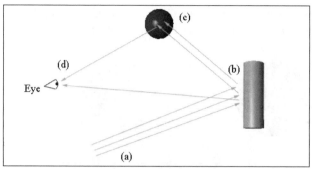

Figure 10.2: (a) Flux of incoming white light. (b) The light strikes the cylinder and some rays are absorbed and other rays are scatter toward the eye and sphere. (c) The light reflecting off the cylinder toward the sphere is absorbed or reflected again and travels into the eye. (d) The eye receives incoming light that determines what the eye "sees."

According to the *trichromatic* theory (see [Santrock03]), the retina contains three kinds of light receptors, each of which is sensitive to red, green, or blue light (with some overlap). The incoming light stimulates its corresponding light receptors to varying intensities based on the strength of the light. As the light receptors are stimulated (or not), neural impulses are sent down the optic nerve toward the brain, where the brain generates an image based on the stimulus of the light receptors. (Of course, if you close/cover your eyes, the receptor cells receive no stimulus and the brain registers this as black.)

For example, consider Figure 10.2 again. Suppose that the material of the cylinder reflects 75% red light and 75% green light, and absorbs the rest; and that the sphere reflects 25% red light and absorbs the rest. Also suppose that pure white light is being emitted from the light source. As the light rays strike the cylinder, all the blue light is absorbed and only 75% of the red and green light is reflected (i.e., a medium-high intensity yellow). This light is then scattered — some of it travels into the eye and some of it travels toward the sphere. The part that travels into the eye primarily stimulates the red and green cone cells to a semi-high degree; hence, the viewer sees the cylinder as a semi-bright shade of yellow. Now, the other light rays travel toward the sphere and strike it. The sphere reflects 25% red light and absorbs the rest; thus, the diluted incoming red light (medium-high intensity red) is diluted further and reflected, and all of the incoming green light is absorbed. This remaining red light then travels into the eye and primarily stimulates the red cone cells to a low degree. Thus, the viewer sees the sphere as a dark shade of red.

The lighting models we adopt in this book (and that most real-time applications use) are called *local illumination models*. With a local model, each object is lit independently of another object, and only the light directly emitted from light sources is taken into account in the lighting process (i.e., light that has bounced off other scene objects to strike the object currently being lit is ignored). Figure 10.3 shows a consequence of this model.

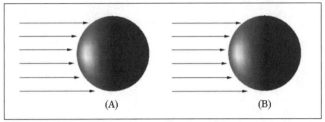

Figure 10.3: Here we have light coming from the left. Physically, sphere (a) should block the light so that sphere (b) receives no light (i.e., sphere (b) is in the shadow of sphere (a)). However, in a local illumination model, each object (more precisely, each vertex) is lit independently, and other objects are not taken into consideration. Thus, sphere (b) is lit exactly like sphere (a) as if sphere (a) was not there.

On the other hand, *global illumination models* light objects by taking into consideration not only the light directly emitted from light sources but also the indirect light that has bounced off other objects in the scene. These are called global illumination models because they take everything in the global scene into consideration when lighting an object. Global illumination models are generally prohibitively expensive for real-time games (but come very close to generating photorealistic scenes).

10.2 **Diffuse Lighting**

In this section, we illustrate a number of concepts using a simple directional light (Figure 10.4). (In later sections we introduce other types of lights.) A *directional light*, or parallel light, approximates a light source that is very far away. Consequently, we can approximate all incoming light rays as parallel to each other. The common example of a real directional light source is the sun (see Figure 10.5).

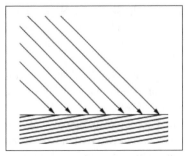

Figure 10.4: With a directional light, the light rays are parallel to each other.

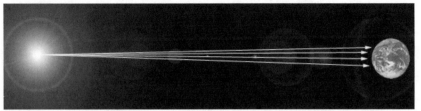

Figure 10.5: The figure is not drawn to scale, but if you selected a small surface area on the Earth, the light rays striking that area are approximately parallel.

10.2.1 Normal Vectors

A *face normal* is a unit vector that describes the direction a polygon is facing (i.e., it is orthogonal to all points on the polygon), as shown in Figure 10.6a. A *vertex normal* is a unit vector that is orthogonal to the tangent plane of a surface at a vertex, as shown in Figure 10.6b. Observe that vertex normals determine the direction a vertex on a surface is facing. For lighting calculations, we need to specify vertex normals so that we can determine the angle at which light strikes a vertex.

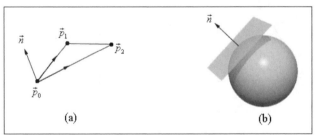

Figure 10.6: (a) The face normal is perpendicular to all points on the face, and can be found by finding two linearly independent vectors on the face and then taking the cross product. (b) The vertex normal is the vector that is perpendicular to all points on the vertex's tangent plane.

To find the face normal of a triangle $\Delta \vec{p}_0 \, \vec{p}_1 \, \vec{p}_2$, we first compute two vectors that lie on the triangle's edges:

$$\vec{u} = \vec{p}_1 - \vec{p}_0$$
$$\vec{v} = \vec{p}_2 - \vec{p}_0$$

Then the face normal is:

$$\vec{n} = (\vec{u} \times \vec{v}) / \|\vec{u} \times \vec{v}\|$$

The following function computes the face normal of a triangle from three vertex points of the triangle. Note that this procedure assumes that the vertices are specified in a clockwise winding order. If they are not, the normal will point in the opposite direction.

```
void ComputeNormal(D3DXVECTOR3* p0,
                   D3DXVECTOR3* p1,
                   D3DXVECTOR3* p2,
                   D3DXVECTOR3* out)
{
    D3DXVECTOR3 u = *p1 - *p0;
    D3DXVECTOR3 v = *p2 - *p0;

    D3DXVec3Cross(out, &u, &v);
    D3DXVec3Normalize(out, out);
}
```

For a differentiable surface, we can use calculus to find the normals of points on the surface. Unfortunately, a triangle mesh is not differentiable. The technique that is generally applied to triangle meshes is called *vertex normal averaging*. Figure 10.7 illustrates the idea.

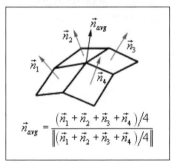

Figure 10.7: The middle vertex is shared by the neighboring four polygons, so we approximate the middle vertex normal by averaging the four polygon face normals.

Essentially, for each vertex, we compute the face normals of the polygons adjacent to the vertex. For example, in Figure 10.7, four polygons share the middle vertex v; thus, the vertex normal for v is given by:

$$\vec{n}_{avg} = \frac{\left(\vec{n}_1 + \vec{n}_2 + \vec{n}_3 + \vec{n}_4\right)/4}{\left\|\left(\vec{n}_1 + \vec{n}_2 + \vec{n}_3 + \vec{n}_4\right)/4\right\|}$$

10.2.1.1 *Transforming Normal Vectors*

Care must be taken when applying nonuniform scaling transformations or shear transformations to normals. Figure 10.8 illustrates the classic problem.

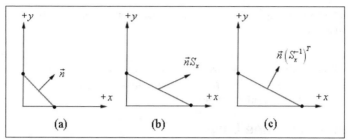

Figure 10.8: (a) Surface normal before transformation. (b) After scaling by 2 units on the *x*-axis the vector is no longer normal to the surface. (c) Surface normal correctly transformed by the inverse-transpose of the scaling transformation.

In other words, the vector is scaled as the transformation dictates, but it is no longer normal to the surface. Thus, given a transformation matrix A that transforms points and vectors (non-normal vectors), we want to find a transformation matrix B that correctly transforms normals. How do we do this? First, note that A transforms tangent vectors correctly since it can be viewed as the difference of two points: $\vec{u}A=(\vec{v}_1-\vec{v}_0)A=\vec{v}_1 A-\vec{v}_0 A$ (i.e., the transformed tangent vector is the difference of the transformed points). Now, let us first start with something we know: We know that the normal $\vec{n}$ vector is perpendicular to the tangent vector $\vec{u}$ (i.e., $\vec{u}\cdot\vec{n}=0$):

$\vec{u}\cdot\vec{n}=0$	Tangent vector perpendicular to normal vector
$\vec{u}(\vec{n})^T=0$	Rewriting the dot product as a matrix multiplication
$\vec{u}(AA^{-1})(\vec{n})^T=0$	Inserting the identity matrix $AA^{-1}=I$
$(\vec{u}A)(A^{-1}(\vec{n})^T)=0$	Associative property
$(\vec{u}A)(\vec{n}(A^{-1})^T)^T=0$	Transpose of a matrix product
$(\vec{u}A)\cdot(\vec{n}(A^{-1})^T)=0$	Rewriting as a dot product
$(\vec{u}A)\cdot(\vec{n}B)=0$	Transformed tangent vector perpendicular to transformed normal vector

That is to say, $B=(A^{-1})^T$ (the inverse-transpose of A) does the job in transforming normal vectors so that they are perpendicular to its associated transformed tangent vector.

Note that if the matrix is orthogonal (i.e., $A^T=A^{-1}$), then $B=(A^{-1})^T=(A^T)^T=A$; that is, we do not need to compute the inverse-transpose, since A does the job in this case. In summary, when transforming a normal vector by a nonuniform or shear transformation, use the inverse-transpose.

━━━━━━━━━━━━━━━━

Note: Even with the inverse-transpose transformation, normal vectors may lose their unit length; thus, they may need to be renormalized after the transformation.

10.2.2 **Lambert's Cosine Law**

Now, obviously the light that strikes a surface point head-on is more intense than light that just glances a surface point (see Figure 10.9).

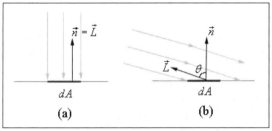

Figure 10.9: Consider a small area element dA. (a) The area dA receives the most light when the normal vector $\vec{n}$ and light vector $\vec{L}$ are aligned. (b) The area dA receives less light as the angle θ between $\vec{n}$ and $\vec{L}$ increases (as depicted by the light rays that miss the surface dA).

So the idea is to come up with a function that returns different intensities based on the alignment of the vertex normal and the *light vector*. (Observe that the light vector is the vector from the vertex to the light source; that is, it is aimed in the opposite direction the light rays travel.) The function should return maximum intensity when the vertex normal and light vector are perfectly aligned (i.e., the angle θ between them is 0°), and it should smoothly diminish in intensity as the angle between the vertex normal and light vector increases. If $\theta > 90°$, then the light strikes the back of a surface and so we set the intensity to zero. *Lambert's cosine law* gives the function we seek, which is given by

$$f(\theta)=\max(\cos\theta,0)=\max\left(\vec{L}\cdot\vec{n},0\right)$$

where $\vec{L}$ and $\vec{n}$ are unit vectors. Figure 10.10 shows a plot of $f(\theta)$ to see how the intensity, ranging from 0.0 to 1.0 (i.e., 0% to 100%), varies with θ.

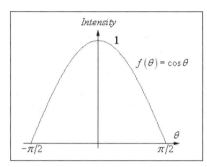

Figure 10.10: Plot of the cosine function for $\theta \in [-\pi/2, \pi/2]$.

10.2.3 **Diffuse Lighting**

Consider a rough surface, as in Figure 10.11. When light strikes such a surface, the light rays scatter in various random directions; this is called a _diffuse reflection_. In our approximation for modeling this kind of light/surface interaction, we stipulate that the light reflects equally in all directions above the surface; consequently, the reflected light will reach the eye no matter the viewpoint, and therefore, we do not need to take the viewpoint into consideration (i.e., the diffuse lighting calculation is viewpoint independent), and the surface brightness will always look the same no matter the viewpoint.

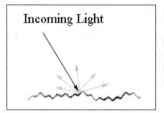

Figure 10.11: Incoming light scatters in random directions when striking a diffuse surface.

We break the calculation of diffuse lighting into two parts. For the first part, we specify a diffuse light color and a diffuse material. The diffuse material specifies the color of incoming diffuse light that the geometry reflects/absorbs on a per-vertex basis (remember, we are doing lighting per-vertex to generate a vertex color, which is then interpolated in rasterization to fill in the pixels of the triangle face); this is handled with a component-wise color multiplication. For example, for some given vertex, suppose that the surface with which the vertex coincides reflects 50% incoming red light, 100% green light, and 75% blue light, and the incoming light color is 80% intensity white light. Then, the incoming diffuse light color is given by $\vec{c}_d = (0.8, 0.8, 0.8)$ and the diffuse material color is given by $\vec{m}_d = (0.5, 1.0, 0.75)$, and the amount of light reflected off the vertex is given by:

$$\vec{c}_d \otimes \vec{m}_d = (0.8, 0.8, 0.8) \otimes (0.5, 1.0, 0.75) = (0.4, 0.8, 0.6)$$

To finish the diffuse lighting calculation, we simply include Lambert's cosine law (which controls how much of the original light the surface receives based on the angle between the vertex normal and light vector). Let $\vec{c}_d = (c_r, c_g, c_b)$ be the diffuse light color, $\vec{m}_d = (m_r, m_g, m_b)$ be the diffuse material color, $\vec{L}$ be the light vector, and $\vec{n}$ be the vertex normal we are lighting. Then the amount of light reflected off the vertex is given by:

$$\max(\vec{L} \cdot \vec{n}, 0) \cdot (\vec{c}_d \otimes \vec{m}_d) \tag{10.1}$$

10.2.4 Diffuse Demo

We now have everything we need to develop our first lighting demo. In this demo we light a teapot. We point out now that the D3DXCreate* functions create vertex data with both position and normal data; thus, we are all set to go. However, note that a Diffuse Pyramid demo and Diffuse Cube demo are available in this chapter's downloadable demo directory as well, which show how to manually specify the vertex normals during vertex creation (i.e., as you are filling out the vertex buffer); we recommend that you take a look at these demos to study the manual specification of vertex normals at least once. Figure 10.12 shows a screenshot of the Diffuse demo.

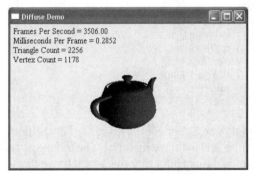

Figure 10.12: Screenshot of the Diffuse demo.

10.2.4.1 *Vertex Structure*

The first thing we need to do is define a new vertex structure (and corresponding vertex declaration):

```
struct VertexPN
{
    VertexPN()
        :pos(0.0f, 0.0f, 0.0f),
         normal(0.0f, 0.0f, 0.0f){}
    VertexPN(float x, float y, float z,
             float nx, float ny, float nz)
        :pos(x,y,z), normal(nx,ny,nz){}
```

```
        VertexPN(const D3DXVECTOR3& v, const D3DXVECTOR3& n)
            :pos(v),normal(n){}

        D3DXVECTOR3 pos;
        D3DXVECTOR3 normal;
        static IDirect3DVertexDeclaration9* Decl;
};

D3DVERTEXELEMENT9 VertexPNElements[] =
{
    {0, 0,  D3DDECLTYPE_FLOAT3, D3DDECLMETHOD_DEFAULT,
                                D3DDECLUSAGE_POSITION, 0},
    {0, 12, D3DDECLTYPE_FLOAT3, D3DDECLMETHOD_DEFAULT,
                                D3DDECLUSAGE_NORMAL, 0},
    D3DDECL_END()
};
HR(gd3dDevice->CreateVertexDeclaration(VertexPNElements,
                                &VertexPN::Decl));
```

Hopefully by now you are becoming comfortable with making vertex structures and declarations. Note that we use the suffix "PN" to denote that the vertex contains position and normal data.

10.2.4.2 *Effect Parameters*

Now let's look at the *diffuse.fx* file. The effect parameters are:

```
uniform extern float4x4 gWorldInverseTranspose;
uniform extern float4x4 gWVP;

uniform extern float4 gDiffuseMtrl;
uniform extern float4 gDiffuseLight;
uniform extern float3 gLightVecW;
```

Four of these parameters are new, as we have already been working with gWVP (combined world, view, and projection matrices) in past demos.

■ gWorldInverseTranspose: Let W be the world matrix. Then this parameter is the inverse-transpose of W; that is, $(W^{-1})^T$. This parameter is used to transform vertex normals into world space (recall from §10.2.1 that care needs to be taken in transforming vertex normals). We need to transform them into world space because this is the space relative to which we define our light sources. Thus, for the lighting calculations to work correctly, we need the lights and vertex normals in the same coordinate system. Note that you could eliminate the necessity of this parameter if you insist on having only uniform scaling transforms.

■ gDiffuseMtrl: A color vector that describes the diffuse material.

■ gDiffuseLight: A color vector that describes the diffuse light color.

■ gLightVecW: The light vector; for a directional light, this is a vector that points in the direction of the light source (i.e., in the opposite direction of the incoming light rays). (Observe we only need a single vector to describe a directional light since all the light rays are parallel; see $\bar{L}$ in Figure 10.9b.)

These parameters are set in the application every frame like so:

```
HR(mFX->SetMatrix(mhWVP, &(mWorld*mView*mProj)));
D3DXMATRIX worldInverseTranspose;
D3DXMatrixInverse(&worldInverseTranspose, 0, &mWorld);
D3DXMatrixTranspose(&worldInverseTranspose, &worldInverseTranspose);
HR(mFX->SetMatrix(mhWorldInverseTranspose, &worldInverseTranspose));
HR(mFX->SetValue(mhLightVecW, &mLightVecW, sizeof(D3DXVECTOR3)));
HR(mFX->SetValue(mhDiffuseMtrl, &mDiffuseMtrl, sizeof(D3DXCOLOR)));
HR(mFX->SetValue(mhDiffuseLight, &mDiffuseLight, sizeof(D3DXCOLOR)));
```

Note that you can change these settings at run time by changing the parameters. For instance, if you wanted to program an animated light, you could update mLightVecW every frame. In addition, you can change the light color and material color anytime you want. Thus we can use the same .fx file for objects and lights of different colors — we just change the effect parameters accordingly before rendering the new object/light.

To facilitate these effect parameters, we obviously need to add some new D3DXHANDLEs:

```
D3DXHANDLE    mhWorldInverseTranspose;
D3DXHANDLE    mhLightVecW;
D3DXHANDLE    mhDiffuseMtrl;
D3DXHANDLE    mhDiffuseLight;
```

These handles are initialized in the DiffuseDemo::buildFX method like so:

```
mhTech = mFX->GetTechniqueByName("DiffuseTech");
mhWVP  = mFX->GetParameterByName(0, "gWVP");
mhLightVecW    = mFX->GetParameterByName(0, "gLightVecW");
mhDiffuseMtrl  = mFX->GetParameterByName(0, "gDiffuseMtrl");
mhDiffuseLight = mFX->GetParameterByName(0, "gDiffuseLight");
mhWorldInverseTranspose =
    mFX->GetParameterByName(0, "gWorldInverseTranspose");
```

10.2.4.3 *The Vertex Shader*

The rest of the C++ application code is only slightly different from the previous chapter's demos, so we do not comment further on it here. However, what has significantly changed is the vertex shader, as we now need to implement Equation 10.1:

```
OutputVS DiffuseVS(float3 posL : POSITION0, float3 normalL : NORMAL0)
{
    // Zero out our output.
    OutputVS outVS = (OutputVS)0;

    // Transform normal to world space.
    float3 normalW = mul(float4(normalL, 0.0f),
                        gWorldInverseTranspose).xyz;
```

```
        normalW = normalize(normalW);

        // Compute the color: Equation 10.1.
        float s = max(dot(gLightVecW, n), 0.0f);
        outVS.color.rgb = s*(gDiffuseMtrl*gDiffuseLight).rgb;
        outVS.color.a   = gDiffuseMtrl.a;

        // Transform to homogeneous clip space.
        outVS.posH = mul(float4(posL, 1.0f), gWVP);

        // Done--return the output.
        return outVS;
}
```

The key lines have been bolded. The first bolded line transforms the normal vector (specified in local space) to world space using the inverse-transpose of the world matrix. The second bolded line normalizes the world space normal vector. This is necessary because a scaling transform can lengthen the normal vector and make it non-unit length. Consequently, because we normalize the normal vector anyway, theoretically it does not originally have to be specified as a normal vector. Note that we can use the HLSL `normalize` intrinsic function to normalize a vector. Also note the `.xyz` syntax. When we transform the normal vector, we do it with a 4D vector and 4×4 matrix; however, after that we only need the 3D part for the lighting calculation. The syntax `.xyz` returns the 3D vector part of the 4D vector. In fact, you can even reshuffle (swizzle) the components around in the HLSL. For example:

```
    float3 u = float3(x, y, z);
    float3 v = u.zyx; v = (z, y, x)
    float3 w = u.xzy; w = (x, z, y)
```

The next three (bolded) lines implement Equation 10.1. The `max` and `dot` functions are HLSL intrinsic functions that return the maximum of two arguments and dot product, respectively. Observe the `.rgb` syntax (red, green, blue). This works just like the `.xyz` syntax (i.e., it returns the RGB part of the color vector) — the HLSL provides both space coordinate syntax and color coordinate syntax since both geometric vectors and colors are represented by coordinate arrays; use the notation that makes sense for the data, however. Note that in the HLSL, `operator*` does a component-wise multiplication for vectors (i.e., $\otimes$).

Finally, observe that the lighting calculation does not touch the material's alpha component; we simply pass the material's alpha component over to the output color's alpha component. The ".a" syntax simply addresses the alpha component; you can access the other components individually by .r, .g, and .b, or, if working with vectors, .x, .y, .z, and .w, or you can use plain array syntax: [0], [1], [2], and [3].

10.2.4.4 *The Pixel Shader and Technique*

For completeness, we present the rest of the *diffuse.fx* contents here; the implementation is obvious.

```
float4 DiffusePS(float4 c : COLOR0) : COLOR
{
    return c;
}


technique DiffuseTech
{
    pass P0
    {
        vertexShader = compile vs_2_0 DiffuseVS();
        pixelShader  = compile ps_2_0 DiffusePS();
    }
}
```

10.3 **Ambient Lighting**

As stated earlier, our lighting model does not take into consideration indirect light that has bounced off other light sources. However, much of the light we see in the real world is indirect. For example, a hallway connected to a room might not be in direct contact with a light source in the room, but the light bounces off the walls in the room and some of it may make it into the hallway, thereby lightening it up a bit. If you ran the Diffuse demo, you may have noticed that the back of the teapot is pitch black. This is unrealistic, for if the teapot were in a room, some indirect light would bounce off some walls and dimly light the back of the teapot. (You have probably noticed that you can see the back sides of objects fine even though light is not directly shined on them.) To sort of hack this indirect light, we introduce an ambient component. All ambient light does is brighten up the object a bit — there is no real physics calculation at all. For flexibility purposes, we want to control ambient lighting separately from diffuse lighting. Thus, we introduce an ambient material component $\vec{m}_a$ and an ambient light component $\vec{c}_a$. Our new lighting equation looks like this:

$$\left(\vec{c}_a \otimes \vec{m}_a\right) + \max\left(\vec{L} \cdot \vec{n}, 0\right) \cdot \left(\vec{c}_d \otimes \vec{m}_d\right) \tag{10.2}$$

Basically, Equation 10.2 just adds the ambient term to the previous diffuse term. As said, this is just a hack, but nevertheless, it gives the artist an extra set of parameters to use for specific looks.

Figure 10.13 shows a screenshot of the Ambient-Diffuse demo; as you can see, the back side of the teapot now shows up. For brevity we omit the C++ application code for this demo and just show the vertex shader. Essentially, the only C++ application code change (from the Diffuse demo) that needs to be made is to add data members for the additional effect

parameters (the ambient components) and initialize them. The vertex
shader is implemented as follows (the new parts have been bolded):

```
uniform extern float4x4 gWorldInverseTranspose;
uniform extern float4x4 gWVP;

uniform extern float4 gAmbientMtrl;
uniform extern float4 gAmbientLight;
uniform extern float4 gDiffuseMtrl;
uniform extern float4 gDiffuseLight;
uniform extern float3 gLightVecW;

struct OutputVS
{
    float4 posH  : POSITION0;
    float4 color : COLOR0;
};

OutputVS AmbientDiffuseVS(float3 posL : POSITION0, float3 normalL :
                          NORMAL0)
{
    // Zero out our output.
    OutputVS outVS = (OutputVS)0;

    // Transform normal to world space.
    float3 normalW = mul(float4(normalL, 0.0f),
                         gWorldInverseTranspose).xyz;
    normalW = normalize(normalW);

    // Compute the color: Equation 10.2.
    float s = max(dot(gLightVecW, normalW), 0.0f);
    float3 diffuse = s*(gDiffuseMtrl*gDiffuseLight).rgb;
    float3 ambient = gAmbientMtrl*gAmbientLight;
    outVS.color.rgb = ambient + diffuse;
    outVS.color.a   = gDiffuseMtrl.a;

    // Transform to homogeneous clip space.
    outVS.posH = mul(float4(posL, 1.0f), gWVP);

    // Done--return the output.
    return outVS;
}
```

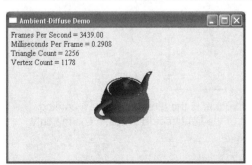

Figure 10.13:
Screenshot of the
Ambient-Diffuse
demo.

10.4 **Specular Lighting**

Consider a smooth surface, as shown in Figure 10.14. When light strikes such a surface, the light rays reflect sharply in a general direction; this is called a *specular reflection*. In contrast to diffuse light, because specular reflected light reflects in a specific direction, it might not travel into the eye; in other words, the specular lighting calculation is viewpoint dependent.

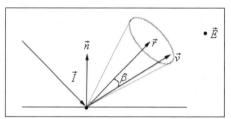

Figure 10.14: Specular reflections do not scatter, but instead reflect in a general cone of reflection whose size we can control with a parameter. If $\vec{v}$ is in the cone, the eye receives specular light; otherwise it does not. The closer $\vec{v}$ is aligned with $\vec{r}$, the more specular light the eye receives.

Essentially, we stipulate that if the angle β between the reflected vector $\vec{r}$ and the *view vector* $\vec{v}$ (i.e., the vector from the vertex point to the eye position) is small, then the specular reflected light makes it into the eye. Moreover, all the specular light in the *cone of reflectance* should not be of equal intensity; the light at the center of the cone should be the most intense and the light intensity should fade to zero as β increases.

Note: The reflection vector is given by $\vec{r} = \vec{i} - (2\vec{i} \cdot \vec{n})\vec{n}$ (see Figure 10.15). However, we can actually use the HLSL intrinsic `reflect` function to compute $\vec{r}$ for us.

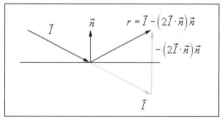

Figure 10.15: Mathematics of reflection.

Observe that $\vec{i}$, the incident vector, is the direction of the incoming light (i.e., opposite direction of the light vector). Thus, if $\vec{L}$ is the light vector, then $\vec{i} = -\vec{L}$.

So how do we control the falloff of the specular light intensity as a function of β? Well, we might start with the same falloff formula we used for diffuse lighting: $f(\beta) = \max(\cos\beta, 0) = \max(\vec{v} \cdot \vec{r}, 0)$. The problem with this formula is that it allows for too wide of a cone of reflectance. That is to say, with $f(\beta) = \max(\vec{v} \cdot \vec{r}, 0)$, some specular light can make it into the eye as long as the eye is within 90° of the reflection vector $\vec{r}$, which means the reflectance cone is just under 180°. Remember, specular light reflects sharply in a general direction — it does not spread out and scatter like diffuse light. Thus, allowing a 180° specular reflectance spread does not make sense! That said, a quick modification can enable us to control the cone of reflectance; specifically, we raise the cosine to a power p:

$$f(\beta) = \left(\max(\cos\beta, 0)\right)^p = \left(\max(\vec{v} \cdot \vec{r}, 0)\right)^p$$

Of course, we take the power after we take the max; otherwise, an even power can make a negative $\vec{v} \cdot \vec{r}$ (i.e., the angle β between the two vectors is greater than 90°) positive, which would be incorrect. (A negative dot product means the light is striking the back of the surface, in which case $f(\beta)$ should evaluate to zero, but if we make a negative dot product become positive by raising it to an even power, then $f(\beta)$ won't evaluate to zero.) Figure 10.16 shows a plot of $\cos^p\beta$ for various powers of p. As you can see, the higher we raise p, the further the cone of reflectance shrinks. Consequently, we have yet another parameter for controlling the shininess of surfaces; that is, highly polished surfaces will have a smaller cone of reflectance (the light reflects more sharply) than less shiny objects.

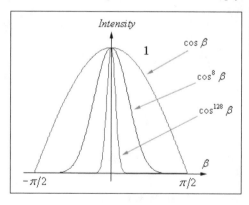

Figure 10.16: Plots of the cosine function to the first, eighth, and 128th power.

For flexibility purposes, we want to control specular lighting separately from diffuse and ambient lighting. To do so, we introduce a specular material component $\vec{m}_s$, a specular light component $\vec{c}_s$, and a specular power exponent p. Thus, our new lighting equation becomes:

$$\left(\vec{c}_a \otimes \vec{m}_a\right) + \max\left(\vec{L} \cdot \vec{n}, 0\right) \cdot \left(\vec{c}_d \otimes \vec{m}_d\right) + \left(\max(\vec{v} \cdot \vec{r}, 0)\right)^p \cdot \left(\vec{c}_s \otimes \vec{m}_s\right) \tag{10.3}$$

Observe that Equation 10.3 requires the view vector (i.e., vector from the vertex to the eye position) and also the reflection vector. Given the world eye position $\vec{e}$ and the world vertex position $\vec{p}$, we can compute $\vec{v}$ as follows: $\vec{v} = (\vec{e} - \vec{p}) / \|\vec{e} - \vec{p}\|$. Consequently, the eye position, in world space, needs to be specified as a parameter to the effect (gEyePosW). Moreover, we also need the world matrix (not just the inverse-transpose) to transform the vertex from local space to world space; thus, the world matrix must also be specified as a parameter (gWorld). As already mentioned, the reflection vector can be obtained via the HLSL reflect function. The vertex shader for implementing Equation 10.3 looks like this (the new parts have been bolded):

```
uniform extern float4x4 gWorld;
uniform extern float4x4 gWorldInverseTranspose;
uniform extern float4x4 gWVP;

uniform extern float4 gAmbientMtrl;
uniform extern float4 gAmbientLight;
uniform extern float4 gDiffuseMtrl;
uniform extern float4 gDiffuseLight;
uniform extern float4 gSpecularMtrl;
uniform extern float4 gSpecularLight;
uniform extern float  gSpecularPower;
uniform extern float3 gLightVecW;
uniform extern float3 gEyePosW;

struct OutputVS
{
    float4 posH  : POSITION0;
    float4 color : COLOR0;
};

OutputVS AmbientDiffuseSpecVS(float3 posL : POSITION0,
                             float3 normalL : NORMAL0)
{
    // Zero out our output.
    OutputVS outVS = (OutputVS)0;

    // Transform normal to world space.
    float3 normalW = mul(float4(normalL, 0.0f),
                         gWorldInverseTranspose).xyz;
    normalW = normalize(normalW);

    // Transform vertex position to world space.
    float3 posW  = mul(float4(posL, 1.0f), gWorld).xyz;

    //===========================================================
    // Compute the color: Equation 10.3.

    // Compute the vector from the vertex to the eye position.
    float3 toEye = normalize(gEyePosW - posW);
```

```
// Compute the reflection vector.
float3 r = reflect(-gLightVecW, normalW);

// Determine how much (if any) specular light makes it
// into the eye.
float t = pow(max(dot(r, toEye), 0.0f), gSpecularPower);

// Determine the diffuse light intensity that strikes the vertex.
float s = max(dot(gLightVecW, normalW), 0.0f);

// Compute the ambient, diffuse, and specular terms separately.
float3 spec = t*(gSpecularMtrl*gSpecularLight).rgb;
float3 diffuse = s*(gDiffuseMtrl*gDiffuseLight).rgb;
float3 ambient = gAmbientMtrl*gAmbientLight;

// Sum all the terms together and copy over the diffuse alpha.
outVS.color.rgb = ambient + diffuse + spec;
outVS.color.a   = gDiffuseMtrl.a;
//=========================================================

// Transform to homogeneous clip space.
outVS.posH = mul(float4(posL, 1.0f), gWVP);

// Done--return the output.
return outVS;
}
```

Note: The position of the eye, in world space, is given in the `buildViewMtx` method, so that is the method in which we set the eye position effect parameter:

```
void AmbientDiffuseSpecularDemo::buildViewMtx()
{
    float x = mCameraRadius * cosf(mCameraRotationY);
    float z = mCameraRadius * sinf(mCameraRotationY);
    D3DXVECTOR3 pos(x, mCameraHeight, z);
    D3DXVECTOR3 target(0.0f, 0.0f, 0.0f);
    D3DXVECTOR3 up(0.0f, 1.0f, 0.0f);
    D3DXMatrixLookAtLH(&mView, &pos, &target, &up);

    HR(mFX->SetValue(mhEyePos, &pos, sizeof(D3DXVECTOR3)));
}
```

Figure 10.17 shows a screenshot of the demo; observe the specular highlight.

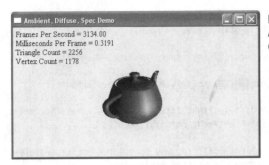

Figure 10.17: Screenshot of the Ambient-Diffuse-Specular demo; observe the specular highlight.

Note: In general, different combinations of diffuse, ambient, and specular lighting are needed to simulate different kinds of real world materials. For example, for matte objects, a strong level of diffuse reflectance and a very low level of specular reflectance works well. On the other hand, for shiny objects, a low level of diffuse reflectance and a high level of specular reflectance works well.

10.5 **Point Lights**

A good physical example of a point light is a lightbulb. It radiates light spherically in *all* directions (see Figure 10.18).

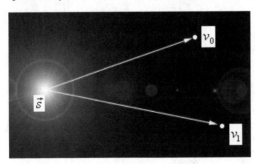

Figure 10.18: Point lights radiate in every direction; in particular, for vertices v_o and v_1, there exists a light ray originating from the point light position $\vec{s}$ and traveling toward v_o and v_1.

In particular, for an arbitrary vertex at position $\vec{p}$, there exists a light ray originating from the point light position $\vec{s}$ traveling toward the vertex. As usual, we define the light vector to go in the opposite direction; that is, $\vec{L} = \left(\vec{s} - \vec{p}\right) / \left\|\vec{s} - \vec{p}\right\|$ (i.e., the direction from the vertex $\vec{p}$ to the point light source $\vec{s}$). Essentially, the only difference between point lights and directional lights is how the light vector is computed — it *varies* from vertex to vertex for point lights, but remains *constant* across all vertices for directional lights.

10.6 **Spotlights**

A good physical example of a spotlight is a flashlight. Essentially, a spotlight has a position $\vec{s}$, is aimed in a direction $\vec{d}$, and radiates light through a cone (see Figure 10.19).

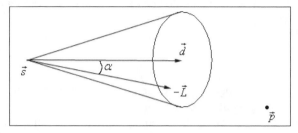

Figure 10.19: A spotlight has a position $\vec{s}$, is aimed in a direction $\vec{d}$, and radiates light through a cone.

Note: As with point lights, the light vector $\vec{L}$ varies per vertex.

To implement a spotlight, we begin as we do with a point light: The light vector is given by $\vec{L} = \left(\vec{s} - \vec{p}\right)/\left\|\vec{s} - \vec{p}\right\|$, where $\vec{p}$ is the position of the vertex being lit and $\vec{s}$ is the position of the spotlight. Observe from Figure 10.19 that $\vec{p}$ is inside the spotlight's cone (and therefore receives light) if and only if the angle α between $-\vec{L}$ and $\vec{d}$ is smaller than the cone angle. Moreover, all the light in the spotlight's cone should not be of equal intensity; the light at the center of the cone should be the most intense and the light intensity should fade to zero as α increases to the boundary of the spotlight's cone.

So how do we control both the intensity falloff as a function of α and the size of the spotlight's cone? Well, we can play the same game we did with the specular cone of reflectance. That is, we use the function:

$$f(\alpha) = \left(\max\left(\cos\alpha, 0\right)\right)^{s} = \left(\max\left(-\vec{L}\cdot\vec{d}, 0\right)\right)^{s}$$

Refer back to Figure 10.16 to see the graph of this function. As you can see, the intensity smoothly fades as α increases, which is one desired characteristic we want, and additionally, by altering the exponent s, we can control at which angle α the intensity drops off to zero; that is to say, we can shrink or expand the spotlight cone by varying s. For example, if we set $s = 8$, the cone has approximately a 45° half angle.

Our lighting equation for a spotlight is:

$$spot\left[\left(\vec{c}_{a}\otimes\vec{m}_{a}\right) + \max\left(\vec{L}\cdot\vec{n}, 0\right)\cdot\left(\vec{c}_{d}\otimes\vec{m}_{d}\right) + \left(\max\left(\vec{v}\cdot\vec{r}, 0\right)\right)^{p}\cdot\left(\vec{c}_{s}\otimes\vec{m}_{s}\right)\right]$$

where,

$$spot = \left(\max\left(-\vec{L}\cdot\vec{d}, 0\right)\right)^{s}$$

10.7 **Attenuation**

Physically, light intensity weakens as a function of distance based on the inverse square law. That is to say, if I_0 is the initial light intensity and d is the distance of the light from its source (for implementation purposes, the distance between the light source and the vertex being lit), then the light intensity is given by:

$$I(d) = \frac{I_0}{d^2}$$

However, this formula does not always give aesthetically pleasing results. Thus, instead of worrying about physical accuracy, we use a more general function that gives the artist/programmer some parameters to control (i.e., the artist/programmer experiments with different parameter values until he is satisfied with the result). The typical formula used is:

$$I(d) = \frac{I_0}{a_0 + a_1 d + a_2 d^2}$$

We call a_0, a_1, and a_2 *attenuation parameters*, and they are to be supplied by the artist or programmer. For example, if you actually want the light intensity to weaken linearly with distance, set $a_0 = 0$, $a_1 = 1$, and $a_2 = 0$. On the other hand, if you actually wanted to use the inverse square law, then set $a_0 = 0$, $a_1 = 0$, and $a_2 = 1$.

For point lights, our lighting equation becomes:

$$\left(\vec{c}_a \otimes \vec{m}_a\right) + \frac{\max\left(\vec{L}\cdot\vec{n}, 0\right)\cdot\left(\vec{c}_d \otimes \vec{m}_d\right) + \max\left(\vec{v}\cdot\vec{r}, 0\right)^p \cdot\left(\vec{c}_s \otimes \vec{m}_s\right)}{a_0 + a_1 d + a_2 d^2} \qquad (10.4)$$

where $d = \left\|\vec{p} - \vec{s}\right\|$ (i.e., the distance between $\vec{p}$ and $\vec{s}$), $\vec{p}$ is the position of the vertex being lit, and $\vec{s}$ is the position of the point light. For a spotlight, we use the same formula, except we multiply Equation 10.4 by the *spot* factor:

$$spot\left[\left(\vec{c}_a \otimes \vec{m}_a\right) + \frac{\max\left(\vec{L}\cdot\vec{n}, 0\right)\cdot\left(\vec{c}_d \otimes \vec{m}_d\right) + \max\left(\vec{v}\cdot\vec{r}, 0\right)^p \cdot\left(\vec{c}_s \otimes \vec{m}_s\right)}{a_0 + a_1 d + a_2 d^2}\right] \qquad (10.5)$$

Note: Attenuation is not applied to directional lights, which are, theoretically, at an infinite distance from the scene.

10.8 **The Point Light Demo**

Figure 10.20 shows a screenshot of the Point Light demo; it builds off of Chapter 8's Mesh demo. As usual, the core code change is replacing our previous lighting equation with Equation 10.4 in the vertex shader. However, there are also some C++ application implementation details worth mentioning.

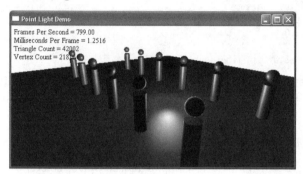

Figure 10.20: Screenshot of the Point Light demo.

10.8.1 **Grid Normals**

The cylinders and spheres have normals already calculated since the D3DXCreate* functions generate them; however, the grid does not. Fortunately, the grid vertex normals are trivial to compute; they are all just (0, 1, 0) (i.e., they just point straight up, which is orthogonal to the xz-plane). Thus, as we are filling the vertex buffer with the grid geometry, we just set the vertex normal to (0, 1, 0):

```
// Now lock it to obtain a pointer to its internal data, and write the
// grid's vertex data.
VertexPN* v = 0;
HR(mVB->Lock(0, 0, (void**)&v, 0));

for(DWORD i = 0; i < numGridVertices; ++i)
{
    v[i].pos = verts[i];
    v[i].normal = D3DXVECTOR3(0.0f, 1.0f, 0.0f);
}

HR(mVB->Unlock());
```

Note: Here we hard coded the normals directly because they had a simple form. However, for an arbitrary mesh where we could not hard code the normals, we could just apply the averaging technique from §10.2.1.

10.8.2 **Animated Light**

To make the demo more interesting, we animate the light by oscillating it up and down along the *z*-axis. This oscillation code is updated every frame (i.e., it exists in the PointLightDemo::updateScene method) and is implemented like so:

```
// Reset the angle every period so that theta
// doesn't get too big.
if(theta >= 2.0f*D3DX_PI)
    theta = 0.0f;

mLightPosW.z = 25.0f*sinf(theta);
```

Observe that we use a sine wave to implement the oscillation effect with an amplitude of 25.0, which means the light oscillates in the range [–25, 25] along the *z*-axis.

10.8.3 **Different Materials**

To facilitate the grouping of material components, as well as colors, we add the following code to *d3dUtil.h*:

```
const D3DXCOLOR WHITE(1.0f, 1.0f, 1.0f, 1.0f);
const D3DXCOLOR BLACK(0.0f, 0.0f, 0.0f, 1.0f);
const D3DXCOLOR RED(1.0f, 0.0f, 0.0f, 1.0f);
const D3DXCOLOR GREEN(0.0f, 1.0f, 0.0f, 1.0f);
const D3DXCOLOR BLUE(0.0f, 0.0f, 1.0f, 1.0f);

struct Mtrl
{
    Mtrl()
            :ambient(WHITE), diffuse(WHITE),
            spec(WHITE), specPower(8.0f){}
    Mtrl(const D3DXCOLOR& a, const D3DXCOLOR& d,
            const D3DXCOLOR& s, float power)
            :ambient(a), diffuse(d), spec(s), specPower(power){}

    D3DXCOLOR ambient;
    D3DXCOLOR diffuse;
    D3DXCOLOR spec;
    float specPower;
};
```

Now the grid, cylinders, and spheres each reflect a different color of light. Thus, each has its own material:

```
Mtrl    mGridMtrl;
Mtrl    mCylinderMtrl;
Mtrl    mSphereMtrl;
```

These are initialized in the application class constructor like so:

```
mGridMtrl     = Mtrl(BLUE, BLUE, WHITE, 16.0f);
mCylinderMtrl = Mtrl(RED, RED, WHITE, 8.0f);
mSphereMtrl   = Mtrl(GREEN, GREEN, WHITE, 8.0f);
```

In order for the correct material to be applied to each object, we must set the appropriate material to the effect before rendering. For example, in the draw cylinders code, we set the cylinder material components before drawing them so that the cylinder material is used during rendering:

```
void PointLightDemo::drawCylinders()
{
    D3DXMATRIX T, R, W, WIT;

    D3DXMatrixRotationX(&R, D3DX_PI*0.5f);

    HR(mFX->SetValue(mhAmbientMtrl, &
        mCylinderMtrl.ambient, sizeof(D3DXCOLOR)));
    HR(mFX->SetValue(mhDiffuseMtrl,
        &mCylinderMtrl.diffuse, sizeof(D3DXCOLOR)));
    HR(mFX->SetValue(mhSpecMtrl,
        &mCylinderMtrl.spec, sizeof(D3DXCOLOR)));
    HR(mFX->SetFloat(mhSpecPower, mCylinderMtrl.specPower));

    ... Other Drawing Code
```

We execute the same code when drawing the grid and spheres, except that we would instead use the grid material and sphere material, respectively.

10.8.4 The Vertex Shader

We now present the effect parameters and vertex shader for the Point Light demo. It may seem like a lot, but really it just breaks up Equation 10.4 over multiple lines.

```
uniform extern float4x4 gWorld;
uniform extern float4x4 gWorldInvTrans;
uniform extern float4x4 gWVP;
uniform extern float3   gEyePosW;

uniform extern float4 gAmbientMtrl;
uniform extern float4 gDiffuseMtrl;
uniform extern float4 gSpecMtrl;
uniform extern float  gSpecPower;

uniform extern float4 gAmbientLight;
uniform extern float4 gDiffuseLight;
uniform extern float4 gSpecLight;
uniform extern float3 gLightPosW;
uniform extern float3 gAttenuation012;

struct OutputVS
{
```

```
        float4 posH  : POSITION0;
        float4 color : COLOR0;
};

OutputVS PointLightVS(float3 posL : POSITION0,
                      float3 normalL : NORMAL0)
{
    // Zero out our output.
    OutputVS outVS = (OutputVS)0;

    // Transform normal to world space.
    float3 normalW = mul(float4(normalL, 0.0f), gWorldInvTrans).xyz;
    normalW = normalize(normalW);

    // Transform vertex position to world space.
    float3 posW = mul(float4(posL, 1.0f), gWorld).xyz;

    // Unit vector from vertex to light source.
    float3 lightVecW = normalize(gLightPosW - posW);

    // Ambient Light Computation.
    float3 ambient = (gAmbientMtrl*gAmbientLight).rgb;

    // Diffuse Light Computation.
    float s = max(dot(normalW, lightVecW), 0.0f);
    float3 diffuse = s*(gDiffuseMtrl*gDiffuseLight).rgb;

    // Specular Light Computation.
    float3 toEyeW   = normalize(gEyePosW - posW);
    float3 reflectW = reflect(-lightVecW, normalW);
    float t = pow(max(dot(reflectW, toEyeW), 0.0f), gSpecPower);
    float3 spec = t*(gSpecMtrl*gSpecLight).rgb;

    // Attentuation.
    float d = distance(gLightPosW, posW);
    float A = gAttenuation012.x + gAttenuation012.y*d +
                                  gAttenuation012.z*d*d;

    // Everything together (Equation 10.4)
    float3 color = ambient + ((diffuse + spec) / A);

    // Pass on color and diffuse material alpha.
    outVS.color = float4(color, gDiffuseMtrl.a);

    // Transform to homogeneous clip space.
    outVS.posH = mul(float4(posL, 1.0f), gWVP);

    // Done--return the output.
    return outVS;
}
```

Note: The attenuation parameters a_0, a_1, and a_2 are stored in the x-, y-, and z-coordinates of gAttenuation012, respectively.

10.9 **The Spotlight Demo**

The Spotlight demo is very similar to the Point Light demo. We outline the major differences here. First, we add an extra gSpotPower effect parameter to control the spotlight cone. This is used in the *spotlight.fx* file to compute the *spot* factor of Equation 10.5:

```
// Spotlight factor.
float spot = pow(max(dot(-lightVecW, gLightDirW), 0.0f), gSpotPower);

// Everything together.
float3 color = spot*(ambient + ((diffuse + spec) / A));
```

We have also added a gLightDirW effect parameter; this is because a spotlight has a position like a point light, but it also has a direction. To simulate the result of the camera "holding a flashlight," we actually set the position of the spotlight and the direction of the spotlight to be the position of the camera and the direction the camera is aimed, respectively. Because the camera's position and direction may change every frame, we must update the spotlight position and direction every frame correspondingly; this is done in the SpotlightDemo::buildViewMtx method:

```
void SpotlightDemo::buildViewMtx()
{
        float x = mCameraRadius * cosf(mCameraRotationY);
        float z = mCameraRadius * sinf(mCameraRotationY);
        D3DXVECTOR3 pos(x, mCameraHeight, z);
        D3DXVECTOR3 target(0.0f, 0.0f, 0.0f);
        D3DXVECTOR3 up(0.0f, 1.0f, 0.0f);
        D3DXMatrixLookAtLH(&mView, &pos, &target, &up);

        HR(mFX->SetValue(mhEyePos, &pos, sizeof(D3DXVECTOR3)));

        // Spotlight position is the same as camera's position.
        HR(mFX->SetValue(mhLightPosW, &pos, sizeof(D3DXVECTOR3)));

        // Spotlight direction is the same as camera's forward direction.
        D3DXVECTOR3 lightDir = target - pos;
        D3DXVec3Normalize(&lightDir, &lightDir);
        HR(mFX->SetValue(mhLightDirW, &lightDir, sizeof(D3DXVECTOR3)));
}
```

Other than that, everything is pretty much the same as the Point Light demo. As always, be sure to study the source code to see all of the details put together in a complete program. Figure 10.21 shows a screenshot of the Spotlight demo.

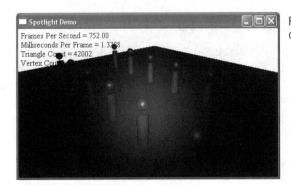

Figure 10.21: Screenshot of the Spotlight demo.

10.10 **Phong Shading**

Thus far we have been doing lighting calculations per vertex to generate a vertex color. This vertex color is then interpolated across the triangle face during rasterization. You might suggest that we instead interpolate vertex normals across the face of the triangle during rasterization, and then do the lighting calculations per pixel; interpolating normals in rasterization is referred to as *Phong shading*; Figure 10.22 illustrates the idea.

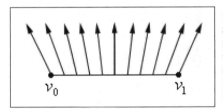

Figure 10.22: The normals at vertices v_0 and v_1 are output from the vertex shader and passed into the rasterization stage where they are interpolated across the face of the triangle (i.e., each pixel of the triangle the vertices make up receive an interpolated normal).

In general, per-pixel lighting gives better results than per-vertex lighting, but it requires more work since we are doing the computations at a finer level of detail (pixel level versus vertex level).

One thing to note is that linearly interpolating normal vectors during rasterization can make them become not normal; thus, we need to renormalize them in the pixel shader. (The interpolation is a step done by the graphics card between the vertex and pixel shaders.) Other than that, the lighting calculation is done exactly the same as it is in the vertex shader; we have just moved the calculations over to the pixel shader stage. The following vertex and pixel shader implements a directional light using Phong shading:

```
struct OutputVS
{
    float4 posH    : POSITION0;
    float3 normalW : TEXCOORD0;
    float3 posW    : TEXCOORD1;
};
```

```
OutputVS PhongVS(float3 posL : POSITIONO, float3 normalL : NORMALO)
{
    // Zero out our output.
    OutputVS outVS = (OutputVS)0;

    // Transform normal to world space.
    outVS.normalW = mul(float4(normalL, 0.0f),
                        gWorldInverseTranspose).xyz;
    outVS.normalW = normalize(outVS.normalW);

    // Transform vertex position to world space.
    outVS.posW  = mul(float4(posL, 1.0f), gWorld).xyz;

    // Transform to homogeneous clip space.
    outVS.posH = mul(float4(posL, 1.0f), gWVP);

    // Done--return the output.
    return outVS;
}


float4 PhongPS(float3 normalW : TEXCOORDO,
               float3 posW : TEXCOORD1) : COLOR
{
    // Compute the color: Equation 10.3.

    // Interpolated normals can become unnormal--so normalize.
    normalW = normalize(normalW);

    // Compute the vector from the vertex to the eye position.
    float3 toEye = normalize(gEyePosW - posW);

    // Compute the reflection vector.
    float3 r = reflect(-gLightVecW, normalW);

    // Determine how much (if any) specular light makes it
    // into the eye.
    float t  = pow(max(dot(r, toEye), 0.0f), gSpecularPower);

    // Determine the diffuse light intensity that strikes the vertex.
    float s = max(dot(gLightVecW, normalW), 0.0f);

    // Compute the ambient, diffuse, and specular terms separately.
    float3 spec = t*(gSpecularMtrl*gSpecularLight).rgb;
    float3 diffuse = s*(gDiffuseMtrl*gDiffuseLight).rgb;
    float3 ambient = gAmbientMtrl*gAmbientLight;

    // Sum all the terms together and copy over the diffuse alpha.
    return float4(ambient + diffuse + spec, gDiffuseMtrl.a);
}
```

Figure 10.23 shows a comparison of per-vertex lighting and per-pixel lighting.

Figure 10.23: The teapot on the left is lit per pixel using Phong shading, and the vertex on the right is lit per vertex. The per-pixel lighting is smoother than the per-vertex lighting.

10.11 **Summary**

- With lighting, we no longer specify per-vertex colors but instead define lights and materials, and then the lighting equation computes a vertex color for us. Materials determine how light interacts with an object, and lights emit colored light of different combinations and intensities, as described by an RGB triplet.

- A directional light, or parallel light, approximates a light source that is very far away. Consequently, we can approximate all incoming light rays as parallel to each other. A physical example of a directional light is the sun relative to the Earth. A point light emits light in *every* direction. A physical example of a point light is a lightbulb. A spotlight emits light through a cone. A physical example of a spotlight is a flashlight.

- Ambient light models light that has reflected off other surfaces and is used to brighten up the overall scene. Diffuse light travels in a particular direction, and when it strikes a surface, it reflects equally in all directions. Diffuse light should be used to model rough and/or matte surfaces. Specular light travels in a particular direction, and when it strikes a surface, it reflects sharply in one general direction, thereby causing a bright shine that can only be seen at some angles. Specular light should be used to model smooth and polished surfaces.

- A face normal is a unit vector that describes the direction a polygon is facing (i.e., it is orthogonal to all points on the polygon). A vertex normal is a unit vector that is orthogonal to the tangent plane of a surface at a vertex. For lighting calculations, we need to specify vertex normals so that we can determine the angle at which light strikes a vertex. For arbitrary triangle meshes, vertex normals are typically approximated via a technique called normal averaging. If the matrix A is used to transform points and vectors (non-normal vectors), then $\left(A^{-1} \right)^{T}$ should be used to transform vertex normals.

■ The directional light, point light, and spotlight lighting equations are given, respectively, by:

$$(\vec{c}_a \otimes \vec{m}_a) + \max(\vec{L} \cdot \vec{n}, 0) \cdot (\vec{c}_d \otimes \vec{m}_d) + (\max(\vec{v} \cdot \vec{r}, 0))^p \cdot (\vec{c}_s \otimes \vec{m}_s)$$

$$(\vec{c}_a \otimes \vec{m}_a) + \frac{\max(\vec{L} \cdot \vec{n}, 0) \cdot (\vec{c}_d \otimes \vec{m}_d) + \max(\vec{v} \cdot \vec{r}, 0)^p \cdot (\vec{c}_s \otimes \vec{m}_s)}{a_0 + a_1 d + a_2 d^2}$$

$$spot \left[(\vec{c}_a \otimes \vec{m}_a) + \frac{\max(\vec{L} \cdot \vec{n}, 0) \cdot (\vec{c}_d \otimes \vec{m}_d) + \max(\vec{v} \cdot \vec{r}, 0)^p \cdot (\vec{c}_s \otimes \vec{m}_s)}{a_0 + a_1 d + a_2 d^2} \right]$$

where $spot = \left(\max(-\vec{L} \cdot \vec{d}, 0) \right)^s$

■ Phong shading refers to interpolating the vertex normals over the pixels covering the triangle face during rasterization, and doing the lighting calculation per pixel rather than per vertex.

10.12 **Exercises**

1. Instead of using $\left(\max(\vec{v} \cdot \vec{r}, 0) \right)^p$ to compute the specular term, Jim Blinn suggests using a *halfway* vector defined by $\vec{h} = (\vec{L} + \vec{v}) / \|\vec{L} + \vec{v}\|$, and using $\left(\max(\vec{n} \cdot \vec{h}, 0) \right)^p$ instead, where $\vec{n}$ is the normal vector, $\vec{L}$ is the light vector, and $\vec{v}$ is the unit vector from the vertex aimed toward the eye point. Why is $\vec{h}$ called the halfway vector? Draw a picture and explain how this variation works. Pick one of the demos that used specular lighting and modify it to use this variation. Describe your results.

2. One characteristic of toon lighting is the abrupt transition from one color shade to the next (in contrast with a smooth transition) as shown in Figure 10.24. This can be implemented by setting $s = \max(\vec{L} \cdot \vec{n}, 0)$ in the vertex shader and then feeding s into the pixel shader. Then, in the pixel shader, instead of using the interpolated s value as the diffuse lighting factor, we use it as a lookup into the following discrete function:

$$f(s) = \begin{cases} 0.4 & \text{if } 0 < s \le 0.25 \\ 0.6 & \text{if } 0.25 < s \le 0.85 \\ 1.0 & \text{if } 0.80 < s \le 1.0 \end{cases}$$

In this way, the light transitions will be abrupt and not smooth, which is the desired effect in toon style rendering. Note that it is important to do the discrete function lookup in the pixel shader — if you don't, the color interpolation done in rasterization will smooth out the abruptness, giving us poor results. Now, redo the Ambient-Diffuse demo (i.e., you do not need to handle specular lighting), but this time using a toon style lighting as described above.

Figure 10.24: Toon lighting is characterized by the abrupt transition from one color shade to the next.

3. Modify the Ambient-Diffuse-Specular demo by animating the directional light. For example, you can have the light vector rotate in a circle to simulate the change from day to night.

4. Modify the Point Light demo by adding another point light to the scene (i.e., two lights).

5. Modify the Ambient-Diffuse-Specular demo by using per-pixel lighting instead of per-vertex lighting.

6. This is a harder exercise in the sense that it requires calculus (so feel free to skip it if your calculus is rusty), but we'll get you started. Modify the Colored Waves demo from Chapter 9 by using a blue material for the grid and doing per-pixel ambient, diffuse, and specular lighting (use white light) with a directional light (see Figure 10.25).

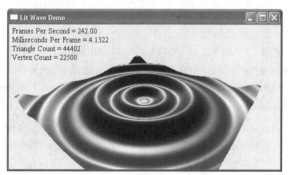

Figure 10.25: Example output for exercise 6.

What makes this exercise a bit more challenging is finding a way to compute the vertex normals in the vertex shader. (Since the mesh is animated in the vertex shader, it does not have fixed normal vectors.) You need to find two tangent vectors at each vertex and then take the cross product to generate the normal vector.

We describe the surface at a time t by a sum of n circular waves; that is,

$$h(x, z, t) = \sum_i a_1 \cdot \sin(k_i r - \omega_i t + \phi_i) = \sum_i a_i \cdot \sin\left(k_i \sqrt{x^2 + z^2} - \omega_i t + \phi_i\right)$$

Taking the partial derivatives in the x- and z-directions, we obtain the formulas:

$$\frac{\partial h}{\partial x}(x, z, t) = \sum_i \frac{a_1 k_i x \cdot \cos\left(k_i \sqrt{x^2 + z^2} - \omega_i t + \phi_i\right)}{\sqrt{x^2 + z^2}} \qquad (10.6)$$

$$\frac{\partial h}{\partial z}(x, z, t) = \sum_i \frac{a_1 k_i z \cdot \cos\left(k_i \sqrt{x^2 + z^2} - \omega_i t + \phi_i\right)}{\sqrt{x^2 + z^2}} \qquad (10.7)$$

An HLSL function to compute the partial derivatives is given as follows (we sum three waves):

```
// Note that in the HLSL we can use the "out" keyword to return more
// than one return value through parameters.
void Partials(float x, float z, out float dhOverdx, out float dhOverdz)
{
    // Distance of vertex from source of waves (which we set
    // as the origin of the local space).
    float d = sqrt(x*x + z*z);

    // Derivative of a sum of functions is the sum of the derivatives.
    dhOverdx = 0.0f;
    dhOverdz = 0.0f;
    for(int i = 0; i < 3; ++i)
    {
        dhOverdx += (a[i]*k[i]*x*cos(k[i]*d - gTime*w[i] + p[i]))/d;
        dhOverdz += (a[i]*k[i]*z*cos(k[i]*d - gTime*w[i] + p[i]))/d;
    }
}
```

Now, the tangent vectors (not of unit length) in the x- and z-directions at (x, z, t), respectively, are just:

$$\vec{v} = \left(1, \frac{\partial h}{\partial x}(x, z, t), 0\right)$$

and

$$\vec{u} = \left(0, \frac{\partial h}{\partial z}(x, z, t), 1\right)$$

To see this, consider Figure 10.26.

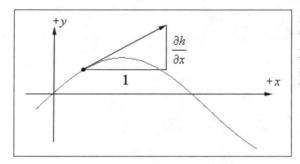

Figure 10.26: Computation of the *x*-tangent vector; the tangent vector in the *z*-direction is found similarly.

Finally, the vertex normal is a simple application of the cross product:

$$\vec{n}=(\vec{u}\times\vec{v})/\|\vec{u}\times\vec{v}\| \tag{10.8}$$

Of course, both of the partial derivatives in Equations 10.6 and 10.7 are undefined for the origin (0, 0, 0). To get around this, we will do the following: If $x^2 = z^2 < 0.01$ (i.e., if the squared distance is close to the origin), then set the normal to be (0, 1, 0). Otherwise, apply Equation 10.8. Although not correct, the visual results are acceptable.

Chapter 11

Texturing

Our demos are getting a little more interesting, but real-world objects are not typically uniformly colored; for example, you probably won't see many perfectly red spheres or green cylinders. What our objects lack is detail and texture. *Texture mapping* is a technique that allows us to map image data onto a triangle, thereby enabling us to increase the details and realism of our scene significantly. For instance, we can build a cube and turn it into a crate by mapping a crate texture on each side (see Figure 11.1).

In Direct3D, a texture is represented by the IDirect3DTexture9 interface. A texture is a matrix of pixels similar to a surface but can be mapped onto triangles and may have several levels of detail (e.g., mipmaps).

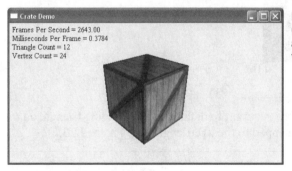

Figure 11.1: The Crate demo creates a cube with a crate texture.

Objectives:

- To learn how to specify the part of a texture that gets mapped to a triangle.
- To find out how to create and enable textures.
- To learn how textures can be filtered to create a smoother image.
- To discover how to tile a texture several times with address modes.
- To learn how multiple textures can be combined to create new textures and special effects.

■ To find out how to texture cylinders and spheres, and how to texture arbitrary meshes by approximating them as cylinders and spheres.

■ To learn how to create some basic effects via texture animation.

11.1 Texture Coordinates

Direct3D uses a texture coordinate system that consists of a u-axis that runs horizontally to the image and a v-axis that runs vertically to the image. The coordinates (u, v) identify an element on the texture called a *texel*. Notice that the v-axis is positive in the "down" direction (see Figure 11.2). Also, notice the normalized coordinate interval, [0, 1], which is used because it gives Direct3D a dimension-independent range with which to work; for example, (0.5, 0.5) always specifies the middle texel no matter if the actual texture dimension is 256×256, 512×512, or 1024×1024 in pixels. Likewise, (0.25, 0.75) identifies the texel a quarter of the total width in the horizontal direction, and three-quarters of the total height in the vertical direction. For now, texture coordinates are always in the range [0, 1], but later we explain what can happen when you go outside this range.

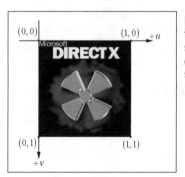

Figure 11.2: The texture coordinate system, sometimes called texture space.

For each 3D triangle, we want to define a corresponding triangle on the texture that is to be mapped to the 3D triangle (see Figure 11.3).

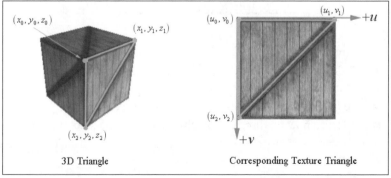

Figure 11.3: On the left is a triangle in 3D space, and on the right we define a 2D triangle on the texture that is going to be mapped onto the 3D triangle.

To do this, we modify our vertex structure once again and add a pair of texture coordinates that identifies a vertex on the texture.

```
struct VertexPNT
{
    VertexPNT()
        :pos(0.0f, 0.0f, 0.0f),
        normal(0.0f, 0.0f, 0.0f),
        tex0(0.0f, 0.0f){}
    VertexPNT(float x, float y, float z,
        float nx, float ny, float nz,
        float u, float v):pos(x,y,z), normal(nx,ny,nz), tex0(u,v){}
    VertexPNT(const D3DXVECTOR3& v,
        const D3DXVECTOR3& n,
        const D3DXVECTOR2& uv)
        :pos(v),normal(n), tex0(uv){}

    D3DXVECTOR3 pos;
    D3DXVECTOR3 normal;
    D3DXVECTOR2 tex0;

    static IDirect3DVertexDeclaration9* Decl;
};

D3DVERTEXELEMENT9 VertexPNTElements[] =
{
    {0, 0,  D3DDECLTYPE_FLOAT3, D3DDECLMETHOD_DEFAULT,
                            D3DDECLUSAGE_POSITION, 0},
    {0, 12, D3DDECLTYPE_FLOAT3, D3DDECLMETHOD_DEFAULT,
                            D3DDECLUSAGE_NORMAL, 0},
    {0, 24, D3DDECLTYPE_FLOAT2, D3DDECLMETHOD_DEFAULT,
                            D3DDECLUSAGE_TEXCOORD, 0},
    D3DDECL_END()
};
HR(gd3dDevice->CreateVertexDeclaration(VertexPNTElements,
                            &VertexPNT::Decl));
```

Thus, every 3D triangle defined by three vertices also defines a 2D triangle
in texture space (i.e., we have associated a 2D texture triangle for every 3D
triangle).

Note: Although we specify a corresponding texture triangle to a
3D triangle, the texture triangle is not mapped onto the 3D triangle
until the rasterization stage where the 3D triangle has been transformed to a 2D screen space triangle. Thus, it is not really mapped
onto a 3D triangle, but rather it is mapped onto the projection of a 3D
triangle in screen space. Texturing is a pixel operation.

11.2 **Creating and Enabling a Texture**

Texture data is usually read from an image file stored on disk and loaded into an IDirect3DTexture9 object. To do this, we can use the following D3DX function:

```
HRESULT D3DXCreateTextureFromFile(
    LPDIRECT3DDEVICE9 pDevice,      // device to create the texture
    LPCSTR pSrcFile,                // filename of image to load
    LPDIRECT3DTEXTURE9* ppTexture   // ptr to receive the created texture
);
```

This function can load any of the following image formats: BMP, DDS, DIB, JPG, PNG, and TGA.

For example, to create a texture from an image called crate.jpg we would write the following:

```
IDirect3Dtexture9* mCrateTex;
HR(D3DXCreateTextureFromFile(gd3dDevice, "crate.jpg", &mCrateTex));
```

Once a texture is loaded, we need to set it as an effect parameter so that it can be used in a pixel shader (or in a vertex shader in newer cards — that is, newer 3D cards can sample textures in a vertex shader for special effects). A texture object in an .fx file is represented by the texture type; for example, we declare a texture effect parameter like so:

```
uniform extern texture gTex;
```

Then, to set a created IDirect3DTexture9 object to a texture effect parameter, we just call ID3DXEffect::SetTexture:

```
HR(mFX->SetTexture(mhTex, mCrateTex));
```

If our scene has triangles that use different textures but are drawn using the same effect, we would have to do something similar to the following code:

```
HR(mFX->SetTexture(mhTex, mTex0));
HR(mFX->CommitChanges());
drawTrisUsingTex0();
HR(mFX->SetTexture(mhTex, mTex1));
HR(mFX->CommitChanges());
drawTrisUsingTex1();
HR(mFX->SetTexture(mhTex, mTex2));
HR(mFX->CommitChanges());
DrawTrisUsingTex2();
```

11.3 **Filters**

As mentioned previously, textures are mapped to triangles in screen space. Usually the texture triangle is not the same size as the screen triangle. When the texture triangle is smaller than the screen triangle, the texture triangle is *magnified* to fit. When the texture triangle is larger than the screen triangle, the texture triangle is *minified* to fit. In both cases distortion occurs. *Filtering* is a technique Direct3D uses to help smooth out these distortions.

Direct3D provides three different types of filters; each one provides a different level of quality. The better the quality, the slower it is, so you must make the trade-off between quality and speed.

- **Nearest Point Sampling:** This is not really a filter at all; what it does is map a texel to the nearest screen pixel. The results of this filter are poor, and it generally should not be used unless you have good reason to do so. However, it requires little additional work.

- **Linear Filtering:** This type of filtering produces pretty good results and can be done very fast on today's hardware. It is recommended that you use linear filtering as a minimum. The filter works by averaging (weighting) the 2×2 texels surrounding a given screen pixel.

- **Anisotropic Filtering:** This type of filter helps alleviate the distortion that occurs when the angle between the polygon normal and the camera's look vector is wide. This is the most expensive filter, but generally gives the best results; still, it should only be used when linear filtering does not suffice. When using anisotropic filtering, we must also set the MAXANISOTROPY level, which determines the quality of the anisotropic filtering. The higher this value, the better the results. Check the D3DCAPS9::MaxAnisotropy data member for the maximum value your device supports.

Texture filters are associated with a texture in an effect file by defining a *sampler*. For example, the following code (which would be located in an .fx file) defines a sampler:

```
uniform extern texture gTex;

sampler TexS = sampler_state
{
        Texture = <gTex>;
        MinFilter = LINEAR;
        MagFilter = LINEAR;
};
```

The above code attaches a texture to a sampler object and specifies the minification and magnification states. A sampler encapsulates a texture along with certain sampler states that control how it is used (such as its filters). Here is another example that uses an anisotropic min filter with `MaxAnisotropy = 4`:

```
uniform extern texture gTex0;

sampler Tex0S = sampler_state
{
      Texture = <gTex0>;
      MinFilter = Anisotropic;
      MagFilter = LINEAR;
      MaxAnisotropy = 4;
};
```

And lastly, using the point filter:

```
sampler TexS = sampler_state
{
      Texture = <gTex>;
      MinFilter = POINT;
      MagFilter = POINT;
};
```

Note: Some cards do not support an anisotropic magnification filter (they only support an anisotropic minification filter); as always, check the device capabilities.

Note: The sampler state definitions (and, incidentally, also the effect pass definitions) are not case sensitive. For example, you can write:

```
sampler TexS = sampler_state
{
      Texture = <gTex>;
      MinFilter = POINT;
      MAGFilter = Point;
};
```

11.4 Mipmaps

As discussed in §11.3, the triangle on the screen is usually not the same size as the texture triangle. In an effort to make the size difference less drastic, we can create a chain of *mipmaps* for a texture. The idea is to take a texture and create a series of smaller, lower-resolution textures, but customizing the filtering for each of these levels so it preserves the detail that is important for us (see Figure 11.4).

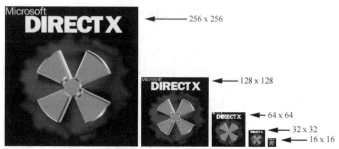

Figure 11.4: A chain of mipmaps; notice that each successive mipmap is half the size, in each dimension, of the previous mipmap level of detail.

11.4.1 Mipmap Filter

The mipmap filter is used to control how Direct3D uses the mipmaps. You can set the mipmap filter by writing the following in a `sampler_state` definition:

```
MipFilter = Filter;
```

Where `Filter` is one of the following three options:

- `NONE`: Disables mipmapping.
- `POINT`: By using this filter, Direct3D chooses the mipmap level that is closest in size to the screen triangle. Once that level is chosen, Direct3D filters that level based on the specified min and mag filters.
- `LINEAR`: By using this filter, Direct3D takes the two mipmap levels that are closest in size to the screen triangle, filters each level with the min and mag filters, and finally linearly combines these two levels to form the final color values.

11.4.2 Using Mipmaps with Direct3D

Using mipmaps with Direct3D is easy. If the device supports mipmaps, `D3DXCreateTextureFromFile` generates a mipmap chain for you. In addition, Direct3D automatically selects the mipmap that best matches the screen triangle based on the specified filter. So mipmapping is pretty much used and set up automatically.

Note: Observe that a key difference between a texture (`IDirect3DTexture9`) and a surface (`IDirect3DSurface9`) is that a texture has a collection of surfaces (one for each mip level).

11.4.3 **Hardware-Generated Mipmaps**

The mipmap levels are usually generated at content creation time (e.g., the *DXTex* utility application that ships with the DirectX SDK [located in *DX9SDK\Utilities\Bin\x86*] can generate a chain of mipmaps and export them to a DDS file (Direct Draw Surface Format), which D3DXCreate-TextureFromFile can load. Then, during application initialization, the program only needs to load the mipmap data.

Alternatively, if no mipmaps are present in the file (many image file formats do not even support the concept of mipmaps), D3DXCreateTexture-FromFile will generate a mipmap chain for you (as previously stated). The D3DXFilterTexture function provides yet another way to generate mipmaps (see the SDK documentation for details). Note that when either D3DXCreateTextureFromFile or D3DXFilterTexture are used to create mipmaps, the mipmaps are generated in software on the CPU. Thus, we would never want to do this at run time, and creating mipmaps for many textures can prolong our initialization times.

Some hardware can generate mipmap levels automatically (i.e., a hardware filter is applied to generate the lower mipmap levels given the base level). This is useful for times when the texture contents change at run time (e.g., dynamic textures, or render target textures, where we draw to a texture instead of the back buffer), and the mipmap levels need to be updated, as generating the mipmap levels on the CPU at run time would be too slow. Note that with hardware mipmapping, mipmap levels are generated as needed by the hardware; to manually force a generation of mipmap levels, call the following function:

```
VOID IDirect3DBaseTexture9::GenerateMipSubLevels();
```

To use hardware mipmaps, we must specify the D3DUSAGE_AUTOGENMIPMAP flag during creation as the Usage argument. Now, the D3DXCreateTextureFromFile function does not give us the option to specify this flag. Instead, we must use the D3DXCreateTextureFromFileEx function, which is more complicated in the sense that it takes many more parameters; we leave it as exercise 2 for you to investigate this function.

To set the filtering technique used to generate subsequent mipmap levels, we use the following method:

```
HRESULT IDirect3DBaseTexture9::SetAutoGenFilterType(
                            D3DTEXTUREFILTERTYPE FilterType);
```

Where FilterType can be D3DTEXF_POINT or D3DTEXF_LINEAR, which denote point and linear filtering, respectively. The default is D3DTEXF_LINEAR.

Note: IDirect3DTexture9 inherits from IDirect3DBaseTexture9.

To detect support for hardware mipmapping, check the D3DCAPS9::Caps2 D3DCAPS2_CANAUTOGENMIPMAP bit, and use the IDirect3D9::CheckDeviceFormat method. For example:

```
bool CanAutoGenMipmaps(D3DFORMAT texFormat)
{
    bool autoMipCap = (gCaps.Caps2 & D3DCAPS2_CANAUTOGENMIPMAP) != 0;

    HRESULT hr = D3D_OK;
    hr = gd3dObject->CheckDeviceFormat(D3DADAPTER_DEFAULT,
            D3DDEVTYPE_HAL, gDisplayFormat, D3DUSAGE_AUTOGENMIPMAP,
            D3DRTYPE_TEXTURE, texFormat);

    return autoMipCap && (hr == D3D_OK);
}
```

11.5 **Crate Demo**

We now review the key points of adding a crate texture to a cube (as shown in Figure 11.1).

11.5.1 **Specifying the Texture Coordinates**

The CrateDemo::buildBoxGeometry method is responsible for creating and filling in the vertex and index buffers mBoxVB and mBoxIB. The index buffer code is unchanged from previous demos that used cubes, and the only change to the vertex buffer code is that we need to add texture coordinates. We use the VertexPNT vertex structure, as defined in §11.1. Because there are 24 vertices, for brevity, we only show the texture coordinates for the front cube face (the other cube faces are done analogously — you just look at the coordinate plane to which the face is parallel). The code is as follows, and we have bolded the texture coordinates:

```
void CrateDemo::buildBoxGeometry()
{
    // Create the vertex buffer.
    HR(gd3dDevice->CreateVertexBuffer(24 * sizeof(VertexPNT),
            D3DUSAGE_WRITEONLY,0, D3DPOOL_MANAGED, &mBoxVB, 0));

    // Write box vertices to the vertex buffer.
    VertexPNT* v = 0;
    HR(mBoxVB->Lock(0, 0, (void**)&v, 0));

    // Fill in the front face vertex data.
    v[0] = VertexPNT(-1.0f, -1.0f, -1.0f, 0.0f, 0.0f, -1.0f, 0.0f, 1.0f);
    v[1] = VertexPNT(-1.0f,  1.0f, -1.0f, 0.0f, 0.0f, -1.0f, 0.0f, 0.0f);
    v[2] = VertexPNT( 1.0f,  1.0f, -1.0f, 0.0f, 0.0f, -1.0f, 1.0f, 0.0f);
    v[3] = VertexPNT( 1.0f, -1.0f, -1.0f, 0.0f, 0.0f, -1.0f, 1.0f, 1.0f);

    ...
```

Refer back to Figure 11.3 if you need help seeing why the texture coordinates are specified this way.

11.5.2 Creating the Texture

We create the texture at initialization time (i.e., in the application constructor) as follows:

```
HR(D3DXCreateTextureFromFile(gd3dDevice, "crate.jpg", &mCrateTex));
```

Here, crate.jpg is an image stored in the application's working directory, and mCrateTex is of type IDirect3DTexture9.

Note: Because IDirect3DTexture9 objects are COM interfaces, they need to be released when done.

11.5.3 Setting and Sampling the Texture

Texture data is typically accessed in a pixel shader. In order for the pixel shader to access it, we need to set the texture (IDirect3DTexture9 object) to a texture object in the .fx file. This is done as follows:

```
HR(mFX->SetTexture(mhTex, mCrateTex));
```

Here, mhTex is a handle to a texture object in the effect file:

```
uniform extern texture gTex;
```

Additionally in the .fx file, we need to define a sampler object, which encapsulates a texture and its filter settings:

```
sampler TexS = sampler_state
{
    Texture = <gTex>;
    MinFilter = LINEAR;
    MagFilter = LINEAR;
    MipFilter = LINEAR;
};
```

Now, the vertex shader for the Crate demo is given as follows:

```
struct OutputVS
{
    float4 posH    : POSITION0;
    float4 diffuse : COLOR0;
    float4 spec    : COLOR1;
    float2 tex0    : TEXCOORD0;
};

OutputVS DirLightTexVS(float3 posL : POSITION0,
                       float3 normalL : NORMAL0,
                       float2 tex0: TEXCOORD0)
{
    // Zero out our output.
```

```
OutputVS outVS = (OutputVS)0;

// Transform normal to world space.
float3 normalW = mul(float4(normalL, 0.0f), gWorldInvTrans).xyz;
normalW = normalize(normalW);

// Transform vertex position to world space.
float3 posW  = mul(float4(posL, 1.0f), gWorld).xyz;

//=========================================================

// Lighting Calculations Omitted...

//=========================================================

outVS.diffuse.rgb = ambient + diffuse;
outVS.diffuse.a   = gDiffuseMtrl.a;
outVS.spec = float4(spec, 0.0f);

// Transform to homogeneous clip space.
outVS.posH = mul(float4(posL, 1.0f), gWVP);

// Pass on texture coordinates to be interpolated in
// rasterization.
outVS.tex0 = tex0;

// Done--return the output.
return outVS;
}
```

After the texture coordinates are output for each vertex, they are interpolated during rasterization. The interpolated texture coordinates are fed in, as input, to the pixel shader for each pixel. A pixel shader *samples* a texture (i.e., fetches a color from the texture at a point in the texture based on the filters) with the tex2D HLSL function. We specify a sampler object (first parameter) that specifies the texture object and its filters, and we specify texture coordinates (second parameter), which indicate the point on the texture map we want to sample.

```
float4 DirLightTexPS(float4 c : COLOR0,
                     float4 spec : COLOR1,
                     float2 tex0 : TEXCOORD0) : COLOR
{
    // Get texel from texture map that gets mapped to this pixel.
    float3 texColor = tex2D(TexS, tex0).rgb;

    // Combine texture color with color generated by lighting.
    float3 diffuse = c.rgb * texColor;

    // Add in the specular term separately.
    return float4(diffuse + spec.rgb, c.a);
}
```

Observe from the vertex shader that with texturing, we pass on the diffuse (combined with ambient) and specular terms independently into the pixel shader. This is because the pixel shader combines the diffuse color lit by vertex lighting and the texture color by a color-multiply. We can think of the texture color as being part of the *diffuse* material but not the *specular* material. Thus, we do not want to multiply the specular light with the texture color, and hence why we pass the terms separately into the pixel shader.

Note: Observe that if we specify a yellow diffuse material, that color is multiplied with the texture color to form a new color (it will look like the texture color with a yellow tint). Often we want to just use the texture color. In this case, use a white material and white light so that the lighting term is basically a grayscale value that will darken or lighten the texture color based on the lighting.

11.6 **Address Modes**

Previously, we stated that texture coordinates must be specified in the range [0, 1]. Technically, that is not correct; they can go outside that range. The behavior for texture coordinates that go outside the [0, 1] range is defined by the Direct3D *address mode*. There are four types of address modes: *wrap*, *border color*, *clamp*, and *mirror*, which are illustrated in Figures 11.5, 11.6, 11.7, and 11.8, respectively.

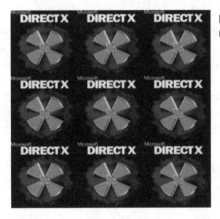

Figure 11.5: Wrap mode.

Figure 11.6: Border color mode.

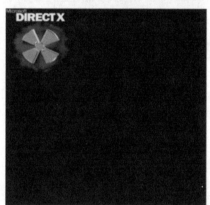

Figure 11.7: Clamp mode.

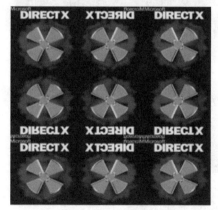

Figure 11.8: Mirror mode.

In these figures, the texture coordinates for the four unique quad vertices are defined as $(0, 0)$, $(0, 3)$, $(3, 0)$, and $(3, 3)$. From the 3 in both the u-axis and v-axis direction, the quad is subdivided into a 3×3 area matrix.

The wrap address mode is the default and probably the most often employed address mode, as it allows us to tile the texture repeatedly over some polygon. This effectively enables us to increase the texture resolution without supplying additional data (although the extra resolution is repetitive). If, for instance, you wanted the texture to be tiled 5×5 across the quad, you would specify the wrap address mode and texture coordinates (0, 0), (0, 5), (5, 0), and (5, 5).

The clamp address mode is also useful if, for example, you want to clamp "out of bounds" texture coordinates to the boundary value of the texture.

As with filters, address modes are states associated with a sampler; as such, they are specified in a `sampler_state` definition block. The following code demonstrates how the four address modes are set:

```
sampler TexS = sampler_state
{
    Texture = <gTex>;
    MinFilter = LINEAR;
    MagFilter = LINEAR;
    MipFilter = LINEAR;
    AddressU  = WRAP;
    AddressV  = WRAP;
};

sampler TexS = sampler_state
{
    Texture = <gTex>;
    MinFilter = LINEAR;
    MagFilter = LINEAR;
    MipFilter = LINEAR;
    AddressU  = BORDER;
    AddressV  = BORDER;
    BorderColor = 0xff0000ff;
};

sampler TexS = sampler_state
{
    Texture = <gTex>;
    MinFilter = LINEAR;
    MagFilter = LINEAR;
    MipFilter = LINEAR;
    AddressU  = MIRROR;
    AddressV  = MIRROR;
};

sampler TexS = sampler_state
{
    Texture = <gTex>;
    MinFilter = LINEAR;
    MagFilter = LINEAR;
    MipFilter = LINEAR;
    AddressU  = CLAMP;
    AddressV  = CLAMP;
};
```

Observe that you can control the address mode separately in the u- and v-axis directions. Furthermore, for the border color mode, a border color value must be specified (e.g., `BorderColor = 0xff0000ff` sets a blue border color).

Tip: Suppose that you do have texture coordinates in the range [0, 1] and that you want to tile the texture 10 times. We can easily transform outside this range by multiplying the texture coordinates by a scaling factor. For example, $10 \cdot [0, 1] = [0, 10]$; so we have just easily altered the texture coordinates so that the texture would tile 10 times (assuming the wrap mode is specified). We can go in the other direction as well; that is, if we have texture coordinates in the range [0, 10], we can shrink the interval by multiplying the texture coordinates with a scaling factor of less than 1: $0.25 \cdot [0, 10] = [0, 2.5]$. The point here is that we can easily control the amount of tiling by adjusting a texture coordinate scaling factor value.

11.7 **Tiled Ground Demo**

For this demo, we tile a ground texture repeatedly over a grid to provide us with a "ground" plane. If we do not tile the texture, then the texture will be stretched over the grid and distortions will occur since the triangle in screen space will generally be much larger than the corresponding texture triangle (if there is not enough resolution, too much magnification occurs). In addition, we employ an anisotropic minification filter because typically the camera will "walk" on the ground and thus the ground plane normal will be almost perpendicular to the camera's look vector direction. (Exercise 3 asks you to experiment with different anisotropic levels, and exercise 4 asks you to experiment with different tiling frequencies.)

Essentially, the only core texture-related change of this demo from the previous demo is that we need to generate the grid texture coordinates in such a way that the texture will be tiled over the grid. Here is the code that does this:

```
VertexPNT* v = 0;
HR(mGridVB->Lock(0, 0, (void**)&v, 0));

float texScale = 0.2f;
for(int i = 0; i < numVertRows; ++i)
{
    for(int j = 0; j < numVertCols; ++j)
    {
        DWORD index = i * numVertCols + j;
        v[index].pos    = verts[index];
        v[index].normal = D3DXVECTOR3(0.0f, 1.0f, 0.0f);
        v[index].tex0 = D3DXVECTOR2((float)j, (float)i) * texScale;
    }
```

```
        }

   HR(mGridVB->Unlock());
```

As you can see, we iterate over each grid point in a nested for-loop fashion. The texture coordinates for the v-axis are just $i = 0, 1, ..., numVertRows - 1$, and the texture coordinates for the u-axis are just $j = 0, 1, ..., numVertCols - 1$. Thus, if we have a 100×100 vertex grid, the texture coordinates in both the u- and v-directions range from [0, 99]. However, that is probably too much tiling; thus we multiply the texture coordinates, as we generate them, by texScale, which scales the texture coordinates down. You can modify this value to experiment with different tiling frequencies.

Also, obviously, we need to set the address modes to wrap so that the texture is tiled:

```
sampler TexS = sampler_state
{
     Texture = <gTex>;
     MinFilter = Anisotropic;
     MagFilter = LINEAR;
     MipFilter = LINEAR;
     MaxAnisotropy = 8;
     AddressU  = WRAP;
     AddressV  = WRAP;
};
```

Note: Our grid vertices are not stored in a matrix data structure; they are stored in a linear array. Thus, when we do the double for-loop, which is the natural way to iterate over a matrix, we have to do a small conversion calculation that converts the ij matrix indices into the corresponding linear array index:

```
DWORD index = i * numVertCols + j;
```

Figure 11.9 shows a screenshot of the demo.

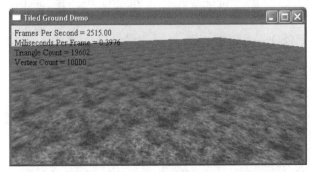

Figure 11.9: Screenshot of the Tiled Ground demo.

11.8 **Multi-texturing**

One annoyance with the previous demo is that we tile the same texture over the grid, which makes it extremely repetitive. We now show how to use multi-texturing to remove some of that repetition. _Multi-texturing_ refers to the technique of combining several texture maps together to form a net texture. Figure 11.10 illustrates the idea (and is also a screenshot of the Multi-texturing demo that we implement).

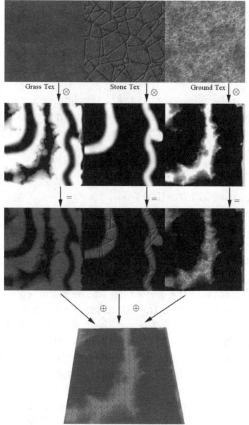

Figure 11.10: We start with three texture maps: grass, stone, and ground textures. We then associate grayscale blend maps with each color texture, which globally mark the regions on the grid where the corresponding texture should show up (bright regions mean more of the texture shows up and dark regions mean less of the texture should show up). (Note that we actually compact three grayscale maps into a single RGB image, where the red, green, and blue color channels are treated independently as grayscale images.) Each texture is color multiplied with its corresponding grayscale blend map, which kills or diminishes the intensity of the colored pixels based on their contribution (i.e., weight) as defined by the blend map. Finally, we add the results to produce a net texture that is mapped over the grid.

As Figure 11.10 shows, we have three textures that provide color. These color textures are tiled over a grid to increase the resolution. A fourth _blend map_ is then used, where each RGB color channel does not contain color data in the usual sense, but rather each RGB channel should be thought of as an 8-bit grayscale percent that controls how much of its corresponding texture shows up in the final image (the red channel is the grayscale blend map for the first color texture, the green channel is the grayscale blend map for the second color texture, and the blue channel is the grayscale blend map for the third color texture). Mathematically, this is expressed as follows: Let $\vec{C}_{1,ij}$, $\vec{C}_{2,ij}$, and $\vec{C}_{3,ij}$ be colors sampled from the three texture maps for the ijth pixel, and let $\vec{B}_{ij}=(B_{r,ij},B_{g,ij},B_{b,ij})$ be the color sampled from the blend map for the ijth pixel. Then the final color of the ijth pixel $\vec{F}_{ij}$ is given by:

$$\vec{F}_{ij}=w_1\vec{C}_{1,ij}+w_2\vec{C}_{2,ij}+w_3\vec{C}_{3,ij} \tag{11.1}$$

where $w_1 = \dfrac{B_{r,ij}}{B_{r,ij}+B_{g,ij}+B_{b,ij}}$, $w_2 = \dfrac{B_{g,ij}}{B_{r,ij}+B_{g,ij}+B_{b,ij}}$,

and $w_3 = \dfrac{B_{b,ij}}{B_{r,ij}+B_{g,ij}+B_{b,ij}}$.

Each scalar w_1, w_2, and w_3 prefixing a color vector is a weight determining how much of that color contributes to the final pixel color. To generate the weights, we divide each component of the blend map color vector by the sum of its components so that the sum of all three weights adds to 1.0. So, for example, if $B_{r,ij} = 5$, $B_{g,ij} = 10$, and $B_{b,ij} = 15$, then $B_{r,ij} + B_{g,ij} + B_{b,ij} = 30$, and $w_1 = 1/6 \approx 0.17 = 17\%$, $w_2 = 1/3 \approx 0.33 = 33\%$, and $w_3 = 1/2 \approx 0.5 = 50\%$. So the weights sum to 1.0 or 100%.

Now note that, unlike the other textures, the blend map is not tiled as we stretch it over the entire grid. This is necessary since we use the blend map to mark regions of the grid where we want a particular texture to show through, so the texture must be global and span the whole grid. You might wonder whether this is acceptable or if excessive magnification occurs. Indeed, magnification will occur and the blend map will be distorted by the texture filtering when it is stretched over the entire grid, but recall that the blend map is not where we get our details (we get them from the tiled textures). The blend map merely marks the general regions of the grid where (and how much) a particular texture contributes. So if the blend map gets distorted and blurred, it will not significantly affect the end result — perhaps a bit of dirt will blend in with a bit of grass, for example, and this actually provides a smoother and more natural transition between textures.

Of course, this is only one way to employ multi-texturing. There are many other ways texture maps can be combined to produce different effects, some of which we will look at toward the end of this book.

11.8.1 Generating Texture Coordinates

We need two sets of texture coordinates: one for the blend map, which is stretched over the entire grid (its texture coordinates are in the [0, 1] range), and one for tiled color textures (texture coordinates outside the range [0, 1]). So what we do is compute the texture coordinates in the [0, 1] range for the blend map, and then scale these texture coordinates outside this range in order to tile the colored textures. Note that we actually do the scaling in the vertex shader (so we can still use the VertexPNT vertex format):

```
// In vertex shader...

// tex0 in the range [0, 1].
outVS.tiledTexC    = tex0 * 16.0f; // Scale tex-coord to tile 16 times
                                   // for colored textures: [0, 16].

outVS.nonTiledTexC = tex0;         // Pass on non-tiled tex-coords
                                   // for blend map.
```

Note that we have hard coded the scaling factor as 16 here, but you could make the scaling factor an effect parameter if you wanted to be able to change it at run time.

So how do we compute the texture coordinates in the [0, 1] range for each vertex in the grid so that the texture stretches over the grid? The texture coordinates for each vertex can be derived in terms of its corresponding vertex position by transforming the grid vertices to the texture coordinate system (see Figure 11.11).

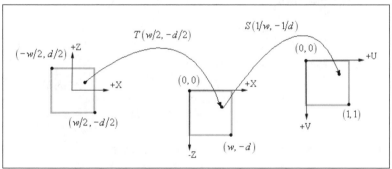

Figure 11.11: The grid centered about the origin, where _w_ is the grid width and _d_ is the grid depth in the _xz_-plane. We first shift the grid vertices into the fourth quadrant by applying a translation transformation. Then we scale the grid vertices to be in the range [0, 1]. Observe that we need to negate the _z_-coordinates since positive _v_ goes "down" in the texture coordinate system.

So if (x, z) (ignore the y-coordinate) is the position of a grid vertex in the xz-plane, then its corresponding texture coordinates (u, v) are found by applying the sequence of transformations shown in Figure 11.11 to (x, z). That is:

$$(u,v)=\left((x,z)+(w/2,-d/2)\right)\otimes(1/w,-1/d)$$

(Recall ⊗ means component-wise multiplication.) The following code generates the texture coordinates using this formula.

```
VertexPNT* v = 0;
HR(mGridVB->Lock(0, 0, (void**)&v, 0));

float w = 99.0f;
float d = 99.0f;
for(int i = 0; i < 100; ++i)
{
    for(int j = 0; j < 100; ++j)
    {
        DWORD index = i * 100 + j;
        v[index].pos    = verts[index];
        v[index].normal = D3DXVECTOR3(0.0f, 1.0f, 0.0f);
        v[index].tex0.x = (v[index].pos.x + (0.5f*w)) / w;
        v[index].tex0.y = (v[index].pos.z - (0.5f*d)) / -d;
    }
}
```

11.8.2 Creating and Enabling the Textures

Our application class has the following texture data members:

```
IDirect3DTexture9* mTex0;
IDirect3DTexture9* mTex1;
IDirect3DTexture9* mTex2;
IDirect3DTexture9* mBlendMap;
```

We create the textures in the constructor:

```
HR(D3DXCreateTextureFromFile(gd3dDevice, "grass0.dds", &mTex0));
HR(D3DXCreateTextureFromFile(gd3dDevice, "stone2.dds", &mTex1));
HR(D3DXCreateTextureFromFile(gd3dDevice, "ground0.dds", &mTex2));
HR(D3DXCreateTextureFromFile(gd3dDevice, "blendmap.jpg", &mBlendMap));
```

We set the textures to the effect parameters like so:

```
HR(mFX->SetTexture(mhTex0, mTex0));
HR(mFX->SetTexture(mhTex1, mTex1));
HR(mFX->SetTexture(mhTex2, mTex2));
HR(mFX->SetTexture(mhBlendMap, mBlendMap));
```

Here, mhTex0, mTex1, mTex2, and mBlendMap are D3DXHANDLEs referencing the texture objects in the .fx file.

11.8.3 Sampler Objects

For each texture in the .fx file, we define a sampler object:

```
uniform extern texture gTex0;
uniform extern texture gTex1;
uniform extern texture gTex2;
uniform extern texture gBlendMap;

sampler Tex0S = sampler_state
```

```
{
    Texture = <gTex0>;
    MinFilter = Anisotropic;
    MagFilter = LINEAR;
    MipFilter = LINEAR;
    MaxAnisotropy = 8;
    AddressU  = WRAP;
    AddressV  = WRAP;
};

sampler Tex1S = sampler_state
{
    Texture = <gTex1>;
    MinFilter = Anisotropic;
    MagFilter = LINEAR;
    MipFilter = LINEAR;
    MaxAnisotropy = 8;
    AddressU  = WRAP;
    AddressV  = WRAP;
};

sampler Tex2S = sampler_state
{
    Texture = <gTex2>;
    MinFilter = Anisotropic;
    MagFilter = LINEAR;
    MipFilter = LINEAR;
    MaxAnisotropy = 8;
    AddressU  = WRAP;
    AddressV  = WRAP;
};

sampler BlendMapS = sampler_state
{
    Texture = <gBlendMap>;
    MinFilter = LINEAR;
    MagFilter = LINEAR;
    MipFilter = LINEAR;
    AddressU  = WRAP;
    AddressV  = WRAP;
};
```

11.8.4 The Vertex and Pixel Shader

The vertex shader does not do anything we have not already seen. As far as texturing goes, it just outputs the texture coordinates.

```
struct OutputVS
{
    float4 posH        : POSITION0;
    float4 diffuse     : COLOR0;
    float4 spec        : COLOR1;
    float2 tiledTexC   : TEXCOORD0;
    float2 nonTiledTexC : TEXCOORD1;
```

```
};

OutputVS TerrainMultiTexVS(float3 posL : POSITION0,
                          float3 normalL : NORMAL0,
                          float2 tex0 : TEXCOORD0)
{
    // Zero out our output.
    OutputVS outVS = (OutputVS)0;

    // Transform normal to world space.
    float3 normalW = mul(float4(normalL, 0.0f), gWorldInvTrans).xyz;
    normalW = normalize(normalW);

    // Transform vertex position to world space.
    float3 posW  = mul(float4(posL, 1.0f), gWorld).xyz;

    //=========================================================

    // Lighting Calculations Omitted...

    //=========================================================

    outVS.diffuse.rgb = ambient + diffuse;
    outVS.diffuse.a   = gDiffuseMtrl.a;
    outVS.spec = float4(spec, 0.0f);

    // Transform to homogeneous clip space.
    outVS.posH = mul(float4(posL, 1.0f), gWVP);

    // Pass on texture coordinates to be interpolated in
    // rasterization.
    outVS.tiledTexC    = tex0 * 16.0f; // Scale tex-coord to
    outVS.nonTiledTexC = tex0;         // tile 16 times.

    // Done--return the output.
    return outVS;
}
```

The pixel shader to do the texture blending is also straightforward, and essentially implements Equation 11.1.

```
float4 TerrainMultiTexPS(float4 diffuse : COLOR0,
                         float4 spec       : COLOR1,
                         float2 tiledTexC : TEXCOORD0,
                         float2 nonTiledTexC : TEXCOORD1) : COLOR
{
    // Layer maps are tiled
    float3 c0 = tex2D(Tex0S, tiledTexC).rgb;
    float3 c1 = tex2D(Tex1S, tiledTexC).rgb;
    float3 c2 = tex2D(Tex2S, tiledTexC).rgb;

    // Blend map is not tiled.
    float3 B = tex2D(BlendMapS, nonTiledTexC).rgb;
```

```
// Find the inverse of all the blend weights so that we can
// scale the total color to the range [0, 1].
float totalInverse = 1.0f / (B.r + B.g + B.b);

// Scale the colors by each layer by its corresponding weight
// stored in the blend map.
c0 *= B.r * totalInverse;
c1 *= B.g * totalInverse;
c2 *= B.b * totalInverse;

// Sum the colors and modulate with the lighting color.
float3 final = (c0 + c1 + c2) * diffuse.rgb;

return float4(final + spec, diffuse.a);
}
```

11.9 **Spherical and Cylindrical Texturing**

Specifying texture coordinates by hand is a chore. Sometimes, as with the grid, we can generate the texture coordinates algorithmically. In addition, there are programs that enable it to be done interactively by an artist. Sphere and cylindrical texture mappings can be used to approximate the texture coordinates for arbitrary meshes that are similar in shape to a sphere or cylinder. For example, the distortions of using texture coordinates generated by a spherical mapping for a round stone, or even a teapot, would be small. On the other hand, a cylindrical mapping would produce good results for objects that are approximately cylinders, such as cups, poles, and columns.

11.9.1 **Spherical Mapping**

The idea of spherical mapping is to take a mesh and convert its 3D rectangular coordinates (x, y, z) to spherical coordinates (ρ, θ, ϕ). Then, we ignore the 3D radius ρ and just look at its surface coordinates θ and ϕ. The conversion formulas are:

$$\rho = \sqrt{x^2 + y^2 + z^2}$$

$$\theta = \begin{cases} \tan^{-1}(z/x) & \text{if } \theta \text{ is in quadrant 1 or 4} \\ \tan^{-1}(z/x) + \pi & \text{if } \theta \text{ is in quadrant 2 or 3} \end{cases}$$

$$\phi = \cos^{-1}\left(y / \sqrt{x^2 + y^2 + z^2}\right)$$

We may derive these equations by examining Figure 11.12 and applying trigonometry.

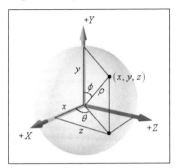

Figure 11.12: Converting rectangular coordinates to spherical coordinates.

The surface coordinates θ and ϕ provide us with a set of 2D coordinates that tell us how to move on the sphere's surface (see Figure 11.13).

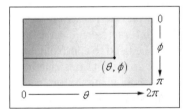

Figure 11.13: 2D rectangular coordinates given by θ and ϕ.

By transforming $\theta \in [0, 2\pi] \rightarrow [0, 1]$ and $\phi \in [0, \pi] \rightarrow [0, 1]$, we obtain rectangular texture coordinates that map over the surface of the sphere. Note, however, that this leads to distortions at the poles, because at the poles $x = 0$ and $y = 1$; hence, $\theta = \tan^{-1}(z/x)$ is undefined.

The code that computes the spherical texture coordinates is given as follows:

```
void SphereCylDemo::genSphericalTexCoords()
{
    // D3DXCreate* functions generate vertices with position
    // and normal data. But for texturing, we also need
    // tex-coords. So clone the mesh to change the vertex
    // format to a format with tex-coords.

    D3DVERTEXELEMENT9 elements[64];
    UINT numElements = 0;
    VertexPNT::Decl->GetDeclaration(elements, &numElements);

    ID3DXMesh* temp = 0;
    HR(mSphere->CloneMesh(D3DXMESH_SYSTEMMEM,
            elements, gd3dDevice, &temp));

    ReleaseCOM(mSphere);
```

```
// Now generate texture coordinates for each vertex.
VertexPNT* vertices = 0;
HR(temp->LockVertexBuffer(0, (void**)&vertices));

for(UINT i = 0; i < temp->GetNumVertices(); ++i)
{
        // Convert to spherical coordinates.
        D3DXVECTOR3 p = vertices[i].pos;

        float theta = atan2f(p.z, p.x);
        float phi   = acosf(p.y / sqrtf(p.x*p.x+p.y*p.y+p.z*p.z));

        // Phi and theta give the texture coordinates, but are
        // not in the range [0, 1], so scale them into that range.

        float u = theta / (2.0f*D3DX_PI);
        float v = phi   / D3DX_PI;

        // Save texture coordinates.

        vertices[i].tex0.x = u;
        vertices[i].tex0.y = v;
}
HR(temp->UnlockVertexBuffer());

// Clone back to a hardware mesh.
HR(temp->CloneMesh(D3DXMESH_MANAGED | D3DXMESH_WRITEONLY,
        elements, gd3dDevice, &mSphere));

ReleaseCOM(temp);
}
```

The above code uses some methods of the ID3DXMesh interface and IDirect3DVertexDeclaration9 interface that we have not discussed. We briefly review, at a conceptual level, what the methods do. The details of the ID3DXMesh methods will be discussed in a later chapter when we actually study the ID3DXMesh interface in depth.

■ IDirect3DVertexDeclaration9::GetDeclaration: This method returns an array of D3DVERTEXELEMENT9 elements that describe the vertex declaration; this data is returned via the first parameter, which serves as a "destination" buffer. The second parameter returns the number of elements in the array and counts the terminating D3DDECL_END element.

■ ID3DXMesh::CloneMesh: This method copies (clones) a mesh. However, besides doing a direct copy, it allows us to change some things about the clone, such as its memory pool, and the vertex structure of its vertices (as described by the D3DVERTEXELEMENT9 array passed into the second parameter). We use this method to clone the sphere to system memory (because we will be reading and writing to it) and to change its vertex format to a format that possesses texture coordinates (recall that the D3DXCreate* functions only generate position and normal data).

After we have cloned it to a format that supports texture coordinates (namely, `VertexPNT`), we generate the texture coordinates based on the previously discussed mathematics. Finally, when we are done, we clone the mesh again, but this time using 3D hardware friendly flags.

■ `ID3DXMesh::LockVertexBuffer/ID3DXMesh::UnlockVertexBuffer`: These methods do what their names imply: They lock/unlock the mesh's internal vertex buffer for access.

11.9.2 Cylindrical Mapping

The idea of cylindrical mapping is to take a mesh and convert its 3D rectangular coordinates (x, y, z) to cylindrical coordinates (r, θ, y). Then, we ignore the 2D radius r and just look at its surface coordinates θ and y. The conversion formulas are:

$$r = \sqrt{x^2 + z^2}$$

$$\theta = \begin{cases} \tan^{-1}(z/x) & \text{if } \theta \text{ is in quadrant 1 or 4} \\ \tan^{-1}(z/x) + \pi & \text{if } \theta \text{ is in quadrant 2 or 3} \end{cases}$$

$$y = y$$

We may derive these equations by examining Figure 11.14 and applying trigonometry.

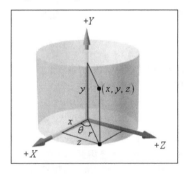

Figure 11.14: Converting rectangular coordinates to cylindrical coordinates.

The surface coordinates θ and y provide us with a set of 2D coordinates that tell us how to move on the cylinder's surface (see Figure 11.15).

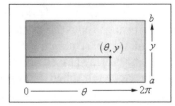

Figure 11.15: 2D rectangular coordinates given by θ and y.

Let a be the minimum coordinate value of all the mesh vertices on the axis with which our cylinder is aligned (e.g., if the cylinder is aligned on the z-axis, then a is the minimum z-coordinate of all the mesh vertices), and let b be the maximum coordinate value of all the mesh vertices on the axis with which our cylinder is aligned. Then the height of a tight cylinder that encapsulates the mesh is given by $h = b - a$. By transforming $\theta \in [0, 2\pi] \rightarrow [0, 1]$ and $y \in [a, b] \rightarrow [a - b, 0] = [-h, 0] \rightarrow [-1, 0] \rightarrow [0, 1]$, we obtain rectangular texture coordinates that map over the surface of the cylinder. The series of transformations on $[a, b]$ may seem complicated, but it only consists of translations of scaling transformations. Recall that a and b mark the end points of the cylinder along its axis. Then $[a, b] \rightarrow [a - b, 0] = [-h, 0]$ translates the cylinder down so that its top is at the origin. The transformation $[-h, 0] \rightarrow [-1, 0]$ is just a normalization found by dividing by h. Finally, the last transformation, $[-1, 0] \rightarrow [0, 1]$, is just a reflection that flips the sign since we want v positive in the down direction for texture coordinates.

The code that computes the cylindrical texture coordinates is given as follows:

```
void SphereCylDemo::genCylTexCoords(AXIS axis)
{
    // D3DXCreate* functions generate vertices with position
    // and normal data. But for texturing, we also need
    // tex-coords. So clone the mesh to change the vertex
    // format to a format with tex-coords.

    D3DVERTEXELEMENT9 elements[64];
    UINT numElements = 0;
    VertexPNT::Decl->GetDeclaration(elements, &numElements);

    ID3DXMesh* temp = 0;
    HR(mCylinder->CloneMesh(D3DXMESH_SYSTEMMEM,
        elements, gd3dDevice, &temp));

    ReleaseCOM(mCylinder);

    // Now generate texture coordinates for each vertex.
    VertexPNT* vertices = 0;
    HR(temp->LockVertexBuffer(0, (void**)&vertices));

    // We need to get the height of the cylinder onto which we are
    // projecting the vertices. That height depends on the axis on
    // which the client has specified that the cylinder lies. The
    // height is determined by finding the height of the bounding
    // cylinder on the specified axis.

    D3DXVECTOR3 maxPoint(-FLT_MAX, -FLT_MAX, -FLT_MAX);
    D3DXVECTOR3 minPoint(FLT_MAX, FLT_MAX, FLT_MAX);

    for(UINT i = 0; i < temp->GetNumVertices(); ++i)
    {
```

```
        D3DXVec3Maximize(&maxPoint, &maxPoint, &vertices[i].pos);
        D3DXVec3Minimize(&minPoint, &minPoint, &vertices[i].pos);
}

float a = 0.0f;
float b = 0.0f;
float h = 0.0f;
switch( axis )
{
case X_AXIS:
    a = minPoint.x;
    b = maxPoint.x;
    h = b-a;
    break;
case Y_AXIS:
    a = minPoint.y;
    b = maxPoint.y;
    h = b-a;
    break;
case Z_AXIS:
    a = minPoint.z;
    b = maxPoint.z;
    h = b-a;
    break;
}

// Iterate over each vertex and compute its texture coordinate.
for(UINT i = 0; i < temp->GetNumVertices(); ++i)
{
    // Get the coordinates along the axes orthogonal to the
    // axis with which the cylinder is aligned.

    float x = 0.0f;
    float y = 0.0f;
    float z = 0.0f;
    switch( axis )
    {
    case X_AXIS:
        x = vertices[i].pos.y;
        z = vertices[i].pos.z;
        y = vertices[i].pos.x;
        break;
    case Y_AXIS:
        x = vertices[i].pos.x;
        z = vertices[i].pos.z;
        y = vertices[i].pos.y;
        break;
    case Z_AXIS:
        x = vertices[i].pos.x;
        z = vertices[i].pos.y;
        y = vertices[i].pos.z;
        break;
    }
```

```
                    // Convert to cylindrical coordinates.

                    float theta = atan2f(z, x);
                    float y2    = y - b; // Transform [a, b]-->[-h, 0]

                    // Transform theta from [0, 2*pi] to [0, 1] range and
                    // transform y2 from [-h, 0] to [0, 1].

                    float u = theta / (2.0f*D3DX_PI);
                    float v = y2 / -h;

                    // Save texture coordinates.
                    vertices[i].tex0.x = u;
                    vertices[i].tex0.y = v;
            }

            HR(temp->UnlockVertexBuffer());

            // Clone back to a hardware mesh.
            HR(temp->CloneMesh(D3DXMESH_MANAGED | D3DXMESH_WRITEONLY,
                    elements, gd3dDevice, &mCylinder));

            ReleaseCOM(temp);
    }
```

11.9.3 **Textural Wrapping**

Suppose that we have a texture triangle defined by the vertices (u_0, v_0), (u_1, v_1), and (u_2, v_2), as in Figure 11.16. The figure shows two ways the triangle can be formed. In Figure 11.16a, we can think of the edge $u = 1$ wrapping around in a cylindrical fashion such that it coincides with $u = 0$. In Figure 11.16b, we can think of the edges as boundaries and just take the triangle that lies in the boundary. If we are texture mapping a cylinder (or sphere, or any other object that wraps around), then we naturally want the cylindrical interpretation; otherwise, we would map the wrong texture triangle (i.e., the one in Figure 11.16b) to the 3D triangle.

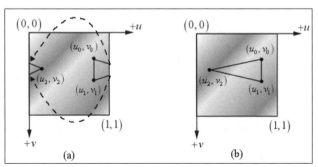

Figure 11.16: (a) The texture wraps around, as it is the surface of a cylinder. (b) The texture does not wrap around; it is a rectangle.

By default, Direct3D interpolates texture coordinates such that the triangle in Figure 11.16b would be used. However, we can change this behavior so that the texture coordinates are interpolates such that the triangle in Figure 11.16a is used by setting the following render state:

```
HR(gd3dDevice->SetRenderState(D3DRS_WRAP0, D3DWRAP_U));
```

This tells Direct3D to wrap texture coordinates in the u-axis direction. We can also wrap in the other coordinate directions by specifying combinations (combined by bitwise OR) of: D3DWRAP_U, D3DWRAP_V, and D3DWRAP_W (equivalently, you can use D3DWRAPCOORD_0, D3DWRAPCOORD_1, and D3DWRAPCOORD_2, respectively). To restore the default behavior, we just pass 0 for the second parameter:

```
HR(gd3dDevice->SetRenderState(D3DRS_WRAP0, 0));
```

Note: You would use D3DWRAP_W, for example, with 3D texture coordinates.

The zero index suffix in D3DRS_WRAP0 means the wrap setting is applied to the texture coordinates with that usage index (i.e., the texture coordinates assigned to the register identified by the semantic TEXCOORD0). If you want the texture coordinates mapped to the register identified by the semantic TEXCOORD2 to be wrapped, then specify D3DRS_WRAP2:

```
HR(gd3dDevice->SetRenderState(D3DRS_WRAP2, D3DWRAP_U));
```

Warning: Do not confuse texture wrapping as described here with the WRAP address mode, which tiles a texture.

11.9.4 Spherical and Cylindrical Texturing Demo

The code for this demo (see the screenshot in Figure 11.17) is essentially the same as what we have seen previously, except some extra initialization work must be done to generate the texture coordinates. In the constructor we have:

```
HR(D3DXCreateCylinder(gd3dDevice, 1.0f, 1.0f, 6.0f,
    20, 20, &mCylinder, 0));
HR(D3DXCreateSphere(gd3dDevice, 1.0f, 20, 20, &mSphere, 0));

genSphericalTexCoords();
genCylTexCoords(Z_AXIS);

HR(D3DXCreateTextureFromFile(gd3dDevice, "crate.jpg", &mSphereTex));
HR(D3DXCreateTextureFromFile(gd3dDevice, "stone2.dds", &mCylTex));
HR(D3DXCreateTextureFromFile(gd3dDevice, "ground0.dds", &mGridTex));
```

In addition, we must set the appropriate texture to the effect file before rendering, and lastly, the D3DRS_WRAP0 render state needs to be set to D3DWRAP_U when rendering the cylinder or sphere.

```
HR(mFX->SetTexture(mhTex, mGridTex));
// ...Draw Grid

HR(gd3dDevice->SetRenderState(D3DRS_WRAP0, D3DWRAP_U));
HR(mFX->SetTexture(mhTex, mCylTex));
// ...Draw Cylinders

HR(mFX->SetTexture(mhTex, mSphereTex));
// ...Draw Spheres
HR(gd3dDevice->SetRenderState(D3DRS_WRAP0, 0));
```

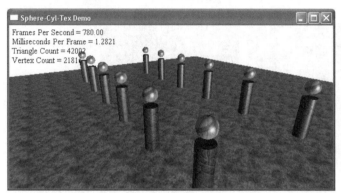

Figure 11.17:
Screenshot of
the Sphere-Cyl-
Tex demo.

11.10 **Texture Animation**

Thus far, in the vertex shader of all of our programs, we have simply passed the texture coordinates on to the rasterization stage for interpolation and input into the pixel shader. For example:

```
// Pass on texture coordinates to be interpolated in
// rasterization.
outVS.tiledTexC    = tex0 * 16.0f;
outVS.nonTiledTexC = tex0;
```

However, some special effects can be achieved by altering the texture coordinates. For instance, we can translate texture coordinates as a function of time to "scroll" the texture over the surface to which it is mapped. In older games, scrolling a water and lava texture map was used to simulate movement. Scrolling cloud textures over a skybox or sky dome to implement moving clouds demonstrates another application for texture animation. You can also rotate or scale texture coordinates as a function of time to animate the textures in a different way.

This section's demo program provides an example of texture animation, as well as another application of multi-texturing. We scroll two cloud maps (see Figure 11.18) at different velocities over a grid and *add* them together along with a blue color (for the sky):

```
float4 CloudsPS(float4 c : COLOR0,
                float2 tex0 : TEXCOORD0,
                float2 tex1 : TEXCOORD1) : COLOR
{
    float3 c0 = tex2D(CloudS0, tex0).rgb;
    float3 c1 = tex2D(CloudS1, tex1).rgb;
    float3 blue = float3(0.0f, 0.0f, 1.0f);
    return float4(c0+c1+blue, 1.0f);
}
```

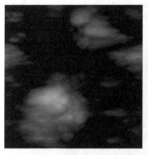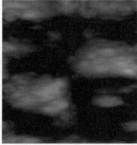

Figure 11.18: Cloud textures we scroll over a grid.

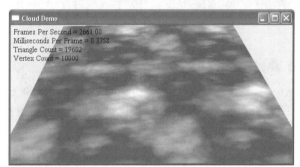

Figure 11.19: Screenshot of the Cloud demo.

So when we add the gray clouds with the blue sky, the net effect is light gray to white colored clouds. Figure 11.19 shows a screenshot of the demo. By scrolling the two cloud layers at different velocities, they animate out of phase, and therefore, for each frame of animation they will intermix in a different way, thereby creating variety in cloud composition and density.

So the question that remains is, How do we translate texture coordinates to implement a scrolling effect? The answer is, The same way we would translate any other coordinates — we just add a small offset value to all the texture coordinates, which is increased as time passes; thus, the texture map is shifted over the polygons by small amounts over time, giving an animated effect. The code that updates the texture coordinate offsets is given as follows:

```
void CloudDemo::updateScene(float dt)
{
    // Other update code removed...

    // Update texture coordinate offsets. These offsets are added
    // to the texture coordinates in the vertex shader to animate
    // them.
    mTexOffset0 += D3DXVECTOR2(0.11f, 0.05f) * dt;
    mTexOffset1 += D3DXVECTOR2(0.25f, 0.1f) * dt;

    // Textures repeat every 1.0 unit, so reset back down to zero
    // so the coordinates do not grow.
    if(mTexOffset0.x >= 1.0f || mTexOffset0.x <= -1.0f)
        mTexOffset0.x = 0.0f;
    if(mTexOffset1.x >= 1.0f || mTexOffset1.x <= -1.0f)
        mTexOffset1.x = 0.0f;
    if(mTexOffset0.y >= 1.0f || mTexOffset0.y <= -1.0f)
        mTexOffset0.y = 0.0f;
    if(mTexOffset1.y >= 1.0f || mTexOffset1.y <= -1.0f)
        mTexOffset1.y = 0.0f;
}
```

Then we set the current offsets to the effect file and use them to offset the texture coordinates in the vertex shader:

```
// Set Effect Parameters
HR(mFX->SetValue(mhTexOffset0, &mTexOffset0, sizeof(D3DXVECTOR2)));
HR(mFX->SetValue(mhTexOffset1, &mTexOffset1, sizeof(D3DXVECTOR2)));

// Selected parts of .fx file.
uniform extern float2  gTexOffset0;
uniform extern float2  gTexOffset1;

struct OutputVS
{
    float4 posH : POSITION0;
    float2 tex0 : TEXCOORD0;
    float2 tex1 : TEXCOORD1;
};

OutputVS CloudsVS(float3 posL : POSITION0, float2 tex0: TEXCOORD0)
{
    // Zero out our output.
    OutputVS outVS = (OutputVS)0;

    // Transform to homogeneous clip space.
    outVS.posH = mul(float4(posL, 1.0f), gWVP);

    // Offset texture coordinates.
    outVS.tex0 = tex0 + gTexOffset0;
    outVS.tex1 = tex0 + gTexOffset1;
```

```
    // Done--return the output.
    return outVS;
}
```

11.11 **Compressed Textures and the DXTex Tool**

The (video) memory requirements for textures add up quickly as your virtual worlds grow with hundreds of textures (remember we need to keep all these textures in video memory to apply them). To help alleviate memory overuse, Direct3D supports five compressed texture formats: D3DFMT_DXT1, D3DFMT_DXT2, D3DFMT_DXT3, D3DFMT_DXT4, and D3DFMT_DXT5 (you can look up the specifics of these formats in the documentation). If the graphics device supports the compressed format as a texture (check if the format is a supported D3DRTYPE_TEXTURE resource with CheckDeviceFormat), then the application can create textures of the compressed format, apply them, and they will be decompressed by the hardware automatically during rasterization. (So note that we are not talking about using compressed texture formats to save disk space, as that is not our problem. We want to store compressed texture data on the video card and then decompress it on the fly when it is needed during rasterization.) Note that for the Direct3D compressed texture coordinates, the dimensions must be powers of 2.

D3DXCreateTextureFromFile does not give the option of specifying the texture format (it is taken from the file) of the texture being created. However, D3DXCreateTextureFromFileEx does provide the option of specifying the texture format of the texture being created. So using D3DXCreateTexture-FromFileEx provides one way to create compressed textures. Alternatively, you can save your texture files to the .dds format (a DirectX format), which supports the Direct3D compressed texture formats (in addition to the other Direct3D surface formats). Then D3DXCreateTextureFromFile may be used (it will see from the file the compressed format type).

You may be wondering how you create .dds files, as they are not very common outside of DirectX development. The DirectX documentation documents the .dds file format, so you could always create your own program that imports image data from popular formats and exports them to .dds (you probably do not want to do this). NVIDIA's developer website (http://developer.nvidia.com/object/nv_texture_tools.html) provides an Adobe Photoshop plug-in that enables Photoshop to export to .dds. The DirectX SDK also ships with a program called DXTex (located at *DX9SDK\Utilities\Bin\x86*), which can load popular image formats and export to .dds. The DXTex tool can also generate mipmap levels, which can be saved and stored in the .dds format; if you do this, then the mipmap levels do not need to be generated at application initialization time, as they can be directly read from the .dds file.

11.12 **Summary**

- Texture coordinates are used to define a triangle on the texture that gets mapped to the 3D triangle.
- We can create textures from image files stored on disk using the `D3DXCreateTextureFromFile` function.
- We can filter textures by using the minification, magnification, and mipmap filter sampler states.
- Address modes define what Direct3D is supposed to do with texture coordinates outside the [0, 1] range. For example, should the texture be tiled, mirrored, clamped, etc.?
- Multi-texturing refers to the technique of combining several texture maps together to form a net texture.
- We can generate texture coordinates that are approximately accurate for objects that are roughly spherical and cylindrical in shape by using a spherical and cylindrical mapping, respectively.
- By modifying texture coordinates in some way (e.g., translating, rotating, scaling), and thereby changing which part of the texture gets mapped to the polygon with respect to time, we can animate the textures.
- By using a compressed Direct3D texture format such as `D3DFMT_DXT1`, `D3DFMT_DXT2`, `D3DFMT_DXT3`, `D3DFMT_DXT4`, or `D3DFMT_DXT5`, we can save a considerable amount of video memory.

11.13 **Exercises**

1. Draw a pyramid-shaped object and apply a segment of the crate texture to each face.

2. Look up `D3DXCreateTextureFromFileEx` in the SDK documentation and explain each parameter in your own words.

3. Modify the Tiled Ground demo by experimenting with different `MaxAnisotropy` values. For `MaxAnisotropy = 1`, `MaxAnisotropy = 2`, `MaxAnisotropy = 4`, `MaxAnisotropy = 8`, and `MaxAnisotropy = 16`, record your frame rate. (You should check `D3DCAPS9::MaxAnisotropy` to see that you support these levels.) Does it change? Make sure that you record it in a consistent way for each trial (e.g., same camera position and orientation).

4. Modify the Tiled Ground demo by experimenting with different scaling factors to change the texture coordinates (more precisely, experiment with the value set to `texScale`). What happens if you tile less and less?

5. Modify the Tiled Ground demo by changing the address modes. Use mirror and clamp instead of the wrap mode. Describe your results. You might want to try using a different texture to see the results more clearly.

6. In this chapter's demo directory there are two textures, as shown in the left and middle images of Figure 11.20. Use multi-texturing to combine them together to produce the image at the right in Figure 11.20. In addition, animate the flare by rotating it as a function of time (rotate the color and grayscale textures at different rates). Display the resultant texture on each face of a cube. (Hint: The center in texture coordinates is not the origin; it is (1/2, 1/2), and thus the rotation will be off because the rotation equations rotate about (0, 0). Therefore, you will need to first translate the texture coordinates so that the center is at the origin, apply the rotation transformation, and then translate back so that the center is back at (1/2, 1/2) for texturing.)

Figure 11.20: Combining textures to make a fireball.

7. Generate texture coordinates for a teapot by using a spherical mapping, and render the teapot with the texture of your choice.

8. Generate texture coordinates for a cone by using a cylindrical mapping, and render the cone with the texture of your choice.

Chapter 12

Blending

Many objects in the real world are semi-transparent, such as water and glass. In this chapter, we examine a technique called *blending* that allows us to blend (combine) the pixels that we are currently rasterizing with the pixels that were previously rasterized to the back buffer; that is, if p_{ij} is the *source* pixel we are currently rasterizing, then p_{ij} is blended with the previous *ij*th *destination* pixel on the back buffer b_{ij}. This technique enables us, among other things, to render semi-transparent objects.

Objectives:

- To understand how blending works and how to use it.
- To learn about the different blend modes that Direct3D supports.
- To find out how the alpha component can be used to control the transparency of a primitive.
- To learn how we can prevent a pixel from being drawn to the back buffer altogether by employing the alpha test.

12.1 The Blending Equation

Consider Figure 12.1, where we have a teapot drawn in front of a wooden crate background.

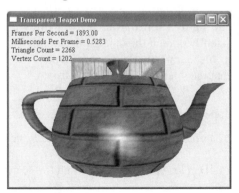

Figure 12.1: An opaque teapot.

Suppose that we want to draw the teapot with a level of transparency such that we could see through the teapot to the background crate behind it (see Figure 12.2).

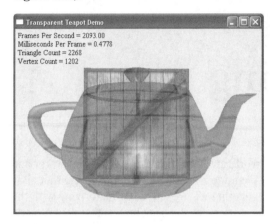

Figure 12.2: A transparent teapot.

How would we accomplish this? As we are rasterizing the teapot's triangles on top of the crate, we need to combine the pixel colors being computed for the teapot with the pixel colors of the crate in such a way that the crate shows through the teapot. The idea of combining the pixel values that are currently being computed (source pixel) with the pixel values previously written on the back buffer (destination pixel) is called *blending*. Note that the effect of blending is not limited to ordinary glass-like transparency. We have a variety of options that specify how the colors will be combined as will be seen in §12.2.

It is important to realize that the triangles currently being rasterized are blended with the pixels that were previously written to the back buffer. In the example figures, the crate image is drawn first, so that the crate's pixels are on the back buffer. We then draw the teapot so that the teapot's pixels will be blended with the crate's pixels. Thus, follow this rule when using blending:

Draw objects that do not use blending first, then sort the objects that use blending by their distance from the camera. This is most efficiently done if the objects are in view space so that you can sort simply by the z-component. Finally, draw the objects that use blending in a back-to-front order.

Direct3D uses the following alpha blending equation to blend pixels:

$$OutputPixel = SourcePixel \otimes SourceBlendFactor + DestPixel \otimes DestBlendFactor$$

Each of the above variables is a 4D color vector (r, g, b, a) and the $\otimes$ symbol denotes component-wise multiplication.

- *OutputPixel*: The resulting blended pixel.
- *SourcePixel*: The pixel currently being computed that is to be blended with the pixel on the back buffer.
- *SourceBlendFactor*: A 4D color vector that is multiplied with *SourcePixel*; by modifying this factor we can customize the blending equation to some degree to achieve different effects.
- *DestPixel*: The pixel currently on the back buffer.
- *DestBlendFactor*: A 4D color vector that is multiplied with *DestPixel*; by modifying this factor we can customize the blending equation to some degree to achieve different effects.

The *source and destination blend factors* let us modify the original source and destination pixels in a variety of ways, allowing for different effects to be achieved. §12.2 covers the predefined values that can be used.

Note: The + operator used in the blending equation can be changed if your graphics device sets the D3DPMISCCAPS_BLENDOP capability bit of D3DCAPS9::PrimitiveMiscCaps. Specifically, the blend operator can be one of the following:

- D3DBLENDOP_ADD: Sets the blending equation to:

  OutputPixel = SourcePixel ⊗ SourceBlendFactor + DestPixel ⊗ DestBlendFactor

- D3DBLENDOP_SUBTRACT: Sets the blending equation to:

  OutputPixel = SourcePixel ⊗ SourceBlendFactor − DestPixel ⊗ DestBlendFactor

- D3DBLENDOP_REVSUBTRACT: Sets the blending equation to:

  OutputPixel = DestPixel ⊗ DestBlendFactor − SourcePixel ⊗ SourceBlendFactor

- D3DBLENDOP_MIN: Sets the blending equation to:

  OutputPixel = min(SourcePixel ⊗ SourceBlendFactor, DestPixel ⊗ DestBlendFactor)

- D3DBLENDOP_MAX: Sets the blending equation to:

  OutputPixel = max(SourcePixel ⊗ SourceBlendFactor, DestPixel ⊗ DestBlendFactor)

The blend operator is set by the D3DRS_BLENDOP render state. For example, to change the blend operator to D3DBLENDOP_REVSUBTRACT we would write:

```
gd3dDevice->SetRenderState(D3DRS_BLENDOP, D3DBLENDOP_REVSUBTRACT);
```

Blending is disabled by default; you can enable it by setting the
D3DRS_ALPHABLENDENABLE render state to `true`, and disable it by setting it to
`false`:

```
Device->SetRenderState(D3DRS_ALPHABLENDENABLE, true);
Device->SetRenderState(D3DRS_ALPHABLENDENABLE, false);
```

Tip: Blending is not a cheap operation and should only be enabled
for the geometry that needs it. When you are done rendering that
geometry, you should disable alpha blending. Also, try to batch triangles that use blending and render them at once, so that you can
avoid turning blending on and off multiple times per frame.

12.2 **Blend Factors**

By setting different combinations for the source and destination blend factors, dozens of different blending effects may be achieved. Experiment with
different combinations to see what they do. The source blend factor and the
destination blend factor are specified by setting the D3DRS_SRCBLEND and
D3DRS_DESTBLEND render states, respectively. For example, we can write:

```
gd3dDevice->SetRenderState(D3DRS_SRCBLEND, Source);
gd3dDevice->SetRenderState(D3DRS_DESTBLEND, Destination);
```

Where Source and Destination can be one of the following blend factors:

- D3DBLEND_ZERO: *blendFactor* = $(0, 0, 0, 0)$
- D3DBLEND_ONE: *blendFactor* = $(1, 1, 1, 1)$
- D3DBLEND_SRCCOLOR: *blendFactor* = (r_s, g_s, b_s, a_s)
- D3DBLEND_INVSRCCOLOR: *blendFactor* = $(1 - r_s, 1 - g_s, 1 - b_s, 1 - a_s)$
- D3DBLEND_SRCALPHA: *blendFactor* = (a_s, a_s, a_s, a_s)
- D3DBLEND_INVSRCALPHA: *blendFactor* = $(1 - a_s, 1 - a_s, 1 - a_s, 1 - a_s)$
- D3DBLEND_DESTALPHA: *blendFactor* = (a_d, a_d, a_d, a_d)
- D3DBLEND_INVDESTALPHA: *blendFactor* = $(1 - a_d, 1 - a_d, 1 - a_d, 1 - a_d)$
- D3DBLEND_DESTCOLOR: *blendFactor* = (r_d, g_d, b_d, a_d)
- D3DBLEND_INVDESTCOLOR: *blendFactor* = $(1 - r_d, 1 - g_d, 1 - b_d, 1 - a_d)$
- D3DBLEND_SRCALPHASAT: *blendFactor* = $(f, f, f, 1)$, where $f = \min(a_s, 1 - a_d)$
- D3DBLEND_BOTHINVSRCALPHA: This blend mode sets the source blend factor
  to $(1 - a_s, 1 - a_s, 1 - a_s, 1 - a_s)$ and the destination blend factor to (a_s, a_s, a_s, a_s). This blend mode is only valid for D3DRS_SRCBLEND.

The default values for the source blend factor and destination blend factor
are D3DBLEND_SRCALPHA and D3DBLEND_INVSRCALPHA, respectively.

Note: You can also set the source and destination blend factors directly in an effect file inside a pass block; in addition, you can enable alpha blending and set the blend operation from here:

```
pass P0
{
    vertexShader = compile vs_2_0 VS();
    pixelShader  = compile ps_2_0 PS();

    AlphaBlendEnable = true;
    SrcBlend = One;
    DestBlend = One;
    BlendOp = RevSubtract
}
```

Note: It is possible to blend the alpha component differently than the RGB components, provided the D3DPMISCCAPS_SEPARATEALPHABLEND capability bit is set in D3DCAPS9::PrimitiveMiscCaps. To enable separate alpha component blending, set the D3DRS_SEPARATEALPHABLEND-ENABLE render state to true. Then set the blend operation and blend factors specific to the alpha component with the D3DRS_BLENDOPALPHA, D3DRS_SRCBLENDALPHA, and D3DRS_DESTBLENDALPHA render states. Here is an example:

```
pass P0
{
    vertexShader = compile vs_2_0 VS();
    pixelShader  = compile ps_2_0 PS();

    // Use these states to blend RGB components.
    AlphaBlendEnable = true;
    SrcBlend = One;
    DestBlend = One;
    BlendOp = RevSubtract;

    // Use these states to blend the alpha component.
    SeparateAlphaBlendEnable = true;
    SrcBlendAlpha = SrcAlpha;
    DestBlendAlpha = InvSrcAlpha;
    BlendOpAlpha = Add;
}
```

> **Aside:** Another useful render state to keep in mind is D3DRS_COLOR-
> WRITEENABLE. This allows you to control which color components the
> graphics device writes to, provided the D3DPMISCCAPS_COLORWRITE-
> ENABLE capability bit is set in D3DCAPS9::PrimitiveMiscCaps. For
> example, you could block rendering to the RGB color channels and
> only write to the alpha channel. This can be useful for certain
> multi-pass rendering techniques. Valid settings for this render state
> are any combination of the D3DCOLORWRITEENABLE_ALPHA,
> D3DCOLORWRITEENABLE_BLUE, D3DCOLORWRITEENABLE_GREEN, or
> D3DCOLORWRITEENABLE_RED flags, where the specified flags indicate
> which color channels to write to. For example, to write only to the
> green and blue channels, you would use:

```
gd3dDevice->SetRenderState(D3DRS_COLORWRITEENABLE,
    D3DCOLORWRITEENABLE_GREEN | D3DCOLORWRITEENABLE_BLUE);
```

The default setting is:

```
gd3dDevice->SetRenderState(D3DRS_COLORWRITEENABLE,
    D3DCOLORWRITEENABLE_GREEN | D3DCOLORWRITEENABLE_BLUE |
    D3DCOLORWRITEENABLE_RED | D3DCOLORWRITEENABLE_ALPHA);
```

which writes to all four color channels.

12.2.1 Blend Factor Example 1

Suppose that you want to keep the original destination pixel exactly as it is
and not overwrite or blend it with the source pixel currently being
rasterized. Then set the source pixel blend factor to D3DBLEND_ZERO and the
destination pixel blend factor to D3DBLEND_ONE. With this setup, the blending
equation reduces to:

$$OutputPixel = SourcePixel \otimes SourceBlendFactor + DestPixel \otimes DestBlendFactor$$
$$OutputPixel = SourcePixel \otimes (0, 0, 0, 0) + DestPixel \otimes (1, 1, 1, 1)$$
$$OutputPixel = (0, 0, 0, 0) + DestPixel$$
$$OutputPixel = DestPixel$$

12.2.2 Blend Factor Example 2

Suppose that you have two images and you want to directly add them
together to form a new image (see Figure 12.3). To do this, set the source
pixel blend factor to D3DBLEND_ONE and the destination pixel blend factor to
D3DBLEND_ONE. With this setup, the blending equation reduces to:

$$OutputPixel = SourcePixel \otimes SourceBlendFactor + DestPixel \otimes DestBlendFactor$$
$$OutputPixel = SourcePixel \otimes (1, 1, 1, 1) + DestPixel \otimes (1, 1, 1, 1)$$
$$OutputPixel = SourcePixel + DestPixel$$

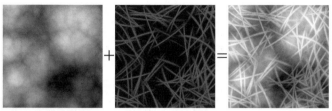
Figure 12.3: Adding source color and destination color.

12.2.3 **Blend Factor Example 3**

Suppose that we want to multiply a source pixel with its corresponding destination pixel (see Figure 12.4). To do this, set the source pixel blend factor to D3DBLEND_ZERO and the destination pixel blend factor to D3DBLEND_SRCCOLOR. With this setup, the blending equation reduces to:

OutputPixel = SourcePixel ⊗ SourceBlendFactor + DestPixel ⊗ DestBlendFactor
OutputPixel = SourcePixel ⊗ (0, 0, 0, 0) + DestPixel ⊗ SourcePixel
OutputPixel = DestPixel ⊗ SourcePixel

Figure 12.4: Multiplying source color and destination color.

12.2.4 **Blend Factor Example 4**

Let the source alpha component a_s be thought of as a percent that controls the transparency of the source pixel (e.g., 0 alpha means 100% transparent, 0.5 means 50% transparent, and 1.0 means 0% transparent or 100% opaque). Now suppose that you want to blend the source and destination pixels based on the transparency percent of the source pixel. To do this, set the source pixel blend factor to D3DBLEND_SRCALPHA and the destination pixel blend factor to D3DBLEND_INVSRCALPHA. With this setup, the blending equation reduces to:

OutputPixel = SourcePixel ⊗ SourceBlendFactor + DestPixel ⊗ DestBlendFactor
OutputPixel = SourcePixel ⊗ (s_a, s_a, s_a, s_a) + DestPixel ⊗
   (1 − s_a, 1 − s_a, 1 − s_a, 1 − s_a)
OutputPixel = s_a · SourcePixel + (1 − s_a) · DestPixel

For example, suppose $a_s = 0.25$. Then we have:

$$OutputPixel = 0.25 \cdot SourcePixel + (1 - 0.25) \cdot DestPixel$$
$$OutputPixel = 0.25 \cdot SourcePixel + (.75) \cdot DestPixel$$

The scalar 0.25 "weakens" the source pixel color by three-fourths, so that the source pixel only contributes 25% of its original value. The scalar 0.75 "weakens" the destination pixel color by one-fourth, so that the destination pixel only contributes 75% of its original value. We then add the 25% source contribution to the 75% destination contribution. (Observe the total is 100%.) Consequently, by construction, we'll see 75% of the destination pixel (background) and only 25% of the source pixel; the net result is that the source object looks only 25% opaque (i.e., 75% transparent).

12.3 **Transparent Teapot Demo**

As described in §12.2.4, we can use the source pixel's alpha component to control its transparency. In this section, we explain the demo that implements the screenshot shown in Figure 12.2. Fortunately, the code we have developed so far has been organized in preparation for blending, so it is very easy to implement. Recall that we have been setting the pixel's alpha component in the pixel shader to that of the diffuse material's alpha component:

```
mTeapotMtrl.ambient   = D3DXCOLOR(1.0f, 1.0f, 1.0f, 1.0f);
mTeapotMtrl.diffuse   = D3DXCOLOR(1.0f, 1.0f, 1.0f, 0.5f);
mTeapotMtrl.spec      = D3DXCOLOR(0.8f, 0.8f, 0.8f, 1.0f);
mTeapotMtrl.specPower = 16.0f;


// In vertex shader we just pass along the alpha component to
// the pixel shader.
outVS.diffuse.a = gDiffuseMtrl.a;


// In pixel shader we just set the pixel's alpha value to the
// interpolated color's alpha component.
float4 DirLightTexPS(float4 c : COLOR0,
                     float4 spec : COLOR1,
                     float2 tex0 : TEXCOORD0) : COLOR
{
    float3 texColor = tex2D(TexS, tex0).rgb;
    float3 diffuse = c.rgb * texColor;
    return float4(diffuse + spec.rgb, c.a);
}
```

So all we need to do to control the transparency of an object is modify the diffuse material's alpha component; this controls the source alpha. In the above code, we set the diffuse material's alpha component to 0.5 so that the teapot will be 50% transparent.

Finally, we just need to enable alpha blending and set the blend factor render states before drawing the teapot so that Direct3D will alpha blend the pixels during rasterization of the teapot:

```
void TeapotDemo::drawTeapot()
{
    // Cylindrically interpolate texture coordinates.
    HR(gd3dDevice->SetRenderState(D3DRS_WRAP0, D3DWRAPCOORD_0));

    // Enable alpha blending.
    HR(gd3dDevice->SetRenderState(D3DRS_ALPHABLENDENABLE, true));
    HR(gd3dDevice->SetRenderState(D3DRS_SRCBLEND,
                                  D3DBLEND_SRCALPHA));
    HR(gd3dDevice->SetRenderState(D3DRS_DESTBLEND,
                                  D3DBLEND_INVSRCALPHA));

    // [...] Set effect parameters/draw teapot

    // Disable alpha blending.
    HR(gd3dDevice->SetRenderState(D3DRS_ALPHABLENDENABLE, false));
}
```

12.4 Transparent Teapot Demo with Texture Alpha Channel

A material is typically applied to a collection of triangles. Thus, for some collection of triangles with an associated material, the level of transparency will be uniformly set for the entire collection by the diffuse material's alpha component. Sometimes we would like to control the transparency at a finer level of detail than at the triangle level. The solution is to obtain the alpha value from a texture, where we can encode an alpha value per texel. For example, in the demo for this section, we use the alpha channel as shown in Figure 12.5. As you can see, by using a texture we can control the transparency of an object at the pixel level, and we can have very complicated patterns of alpha values.

Figure 12.5: An alpha channel.

To add alpha information to a texture, we create a fourth channel called the *alpha channel*. That is, a texture will have RGB channels and an additional alpha channel. You can generally add an alpha channel in any popular image editing software, such as Adobe Photoshop, and then save the image to a format that supports an alpha channel (e.g., 32-bit .bmp format). However, here we show an alternative way to insert an alpha channel using the DXTex utility program that was discussed in the previous chapter.

We start by assuming we have two images — a color RGB image and a grayscale image that will be inserted into the alpha channel (see Figure 12.6).

RGB Channels   Alpha Channel

Figure 12.6: An RGB image (left) and a grayscale image (right). The grayscale image will be inserted into the alpha channel of the texture.

Now, open the DXTex tool and open the brick.jpg file located in this chapter's sample folder on the book's website. The brick texture is automatically loaded in as a 24-bit RGB texture (i.e., D3DFMT_R8G8B8), with 8 bits of red, 8 bits of green, and 8 bits of blue per pixel. We need to change the format to a format that supports an alpha channel, such as a 32-bit ARGB texture format D3DFMT_A8R8G8B8 or with a compressed format that supports alpha like D3DFMT_DXT3. Select **Format** from the menu bar and choose **Change Surface Format**. A dialog box pops up as shown in Figure 12.7; select the **DXT3** format and press **OK**.

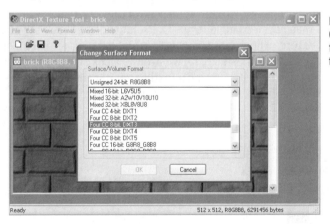

Figure 12.7: Changing the format of the texture.

This creates a compressed texture with an alpha channel. Our next task is to load data into the alpha channel. We will load the 8-bit grayscale map shown in Figure 12.6 into the alpha channel. Select **File** from the menu bar, and then choose **Open Onto Alpha Channel Of This Texture**. A dialog box will pop up, asking you to locate the image file that contains the data you want to load into the alpha channel. Select the alpha.jpg file that is located in this chapter's demo folder. Figure 12.8 shows the program after the alpha channel data has been inserted.

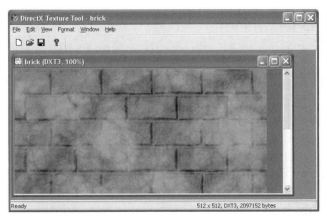

Figure 12.8: Resulting texture with an alpha channel.

Now save the texture with the name of your choice; we used the name bricka.dds.

Now for the demo, we need to make one small change to the pixel shader since we are taking our alpha data from another source:

```
float4 DirLightTexPS(float4 c : COLOR0,
                     float4 spec : COLOR1,
                     float2 tex0 : TEXCOORD0) : COLOR
{
    float4 texColor = tex2D(TexS, tex0);
    float3 diffuse = c.rgb * texColor.rgb;
    return float4(diffuse + spec.rgb, texColor.a*c.a);
}
```

That is, we multiply the texture alpha with the diffuse alpha. Generally, when using an alpha channel, we will just set the diffuse material's alpha component to 1.0 so that it simplifies out and just the texture alpha is used. Figure 12.9 shows a screenshot of the Transparent Teapot demo with texture alpha.

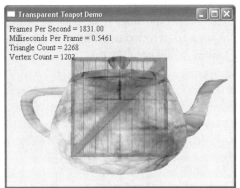

Figure 12.9: Teapot transparency is no longer uniform, but is specified per pixel with the texture's alpha channel.

12.5 **The Alpha Test**

The alpha test allows us to discard a pixel (i.e., not render it) based on its alpha value in comparison to some reference value. Let a_s be the source alpha component, and let *ref* be an application-defined reference value. Then, the alpha test is given as follows:

> IF a_s ⊙ *ref* == *true* THEN *accept pixel*
>
> ELSE *reject pixel*

Here, ⊙ is an operation specified by the D3DCMPFUNC enumerated type:

```
typedef enum _D3DCMPFUNC {
    D3DCMP_NEVER = 1,
    D3DCMP_LESS = 2,
    D3DCMP_EQUAL = 3,
    D3DCMP_LESSEQUAL = 4,
    D3DCMP_GREATER = 5,
    D3DCMP_NOTEQUAL = 6,
    D3DCMP_GREATEREQUAL = 7,
    D3DCMP_ALWAYS = 8,
    D3DCMP_FORCE_DWORD = 0x7fffffff
} D3DCMPFUNC;
```

- D3DCMP_NEVER: Alpha test always fails — the pixel is always rejected.
- D3DCMP_LESS: Replace ⊙ with < operator.
- D3DCMP_EQUAL: Replace ⊙ with == operator.
- D3DCMP_LESSEQUAL: Replace ⊙ with ≤ operator.
- D3DCMP_GREATER: Replace ⊙ with > operator.
- D3DCMP_NOTEQUAL: Replace ⊙ with != operator.
- D3DCMP_GREATEREQUAL: Replace ⊙ with ≥ operator.
- D3DCMP_ALWAYS: Alpha test always succeeds — the pixel is always drawn.
- D3DCMP_FORCE_DWORD: Not used, but included to make enumerated type instances 32 bits.

For example, the following code enables the alpha test, sets the reference value to 100, and sets the comparison operation to D3DCMP_GREATEREQUAL. Thus, only pixels with alpha values ≥ 100 are drawn.

```
HR(gd3dDevice->SetRenderState(D3DRS_ALPHATESTENABLE, true));
HR(gd3dDevice->SetRenderState(D3DRS_ALPHAFUNC, D3DCMP_GREATEREQUAL));
HR(gd3dDevice->SetRenderState(D3DRS_ALPHAREF, 100));
```

Note: The alpha test can also be set in an effect file in a pass block. For example:

```
pass P0
{
    vertexShader = compile vs_2_0 VS();
    pixelShader  = compile ps_2_0 PS();

    AlphaTestEnable = true;
    AlphaFunc = GreaterEqual;
    AlphaRef = 220;
}
```

So why is the alpha test useful? Consider the following: By setting the alpha test up as we did in the above example, we can implement a gate by texturing a quad with the texture shown in Figure 12.10.

RGB Channels   Alpha Channel

Figure 12.10: A gate texture with its alpha channel. The pixels with black alpha values will be rejected by the alpha text and not drawn; hence, only the gate remains. Essentially, the alpha test enables us to mask out certain pixels.

Modeling the individual gate pieces out of triangles would eat up processing power that could be better spent elsewhere. So for things like fences, chicken wire, gates, nets, etc., a quad with a texture and alpha channel works quite well. Figure 12.11 shows a screenshot of the Gate demo.

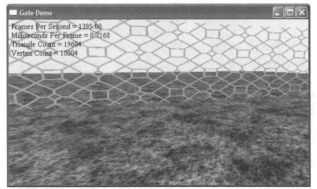

Figure 12.11: Screenshot of the Gate demo.

12.6 **Summary**

■ Let p_{ij} be the *source* pixel we are currently rasterizing to the ijth back buffer location, and let b_{ij} be the ijth *destination* pixel on the back buffer b_{ij}. If alpha blending is enabled, Direct3D blends p_{ij} and b_{ij} together with the following equation:

OutputPixel = SourcePixel ⊗ SourceBlendFactor + DestPixel ⊗ DestBlendFactor

■ The blend factors *SourceBlendFactor* and *DestBlendFactor* enable us to customize how the source and destination pixels are blended together in the blending equation.

■ Alpha information can come from the diffuse component of the material or from the alpha channel of the primitive's texture.

■ The alpha test enables us to accept or reject a pixel based on its alpha value in comparison with some defined reference value.

12.7 **Exercises**

1. The Transparent Teapot demo uses the source and destination blend factors used in Blend Factor Example 4 (§12.2.4) to achieve transparency. Modify the Transparent Teapot demo to use the source and destination factors used in Blend Factor Example 1 (§12.2.1), Blend Factor Example 2 (§12.2.2), and Blend Factor Example 3 (§12.2.3). You should experiment further with the other possible blend combinations. In addition, experiment with different D3DBLENDOP settings. Lastly, try out the D3DRS_COLORWRITEENABLE render state by only rendering to the green color channel.

2. Modify the Transparent Teapot demo by reversing the drawing order; that is, draw the teapot first and the crate second. Explain the results.

3. Multi-texturing can be implemented via blending using a multi-pass technique. The idea is as follows: We draw the geometry once on the first pass with a base texture; we then draw the geometry again with alpha blending enabled and a second texture, where the alpha channel and blend operations specify how the secondary texture should be blended with the geometry drawn in the first pass; we next draw the geometry again with alpha blending enabled and a third texture, where the alpha channel and blend operations specify how the third texture should be blended with the previously drawn geometry. We can keep doing this repeatedly, each pass layering on more and more details. The benefit of this technique is that you are not limited by any hardware restrictions that might limit how many textures you can sample simultaneously in a single pass. The downside of this technique is that it requires you to render the same geometry repeatedly.

Reimplement the Multi-texturing demo from Chapter 11, but instead of sampling multiple textures simultaneously in one pass, use a multi-pass technique as described above (i.e., you can only use one texture per pass).

4. When trees are far away, a _billboarding_ technique is used for efficiency. That is, instead of rendering the geometry for a fully 3D tree, a 2D polygon is used with a picture of a 3D tree painted on it (see Figure 12.12). From a distance, you cannot tell that a billboard is being used. However, the trick is to make sure that the billboard always faces the camera (otherwise the illusion would break). For trees, assuming the y-axis is up, billboards will generally be aligned with the y-axis and just face the camera in the xz-plane. For other kinds of billboards, such as particles, the billboards may fully face the camera.

Recall that the world matrix for an object has the following form:

$$\begin{bmatrix} r_x & r_y & r_z & 0 \\ u_x & u_y & u_z & 0 \\ f_x & f_y & f_z & 0 \\ p_x & p_y & p_z & 1 \end{bmatrix}$$

Let $\vec{c}$ be the position of the camera in world space. Then, assuming a y-axis aligned billboard, and that the billboard's world space position $\vec{p}$ is given, we have

$$\vec{f} = \frac{\left(c_x - p_x, 0, c_z - p_z \right)}{\left\| \left(c_x - p_x, 0, c_z - p_z \right) \right\|}$$

$$\vec{u} = \left(0, 1, 0 \right)$$

$$\vec{r} = \vec{u} \times \vec{f}$$

Note that $\vec{f}$ is aimed toward the camera in the xz-plane.

In general, each tree has a different world matrix, which makes it face the camera at its position in world space. A naïve approach to rendering a collection of billboards would be one by one, and setting the respective world matrix each time. However, rendering small numbers of polygons per draw call is inefficient — the hardware likes to draw large batches at a time, and draw primitive calls should be limited to avoid driver overhead. So to avoid this cost, we compute the world matrix of a vertex in the vertex shader:

```
OutputVS AABillBoardVS(
        float3 posL : POSITION0,
        float3 bbOffset : TEXCOORD0, // Offsets to world space position.
        float2 tex0: TEXCOORD1)
{
        // Zero out our output.
        OutputVS outVS = (OutputVS)0;

        // Vertex world position without rotation applied to make
        // face the camera.
        float3 tempPosW = posL + bbOffset;

        float3 look = gEyePosW - tempPosW;
        look.y = 0.0f;  // axis-aligned, so keep look in xz-plane.
        look = normalize(look);
        float3 up    = float3(0.0f, 1.0f, 0.0f);
        float3 right = cross(up, look);

        // Rotate to make face the camera.
        float3x3 R;
        R[0] = right;
        R[1] = up;
        R[2] = look;

        // Offset to world position.
        float3 posW = mul(posL, R) + bbOffset;

        // Transform to homogeneous clip space.
        outVS.posH = mul(float4(posW, 1.0f), gViewProj);

        // Pass on texture coordinates to be interpolated in
        // rasterization.
        outVS.tex0 = tex0;

        // Done--return the output.
        return outVS;
}
```

Observe that, for each vertex, we have to specify the translation offset that positions the billboard the vertex is part of in world space, so that we can compute the rotation part and translation part of the world transformation.

With this setup, we can render all of the billboards in one draw primitive call, and the correct billboard world matrix is generated in the vertex shader for each vertex.

Use the above described billboarding technique to render some trees with the tree textures available in this chapter's demo folder and shown in Figure 12.13.

Figure 12.12: Example output for this exercise.

Figure 12.13: Tree texture with alpha channel.

RGB Channels   Alpha Channel

Chapter 13

Stenciling

This chapter brings us to the study of the stencil buffer and is the concluding chapter of Part II of this text. The stencil buffer is an off-screen buffer we can use to achieve special effects. The stencil buffer has the same resolution as the back buffer and depth buffer, such that the ijth pixel in the stencil buffer corresponds with the ijth pixel in the back buffer and depth buffer. As the name suggests, the stencil buffer works as a stencil and allows us to block rendering to certain parts of the back buffer.

For instance, when implementing a mirror we simply need to reflect a particular object across the plane of the mirror; however, we only want to draw the reflection into a mirror. We can use the stencil buffer to block the rendering of the reflection unless it is in a mirror. Figure 13.1 should make this clear.

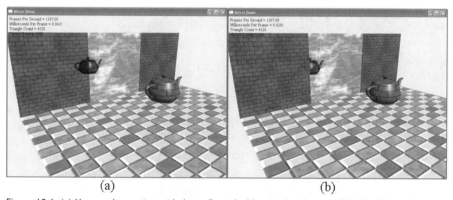

(a)   (b)

Figure 13.1: (a) Here we have a teapot being reflected without using the stencil buffer. We see that the reflected teapot is always rendered regardless of whether it is in front of the mirror or a wall. (b) By using the stencil buffer we can block the reflected teapot from being rendered unless it is being drawn in the mirror.

The stencil buffer is a small part of Direct3D and is controlled through a simple interface. But like blending, the simple interface offers a flexible and powerful set of capabilities. Learning to use the stencil buffer effectively comes best by studying existing applications. Once you understand a few applications of the stencil buffer, you will have a better idea of how it can be applied for your own specific needs. For this reason, this chapter puts special emphasis on the study of two specific applications using stencils: implementing mirrors and planar shadows.

Objectives:

■ To gain an understanding of how the stencil buffer works, how to create a stencil buffer, and how we can control the stencil buffer.

■ To learn how to implement mirrors by using the stencil buffer to prevent reflections from being drawn to non-mirror surfaces.

■ To discover how to render shadows and prevent "double blending" by using the stencil buffer.

13.1 **Using the Stencil Buffer**

To use the stencil buffer, we must first request one when we initialize Direct3D and then we must enable it. We describe requesting a stencil buffer in section 13.1.1. To enable the stencil buffer we must set the D3DRS_STENCILENABLE render state and specify true. To disable the stencil buffer we specify false for the D3DRS_STENCILENABLE render state. The following code snippet enables the stencil buffer and then disables it:

```
gd3dDevice->SetRenderState(D3DRS_STENCILENABLE, true);

... // do stencil work

gd3dDevice->SetRenderState(D3DRS_STENCILENABLE, false);
```

Note: Although not used in this book, DirectX 9.0 has added a *two-sided stencil* feature that speeds up shadow volume rendering by reducing the number of rendering passes required to draw the shadow volume. See the SDK documentation for details.

We can clear the stencil buffer to a default value using the IDirect3DDevice9::Clear method. Recall this is the same method used to clear the back buffer and depth buffer as well.

```
gd3dDevice->Clear(0, 0,
        D3DCLEAR_TARGET | D3DCLEAR_ZBUFFER | D3DCLEAR_STENCIL,
        0xff000000, 1.0f, 0 );
```

Note that we have added D3DCLEAR_STENCIL to the third argument, indicating that we want to clear the stencil buffer as well as the target (back buffer) and depth buffer. Argument six is used to specify the value to which to clear the stencil buffer; in this example, we clear it to zero.

Note: Using the stencil buffer can be considered as a "free" operation in hardware if you are already using depth buffering, according to [Kilgard99].

13.1.1 Requesting a Stencil Buffer

A stencil buffer can be created at the time we create the depth buffer. When specifying the format of the depth buffer, we can also specify the format of the stencil buffer. In actuality, the stencil buffer and depth buffer share the same off-screen surface buffer, but a segment of memory in each pixel is designated to each particular buffer. For instance, consider the following three depth/stencil formats:

- `D3DFMT_D24S8`: This format says to create a 32-bit depth/stencil buffer and designate 24 bits per pixel to the depth buffer and 8 bits per pixel to the stencil buffer.

- `D3DFMT_D24X4S4`: This format says to create a 32-bit depth/stencil buffer and designate 24 bits per pixel to the depth buffer and 4 bits per pixel to the stencil buffer. Four of the bits will not be used.

- `D3DFMT_D15S1`: This format says to create a 16-bit depth/stencil buffer and designate 15 bits per pixel to the depth buffer and 1 bit per pixel to the stencil buffer.

Note that there are formats that do not allocate any bits to the stencil buffer. For example, the `D3DFMT_D32` format says to create a 32-bit depth buffer only.

Also, the support of stenciling varies among the various graphics cards. Some cards may not support an 8-bit stencil buffer, for example.

In our sample application framework, we specify the `D3DFMT_D24S8` format:

```
md3dPP.AutoDepthStencilFormat = D3DFMT_D24S8;
```

13.1.2 The Stencil Test

As previously stated, we can use the stencil buffer to block rendering to certain areas of the back buffer. The decision to block a particular pixel from being written is decided by the *stencil test*, which is given by the following:

IF *ref* & *mask* $\odot$ *value* & *mask* == *true* THEN *accept pixel*

ELSE *reject pixel*

The stencil test is performed as pixels get rasterized, assuming stenciling is enabled, and takes two operands:

- A left-hand-side operand (*LHS* = *ref* & *mask*) that is determined by ANDing an application-defined *stencil reference value* (*ref*) with an application-defined *masking value* (*mask*).

- A right-hand-side operand (*RHS* = *value* & *mask*) that is determined by ANDing the entry in the stencil buffer for the particular pixel we are testing (*value*) with an application-defined masking value (*mask*).

The stencil test then compares the *LHS* with the *RHS* as specified by an application-chosen *comparison operation* $\odot$. ($\odot$ is just a dummy comparison operation we fill in later — we have several options as we did with the alpha test.) The entire expression evaluates to a true or false value. We write the pixel to the back buffer if the test evaluates to true (passes). If the test evaluates to false (fails), then we block the pixel from being written to the back buffer. And of course, if a pixel isn't written to the back buffer, it isn't written to the depth buffer either.

13.1.3 **Controlling the Stencil Test**

To give us flexibility, Direct3D allows us to control the variables used in the stencil test. In other words, we get to specify the stencil reference value, the mask value, and even the comparison operation. Although, we do not get to explicitly set the stencil value, we do have some control over what values get written to the stencil buffer (in addition to clearing the stencil buffer).

13.1.3.1 *Stencil Reference Value*

The stencil reference value *ref* is zero by default, but we can change it with the D3DRS_STENCILREF render state. For example, the following code sets the stencil-reference value to one:

```
gd3dDevice->SetRenderState(D3DRS_STENCILREF, 0x1);
```

Note that we tend to use hexadecimal because it makes it easier to see the bit alignment of an integer and this is useful to see when doing bitwise operations such as ANDing.

13.1.3.2 *Stencil Mask*

The stencil masking value *mask* is used to mask (hide) bits in both the *ref* and *value* variables. The default mask is 0xffffffff, which does not mask any bits. We can change the mask by setting the D3DRS_STENCILMASK render state. The following example masks the 16 high bits:

```
gd3dDevice->SetRenderState(D3DRS_STENCILMASK, 0x0000ffff);
```

Note: If you do not understand this talk of bits and masking, it most likely means that you need to brush up on your binary, hexadecimal, and bitwise operations.

13.1.3.3 *Stencil Value*

As stated previously, this is the value in the stencil buffer for the current pixel we are stencil testing. For example, if we are performing the stencil test on the *ij*th pixel, then *value* will be the value in the *ij*th entry of the stencil buffer. We cannot explicitly set individual stencil values, but recall that we can clear the stencil buffer. In addition, we can use the stencil render states to control what gets written to the stencil buffer. The stencil-related render states will be covered shortly.

13.1.3.4 *Comparison Operation*

Recall the stencil test:

IF *ref* & *mask* $\odot$ *value* & *mask* == *true* THEN *accept pixel*

ELSE *reject pixel*

We can set the comparison operation $\odot$ by setting the D3DRS_STENCIL-FUNC render state. The comparison operation can be any member of the D3DCMPFUNC enumerated type:

```
typedef enum _D3DCMPFUNC {
    D3DCMP_NEVER = 1,
    D3DCMP_LESS = 2,
    D3DCMP_EQUAL = 3,
    D3DCMP_LESSEQUAL = 4,
    D3DCMP_GREATER = 5,
    D3DCMP_NOTEQUAL = 6,
    D3DCMP_GREATEREQUAL = 7,
    D3DCMP_ALWAYS = 8,
    D3DCMP_FORCE_DWORD = 0x7fffffff
} D3DCMPFUNC;
```

- D3DCMP_NEVER: Stencil test always fails — the pixel is always rejected.
- D3DCMP_LESS: Replace $\odot$ with < operator.
- D3DCMP_EQUAL: Replace $\odot$ with == operator.
- D3DCMP_LESSEQUAL: Replace $\odot$ with $\leq$ operator.
- D3DCMP_GREATER: Replace $\odot$ with > operator.
- D3DCMP_NOTEQUAL: Replace $\odot$ with != operator.
- D3DCMP_GREATEREQUAL: Replace $\odot$ with $\geq$ operator.
- D3DCMP_ALWAYS: Stencil test always succeeds — the pixel is always drawn.
- D3DCMP_FORCE_DWORD: Not used, but included to make enumerated type instances 32 bits.

13.1.4 **Updating the Stencil Buffer**

In addition to deciding whether to write or block a particular pixel from being written to the back buffer, we can define how the stencil buffer entry should be updated based on three possible cases:

- The stencil test fails for the ijth pixel. We can define how to update the ijth entry in the stencil buffer in response to this case by setting the D3DRS_STENCILFAIL render state:

  ```
  gd3dDevice->SetRenderState(D3DRS_STENCILFAIL, StencilOperation);
  ```

- The depth test fails for the ijth pixel. We can define how to update the ijth entry in response to this case by setting the D3DRS_STENCILZFAIL render state:

  ```
  gd3dDevice->SetRenderState(D3DRS_STENCILZFAIL, StencilOperation);
  ```

- The depth test and stencil test succeed for the ijth pixel. We can define how to update the ijth entry in response to this case by setting the D3DRS_STENCILPASS render state:

  ```
  gd3dDevice->SetRenderState(D3DRS_STENCILPASS, StencilOperation);
  ```

Where StencilOperation can be one of the following predefined constants:

D3DSTENCILOP_KEEP: Specifies to not change the stencil buffer; that is, keep the value currently there.

D3DSTENCILOP_ZERO: Specifies to set the stencil buffer entry to zero.

D3DSTENCILOP_REPLACE: Specifies to replace the stencil buffer entry with the stencil-reference value.

D3DSTENCILOP_INCRSAT: Specifies to increment the stencil buffer entry. If the incremented value exceeds the maximum allowed value, then we clamp the entry to that maximum.

D3DSTENCILOP_DECRSAT: Specifies to decrement the stencil buffer entry. If the decremented value is less than zero, then we clamp the entry to zero.

D3DSTENCILOP_INVERT: Specifies to invert the bits of the stencil buffer entry.

D3DSTENCILOP_INCR: Specifies to increment the stencil buffer entry. If the incremented value exceeds the maximum allowed value, then we wrap to zero.

D3DSTENCILOP_DECR: Specifies to decrement the stencil buffer entry. If the decremented value is less than zero, then we wrap to the maximum allowed value.

13.1.5 **Stencil Write Mask**

In addition to the mentioned stencil render states, we can set a *write mask* that masks off bits of any value we write to the stencil buffer. We can set the write mask with the D3DRS_STENCILWRITEMASK render state. The default value is 0xffffffff. The following example masks the top 16 bits:

```
gd3dDevice->SetRenderState(D3DRS_STENCILWRITEMASK, 0x0000ffff);
```

13.2 **Mirror Demo**

Many surfaces in nature serve as mirrors and allow us to see the reflections of objects. This section describes how we can simulate mirrors for our 3D applications. Note that for simplicity, we reduce the task of implementing mirrors to planar surfaces only. For instance, a shiny car can display a reflection; however, a car's body is smooth, round, and not planar. Instead, we render reflections such as those that are displayed in a shiny marble floor or in a mirror hanging on a wall — in other words, mirrors that lie on a plane.

Implementing mirrors programmatically requires us to solve two problems. First, we must learn how to reflect an object about an arbitrary plane so that we can draw the reflection correctly. Second, we must only display the reflection in a mirror; that is, we must somehow "mark" a surface as a mirror and then, as we are rendering, only draw the reflected object if it is in a mirror. Refer to Figure 13.1, which first introduced this concept.

The first problem is easily solved with some analytical geometry. We can solve the second problem with the stencil buffer. The next two subsections explain the solutions to these problems individually. The third subsection ties them together and reviews the relevant code to the first demo application for this chapter.

13.2.1 **The Mathematics of Reflection**

We now show how to compute the reflection point $\vec{v}'=\left(v'_x,v'_y,v'_z\right)$ of a point $\vec{v}=\left(v_x,v_y,v_z\right)$ about an arbitrary plane $(\vec{n},d)$. (Note that we assume $\vec{n}$ is of unit length.) Refer to Figure 13.2 throughout this discussion.

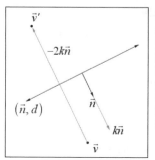

Figure 13.2: Reflection about an arbitrary plane. Note k is the shortest signed distance from $\vec{v}$ to the plane and is positive in this figure since $\vec{v}$ lies in the positive half-space of the plane.

From Figure 13.2, we see that $\vec{v}' = \vec{v} - 2k\vec{n}$, where k is the shortest signed distance from $\vec{v}$ to the plane; but that is just $k = \vec{n} \cdot \vec{v} + d$. Therefore:

$$\vec{v}' = \vec{v} - 2(\vec{n} \cdot \vec{v} + d)\vec{n}$$

We can represent this transformation from $\vec{v}$ to $\vec{v}'$ with the following matrix:

$$R = \begin{bmatrix} -2n_x n_x + 1 & -2n_y n_x & -2n_z n_x & 0 \\ -2n_x n_y & -2n_y n_y + 1 & -2n_z n_y & 0 \\ -2n_x n_z & -2n_y n_z & -2n_z n_z + 1 & 0 \\ -2n_x d & -2n_y d & -2n_z d & 1 \end{bmatrix}$$

The D3DX library provides the following function to create the reflection matrix as shown by R about an arbitrary plane:

```
D3DXMATRIX *D3DXMatrixReflect(
    D3DXMATRIX *pOut,        // The resulting reflection matrix.
    CONST D3DXPLANE *pPlane  // The plane to reflect about.
);
```

Since we are on the topic of reflection transformations, we present the matrices representing three other special case reflection transformations. They are the reflections about the three standard coordinate planes — the yz-plane, xz-plane, and xy-plane, and are represented by the following three matrices respectively:

$$R_{yz} = \begin{bmatrix} -1 & 0 & 0 & 0 \\ 0 & 1 & 0 & 0 \\ 0 & 0 & 1 & 0 \\ 0 & 0 & 0 & 1 \end{bmatrix} \quad R_{xz} = \begin{bmatrix} 1 & 0 & 0 & 0 \\ 0 & -1 & 0 & 0 \\ 0 & 0 & 1 & 0 \\ 0 & 0 & 0 & 1 \end{bmatrix} \quad R_{xy} = \begin{bmatrix} 1 & 0 & 0 & 0 \\ 0 & 1 & 0 & 0 \\ 0 & 0 & -1 & 0 \\ 0 & 0 & 0 & 1 \end{bmatrix}$$

To reflect a point across the yz-plane we simply take the opposite of the x-component. Similarly, to reflect a point across the xz-plane we take the opposite of the y-component. And finally, to reflect a point across the xy-plane we take the opposite of the z-component. These reflections are readily seen by observing the symmetry on each of the standard coordinate planes.

13.2.2 Mirror Implementation Overview

When implementing a mirror, it follows that an object is only reflected if it is in front of the mirror. However, we don't want to test spatially if an object is in front of a mirror, as it could get complicated. Therefore, to simplify things, we will always reflect the object and render it no matter where it is. But this introduces problems, as seen in Figure 13.1 at the beginning of this chapter. Namely, the reflection of the object (the teapot in this case) is rendered into surfaces that are not mirrors (like the walls, for example). We can solve this problem using the stencil buffer because the stencil buffer allows us to block rendering to certain areas on the back buffer. Thus, we can use the stencil buffer to block the rendering of the reflected teapot if it is not being rendered into the mirror. The following outline briefly explains the steps of how this can be accomplished:

1. Render the entire scene as normal — the floor, walls, mirror, and teapot — but *not* the teapot's reflection. Note that this step does not modify the stencil buffer.

2. Clear the stencil buffer to 0. Figure 13.3 shows the back buffer and stencil buffer up to this point.

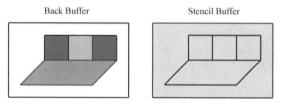

Figure 13.3: The scene rendered to the back buffer and the stencil buffer cleared to 0. The light gray on the stencil buffer denotes pixels cleared to 0.

3. Render the primitives that make up the mirror into the *stencil buffer only*. Set the stencil test to always succeed and specify that the stencil buffer entry should be replaced with 1 if the test passes. Since we are only rendering the mirror, it follows that all the pixels in the stencil buffer will be 0 except for the pixels that correspond to the mirror — they will have a 1. Figure 13.4 shows the updated stencil buffer. Essentially, we are marking the pixels of the mirror in the stencil buffer.

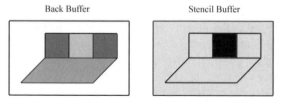

Figure 13.4: Rendering the mirror to the stencil buffer, essentially marking the pixels in the stencil buffer that correspond to the mirror. The black on the stencil buffer denotes pixels set to 1.

4. Now we render the reflected teapot to the back buffer and stencil buffer. But recall that we only will render to the back buffer if the stencil test passes. This time we set the stencil test to only succeed if the value in the stencil buffer is a 1. In this way, the teapot will only be rendered to areas that have a 1 in their corresponding stencil buffer entry.

Since the areas in the stencil buffer that correspond to the mirror are the only entries that have a 1, it follows that the reflected teapot will only be rendered into the mirror.

13.2.3 **Code and Explanation**

The code relevant to this sample lies in the `MirrorDemo::drawReflectedTeapot` function, which first renders the mirror primitives to the stencil buffer and then renders the reflected teapot only if it is being rendered into the mirror. We walk through this function almost line-by-line and explain what is occurring and, more importantly, why.

If you are using the steps outlined in §13.2.2 to serve as an overall guide to the code, note that we are starting at step 3 since steps 1 and 2 have nothing to do with the stencil buffer. We divide this explanation up into parts for no other reason than to offer a more modular discussion.

13.2.3.1 *Code Part I*

We begin by enabling the stencil buffer and setting the related render states:

```
void MirrorDemo::drawReflectedTeapot()
{
HR(gd3dDevice->SetRenderState(D3DRS_STENCILENABLE, true));
HR(gd3dDevice->SetRenderState(D3DRS_STENCILFUNC, D3DCMP_ALWAYS));
HR(gd3dDevice->SetRenderState(D3DRS_STENCILREF, 0x1));
HR(gd3dDevice->SetRenderState(D3DRS_STENCILMASK, 0xffffffff));
HR(gd3dDevice->SetRenderState(D3DRS_STENCILWRITEMASK, 0xffffffff));
HR(gd3dDevice->SetRenderState(D3DRS_STENCILZFAIL, D3DSTENCILOP_KEEP));
HR(gd3dDevice->SetRenderState(D3DRS_STENCILFAIL, D3DSTENCILOP_KEEP));
HR(gd3dDevice->SetRenderState(D3DRS_STENCILPASS, D3DSTENCILOP_REPLACE));
```

This is fairly straightforward. We set the stencil comparison operation to `D3DCMP_ALWAYS`, which specifies that the stencil test will always pass.

If the depth test fails, we specify `D3DSTENCILOP_KEEP`, which indicates to not update the stencil buffer entry; that is, we keep its current value. We do this because if the depth test fails, it means the pixel is obscured, and we do not want to render part of the reflection to a pixel that is obscured.

We also specify `D3DSTENCILOP_KEEP` if the stencil test fails. But this is not really necessary because the test will never fail since we specified `D3DCMP_ALWAYS`. However, we change the comparison operation a little later, so setting the stencil fail render state will be required eventually.

If the depth and stencil tests pass, we specify `D3DSTENCILOP_REPLACE`, which replaces the stencil buffer entry with the stencil reference value — `0x1`.

13.2.3.2 *Code Part II*

This next block of code renders the mirror, but only to the stencil buffer. We can stop writes to the depth buffer by setting the `D3DRS_ZWRITEENABLE` render state to `false`. We can prevent updating the back buffer with blending and setting the source blend factor to D3DBLEND_ZERO and the destination blend factor to D3DBLEND_ONE. Plugging these blend factors into the blending equation, we show that the back buffer is left unchanged:

$$FinalPixel = sourcePixel \otimes (0, 0, 0, 0) + DestPixel \otimes (1, 1, 1, 1)$$
$$= (0, 0, 0, 0) + DestPixel$$
$$= DestPixel$$

```
// Disable writes to the depth and back buffers
HR(gd3dDevice->SetRenderState(D3DRS_ZWRITEENABLE, false));
HR(gd3dDevice->SetRenderState(D3DRS_ALPHABLENDENABLE, true));
HR(gd3dDevice->SetRenderState(D3DRS_SRCBLEND, D3DBLEND_ZERO));
HR(gd3dDevice->SetRenderState(D3DRS_DESTBLEND, D3DBLEND_ONE));

// Draw mirror to stencil only.
drawMirror();

// Re-enable depth writes
HR(gd3dDevice->SetRenderState( D3DRS_ZWRITEENABLE, true));
```

13.2.3.3 *Code Part III*

At this point, the pixels in the stencil buffer that correspond to the visible pixels of the mirror will have an entry of 0x1, thus marking the area to which the mirror has been rendered. We now will prepare to render the reflected teapot. Recall that we only want to render the reflection into pixels that correspond to the mirror. We can do this easily now that we have marked those pixels in the stencil buffer.

We set the following render states:

```
// Only draw reflected teapot to the pixels where the mirror
// was drawn.
HR(gd3dDevice->SetRenderState(D3DRS_STENCILFUNC, D3DCMP_EQUAL));
HR(gd3dDevice->SetRenderState(D3DRS_STENCILPASS, D3DSTENCILOP_KEEP));
```

With the new comparison operation set (i.e., D3DCMP_EQUAL), we get the following stencil test:

ref & $mask$ $\odot$ $value$ & $mask$
0×1 & $0\times$ffffffff $==$ $value$ & $0\times$ffffffff
0×1 $==$ $value$

This shows that the stencil test only succeeds if *value* equals 0x1. Since *value* is only 0x1 in areas of the stencil buffer that correspond to the mirror, the test only succeeds if we are rendering to those areas. Thus, the reflected teapot is only drawn into the mirror and will *not* be drawn into other surfaces.

Note that we have changed the D3DRS_STENCILPASS render state to D3DSTENCILOP_KEEP, which simply says to keep the value in the stencil buffer if the test passed. Therefore, in this second rendering pass we do not change the values in the stencil buffer (all states are D3DSTENCILOP_KEEP); in the second rendering pass, we just use the stencil buffer to accept or reject pixels from being drawn based on the stencil test (we do not modify the stencil buffer).

13.2.3.4 *Code Part IV*

The next part of the `MirrorDemo::drawReflectedTeapot` function computes the matrix that positions the reflection in the scene:

```
// Build reflection transformation.
D3DXMATRIX R;
D3DXPLANE plane(0.0f, 0.0f, 1.0f, 0.0f); // xy-plane
D3DXMatrixReflect(&R, &plane);

// Save the original teapot world matrix.
D3DXMATRIX oldTeapotWorld = mTeapotWorld;

// Add reflection transform.
mTeapotWorld = mTeapotWorld * R;

// Reflect light vector also.
D3DXVECTOR3 oldLightVecW = mLightVecW;
D3DXVec3TransformNormal(&mLightVecW, &mLightVecW, &R);
HR(mFX->SetValue(mhLightVecW, &mLightVecW, sizeof(D3DXVECTOR3)));
```

Notice that we first translate to where the non-reflection teapot is positioned. Then, once positioned there, we reflect across the *xy*-plane. This order of transformation is specified by the order in which we multiply the matrices. Also note that we need to reflect the light vector as well; otherwise, the lighting of the reflected teapot would not be consistent.

13.2.3.5 *Code Part V*

We are almost ready to render the reflected teapot. However, if we render it now it will not be displayed. Why? Because the reflected teapot's depth is greater than the mirror's depth, and thus the mirror primitives technically obscure the reflected teapot. To get around this, we disable the depth buffer before rendering:

```
// Disable depth buffer and render the reflected teapot. We also
// disable alpha blending since we are done with it.
HR(gd3dDevice->SetRenderState(D3DRS_ZENABLE, false));
HR(gd3dDevice->SetRenderState(D3DRS_ALPHABLENDENABLE, false));

HR(gd3dDevice->SetRenderState(D3DRS_CULLMODE, D3DCULL_CW));
drawTeapot();
```

Observe that we change the backface cull mode. We must do this because when an object is reflected, its front faces will be swapped with its back faces; however, the winding order will not be changed. Thus, the "new" front faces will have a winding order that indicates to Direct3D that they are back facing. And similarly, the "new" back facing triangles will have a winding order that indicates to Direct3D that they are front facing. There-fore, to correct this we must change our backface culling condition.

And cleaning up, we restore the old teapot world matrix and light vec-tor, and re-enable the depth buffer, disable stenciling, and restore the usual cull mode:

```
// Restore original teapot world matrix and light vector.
mTeapotWorld = oldTeapotWorld;
mLightVecW   = oldLightVecW;

// Restore render states.
HR(gd3dDevice->SetRenderState(D3DRS_ZENABLE, true));
HR(gd3dDevice->SetRenderState( D3DRS_STENCILENABLE, false));
HR(gd3dDevice->SetRenderState(D3DRS_CULLMODE, D3DCULL_CCW));
}
```

13.3 Sample Application: Planar Shadows

Shadows aid in our perception of where light is being emitted in a scene and ultimately make the scene more realistic. In this section, we will show how to implement planar shadows; that is, shadows that lie on a plane (see Fig-ure 13.5).

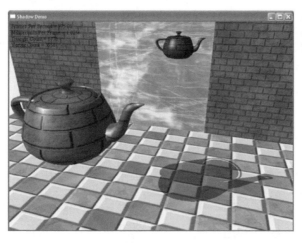

Figure 13.5: A screenshot from the Shadow demo.

To implement planar shadows we must first find the shadow an object casts to a plane and model it geometrically so that we can render it. This can eas-ily be done with some 3D math. We then render the polygons that describe the shadow with a black material at 50% transparency. Rendering the shadow like this can introduce some artifacts, namely "double blending," which we explain in §13.3.4. We employ the stencil buffer to prevent double blending from occurring.

13.3.1 **Parallel Light Shadows**

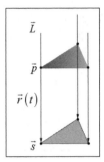

Figure 13.6: The shadow cast with respect to a parallel light source.

Figure 13.6 shows the shadow an object casts with respect to a parallel light source. The light ray from a parallel light, with direction vector $\vec{L}$, through any vertex $\vec{p}$ is given by $\vec{r}(t) = \vec{p} + t\vec{L}$. The intersection of the ray $\vec{r}(t)$ with the plane $(\vec{n}, d)$ gives $\vec{s}$. The set of intersection points found by shooting $\vec{r}(t)$ through each of the object's vertices with the plane defines the projected geometry of the shadow. An intersection point $\vec{s}$ is easily found with a ray/plane intersection test:

$$\vec{n} \cdot \left(\vec{p} + t\vec{L} \right) + d = 0 \qquad \text{Plugging } \vec{r}(t) \text{ into the plane equation } \vec{n} \cdot \vec{p} + d = 0$$

$$\vec{n} \cdot \vec{p} + t \left(\vec{n} \cdot \vec{L} \right) = -d$$

$$t \left(\vec{n} \cdot \vec{L} \right) = -d - \vec{n} \cdot \vec{p} \qquad \text{Solving for } t$$

$$t = \frac{-d - \vec{n} \cdot \vec{p}}{\vec{n} \cdot \vec{L}}$$

Then:

$$\vec{s} = \vec{p} + \left[\frac{-d - \vec{n} \cdot \vec{p}}{\vec{n} \cdot \vec{L}} \right] \vec{L}$$

13.3.2 **Point Light Shadows**

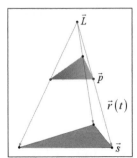

Figure 13.7: The shadow cast with respect to a point light source.

Figure 13.7 shows the shadow an object casts with respect to a point light source whose position is described by the point $\bar{L}$. The light ray from a point light through any vertex $\vec{p}$ is given by $\vec{r}(t) = \vec{p} + t(\vec{p} - \bar{L})$. The intersection point of the ray $\vec{r}(t)$ with the plane $(\vec{n}, d)$ gives $\vec{s}$. The set of intersection points found by shooting $\vec{r}(t)$ through each of the object's vertices with the plane defines the geometry of the shadow. And $\vec{s}$ can be solved for using the same technique (plane/ray intersection) used in §13.3.1.

Note: Notice that $\bar{L}$ serves different purposes for point and parallel lights. For point lights we use $\bar{L}$ to define the position of the point light. For parallel lights we use $\bar{L}$ to define the direction of the parallel light rays.

13.3.3 The Shadow Matrix

Notice from Figure 13.6 that for a parallel light, the shadow is essentially a _parallel_ projection of the object onto the plane $(\vec{n}, d)$ in the specified light direction. Similarly, Figure 13.7 shows that for a point light, the shadow is essentially a _perspective_ projection of the object onto the plane $(\vec{n}, d)$ from the viewpoint of the light source.

We can represent the transformation from a vertex $\vec{p}$ to its projection $\vec{s}$ with the plane $(\vec{n}, d)$ with a matrix. Moreover, we can represent both an orthogonal projection and a perspective projection with the same matrix using some ingenuity.

Let (n_x, n_y, n_z, d) be a 4D vector representing the coefficients of the general plane equation describing the plane onto which we wish to cast the shadow. Let $\bar{L} = (L_x, L_y, L_z, L_w)$ be a 4D vector describing either the direction of a parallel light or the location of a point light. We use the w coordinate to denote which:

■ If $w = 0$, then $\bar{L}$ describes the direction of the parallel light.
■ If $w = 1$, then $\bar{L}$ describes the location of the point light.

Assuming the normal of the plane is normalized, we let $k = (n_x, n_y, n_z, d) \cdot (L_x, L_y, L_z, L_w) = n_x L_x + n_y L_y + n_z L_z + dL_w$.

Then we represent the transformation from a vertex $\vec{p}$ to its projection $\vec{s}$ with the following _shadow matrix_:

$$S = \begin{bmatrix} n_x L_x + k & n_x L_y & n_x L_z & n_x L_w \\ n_y L_x & n_y L_y + k & n_y L_z & n_y L_w \\ n_y L_x & n_z L_y & n_z L_z + k & n_z L_w \\ dL_x & dL_y & dL_z & dL_w + k \end{bmatrix}$$

Note: Because it has been done elsewhere and it is not of significant importance to us, we do not show how to derive this matrix.
However, for the interested reader, we refer you to Chapter 6, "Me
and My (Fake) Shadow," of [Blinn96], which shows how this matrix
can be derived.

The D3DX library provides the following function to build the shadow
matrix given the plane we wish to project the shadow into and a vector
describing a parallel light if $w = 0$ or a point light if $w = 1$:

```
D3DXMATRIX *D3DXMatrixShadow(
    D3DXMATRIX *pOut,
    CONST D3DXVECTOR4 *pLight,     // L
    CONST D3DXPLANE *pPlane        // plane to cast shadow onto
);
```

13.3.4 **Using the Stencil Buffer to Prevent Double Blending**

When we flatten out the geometry of an object onto the plane to describe its
shadow, it is possible that two or more of the flattened triangles will overlap. When we render the shadow with transparency (using blending), these
areas that have overlapping triangles will get blended multiple times and
thus appear darker. Figure 13.8 shows this.

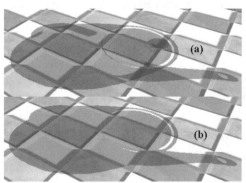

Figure 13.8: Notice
the "black" areas of
the shadow in (a).
These correspond to
areas where parts of
the flattened teapot
overlapped, thus
causing a "double
blend." Image (b)
shows the shadow
rendered correctly,
without double
blending.

We can solve this problem using the stencil buffer. We set the stencil test to
only accept pixels the first time they are rendered. That is, as we render
the shadow's pixels to the back buffer, we will mark the corresponding stencil buffer entries. Then, if we attempt to write a pixel to an area that has
already been rendered to (marked in the stencil buffer), the stencil test will
fail. In this way, we prevent writing overlapping pixels, and therefore, avoid
double blending artifacts.

13.3.5 **Code and Explanation**

The code relevant to this sample lies in the `ShadowDemo::drawTeapotShadow` function. Note that we assume the stencil buffer has already been cleared to zero.

We begin by setting the stencil render states. We set the stencil comparison function to `D3DCMP_EQUAL`, and the `D3DRS_STENCILREF` render state to `0x0`, thereby specifying to render the shadow to the back buffer if the corresponding entry in the stencil buffer equals `0x0`.

Since the stencil buffer is cleared to zero (`0x0`), this is always true the first time we write a particular pixel of the shadow. But, because we set `D3DRS_STENCILPASS` to `D3DSTENCILOP_INCR`, the test will fail if we try to write to a pixel we have already written to again. This is because the pixel's stencil entry will have been incremented to `0x1` the first time it was drawn, and thus the stencil test will fail if we try to write to it again (it no longer equals `0x0`). Hence, we avoid overwriting a pixel, and thus avoid double blending.

```
void ShadowDemo::drawTeapotShadow()
{
HR(gd3dDevice->SetRenderState(D3DRS_STENCILENABLE, true));
HR(gd3dDevice->SetRenderState(D3DRS_STENCILFUNC, D3DCMP_EQUAL));
HR(gd3dDevice->SetRenderState(D3DRS_STENCILREF, 0x0));
HR(gd3dDevice->SetRenderState(D3DRS_STENCILMASK, 0xffffffff));
HR(gd3dDevice->SetRenderState(D3DRS_STENCILWRITEMASK, 0xffffffff));
HR(gd3dDevice->SetRenderState(D3DRS_STENCILZFAIL, D3DSTENCILOP_KEEP));
HR(gd3dDevice->SetRenderState(D3DRS_STENCILFAIL, D3DSTENCILOP_KEEP));
HR(gd3dDevice->SetRenderState(D3DRS_STENCILPASS, D3DSTENCILOP_INCR));
```

Next, we compute the shadow transformation and translate the shadow into the appropriate place in the scene.

```
// Position shadow.
D3DXVECTOR4 lightDirection(0.577f, -0.577f, 0.577f, 0.0f);
D3DXPLANE groundPlane(0.0f, -1.0f, 0.0f, 0.0f);

D3DXMATRIX S;
D3DXMatrixShadow(&S, &lightDirection, &groundPlane);

// Offset the shadow up slightly so that there is no
// z-fighting with the shadow and ground.
D3DXMATRIX eps;
D3DXMatrixTranslation(&eps, 0.0f, 0.001f, 0.0f);

// Save the original teapot world matrix.
D3DXMATRIX oldTeapotWorld = mTeapotWorld;

// Add shadow projection transform.
mTeapotWorld = mTeapotWorld * S * eps;
```

Observe that we slightly translate the teapot shadow up on the *y*-axis; this is so that the shadow does not coincide with the floor plane. We do this because if they did coincide, then a phenomenon called z-fighting may occur. *Z-fighting* occurs when two pixels corresponding to different polygons have the same depth values; the depth buffer doesn't know which one is in front of the other, and an annoying flickering results as the two pixels compete to be drawn.

Lastly, we set a black material at 50% transparency (not shown), render the shadow, and then clean up by disabling alpha blending and stencil testing.

```
// Alpha blend the shadow.
HR(gd3dDevice->SetRenderState(D3DRS_ALPHABLENDENABLE, true));
HR(gd3dDevice->SetRenderState(D3DRS_SRCBLEND, D3DBLEND_SRCALPHA));
HR(gd3dDevice->SetRenderState(D3DRS_DESTBLEND, D3DBLEND_INVSRCALPHA));

// Recall that the teapot's world matrix has been modified to
// include the shadow projection transform; so this draw call
// draws the shadow projection of the teapot. (The world matrix
// is set to the FX file internally in drawTeapot.)
drawTeapot();

// Restore settings.
mTeapotWorld = oldTeapotWorld;
HR(gd3dDevice->SetRenderState(D3DRS_ALPHABLENDENABLE, false));
HR(gd3dDevice->SetRenderState(D3DRS_STENCILENABLE, false));
}
```

13.4 Summary

- The stencil buffer and depth buffer share the same surface and are therefore created at the same time. We specify the format of the depth/stencil surface using the D3DFORMAT types.

- Stenciling is used to block certain pixels from being rasterized. As we have seen in this chapter, this ability is useful for implementing such things as mirrors and shadows.

- We can control stenciling operations and how the stencil buffer is updated through the D3DRS_STENCIL* render states.

13.5 Exercises

1. If you run the Shadow demo and move the teapot (using the "A" and "D" keys) such that the shadow goes off the floor, you will observe that the shadow is still drawn. This can be fixed by employing the stencil technique used for the Mirror demo; that is, mark the stencil buffer pixels that correspond with the floor and then only render the shadow pixels that coincide with the floor. Modify the Shadow demo by applying this described fix.

2. Modify the Shadow demo program to render a point light shadow instead of a parallel light shadow.

3. *Depth complexity* refers to the number of pixels that compete, via the depth test, to be written to a particular entry in the back buffer. For example, a pixel we have drawn may be overwritten by a pixel that is closer to the camera (and this can happen several times before the closest pixel is actually figured out once the entire scene has been drawn). Thus, potentially, the graphics card could fill a pixel several times each frame. This *overdraw* has performance implications, as the graphics card is wasting time processing pixels that eventually get overridden and are never seen. Consequently, it is useful to measure the depth complexity in a scene for performance analysis. In addition, some games have used depth complexity to render obscured pixels in a special way; for instance, in a strategy game, if some of your troops are behind a tree or building, you do not want to forget about them, and therefore, the game might render those obscured objects in a special way so that you can still see them, but it is implied that they are behind another object (the depth complexity can be used to indicate which pixels need to be specially rendered).

   You can measure the depth complexity as follows: Render the scene and use the stencil buffer as a counter; that is, each pixel in the stencil buffer is originally cleared to zero, and every time a pixel is processed, you increment its count with the D3DSTENCILOP_INCR state. Then, for example, after the frame has been drawn, if the *ij*th pixel has a corresponding entry of five in the stencil buffer, then you know that that pixel was processed five times that frame (i.e., the pixel has a depth complexity of five).

   To visualize the depth complexity (stored in the stencil buffer), proceed as follows:

   a. Associate a color c_k for each level of depth complexity k. For example, blue for a depth complexity of one, green for a depth complexity of two, red for a depth complexity of three, and so on. (In very complex scenes where the depth complexity for a pixel could get very large, you probably do not want to associate a color for each level. Instead, you could associate a color for a range of disjoint levels. For example, pixels with depth complexity 1-10 are colored blue, pixels with depth complexity 11-20 are colored green, and so on.)

   b. Set the stencil buffer operation to keep so that we do not modify it anymore. (We modify the stencil buffer with D3DSTENCILOP_INCR when we are counting the depth complexity as the scene is rendered, but when writing the code to visualize the stencil buffer, we only need to *read* from the stencil buffer and we should not *write* to it.) This is done as follows:

```
HR(gd3dDevice->SetRenderState(D3DRS_STENCILPASS, D3DSTENCILOP_KEEP));
```

c. For each level of depth complexity k:

1) Set the stencil buffer such that only pixels with k depth complexity can be drawn to; that is:
```
HR(gd3dDevice->SetRenderState(D3DRS_STENCILFUNC, D3DCMP_EQUAL));
HR(gd3dDevice->SetRenderState(D3DRS_STENCILREF, 0xk));
```

2) Draw a quad of color c_k that covers the entire projection window. Note that this only colors the pixels that have a depth complexity of k because of the preceding set stencil function and reference value.

With this setup, we have colored each pixel based on its depth complexity uniquely, and so we can easily study the depth complexity of the scene. For this exercise, render the depth complexity of a scene. In particular, try it with the ground plane, cylinder, and sphere scene we have used in past demos. Figure 13.9 shows a sample output.

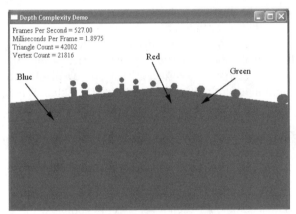

Figure 13.9: Blue denotes pixels with a depth complexity of one, green denotes pixels with a depth complexity of two, and red denotes pixels with a depth complexity of three. Based on the scene, are the colors drawn in the figure justified?

Note: On a performance note, you should try to render your non-blended game objects in front-to-back order with respect to the camera. In this way, the nearest objects will be drawn first, and objects behind them will fail the depth test and not be processed further. The opposite of this strategy is to render in back-to-front order, which would mean every pixel would be processed only to be overwritten by a pixel in front of it.

Part III

Applied Direct3D and the D3DX Library

In this part, we focus on applying Direct3D to implement several 3D applications, demonstrating techniques such as terrain rendering, mesh hierarchies, character animation using vertex blending, fog, grass rendering, sky rendering, water rendering, particle systems, picking, environment mapping, and normal mapping. In addition, we spend some time further exploring the D3DX library (in particular, the mesh-related components). A brief description of the chapters in this part follows.

Chapter 14, "Meshes"

This chapter shows how to work with .X files and the ID3DXMesh interface. In addition, many of the D3DX mesh functions are surveyed. We also show how to compute the bounding box and sphere of a mesh.

Chapter 15, "Mesh Hierarchy Animation Part I — Rigid Meshes"

In this chapter, we learn the relationship between a child mesh and its parent mesh, and how to model this hierarchy relationship in code. To demonstrate the ideas, we create and animate some simple mesh hierarchies, namely a robot arm and a solar system.

Chapter 16, "Mesh Hierarchy Animation Part II — Skinned Meshes"

With the theory of mesh hierarchies covered in the previous chapter, we focus now on implementing the vertex blending algorithm to model elastic skin. We demonstrate this technique by loading the animation and skinning data from an .X file, and then animating it with vertex blending. We use the D3DX animation interfaces.

Chapter 17, "Terrain Rendering — Part I"

This chapter shows how to create, texture, light, and render 3D terrains using heightmaps and a multi-texturing technique. Furthermore, we show how to smoothly "walk" the camera over the terrain. We also learn how to divide the terrain mesh into sub-grid chunks in preparation for frustum culling.

Chapter 18, "Terrain Rendering — Part II"

In this chapter, we show how to implement frustum culling. In addition, we embellish our terrain scene by adding trees, a castle, fog, and animated grass. As always, all of our work is done in the programmable pipeline with vertex and pixel shaders.

Chapter 19, "Particle Systems"

In this chapter, we learn how to model systems that consist of many small particles that all behave in a similar manner. For example, particle systems can be used to model falling snow and rain, fire and smoke, rocket trails and particle guns, and sprinklers and fountains.

Chapter 20, "Picking"

This chapter shows how to determine the particular 3D object (or 3D primitive) that the user has selected with the mouse. Picking is often a necessity in 3D games and applications where the user interacts with the 3D world by using the mouse.

Chapter 21, "Advanced Texturing — Part I"

In this chapter we examine some more advanced texture methods. In particular, we show how to reflect environments onto arbitrary meshes with environment mapping. In addition, we use an environment map to texture a sky sphere. We also show how to get detailed real-time lighting using normal maps, which can also be used to simulate water waves. Finally, we implement a radar map by rendering the scene to a texture from a bird's-eye view directly above the camera.

Chapter 22, "Advanced Texturing — Part II"

In this final chapter we continue our exploration of texturing techniques. Here, we discuss projective texturing, which can be used like a slide projector or as an intermediate step for other techniques such as shadow mapping. Also included is a discussion of the general techniques used to cast shadows on arbitrary meshes with spotlights using the shadow mapping algorithm. The final topic discussed in the chapter covers the technique of displacement mapping by animating realistic ocean waves.

Chapter 14

Meshes

We have already worked with the ID3DXMesh interface using the D3DXCreate* routines; in this chapter, we examine this interface in more detail. This chapter is largely a survey of the data and methods related to the ID3DXMesh interface.

Before starting, let us point out that the ID3DXMesh interface inherits the majority of its functionality from its parent, ID3DXBaseMesh. This is important to know because other D3DX mesh interfaces such as ID3DXPMesh (progressive mesh) and ID3DXSPMesh (simplified mesh) also inherit from ID3DXBaseMesh; therefore, the topics covered in this chapter are also relevant when working with the other mesh types.

Objectives:

- To gain an understanding of the internal data organization of an ID3DXMesh object.
- To find out how to create, optimize, and render an ID3DXMesh object.
- To learn how to load the data of an .X file into an ID3DXMesh object.
- To become familiar with several D3DX mesh-related utility functions.
- To learn about bounding volumes, why they are useful, and how to create them using the D3DX functions.

14.1 Geometry Info

The ID3DXBaseMesh interface contains a vertex buffer that stores the vertices of the mesh, and an index buffer that defines how these vertices are put together to form the triangles of the mesh. We can get a pointer to these buffers using the following methods:

```
HRESULT ID3DXMesh::GetVertexBuffer(LPDIRECT3DVERTEXBUFFER9* ppVB);
HRESULT ID3DXMesh::GetIndexBuffer(LPDIRECT3DINDEXBUFFER9* ppIB);
```

Here is an example of how these methods are called:

```
IDirect3DVertexBuffer9* vb = 0;
Mesh->GetVertexBuffer(&vb);

IDirect3DIndexBuffer9* ib = 0;
Mesh->GetIndexBuffer(&ib);
```

Note: For its primitive type, the ID3DXMesh interface supports indexed triangle lists only; that is, ID3DXMesh::DrawSubset internally calls IDirect3DDevice9::DrawIndexedPrimitive with the D3DPT_TRIANGLELIST member of the D3DPRIMITIVETYPE enumerated type.

Alternatively, if we just want to lock the buffers to read or write to them, then we can use this next pair of methods. Note that these methods lock the entire vertex/index buffer.

```
HRESULT ID3DXMesh::LockVertexBuffer(DWORD Flags, BYTE** ppData);
HRESULT ID3DXMesh::LockIndexBuffer(DWORD Flags, BYTE** ppData);
```

The Flags parameter describes how the lock is done. Locking flags for a vertex/index buffer were explained in Chapter 7 when we first introduced vertex and index buffers. The ppData argument is the address of a pointer that is to point to the locked memory when the function returns.

Remember to call the appropriate unlock method when you are done with the lock:

```
HRESULT ID3DXMesh::UnlockVertexBuffer();
HRESULT ID3DXMesh::UnlockIndexBuffer();
```

Below is a list of additional ID3DXMesh methods used to obtain various information about a mesh:

■   HRESULT GetDeclaration(D3DVERTEXELEMENT9
        Declaration[MAX_FVF_DECL_SIZE]);

Returns an array of D3DVERTEXELEMENT9 elements that describe the vertex format of the mesh (the D3DDECL_END element is included). MAX_FVF_DECL_SIZE is defined as:

```
typedef enum {
    MAX_FVF_DECL_SIZE = MAXD3DDECLLENGTH + 1
} MAX_FVF_DECL_SIZE;
```

And MAXD3DDECLLENGTH is defined in *d3d9types.h* as:

```
#define MAXD3DDECLLENGTH        64
```

■   DWORD GetNumVertices();

Returns the number of vertices in the vertex buffer.

■   DWORD GetNumBytesPerVertex();

Returns the number of bytes per vertex.

- DWORD GetNumFaces();

  Returns the number of faces (triangles) in the mesh.

- DWORD GetOptions();

  Returns a DWORD whose bits are bit-flags that describe various options about the mesh such as what memory pool it is stored in, the format of the indices, and/or whether it is static or dynamic. We'll look at mesh options in more detail later on in this chapter.

14.2 **Subsets and the Attribute Buffer**

A mesh consists of one or more subsets. A _subset_ is a group of triangles in a mesh that can all be rendered using the same attribute. By _attribute_ we mean material, texture, and render states. Figure 14.1 illustrates how a mesh representing a car may be divided into several subsets.

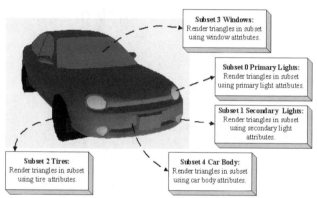

Figure 14.1: A car broken up by subset. Here only the materials per subset differ, but we could also imagine textures being added and differing as well. In addition, the render states may differ; for example, the glass windows may be rendered with alpha blending for transparency.

We label each subset by specifying a unique positive integer value for that subset. This value can be any number that can be stored in a DWORD. For instance, in Figure 14.1 we labeled the subsets 0, 1, 2, 3, and 4.

Each triangle in a mesh is given an _attribute ID_ that specifies the subset in which the triangle lives. For example, in Figure 14.1, the triangles that make up the tires of the car have an attribute ID of 2 to indicate they live in subset 2. Similarly, the triangles that make up the body of the car have an attribute ID equal to 4 to indicate they live in subset 4.

The attribute IDs for the triangles are stored in a mesh's _attribute buffer_, which is a DWORD array. Since each face has an entry in the attribute buffer, the number of elements in the attribute buffer is equal to the number of faces in the mesh. The entries in the attribute buffer and the triangles defined in the index buffer have a one-to-one correspondence; that is, entry i in the attribute buffer corresponds with triangle i in the index buffer. Triangle i is defined by the following three indices in the index buffer:

$$A = i \cdot 3$$
$$B = i \cdot 3 + 1$$
$$C = i \cdot 3 + 2$$

Figure 14.2 shows this correspondence:

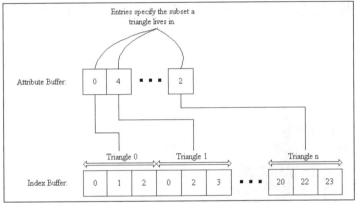

Figure 14.2: The correspondence between the triangles defined in the index buffer and the entries in the attribute buffer. We see that triangle 0 exists in subset 0, triangle 1 exists in subset 4, and triangle *n* exists in subset 2.

We can access the attribute buffer by locking it as this next code snippet illustrates:

```
DWORD* buffer = 0;
Mesh->LockAttributeBuffer(lockingFlags, &buffer);

    // Read or write to attribute buffer...

Mesh->UnlockAttributeBuffer();
```

14.3 **Drawing**

The ID3DXMesh interface provides the DrawSubset(DWORD AttribId) method to draw the triangles of a particular subset specified by the AttribId argument. For instance, to draw all the triangles that live in subset 0 we would write:

```
Mesh->DrawSubset(0);
```

Therefore, to draw an entire mesh, we must draw all the subsets of the mesh. It is convenient to label subsets in the order 0, 1, 2, ..., $n-1$, where n is the number of subsets, and to have a corresponding material and texture array such that index i refers to the material and texture associated with subset i. This allows us to render the entire mesh using a simple loop:

```
HR(mFX->BeginPass(0));

for(int j = 0; j < mMtrl.size(); ++j)
{
    HR(mFX->SetValue(mhMtrl, &mMtrl[j], sizeof(Mtrl)));

    if(mTex[j] != 0)
    {
        HR(mFX->SetTexture(mhTex, mTex[j]));
    }
    else
    {
        HR(mFX->SetTexture(mhTex, mWhiteTex));
    }

    HR(mFX->CommitChanges());
    HR(mMesh->DrawSubset(j));
}
HR(mFX->EndPass());
```

In the above code, we check to see if the subset has a texture (i.e., the ith texture corresponding to the ith subset is not null). If it does, then we set its texture; otherwise, we set a default white texture. The reason for this is so that we can use the same effect files for subsets that use textures and those that do not. Recall that for our lighting and texturing effect file, we've been doing something like the following:

```
// Combine the color from lighting with the texture color.
float3 color = (ambient + diffuse)*texColor.rgb + spec;
```

So if a subset did not have a texture, what would `texColor` be? By defaulting to a white texture in that case, `texColor` essentially drops out since multiplying a color by white is like multiplying a number by one, and we end up with just the light/material calculated color, which is what we want if a subset does not have a texture.

Remark: The meshes created with the `D3DXCreate*` functions only have one subset (specifically, subset 0). Hence, we could draw the mesh with `DrawSubset(0)`.

14.4 **Adjacency Info**

For certain mesh operations, such as optimizing, it is necessary to know the triangles that are adjacent to a given triangle. A mesh's _adjacency array_ stores this information.

The adjacency array is a DWORD array, where each entry contains an index identifying a triangle in the mesh. For example, an entry *i* refers to the *i*th triangle formed by indices:

$$A = i \cdot 3$$
$$B = i \cdot 3 + 1$$
$$C = i \cdot 3 + 2$$

Note that an entry of ULONG_MAX = 4294967295 as its value indicates that the particular edge does not have an adjacent triangle. We can also use –1 to denote this because assigning –1 to a DWORD results in ULONG_MAX. (Recall that a DWORD is an *unsigned* 32-bit integer.)

Since each triangle has three edges, it can have up to three adjacent triangles, as shown in Figure 14.3.

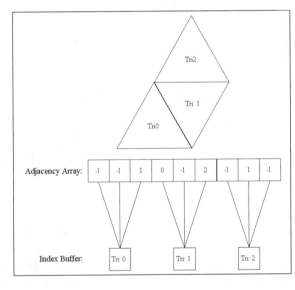

Figure 14.3: We see that each triangle has three entries in the adjacency array that identify the triangles adjacent to it. For instance, Tri: 1 has two adjacent triangles — Tri: 0 and Tri: 2. Thus, for Tri: 1 there is a "0", "2", and "–1" in its corresponding adjacency entries, specifying that Tri: 0 and Tri: 2 are adjacent. The "–1" indicates that one edge of Tri: 1 doesn't have an adjacent triangle.

Therefore, the adjacency array must have ID3DXBaseMesh::GetNumFaces() * 3 many elements — three possible adjacent triangles for every triangle in the mesh.

Many of the D3DX mesh creation functions can output the adjacency info, but the following method can also be used:

```
HRESULT ID3DXMesh::GenerateAdjacency(
    FLOAT fEpsilon,
    DWORD* pAdjacency
);
```

■ fEpsilon: Let $\vec{v}_0$ and $\vec{v}_1$ be two vertex positions. The ID3DXMesh::GenerateAdjacency method treats $\vec{v}_0$ and $\vec{v}_1$ as coincident (i.e., overlapping/at the same position) if and only if $\|\vec{v}_0 - \vec{v}_1\| < \varepsilon$. In other words, ε (epsilon) specifies how far two vertices can differ in position and still be considered equal. This info is needed because we need to know when face edges coincide to build the adjacency array (knowing when vertices coincide enables us to figure out when edges coincide).

■ pAdjacency: A pointer to an array of DWORDs that is to be filled with the adjacency info. This array must have ID3DXBaseMesh::GetNumFaces() * 3 many elements.

Here is an example of how this function could be called:

```
DWORD* adjacencyInfo = new DWORD[Mesh->GetNumFaces() * 3];
Mesh->GenerateAdjacency(0.001f, adjacencyInfo);
```

14.5 **Optimizing**

The vertices and indices of a mesh can be reorganized to render the mesh more efficiently. When we do this, we say that we are *optimizing* a mesh and we use the following method to do this:

```
HRESULT ID3DXMesh::Optimize(
    DWORD Flags,
    CONST DWORD *pAdjacencyIn,
    DWORD *pAdjacencyOut,
    DWORD *pFaceRemap,
    LPD3DXBUFFER *ppVertexRemap,
    LPD3DXMESH *ppOptMesh
);
```

■ Flags: A combination of bit-flags that tell the method what kind of optimizations to perform and the properties of the output mesh (e.g., the memory pool to place it in, whether the mesh is static or dynamic). Here are some commonly used optimization flags:

D3DXMESHOPT_COMPACT: Removes unused geometry that the mesh may contain.

D3DXMESHOPT_ATTRSORT: Sorts the geometry by attribute and generates an attribute table. This allows DrawSubset to be more efficient; see §14.6. Observe that a triangle can belong to only one subset, but a vertex could belong to more than one; this is because ID3DXMesh uses indexed triangle lists, and so a vertex could be referenced by triangles in different subsets. In order to sort the vertices by subset then, D3DXMESHOPT_ATTRSORT duplicates vertices that are shared among different subsets so that each vertex belongs to only one subset.

D3DXMESHOPT_VERTEXCACHE: A vertex cache is a hardware buffer that saves processed vertices. If a vertex is referenced again by other indices and it is in the cache, then it does not need to be processed again. This optimization reorganizes the geometry of the mesh to take better advantage of the vertex cache.

D3DXMESHOPT_STRIPREORDER: Reorganizes the geometry so that triangle strips can be as long as possible.

D3DXMESHOPT_IGNOREVERTS: Optimize index info only; ignore vertices.

D3DXMESHOPT_DONOTSPLIT: Stops the vertex duplication that D3DXMESHOPT_ATTRSORT does if a vertex belongs to more than one subset. With this flag, only the indices will be sorted by subset — the vertices cannot be sorted since a vertex may belong to more than one subset if this flag is specified.

Note: The D3DXMESHOPT_VERTEXCACHE and D3DXMESHOPT_STRIPREORDER flags cannot be used together because they ask the mesh to reorganize in different ways and so are incompatible.

For the output mesh properties, we have the following abridged listing:

D3DXMESH_SYSTEMMEM: Place the mesh in system memory.

D3DXMESH_MANAGED: Place the mesh in the managed memory pool.

D3DXMESH_DYNAMIC: The mesh buffers are dynamic.

Note: The SDK documentation mentions that D3DXMESH_32BIT, D3DXMESH_IB_WRITEONLY, and D3DXMESH_WRITEONLY are not valid flags for this method.

- pAdjacencyIn: Pointer to an array containing the adjacency info of the mesh object invoking this method.

- pAdjacencyOut: Pointer to a DWORD array to be filled with the adjacency info of the optimized mesh. The array must have ID3DXMesh::GetNumFaces() * 3 elements. If you do not need this info, pass zero.

- pFaceRemap: Pointer to a DWORD array to be filled with the face remap info. The array should be of size ID3DXMesh::GetNumFaces() (i.e., one element for each face). When a mesh is optimized, its faces may be moved around in the index buffer. The face remap info tells where the original faces have moved; that is, the ith entry in pFaceRemap provides a face index (relative to the optimized mesh) identifying where the ith original face has moved in the optimized mesh. If you do not need this info, pass zero.

- ppVertexRemap: Address of a pointer to an ID3DXBuffer that will be filled with the vertex remap info. This buffer should contain ID3DXMesh::GetNumVertices() many vertices. When a mesh is optimized, its vertices may be moved around in the vertex buffer. The vertex remap info tells where the original vertices have moved; that is, the ith entry in ppVertexRemap provides the vertex index (relative to the optimized mesh) identifying where the ith original vertex has moved in the optimized mesh. If you do not need this info, pass zero.

■   ppOptMesh: Outputs the optimized mesh.

Here is an example call:

```
// Get the adjacency info of the non-optimized mesh.
DWORD* adjacencyInfo = new DWORD[Mesh->GetNumFaces() * 3];
Mesh->GenerateAdjacency(0.0f, adjacencyInfo);

// Array to hold optimized adjacency info.
DWORD* optimizedAdjacencyInfo = new DWORD[Mesh->GetNumFaces() * 3];

ID3DXMesh* meshOut = 0;
HR(Mesh->Optimize(D3DXMESH_MANAGED | D3DXMESHOPT_COMPACT |
D3DXMESHOPT_ATTRSORT | D3DXMESHOPT_VERTEXCACHE,
adjacencyInfo, optimizedAdjacencyInfo, 0, 0, &meshOut));
```

A similar method is the ID3DXMesh::OptimizeInplace method, which actually
optimizes the calling mesh object instead of outputting an optimized mesh.
Its prototype is given as follows:

```
HRESULT ID3DXMesh::OptimizeInplace(
    DWORD Flags,
    CONST DWORD *pAdjacencyIn,
    DWORD *pAdjacencyOut,
    DWORD *pFaceRemap,
    LPD3DXBUFFER *ppVertexRemap
);
```

14.6 **The Attribute Table**

When a mesh is optimized with the D3DXMESHOPT_ATTRSORT flag (and assuming
D3DXMESHOPT_DONOTSPLIT was not specified), the geometry of the mesh is
sorted by its attribute so that the geometry of a particular subset exists as a
contiguous block in the vertex/index buffers (see Figure 14.4).

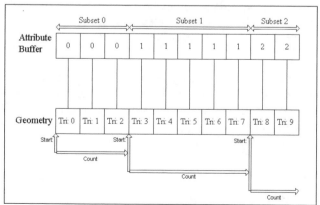

Figure 14.4: Notice that the geometry and attribute buffer are sorted by
attribute such that the geometry of a particular subset is contiguous.
We can now easily mark where the geometry of one subset begins and
ends.

In addition to sorting the geometry, the D3DXMESHOPT_ATTRSORT optimization builds an attribute table. The attribute table is an array of D3DXATTRIBUTERANGE structures. Each entry in the attribute table corresponds to a subset of the mesh and specifies the block of memory in the vertex/index buffers where the geometry for the subset resides. The D3DXATTRIBUTERANGE structure is defined as:

```
typedef struct _D3DXATTRIBUTERANGE {
    DWORD  AttribId;
    DWORD  FaceStart;
    DWORD  FaceCount;
    DWORD  VertexStart;
    DWORD  VertexCount;
} D3DXATTRIBUTERANGE;
```

- AttribId: The subset ID.
- FaceStart: An offset into the index buffer (FaceStart * 3) identifying the start of the triangles that are associated with this subset.
- FaceCount: The number of faces (triangles) in this subset.
- VertexStart: An offset into the vertex buffer identifying the start of the vertices that are associated with this subset.
- VertexCount: The number of vertices in this subset.

We can easily see the members of the D3DXATTRIBUTERANGE structure at work graphically in Figure 14.4. The attribute table for the mesh in Figure 14.4 would have three entries — one to correspond with each subset.

Note: If D3DXMESHOPT_DONOTSPLIT was specified, then it is possible that the vertex ranges for each subset would overlap (i.e., not be disjoint). In this case, the vertex range, [VertexStart, VertexStart + VertexCount], includes all the vertices for a subset, but it could additionally include vertices that are not part of the subset. This follows from the fact that the vertices cannot be sorted by subset if a vertex can belong to more than one subset, which it can when D3DXMESHOPT_DONOTSPLIT is specified.

With the attribute table built, rendering a subset can be done very efficiently, for only a quick lookup in the attribute table is required to find all the geometry of a particular subset. Note that without an attribute table, rendering a subset would require a linear search of the entire attribute buffer to find the geometry that exists in the particular subset we are drawing.

To access the attribute table of a mesh we use the following method:

```
HRESULT ID3DXMesh::GetAttributeTable(
    D3DXATTRIBUTERANGE* pAttribTable,
    DWORD* pAttribTableSize
);
```

This method can do two things: It can return the number of attributes in the attribute table, and it can fill an array of D3DXATTRIBUTERANGE structures with the attribute data.

To get the number of elements in the attribute table, we pass in zero as the first argument:

```
// Assume mesh is of type ID3DXMesh*
DWORD numSubsets = 0;
mesh->GetAttributeTable(0, &numSubsets);
```

Once we know the number of elements in the attribute table, we can fill a D3DXATTRIBUTERANGE array with the actual attribute table by writing:

```
D3DXATTRIBUTERANGE table = new D3DXATTRIBUTERANGE[numSubsets];
mesh->GetAttributeTable( table, &numSubsets );
```

We can directly set the attribute table using the ID3DXMesh::SetAttribute-Table method. The following example sets an attribute table with 12 subsets.

```
D3DXATTRIBUTERANGE attributeTable[12];
// ...manually define and fill the attributeTable array with data
mesh->SetAttributeTable( attributeTable, 12);
```

14.7 **Cloning**

Sometimes we will need to copy the data from one mesh to another. This is accomplished with the ID3DXMesh::CloneMesh method.

```
HRESULT ID3DXMesh::CloneMesh(
    DWORD Options,
    const D3DVERTEXELEMENT9 *pDeclaration,
    LPDIRECT3DDEVICE9 pDevice,
    LPD3DXMESH *ppCloneMesh
);
```

- Options: One or more creation flags that will be used to create the cloned mesh. See the D3DXMESH enumerated type in the SDK documentation for a complete list of option flags. Some common flags are:

   D3DXMESH_32BIT: The mesh will use 32-bit indices.

   D3DXMESH_SYSTEMMEM: The mesh will be placed in the system memory pool.

   D3DXMESH_MANAGED: The mesh will be placed in the managed memory pool.

   D3DXMESH_WRITEONLY: The mesh's data will only be written to and not read from.

   D3DXMESH_DYNAMIC: The mesh's buffers will be made dynamic.

- pDeclaration: A pointer to the first element in a D3DVERTEXELEMENT9 array that describes the vertex format we want for the new cloned mesh.
- pDevice: The device to be associated with the cloned mesh.
- ppCloneMesh: Outputs the cloned mesh.

Notice that this method allows the creation options and vertex format of the destination mesh to be different from that of the source mesh. Thus, in addition to just copying a mesh, this function is useful if the options or vertex format need to be changed.

The following code snippet shows how this method might be invoked:

```
D3DVERTEXELEMENT9 elements[] =
{
{0, 0, D3DDECLTYPE_FLOAT3, D3DDECLMETHOD_DEFAULT, D3DDECLUSAGE_POSITION, 0},
{0, 12, D3DDECLTYPE_FLOAT3, D3DDECLMETHOD_DEFAULT, D3DDECLUSAGE_NORMAL, 0},
{0, 24, D3DDECLTYPE_FLOAT2, D3DDECLMETHOD_DEFAULT, D3DDECLUSAGE_TEXCOORD, 0},
D3DDECL_END()
};

// Assume meshSys is of type ID3DXMesh*.
ID3DXMesh* temp = 0;
HR(meshSys->CloneMesh(D3DXMESH_SYSTEMMEM,
    elements, gd3dDevice, &temp));
```

14.8 Creating a Mesh (D3DXCreateMesh)

Thus far, we have created mesh objects using the D3DXCreate* functions. However, we can also create an "empty" mesh using the D3DXCreateMesh function. By empty mesh, we mean that we specify the number of faces and vertices (of some specified format) we want the mesh to be able to hold, then D3DXCreateMesh allocates the appropriately sized vertex, index, and attribute buffers. Once we have the mesh's buffers allocated, we manually fill in the mesh's data contents; that is, we must write the vertices, indices, and attributes to the vertex buffer, index buffer, and attribute buffer, respectively.

As said, to create an empty mesh we use the D3DXCreateMesh function:

```
HRESULT WINAPI D3DXCreateMesh(
    DWORD NumFaces,
    DWORD NumVertices,
    DWORD Options,
    const LPD3DVERTEXELEMENT9 *pDeclaration,
    LPDIRECT3DDEVICE9 pD3DDevice,
    LPD3DXMESH *ppMesh
);
```

- NumFaces: The number of faces the mesh will have. This must be greater than zero.
- NumVertices: The number of vertices the mesh will have. This must be greater than zero.

- Options: One or more creation flags that will be used to create the mesh. See the D3DXMESH enumerated type in the SDK documentation for a complete list of option flags. Some common flags are:

    D3DXMESH_32BIT: The mesh will use 32-bit indices.

    D3DXMESH_SYSTEMMEM: The mesh will be placed in the system memory pool.

    D3DXMESH_MANAGED: The mesh will be placed in the managed memory pool.

    D3DXMESH_WRITEONLY: The mesh's data will only be written to and not read from.

    D3DXMESH_DYNAMIC: The mesh's buffers will be made dynamic.

- pDeclaration: A pointer to the first element in a D3DVERTEXELEMENT9 array that describes the vertex format of the mesh vertices.

- pD3DDevice: The device associated with the mesh.

- ppMesh: Outputs the created mesh.

Here is an example of how to use this method:

```
D3DVERTEXELEMENT9 elements[] =
{
{0, 0, D3DDECLTYPE_FLOAT3, D3DDECLMETHOD_DEFAULT, D3DDECLUSAGE_POSITION, 0},
{0, 12, D3DDECLTYPE_FLOAT3, D3DDECLMETHOD_DEFAULT, D3DDECLUSAGE_NORMAL, 0},
{0, 24, D3DDECLTYPE_FLOAT2, D3DDECLMETHOD_DEFAULT, D3DDECLUSAGE_TEXCOORD, 0},
D3DDECL_END()
};

ID3DXMesh* mesh = 0;
HR(D3DXCreateMesh(12, 24, D3DXMESH_MANAGED, elements,
    gd3dDevice, &mesh));
```

14.9 .X Files

Thus far, we have worked with simple geometric objects such as spheres, cylinders, and cubes using the D3DXCreate* functions. If you have attempted to construct your own 3D object by manually specifying the vertices, you have, no doubt, found it quite tedious. To avoid the tiresome task of constructing the data of 3D objects, special applications called *3D modelers* have been developed. These modelers allow the user to build complex and realistic meshes in a visual and interactive environment with a rich tool set, thereby making the entire modeling process much easier. Examples of popular modelers used for game development are 3D Studio MAX (www.discreet.com), LightWave 3D (www.newtek.com), Maya (www.alias.com/eng/index.shtml), and Softimage|XSI (www.softimage.com).

These modelers, of course, can export the created mesh data (geometry, materials, animations, and other possible useful data) to a file. Thus, we could write a file reader to extract the mesh data and use it in our Direct3D applications. This is certainly a viable solution. However, an even more convenient solution exists. There is a particular mesh file format called the .X (X-file) format. Many 3D modelers can export to this format (or use plug-ins for exporting to the .X format) and there are converters that can convert other popular 3D file formats to .X (e.g., PolyTrans [http://www.okino.com/conv/conv.htm] and Deep Exploration [http://www.righthemisphere.com/products/dexp/]). What makes .X files convenient is that they are a DirectX defined format, and therefore, the D3DX library readily supports .X files; that is, the D3DX library provides functions for loading and saving .X files. Thus, we avoid having to write our own file loading/saving routines if we use this format.

In this section, we show how to load the geometry stored in an .X file and render it. The DirectX SDK contains a small collection of .X file models, which can be found in the subdirectories of the media folder: *\DX9 (August2005)\Samples\Media*. Figure 14.5 shows a screenshot of the *skullocc.x* file, and Figure 14.6 shows a screenshot of the *dwarf.x* file.

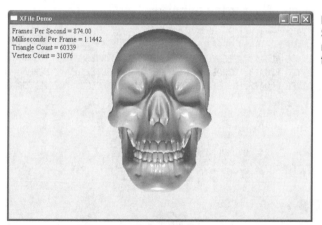

Figure 14.5: Screenshot of the rendered *skullocc.x* file.

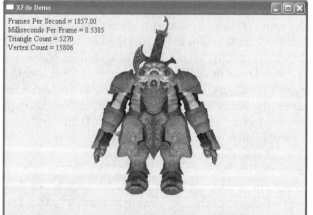

Figure 14.6: Screenshot of the rendered *dwarf.x* file.

14.9.1 **Loading an .X File**

To facilitate loading .X files, we implement the following function in *d3dUtil.h*:

```
void LoadXFile(
      const std::string& filename,
      ID3DXMesh** meshOut,
      std::vector<Mtrl>& mtrls,
      std::vector<IDirect3DTexture9*>& texs);
```

- `filename`: The filename of the .X file we wish to load.
- `meshOut`: Address of the pointer to receive the newly created mesh (i.e., we create an `ID3DXMesh` object by loading the .X file geometry into it).
- `mtrls`: Fills in a vector with the materials of the mesh — one for each subset such that the ith material corresponds with the ith subset.
- `texs`: Fills in a vector with the textures of the mesh — one for each subset such that the ith texture corresponds with the ith subset.

To actually load the .X file data into an `ID3DXMesh` object, we utilize the following D3DX function:

```
HRESULT D3DXLoadMeshFromX(
      LPCSTR pFilename,
      DWORD Options,
      LPDIRECT3DDEVICE9 pDevice,
      LPD3DXBUFFER *ppAdjacency,
      LPD3DXBUFFER *ppMaterials,
      LPD3DXBUFFER* ppEffectInstances,
      PDWORD pNumMaterials,
      LPD3DXMESH *ppMesh
);
```

- `pFilename`: The filename of the .X file to load.
- `Options`: One or more creation flags (combined by a bitwise OR) that are used to create the mesh. See the `D3DXMESH` enumerated type in the SDK documentation for a complete list of option flags. Some common flags are:

  `D3DXMESH_32BIT`: The mesh will use 32-bit indices.

  `D3DXMESH_MANAGED`: The mesh will be placed in the managed memory pool.

  `D3DXMESH_WRITEONLY`: The mesh's data will only be written to and not read from. (You have to be careful with this flag since some of the mesh's internal methods may need to read the geometry — for example, to generate adjacency info, compute normal vectors, or optimize the mesh. So typically, a mesh is first created in system memory, then optimized and cloned to whatever format you want, and finally, once you are done accessing the mesh data, it is cloned once again to a "hardware" mesh with the options [this is an example — the flags you use may vary] D3DXMESH_MANAGED and D3DXMESH_WRITEONLY.)

D3DXMESH_DYNAMIC: The mesh's buffers will be made dynamic.

- pDevice: The device to be associated with the mesh.

- ppAdjacency: Returns an ID3DXBuffer containing a DWORD array that describes the adjacency info of the mesh.

- ppMaterials: Returns an ID3DXBuffer containing an array of D3DXMATERIAL structures that contains the material data for this mesh. We cover the mesh materials in §14.9.6.

- ppEffectInstances: Returns an ID3DXBuffer containing an array of D3DXEFFECTINSTANCE structures; there is one effect instance per subset. A D3DXEFFECTINSTANCE stores an .fx filename and the data needed to initialize the effect parameters. This is useful if your 3D modeler can export effect data information to the .X file, as you can then get all the effect information associated with a subset from the .X file. The .X files we use in this book do not carry effect information, so we ignore this parameter by specifying zero.

- pNumMaterials: Returns the number of materials for the mesh; that is, the number of elements in the D3DXMATERIAL array output by ppMaterials.

- ppMesh: Returns the created ID3DXMesh object filled with the .X file geometry.

So, for example, the first step in LoadXFile loads the .X file like so:

```
// Step 1: Load the .X file from file into a system memory mesh.

ID3DXMesh* meshSys       = 0;
ID3DXBuffer* adjBuffer   = 0;
ID3DXBuffer* mtrlBuffer  = 0;
DWORD numMtrls           = 0;


HR(D3DXLoadMeshFromX(filename.c_str(), D3DXMESH_SYSTEMMEM,
        gd3dDevice, &adjBuffer, &mtrlBuffer, 0, &numMtrls, &meshSys));
```

14.9.2 Testing for Vertex Normals

When an .X file is loaded into an ID3DXMesh, the ID3DXMesh's vertex format matches that of the .X file. The effect file we are going to use to render the meshes assumes that the vertex format has a position, normal, and one set of 2D texture coordinates. However, the geometry stored in the .X file may not have all this information (it will have position information, but not necessarily normal or texture coordinates). (The .X file could actually store additional data as well, which we would ignore here, such as tangent vectors or multiple texture coordinates. Note that you can extend the .X file format; thus, you can extend the .X file format to include any extra data you want it to store.) In any case, we clone the mesh so that its vertices have the VertexPNT (position, normal, 2D texture coordinates) format so that it can be processed by our effect. If the mesh did not have vertex normals, then we generate them procedurally using the normal averaging technique discussed in §10.2.1. If the mesh did not have texture coordinates, we just leave the data uninitialized and apply the white texture in §14.3 (regardless of what the texture coordinates are, white will always be the texel color).

Now, we need to check if the mesh already has normal data, as we do not want to blindly overwrite its normal data with our procedurally generated vertex normals (i.e., we only generate procedural vertex normals if there were no vertex normals in the mesh to begin with). The following code does this:

```
// Step 2: Find out if the mesh already has normal info.

D3DVERTEXELEMENT9 elems[MAX_FVF_DECL_SIZE];
HR(meshSys->GetDeclaration(elems));

bool hasNormals = false;
for(int i = 0; i < MAX_FVF_DECL_SIZE; ++i)
{
    // Did we reach D3DDECL_END() {0xFF,0,D3DDECLTYPE_UNUSED, 0,0,0}?
    if(elems[i].Stream == 0xff)
        break;

    if( elems[i].Type == D3DDECLTYPE_FLOAT3 &&
        elems[i].Usage == D3DDECLUSAGE_NORMAL &&
        elems[i].UsageIndex == 0 )
    {
        hasNormals = true;
        break;
    }
}
```

The code is not tricky; it does a simple linear search of the vertex element array corresponding to the vertex format we are using. If we find a 3D vector with normal usage and usage index 0, then we conclude that the mesh already had vertex normal information.

14.9.3 Changing the Vertex Format

As stated in the preceding section, we clone the mesh so that its vertices have the VertexPNT (position, normal, 2D texture coordinates) format so that it can be processed by our effect. The following code demonstrates how this is done:

```
// Step 3: Change vertex format to VertexPNT.

D3DVERTEXELEMENT9 elements[64];
UINT numElements = 0;
VertexPNT::Decl->GetDeclaration(elements, &numElements);

ID3DXMesh* temp = 0;
```

```
HR(meshSys->CloneMesh(D3DXMESH_SYSTEMMEM,
    elements, gd3dDevice, &temp));
ReleaseCOM(meshSys);
meshSys = temp;
```

14.9.4 Generating Normals

At this point, we have cloned the mesh to reserve room for vertex normals (if there wasn't room to begin with), and we know whether or not the mesh has vertex normals already (see `hasNormals` from §14.9.2). So at this point, we can compute the vertex normals by normal averaging. We do not need to do this ourselves, as the D3DX library provides a function to do it. In our code, we have:

```
// Step 4: If the mesh did not have normals, generate them.

if( hasNormals == false)
    HR(D3DXComputeNormals(meshSys, 0));
```

The first parameter to `D3DXComputeNormals` is a pointer to the mesh to compute the normals of — this mesh must have space reserved for vertex normals in the vertex structure. The second parameter is a pointer to the input mesh's adjacency array. This can be set to null, but if not, it takes adjacent face information into account to smooth the normals at duplicate vertices.

14.9.5 Optimizing

The next step is to optimize the mesh to improve rendering speed; review §14.5 if necessary.

```
// Step 5: Optimize the mesh.

HR(meshSys->Optimize(D3DXMESH_MANAGED | D3DXMESHOPT_COMPACT |
    D3DXMESHOPT_ATTRSORT | D3DXMESHOPT_VERTEXCACHE,
    (DWORD*)adjBuffer->GetBufferPointer(), 0, 0, 0, meshOut));
ReleaseCOM(meshSys);    // Done w/ system mesh.
ReleaseCOM(adjBuffer);  // Done with buffer.
```

14.9.6 .X File Materials

Argument seven of `D3DXLoadMeshFromX` returns the number of materials the mesh contains and argument five returns an array of `D3DXMATERIAL` structures containing the material data. The `D3DXMATERIAL` structure is defined as follows:

```
typedef struct D3DXMATERIAL {
    D3DMATERIAL9 MatD3D;
    LPSTR pTextureFilename;
} D3DXMATERIAL;
```

```
typedef struct _D3DMATERIAL9 {
    D3DCOLORVALUE Diffuse;
    D3DCOLORVALUE Ambient;
    D3DCOLORVALUE Specular;
    D3DCOLORVALUE Emissive;
    float Power;
} D3DMATERIAL9;
```

Note: The D3DMATERIAL9 structure is very similar to the Mtrl structure that we have defined in the source code (d3dUtil.h); the difference being that we do not include an emissive factor. We did not require an emissive factor in this book and so left it out. Briefly, the *emissive factor* just adds color to the lighting equation to increase the brightness in order to simulate that the surface is emitting light.

D3DXMATERIAL is a simple structure; it contains the basic D3DMATERIAL9 structure and a pointer to a null terminating string that specifies the associative texture filename. An .X file does not embed the texture data; rather, it embeds the filename, which is then used as a reference to the image file that contains the actual texture data. Thus, after we load an .X file with D3DXLoadMeshFromX, we must load the texture data given the texture filenames.

It is worth noting that the D3DXLoadMeshFromX function loads the .X file data so that the *i*th entry in the returned D3DXMATERIAL array corresponds with the *i*th subset. Thus, the subsets are labeled in the order 0, 1, 2, ..., *n–1*, where *n* is the number of subsets and materials. This allows the mesh to be rendered as a simple loop that iterates through each subset and renders it.

The following code shows how material and texture data is extracted and returned via the last two parameters of LoadXFile, whose prototype we repeat here:

```
void LoadXFile(
    const std::string& filename,
    ID3DXMesh** meshOut,
    std::vector<Mtrl>& mtrls,
    std::vector<IDirect3DTexture9*>& texs);
```

Now the material extraction and texture loading code is given as follows:

```
// Step 6: Extract the materials and load the textures.

if( mtrlBuffer != 0 && numMtrls != 0 )
{
    D3DXMATERIAL* d3dxmtrls =
        (D3DXMATERIAL*)mtrlBuffer->GetBufferPointer();

    for(DWORD i = 0; i < numMtrls; ++i)
    {
        // Save the ith material.  Note that the MatD3D property
```

```
                        // does not have an ambient value set when it's loaded, so
                        // just set it to the diffuse value.
                        Mtrl m;
                        m.ambient   = d3dxmtrls[i].MatD3D.Diffuse;
                        m.diffuse   = d3dxmtrls[i].MatD3D.Diffuse;
                        m.spec      = d3dxmtrls[i].MatD3D.Specular;
                        m.specPower = d3dxmtrls[i].MatD3D.Power;
                        mtrls.push_back( m );

                        // Check if the ith material has an associative texture
                        if( d3dxmtrls[i].pTextureFilename != 0 )
                        {
                                // Yes, load the texture for the ith subset
                                IDirect3DTexture9* tex = 0;
                                char* texFN = d3dxmtrls[i].pTextureFilename;
                                HR(D3DXCreateTextureFromFile(gd3dDevice,
                                                             texFN, &tex));

                                // Save the loaded texture
                                texs.push_back( tex );
                        }
                        else
                        {
                                // No texture for the ith subset
                                texs.push_back( 0 );
                        }
                }
        }
}
ReleaseCOM(mtrlBuffer); // done w/ buffer
```

14.9.7 The .X File Demo

The following shows the relevant application code for loading an .X file
mesh and rendering it.

```
// Application data members.
ID3DXMesh* mMesh;
std::vector<Mtrl> mMtrl;
std::vector<IDirect3DTexture9*> mTex;

// In application constructor:
LoadXFile("skullocc.x", &mMesh, mMtrl, mTex);

// Rendering code:

HR(mFX->BeginPass(0));

for(int j = 0; j < mMtrl.size(); ++j)
{
        HR(mFX->SetValue(mhMtrl, &mMtrl[j], sizeof(Mtrl)));

        // If there is a texture, then use.
        if(mTex[j] != 0)
        {
```

```
            HR(mFX->SetTexture(mhTex, mTex[j]));
    }

    // But if not, then set a pure white texture.
    else
    {
            HR(mFX->SetTexture(mhTex, mWhiteTex));
    }

    HR(mFX->CommitChanges());
    HR(mMesh->DrawSubset(j));
}
HR(mFX->EndPass());
```

Finally, in the cleanup stage, we release the mesh and each of its textures:

```
ReleaseCOM(mMesh);
for(int i = 0; i < mTex.size(); ++i)
    ReleaseCOM(mTex[i]);
```

14.10 **Bounding Volumes**

Sometimes we want to compute a bounding volume of a mesh. Two common examples of bounding volumes used are spheres and axis-aligned bounding boxes (AABB). Other examples include cylinders, ellipsoids, lozenges, and capsules. Figure 14.7 shows a mesh with a bounding sphere and the same mesh with an AABB. In this section we work only with AABBs and bounding spheres.

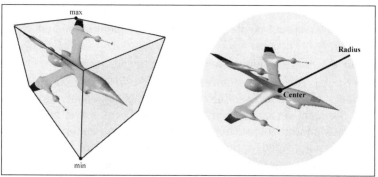

Figure 14.7: A mesh rendered with its bounding sphere and AABB. A sphere can be defined by its center point and radius. An AABB can be defined by its minimum and maximum points.

AABBs/spheres are often used to speed up visibility tests and collision tests, among other things. For example, we can say a mesh is not visible if its bounding AABB/sphere is not visible. An AABB/sphere visibility test is much cheaper than individually testing the visibility of each triangle in the mesh, as a bounding AABB/sphere test allows us to reject a collection of triangles with one test. For a collision example, suppose a missile is fired in the scene and we want to determine if the missile hit an object in the scene. Since the objects are made up of triangles, we could iterate through each triangle of each object and test if the missile (modeled mathematically by a ray) hit a triangle of the object. This approach would require many ray/triangle intersection tests — one for each triangle of each object in the scene. A more efficient approach would be to compute the bounding AABB/sphere of each mesh and then do one ray/AABB or ray/sphere intersection test per object. We can then say the object is hit if the ray intersected its bounding volume. This is a fair approximation; if more precision is necessary, we can use the ray/AABB or ray/sphere to quickly reject objects that are obviously not going to be hit and then apply a more precise test (e.g., ray/triangle intersection) to objects that have a good chance of being hit. (Objects that have a good chance of being hit are objects whose bounding volumes were hit.)

The D3DX library provides functions to calculate the bounding sphere of a mesh and the AABB of a mesh. These functions take an array of vertices as input to compute the bounding sphere or AABB. These functions are designed to be flexible and can work with various vertex formats.

```
HRESULT D3DXComputeBoundingSphere(
    LPD3DXVECTOR3 pFirstPosition,
    DWORD NumVertices,
    DWORD dwStride,
    D3DXVECTOR3* pCenter,
    FLOAT* pRadius
);
```

- `pFirstPosition`: A pointer to the position element in the first vertex of an array of vertices.

- `NumVertices`: The number of vertices in the vertex array.

- `dwStride`: The size of each vertex in bytes. With this information, the function can offset from the first vertex position element to the subsequent vertex position; this is needed to skip over additional vertex information, such as a normal vector and texture coordinates, that is not needed for the bounding sphere function.

- `pCenter`: Returns the center of the bounding sphere.

- `pRadius`: Returns the radius of the bounding sphere.

```
HRESULT D3DXComputeBoundingBox(
    LPD3DXVECTOR3 pFirstPosition,
    DWORD NumVertices,
    DWORD dwStride,
    D3DXVECTOR3* pMin,
    D3DXVECTOR3* pMax
);
```

The first three parameters are the same as the first three in D3DXCompute-BoundingSphere. The last two parameters are used to return the AABB's minimum and maximum points, respectively.

14.10.1 **Some New Special Constants**

Let us introduce two constants (we define them in *d3dUtil.h*) that prove useful in various parts of the rest of this book:

```
const float INFINITY = FLT_MAX;
const float EPSILON  = 0.001f;
```

The INFINITY constant is simply used to represent the largest number we can store in a float. Since we cannot have a float bigger than FLT_MAX, we can conceptualize it as infinity, which makes for more readable code that signifies ideas of infinity. The EPSILON constant is a small value we define such that we consider any number smaller than it equal to zero. This is necessary because due to floating-point imprecision, a number that should really be zero may be off slightly. Thus, comparing it to zero would give the incorrect result. We therefore test if a floating-point variable is zero by testing if its absolute value is less than EPSILON. The following function illustrates how EPSILON can be used to test if two floating-point values are equal:

```
bool Equals(float lhs, float rhs)
{
    // if lhs == rhs their difference should be zero
    return fabs(lhs - rhs) < EPSILON ? true : false;
}
```

14.10.2 **Bounding Volume Types**

To facilitate work with bounding spheres and AABBs, it is natural to implement classes representing each. We define the following classes in *d3dUtil.h*:

```
struct AABB
{
    // Initialize to an infinitely small AABB.
    AABB()
        : minPt(INFINITY, INFINITY, INFINITY),
          maxPt(-INFINITY, -INFINITY, -INFINITY){}

    D3DXVECTOR3 center()
    {
        return 0.5f*(minPt+maxPt);
    }

    D3DXVECTOR3 minPt;
    D3DXVECTOR3 maxPt;
};
```

```
struct BoundingSphere
{
    BoundingSphere()
        : pos(0.0f, 0.0f, 0.0f), radius(0.0f){}

    D3DXVECTOR3 pos;
    float radius;
};
```

14.10.3 Bounding Box Demo

The Bounding Box demo shows how to use the D3DXComputeBoundingBox function; we ask you to try out D3DXComputeBoundingSphere in the exercises. What follows now is a description of the bounding box-related code.

After the mesh has been created, we lock its vertex buffer so that we can access its vertices and feed them into the D3DXComputeBoundingBox function. Note that the function we wrote, LoadXFile, clones the mesh vertices to the VertexPNT format; thus, we know the underlying vertex format of the mesh and can safely cast the vertex data to this format. Now we just pass in our info into the parameters of D3DXComputeBoundingBox:

```
LoadXFile("skullocc.x", &mMesh, mMtrl, mTex);
D3DXMatrixIdentity(&mWorld);

// Compute the bounding box.
VertexPNT* v = 0;
HR(mMesh->LockVertexBuffer(0, (void**)&v));

HR(D3DXComputeBoundingBox(&v[0].pos, mMesh->GetNumVertices(),
    sizeof(VertexPNT), &mBoundingBox.minPt, &mBoundingBox.maxPt));

HR(mMesh->UnlockVertexBuffer());
```

We pass in a pointer to the position element of the first vertex (&v[0].pos), the number of vertices in the mesh (mMesh->GetNumVertices()), the stride of the mesh vertices (sizeof(VertexPNT)), and the vectors to receive the minimum (&mBoundingBox.minPt) and maximum (&mBoundingBox.maxPt) points defining the bounding box. Note that mMesh is an ID3DXMesh object and mBoundingBox is of type AABB; both data members are part of the application class.

We next compute the width, height, and depth of the bounding box while in local space, and use this info to compute a box mesh, which we use to visually render the bounding box:

```
float width  = mBoundingBox.maxPt.x - mBoundingBox.minPt.x;
float height = mBoundingBox.maxPt.y - mBoundingBox.minPt.y;
float depth  = mBoundingBox.maxPt.z - mBoundingBox.minPt.z;

// Build a box mesh so that we can render the bounding box visually.
HR(D3DXCreateBox(gd3dDevice, width, height, depth, &mBox, 0));
```

Again, mBox is an ID3DXMesh object that is an application class data member.

Note: A bounding volume should be transformed with its coupled mesh so that they are consistent. Also note that transforming a mesh may mean the bounding volume needs to be adjusted.

Next, we compute the center of the mesh, which is found by averaging the minimum and maximum points. We use this to offset the bounding box *mesh* (distinguish the mesh from the mathematical bounding box) so that its center matches the mathematical AABB center. We must do this because D3DXCreateBox creates the box mesh centered about the origin, but the AABB's center might not be at the origin. Thus we need to offset the box mesh so that it matches the mathematical AABB.

```
D3DXVECTOR3 center = mBoundingBox.center();
    D3DXMatrixTranslation(&mBoundingBoxOffset,
        center.x, center.y, center.z);
```

We also define a material for the bounding box:

```
// Define the box material--make semi-transparent.
mBoxMtrl.ambient   = D3DXCOLOR(0.0f, 0.0f, 1.0f, 1.0f);
mBoxMtrl.diffuse   = D3DXCOLOR(0.0f, 0.0f, 1.0f, 0.5f);
mBoxMtrl.spec      = D3DXCOLOR(0.5f, 0.5f, 0.5f, 1.0f);
mBoxMtrl.specPower = 8.0f;
```

Now, in BoundingBoxDemo::drawScene, we draw the bounding box with alpha blending as follows:

```
// Draw the bounding box with alpha blending.
HR(gd3dDevice->SetRenderState(D3DRS_ALPHABLENDENABLE, true));
HR(gd3dDevice->SetRenderState(D3DRS_SRCBLEND, D3DBLEND_SRCALPHA));
HR(gd3dDevice->SetRenderState(D3DRS_DESTBLEND, D3DBLEND_INVSRCALPHA));
HR(mFX->SetMatrix(mhWVP, &(mBoundingBoxOffset*mView*mProj)));
D3DXMatrixInverse(&worldInvTrans, 0, &mBoundingBoxOffset);
D3DXMatrixTranspose(&worldInvTrans, &worldInvTrans);
HR(mFX->SetMatrix(mhWorldInvTrans, &worldInvTrans));
HR(mFX->SetMatrix(mhWorld, &mBoundingBoxOffset));
HR(mFX->SetValue(mhMtrl, &mBoxMtrl, sizeof(Mtrl)));
HR(mFX->SetTexture(mhTex, mWhiteTex));
HR(mFX->CommitChanges());
HR(mBox->DrawSubset(0));
HR(gd3dDevice->SetRenderState(D3DRS_ALPHABLENDENABLE, false));
```

14.11 **Survey of Other D3DX Mesh Functions**

In this section, we briefly describe some additional D3DX mesh-related functions that may be useful to you. We do not go into details here, as our aim is to merely introduce the functions so that you know they exist; some of the exercises ask you to further experiment with these functions.

14.11.1 **D3DXSplitMesh**

```
void WINAPI D3DXSplitMesh(
    LPD3DXMESH pMeshIn,
    const DWORD *pAdjacencyIn,
    const DWORD MaxSize,
    const DWORD Options,
    DWORD *pMeshesOut,
    LPD3DXBUFFER *ppMeshArrayOut,
    LPD3DXBUFFER *ppAdjacencyArrayOut,
    LPD3DXBUFFER *ppFaceRemapArrayOut,
    LPD3DXBUFFER *ppVertRemapArrayOut
);
```

This function is used to break up a mesh into smaller meshes. As the SDK documentation points out, one reason for this would be to break a large mesh that required 32-bit indices into several smaller meshes so that 16-bit indices could be used for each of the smaller meshes.

- pMeshIn: Pointer to the input mesh to split.

- pAdjacencyIn: Pointer to the adjacency array of the input mesh.

- MaxSize: Specifies the maximum number of vertices any of the split meshes can have.

- Options: Mesh options of the output meshes; see the Options parameter for D3DXLoadMeshFromX.

- pMeshesOut: Returns the number of output meshes.

- ppMeshArrayOut: Returns a buffer that contains an array of the output ID3DXMesh* types (cast to ID3DXMesh**).

- ppAdjacencyArrayOut: Returns a buffer that contains an array of adjacency arrays (array of arrays — cast to DWORD**), one adjacency array for each output mesh. If you do not need this information, specify 0.

- ppFaceRemapArrayOut: Returns a buffer that contains an array of face remap arrays (array of arrays — cast to DWORD**), one face remap array for each output mesh. If you do not need this information, specify 0.

- ppVertRemapArrayOut: Returns a buffer that contains an array of vertex remap arrays (array of arrays — cast to DWORD**), one vertex remap array for each output mesh.

14.11.2 **D3DXConcatenateMeshes**

The opposite of splitting meshes is concatenating them. To merge several mesh objects together into one larger mesh, use the D3DXConcatenateMeshes function.

```
HRESULT WINAPI D3DXConcatenateMeshes(
    LPD3DXMESH * ppMeshes,
    UINT NumMeshes,
    DWORD Options,
```

```
        CONST D3DXMATRIX * pGeomXForms,
        CONST D3DXMATRIX * pTextureXForms,
        CONST D3DVERTEXELEMENT9 * pDecl,
        LPDIRECT3DDEVICE9 pD3DDevice,
        LPD3DXMESH * ppMeshOut
    );
```

- **ppMeshes**: Pointer to an array of ID3DXMesh* types; that is, the array of meshes to concatenate.

- **NumMeshes**: The number of meshes to concatenate (i.e., the size of the array to which ppMeshes points).

- **Options**: Mesh options of the concatenated mesh; see the Options parameter for D3DXLoadMeshFromX.

- **pGeomXForms**: Pointer to the first element in an array (of size NumMeshes — one for each input mesh) of transformation matrices. The ith transformation matrix is applied to the ith input mesh before concatenation to transform its geometry. This provides the option of transforming the geometry of an input mesh before concatenating it with the other meshes. If 0 is specified, then the identity transformation is applied.

- **pTextureXForms**: Pointer to the first element in an array (of size NumMeshes — one for each input mesh) of transformation matrices. The ith transformation matrix is applied to the ith input mesh before concatenation to transform its texture coordinates. This provides the option of transforming the texture coordinates of an input mesh before concatenating it with the other meshes. If 0 is specified, then the identity transformation is applied.

- **pDecl**: Pointer to the first element in a D3DVERTEXELEMENT9 array describing the vertex declaration of the concatenated mesh. If 0 is specified, then the vertex declarations of each input mesh are combined together to form the vertex declaration of the concatenated mesh.

- **pD3DDevice**: The device to be associated with the concatenated mesh.

- **ppMeshOut**: Outputs the concatenated mesh.

14.11.3 **D3DXValidMesh**

```
    HRESULT WINAPI D3DXValidMesh(
        LPD3DXMESH pMeshIn,
        const DWORD *pAdjacency,
        LPD3DXBUFFER *ppErrorsAndWarnings
    );
```

This function checks to see if a mesh is valid. Things that can make a mesh invalid are bowties (see Figure 14.8), and triangles that are duplicates except for their winding order (i.e., the face normals of the duplicate triangles are opposite); such duplicate triangles create conflicting adjacency info. The function returns D3DXERR_INVALIDMESH if the mesh is invalid.

- pMeshIn: Pointer to the mesh for which to check validity.

- pAdjacency: Pointer to the adjacency array of the input mesh.

- ppErrorsAndWarnings: Returns a description on the invalidities in the mesh (cast this buffer's data to a char* to obtain the string).

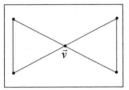

Figure 14.8: This configuration is called a bowtie (for obvious reasons), where the middle vertex $\bar{v}$ is shared between the two triangles. Thus, if $\bar{v}$ is modified in a mesh operation (e.g., removed), it affects two triangles, which may be incorrect. To fix this, the vertex $\bar{v}$ is duplicated so that each triangle has its own copy. In this way, any mesh operations affecting the vertex will only affect one triangle.

14.11.4 **D3DXCleanMesh**

```
HRESULT WINAPI D3DXCleanMesh(
    D3DXCLEANTYPE CleanType,
    LPD3DXMESH pMeshIn,
    const DWORD *pAdjacencyIn,
    LPD3DXMESH *ppMeshOut,
    DWORD *pAdjacencyOut,
    LPD3DXBUFFER *ppErrorsAndWarnings
);
```

This function can fix the problems identified by D3DXValidMesh.

- CleanType: One of the following enumerated types (or a combination of types):

    D3DXCLEAN_BACKFACING: Merges triangles that are duplicates except for their winding order (i.e., the face normals of the duplicate triangles are opposite).

    D3DXCLEAN_BOWTIES: Removes bowties from the mesh.

    D3DXCLEAN_SKINNING: This is just defined as D3DXCLEAN_BACKFACING, and should be specified to clean the mesh before skinned mesh operations (i.e., bowties are not problematic for skinned mesh operations).

    D3DXCLEAN_OPTIMIZATION: This is just defined as D3DXCLEAN_BACKFACING, and should be specified to clean the mesh before optimizing the mesh (i.e., bowties are not problematic for mesh optimization operations). Note that we did not clean the mesh before our mesh optimization calls, but we should have. It turned out okay since the .X file meshes we used didn't have any backfacing triangles.

    D3DXCLEAN_SIMPLIFICATION: This is defined as D3DXCLEAN_BACKFACING | D3DXCLEAN_BOWTIES, and should be specified to clean the mesh before subjecting it to any simplification operations.

- pMeshIn: Input mesh.

- **pAdjacencyIn**: Pointer to an array containing the adjacency info of the input mesh.

- **ppMeshOut**: Outputs the cleaned mesh.

- **pAdjacencyOut**: Pointer to a `DWORD` array to be filled with the adjacency info of the output mesh. The array must have `ID3DXMesh::GetNumFaces()` `* 3` elements. If you do not need this info, pass zero.

- **ppErrorsAndWarnings**: Returns a description on the invalidities in the mesh (cast this buffer's data to a `char*` to obtain the string).

14.11.5 **D3DXWeldVertices**

```
HRESULT WINAPI D3DXWeldVertices(
    LPD3DXMESH pMesh,
    DWORD Flags,
    CONST D3DXWELDEPSILONS * pEpsilons,
    CONST DWORD * pAdjacencyIn,
    DWORD *pAdjacencyOut,
    DWORD * pFaceRemap,
    LPD3DXBUFFER * ppVertexRemap
);
```

This function combines (welds) duplicate vertices and readjusts the index buffer accordingly. When we think of duplicate vertices, we probably first think of duplicate position information, but we must also recall the other possible vertex components. For example, two vertices may be coincident in position, but have vastly different texture coordinates or normal vectors. Such vertices should not be welded because, even though they have the same position data, their other vertex components differ — thus they are not really the same.

How do we determine if a vertex is duplicated? How much can two vertices differ and still be considered the same? To answer these questions, we define a `D3DXWELDEPSILONS` structure:

```
typedef struct _D3DXWELDEPSILONS {
    FLOAT Position;
    FLOAT BlendWeights;
    FLOAT Normal;
    FLOAT PSize;
    FLOAT Specular;
    FLOAT Diffuse;
    FLOAT Texcoord[8];
    FLOAT Tangent;
    FLOAT Binormal;
    FLOAT Tess Factor;
} D3DXWELDEPSILONS;
```

This structure has data members for just about every vertex component you can think of — many of which we have not seen or discussed. However, some should look familiar. Each vertex component in the `D3DXWELDEPSILONS` structure defines a tolerance (or "distance"), which says how far a vertex component of two vertices can differ, yet still be considered the same. For example, if two normal vectors of a vertex structure differ by an amount less than the specified eps.Normal value (where eps is an instance of D3DXWELDEPSILONS), then the normal vector components are considered "equal." If all of the vertex components are equal, then the vertices are equal and can be welded together. Note that the D3DXWELDEPSILONS structure probably has more vertex components than you will ever use in a real vertex structure at one time; for the vertex components you are not using, you can just set the epsilon value to zero.

Note: The tolerance for each vertex component, or how far things can differ and still be considered the same, depends on the specifics of your application (i.e., scale of your data), as distances are relative and depend on the scale of your data. So you will need to pick tolerance values that make sense for your application. In other words, you want to look at relative distances, not absolute distances.

- pMesh: Pointer to the mesh for which we are going to weld the vertices.
- Flags: One or more of the following flags that determine how to weld the vertices and how to determine duplicate vertices (combined by bitwise OR):

    D3DXWELDEPSILONS_WELDALL: Looks at vertex position info only to determine whether or not to weld vertices.

    D3DXWELDEPSILONS_WELDPARTIALMATCHES: Given two vertices in the input mesh to possibly weld, this flag goes vertex component-by-vertex component checking to see if the vertex components are equal (i.e., within the specified tolerance). If a vertex component does match between the two vertices, then both components are updated to equal each other. If all the vertex components are equal (i.e., within the specified tolerance), then the entire vertices are equal, and therefore, they are welded together.

    D3DXWELDEPSILONS_DONOTREMOVEVERTICES: This flag is designed to be set only if D3DXWELDEPSILONS_WELDPARTIALMATCHES is also set. This flag instructs the weld function not to weld vertices — vertex components will only be updated to equal each other if they are within the specified tolerance.

    D3DXWELDEPSILONS_DONOTSPLIT: Same idea as D3DXMESHOPT_DONOTSPLIT; see ID3DXMesh::Optimize in §14.5 for details.

- pEpsilons: The address of a D3DXWELDEPSILONS object that provides a tolerance value describing how far two vertices can differ and still be considered the same.
- pAdjacencyIn: Pointer to an array containing the adjacency info of the input mesh.

- pAdjacencyOut: Pointer to a DWORD array to be filled with the adjacency info of the output mesh. The array must have ID3DXMesh::GetNumFaces() * 3 elements. If you do not need this info, pass zero.

- pFaceRemap: Pointer to a DWORD array to be filled with the face remap info; see ID3DXMesh::Optimize in §14.5 for details.

- ppVertexRemap: Pointer to a DWORD array to be filled with the vertex remap info; see ID3DXMesh::Optimize in §14.5 for details.

14.11.6 **D3DXSimplifyMesh**

```
HRESULT WINAPI D3DXSimplifyMesh(
    LPD3DXMESH pMesh,
    const DWORD *pAdjacency,
    const D3DXATTRIBUTEWEIGHTS *pVertexAttributeWeights,
    const FLOAT *pVertexWeights,
    DWORD MinValue,
    DWORD Options,
    LPD3DXMESH *ppMesh
);
```

This function can be used to reduce the vertex and triangle count of a mesh, while still preserving the general structure. So if you have a mesh with a high triangle count and you determine that such a high triangle count is unnecessary (i.e., you could get by with a lower triangle count), then you can run the mesh through this function to simplify it. The idea is analogous to creating textures at lower resolution. Just like we might have high- and low-resolution textures, we may want high-resolution meshes (high triangle density) and low-resolution meshes (low triangle density).

- pMesh: Pointer to the mesh we want to simplify.

- pAdjacency: Pointer to an array containing the adjacency info of the input mesh.

- pVertexAttributeWeights: Pointer to a D3DXATTRIBUTEWEIGHTS array of size pMesh->GetNumVertices(), where the *i*th entry corresponds with the *i*th vertex in pMesh and specifies its attribute weight. The attribute weights are used to determine the chance a vertex is removed during simplification. You can pass in 0 for this parameter and a default vertex attribute weight will be used for each vertex. D3DXATTRIBUTEWEIGHTS is defined as follows:

```
typedef struct _D3DXATTRIBUTEWEIGHTS {
    FLOAT Position;
    FLOAT Boundary;
    FLOAT Normal;
    FLOAT Diffuse;
    FLOAT Specular;
    FLOAT Texcoord[8];
    FLOAT Tangent;
```

```
    FLOAT Binormal;
} D3DXATTRIBUTEWEIGHTS;
```

The vertex weight structure allows us to specify a weight for each possible component of a vertex. A value of 0.0 would indicate the component carries no weight. The higher the weights for the vertex components, the less likely the vertex will be removed in simplification. Typically, an application will only consider the position and normal vector components (i.e., the other components have a weight of 0.0).

■ pVertexWeights: Pointer to a float array of size pMesh->GetNumVertices(), where the *i*th entry corresponds to the *i*th vertex in pMesh and specifies its vertex weight. The higher a vertex weight, the less chance it has of being removed during simplification. You can pass in 0 for this parameter and a default vertex weight of 1.0 will be used for each vertex. The weight parameters are useful because they allow you to have some control over which vertices get simplified; obviously some vertices are more important to the overall structure of the object than others.

■ MinValue: The minimum number of vertices or faces (determined by the next parameter — Options) we want to simplify down to. Note that this is a request and, depending on vertex/attribute weights, the resulting mesh might not match this value.

■ Options: This can be either D3DXMESHSIMP_VERTEX or D3DXMESHSIMP_FACE, but not both. If D3DXMESHSIMP_VERTEX is specified, then the previous parameter, MinValue, refers to vertices. If D3DXMESHSIMP_FACE is specified, then MinValue refers to faces.

■ ppMesh: Outputs the simplified mesh.

Note: For a more powerful simplification mechanism, the reader may want to investigate ID3DXSPMesh and D3DXCreateSPMesh in the DirectX SDK documentation.

14.11.7 **D3DXGeneratePMesh**

Progressive meshes, represented by the ID3DXPMesh interface, allow us to simplify a mesh by applying a sequence of *edge collapse transformations* (ECT). Each ECT removes one vertex and one or two faces. Because each ECT is invertible (its inverse is called a *vertex split*), we can reverse the simplification process and restore the mesh to its exact original state. This, of course, means that we cannot obtain a mesh more detailed than the original; we can only simplify and then reverse those simplification operations. Figure 14.9 shows a mesh at three different *levels of detail* (LOD) — a high, medium, and low LOD.

Figure 14.9: A mesh shown at three different resolutions.

The idea of progressive meshes is analogous to using mipmaps for textures. When texturing, we noticed that it was wasteful to use a high-resolution texture for a small, faraway primitive where the extra detail would go unnoticed. The same goes for meshes; a small, faraway mesh does not need as high a triangle count as a large, close-up mesh because the extra triangle detail for the small mesh would go unnoticed. Thus, we would end up spending time rendering a high triangle count model when a simpler, low triangle count model would suffice.

One way we can use progressive meshes is to adjust the LOD of a mesh based on its distance from the camera. That is, as the distance decreases we would add detail (triangles) to the mesh, and as the distance increased we would remove detail.

Note: For those readers interested in the implementation details, you can find the original progressive mesh papers at Hugues Hoppe's website: http://research.microsoft.com/~hoppe/.

We can construct a progressive mesh with the following function:

```
HRESULT WINAPI D3DXGeneratePMesh(
    LPD3DXMESH pMesh,
    const DWORD *pAdjacency,
    const D3DXATTRIBUTEWEIGHTS *pVertexAttributeWeights,
    const FLOAT *pVertexWeights,
    DWORD MinValue,
    DWORD Options,
    LPD3DXPMESH *ppPMesh
);
```

We omit parameter explanations because they are exactly the same as in D3DXSimplifyMesh, except that the function outputs a progressive mesh (ID3DXPMesh).

As shown above, D3DXGeneratePMesh allows us to simplify the mesh LOD during creation. Thus, so far it seems quite similar to D3DXSimplifyMesh; however, the big difference is that D3DXGeneratePMesh outputs an ID3DXPMesh. Through this class, we can control the LOD of the mesh. In particular, we can restore back to the original mesh resolutions or intermediate resolutions, or perhaps, even lower resolutions. The key methods behind the progressive mesh class are:

```
HRESULT ID3DXPMesh::SetNumFaces(DWORD Faces);
HRESULT ID3DXPMesh::SetNumVertices(DWORD Vertices);
```

These methods allow us to adjust the LOD by setting a new face/vertex count. For example, suppose the mesh, in its current LOD, has 500 faces. We can simplify it by writing:

```
pmesh->SetNumFaces(200);
```

Note that there exist minimum and maximum values for the face and vertex count settings. These maximums and minimums can be obtained with the following methods:

- ■ DWORD GetMaxFaces();
- ■ DWORD GetMaxVertices();
- ■ DWORD GetMinFaces();
- ■ DWORD GetMinVertices();

Note: Sometimes we must add more than one face to invert an ECT because of the internal implementation details of the ID3DXPMesh interface. In other words, adding one face may possibly result in a mesh with the same number of faces as before. Thus, to increase the face count we may sometimes have to add two faces at once.

14.12 **Summary**

- ■ An ID3DXMesh contains vertex, index, and attribute buffers. The vertex and index buffers hold the geometry of the mesh (vertices and triangles). The attribute buffer contains a corresponding entry for each triangle and specifies the subset to which a triangle belongs. The ID3DXMesh class uses indexed triangle lists internally.

- ■ A mesh can be optimized with the OptimizeInplace or Optimize methods. Optimization reorganizes the geometry of the mesh to make rendering more efficient. Optimizing a mesh with D3DXMESHOPT_ATTRSORT generates an attribute table, which allows the mesh to render an entire subset using a simple lookup into the attribute table.

- ■ The adjacency info of a mesh is a DWORD array that contains three entries for every triangle in the mesh. The three entries corresponding to a particular triangle specify the triangles that are adjacent to that triangle.

- ■ A mesh can be copied with the Clone method. In addition to simply copying the mesh, the Clone method allows us to change the mesh options and vertex format of the output mesh.

- We can create an empty mesh using the D3DXCreateMesh function. We can then manually write data to the mesh using the appropriate locking methods: LockVertexBuffer, LockIndexBuffer, and LockAttributeBuffer. We can manually set an attribute table with the ID3DXMesh::SetAttribute-Table method.

- We can construct complex triangle meshes using 3D modeling programs and either export or convert them to .X files. Then, using the D3DXLoadMeshFromX function, we can load the mesh data stored in an .X file into an ID3DXMesh object, which we can use in our Direct3D applications.

- Use:
  - D3DXSplitMesh to break a mesh up into multiple submeshes.
  - D3DXConcatenateMeshes to combine multiple meshes into a net mesh.
  - D3DXValidMesh to check for characteristics in the mesh that could cause problems for simplification, optimization, and skinning algorithms.
  - D3DXCleanMesh to fix the problems identified by D3DXValidMesh.
  - D3DXWeldVertices to combine vertices that are approximately the same.
  - D3DXSimplifyMesh to reduce the geometry count of a mesh.
  - D3DXGeneratePMesh to generate a progressive mesh, through which you can adjust the LOD of the mesh.

- We can compute the bounding sphere and bounding box using the D3DXComputeBoundingSphere and D3DXComputeBoundingBox functions. Bounding volumes are useful because they approximate the volume of a mesh, and therefore, can be used to speed up calculations related to the volume of space a mesh occupies.

14.13 Exercises

1. In the past, we have been manually maintaining the geometry of a grid and rendering it. For this exercise, create an empty mesh with D3DXCreateMesh and manually write the grid geometry to the created ID3DXMesh. Then render the created ID3DXMesh.

2. You can save the contents of an ID3DXMesh (and its materials and texture filenames) to file with D3DXSaveMeshToX (see the SDK documentation for details). Starting from the previous exercise, modify the program to save the grid geometry and its materials and texture filename to an .X file. Then use the .X File demo program to load and render the saved grid .X file in order to verify that it was saved correctly. (You do not need to write the code to generate the grid in the program; you can just load a precomputed grid from the .X file.)

3. Rewrite the Bounding Box demo, but this time, compute the bounding sphere and render it along with the mesh.

4. Write a program that loads two distinct .X file meshes. Combine the meshes using D3DXConcatenateMeshes, and then render the combined mesh only to verify that the meshes were concatenated correctly.

5. Load an .X file and then convert it to a progressive mesh. Write a program that allows the user to interactively adjust the LOD of the mesh via keyboard input. For example, if the user presses the "–" key, then remove faces; if the user presses the "+" key, then add faces. Because you will be applying a simplification operation, you should clean the mesh first.

Chapter 15

Mesh Hierarchy Animation Part I — Rigid Meshes

Many objects are composed of parts, with a parent-child relationship, where one or more child objects can move independently on their own (with possible physical motion constraints — e.g., human joints have a particular range of motion) — but are also forced to move when their parent moves. For example, consider an arm divided into its parts: upper arm, forearm, and hand. The hand can rotate in isolation about its wrist joint; however, if the forearm rotates about its elbow joint, then the hand must rotate with it. Similarly, if the upper arm rotates about the shoulder joint, the forearm rotates with it; and if the forearm rotates, then the hand rotates with it (see Figure 15.1). Thus we see a definite object hierarchy: The hand is a child of the forearm, the forearm is a child of the upper arm, and if we extended our situation, the upper arm would be a child of the torso, and so on and so forth, until we have completed the skeleton. (Figure 15.2 shows a more complex hierarchy example.)

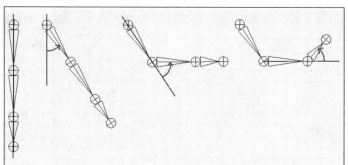

Figure 15.1: Hierarchy transforms; observe that the parent transformation of a bone influences itself and all of its children.

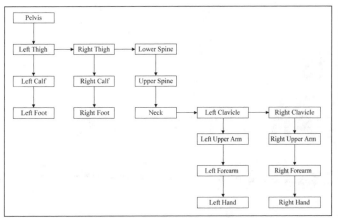

Figure 15.2: A more complex object hierarchy to model a bipedal humanoid character.

In this chapter, we show how to construct a simple hierarchal mesh animation system. The key idea of this chapter is how to place an object in the scene based on its motion and also the motion of its *ancestors* (i.e., its parent, grandparent, great-grandparent, etc.).

Objectives:

- To discover why mesh hierarchies are important for object modeling.
- To understand the mathematics of mesh hierarchy transformations.
- To become familiar with creating and traversing tree-based mesh hierarchies.
- To learn how to implement a robot arm and fictitious solar system using mesh hierarchies.
- To understand the basic idea of keyframes and animation interpolation.

15.1 **Robot Arm Demo**

In this section, we show how to implement a simple robot arm, where the user can select a "bone" and rotate it; see Figure 15.3 for a screenshot.

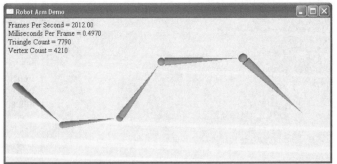

Figure 15.3: A screenshot of the Robot Arm demo. The user can select a bone and rotate it; the rotation will rotate the selected bone and all of its children.

15.1.1 **Mathematical Formulation**

Note: At this point, the reader may wish to review Part I of this book, specifically the topic of change-of-coordinate transformations.

To keep things simple and concrete, we work with the upper arm (the root), forearm, and hand hierarchy, which we label as Bone 0, Bone 1, and Bone 2, respectively (see Figure 15.4).

Figure 15.4: A simple hierarchy.

Once the basic concept is understood, a straightforward generalization is used to handle more complex situations. So given an object in the hierarchy, how do we correctly transform it to world space? Obviously, we cannot just transform it directly into the world space because we must also take into consideration the transformations of its ancestors since they also influence its placement in the scene. The problem is a mathematical one, as there are no new Direct3D concepts to be discussed.

Each object in the hierarchy is modeled about its own local coordinate system with its pivot joint at the origin to facilitate rotation (see Figure 15.5).

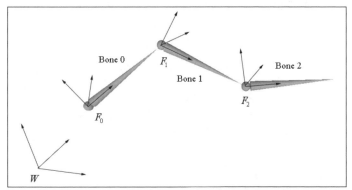

Figure 15.5: The geometry of each bone is described relative to its own local coordinate system. Furthermore, because all the coordinate systems exist in the same universe, we can relate them to one another.

Because all the coordinate systems exist in the same universe, we can relate them; in particular, for an arbitrary instant in time (we fix time and study a snapshot because, in general, these mesh hierarchies are animated and so these relationships change as a function of time), we describe each coordinate system relative to its parent coordinate system. (The parent coordinate system of the root frame F_0 is the world space coordinate system W; that is, the coordinate system F_0 is described relative to the world coordinate system.) Now that we have related the child and parent coordinate systems, we can transform from a child's space to its parent's space with a transformation matrix. (This is the same idea as the local-to-world transformation. However, instead of transforming from local space to world space, we transform from the local space to the space of the parent.) Let A_2 be a matrix that transforms geometry from frame F_2 into F_1, let A_1 be a matrix that transforms geometry from frame F_1 into F_0, and let A_0 be a matrix that transforms geometry from frame F_0 into W. (We call A_i a *to-parent* matrix since it transforms geometry from a child's coordinate system into its parent's coordinate system.) Then, we can transform the ith object in the arm hierarchy into world space by the matrix M_i defined as follows:

$$M_i = A_i A_{i-1} \dots A_1 A_0 \tag{15.1}$$

Specifically, in our example, $M_2 = A_2 A_1 A_0$, $M_1 = A_1 A_0$, and $M_0 = A_0$ transforms the hand into world space, the forearm into world space, and the upper arm into world space, respectively. Observe that an object inherits the transformations of its ancestors; this is what will make the hand move if the upper arm moves, for example.

Figure 15.6 illustrates what Equation 15.1 says graphically; essentially, to transform an object in the arm hierarchy, we just apply the to-parent transform of the object and all of its ancestors (in ascending order) to percolate up the coordinate system hierarchy until the object arrives in the world space.

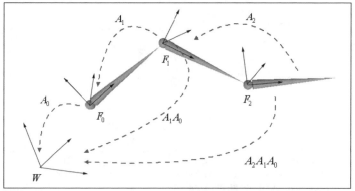

Figure 15.6: Because the coordinate systems exist in the same universe we can relate them, and therefore transform from one to the other. In particular, we relate them by describing each bone's coordinate system relative to its parent's coordinate system. From that, we can construct a to-parent transformation matrix that transforms the geometry of a bone from its local coordinate system to its parent's coordinate system. Once in the parent's coordinate system, we can then transform by the parent's to-parent matrix to transform to the grandparent's coordinate system, and so on and so forth, until we have visited each ancestors' coordinate system and finally reached the world space.

15.1.2 **Implementation**

15.1.2.1 *Bone Mesh*

Figure 15.7 shows the mesh we use to render a bone in the arm; it resembles how bones are displayed in popular 3D modeling programs. Note that we only need one bone mesh; to draw several bones we draw the same bone mesh several times in different places (i.e., with a different world transformation).

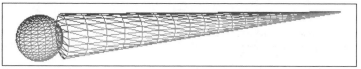

Figure 15.7: The mesh we use to represent a bone.

15.1.2.2 *Bone Data Structure*

In addition to the geometry, there are a few other things we need to know about a bone in the hierarchy, such as its orientation and position relative to its parent and its transformation matrices. These values are captured by the following structure:

```
struct BoneFrame
{
    // Note: The root bone's "parent" frame is the world space.

    D3DXVECTOR3 pos; // Relative to parent frame.
    float zAngle;    // Relative to parent frame.

    D3DXMATRIX toParentXForm;
    D3DXMATRIX toWorldXForm;
};
```

In general, a tree data structure is needed to model a hierarchy, as they may be like that in Figure 15.2. However, for our robot arm model, the hierarchy has a very simple form that is essentially a linked list, which we can model with the following array, where the parent of the ith bone is just the $i - 1$th bone (except the root with index 0; see Figure 15.8).

```
static const int NUM_BONES = 5;
BoneFrame mBones[NUM_BONES];
```

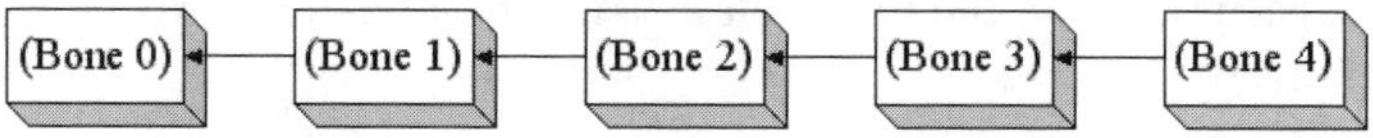

(Bone 0) ◄— (Bone 1) ◄— (Bone 2) ◄— (Bone 3) ◄— (Bone 4)

Figure 15.8: The bone hierarchy for the Robot Arm demo. We can store these bones in an array, and then the parent of the ith bone is just the previous $i - 1$th bone.

In the application constructor, we initialize this array to set up the coordinate system relationships of the bones; this is done like so (recall though that the root is special and its frame is described relative to the world frame):

```
for(int i = 1; i < NUM_BONES; ++i) // Ignore root.
{
    // Describe each bone frame relative to its parent frame.
    mBones[i].pos    = D3DXVECTOR3(2.0f, 0.0f, 0.0f);
    mBones[i].zAngle = 0.0f;
}
// Root frame at center of world.
mBones[0].pos    = D3DXVECTOR3(0.0f, 0.0f, 0.0f);
mBones[0].zAngle = 0.0f;
```

The bone model (§15.1.2.1) was constructed so that the length from joint to joint of two connected bones is two units; that is where the magic number 2 comes from in the above code. That is, if you picked another number, then the bones won't connect. Also observe that initially the bone coordinate systems are not rotated relative to each other on the z-axis.

As said, in this demo the user will be able to select a bone to rotate. To keep track of the currently selected bone, we add the following data member to the application class:

```
// Index into the bone array to the currently selected bone.
// The user can select a bone and rotate it.
int mBoneSelected;
```

15.1.2.3 *Building the Bone World Matrices*

Note: As mentioned earlier, if you are not fully comfortable with the mathematics of change-of-coordinate transformations, you may wish to review the relevant topics from Part I.

The first part of the `RobotArmDemo::buildBoneWorldTransforms` function generates the to-parent transformation matrix for each object. We construct this matrix by using the position and z-rotation angle values of the object (which describe how the object's local coordinate system is relative to its parent's coordinate system) to obtain a rotation matrix R and translation matrix T. The homogeneous row vectors of the combined matrix, RT, describe the object's local coordinate system relative to its parent's coordinate system; thus, this matrix transforms geometry from the object's local space to the parent's space (i.e., it is the to-parent matrix [see Equation 2.3]).

```
void RobotArmDemo::buildBoneWorldTransforms()
{
    // First, construct the transformation matrix that transforms
    // the ith bone into the coordinate system of its parent.

    D3DXMATRIX R, T;
    D3DXVECTOR3 p;
    for(int i = 0; i < NUM_BONES; ++i)
    {
        p = mBones[i].pos;
        D3DXMatrixRotationZ(&R, mBones[i].zAngle);
        D3DXMatrixTranslation(&T, p.x, p.y, p.z);
        mBones[i].toParentXForm = R * T;
    }
}
```

Now to obtain the world transforms for each bone, we just apply Equation 15.1:

```
// The ith object's world transform is given by its
// to-parent transform, followed by its parent's to-parent
// transform, followed by its grandparent's to-parent transform,
// and so on, up to the root's to-parent transform.

    // For each bone...
    for(int i = 0; i < NUM_BONES; ++i)
    {
        // Initialize to identity matrix.
        D3DXMatrixIdentity(&mBones[i].toWorldXForm);

        // Combine  W[i] = W[i]*W[i-1]*...*W[0].
        for(int j = i; j >= 0; --j)
        {
            mBones[i].toWorldXForm *= mBones[j].toParentXForm;
        }
    }
}
```

The above function needs to be called either in `RobotArmDemo::updateScene` or `RobotArmDemo::drawScene`, for as we show in the next section, the relative coordinate system relationships can change each frame and thus the to-parent matrices change, which causes the world matrices to change. Thus, the to-world matrix for each bone needs to be rebuilt every frame.

15.1.2.4 *Animating and Rendering the Bones*

As stated, we allow the user to select a bone to rotate (which animates all of its children as well — that's the whole point of mesh hierarchies). Our demo model consists of five bones, and the user can select one by pressing the number keys 1 to 5. The following code comes from the `RobotArmDemo::updateScene` function:

```
// Allow the user to select a bone (zero-based index)
if( gDInput->keyDown(DIK_1) ) mBoneSelected = 0;
```

```
if( gDInput->keyDown(DIK_2) ) mBoneSelected = 1;
if( gDInput->keyDown(DIK_3) ) mBoneSelected = 2;
if( gDInput->keyDown(DIK_4) ) mBoneSelected = 3;
if( gDInput->keyDown(DIK_5) ) mBoneSelected = 4;
```

Once a bone is selected, the user can rotate it by pressing the "A" or "D" keys:

```
// Allow the user to rotate a bone.
if( gDInput->keyDown(DIK_A) )
     mBones[mBoneSelected].zAngle += 1.0f * dt;
if( gDInput->keyDown(DIK_D) )
     mBones[mBoneSelected].zAngle -= 1.0f * dt;

// If we rotate over 360 degrees, just roll back to 0
if( fabsf(mBones[mBoneSelected].zAngle) >= 2.0f*D3DX_PI)
     mBones[mBoneSelected].zAngle = 0.0f;
```

We omit the rendering code because it contains nothing you have not seen before. At this point, we have constructed a world transformation matrix for each bone. So we just render the bones as we would any other object: For each bone, set its world matrix and other effect parameters and draw it.

15.2 Solar System Demo

In this section, we provide another example of animated mesh hierarchies by animating a fictitious solar system. Figure 15.9 shows the hierarchy for this case.

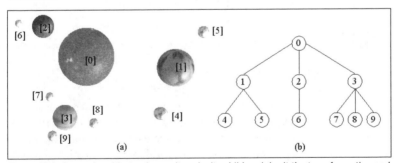

Figure 15.9: As a solar object spins on its axis, its children inherit the transformation and orbit around the object.

As you can see, it is a bit more complicated than the robot arm because we now have a full tree data structure instead of a simple linked list. Nevertheless, the theory developed in the previous section applies; that being, for any object in the hierarchy, its world space transformation is found by just applying the to-parent transform of the object and all of its ancestors (in ascending order) to percolate up the coordinate system hierarchy until the object arrives in the world space (we again stipulate that the parent coordinate system of the root is the world space). The only real difference is that we just have a more complicated tree data structure instead of a linked list.

Note: Like the Robot Arm demo, we only need to maintain one sphere mesh (to represent a solar object) since we can draw several solar objects by drawing the same sphere mesh several times in different places (i.e., with a different world transformation).

15.2.1 Solar Object Data Structure

We classify the solar objects as either a sun, planet, or moon; the following enumerated type is used for this classification:

```
// We classify the objects in our scene as one of three types.
enum SolarType
{
    SUN,
    PLANET,
    MOON
};
```

As with the robot arm example, there are a few other things we need to know about a solar object in the hierarchy in addition to the geometry, such as its orientation and position relative to its parent, size (relative to the *world* space), parent, type, texture, and transformation matrices. These values are captured by the following structure:

```
struct SolarObject
{
    void set(SolarType type, D3DXVECTOR3 p, float yRot,
             int parentIndex, float s, IDirect3DTexture9* t)
    {
        typeID = type;
        pos    = p;
        yAngle = yRot;
        parent = parentIndex;
        size   = s;
        tex    = t;
    }

    // Note: The root's "parent" frame is the world space.

    SolarType typeID;
    D3DXVECTOR3 pos;    // Relative to parent frame.
    float yAngle;       // Relative to parent frame.
    int parent;         // Index to parent frame (-1 if root)
    float size;         // Relative to world frame.
    IDirect3DTexture9* tex;
    D3DXMATRIX toParentXForm;
    D3DXMATRIX toWorldXForm;
};
```

The parent data member is key to setting up the hierarchy. To understand it, note that we store the tree nodes in an array like this:

```
static const int NUM_OBJECTS = 10;
SolarObject mObject[NUM_OBJECTS];
```

The parent of mObject[j] is given by mObject[mObject[j].parent] (i.e., mObject[j].parent is the array index of the parent object of mObject[j]). For example, suppose mObject[5].parent == 2. Then mObject[2] is the parent of mObject[5]. By including the index to the parent of each object, we are able to percolate up the ancestry of an object.

In the application constructor, we manually set up the mesh hierarchy and specify how the solar object frames are related:

```
// Create the textures.
HR(D3DXCreateTextureFromFile(gd3dDevice, "sun.dds", &mSunTex));
HR(D3DXCreateTextureFromFile(gd3dDevice, "planet1.dds", &mPlanet1Tex));
HR(D3DXCreateTextureFromFile(gd3dDevice, "planet2.dds", &mPlanet2Tex));
HR(D3DXCreateTextureFromFile(gd3dDevice, "planet3.dds", &mPlanet3Tex));
HR(D3DXCreateTextureFromFile(gd3dDevice, "moon.dds", &mMoonTex));

D3DXVECTOR3 pos[NUM_OBJECTS] =
{
        D3DXVECTOR3(0.0f, 0.0f, 0.0f),
        D3DXVECTOR3(7.0f, 0.0f, 7.0f),
        D3DXVECTOR3(-9.0f, 0.0f, 0.0f),
        D3DXVECTOR3(7.0f, 0.0f, -6.0f),
        D3DXVECTOR3(5.0f, 0.0f, 0.0f),
        D3DXVECTOR3(-5.0f, 0.0f, 0.0f),
        D3DXVECTOR3(3.0f, 0.0f, 0.0f),
        D3DXVECTOR3(2.0f, 0.0f, -2.0f),
        D3DXVECTOR3(-2.0f, 0.0f, 0.0f),
        D3DXVECTOR3(0.0f, 0.0f, 2.0f)
};

mObject[0].set(SUN, pos[0], 0.0f, -1, 2.5f, mSunTex);        // Sun
mObject[1].set(PLANET, pos[1], 0.0f, 0, 1.5f, mPlanet1Tex); // P1
mObject[2].set(PLANET, pos[2], 0.0f, 0, 1.2f, mPlanet2Tex); // P2
mObject[3].set(PLANET, pos[3], 0.0f, 0, 0.8f, mPlanet3Tex); // P3

mObject[4].set(MOON, pos[4], 0.0f, 1, 0.5f, mMoonTex); // M1P1
mObject[5].set(MOON, pos[5], 0.0f, 1, 0.5f, mMoonTex); // M2P1
mObject[6].set(MOON, pos[6], 0.0f, 2, 0.4f, mMoonTex); // M1P2
mObject[7].set(MOON, pos[7], 0.0f, 3, 0.3f, mMoonTex); // M1P3
mObject[8].set(MOON, pos[8], 0.0f, 3, 0.3f, mMoonTex); // M2P3
mObject[9].set(MOON, pos[9], 0.0f, 3, 0.3f, mMoonTex); // M3P3
```

In order to convince yourself that the above code does set up the solar system tree hierarchy of Figure 15.9, it may be helpful to reconstruct the tree diagram from the code only.

15.2.2 **Building the Solar Object World Matrices**

We build the transformation matrices for each solar object the same way we built them for each bone object in the Robot Arm demo. However, building the to-world matrices may seem a bit trickier, since the mesh hierarchy is a tree instead of a linked list. But recall that we gave each object an index to its parent object; thus, moving up the ancestry chain of an object is actually not complicated.

```
void SolarSysDemo::buildObjectWorldTransforms()
{
    // First, construct the transformation matrix that transforms
    // the ith bone into the coordinate system of its parent.

    D3DXMATRIX R, T;
    D3DXVECTOR3 p;
    for(int i = 0; i < NUM_OBJECTS; ++i)
    {
        p = mObject[i].pos;
        D3DXMatrixRotationY(&R, mObject[i].yAngle);
        D3DXMatrixTranslation(&T, p.x, p.y, p.z);
        mObject[i].toParentXForm = R * T;
    }

    // For each object...
    for(int i = 0; i < NUM_OBJECTS; ++i)
    {
        // Initialize to identity matrix.
        D3DXMatrixIdentity(&mObject[i].toWorldXForm);

        // The ith object's world transform is given by its
        // to-parent transform, followed by its parent's
        // to-parent transform, followed by its grandparent's
        // to-parent transform, and so on, up to the root's
        // to-parent transform.
        int k = i;
        while( k != -1 ) // While there exists an ancestor.
        {
            mObject[i].toWorldXForm *= mObject[k].toParentXForm;
            k = mObject[k].parent; // Move up the ancestry chain.
        }
    }
}
```

Let's go through a small example just to make sure that we understand how the while-loop traverses a nodes ancestry. Suppose $i = 8$. Looking back at Figure 15.9, we see that node $i = 8$ is a moon of the planet at node $i = 3$. Initially, we just set $k = i = 8$, and set $M_8 = I$ (i.e., we set the world transformation matrix of node $i = 8$ to the identity matrix). Then we do an iteration of the while-loop, which makes $M_8 = toParent[8]$, and we move up one node along the node's ancestry: $k = mObject[8].parent = 3$ since node 3 is the parent of node $i = 8$. The condition of the while-loop is satisfied, so we iterate again. In this iteration, we set $M_8 = toParent[8] \cdot toParent[3]$, and $k = mObject[3].parent = 0$ because, as can be seen from Figure 15.9, node 0 is the parent of node 3. On the next iteration we have: $M_8 = toParent[8] \cdot toParent[3] \cdot toParent[0]$ and $k = mObject[0].parent = -1$. Since $k = -1$ at this point, the loop will not iterate again, and we see that M_8 is what it should be — a sequence of transformations that transforms the object into each of its ancestors' coordinate systems (in ascending order) until the object arrives in world space.

15.2.3 Animating the Solar System

To animate the solar objects, we spin them at different speeds based on their classification type. The following code shows how this is done:

```
void SolarSysDemo::updateScene(float dt)
{
    .
    .
    .

    // Animate the solar objects with respect to time.

    for(int i = 0; i < NUM_OBJECTS; ++i)
    {
        switch(mObject[i].typeID)
        {
        case SUN:
            mObject[i].yAngle += 1.5f * dt;
            break;
        case PLANET:
            mObject[i].yAngle += 2.0f * dt;
            break;
        case MOON:
            mObject[i].yAngle += 2.5f * dt;
            break;
        }

        // If we rotate over 360 degrees, just roll back to 0.
        if(mObject[i].yAngle >= 2.0f*D3DX_PI)
            mObject[i].yAngle = 0.0f;
    }
}
```

Note: As with the Robot Arm demo, once the world transformations for each object in the mesh hierarchy are built, rendering the mesh hierarchy is a simple matter of iterating over each object in the hierarchy, setting its world transformation and other effect parameters, and drawing it.

15.3 **Keyframes and Animation**

Before closing this chapter, we introduce the topic of keyframes, which will
be put to use in the next chapter. The idea of keyframes is to prerecord animation data of a hierarchy. In the Robot Arm and Solar System demos, we
did the opposite: We animated the mesh hierarchy at run time. In practice,
however, animations are prerecorded by a 3D animator or recorded from a
motion capture system.

To keep things concrete, we work with a specific example. Suppose that
a 3D artist is assigned the job of creating a robot arm animation sequence
that lasts for five seconds. The robot's upper arm should rotate on its shoulder joint 60°, and the forearm should not move locally during the time
interval [0.0s, 2.5s]. Then, during the time interval (2.5s, 5.0s], the upper
arm should rotate on its shoulder joint −30°, and the forearm should not
move locally. To create this sequence, the artist roughly approximates this
animation with three keyframes for the upper arm bone, taken at the times
the skeleton reaches critical poses in the animation, namely, at times
$t_0 = 0$s, $t_1 = 2.5$s, and $t_2 = 5$s, respectively — see Figure 15.10.

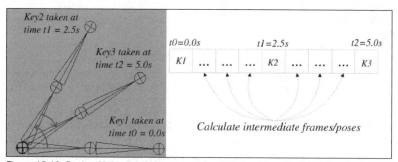

Figure 15.10: During [0.0s, 2.5s] the arm rotates 60° about the shoulder joint. During
(2.5s, 5.0s] the arm rotates −30° about the shoulder joint.

Note: This is a trivial example; in practice, many keyframes are
required to approximate complex animations such as a human character running or swinging a sword. Moreover, since the forearm does
not rotate about its local pivot joint, it does not need its own set of
keyframes. But, in the case that it did move about its local pivot joint,
then the artist would have to define keyframes for the forearm as
well. In general, a set of keyframes will be defined for every bone
that is animated.

A *keyframe* is a significant pose (by *pose* we mean how the object's coordinate system is relative to its parent's coordinate system) of an object in the
mesh hierarchy at some instance in time. Each mesh in the hierarchy typically has several keyframes in an animation sequence, and usually, its pose

is described by a rotation quaternion, scaling vector, and translation vector, but it can also be by a to-parent matrix.

Observe that the keyframes define the *extreme* poses of the animation; that is to say, all the other poses in the animation lie in between some pair of keyframes. Now obviously three keyframes per object is not enough to smoothly represent a five-second animation sequence; that is, three frames per five seconds will result in an extremely choppy animation. However, the idea is this: Given the keyframes, the computer can calculate the correct intermediate object poses between keyframes at any time in the five-second sequence. By calculating enough of these intermediate poses (say 60 poses per second), we can create a smooth, continuous (to the eye) animation. Figure 15.11 shows some of the intermediate poses the computer generated for our robot arm.

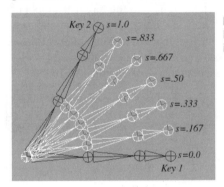

Figure 15.11:
Keyframe
interpolation.

Returning to our original example shown in Figure 15.10, during the time [0.0s, 2.5s] the arm will animate from Key 1 to Key 2. Then during the time (2.5s, 5.0s], the arm will animate from Key 2 to Key 3. The intermediate poses are calculated by interpolating between keyframes. That is, given keyframes K_0 and K_1, we can calculate the intermediate poses by mathematically interpolating from the bone pose described by K_0 to the bone pose described by K_1. Figure 15.11 shows several intermediate poses calculated via interpolating between keyframes K_0 (Key 1) and K_1 (Key 2), for different interpolation parameters taken for s $\in$ [0, 1]. We see that as the interpolation parameter s moves from zero to one, the intermediate pose moves from K_0 to K_1, respectively. Thus s acts like a percentage, indicating how far to blend from one keyframe to the other.

How do we interpolate between bones? As [Parent02] points out, we cannot use matrices because we cannot directly interpolate the rotation part of a matrix — the rows might become un-orthonormal or meaningless. Typically, the to-parent matrix of a bone is decomposed into its rotation, scaling, and translation components (*RST-values*), interpolated independently, and then recombined into the to-parent matrix after interpolation. For the translation and scaling components, linear interpolation works well (although higher order interpolation schemes can be used if greater smoothness is required). Rotations in 3-space are a bit more complex; quaternions are favored to represent rotations to avoid gimbal lock, and spherical interpolation is used to smoothly interpolate quaternion-based rotations. The following D3DX functions perform these interpolation techniques: D3DXVec3Lerp (linear interpolation) and D3DXQuaternionSlerp (spherical interpolation).

Note: A transformation matrix can be decomposed into its rotation, scaling, and translation parts with the D3DXMatrixDecompose function.

Now that we know how to calculate intermediate poses, let's review the overall process. Given a time t to calculate the intermediate pose, the first step is to find the two keyframes K_i and K_{i+1} taken at times t_0 and t_1, respectively, such that $t_0 \le t \le t_1$. These are the two keyframes to interpolate between for the given time t. The second step is to transform $t \in [t_0, t_1]$ to the range $t \in [0, 1]$ so that it acts as a percent value indicating how far to interpolate from K_i to K_{i+1}. Next, we iterate over each object, decompose the to-parent matrix into RST values if it's not already, and compute the interpolated RST-values for each bone. (Depending on the .X file exporter, the keyframes for a bone may be saved as a to-parent matrix, or directly as RST values; see the AnimationKey .X file template — *Documentation\ DirectX9\directx9_c.chm::/directx/graphics/reference/fileformat/templates/ animationkey.htm*.) Finally, we iterate over the interpolated RST values and update the to-parent matrix of each object to reflect the current interpolated object pose for this animation frame.

Given a time t to calculate the intermediate pose, the following pseudocode interpolates between two keyframes K_0 and K_1 of some bone taken at times t_0 and t_1, respectively, that satisfy $t_0 \le t \le t_1$:

```
struct Keyframe
{
    float time;
    D3DXQUATERNION R;
    D3DXVECTOR3    S;
    D3DXVECTOR3    T;
};

void interpolateBone(Keyframe& K0, Keyframe& K1, D3DXMATRIX& L)
{
    // Transform to [0, 1]
    float t0 = K0.time;
    float t1 = K1.time;
    float lerpTime = (t - t0) / (t1 - t0);

    // Compute interpolated RST values.
    D3DXVECTOR3 lerpedT;
```

```
D3DXVECTOR3 lerpedS;
D3DXQUATERNION lerpedR;
D3DXVec3Lerp(&lerpedT, &K0.T, &K1.T, lerpTime);
D3DXVec3Lerp(&lerpedS, &K0.S, &K1.S, lerpTime);
D3DXQuaternionSlerp(&lerpedR, &K0.R, &K1.R, lerpTime);

// Build and return the interpolated to-parent
// matrix for this bone.
D3DXMATRIX T, S, R;
D3DXMatrixTranslation(&T, lerpedT.x, lerpedT.y, lerpedT.z);

D3DXMatrixScaling(&S, lerpedS.x, lerpedS.y, lerpedS.z);
D3DXMatrixRotationQuaternion(&R, &lerpedQ);

L = R * S * T;
}
```

Note: It is usually the case that the translation and scaling keys are constant, and therefore do not need to be interpolated.

The above code just interpolates one object in the hierarchy. Of course, in order to animate the entire mesh hierarchy, we must perform an interpolation *for each object* in the hierarchy.

All that said, in this book we do not have to calculate any intermediate poses ourselves, as that will be handled by the D3DX ID3DXAnimationController interface (discussed in the next chapter).

Note: It would be a good idea for the reader to try out a 3D modeling/animation program and experiment directly with keyframes. It is one thing to read about keyframes and interpolation, but it is really recommended to try it and see it in action. Some professional 3D modelers have free educational versions (e.g., Maya has the Maya Personal Learning Edition), or you could try out a program like MilkShape3D (http://www.swissquake.ch/chumbalum-soft/).

15.4 **Summary**

■ Many real-world objects we wish to model graphically in a computer program consist of parts with a parent-child-relationship, where a child object can move independently on its own but is also forced to move when its parent moves. For example, a tank turret can rotate independently of the tank, but it is still fixed to the tank and moves with the tank. Another classic example is a skeleton, in which bones are attached to other bones and must move when they move (as we saw with the Robot Arm demo). Consider game characters on a train. The characters can move independently inside the train, but they also move as the train moves. This example illustrates how, in a game, the hierarchy can change dynamically and must be updated. That is, before a character enters a train, the train is not part of the character's hierarchy, but once the player does enter a train, the train becomes part of the character's hierarchy (the character inherits the train transformation).

■ Each object in a mesh hierarchy is modeled about its own local coordinate system with its pivot joint at the origin to facilitate rotation. Because the coordinate systems exist in the same universe we can relate them, and therefore transform from one to the other. In particular, we relate them by describing each object's coordinate system relative to its parent's coordinate system. From that, we can construct a to-parent transformation matrix that transforms the geometry of an object from its local coordinate system to its parent's coordinate system. Once in the parent's coordinate system, we can then transform by the parent's to-parent matrix to transform to the grandparent's coordinate system, and so on, until we have visited each ancestors' coordinate system and finally reach the world space. In other words, to transform an object in a mesh hierarchy from its local space to world space, we apply the to-parent transform of the object and all of its ancestors (in ascending order) to percolate up the coordinate system hierarchy until the object arrives in the world space. In this way, the object inherits the transformations of its parents and moves when they move.

■ When constructing an animation, artists specify the keyframes of each bone. Then an interpolation algorithm is used to generate the intermediate bone poses.

15.5 **Exercises**

1. In the Robot Arm demo, you can only rotate each bone along the z-axis. Modify the program so that you can also rotate a bone along the y-axis.

2. In the Robot Arm demo, there is no visual mechanism to show which bone is currently selected. Modify the demo so that the currently selected bone is highlighted. You can implement the highlight any way you want as long as the selected bone is distinguishable from the non-selected bones. For example, you might make the selected bone use a different material.

3. Modify the Robot Arm demo to draw the bone hierarchy shown in Figure 15.12. Allow the user to animate the bones as follows: rotate bone 0 on the y-axis; rotate bones 1 and 2 on the z-axis; and rotate bones 3, 4, 5, and 6 on the x-axis.

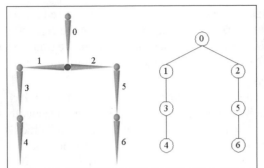

Figure 15.12:
Skeleton hierarchy
for exercise 3.

4. Modify the Robot Arm demo to draw the bone hierarchy shown in Figure 15.13. Allow the user to animate the bones as follows: rotate bone 0 on the z-axis; rotate bones 1 and 2 on the y-axis; rotate bones 2 and 6 on the x-axis; and rotate bones 3, 4, 7, and 8 on the z-axis.

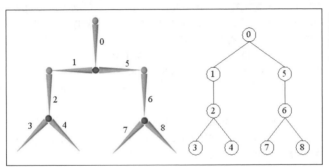

Figure 15.13:
Skeleton
hierarchy for
exercise 4.

5. The bottom-up approach we have used to compute each hierarchy object's world transformation matrix is not the most efficient. Can you find a more efficient top-down approach?

Chapter 16

Mesh Hierarchy Animation Part II — Skinned Meshes

In the last chapter, we linked *separate* mesh parts together into a hierarchy to form a larger object. For some things, like the Solar System demo, this technique works fine. However, for objects like a human character, it does not work out so well, as Figure 16.1 illustrates. The problem is that humans and animals (and some other objects you can think of) have a flexible skin covering the underlying bone structure that stretches and contracts as the bones (and also muscles, but we do not consider that here) that influence it move. The breaking up of the skin (modeled with vertices and triangles) into separate parts for each bone leads to the unnatural discontinuity shown in Figure 16.1. In this chapter, we study a popular solution to this discontinuity problem — *vertex blending*.

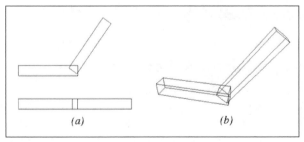

(a)   *(b)*

Figure 16.1: (a) Observe the sharp unnatural bending that occurs when we rotate a bone using two separate meshes. (b) A perspective view of the unnatural bending.

Objectives:

- To become familiar with the terminology of animated skinned meshes.
- To understand the idea and mathematics of vertex blending.
- To learn the basics of the D3DX animation API and how to use it to animate a skinned mesh.

16.1 Overview of Skinned Meshes

16.1.1 Definitions

Figure 16.2 shows a character mesh. The highlighted chain of bones in the figure is called a *skeleton*. A skeleton provides a natural hierarchal structure for driving a character animation system. The skeleton is surrounded by an exterior skin, which we model as 3D geometry (vertices and polygons). Initially, the skin vertices are relative to the *bind space*, which is the local coordinate system relative to which the entire skin is defined (usually the root coordinate system). Each bone in the skeleton influences the shape and position of the subset of skin it influences (i.e., the vertices it influences), just like in real life. Thus, as we animate the skeleton, the attached skin is animated accordingly to reflect the current pose of the skeleton.

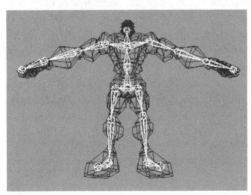

Figure 16.2: A character mesh. The highlighted bone chain represents the character's skeleton. The dark colored polygons represent the character's skin. The skin vertices are relative to the *bind space*, which is the coordinate system in which the mesh was modeled.

16.1.2 Reformulating a Bone's To-Root Transform

One difference from the last chapter is that here we will transform from the root coordinate system to the world coordinate system in a separate step. So rather than finding the to-world matrix for each bone, we find the *to-root* (i.e., the transformation that transforms from the bone's local coordinate system to the root bone's coordinate system) matrix for each bone.

A second difference is that in the previous chapter, we traversed the ancestry of a node in a bottom-up fashion, where we started at a bone and moved up its ancestry. However, it is actually more efficient to take a top-down approach (see Equation 16.1), where we start at the root and move down the tree. Labeling the n bones with an integer number 0, 1, ..., $n - 1$, we have the following formula for expressing the ith bone's to-root transformation:

$$toRoot_i = toParent_i \cdot toRoot_p \qquad\qquad (16.1)$$

Here, p is the bone label of the parent of bone i. Does this make sense? Indeed, $toRoot_p$ gives us a direct map that sends geometry from the coordinate system of bone p to the coordinate system of the root. So to get to the root coordinate system, it follows that we just need to get geometry from the coordinate system of bone i to the coordinate system of its parent bone p, and $toParent_i$ does the job.

Now, we can also see why this is more efficient. With the top-down approach, for any bone i, we already have the to-root transformation matrix of its parent; thus, we are only one step away from the to-root transformation for bone i. With a bottom-up technique, we'd traverse the entire ancestry for each bone, and many matrix multiplications would be duplicated when bones share common ancestors.

16.1.3 The Offset Transform

There is a small subtlety that comes from the fact that the vertices influenced by a bone are not relative to the coordinate system of the bone (they are relative to the bind space). So before we apply Equation 16.1, we first need to transform the vertices from bind space to the space of the bone that influences it. A so-called *offset transformation* does this (see Figure 16.3).

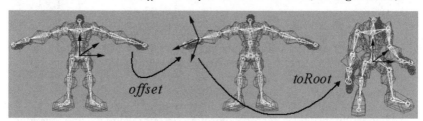

Figure 16.3: We first transform the vertices influenced by a bone from bind space to the space of the influencing bone via the offset transform. Then, once in the space of the bone, we apply the bone's to-root transformation to transform the vertices from the space of the bone to the space of the root bone. The final transformation is the combination of the offset transform, followed by the to-root transform.

Thus, by transforming the vertices by the offset matrix of some arbitrary bone B, we move the vertices from the bind space to the bone space of B. Then, once we have the vertices in bone space of B, we can use B's to-root transform to position it back in character space in its current animated pose.

We now introduce a new transform, which we'll call the *final transform*, that combines a bone's offset transform with its to-root transform. Mathematically, the final transformation matrix of the *i*th bone F_i is given by:

$$F_i = offset_i \cdot toRoot_i \tag{16.2}$$

16.1.4 Vertex Blending

The strategy of vertex blending is as follows: We have an underlying bone hierarchy, but the skin itself is one continuous mesh (i.e., we do not break the mesh up into parts to correspond with each bone and animate them individually as we did in the preceding chapter). Moreover, one or more bones can influence a vertex of the skin, with the net result being determined by a weighted average of the influencing bones' final transforms (the weights are specified by an artist when the skinned mesh is being made and saved in the .X file). With this setup, a smooth transitional blend can be achieved at joints (which are typically the trouble areas), thereby making the skin appear elastic (see Figure 16.4).

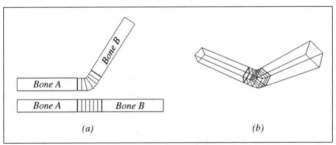

Figure 16.4: The skin is one continuous mesh that covers both bones. Observe that the vertices near the joint are influenced by both bone *A* and bone *B* to create a smooth transitional blend to simulate a flexible skin.

In practice, [Möller02] notes that we usually do not need more than four bone influences per vertex. Therefore, in our design we will consider a maximum of four influential bones per vertex. So to implement vertex blending, we now model the character mesh's skin as one continuous mesh. Each vertex contains up to four indices that index into a *bone matrix palette*, which is the array of final transformation matrices (one entry for each bone in the skeleton). Additionally, each vertex also has up to four weights that describe the respective amount of influence each of the four influencing ones has on that vertex. Thus, we have the vertex structure for vertex blending shown in Figure 16.5:

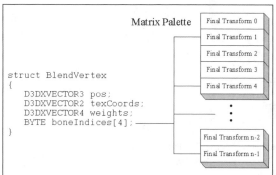

Figure 16.5: The matrix palette stores the final transformation for each bone. Observe how the four bone indices index into the matrix palette. The bone indices identify the bones that influence the vertex. Note that the vertex is not necessarily influenced by four bones; for instance, only two of the four indices might be used, thereby indicating that only two bones influence the vertex.

A continuous mesh whose vertices have this format is ready for vertex blending, and we call it a *skinned mesh*.

The vertex-blended position $\vec{v}^*$ of any vertex $\vec{v}$, relative to the root frame (remember we perform the world transformation as a last step once we have everything in the root coordinate system), can be calculated with the following weighted average formula:

$$\vec{v}^* = w_0\vec{v}F_0 + w_1\vec{v}F_1 + \ldots + w_{n-1}\vec{v}F_{n-1} \tag{16.3}$$

where $w_0 + w_1 + \ldots + w_{n-1} = 1$; that is, the sum of the weights equals one.

Observe that in this equation, we transform a given vertex $\vec{v}$ individually by all of the final bone transforms that influence it (i.e., matrices F_0, ..., F_{n-1}). We then take a weighted average of these individually transformed points to compute the final vertex-blended position $\vec{v}^*$.

Transforming normals is done similarly:

$$\vec{n}^* = normalize\left(w_0\vec{n}F_0 + w_1\vec{n}F_1 + \ldots + w_{n-1}\vec{n}F_{n-1}\right) \tag{16.4}$$

Here we assume that for each i, F_i is its own inverse-transpose; that is, $F_i = \left(F_i^{-1}\right)^T$. If this is not the case (e.g., F_i has non-uniform scaling transformations), then we must replace F_i with $\left(F_i^{-1}\right)^T$ to transform normals correctly.

The following vertex shader fragment shows the key code that does vertex blending with a maximum of two bone influences per vertex:

```
uniform extern float4x4 gWorld;
uniform extern float4x4 gWorldInvTrans;
uniform extern float4x4 gWVP;

// The matrix palette.
uniform extern float4x4 gFinalXForms[35];

OutputVS VBlend2VS(float3 posL    : POSITIONO,
                   float3 normalL : NORMALO,
```

```
                    float2 tex0    : TEXCOORD0,
                    float weight0  : BLENDWEIGHT0,
                    int4 boneIndex : BLENDINDICES0)
{
    // Zero out our output.
    OutputVS outVS = (OutputVS)0;

    // Equation 16.3.
    float weight1 = 1.0f - weight0;

    float4 p = weight0 * mul(float4(posL, 1.0f),
        gFinalXForms[boneIndex[0]]);
    p       += weight1 * mul(float4(posL, 1.0f),
        gFinalXForms[boneIndex[1]]);
    p.w = 1.0f;

    // Equation 16.4.  Note that we do not normalize here - we
    // do it in the pixel shader.
    float4 n = weight0 * mul(float4(normalL, 0.0f),
        gFinalXForms[boneIndex[0]]);
    n       += weight1 * mul(float4(normalL, 0.0f),
        gFinalXForms[boneIndex[1]]);
    n.w = 0.0f;

    // Transform normal to world space.
    outVS.normalW = mul(n, gWorldInvTrans).xyz;

    // Transform vertex position to world space.
    float3 posW  = mul(p, gWorld).xyz;

    // Transform to homogeneous clip space.
    outVS.posH = mul(p, gWVP);
    .
    . // Non-vertex blending code snipped.
    .
}
```

Observe the semantic `BLENDWEIGHT0` for the vertex blend weights, and the semantic `BLENDINDICES0` for the bone matrix palette indices.

If the above vertex shader does vertex blending with a maximum of two bone influences per vertex, then why do we only input one vertex weight per vertex instead of two? Well, recall that the total weight must sum to one; thus, for two weights we have: $w_0 + w_1 \Rightarrow w_1 = 1 - w_0$. In other words, for two blend weights, we only need to know one of them, as the other one can be solved for in terms of the given one. (If the skinned mesh used four bones per vertex, then there would be three blend weights given and the fourth blend weight could be solved in terms of the other three given ones: $w_0 + w_1 + w_2 + w_3 = 1 \Rightarrow w_3 = 1 - w_0 - w_1 - w_2$.)

16.1.5 **D3DXFRAME**

We now introduce a D3DX hierarchical data structure called D3DXFRAME. We use this structure to represent the bones of the character. By assigning some pointers we can connect these bones to form a skeleton. For example, Figure 16.6 shows the pointer connection that forms the bone hierarchy tree (skeleton) of the character shown in Figure 16.2.

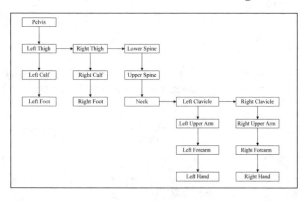

Figure 16.6: Tree hierarchy of the skeleton of the character depicted in Figure 16.2. Down arrows represent "first child" relationships, and right arrows represent "sibling" relationships.

Admittedly, in the context of character animation, the name BONE is preferred to D3DXFRAME. However, we must remember that D3DXFRAME is a generic data structure that can describe non-character mesh hierarchies as well. In any case, in the context of character animation we can use "bone" and "frame" interchangeably.

```
typedef struct _D3DXFRAME {
    LPSTR Name;
    D3DXMATRIX TransformationMatrix;
    LPD3DXMESHCONTAINER pMeshContainer;
    struct _D3DXFRAME *pFrameSibling;
    struct _D3DXFRAME *pFrameFirstChild;
} D3DXFRAME, *LPD3DXFRAME;
```

- Name: The name of the node.
- TransformationMatrix: The to-parent matrix of this node.
- pMeshContainer: Pointer to a D3DXMESHCONTAINER. This member is used in the case that you want to associate a container of meshes with this frame. If no mesh container is associated with this frame, set this pointer to null.
- pFrameSibling: Pointer to this frame's sibling frame; one of two pointers used to connect this node to the mesh hierarchy — see Figure 16.6.
- pFrameFirstChild: Pointer to this frame's first child frame; one of two pointers used to connect this node to the mesh hierarchy — see Figure 16.6.

> **Note:** If you are not comfortable with representing and traversing
> tree/graph data structures, then you might want to review them in
> your favorite data structure book.

The immediate problem with D3DXFRAME is that it does not have a to-root data member. To remedy this we extend D3DXFRAME as follows:

```
struct FrameEx : public D3DXFRAME
{
    D3DXMATRIX toRoot;
};
```

We can compute the to-root transform for each node in the hierarchy by recursively traversing the tree top-down. The following C++ code implements this process:

```
void SkinnedMesh::buildToRootXForms(FrameEx* frame,
                                    D3DXMATRIX& parentsToRoot)
{
    // Save some references to economize line space.
    D3DXMATRIX& toParent = frame->TransformationMatrix;
    D3DXMATRIX& toRoot   = frame->toRoot;

    toRoot = toParent * parentsToRoot;

    FrameEx* sibling   = (FrameEx*)frame->pFrameSibling;
    FrameEx* firstChild = (FrameEx*)frame->pFrameFirstChild;

    // Recurse down siblings.
    if( sibling )
        buildToRootXForms(sibling, parentsToRoot);

    // Recurse to first child.
    if( firstChild )
        buildToRootXForms(firstChild, toRoot);
}
```

And to start off the recursion we would write:

```
D3DXMATRIX identity;
D3DXMatrixIdentity(&identity);
buildToRootXForms((FrameEx*)mRoot, identity);
```

Because the root does not have a parent, we pass in an identity matrix for its parent's to-parent transform.

16.2 Skinned Mesh Demo

In this section, we put the theory of the previous sections into practice by using vertex blending to animate a skinned mesh with the D3DX animation API (Figure 16.7). We make the following assumptions:

- The .X file contains exactly one skinned mesh (we do not load more if there exists more than one).

- The skinned mesh uses a maximum of two bone influences per vertex since our vertex shader defined in §16.1.4 is hard coded for two. It is a simple exercise to write additional vertex shaders that support three and four bone influences per vertex, and if your video card supports static branching, you could write one generalized shader that supports two to four bone influences per vertex.

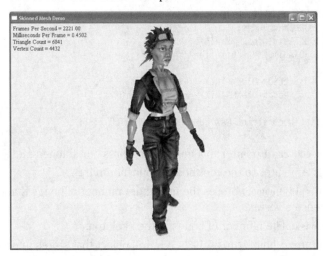

Figure 16.7: A screenshot of the Skinned Mesh demo.

Before continuing, let's briefly recapitulate the components needed for vertex blending to work:

- First and foremost, we need a hierarchy of bones and a skinned mesh (i.e., a mesh with vertices that possess bone weights, and indices — which identify the bones that influence the vertex — that index into the bone matrix palette).

- Additionally, in order to compute the final transform for each bone based on the current animated pose, we need the offset transformation matrix (which transforms the vertices from the mesh's local coordinate system to the space of the bone that influences it), and we need the updated to-root matrix (updated in the sense that it has been rebuilt after keyframe interpolation occurs).

- For animation, we require keyframes for each bone; the keyframe data is loaded from the .X file (it is worth mentioning though, that not all .X files contain animation data/keyframes); moreover, we need functionality to interpolate bones between keyframes.

Given the preceding data and functionality, we can animate a skinned mesh using the vertex blending algorithm. The subsequent sections describe the details for obtaining, building, and using this data and functionality.

16.2.1 **SkinnedMesh Overview**

We begin by providing an overview of the data members and methods of the SkinnedMesh class, which we write in order to facilitate loading and animating a skinned mesh (you already saw the implementation to SkinnedMesh::build-ToRootXForms in §16.1.5). We start with the data members:

```
protected:
    ID3DXMesh* mSkinnedMesh;
    D3DXFRAME* mRoot;
    DWORD mMaxVertInfluences;
    DWORD mNumBones;
    ID3DXSkinInfo* mSkinInfo;
    ID3DXAnimationController* mAnimCtrl;

    std::vector<D3DXMATRIX> mFinalXForms;
    std::vector<D3DXMATRIX*> mToRootXFormPtrs;

    static const int MAX_NUM_BONES_SUPPORTED = 35;
};
```

- mSkinnedMesh: A pointer to a mesh that stores our skinned mesh.

- mRoot: A pointer to the root node in our hierarchy.

- mMaxVertInfluences: Stores the maximum number of bones that can influence a vertex.

- mNumBones: The number of bones in the skeleton.

- mSkinInfo: A pointer to an ID3DXSkinInfo object that stores information related to skinning, such as the offset transformation for each bone, vertex weights, and bone matrix palette indices.

- mAnimCtrl: A pointer to an ID3DXAnimationController object that is used to interpolate bones as a function of time (i.e., animate them), as well as some more advanced things like animation blending and animation callbacks.

- mFinalXForms: The matrix palette that stores the final transformation of each bone.

- mToRootXFormPtrs: An array of pointers, one for each bone, that points to the to-root transformation matrix of each frame. This gives us quick random access to a frame's to-root transformation matrix without having to traverse the tree hierarchy. In addition, we organize these pointers so that the ith to-root matrix corresponds with the ith offset matrix.

- MAX_NUM_BONES_SUPPORTED: A predefined value that specifies the maximum number of bones a skinned mesh can have. You can change this, but remember that we need to set the bone matrix palette to the effect file, which is stored in the vertex shader's limited constant memory; see the SDK documentation for the constant table limits for the various vertex shader models.

We now outline the key methods of `SkinnedMesh`.

```
class SkinnedMesh
{
public:
    .
    . Trivial methods snipped
    .
    const D3DXMATRIX* getFinalXFormArray();

    void update(float deltaTime);
    void draw();

protected:
    D3DXFRAME* findNodeWithMesh(D3DXFRAME* frame);
    bool hasNormals(ID3DXMesh* mesh);
    void buildSkinnedMesh(ID3DXMesh* mesh);
    void buildToRootXFormPtrArray();
    void buildToRootXForms(FrameEx* frame,
                           D3DXMATRIX& parentsToRoot);
```

■ `getFinalXFormArray`: Returns a pointer to the final transformation matrix array; this is needed to set the array to an effect parameter so that the vertices can index into the array.

■ `update`: Animates the skinned mesh.

■ `draw`: Draws the skinned mesh.

■ `findNodeWithMesh`: Searches the hierarchy for the node that contains the one and only mesh.

■ `hasNormals`: Returns `true` if the original mesh loaded from the .X file already has normal data computed.

■ `buildSkinnedMesh`: Reformats the vertex format of the mesh to contain room for blend weights and indices into the matrix palette; besides allocating room for the data, it also fills in the data.

■ `buildToRootXFormPtrArray`: Traverses the tree and obtains pointers to the to-root transformation matrix for each node.

■ `buildToRootXForms`: Recursively traverses the tree and builds the to-root transformation matrix for each node.

16.2.2 **D3DXMESHCONTAINER**

It was mentioned in §16.1.5 that the D3DXFRAME structure contains a pointer to a D3DXMESHCONTAINER structure, which allowed us to associate a container (linked list) of meshes with a frame. At the time we did not elaborate on D3DXMESHCONTAINER, so we do that now. The D3DXMESHCONTAINER structure is defined as follows:

```
typedef struct _D3DXMESHCONTAINER {
    LPSTR Name;
    D3DXMESHDATA MeshData;
```

```
        LPD3DXMATERIAL pMaterials;
        LPD3DXEFFECTINSTANCE pEffects;
        DWORD NumMaterials;
        DWORD *pAdjacency;
        LPD3DXSKININFO pSkinInfo;
        struct _D3DXMESHCONTAINER *pNextMeshContainer;
} D3DXMESHCONTAINER, *LPD3DXMESHCONTAINER;
```

■ Name: The name of the mesh.

■ MeshData: A D3DXMESHCONTAINER is a general structure and can be an
  ID3DXMesh, ID3DXPMesh (progressive mesh), or ID3DXPatchMesh (we do not
  cover patch meshes in this book). The D3DXMESHDATA structure (defined
  below) specifies what type of mesh it is and contains a valid pointer to
  that type of mesh.

```
typedef struct D3DXMESHDATA {
        D3DXMESHDATATYPE Type;
        union
        {
                LPD3DXMESH pMesh;
                LPD3DXPMESH pPMesh;
                LPD3DXPATCHMESH pPatchMesh;
        }

} D3DXMESHDATA, *LPD3DXMESHDATA;
```

The Type member is one of the following: D3DXMESHTYPE_MESH,
D3DXMESHTYPE_PMESH, or D3DXMESHTYPE_PATCHMESH. In this book, we are only
concerned with regular meshes (i.e., D3DXMESHTYPE_MESH).

■ pMaterials: Pointer to an array of D3DXMATERIAL structures.

■ pEffects: Pointer to a D3DXEFFECTINSTANCE structure, which contains
  effect file information. Recall that a D3DXEFFECTINSTANCE stores an .fx
  filename and the data needed to initialize the effect parameters. This is
  useful if your 3D modeler can export effect data information to the .X
  file, as you can then get all the effect information associated with a
  subset from the .X file. We will not be loading any effect data from the
  .X file, and therefore we can ignore this variable.

■ NumMaterials: The number of elements in the material array to which
  pMaterials points.

■ pAdjacency: Pointer to the adjacency info of the mesh.

■ pSkinInfo: Pointer to an ID3DXSkinInfo interface, which contains
  information needed for performing vertex blending. That is, it contains
  offset matrices for each bone, vertex weights, and vertex bone indices.
  The important methods of ID3DXSkinInfo will be discussed later on at
  the time they are used. You may be wondering where this class gets its
  data; it actually just comes from the .X file, which contains all the
  skinning info (assuming the .X file contains a skinned mesh — not all
  .X files contain skinned meshes or are animated). ID3DXSkinInfo is just

the class into which the D3DX library chooses to load the skinning-related data.

■   pNextMeshContainer: Pointer to the next mesh in the container (thereby forming a linked list). If this value is null, then we are at the end of the mesh container. This is used because there may be several meshes associated with a frame.

16.2.3 **ID3DXAnimationController**

The ID3DXAnimationController interface is responsible for animation. For each animation sequence (e.g., you may have animation sequences for running, walking, idle, and/or sword swinging), it stores all the keyframes for each bone. (The keyframes for all the bones in a skeleton for a distinct animation sequence are stored in what is called an *animation set*.) It also contains the functionality for interpolating between keyframes, and some more advanced features like animation blending and animation callbacks.

To render a smooth animation we must incrementally update the character from its current pose at time t in the animation sequence to its next pose, some Δt seconds later ($t + \Delta t$). By making Δt small enough (e.g., $1/60^{th}$ of a second), the illusion of a smooth continuous animation is achieved. The ID3DXAnimationController::AdvanceTime method does exactly this. Using keyframe interpolation, it updates the bones of a character from its current pose at time t in the animation sequence to the next pose in the animation sequence at time $t + \Delta t$. The method prototype is:

```
HRESULT ID3DXAnimationController::AdvanceTime(
    DOUBLE TimeDelta,
    LPD3DXANIMATIONCALLBACKHANDLER pCallbackHandler);
```

TimeDelta is Δt, and we will ignore pCallbackHandler by passing in null for it (animation callbacks are explored in the exercises). Note that when the animation sequence reaches the end, the current track timer resets and loops back to the beginning of the animation sequence by default.

Once the animation controller has interpolated the bones to reflect the updated pose, we need access to them. Where do we get the interpolated bones? An important fact about the animation controller is that it contains pointers to the D3DXFRAME::TransformationMatrix variables of all the frames in the hierarchy. This is significant because when the animation controller interpolates the bones, it writes the interpolated bones to their respective D3DXFRAME::TransformationMatrix variable. Thus, we have direct access to the interpolated bones at any time via the D3DXFRAME::TransformationMatrix variables, stored in the frame hierarchy. Where do we get the interpolated bones? The answer is that we already have them via the tree hierarchy.

16.2.4 **ID3DXAllocateHierarchy**

In order to create and destroy a mesh hierarchy using the D3DX functions, we must implement an ID3DXAllocateHierarchy interface, which consists of four abstract methods. In doing so, we are able to define how meshes and frames are created and destroyed, thereby giving the application some flexibility in the construction and destruction process. For example, in our implementation of CreateMeshContainer, we elect to ignore meshes that are not skinned meshes, but some other implementation could choose to handle any type of mesh. The following code shows the child class we define to implement the ID3DXAllocateHierarchy interface:

```
class AllocMeshHierarchy : public ID3DXAllocateHierarchy
{
public:
    HRESULT STDMETHODCALLTYPE CreateFrame(
            THIS_ PCSTR Name,
            D3DXFRAME** ppNewFrame);

    HRESULT STDMETHODCALLTYPE CreateMeshContainer(
            PCSTR Name,
            const D3DXMESHDATA* pMeshData,
            const D3DXMATERIAL* pMaterials,
            const D3DXEFFECTINSTANCE* pEffectInstances,
            DWORD NumMaterials,
            const DWORD *pAdjacency,
            ID3DXSkinInfo* pSkinInfo,
            D3DXMESHCONTAINER** ppNewMeshContainer);

    HRESULT STDMETHODCALLTYPE DestroyFrame(
            THIS_ D3DXFRAME* pFrameToFree);

    HRESULT STDMETHODCALLTYPE DestroyMeshContainer(
            THIS_ D3DXMESHCONTAINER* pMeshContainerBase);
};
```

The implementation of these functions is straightforward, so it will not be discussed or shown here; it is really just bookkeeping work on allocating and deleting memory.

Refer to the Skinned Mesh demo for details in the *AllocMeshHierarchy/.cpp* files — the implementation has been heavily commented.

16.2.5 **D3DXLoadMeshHierarchyFromX and D3DXFrameDestroy**

After we have implemented an ID3DXAllocateHierarchy interface, we can use the following D3DX function to load the mesh hierarchy from an .X file:

```
HRESULT WINAPI D3DXLoadMeshHierarchyFromX(
    LPCSTR Filename,
    DWORD MeshOptions,
```

```
LPDIRECT3DDEVICE9 pDevice,
LPD3DXALLOCATEHIERARCHY pAlloc,
LPD3DXLOADUSERDATA pUserDataLoader,
LPD3DXFRAME* ppFrameHierarchy,
LPD3DXANIMATIONCONTROLLER* ppAnimController);
```

■ Filename: The filename of the .X file that contains a mesh hierarchy.

■ MeshOptions: One or more creation flags that will be used to create the mesh. See the D3DXMESH enumerated type in the SDK documentation for a complete list of option flags. Some common flags are:

   D3DXMESH_32BIT: The mesh will use 32-bit indices.

   D3DXMESH_SYSTEMMEM: The mesh will be placed in the system memory pool.

   D3DXMESH_MANAGED: The mesh will be placed in the managed memory pool.

   D3DXMESH_WRITEONLY: The mesh's data will only be written to and not read from.

   D3DXMESH_DYNAMIC: The mesh's buffers will be made dynamic.

■ pDevice: The device associated with the mesh.

■ pAlloc: A pointer to an instance of a class that implements the ID3DXAllocateHierarchy interface. By implementing this interface, the application can define how the hierarchy and its components are created and destroyed.

■ pUserDataLoader: A pointer to an instance of a class that implements the ID3DXLoadUserData interface. By implementing this interface, the application can load custom data templates from .X files. Since we are using standard .X file templates, we ignore this parameter.

■ ppFrameHierarchy: Returns a pointer to the root of the loaded mesh hierarchy.

■ ppAnimController: Returns a pointer to an allocated ID3DXAnimationController interface instance that contains all the animation data from the .X file.

Below is an example of how this function might be called:

```
D3DXFRAME* mRoot;
ID3DXAnimationController* mAnimCtrl;
AllocMeshHierarchy allocMeshHierarchy;
HR(D3DXLoadMeshHierarchyFromX(XFilename.c_str(), D3DXMESH_SYSTEMMEM,
    gd3dDevice, &allocMeshHierarchy, 0, /* ignore user data */
    &mRoot, &mAnimCtrl));
```

To destroy the frame hierarchy, we can use the D3DXFrameDestroy function:

```
if( mRoot )
{
    AllocMeshHierarchy allocMeshHierarchy;
    HR(D3DXFrameDestroy(mRoot, &allocMeshHierarchy));
```

```
            mRoot = 0;
    }
```

16.2.6 Finding the One and Only Mesh

For simplification purposes, we make the following assumption: We assume
that the input .X file contains exactly one skinned mesh. From this assumption, and from the fact that we ignored non-skinned mesh types in
CreateMeshContainer, we can infer that there exists exactly one frame in the
hierarchy that has a pointer to a D3DXMESHCONTAINER with a valid pMesh variable; additionally, because we only read in skinned meshes, that mesh
container also contains skinning info (i.e., a non-null pSkinInfo pointer).

   So let us now find the one and only mesh container. The following
method recursively searches the hierarchy for the frame that has the one
and only mesh:

```
D3DXFRAME* SkinnedMesh::findNodeWithMesh(D3DXFRAME* frame)
{
    if( frame->pMeshContainer )
        if( frame->pMeshContainer->MeshData.pMesh != 0 )
            return frame;

    D3DXFRAME* f = 0;
    if(frame->pFrameSibling)
        if( f = findNodeWithMesh(frame->pFrameSibling) )
            return f;

    if(frame->pFrameFirstChild)
        if( f = findNodeWithMesh(frame->pFrameFirstChild) )
            return f;

    return 0;
}
```

And the subsequent code that starts off the recursion, saves a local pointer
to the mesh container, and saves a member pointer to the skin info:

```
// In this demo we assume that the input .X file contains only one
// mesh.  So search for that one and only mesh.
D3DXFRAME* f = findNodeWithMesh(mRoot);
if( f == 0 ) HR(E_FAIL);
D3DXMESHCONTAINER* meshContainer = f->pMeshContainer;
mSkinInfo = meshContainer->pSkinInfo;
mSkinInfo->AddRef();
```

Note that we just save a pointer to the mesh container, and moreover we do
not take responsibility for freeing it. Because the mesh stays in the hierarchy, it will be freed when we destroy the hierarchy. Conversely, since we
AddRef the skin info object, we do take responsibility for releasing that interface in the SkinnedMesh destructor.

16.2.7 **Converting to a Skinned Mesh**

So far we have a pointer to the one and only mesh container (which contains the one and only mesh). However, at this point, the vertex format of the mesh does not include vertex weights or bone index data, both of which are needed for vertex blending. In addition, the mesh may also not contain vertex normals or texture coordinates, both of which our vertex shader assumes are present. Therefore, we need to do two things: First, we clone the mesh to a vertex format that includes positions and textures, and second, we convert the mesh to an *indexed-blended-mesh* or what is also known as a *skinned mesh*, which does have the necessary vertex format for vertex blending (i.e., also includes blend weights and bone indices). The following code implements the first part, where the parameter mesh is a pointer to the one and only mesh we found in §16.2.6 (i.e., meshContainer->MeshData.pMesh):

```
void SkinnedMesh::buildSkinnedMesh(ID3DXMesh* mesh)
{
    // First add a normal component and 2D texture
    // coordinates component.

    D3DVERTEXELEMENT9 elements[64];
    UINT numElements = 0;
    VertexPNT::Decl->GetDeclaration(elements, &numElements);

    ID3DXMesh* tempMesh = 0;
    HR(mesh->CloneMesh(D3DXMESH_SYSTEMMEM, elements,
        gd3dDevice, &tempMesh));

    if( !hasNormals(tempMesh) )
        HR(D3DXComputeNormals(tempMesh, 0));
```

The method we implement, hasNormals, just does a search of the vertex declaration to see if vertex normals are already present — if not, then we generate them.

Now, before we add the blend weights and bone indices into the vertex format, let us first optimize the mesh for the vertex cache.

```
DWORD* adj = new DWORD[tempMesh->GetNumFaces()*3];
ID3DXBuffer* remap = 0;
HR(tempMesh->GenerateAdjacency(EPSILON, adj));
ID3DXMesh* optimizedTempMesh = 0;
HR(tempMesh->Optimize(D3DXMESH_SYSTEMMEM | D3DXMESHOPT_VERTEXCACHE |
    D3DXMESHOPT_ATTRSORT, adj, 0, 0, &remap, &optimizedTempMesh));

ReleaseCOM(tempMesh);    // Done with this mesh.
delete[] adj;            // Done with buffer.

HR(mSkinInfo->Remap(optimizedTempMesh->GetNumVertices(),
    (DWORD*)remap->GetBufferPointer()));
ReleaseCOM(remap);       // Done with remap info.
```

The `ID3DXSkinInfo::Remap` function deserves some elaboration. In the .X file (specifically the `array DWORD vertexIndices[nWeights]` data member of the `SkinWeights` template), each bone has an array of indices that identify the vertices of the mesh that the bone influences. Because we have just rearranged the vertex array (via optimization), the vertex indices of a bone are obviously no longer correct (i.e., they index to vertices the bone does not influence since we moved the vertices around). In order to update a bone's vertex indices to the vertices the bone *does* influence, we simply need to specify where we remapped the vertices, so that the vertex indices can be updated to match. This is done with the `ID3DXSkinInfo::Remap` method. (Recall that the `Optimize` method can output the vertex remap info.)

Note: An .X file template defines a data block in an .X file. The `SkinWeights` template looks like this:

```
template SkinWeights
{
    < 6F0D123B-BAD2-4167-A0D0-80224F25FABB >
    STRING transformNodeName;
    DWORD nWeights;
    array DWORD vertexIndices[nWeights];
    array float weights[nWeights];
    Matrix4x4 matrixOffset;
}
```

Now, the last step is to modify the vertex format of the mesh to include room for the blend weights and bone indices, and to also write the blend weight and bone index data to the mesh once space is allocated for them. `ID3DXSkinInfo::ConvertToIndexedBlendedMesh` does this; it modifies the vertex format, but it also writes the per-vertex blend weights and per-vertex bone indices to the mesh.

```
DWORD numBoneComboEntries = 0;
ID3DXBuffer* boneComboTable = 0;
HR(mSkinInfo->ConvertToIndexedBlendedMesh(optimizedTempMesh,
    D3DXMESH_MANAGED | D3DXMESH_WRITEONLY,
    MAX_NUM_BONES_SUPPORTED, 0, 0, 0, 0, &mMaxVertInfluences,
    &numBoneComboEntries, &boneComboTable, &mSkinnedMesh));

ReleaseCOM(optimizedTempMesh);    // Done with tempMesh.
ReleaseCOM(boneComboTable);       // Don't need bone table.
```

Recall that the `ID3DXSkinInfo` interface contains the offset matrices for each bone, vertex weights, and vertex bone indices; hence, `ID3DXSkinInfo` is the interface capable of converting an input mesh into a skinned mesh.

Most of the parameters of `ID3DXSkinInfo::ConvertToIndexedBlendedMesh` are self explanatory from the example given. However, a few of them deserve some elaboration. The two parameters related to the bone combination table can be ignored since we do not use the bone combination table in this book. The value returned through mMaxVertInfluences specifies the maximum number of bones that influence a vertex in the skinned mesh (this is usually less than or equal to four — i.e., no more than four bones influence a given vertex). Lastly, observe that we save the resulting skinned mesh into the member variable mSkinnedMesh, which is just an ID3DXMesh data member of the SkinnedMesh class.

For insight into just how ID3DXSkinInfo::ConvertToIndexedBlendedMesh modifies the vertex format, we also include some code that dumps the format of the mesh to the debug output window:

```
#if defined(DEBUG) | defined(_DEBUG)

D3DVERTEXELEMENT9 elems[MAX_FVF_DECL_SIZE];
HR(mSkinnedMesh->GetDeclaration(elems));

OutputDebugString("\nVertex Format After
                   ConvertToIndexedBlendedMesh\n");
int i = 0;
while( elems[i].Stream != 0xff ) // While not D3DDECL_END()
{
    if( elems[i].Type == D3DDECLTYPE_FLOAT1)
        OutputDebugString("Type = D3DDECLTYPE_FLOAT1; ");
    if( elems[i].Type == D3DDECLTYPE_FLOAT2)
        OutputDebugString("Type = D3DDECLTYPE_FLOAT2; ");
    if( elems[i].Type == D3DDECLTYPE_FLOAT3)
        OutputDebugString("Type = D3DDECLTYPE_FLOAT3; ");
    if( elems[i].Type == D3DDECLTYPE_UBYTE4)
        OutputDebugString("Type = D3DDECLTYPE_UBYTE4; ");

    if( elems[i].Usage == D3DDECLUSAGE_POSITION)
        OutputDebugString("Usage = D3DDECLUSAGE_POSITION\n");
    if( elems[i].Usage == D3DDECLUSAGE_BLENDWEIGHT)
        OutputDebugString("Usage = D3DDECLUSAGE_BLENDWEIGHT\n");
    if( elems[i].Usage == D3DDECLUSAGE_BLENDINDICES)
        OutputDebugString("Usage = D3DDECLUSAGE_BLENDINDICES\n");
    if( elems[i].Usage == D3DDECLUSAGE_NORMAL)
        OutputDebugString("Usage = D3DDECLUSAGE_NORMAL\n");
    if( elems[i].Usage == D3DDECLUSAGE_TEXCOORD)
        OutputDebugString("Usage = D3DDECLUSAGE_TEXCOORD\n");
    ++i;
}
#endif
```

For the .X file *tiny.x*, the output is as follows:

```
Vertex Format After ConvertToIndexedBlendedMesh
Type = D3DDECLTYPE_FLOAT3; Usage = D3DDECLUSAGE_POSITION
Type = D3DDECLTYPE_FLOAT1; Usage = D3DDECLUSAGE_BLENDWEIGHT
Type = D3DDECLTYPE_UBYTE4; Usage = D3DDECLUSAGE_BLENDINDICES
Type = D3DDECLTYPE_FLOAT3; Usage = D3DDECLUSAGE_NORMAL
Type = D3DDECLTYPE_FLOAT2; Usage = D3DDECLUSAGE_TEXCOORD
```

Observe that only a 1D float is used for the blend weight because the second blend weight is given by $w_1 = 1 - w_0$. Also note that four unsigned bytes (D3DDECLTYPE_UBYTE4) are used for the bone matrix palette indices; thus we can have up to four bone influences per vertex, and index into a matrix palette with up to 256 entries.

In general, the output will vary depending on the skinned mesh contained in the .X file (e.g., different skinned meshes may use a different number of blend weights). In the above example output, the skinned mesh-related components have been bolded. Observe that the above vertex declaration matches the input vertex for our vertex shader from §16.1.4.

16.2.8 Building the To-Root Transform Matrix Array

Because we eventually need to set the bone matrix palette array (§16.1.4) to the effect for use in the vertex shader, it is convenient to have the to-root transforms in an array format. However, we neither need nor want copies of the to-root transforms because that would duplicate memory and would mean that we would have to update our array copy whenever the to-root transformation matrices in the hierarchy change (and they change every frame). By using an array of pointers to the to-root transformation matrices, we avoid duplication and have direct access to the updated to-root transformation matrices. The subsequent function saves pointers to the to-root transformation matrices:

```
void SkinnedMesh::buildToRootXFormPtrArray()
{
    for(UINT i = 0; i < mNumBones; ++i)
    {
        // Find the frame that corresponds with the ith bone
        // offset matrix.
        const char* boneName = mSkinInfo->GetBoneName(i);
        D3DXFRAME* frame = D3DXFrameFind(mRoot, boneName);
        if( frame )
        {
            FrameEx* frameEx = static_cast<FrameEx*>( frame );
            mToRootXFormPtrs[i] = &frameEx->toRoot;
        }
    }
}
```

Observe that we store the pointers to the to-root transformations such that the ith pointer corresponds with the ith offset matrix. Thus, given the ith bone, we can obtain its ith offset matrix and ith to-root transformation matrix.

16.2.9 Initialization Summarized

Let's summarize the initialization steps taken to create and prepare a skinned mesh for rendering. We first implemented an ID3DXAllocate-Hierarchy interface so that we can use the D3DXLoadMeshHierarchyFromX and

D3DXFrameDestroy functions to create and destroy the bone hierarchy, respectively. Next, we called D3DXLoadMeshHierarchyFromX to actually load the animated character mesh data from the .X file. We then searched the hierarchy for the one frame that contained the character's skin data (i.e., mesh container). Fourth, because the vertex format of the mesh stored in the mesh container was not a skinned mesh (i.e., it did not have vertex weights or bone indices), we had to convert it to a skinned mesh using the ID3DXSkinInfo::ConvertToIndexedBlendedMesh method. Lastly, we built an array of pointers to the to-root transformation matrices of the bones, so that we have a fast data structure from which to access the to-root transforms. We are now ready for animating and rendering the skinned mesh.

16.2.10 **Animating the Skinned Mesh**

After initialization, we have the offset matrices (stored in ID3DXSkinInfo), pointers to the to-root transforms of each bone, an animation controller to interpolate the bones to the current pose in the animation sequence, and a skinned mesh configured for vertex blending. That is to say, we have all the data necessary to animate and render the skinned mesh.

We can break the animation and rendering tasks into five steps:

1. Interpolate the bones to the current pose using the ID3DXAnimation-Controller::AdvanceTime method. Recall that the animation controller has pointers to the hierarchy frame transformation matrices (D3DXFRAME::TransformationMatrix). The animation controller updates these matrices to reflect the pose, at the current time, of the animation sequence by interpolating between keyframes.

2. Now that the frames are updated to the current pose, recurse down the tree, computing the to-root transformation matrices for each bone from the interpolated D3DXFRAME::TransformationMatrixes, like we showed in §16.1.5.

3. For each bone, fetch the ith offset matrix and ith to-root transformation matrix, and concatenate them to build the final transformation matrix of the ith bone (Equation 16.2).

4. Pass the final transformation matrix array, which includes all the transformations to correctly transform the skin to the current pose of the character, to the vertex shader.

5. Finally, render the character mesh in its current pose.

The code for the first three steps is given by the SkinnedMesh::update method:

```
void SkinnedMesh::update(float deltaTime)
{
    // Animate the mesh. The AnimationController has pointers to
    // the hierarchy frame transform matrices. The
    // AnimationController updates these matrices to reflect
```

```
// the given pose at the current time by interpolating between
// animation keyframes.

HR(mAnimCtrl->AdvanceTime(deltaTime, 0));


// Recurse down the tree and generate a frame's toRoot
// transform from the updated pose.
D3DXMATRIX identity;
D3DXMatrixIdentity(&identity);
buildToRootXForms((FrameEx*)mRoot, identity);


// Build the final transforms for each bone (Equation 16.2)
D3DXMATRIX offsetTemp, toRootTemp;
for(UINT i = 0; i < mNumBones; ++i)
{
        offsetTemp = *mSkinInfo->GetBoneOffsetMatrix(i);
        toRootTemp = *mToRootXFormPtrs[i];
        mFinalXForms[i] = offsetTemp * toRootTemp;
}
}
```

The code to implement steps four and five are done outside the SkinnedMesh class in the drawScene method:

```
// Set the matrix palette of final transformations to the effect.
HR(mFX->SetMatrixArray(mhFinalXForms,
    mSkinnedMesh->getFinalXFormArray(),
    mSkinnedMesh->numBones()));

// Set other effect parameters...

// Draw the skinned mesh.
mSkinnedMesh->draw();
```

16.3 Summary

- We can express the to-root transformation of the ith bone with the recurrence relation: $toRoot_i = toParent_i \cdot toRoot_p$, where p refers to the parent bone of the ith bone.

- The bone-offset transformation transforms vertices from bind space to the space of the bone. There is an offset transformation for each bone in the skeleton.

- In vertex blending, we have an underlying bone hierarchy, but the skin itself is one continuous mesh, and one or more bones can influence a vertex. The magnitude by which a bone influences a vertex is determined by a bone weight. The transformed vertex $\vec{v}^*$, relative to the root of the skeleton, is given by the weighted averaging formula $\vec{v}^* = w_0 \vec{v} F_0 + w_1 \vec{v} F_1 + \ldots + w_{n-1} \vec{v} F_{n-1}$. By using a continuous mesh, and several weighted bone influences per vertex, a more natural elastic skin effect is achieved.

■ To implement vertex blending, we store an array of final transformation matrices for each bone (the array is called a *matrix palette*). (The ith bone's final transformation is defined as $F_i = offset_i \cdot toRoot_i$ — that is, the bone's offset transformation followed by its to-root transformation.) Then, for each vertex, we store a list of vertex weights and matrix palette indices. The matrix palette indices of a vertex identify the final transformations of the bones that influence the vertex.

■ The ID3DXSkinInfo interface stores skinning-related data loaded from the .X file, such as bone-offset transformations, vertex weights, and the bones that influence each vertex. The ID3DXAnimationController is responsible for interpolating between keyframes to generate intermediate bone poses. In addition, it handles animation blending and animation callbacks.

■ To load a mesh hierarchy from an .X file using D3DXLoadMeshHierarchy-FromX and to destroy a mesh hierarchy using D3DXFrameDestroy, we must implement an ID3DXAllocateHierarchy interface and define how frames and meshes are to be created and destroyed. By implementing this interface, some flexibility is gained in the construction and destruction process of the hierarchy.

■ When a mesh is loaded with D3DXLoadMeshHierarchyFromX, the skinning info (i.e., vertex weights and matrix palette indices) are not automatically embedded in the mesh vertex format. Restructuring the vertex format of a mesh to include the vertex weights and matrix palette indices is done in a separate step with the ID3DXSkinInfo:: ConvertToIndexedBlendedMesh function.

16.4 **Exercises**

1. An animated character can contain the data for several animation sequences, which we recall the D3DX animation API calls *animation sets*. For example, a character may have walking, running, gun firing, jumping, and death sequences. Of course, to play multiple animation sequences, the .X file must contain the animation sets defining each sequence. The DirectX SDK *MultiAnimation* sample comes with a file called *tiny_4anim.x*, which contains four different animation sequences (animation sets) as shown in Figure 16.10.

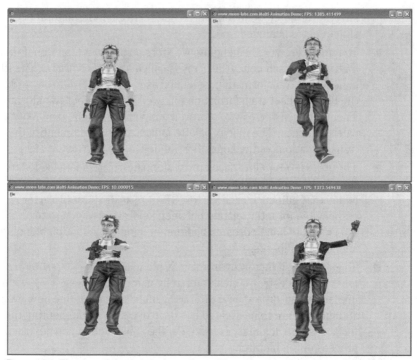

Figure 16.8: The upper-left window shows the walking animation, the upper-right window shows the jogging animation, the bottom-left window shows the loitering animation, and the bottom-right window shows the wave animation.

For this exercise, load *tiny_4anim.x*, and allow the user to switch between the four animation sequences using keyboard input (i.e., key 1 plays the first sequence, key 2 plays the second sequence, key 3 plays the third sequence, and key 4 plays the fourth sequence). The following methods will help you (research them in the DirectX documentation):

■ ID3DXAnimationController::SetTrackAnimationSet

■ ID3DXAnimationController::GetAnimationSet

■ ID3DXAnimationController::ResetTime

2. Suppose your game character has a running sequence and a gun firing sequence. It is probably the case that you would like your character to be able to fire his gun as he is running. Now obviously, you could have your 3D artist create a separate running-firing sequence, but why not save some content production time and memory by letting the computer create the mixed sequence by mathematically blending between the two animations? This is, in fact, what *animation blending* allows you to do: It allows you to take existing animation sequences and mix them together to create new sequences, as shown in Figure 16.11.

Figure 16.9: The upper-left window shows a blend of the loitering and walking animation, the upper-right window shows a blend of the loitering and wave animation, the lower-left window shows a blend of the walking and waving animation, and the lower-right window shows a blend of the running and waving animation.

Conveniently, the D3DX animation API readily supports animation blending. If you completed the previous exercise, then you know that the animation controller has several different tracks that you can attach an animation set to, but thus far, we only have been using the first track — track zero. The key idea to using animation blending, with D3DX is that *the animation controller automatically blends all the enabled track animations together.* Therefore, to perform animation blending, all we need to do is attach several animation sets to several different tracks, and enable the tracks. Then when ID3DXAnimationController::Advance-Time animates the bones, it will do so using a blend of all the animation tracks.

For this exercise, use the four animation sequences from *tiny_4anim.x* to create and play the following new animations: run-wave, by blending the running animation with the wave animation; loiter-wave, by blending the loiter animation with the wave animation; and walk-wave, by blending the walk animation with the wave animation. Note that you can also specify how much weight each track contributes to the final blended animation; for example, you may want one track to contribute 30% and another track to contribute 70% to the final blended animation. The following methods will help you (research them in the DirectX documentation):

- `ID3DXAnimationController::SetTrackAnimationSet`
- `ID3DXAnimationController::GetAnimationSet`
- `ID3DXAnimationController::ResetTime`
- `ID3DXAnimationController::SetTrackEnable`
- `ID3DXAnimationController::SetTrackSpeed`
- `ID3DXAnimationController::SetTrackWeight`
- `ID3DXAnimationController::SetTrackPriority`

3. Sometimes we would like to execute some code at a certain time in an animation sequence; for example, the DirectX SDK sample *Multi-Animation* plays footstep sounds at the particular times *tiny_4anim.x*'s feet land on the ground. We can set the animation up to execute this code automatically by inserting animation callback keys into the animation, which are triggered at certain specified time periods and invoke a callback handler function that contains the code to be executed.

   For this exercise, add a callback key to an animation that does some visual effect so that you can verify that the callback handler was invoked (e.g., flash the screen, move the camera). The following interfaces, structures, and methods will help you (research them in the DirectX documentation):

   - `ID3DXKeyframedAnimationSet`
   - `ID3DXKeyframedAnimationSet::GetSourceTicksPerSecond`
   - `ID3DXKeyframedAnimationSet::GetPeriod`
   - `ID3DXKeyframedAnimationSet::Compress`
   - `D3DXKEY_CALLBACK`
   - `ID3DXAnimationCallbackHandler`
   - `ID3DXAnimationController::AdvanceTime`
   - `D3DXCreateCompressedAnimationSet`
   - `ID3DXAnimationController::UnregisterAnimationSet`
   - `ID3DXAnimationController::RegisterAnimationSet`
   - `ID3DXAnimationController::SetTrackAnimationSet`

4. Investigate the following .X file templates and summarize, in your own words, what each template is used for.

   - `Animation`
   - `AnimationKey`
   - `AnimationOptions`
   - `AnimationSet`

- ■ AnimTicksPerSecond
- ■ CompressedAnimationSet
- ■ FloatKeys
- ■ SkinWeights
- ■ TimedFloatKeys
- ■ XSkinMeshHeader

The information can be found in the DirectX SDK documentation under the URL: *\Documentation\DirectX9\directx9_c.chm::/dx9_graphics_reference_x_file_format_templates.htm*.

Chapter 17

Terrain Rendering — Part I

The idea of terrain rendering is to start off with a flat grid (top of Figure 17.1). Then we adjust the heights (i.e., the y-coordinates) of the vertices in such a way that the mesh models smooth transitions from mountain to valley, thereby simulating a terrain (middle of Figure 17.1). And, of course, we apply a nice texture to render sandy beaches, grassy hills, rocky cliffs, and snowy mountains (bottom of Figure 17.1).

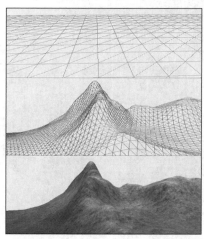

Figure 17.1: (Top) A triangle grid. (Middle) A triangle grid with smooth height transitions used to create hills and valleys. (Bottom) A lit and textured terrain.

In addition to learning how to create terrains in this chapter, we also implement a camera class whose interface enables movement in a game-style manner, rather than our previous orbiting camera.

Objectives:

- To learn how to generate height info for a terrain that results in smooth transitions between mountains and valleys.
- To find out how to light and texture the terrain.
- To learn how to implement a camera whose interface provides control suited for first-person perspective games.
- To discover a way to keep the camera planted on the terrain so that walking or running on the terrain is simulated.

17.1 **Heightmaps**

We use a heightmap to describe the hills and valleys of our terrain. A *heightmap* is a matrix in which each element specifies the height of a particular vertex in the terrain grid. That is, there exists an entry in the heightmap for each grid vertex, and the *ij*th heightmap entry provides the height for the *ij*th vertex. Typically, a heightmap is graphically represented as a grayscale map in an image editor, where black denotes the smallest height, white denotes the largest height, and shades of gray represent in-between heights. Figure 17.2 shows a few examples of heightmaps and the corresponding terrains they construct.

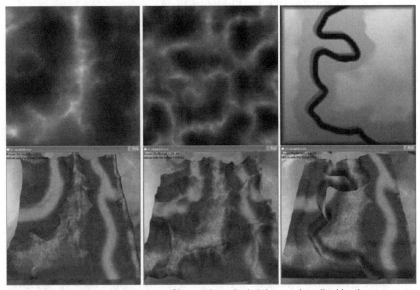

Figure 17.2: Examples of heightmaps. Observe how the heights, as described by the heightmaps, build different terrain surfaces.

When we store our heightmaps on disk, we usually allocate a byte of memory for each element in the heightmap, so the height can range from 0 to 255. The range 0 to 255 is enough to preserve the transition between heights of our terrain, but in our application we may need to scale beyond the 0 to 255 range in order to match the scale of our 3D world. For example, if our unit of measure in the 3D world is feet, then 0 to 255 does not give us enough values to represent anything interesting. For this reason, when we load the data into our applications, we allocate a float for each height element. This allows us to then scale well outside the 0 to 255 range to match any scale necessary; moreover, it also enables us to filter the heightmap and generate height values in between integer numbers.

17.1.1 Creating a Heightmap

Heightmaps can be generated either procedurally or with an image editor such as Adobe Photoshop. Using paint filters to generate different chaotic heightmap patterns can prove to be a good start, and then the heightmap can be manually tweaked by taking advantage of your paint editor's tools. Note that applying the blur filter is useful to smooth out rough edges in the heightmap.

The program Terragen (http://www.planetside.co.uk/terragen/) can generate heightmaps procedurally, and it also provides tools for modifying the heightmap (or the heightmap can be exported, and then imported and modified in a separate paint program like Photoshop). The program Bryce 5.5 (http://bryce.daz3d.com/55index.php) also has many procedural algorithms for generating heightmaps, as well as a built-in heightmap editor.

Once you have finished drawing your heightmap, you need to save it as an 8-bit RAW file. RAW files simply contain the bytes of the image one after another. This makes it very easy to read the image into our programs. If your software asks you to save the RAW file with a header, specify no header. Figure 17.3 shows the Terrain Export dialog for Terragen.

Figure 17.3: (Left) The landscape generator allows you to generate a random terrain procedurally and also to manually sculpt the terrain with brush tools. (Right) The Terrain Export dialog for Terragen. Observe the export method selected is the 8-bit RAW format.

Note: You do not have to use the RAW format to store your heightmaps; you can use any format that suits your needs. The RAW format is just one example of a format that we can use. We decided to use the RAW format because many image editors can export to this format and it is very easy to load the data in a RAW file into our program demos. The demos in this book use 8-bit RAW files (i.e., each element in the heightmap is an 8-bit integer).

Note: If 256 height steps is too coarse for your needs, you may consider storing 16-bit heightmaps, where each height entry is described by a 16-bit integer. Terragen can also export 16-bit RAW heightmaps.

17.1.2 Heightmap Class Overview

To handle heightmaps in code, we define and implement a `Heightmap` class:

```
class Heightmap
{
public:
    Heightmap();
    Heightmap(int m, int n);
    Heightmap(int m, int n,
        const std::string& filename,
        float heightScale, float heightOffset);

    void recreate(int m, int n);

    void loadRAW(int m, int n,
        const std::string& filename,
        float heightScale, float heightOffset);

    int numRows()const;
    int numCols()const;

    // For non-const objects
    float& operator()(int i, int j);

    // For const objects
    const float& operator()(int i, int j)const;

private:
    bool  inBounds(int i, int j);
    float sampleHeight3x3(int i, int j);
    void  filter3x3();
private:
    std::string  mHeightMapFilename;
    Table<float> mHeightMap;
    float        mHeightScale;
    float        mHeightOffset;
};
```

We'll briefly outline the methods and data members here; the key methods loadRAW and filter3x3 are discussed in the subsequent sections. The other methods are trivial, so we do not discuss them further, but be sure to examine the source code to see how it all fits together.

We start with the data members:

- mHeightMapFilename: The name of the heightmap from which the data was loaded.

- mHeightMap: A table (i.e., matrix) of floats, which stores the heightmap data. The Table class template is a class we implement.

- mHeightScale: A scaling value that scales the heightmap entries when the data is loaded.

- mHeightOffset: A translation value that offsets the heightmap entries when the data is loaded. For example, suppose we have scaled the heights to the range [0, 100], but we really want the range to be [–50, 50]. To achieve this, we just shift the range by –50.

We now outline the member functions:

- The first constructor creates an empty heightmap, the second constructor simply calls recreate, and the third constructor simply calls loadRAW.

- recreate: Creates an $m \times n$ heightmap, with heights initialized to zero.

- loadRAW: Creates a heightmap object by loading the data from an external RAW file.

- numRows: Returns the number of rows of the heightmap.

- numCols: Returns the number of columns of the heightmap.

- operator(): Returns the ijth heightmap element.

- inBounds: Returns true if the specified indices reference a heightmap entry; else returns false.

- sampleHeight3x3: This is a helper function for filter3x3 that returns a filtered heightmap element.

- filter3x3: Filters every element in the heightmap.

17.1.3 Loading a RAW File

Since a RAW file is nothing more than a contiguous block of bytes (where each byte is a heightmap entry), we can easily read in the block of memory with one std::ifstream::read call, as is done in this next method:

```
void Heightmap::loadRAW(int m, int n, const string& filename,
                        float heightScale, float heightOffset)
{
    mHeightMapFilename = filename;
    mHeightScale       = heightScale;
    mHeightOffset      = heightOffset;
```

```
// A height for each vertex
std::vector<unsigned char> in( m * n );

// Open the file.
std::ifstream inFile;
inFile.open(filename.c_str(), ios_base::binary);
if(!inFile) HR(E_FAIL);

// Read all the RAW bytes in one go.
inFile.read((char*)&in[0], (streamsize)in.size());

// Done with file.
inFile.close();

// Copy the array data into a float table format, and scale
// and offset the heights.
mHeightMap.resize(m, n, 0);
for(int i = 0; i < m; ++i)
{
    for(int j = 0; j < n; ++j)
    {
        int k = i * n + j;
        mHeightMap(i, j) = (float)in[k] *
                            heightScale +
                            heightOffset;
    }
}

filter3x3();
}
```

Note: The specified heightmap dimensions should match the vertex dimensions of the grid.

17.1.4 Filtering

One of the problems of using an 8-bit heightmap is that it means we can only represent 256 discrete height steps. Consequently, the terrain may be rough because there is a large step size from one height level to the next. Moreover, these step sizes are magnified if the terrain is scaled. Of course, the degree of roughness also varies depending on the triangle density of the terrain. The roughness can be desirable in some cases where you would want a rough terrain, but more often than not, you will want to smooth out these rough step sizes.

So what we do is load the heightmap into memory and use floats to represent each height element. Then we apply a filter to the heightmap (which has been loaded into memory), which smoothes out the heightmap, making the difference in heights between adjacent elements less drastic. The filtering algorithm we use is quite basic. A new filtered heightmap pixel is computed by averaging itself along with its eight neighboring pixels (Figure 17.4):

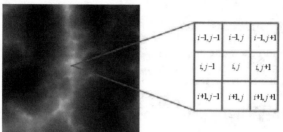

Figure 17.4: The heights of the _ij_th vertex is found by averaging the _ij_th heightmap entry together with its eight neighbor heights.

$$\widetilde{h}_{i,j} = \frac{h_{i-1,j-1} + h_{i-1,j} + h_{i-1,j+1} + h_{i,j-1} + h_{i,j} + h_{i,j+1} + h_{i+1,j-1} + h_{i+1,j} + h_{i+1,j+1}}{9}$$

In all, we take the average of nine pixels in a 3x3 block; hence we term the filter a 3x3 filter (also called a _box filter_).

In the case that we are on the edge of the heightmap, where a pixel does not have eight neighbor pixels, then we just take the average of the pixel itself with as many neighboring pixels as possible.

Here is the implementation of the function that filters the _ij_th pixel in the heightmap:

```
float Heightmap::sampleHeight3x3(int i, int j)
{
    float avg = 0.0f;
    float num = 0.0f;

    for(int m = i-1; m <= i+1; ++m)
    {
        for(int n = j-1; n <= j+1; ++n)
        {
            if( inBounds(m,n) )
            {
                avg += mHeightMap(m,n);
                num += 1.0f;
            }
        }
    }

    return avg / num;
}
```

Recall that `inBounds` returns `true` if the entry is on the heightmap, and `false` otherwise. So if we try to sample an element adjacent to an entry on an edge that is not part of the heightmap, then `inBounds` returns `false`, and we do not include it in our average — it doesn't exist!

To filter the entire heightmap, we just apply `sampleHeight3x3` to each heightmap entry:

```
void Heightmap::filter3x3()
{
    Table<float> temp(mHeightMap.numRows(), mHeightMap.numCols());

    for(int i = 0; i < mHeightMap.numRows(); ++i)
        for(int j = 0; j < mHeightMap.numCols(); ++j)
            temp(i,j) = sampleHeight3x3(i,j);

    mHeightMap = temp;
}
```

17.2 Basic Terrain Demo

Note that generating the grid geometry is already taken care of, as we've been generating triangle grids with `GenTriGrid` (see *d3dUtil.h/.cpp*) since Chapter 8. Also note that in this book, we specify the vertices of the terrain directly in (and centered about) the world space coordinate system.

17.2.1 Building the Terrain Geometry

We already know how to generate a grid with `GenTriGrid`, but in addition, to generate the terrain heights, we must modify the *y*-coordinate of each vertex by setting it to its corresponding heightmap entry. Furthermore, observe that we now use `D3DXCreateMesh` to store our grid instead of managing our own vertex and index buffers. The advantage of this is that we can use the D3DX mesh optimization and utility functions (e.g., `D3DXComputeNormals`). The following code shows how the terrain grid geometry is generated. The key line where we modify each vertex's *y*-coordinate has been bolded.

```
// BasicTerrainDemo data members.
Heightmap mHeightmap;
ID3DXMesh* mTerrainMesh;

// In constructor, load the heightmap.
mHeightmap.loadRAW(129, 129, "heightmap17_129.raw", 0.25f, 0.0f);

void BasicTerrainDemo::buildGridGeometry()
{
    std::vector<D3DXVECTOR3> verts;
    std::vector<DWORD> indices;

    int vertRows = 129;
    int vertCols = 129;
    float dx = 1.0f;
    float dz = 1.0f;

    GenTriGrid(vertRows, vertCols, dx, dz,
```

```
        D3DXVECTOR3(0.0f, 0.0f, 0.0f), verts, indices);

int numVerts = vertRows*vertCols;
int numTris  = (vertRows-1)*(vertCols-1)*2;

// Create the mesh.
D3DVERTEXELEMENT9 elems[MAX_FVF_DECL_SIZE];
UINT numElems = 0;
HR(VertexPNT::Decl->GetDeclaration(elems, &numElems));
HR(D3DXCreateMesh(numTris, numVerts, D3DXMESH_MANAGED, elems,
                  gd3dDevice, &mTerrainMesh));

// Write the vertices.
VertexPNT* v = 0;
HR(mTerrainMesh->LockVertexBuffer(0,(void**)&v));

// width/depth
float w = (vertCols-1) * dx;
float d = (vertRows-1) * dz;
for(int i = 0; i < vertRows; ++i)
{
    for(int j = 0; j < vertCols; ++j)
    {
        DWORD index = i * vertCols + j;
        v[index].pos    = verts[index];
        v[index].pos.y  = mHeightmap(i, j);
        v[index].normal = D3DXVECTOR3(0.0f, 1.0f, 0.0f);
        v[index].tex0.x = (v[index].pos.x + (0.5f*w)) / w;
        v[index].tex0.y = (v[index].pos.z - (0.5f*d)) / -d;
    }
}

HR(mTerrainMesh->UnlockVertexBuffer());


// Write the indices and attribute buffer.
WORD* k = 0;
HR(mTerrainMesh->LockIndexBuffer(0, (void**)&k));
DWORD* attBuffer = 0;
HR(mTerrainMesh->LockAttributeBuffer(0, &attBuffer));

// Compute the indices for each triangle.
for(int i = 0; i < numTris; ++i)
{
    k[i*3+0] = (WORD)indices[i*3+0];
    k[i*3+1] = (WORD)indices[i*3+1];
    k[i*3+2] = (WORD)indices[i*3+2];

    attBuffer[i] = 0; // Always subset 0
}

HR(mTerrainMesh->UnlockIndexBuffer());
HR(mTerrainMesh->UnlockAttributeBuffer());
```

```
// Generate normals and then optimize the mesh.
HR(D3DXComputeNormals(mTerrainMesh, 0));

DWORD* adj = new DWORD[mTerrainMesh->GetNumFaces()*3];
HR(mTerrainMesh->GenerateAdjacency(EPSILON, adj));
HR(mTerrainMesh->OptimizeInplace(D3DXMESHOPT_VERTEXCACHE|
                 D3DXMESHOPT_ATTRSORT, adj, 0, 0, 0));
delete[] adj;
}
```

17.2.2 Lighting and Texturing the Terrain

In the past, we've been using our standard generic lighting models to light objects either in a vertex shader or pixel shader. Well first of all, a terrain is not very specular — it is mostly a diffuse surface. So we can simplify our model by taking the specular lighting calculation out. In addition, there is not much point in using a colored material, as the terrain color comes from the textures. Thus, for lighting, all we really need to do is a simple diffuse and ambient calculation to generate a shading factor in the range [0, 1].

We compute the shade factor in the vertex shader as follows:

```
outVS.shade = saturate(max(0.0f, dot(normalW, gDirToSunW)) + 0.3f);
```

We use a directional light (the sun is the light source), and gDirToSunW is the unit light vector directed toward the sun (it is set as an effect parameter). The normalized vertex normal in world space is normalW. The 0.3f is essentially our ambient light addition used to brighten up the shade. The saturate intrinsic HLSL function simply clamps the result to [0, 1] (the shade factor could go outside this range due to adding the ambient factor 0.3, so we need to clamp it).

Note: If necessary, review the mathematics behind the diffuse lighting calculation from Chapter 10.

You can think of this shade value as a grayscale color which, when multiplied with a color vector, darkens or brightens the color. For example, if the shade factor is 0.25, then multiplying it with a color will reduce the color to one-fourth its intensity; if the shade factor is 1.0, then multiplying it with a color leaves the original color unmodified. So basically, the shade factor is a percent based on the diffuse and ambient lighting calculation (i.e., how much incoming light the surface receives) that specifies how much of a pixel color to keep or discard.

The shading factor is output from the vertex shader, interpolated, and then fed into the pixel shader, where it is multiplied against the texture color to form the final pixel color.

So, what about texturing the terrain? Well, we are already done! Recall the Multi-texturing demo from Chapter 11, where we blended three colored textures via a blend map over a grid. We use the same technique here; the only difference is that our geometry is different: We no longer have a flat grid, but a grid with modified heights to create the hills and valleys of the terrain. Nevertheless, the same texturing technique can be applied without modification. Figure 17.5 summarizes the main idea behind the multi-texturing technique employed, but you should still go back and review the Multi-texturing demo of Chapter 11 for the details.

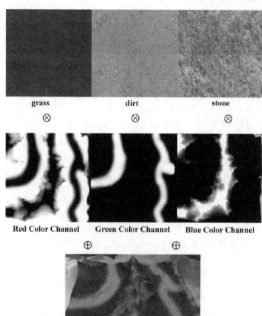

Figure 17.5: Each of the three textures corresponds with a color channel in the blend map. The blend map's color channel for each texture specifies how much the texture contributes to the final image. This is seen clearly when we look at the end result.

17.2.3 The Vertex and Pixel Shaders

The rest of the Basic Terrain demo code is nothing that you have not seen before, so you should be in good shape to study the source code. However, before concluding this section, for completeness we include the vertex and pixel shaders used to render the terrain:

```
uniform extern float4x4 gViewProj;
uniform extern float3 gDirToSunW;
uniform extern texture gTex0;
uniform extern texture gTex1;
uniform extern texture gTex2;
uniform extern texture gBlendMap;

static float gTexScale = 16.0f;
```

```
// [...] Sampler definitions snipped for brevity.

sampler Tex0S = sampler_state{};
sampler Tex1S = sampler_state{};
sampler Tex2S = sampler_state{};
sampler BlendMapS = sampler_state{};
struct OutputVS
{
    float4 posH        : POSITION0;
    float2 tiledTexC   : TEXCOORD0;
    float2 nonTiledTexC : TEXCOORD1;
    float  shade       : TEXCOORD2;
};

// We assume terrain geometry is specified directly in world space.
OutputVS TerrainVS(float3 posW : POSITION0,
                   float3 normalW : NORMAL0,
                   float2 tex0: TEXCOORD0)
{
    // Zero out our output.
    OutputVS outVS = (OutputVS)0;

    // Just compute a grayscale diffuse and ambient lighting
    // term--terrain has no specular reflectance.  The color
    // comes from the texture.
    outVS.shade = saturate(max(0.0f, dot(normalW, gDirToSunW)) + 0.3f);

    // Transform to homogeneous clip space.
    outVS.posH = mul(float4(posW, 1.0f), gViewProj);

    // Pass on texture coordinates to be interpolated in rasterization.
    outVS.tiledTexC    = tex0 * gTexScale; // Scale tex-coords to tile.
    outVS.nonTiledTexC = tex0;             // Blend map not tiled.

    // Done--return the output.
    return outVS;
}


float4 TerrainPS(float2 tiledTexC : TEXCOORD0,
                 float2 nonTiledTexC : TEXCOORD1,
                 float shade : TEXCOORD2) : COLOR
{
    // Layer maps are tiled
    float3 c0 = tex2D(Tex0S, tiledTexC).rgb;
    float3 c1 = tex2D(Tex1S, tiledTexC).rgb;
    float3 c2 = tex2D(Tex2S, tiledTexC).rgb;

    // Blend map is not tiled.
    float3 B = tex2D(BlendMapS, nonTiledTexC).rgb;

    // Find the inverse of all the blend weights so that we can
    // scale the total color to the range [0, 1].
```

```
    float totalInverse = 1.0f / (B.r + B.g + B.b);

    // Scale the colors by each layer by its corresponding weight
    // stored in the blend map.
    c0 *= B.r * totalInverse;
    c1 *= B.g * totalInverse;
    c2 *= B.b * totalInverse;

    // Sum the colors and modulate with the shade to brighten/darken
    // based on lighting.
    float3 final = (c0 + c1 + c2) * shade;

    return float4(final, 1.0f);
}
```

17.3 **Multi-Sub-Grid Terrain**

For reasons that will primarily be made clear in the next chapter, it is useful to break the terrain grid up into a rectangular array of sub-grids. The code to do this is mainly bookkeeping; therefore, we just outline the overall strategy steps, and the details can be examined in the demo program called Terrain demo. (Note that we have moved all the terrain-related code to a `Terrain` class defined and implemented in *Terrain.h/.cpp*.)

1. Initially, create the entire grid (call this the global grid) as we did in the last section, but in system memory.

2. Define the vertex dimensions of the sub-grids and compute the number of sub-grid rows and the number of sub-grid columns.

3. For each sub-grid:

    a. Create a sub-grid mesh.

    b. Copy the portion of vertices that make up this sub-grid from the global grid mesh into the sub-grid mesh (see Figure 17.6).

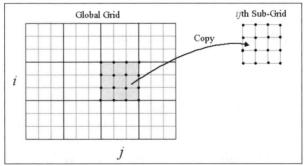

Figure 17.6: Copying a rectangle of vertices from the global mesh to the sub-grid mesh. The portion of vertices on the global grid that form the *ij*th sub-grid have indices contained by the rectangle: $R = \{j \cdot (n-1), i \cdot (m-1), (j+1) \cdot (n-1), (i+1) \cdot (m-1)\}$ where *m* is the number of sub-grid vertex rows and *n* is the number of sub-grid vertex columns, and the rectangle is defined in the usual Win32 way (i.e., $R = \{left, top, right, bottom\}$.

c. Compute the AABB of the sub-grid (this is used in the next chapter).

d. Generate the index buffer and attribute buffer for the sub-grid.

e. Optimize the sub-grid mesh.

4. Release the global grid; to draw the terrain we draw all of the sub-grids.

Remark: It is convenient to stipulate restrictions on the vertex dimensions of the terrain and sub-grids so that the vertex dimensions of the terrain are divisible by the vertex dimensions of the sub-grids. In this book, we require the terrain vertex dimensions to be of the form $(2^m + 1) \times (2^n + 1)$, and we define the vertex dimensions of the sub-grid to be 33×33. Then with this setup, there are $(2^m/32) \times (2^n/32)$ sub-grids. (And, of course, m and n are chosen so that there is at least one sub-grid.) Observe that a power of 2 is always divisible by a power of 2.

Note that sub-grids that are adjacent to each other have intersecting edges; the vertices on these edges need to be duplicated so that each sub-grid has its own copy. In this way, each sub-grid is self-contained.

To generate the indices for a sub-grid, we can actually just use GenTriGrid to generate the vertices and indices for a 33×33 grid. We ignore the vertices here (we extract them from the global grid instead), and just use the returned indices as the indices for the sub-grid. By examining Figure 17.6 it should not be difficult to see why this works. Note that the attribute buffer entries are all zero (i.e., we only use subset zero.)

17.4 **Building a Flexible Camera**

The orbiting camera we have been using has served its purpose well for our demos; however, now that we have a terrain, it would be nice to control the camera in a more game-like fashion.

17.4.1 **View Transformation Recapitulation**

First, let us recapitulate the basic ideas of the camera and coordinate systems; you may also wish to reread §6.4.2. The camera is an object in our universe. As with any other object in the universe, we can make it a frame of reference and describe other objects relative to it; we call the camera frame of reference the *view space* or *camera space*. In view space, the camera is positioned at the origin and looking down the positive z-axis, the x-axis extends out from the right side of the camera, and the y-axis extends upward (see Figure 17.7).

We can pick another point and three axes to form another coordinate system — call it the *world space*. Because the world coordinate system and view coordinate system exist in the same universe, we can describe one

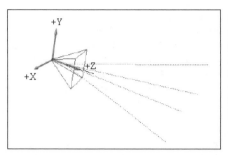

Figure 17.7: The camera coordinate system. Relative to its own coordinate system, the camera sits at the origin looking down the positive z-axis.

relative to the other, and change coordinates relative to one and make them relative to the other. Suppose $\vec{r}$, $\vec{u}$, and $\vec{f}$ describe the axes of the camera space relative to the world space (we often call these vectors the _right vector_, _up vector_, and _look vector_, respectively), and $\vec{p}$ is the position of the origin of the camera space relative to the world space. Then, from Part I of this book, we know the following matrix changes the coordinates of geometry from being relative to camera space to being relative to world space:

$$W = \begin{bmatrix} r_x & r_y & r_z & 0 \\ u_x & u_y & u_z & 0 \\ f_x & f_y & f_z & 0 \\ p_x & p_y & p_z & 1 \end{bmatrix}$$

Then the reverse transformation (i.e., the matrix that changes coordinates of geometry relative to world space and makes them relative to camera space) is just the inverse:

$$V = W^{-1} = \begin{bmatrix} r_x & u_x & f_x & 0 \\ r_y & u_y & f_y & 0 \\ r_x & u_z & f_z & 0 \\ -\vec{p}\cdot\vec{r} & -\vec{p}\cdot\vec{u} & -\vec{p}\cdot\vec{f} & 1 \end{bmatrix} \tag{17.1}$$

We call $V = W^{-1}$ the view matrix (see Figure 17.8).

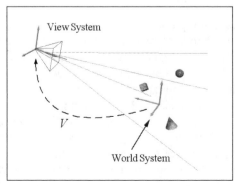

Figure 17.8: The view matrix transforms vertices relative to the world coordinate system and makes them relative to the camera coordinate system. Note that no objects are "physically" moved; we are simply changing the frame of reference relative to which we describe objects.

> **Note:** Section 6.4.2 showed a method for finding the inverse of *W* by realizing *W* is a combination of rotation and translation transforms. You could also use another inverse finding technique and apply it to *W* to obtain *V*, or you could even just use `D3DXMatrixInverse`. However, Equation 17.1 is nice because the problem is already solved — we just have to plug in the numbers.

17.4.2 Camera Functionality

The previous discussion made it clear that to move/rotate the camera, we just need to move/rotate the coordinate system vectors of the camera (described relative to the world space), and then use these updated vectors to rebuild the view matrix using Equation 17.1. For first-person shooter style games, the following camera properties are desirable:

- Property 1: To move the camera along its look vector (running)
- Property 2: To move the camera along its right vector (strafing)
- Property 3: To rotate the camera around its right vector (looking up/down)
- Property 4: To rotate the camera around the world *y*-axis (looking left/right)
- Property 5: No yaw (rotating around the camera's up vector is unnatural for a humanoid character)
- Property 6: No roll (rotating around the camera's look vector is unnatural for a humanoid character)
- Property 7: No moving the camera along its up vector (unnatural for a humanoid character); however, moving the player up/down the world *y*-axis would be acceptable to implement crouching and jumping (although this is better implemented by just making a crouch/jump animation sequence — see Chapter 16 on skinned meshes).

> **Note:** In §17.5 we'll add two more desired properties: that the camera remain planted on the terrain ground, and that the camera always moves tangent to the terrain surface.

Figure 17.9 illustrates the first three properties in action.

Note that we really only need to implement the first four properties. We gain the last three properties by doing nothing. So how do we implement properties 1 through 4? Well, if you have not already figured it out, it turns out to be uncomplicated. Observe Figure 17.9 again, and notice that properties 1 and 2 can be implemented simply by translating the camera along its look and right vectors, respectively. Property 3 can be achieved by simply rotating the camera's look and up vectors around its right vector (and we can rotate vectors around an arbitrary vector with the `D3DXMatrixRotationAxis` function). And finally, to implement property 4, we just rotate all the basis vectors around the world's y-axis (which can be done simply with D3DXMatrixRotationY).

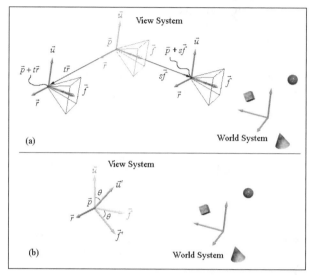

Figure 17.9: (a) To move the camera along its look vector, we compute a vector $s\vec{f}$, where the scalar s determines how far to move along $\vec{f}$, and then we add this vector to the camera position vector $\vec{p}$ to offset the position in the look direction. The idea is analogous to moving the camera along its right vector. (b) To rotate the camera about its right vector by an angle θ, we rotate the camera's up and look vectors about the right vector by the angle θ. Note again that the four camera vectors remain relative to the world system.

17.4.3 **The Camera Class**

To encapsulate our camera-related code, we define and implement a Camera class. Most of the methods are trivial (e.g., simple access methods). See the comments below for an overview of the methods and data members.

```
class Camera
{
public:
    // By default, the camera starts out with its basis vectors
    // aligned with the world space axes, and its origin positioned
    // at the world space origin.
    Camera();

    // Read only accessor functions.
    const D3DXMATRIX& view() const;
    const D3DXMATRIX& proj() const;
    const D3DXMATRIX& viewProj() const;

    const D3DXVECTOR3& right() const;
    const D3DXVECTOR3& up() const;
    const D3DXVECTOR3& look() const;

    // Read/write access to the camera position.
    D3DXVECTOR3& pos();

    // Our implementation of D3DXMatrixLookAtLH
    void lookAt(D3DXVECTOR3& pos,
                D3DXVECTOR3& target,
```

```
                D3DXVECTOR3& up);

        // Perspective projection parameters.
        void setLens(float fov, float aspect, float nearZ, float farZ);

        // Sets the camera speed.
        void setSpeed(float s);

        // Updates the camera's basis vectors and origin, relative to
        // the world space, based on user input.

        void update(float dt);

protected:
        // Constructs the view matrix based on the camera's basis
        // vectors and origin, relative to the world space.
        void buildView();

protected:
        // Save camera-related matrices.
        D3DXMATRIX mView;
        D3DXMATRIX mProj;
        D3DXMATRIX mViewProj;

        // Camera coordinate system relative to world space.
        D3DXVECTOR3 mPosW;
        D3DXVECTOR3 mRightW;
        D3DXVECTOR3 mUpW;
        D3DXVECTOR3 mLookW;

        // Camera speed.
        float mSpeed;
};
```

Remark: Observe that we've included projection-related quantities in the camera class. If you think about it, the perspective projection matrix determines the "lens" of the camera by controlling the field of view, and near and far planes. So it makes sense that a camera class also constructs and contains the projection matrix.

Remark: The camera speed member is important mainly because it will depend on the scale of the application. For example, if you are writing a car racing game, then you probably want to define speed in kilometers per hour. On the other hand, if you are writing a space simulator, you might rather have speed be defined in kilometers per second. So the speed needs to be adjusted such that it makes sense for the scale of your virtual world.

17.4.4 **Updating the Camera**

The real work of the camera class is contained in the update method. This method updates the camera coordinate system relative to the world space based on user input (remember we made our one and only Direct Input object global, so we can access it in the camera class to check input). Its implementation is as follows:

```
void Camera::update(float dt)
{
    // Find the net direction the camera is traveling (since the
    // camera could be running and strafing).
    D3DXVECTOR3 dir(0.0f, 0.0f, 0.0f);

    if( gDInput->keyDown(DIK_W) )
        dir += mLookW;
    if( gDInput->keyDown(DIK_S) )
        dir -= mLookW;
    if( gDInput->keyDown(DIK_D) )
        dir += mRightW;
    if( gDInput->keyDown(DIK_A) )
        dir -= mRightW;

    // Move at mSpeed along net direction.
    D3DXVec3Normalize(&dir, &dir);
    mPosW += dir*mSpeed*dt;

    // Angle to rotate around right vector.
    float pitch  = gDInput->mouseDY() / 150.0f;

    // Angle to rotate around world y-axis.
    float yAngle = gDInput->mouseDX() / 150.0f;

    // Rotate camera's look and up vectors around the
    // camera's right vector.
    D3DXMATRIX R;
    D3DXMatrixRotationAxis(&R, &mRightW, pitch);
    D3DXVec3TransformCoord(&mLookW, &mLookW, &R);
    D3DXVec3TransformCoord(&mUpW, &mUpW, &R);

    // Rotate camera axes about the world's y-axis.
    D3DXMatrixRotationY(&R, yAngle);
    D3DXVec3TransformCoord(&mRightW, &mRightW, &R);
    D3DXVec3TransformCoord(&mUpW, &mUpW, &R);
    D3DXVec3TransformCoord(&mLookW, &mLookW, &R);

    // Rebuild the view matrix to reflect changes.
    buildView();
```

```
        mViewProj = mView * mProj;
    }
```

The implementation is straightforward based on what we discussed at the end of §17.4.2. The final method call, `buildView`, is discussed next.

17.4.5 Building the View Matrix

After we have updated the camera coordinate system (which is described relative to the world space), we need to rebuild the view matrix for this rendering frame. To do this, all we need to do is calculate the matrix in Equation 17.1, and note that we have everything we need — the matrix is completely determined by the vectors describing the camera space relative to the world space. The following implementation builds the view matrix:

```
void Camera::buildView()
{
    // Keep camera's axes orthogonal to each other and
    // of unit length.
    D3DXVec3Normalize(&mLookW, &mLookW);

    D3DXVec3Cross(&mUpW, &mLookW, &mRightW);
    D3DXVec3Normalize(&mUpW, &mUpW);

    D3DXVec3Cross(&mRightW, &mUpW, &mLookW);
    D3DXVec3Normalize(&mRightW, &mRightW);

    // Fill in the view matrix entries.

    float x = -D3DXVec3Dot(&mPosW, &mRightW);
    float y = -D3DXVec3Dot(&mPosW, &mUpW);
    float z = -D3DXVec3Dot(&mPosW, &mLookW);

    mView(0,0) = mRightW.x;
    mView(1,0) = mRightW.y;
    mView(2,0) = mRightW.z;
    mView(3,0) = x;

    mView(0,1) = mUpW.x;
    mView(1,1) = mUpW.y;
    mView(2,1) = mUpW.z;
    mView(3,1) = y;

    mView(0,2) = mLookW.x;
    mView(1,2) = mLookW.y;
    mView(2,2) = mLookW.z;
    mView(3,2) = z;

    mView(0,3) = 0.0f;
    mView(1,3) = 0.0f;
    mView(2,3) = 0.0f;
    mView(3,3) = 1.0f;
}
```

The first few lines deserve some explanation (the rest just builds the matrix shown in Equation 17.1). After several rotation transformations, the right, up, and look vectors can become non-orthonormal to each other due to floating-point errors. Therefore, every time this function is called, we recompute the up and right vectors with respect to the look vector to ensure that they are all mutually orthonormal to each other. To see how this works, we first normalize the look vector. Then we compute a new up vector by normalizing $up = look \times right$. At this point, we know the look and up vectors are of unit length and are orthogonal. The last step is to compute a new right vector that is of unit length and orthogonal to both the look and up vectors; this is done by normalizing the vector $right = up \times look$.

17.4.6 Camera Demo Comments

The project demonstrating our new camera is in the folder called Camera Demo located in the Chapter 17 sample directory, which can be downloaded from both the publisher's and book's websites.

We declare the camera as a global variable in *d3dUtil.h*:

```
class Camera; // Forward declaration.
extern Camera* gCamera;
```

This is useful particularly because we can now get the current view and projection matrix from anywhere in the source code, and do not have to pass references to the view and projection matrix all over the place. Note that for some games that employ multiple cameras, you may want a container of cameras (e.g., a camera stack) instead of just one camera.

We construct a camera and initialize gCamera in WinMain:

```
Camera camera;
gCamera = &camera;
```

One thing to note is that the camera needs to be constructed before the application class, as the application uses the camera. For instance, we set the camera's starting position and speed in the constructor of the application class.

There are a few other differences between the Camera demo and the previous demos. For example, we no longer explicitly build the projection matrix every time the device is reset; we just call setLens:

```
void CameraDemo::onResetDevice()
{
    mGfxStats->onResetDevice();
    mTerrain->onResetDevice();

    float w = (float)md3dPP.BackBufferWidth;
    float h = (float)md3dPP.BackBufferHeight;
    gCamera->setLens(D3DX_PI * 0.25f, w/h, 1.0f, 5000.0f);
}
```

Furthermore, the application class no longer needs to handle the building of the view matrix, as it is all taken care of by the camera class. Lastly, we have also moved user input detection that controls the camera from the application class to the `Camera::update` method. As a result of these changes, the application code is much cleaner since all the camera-related code has been moved to the camera class.

When we are ready to render something and need to set the view/projection matrix as an effect parameter, we just call one of the camera access functions. For example:

```
HR(mFX->SetMatrix(mhViewProj, &gCamera->viewProj()));
```

17.5 **"Walking" on the Terrain**

In this section we introduce methods of adjusting the camera height and movement to simulate that we are walking on the terrain.

17.5.1 **Getting the Terrain Height**

The camera implemented in the last section is useful for flying around your scene, and many first-person shooter games give you such a camera before you spawn into the world. However, once the game starts, gravity should keep the camera fixed to the ground. That is, given the x- and z-coordinates of the camera position, we want to know how to adjust the y-coordinate of the camera so that the camera stands on top of the terrain.

In order to solve this problem, we first define the function $h(x, z)$ to return the height (y-coordinate) of a point on the terrain given the point's x- and z-coordinates. Now, let $\vec{p} = (p_x, p_y, p_z)$ be the current position of the camera. Observe that if we set $p_y = h(p_x, p_z)$, then the camera sits exactly on the terrain. In practice, we actually set $p_y = h(p_x, p_z) + q$, where q is an offset value that slightly elevates the camera so that the camera does not sit exactly on the ground of the terrain. (Presumably, if we are writing a first-person shooter and the players are humans, then the camera should be at or near eye level and sit six or so feet off the ground.)

So the real trick to this problem is how to implement the function $h(x, z)$. (Incidentally, in code we do not call the function h; rather, we call it `getHeight`.) To begin to solve this, our first goal is to figure out in which cell the x- and z-coordinates lie. The following code does this; it tells us the row and column of the cell in which the x- and z-coordinates are located.

```
float Terrain::getHeight(float x, float z)
{
        // Transform from terrain local space to "cell" space.
        float c = (x + 0.5f*mWidth) / mDX;
        float d = (z - 0.5f*mDepth) / -mDZ;
        // Get the row and column we are in.
        int row = (int)floorf(d);
int col = (int)floorf(c);
```

Figure 17.10 explains what this code does. Essentially, we are transforming to a new coordinate system where the origin is at the upper-leftmost terrain vertex, the positive z-axis goes down, and each unit is scaled so that it corresponds to one cell space. In this coordinate system, it is clear by looking at Figure 17.10b that the row and column of the cell is just given by *floor*(z) and *floor*(x), respectively. In the figure example, the point is in row four and column one. (Recall that *floor*(t) evaluates to the greatest integer less than or equal to t.) Observe also that row and col give the indices of the upper-left vertex of the cell.

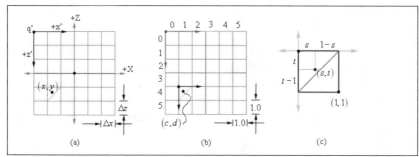

Figure 17.10: (a) The point in the *xz*-plane relative to the terrain coordinate system. We pick a new coordinate where the origin is the upper-left vertex, the positive *z*-axis goes down, and each unit is scaled so that it corresponds to one cell space. (b) The geometry after we have transformed to the new coordinate system. This transformation involves a translation, scaling, and reflection (reflect to make positive *z* go down). As you can see, once in this new coordinate system, finding the row and column of the cell we are in is trivial. Once in this coordinate system, we introduce a third coordinate system, which has its origin at the upper-left vertex of the cell in which the point lies. Transforming the coordinates into this system involves only a simple translation to offset the coordinates. (c) The coordinates after being transformed into the space of the cell. Observe that if *t* < 1.0 − *s*, we are in the "upper" triangle; else we are in the "lower" triangle.

Now that we know the cell we are in, we grab the heights of the four cell vertices from the heightmap:

```
// Grab the heights of the cell we are in.
    // A*--*B
    // | /|
    // |/ |
    // C*--*D
    float A = mHeightmap(row, col);
    float B = mHeightmap(row, col+1);
    float C = mHeightmap(row+1, col);
    float D = mHeightmap(row+1, col+1);
```

At this point we know the cell we are in and we know the heights of the four vertices of that cell. Now we need to find the height (y-coordinate) of the cell at the particular x- and z-coordinates of the camera location. This is a little tricky since the cell can be slanted in a couple of directions (see Figure 17.11).

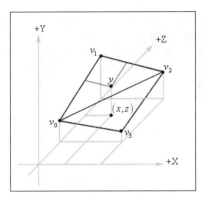

Figure 17.11: The height (y-coordinate) of the quad at the particular x- and z-coordinates of the camera's position.

In order to find the height, we need to know in which triangle of the cell we are located (recall our cells are rendered as two triangles). To find the triangle, we are going to change our coordinates so that the coordinates (c, d) are described relative to the cell coordinate system (see Figure 17.10c). This simple change of coordinates involves only translations and is done as follows:

```
float s = c - (float)col;
float t = d - (float)row;
```

Then, if $t < 1.0 - s$, we are in the "upper" triangle, ΔABC; else we are in the "lower" triangle, ΔDCB.

Now we explain how to find the height if we are in the "upper" triangle. The process is similar for the "lower" triangle, and, of course, the code for both follows shortly. To find the height if we are in the "upper" triangle, we first construct two vectors $\vec{u} = (\Delta x, B - A, 0)$ and $\vec{v} = (0, C - A, \Delta z)$ on the sides of the triangle and originating at the terminal point of the vector $\vec{q} = (q_x, A, q_z)$ as Figure 17.12 shows. Then we linearly interpolate along $\vec{u}$ by s, and we linearly interpolate along $\vec{v}$ by t. Figure 17.12b illustrates these interpolations. The y-coordinate of the vector $\vec{q} + s\vec{u} + t\vec{v}$ gives the height based on the given x- and z-coordinates (recall the geometric interpretation of vector addition to see this).

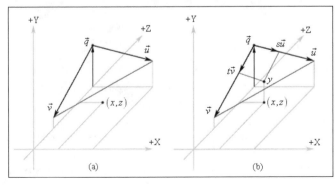

Figure 17.12: (a) Computing two vectors on the upper triangle edges. (b) The height is the y-coordinate of the vector.

Note that since we are only concerned about the interpolated height value we can just interpolate the y-components and ignore the other components. Thus, the height is obtained by the sum $A + s \cdot u_y + t \cdot v_y$.

Thus, the conclusion of the `Terrian::getHeight` code is:

```
// If upper triangle ABC.
if(t < 1.0f - s)
{
        float uy = B - A;
        float vy = C - A;
        return A + s*uy + t*vy;
}
else // lower triangle DCB.
{
        float uy = C - D;
        float vy = B - D;
        return D + (1.0f-s)*uy + (1.0f-t)*vy;
}
}
```

17.5.2 Moving Tangent to the Terrain

As stated earlier, in addition to adjusting the camera height to simulate that we are walking on the terrain, we also want to move tangent to the terrain surface. To see why, consider Figure 17.13.

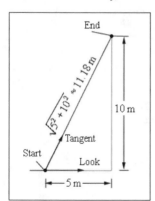

Figure 17.13: Suppose the camera is positioned at "Start" and moving in the "Look" direction. Also suppose that the camera has a speed of 5 m/s (meters per second). In one second, the camera will have traveled 5 m in the "Look" direction, but then the height will be adjusted to "End" so the camera stays on top of the terrain. In reality, then, the camera did not move 5 m in one second; it traveled a total distance of 11.18 m in one second, which is incorrect — the camera unnaturally sped up. To fix this, we always move the camera 5 m/s in a direction tangent to the surface.

We find an approximation for the tangent vector in the direction the camera is moving in the following way: For a fixed frame, let $\vec{p}$ be the camera's current position on the terrain's surface, and based on user input for this frame, we update $\vec{p}$ to $\vec{q}$, as we did in §17.4.4; the updated point $\vec{q}$ may not lie on the terrain surface since there is no such enforcement in the camera update code of §17.4.4. However, using the `Terrain::getHeight` method, we can project $\vec{q}$ onto the surface of the terrain to a new projected point $\vec{q}_p$. Then the vector, *normalize*$(\vec{q}_p - \vec{p})$, is approximately tangent to the terrain in the direction the camera is moving.

Implementing this in code only requires a slight modification to the `Camera::update` method (the new code pertaining to moving along the tangent is in bold):

```
void Camera::update(float dt, Terrain* terrain, float offsetHeight)
{
    // Find the net direction in which the camera is traveling (since
    // the camera could be running and strafing).
    D3DXVECTOR3 dir(0.0f, 0.0f, 0.0f);
    if( gDInput->keyDown(DIK_W) )
        dir += mLookW;
    if( gDInput->keyDown(DIK_S) )
        dir -= mLookW;
    if( gDInput->keyDown(DIK_D) )
        dir += mRightW;
    if( gDInput->keyDown(DIK_A) )
        dir -= mRightW;

    // Move at mSpeed along net direction.
    D3DXVec3Normalize(&dir, &dir);
    D3DXVECTOR3 newPos = mPosW + dir*mSpeed*dt;

    if( terrain != 0)
    {
        // New position might not be on terrain, so project the
        // point onto the terrain.
        newPos.y = terrain->getHeight(newPos.x, newPos.z)
                        + offsetHeight;

        // Now the difference of the new position and old (current)
        // position approximates a tangent vector on the terrain.
        D3DXVECTOR3 tangent = newPos - mPosW;
        D3DXVec3Normalize(&tangent, &tangent);

        // Now move camera along tangent vector.
        mPosW += tangent*mSpeed*dt;

        // After update, there may be errors in the camera
        // height since our tangent is only an approximation.
        // So force camera to correct height, and offset by
        // the specified amount so that camera does not sit
        // exactly on terrain, but instead slightly above it.
        mPosW.y = terrain->getHeight(mPosW.x, mPosW.z)
                        + offsetHeight;
    }
    else
    {
        mPosW = newPos;
    }


    // We rotate at a fixed speed.
    float pitch  = gDInput->mouseDY() / 150.0f;
```

```
    float yAngle = gDInput->mouseDX() / 150.0f;


    // Rotate camera's look and up vectors around the
    // camera's right vector.
    D3DXMATRIX R;
    D3DXMatrixRotationAxis(&R, &mRightW, pitch);
    D3DXVec3TransformCoord(&mLookW, &mLookW, &R);
    D3DXVec3TransformCoord(&mUpW, &mUpW, &R);


    // Rotate camera axes about the world's y-axis.
    D3DXMatrixRotationY(&R, yAngle);
    D3DXVec3TransformCoord(&mRightW, &mRightW, &R);
    D3DXVec3TransformCoord(&mUpW, &mUpW, &R);
    D3DXVec3TransformCoord(&mLookW, &mLookW, &R);


    // Rebuild the view matrix to reflect changes.
    buildView();

    mViewProj = mView * mProj;
}
```

Observe that if you specify null for the `terrain`, then the camera is "free-flying" and not fixed to the terrain (i.e., it works like the camera in §17.4.4). In this way, the `Camera` class supports both a free-flying camera and a "walking" camera.

17.6 **Summary**

- We can model terrains using triangle grids where the height of each vertex is specified in such a way that hills and valleys are simulated.

- A heightmap is a matrix where each element specifies the height of a particular vertex in the terrain grid. There exists an entry in the heightmap for each grid vertex, and the ijth heightmap entry provides the height for the ijth vertex. A heightmap is commonly represented visually as a grayscale map, where black denotes the smallest height, white denotes the largest height, and shades of gray represent in-between heights.

- We describe the position and orientation of our camera in the world coordinate system by maintaining four vectors: right, up, look, and position. We then apply transformations to these vectors to move/rotate the camera in the world space. Once the camera has been updated and repositioned relative to the world, we can build the view matrix, which changes coordinates relative to the world coordinate system so that they are relative to the camera coordinate system.

- We can force the camera to "walk" on top of the terrain by first defining the function $h(x, z)$ to return the height (y-coordinate) of a point on the terrain given the point's x- and z-coordinates. Then, letting $\vec{p} = (p_x, p_y, p_z)$ be the camera's position, if we set the camera's y-coordinate to $p_y = h(p_x, p_z) + q$, where q is an offset value that slightly elevates the camera so that the camera does not sit exactly on the ground of the terrain, then the camera will stand on the terrain.

- When walking on the terrain, we want to move tangent to the terrain surface so that unrealistic speedups and slowdowns do not occur.

17.7 **Exercises**

1. Load the *tiny.x* model into the Basic Terrain demo and have the model walk around on the terrain.

2. Modify the Camera demo (the one where the camera is not fixed to the ground) so that the camera behaves more like an aircraft; that is, the camera can yaw and roll.

3. Modify the Walk Terrain Demo so that the camera jumps when the Spacebar key is pressed and then returns to ground level. The acceleration due to gravity is $\vec{g} = (0, -9.8, 0)\, m/s^2$.

4. Given a "slip" angle θ, design a method that makes the player slide down the terrain if the player walks onto a terrain point whose slope's angle of inclination is greater than θ.

Chapter 18

Terrain Rendering — Part II

In this chapter, we wish to embellish our terrain scene by adding trees, a castle, grass, and fog; in addition, we introduce a simple optimization technique that can be extended and modified to different situations. Figure 18.1 shows a screenshot of the application we build in this chapter.

Figure 18.1:
Screenshot of the
demo we make in
this chapter.

Objectives:

- To become familiar with the idea of culling, which is discarding entire objects at a time from processing.
- To see how trees and a castle can be added to the scene.
- To learn how to draw and animate grass.
- To find out how to simulate fog in the scene to add atmosphere.

18.1 **Sub-Grid Culling and Sorting**

Recall from the last chapter that we partitioned the terrain grid into square sub-grids. At first, this approach may have seemed counterintuitive as it increases the number of draw primitive calls, which have some driver overhead, needed to render the terrain. Nevertheless, by breaking the terrain up into sub-grids, we can take advantage of an optimization technique called frustum culling.

The idea of *frustum culling* is this: For each sub-grid, we construct an AABB (you could use another bounding volume as well). Then, if the AABB of the sub-grid does not intersect the frustum (i.e., no part of the sub-grid's AABB is visible to the frustum), then do not even bother drawing the sub-grid at all (see Figure 18.2). In this way, we can discard an entire sub-grid from processing with *one* frustum/AABB intersection test.

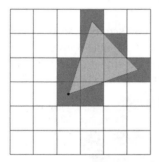

Figure 18.2: Each square represents a sub-grid. The shaded squares correspond with the sub-grids that intersect the frustum, and hence are rendered.

The alternative to frustum culling would be to just throw all the triangles of the terrain at the graphics card and let the graphics card clip the triangles that are not in the frustum. But remember that before the clipping stage, vertices pass through the vertex shader. Thus, we still do vertex processing work on geometry that is outside the frustum and unseen before it is clipped. (Moreover, clipping requires work also.) Thus, by not feeding sub-grids that are not seen into the graphics pipeline, we prevent the GPU from doing a lot of wasteful vertex processing work. Note that the cost of frustum culling is quite cheap to us: a simple frustum/AABB per sub-grid.

It is also important not to micromanage your culling system to the point of diminishing returns. For example, if you look at Figure 18.2, you will notice that some of the geometry in the visible sub-grids is outside the frustum (i.e., the dark shaded regions of Figure 18.2). You might suggest that if we refine the sub-grid sizes (see Figure 18.3), then we will get more accurate culling (because the dark shaded area shrinks) and save further processing. This is true, but the savings are relatively small compared to the large chunks of geometry that we have already culled. Moreover, refining the sub-grid sizes costs us more; specifically, as we make the sub-grids smaller, we increase our draw primitive calls (because there are more sub-grids to draw) and we also have to perform more frustum/AABB intersection tests. Thus, there comes a point where the disadvantages of refinement offset any gain, and it would have been faster to just let the graphics card discard the geometry during clipping. As a general rule, culling should be used to eliminate large chunks of geometry quickly; it is not worthwhile to spend time culling small collections of geometry — the graphics card can handle these.

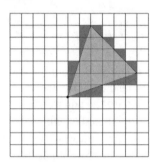

Figure 18.3: Refined sub-grids.

On the other hand, you also do not want to make the sub-grid size too large, because then you lose some of the benefits of frustum culling. A balance must be found. On the author's system, 33×33 and 65×65 size sub-grids seem to work well.

We point out that culling only saves vertex processing work. So if pixel processing is the application bottleneck, then more aggressive culling won't help. Thus, for example, if you are doing some heavy pixel processing, say, due to a lot of overdraw from a particle system, then you may see no improvement from culling.

18.1.1 The SubGrid Structure

We slightly modify the sub-grid structure from the demo applications used in the previous chapter as follows:

```
struct SubGrid
{
    ID3DXMesh* mesh;
    AABB box;

    // For sorting.
    bool operator<(const SubGrid& rhs)const;

    const static int NUM_ROWS  = 33;
    const static int NUM_COLS  = 33;
    const static int NUM_TRIS  = (NUM_ROWS-1)*(NUM_COLS-1)*2;
    const static int NUM_VERTS = NUM_ROWS*NUM_COLS;
};
```

Our new sub-grid structure stores the sub-grid mesh, its AABB, as well as its dimensions (static members since they do not change from sub-grid to sub-grid). In addition, we overload the less than operator so that we have a comparison function in which to sort our sub-grids; this is implemented as follows:

```
bool Terrain::SubGrid::operator<(const SubGrid& rhs) const
{
    D3DXVECTOR3 d1 = box.center() - gCamera->pos();
    D3DXVECTOR3 d2 = rhs.box.center() - gCamera->pos();
    return D3DXVec3LengthSq(&d1) < D3DXVec3LengthSq(&d2);
}
```

This comparison operator allows us to sort our sub-grids from the camera, based on the squared distance, from nearest to farthest. (We use the squared distance so that we do not have to compute the square root; if $d_1^2 < d_2^2$, then $d_1 < d_2$, whenever d_1 and d_2 are nonnegative, and distances are nonnegative.) Once the sub-grids are sorted in this way, we can draw them in front-to-back order to prevent overdraw (see the note at the end of Exercise 3 in §12.5).

Note: The benefits of sorting objects in front-to-back order to reduce overdraw is only seen if your application is fill rate limited (i.e., pixel processing is the bottleneck). If the CPU or vertex processing stage is the bottleneck, then reducing overdraw won't help your frame rates.

18.1.2 Extracting Frustum Planes

In order to determine whether an AABB intersects the frustum, we need the six planes of the frustum. It turns out that the planes can be extracted from the projection matrix, which makes sense since the projection matrix defines the frustum. Because the frustum is the viewing volume of the camera, we place the frustum extraction code in the Camera class:

```
void Camera::buildWorldFrustumPlanes()
{
    // Note: Extract the frustum planes in world space.

    D3DXMATRIX VP = mView * mProj;

    D3DXVECTOR4 col0(VP(0,0), VP(1,0), VP(2,0), VP(3,0));
    D3DXVECTOR4 col1(VP(0,1), VP(1,1), VP(2,1), VP(3,1));
    D3DXVECTOR4 col2(VP(0,2), VP(1,2), VP(2,2), VP(3,2));
    D3DXVECTOR4 col3(VP(0,3), VP(1,3), VP(2,3), VP(3,3));

    // Planes face inward.
    mFrustumPlanes[0] = (D3DXPLANE)(col2);          // near
    mFrustumPlanes[1] = (D3DXPLANE)(col3 - col2); // far
    mFrustumPlanes[2] = (D3DXPLANE)(col3 + col0); // left
```

```
mFrustumPlanes[3] = (D3DXPLANE)(col3 - col0); // right
mFrustumPlanes[4] = (D3DXPLANE)(col3 - col1); // top
mFrustumPlanes[5] = (D3DXPLANE)(col3 + col1); // bottom

for(int i = 0; i < 6; i++)
    D3DXPlaneNormalize(&mFrustumPlanes[i],
                       &mFrustumPlanes[i]);
}
```

So where does this code come from? We will actually omit the mathematical derivation and instead refer the reader to [Lengyel02] or [Möller02].

Notes: In the camera class definition, we add data members to store the six frustum planes:

```
// Frustum planes
    D3DXPLANE mFrustumPlanes[6]; // [0] = near
                                 // [1] = far
                                 // [2] = left
                                 // [3] = right
                                 // [4] = top
                                 // [5] = bottom
```

A plane has two sides, so there are two opposite directions we can pick to have the plane normals face. The frustum planes we extract have normals that face inward (i.e., they point inside the frustum volume). The direction the planes face is important when we implement the frustum/AABB intersection test.

The above code extracts the frustum planes in world space.

The above code is called every frame, as the camera potentially moves about the world each frame.

18.1.3 **Frustum/AABB Intersection Test**

We can test if an AABB is strictly in the negative half-space of a plane as follows: From the AABB vertices, we find new box vertices P and Q which form a diagonal PQ passing through the center of the box that is most aligned with the plane normal (see Figure 18.4). (So note PQ has a direction associated with it also, which always points roughly in the same direction as the plane normal — you can think of it as a vector from P to Q.) Thus, if Q is in the negative half-space of the plane, then P must be also; therefore, the entire box must be also in the negative half-space.

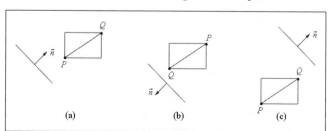

Figure 18.4: The diagonal *PQ* is always the diagonal most directed with the plane normal. Consequently, if *Q* is behind the plane, then *P* must be also.

Now, to test whether an AABB is outside the frustum, we simply test the AABB against each of the six frustum half-spaces. If there exists a frustum plane p_i for $i = \{0, 1, 2, 3, 4, 5\}$ such that the AABB is in the negative half-space of p_i, then we can conclude that the AABB is completely outside the frustum. If such a plane does not exist, then we conclude that the AABB intersects the frustum. The code is as follows:

```
bool Camera::isVisible(const AABB& box)const
{
    // Test assumes frustum planes face inward.

    D3DXVECTOR3 P;
    D3DXVECTOR3 Q;

    //      N  *Q                     *P
    //      | /                      /
    //      |/                      /
    // -----/----- Plane    -----/----- Plane
    //     /                   / |
    //    /                   /  |
    //   *P                 *Q  N
    //
    // PQ forms diagonal most closely aligned with plane normal.
    // For each frustum plane, find the box diagonal (there are
    // four main diagonals that intersect the box center point)
    // that points in the same direction as the normal along each
    // axis (i.e., the diagonal that is most aligned with the
    // plane normal). Then test if the box is in front of the
    // plane or not.
    for(int i = 0; i < 6; ++i)
    {
        // For each coordinate axis x, y, z...
        for(int j = 0; j < 3; ++j)
        {
            // Make PQ point in the same direction as
            // the plane normal on this axis.
            if( mFrustumPlanes[i][j] >= 0.0f )
            {
                P[j] = box.minPt[j];
                Q[j] = box.maxPt[j];
            }
            else
            {
                P[j] = box.maxPt[j];
                Q[j] = box.minPt[j];
            }
        }

        // If box is in negative half-space, it is behind
        // the plane, and thus, completely outside the
        // frustum. Note that because PQ points roughly in
        // the direction of the plane normal, we can deduce
        // that if Q is outside, then P is also outside--thus we
```

```
                    // only need to test Q.

                    // outside
                    if(D3DXPlaneDotCoord(&mFrustumPlanes[i], &Q) < 0.0f)
                            return false;
        }
        // If we got here, then the AABB is not in the negative
        // space of any of the six frustums; therefore, it must
        // intersect the frustum.
        return true;
    }
```

18.1.4 Experiments

As stated, the benefits of frustum culling are best seen when the geometric processing stage is the bottleneck. To informally test out our frustum culling strategy, we render a 1025×1025 vertex terrain grid (2,097,152 triangles) at different sub-grid sizes in release mode at 800×600 resolution with a Geforce 6800 GT. The following table summarizes the results:

Sub-Grid Size	FPS	Number of Sub-Grids for 1025×1025 Vertices
9×9	64	128×128
17×17	220	64×64
33×33	255	32×32
65×65	250	16×16
129×129	210	8×8
257×257	135	4×4
513×513	80	2×2

Note: Although we do not discuss it here, bounding volume hierarchies can be used to speed up culling tests, as well as other types of calculations like collision detection. The general idea is analogous to the binary search algorithm. By organizing space in certain ways (by building a spatial data structure), we can come up with algorithms that enable us to discard entire collections of objects with one test. For example, with our terrain scenario, we would be able to discard a large number of sub-grids with a single test. For a discussion of bounding volume hierarchies and spatial data structures, see [Möller02]. In addition, spatial data structures are often needed to come up with efficient computational geometry problems; thus, computational geometry books, such as [DeBerg00], also provide in-depth explanations of various spatial data structures like binary space partitioning trees, quadtrees, and KD-trees.

18.2 **Trees and Castle**

To add trees to our scene we load four tree models from .X files. We then draw these trees several times per frame in different locations to draw hundreds of trees. Most of this is straightforward, but manually specifying the location of hundreds of trees by hand can be tedious. Therefore, we use random numbers to randomly generate the positions of the trees. In order to prevent trees from being randomly placed on top of mountain peaks or other places where trees would look oddly placed, we stipulate that trees can only be generated in a certain height interval (see the PropsDemo:: buildTrees method in this chapter's Props demo). This interval was found by experimenting and would depend on the scale of the world and heightmap used.

Note: To facilitate random numbers, we define the following functions in *d3dUtil.h/.cpp*:

```
float GetRandomFloat(float a, float b)
{
        if( a >= b ) // bad input
                return a;

        // Get random float in [0, 1] interval.
        float f = (rand()%10001) * 0.0001f;

        return (f*(b-a))+a;
}

void GetRandomVec(D3DXVECTOR3& out)
{
        out.x = GetRandomFloat(-1.0f, 1.0f);
        out.y = GetRandomFloat(-1.0f, 1.0f);
        out.z = GetRandomFloat(-1.0f, 1.0f);

        // Project onto unit sphere.
        D3DXVec3Normalize(&out, &out);
}
```

Note: Randomly generating tree positions can have the side effect of some trees being generated at the same position or so near each other that they intersect, which is incorrect. In a real application, you'd want to take the steps necessary to prevent this (or not use random positions at all but have an artist manually specify the position of each tree in a level editor). However, for a demo application, this flaw is not too distracting.

The castle is also just loaded from an .X file, and its position in the scene was determined by experimenting. In a real application, it is convenient to have "level editors" interactively place objects in the scene.

The trees and castle are objects, and we can compute their AABBs to use for frustum culling. For example, if a tree's AABB is not visible, then we do not bother drawing the tree at all. So, for example, in the sample code for this chapter, you will see code like the following:

```
void PropsDemo::drawObject(Object3D& obj, const D3DXMATRIX& toWorld)
{
    // Transform AABB into the world space.

    AABB box;
    obj.box.xform(toWorld, box);

    // Only draw if AABB is visible.
    if( gCamera->isVisible( box ) )
    {
        // It is visible, so go ahead and draw it
        // [...]
    }
}
```

Note: In the previous chapters, we have generally been doing per-pixel lighting. For this chapter's demos, we switch back to vertex lighting. We do this primarily because the leaves of the trees can induce overdraw, which can potentially eat up a lot of pixel processing power. Moreover, doing per-pixel lighting for the trees does not get us any better results, so it would largely be a waste to do per-pixel lighting unless we were using normal maps.

18.3 **Fog**

To simulate certain types of weather conditions in our games, we need to be able to implement a fog effect (see Figure 18.5). In addition to the obvious purposes of fog, fog provides some fringe benefits. For example, it can mask distant rendering artifacts and prevent popping. *Popping* refers to a situation in which an object that was previously behind the far plane all of a sudden comes in front of the frustum due to camera movement, and thus becomes visible, seeming to "pop" into the scene abruptly. By having a layer of fog in the distance, the popping is hidden. Note that even if your scene takes place on a clear day, you may still wish to include a subtle amount of fog at far distances. Even on clear days, distant objects such as mountains appear hazy and lose contrast as a function of depth, and we can use fog to simulate this atmospheric perspective phenomenon.

Figure 18.5:
Observe the fog in
the background
mountains.

Intuitively, the strategy for implementing fog works as follows: We specify a
fog color, a fog start distance from the camera, and a fog range (i.e., the
range from the start distance until the fog is so thick it completely hides
any objects). Then the color of a vertex is a linear interpolation of its usual
color and the fog color:

$$finalColor = color + s(fogColor - color) \qquad\qquad (18.1)$$

The parameter s varies from vertex to vertex in the range 0 to 1, and is a
function of the distance between the camera position and the vertex. In this
way, we can control the fog thickness with respect to distance from the
camera, which makes sense physically. The parameter s is defined as
follows:

$$s = saturate\left(\frac{dist(\vec{v}, \vec{p}) - fogStart}{fogRange}\right) \qquad\qquad (18.2)$$

where $dist(\vec{v}, \vec{p})$ is the distance between the vertex position $\vec{v}$ and the camera position $\vec{p}$. (Recall that the saturate function clamps the argument to the
range [0, 1].) We now show an example to illustrate how Equations 18.1 and
18.2 work.

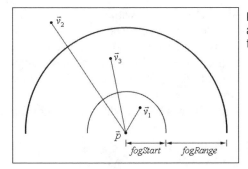

Figure 18.6: Vertices at different distances from the camera.

Figure 18.6 shows the setup. For $\vec{v}_1$, we have $dist(\vec{v}_1, \vec{p}) < fogStart$, which implies the numerator is negative and will be clamped to 0 by the saturate function. Thus, $s = 0$ and the final color for $\vec{v}_1$ is given by:

$$finalColor = color + 0(fogColor - color) = color$$

In other words, the fog does not modify the color of vertices whose distance from the camera is less than *fogStart*. This makes sense based on the name "*fogStart*"; the fog does not start affecting the color of vertices until the distance from the camera is at least that of *fogStart*.

For $\vec{v}_2$, we have $dist(\vec{v}_2, \vec{p}) > fogStart + fogRange$, which implies the argument to saturate is greater than 1, and hence, the saturate function will clamp the argument to 1. Thus, $s = 1$ and the final color for $\vec{v}_2$ is given by:

$$finalColor = color + 1(fogColor - color) = fogColor$$

In other words, the fog is so thick at distances greater than or equal to *fogStart* + *fogRange* that none of the original color shows up — all you see is the fog color.

For $\vec{v}_3$, we have $fogStart < dist(\vec{v}_3, \vec{p}) < fogStart + fogRange$. For the sake of example, let's suppose $dis(\vec{v}_3, \vec{p}) = 110$, $fogStart = 10$, and $fogRange = 200$. Then,

$$s = saturate\left(\frac{110 - 10}{200}\right) = 0.5$$

The final color for $\vec{v}_3$ is then given by:

$$finalColor = color + 0.5(fogColor - color) = (0.5)color + (0.5)fogColor$$

In other words, the final color is an average of the original color and the fog color. As an exercise, consider what the final color would be if you instead supposed $dist(\vec{v}_3, \vec{p}) = 60$ and $dist(\vec{v}_3, \vec{p}) = 160$. Does this agree with how you'd expect fog to behave physically with distance?

In the above discussion we worked strictly with vertices for simplicity in discourse. However, in our implementation, we actually compute the interpolation parameter *s* in the vertex shader, and then do the color interpolation (Equation 18.1) in the pixel shader. The main reason we do the color interpolation in the pixel shader is because we don't know what *color* is until we sample textures, which is done in the pixel shader.

Here is how the terrain effect file has been modified to include fog (see the bolded lines):

```
static float3 gFogColor = {0.5f, 0.5f, 0.5f}; // Grayish
static float  gFogStart = 1.0f;
static float  gFogRange = 200.0f;

OutputVS TerrainVS(
        float3 posW : POSITION0,  // directly in world space.
        float3 normalW : NORMAL0, // directly in world space.
        float2 tex0: TEXCOORD0)
{
        // Zero out our output.
        OutputVS outVS = (OutputVS)0;

        // Just compute a grayscale diffuse and ambient lighting
        // term--terrain has no specular reflectance.  The color
        // comes from the texture.
        outVS.shade = saturate(max(0.0f,
                        dot(normalW, gDirToSunW)) + 0.25f);

        // Transform to homogeneous clip space.
        outVS.posH = mul(float4(posW, 1.0f), gViewProj);

        // Pass on texture coordinates to be interpolated
        // in rasterization.
        outVS.tiledTexC = tex0 * gTexScale; // Scale tex-coord to tile.
        outVS.nonTiledTexC = tex0;          // Blend map not tiled.

        // Compute vertex distance from camera in world
        // space for fog calculation (Equation 18.2).
        float dist = distance(posW, gEyePosW);
        outVS.fogLerpParam = saturate((dist - gFogStart) / gFogRange);

        // Done--return the output.
        return outVS;
}

float4 TerrainPS(float2 tiledTexC : TEXCOORD0,
                 float2 nonTiledTexC : TEXCOORD1,
                 float shade : TEXCOORD2,
                 float fogLerpParam : TEXCOORD3) : COLOR
{
        // Layer maps are tiled
        float3 c0 = tex2D(Tex0S, tiledTexC).rgb;
        float3 c1 = tex2D(Tex1S, tiledTexC).rgb;
```

```
    float3 c2 = tex2D(Tex2S, tiledTexC).rgb;

    // Blend map is not tiled.
    float3 B = tex2D(BlendMapS, nonTiledTexC).rgb;

    // Find the inverse of all the blend weights so that we can
    // scale the total color to the range [0, 1].
    float totalInverse = 1.0f / (B.r + B.g + B.b);

    // Scale the colors by each layer by its corresponding weight
    // stored in the blend map.
    c0 *= B.r * totalInverse;
    c1 *= B.g * totalInverse;
    c2 *= B.b * totalInverse;

    // Sum the colors and modulate with the shade to brighten/darken.
    float3 texColor = (c0 + c1 + c2) * shade;

    // Add fog (Equation 18.1).
    float3 final = lerp(texColor, gFogColor, fogLerpParam);

    return float4(final, 1.0f);
}
```

Note that we will need to modify each effect file to include the fog code, which shades objects that should be fogged. For example, we add the fog code to all of our shaders in the demo application since they all shade outdoor objects that are influenced by the fog. On the other hand, we would not add the fog code to an effect file that is used to shade the inside of a house, as fog generally does not come indoors.

You might observe that this sounds like a maintenance nightmare, as the number of effect files you have could easily double: those with fog and those without. Moreover, what if a new technique comes along that you want to add into your existing effects? Your number of effects could again double to add the new feature. With 3D cards that support branching, you can write generalized shaders with branch statements that only execute the appropriate code; this can help alleviate the problem a bit, as you could just set a flag to have fog skipped. Another solution is to write shader fragments, and link them together on the fly to assemble your shaders; see ID3DXFragment in the SDK (the DirectX SDK also ships with a sample illustrating this interface). The ID3DXFragment interface is beyond the scope of this book, and we do not really need it since we are just writing demos and thus do not have the escalation problem. However, hopefully this discussion illustrates some of the things you need to think about from a software engineering viewpoint when you increase the scope of your project.

18.4 **Grass**

To render grass, we use a billboarding technique with a grass clump texture and alpha mask (see Figure 18.7). By increasing the density of the billboards, we can simulate fields of grass (see Figure 18.8).

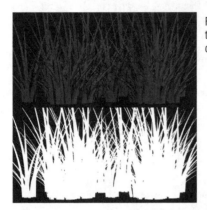

Figure 18.7: A grass texture and its alpha channel.

Figure 18.8: A screenshot of the grass field rendered in the demo.

Note: Sometimes we call a grass billboard a *fin*.

18.4.1 **The Billboard Matrix**

Recall that a billboard is a textured quad that always faces the camera. In order to construct the billboard's world matrix, we need to describe the billboard's local frame relative to the world frame such that the local frame is looking at the camera. (The idea is analogous to how we constructed the look-at matrix for the camera in §6.4.2.) Figure 18.9 shows the setup. Let $\vec{p}$ be the quad center point in world space and let $\vec{e}$ be the camera position in world space. The look vector is given by $\vec{l} = normalize(\vec{e} - \vec{p})$, where *normalize* returns the unit vector of the argument. Once we have the look vector, we can get a right vector $\vec{r}$ by crossing the world space up vector (generally $(0, 1, 0)$) with the look vector $\vec{l}$: $\vec{r} = normalize((0, 1, 0) \times \vec{l})$.

Finally, the up vector is given by $\vec{u} = \vec{l} \times \vec{r}$. Now we have the billboard's local frame basis vectors $\vec{r}$, $\vec{u}$, and $\vec{l}$ relative to the world coordinate system such that the local frame is looking at the camera. (And, of course, the origin of the local billboard frame relative to the world coordinate system is just $\vec{p}$.) Thus the matrix that transforms a billboard from local space to world space is given by:

$$W = \begin{bmatrix} r_x & r_y & r_z & 0 \\ u_x & u_y & u_z & 0 \\ l_x & l_y & l_z & 0 \\ p_x & p_y & p_z & 1 \end{bmatrix}$$

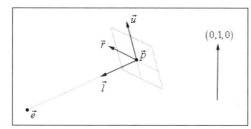

Figure 18.9: The billboard's local coordinate system is constructed relative to the world space such that the billboard always faces the camera.

We do *not* want to render billboards in the following manner:

```
For Each Billboard b
    Set Billboard Matrix for b
    Render b
```

(Note that distinct billboards have their own distinct billboard matrix.) Rendering the billboards one by one in this fashion would be inefficient, as the graphics card performs most efficiently with large primitive batches.

To avoid the above algorithm, we will instead compute the billboard matrix in the vertex shader. Based on the above discussion, if, for each vertex, we store the world space quad position $\vec{p}$ of the billboard to which the vertex belongs, and we know the camera position (we pass it in as an effect parameter), then we can compute the billboard matrix in the vertex shader for each vertex:

```
// Effect parameter
uniform extern float3   gEyePosW;

OutputVS GrassVS(float3 posL : POSITION0,
                 float3 quadPosW : TEXCOORD0,
                 float2 tex0 : TEXCOORD1,
```

```
                float amplitude : TEXCOORD2,
                float4 colorOffset: COLOR0)
{
    // Zero out our output.
    OutputVS outVS = (OutputVS)0;

    // Compute billboard matrix.
    float3 look = normalize(gEyePosW - quadPosW);
    float3 right = normalize(cross(float3(0.0f, 1.0f, 0.0f), look));
    float3 up    = cross(look, right);

    // Build look-at rotation matrix that makes the
    // billboard face the camera.
    float4x4 lookAtMtx;
    lookAtMtx[0] = float4(right, 0.0f);
    lookAtMtx[1] = float4(up, 0.0f);
    lookAtMtx[2] = float4(look, 0.0f);
    lookAtMtx[3] = float4(quadPosW, 1.0f);

    // Transform to world space.
    float4 posW = mul(float4(posL, 1.0f), lookAtMtx);
```

In this way, we can store all of the billboards in a vertex buffer and render them all with one draw primitive call. The world billboard matrix for each vertex is built on the fly in the vertex shader.

18.4.2 Animating the Grass

We would like the grass to animate as if the wind were blowing. A simple hack to simulate this illusion is to simply oscillate the top two vertices of the billboard with a sine function in the vertex shader:

```
// Oscillate the vertices based on their amplitude factor. Note that
// the bottom vertices of the grass fins (i.e., the vertices fixed to
// the ground) have zero amplitude, hence they do not move, which
// is what we want since they are fixed.
float sine = amplitude*sin(amplitude*gTime);

// Oscillate along right vector.
posW.xyz += sine*right;
```

In addition, we oscillate the color slightly, focusing mainly on the green color channel to give the grass various tints of green color. This gives variation and also simulates the grass changing color due to lighting as it is blowing in the wind.

```
// Oscillate the color channels as well for variety (we add this
// color perturbation to the color of the texture to offset it).
outVS.colorOffset.r = colorOffset + 0.1f*sine;
outVS.colorOffset.g = colorOffset + 0.2f*sine;
outVS.colorOffset.b = colorOffset + 0.1f*sine;
```

This output color is not multiplied with the texture color; rather, it is added to the texture color in the pixel shader to slightly offset it for variation.

18.4.3 **The Grass Vertex Structure**

The grass vertex structure we use is defined as follows:

```
struct GrassVertex
{
    GrassVertex()
        :pos(0.0f, 0.0f, 0.0f),
        tex0(0.0f, 0.0f),
        amplitude(0.0f){}
    GrassVertex(const D3DXVECTOR3& v,
        const D3DXVECTOR2& uv, float amp)
        :pos(v), tex0(uv), amplitude(amp){}
    D3DXVECTOR3 pos;
    D3DXVECTOR3 quadPos;
    D3DXVECTOR2 tex0;
    float amplitude; // for wind oscillation.
    D3DCOLOR colorOffset;

    static IDirect3DVertexDeclaration9* Decl;
};
```

- `pos`: The position of the vertex in the *local* space of the billboard the vertex is part of.

- `quadPos`: The center position (i.e., origin) of the billboard the vertex is part of relative to the *world* space.

- `tex0`: The texture coordinates of the vertex for texturing.

- `amplitude`: An amplitude factor for the sine function used in the vertex shader to oscillate the top vertices of the billboard in order to simulate wind. The higher the amplitude, the farther the top vertices move, and vice versa. Set the amplitude to zero if you do not want a vertex to oscillate (e.g., we do not want the bottom vertices that are fixed to the ground to move).

- `colorOffset`: A randomized color value used to offset the texture color. In this way, the different grass billboards have a slightly different green tint.

18.4.4 **Building the Grass Fin**

Now that we see how the grass system works, we'll demonstrate how a grass fin is built.

```
void PropsDemo::buildGrassFin(GrassVertex* v, WORD* k,
    int& indexOffset, D3DXVECTOR3& worldPos, D3DXVECTOR3& scale)
{
    // The pointer v specifies the position in the vertex buffer of
    // where to write the new fin vertices.

    // Only top vertices have non-zero amplitudes.
    // The bottom vertices are fixed to the ground.
    float amp = GetRandomFloat(0.5f, 1.0f);
```

```
v[0] = GrassVertex(D3DXVECTOR3(-1.0f,-0.5f, 0.0f),
                   D3DXVECTOR2(0.0f, 1.0f), 0.0f);
v[1] = GrassVertex(D3DXVECTOR3(-1.0f, 0.5f, 0.0f),
                   D3DXVECTOR2(0.0f, 0.0f), amp);
v[2] = GrassVertex(D3DXVECTOR3( 1.0f, 0.5f, 0.0f),
                   D3DXVECTOR2(1.0f, 0.0f), amp);
v[3] = GrassVertex(D3DXVECTOR3( 1.0f,-0.5f, 0.0f),
                   D3DXVECTOR2(1.0f, 1.0f), 0.0f);

// The pointer k specifies the position in the index buffer of
// where to write the new fin indices.

// Set indices of fin.
k[0] = 0 + indexOffset;
k[1] = 1 + indexOffset;
k[2] = 2 + indexOffset;
k[3] = 0 + indexOffset;
k[4] = 2 + indexOffset;
k[5] = 3 + indexOffset;

// Offset the indices by four to have the indices index into
// the next four elements of the vertex buffer for the next fin.
indexOffset += 4;

// Scale the fins and randomize green color intensity.
for(int i = 0; i < 4; ++i)
{
    v[i].pos.x *= scale.x;
    v[i].pos.y *= scale.y;
    v[i].pos.z *= scale.z;

    // Generate random offset color (mostly green).
    v[i].colorOffset = D3DXCOLOR(
        GetRandomFloat(0.0f, 0.1f),
        GetRandomFloat(0.0f, 0.2f),
        GetRandomFloat(0.0f, 0.1f),
        0.0f);
}

// Add offset so that the bottom of fin touches the ground
// when placed on terrain.  Otherwise, the fin's center point
// will touch the ground and only half of the fin will show.
float heightOver2 = (v[1].pos.y - v[0].pos.y) / 2;
worldPos.y += heightOver2;

// Set world center position for the quad.
v[0].quadPos = worldPos;
v[1].quadPos = worldPos;
v[2].quadPos = worldPos;
v[3].quadPos = worldPos;
}
```

In the demo application, we call this function several times depending on how many grass billboards we want to create, and the world position and scale is randomized for each billboard. Moreover, we employ the same height interval restriction trick we did with the trees, so that we do not have grass blades on the slopes or tops of mountains.

18.4.5 **Grass Effect**

The entire grass effect is as follows:

```
uniform extern float4x4 gViewProj;
uniform extern texture  gTex;
uniform extern float    gTime;
uniform extern float3   gEyePosW;
uniform extern float3   gDirToSunW;

static float3 gFogColor = {0.5f, 0.5f, 0.5f};
static float  gFogStart = 1.0f;
static float  gFogRange = 200.0f;

sampler TexS = sampler_state
{
    Texture = <gTex>;
    MinFilter = LINEAR;
    MagFilter = LINEAR;
    MipFilter = LINEAR;
    AddressU  = WRAP;
    AddressV  = WRAP;
};

struct OutputVS
{
    float4 posH    : POSITION0;
    float2 tex0    : TEXCOORD0;
    float  fogLerpParam : TEXCOORD1;
    float4 colorOffset: COLOR0;
};

OutputVS GrassVS(float3 posL : POSITION0,
                 float3 quadPosW : TEXCOORD0,
                 float2 tex0 : TEXCOORD1,
                 float amplitude : TEXCOORD2,
                 float4 colorOffset : COLOR0)
{
    // Zero out our output.
    OutputVS outVS = (OutputVS)0;

    // Compute billboard matrix.
    float3 look = normalize(gEyePosW - quadPosW);
    float3 right = normalize(cross(float3(0.0f, 1.0f, 0.0f), look));
    float3 up    = cross(look, right);

    // Build look-at rotation matrix that makes the billboard
```

```
            // face the camera.
            float4x4 lookAtMtx;
            lookAtMtx[0] = float4(right, 0.0f);
            lookAtMtx[1] = float4(up, 0.0f);
            lookAtMtx[2] = float4(look, 0.0f);
            lookAtMtx[3] = float4(quadPosW, 1.0f);

            // Transform to world space.
            float4 posW = mul(float4(posL, 1.0f), lookAtMtx);

            // Oscillate the vertices based on their amplitude factor.
            // Note that the bottom vertices of the grass fins (i.e., the
            // vertices fixed to the ground) have zero amplitude, hence
            // they do not move, which is what we want since they are fixed.
            float sine = amplitude*sin(amplitude*gTime);

            // Oscillate along right vector.
            posW.xyz += sine*right;

            // Oscillate the color channels as well for variety (we add this
            // color perturbation to the color of the texture to offset it).
            outVS.colorOffset.r = colorOffset.r + 0.1f*sine;
            outVS.colorOffset.g = colorOffset.g + 0.2f*sine;
            outVS.colorOffset.b = colorOffset.b + 0.1f*sine;

            // Transform to homogeneous clip space.
            outVS.posH = mul(posW, gViewProj);

            // Pass on texture coordinates to be interpolated
            // in rasterization.
            outVS.tex0 = tex0;

            // Compute vertex distance from camera in world space
            // for fog calculation.
            float dist = distance(posW, gEyePosW);
            outVS.fogLerpParam = saturate((dist - gFogStart) / gFogRange);

            // Done--return the output.
            return outVS;
}

float4 GrassPS(float2 tex0 : TEXCOORD0,
               float fogLerpParam : TEXCOORD1,
               float4 colorOffset : COLOR0) : COLOR
{
            // Get the texture color.
            float4 texColor = tex2D(TexS, tex0);

            texColor += colorOffset; // Add in color.

            // Add fog.
            float3 final = lerp(texColor.rgb, gFogColor, fogLerpParam);
```

```
            return float4(final, texColor.a);
}

technique GrassTech
{
        pass P0
        {
                vertexShader = compile vs_2_0 GrassVS();
                pixelShader  = compile ps_2_0 GrassPS();

                // Alpha test to mask out parts of texture from showing up.
                AlphaRef = 200;
                AlphaFunc = GreaterEqual;
                AlphaTestEnable = true;

                // We want to be able to see both sides of grass fins.
                CullMode = None;
        }
}
```

18.5 **Water**

The water we set up in this chapter's demo is very basic: We simply use a transparent water plane colored blue. This is very unconvincing, and, for the time being, serves merely as a placeholder until we learn some new techniques that will allow us to implement better-looking water.

18.6 **Summary**

- Use frustum culling to prevent geometry outside the frustum from being sent to the graphics card. Sort objects in front-to-back order to reduce overdraw.

- Because frustum culling reduces vertex processing, the benefits are seen when vertex processing is the application bottleneck. On the other hand, drawing objects from front to back to reduce overdraw reduces the amount of pixel processing work. Thus, the benefits of this optimization are seen when pixel processing is the application bottleneck.

- Use fog to model various weather effects and atmospheric perspective, to hide distant rendering artifacts, and to hide popping.

- To simulate grass, we render a grass texture with alpha mask to quads that always face the camera (billboards). We model grass blowing in the wind by oscillating only the top two vertices of the grass quad in the vertex shader.

18.7 **Exercises**

1. In this book, the castle mesh is one mesh for simplicity. However, when it was originally modeled, it was modeled in parts; for example, each tower and wall was its own model, and then these models were duplicated, transformed, and merged to form the castle mesh. What might be an advantage of leaving the castle mesh as a collection of sub-meshes?

2. Experiment with the fog by varying the fog start and fog range values. In order to see exactly what is happening, only vary one value at a time.

3. The fog model we described in this chapter is called *linear fog*, since we used a linear function for the parameter *s*. You can use other functions such as an exponential function:

    $$s = saturate\left(\alpha e^{d\rho} + \beta\right)$$

    where d is the distance of the vertex from the camera, and α, β, and ρ are constants you specify to customize the exponential curve to the one you want based on how you want the fog to behave. For this exercise, modify the fog demo code to use an exponential function. Experiment with the constants α, β, and ρ to get an idea of how they can be used to control the fog and get the results you want. (Hint: It might be useful to use a graphing utility to plot the exponential function you make to better see its behavior.)

4. In the demo application we render the trees in an arbitrary order. Modify the program to sort and render the trees in front-to-back order with respect to the camera.

5. In §18.1.3 we explained a way to figure out if an AABB is behind a plane. Can you figure out a way to test whether a bounding sphere is behind a plane? Can you find a frustum/sphere intersection test?

Chapter 19

Particle Systems

In this chapter, we concern ourselves with the task of modeling a collection of particles (usually small) that all behave in a similar yet somewhat random manner; we call such a collection of particles a *particle system*. Particle systems can be utilized to simulate a wide range of phenomena such as fire, rain, smoke, explosions, sprinklers, magic spell effects, and projectiles.

Objectives:

- To learn how to render a special Direct3D primitive called a point sprite, which is efficient for drawing particle systems.
- To find out how we can make our particles move in a physically realistic way using basic physics concepts.
- To design a flexible particle system base class that makes it easy to create new custom particle systems.

19.1 Particles and Point Sprites

A *particle* is a very small object that is usually modeled as a point mathematically. It follows then that a point primitive (D3DPT_POINTLIST of D3DPRIMITIVETYPE) would be a good candidate to display particles. However, point primitives are rasterized as a single pixel. This does not give us much flexibility, as we would like to have particles of various sizes and even map entire textures to these particles. Before Direct3D 8.0, the way to get around the limitations of point primitives was to not use them at all. Instead, programmers would use a *billboard* to display a particle. (Recall that a billboard is a quad whose world matrix orients it so that it always faces the camera.)

Direct3D 8.0 introduced a special point primitive called a *point sprite* that is most applicable to particle systems. Unlike ordinary point primitives, point sprites can have textures mapped to them and can change size. And, unlike billboards, we can describe a point sprite by a single point; this saves

483

memory and processing time because we only have to store and process one vertex rather than the four needed to store a billboard (quad).

19.1.1 **Using Point Sprites**

To enable point sprites, set the D3DRS_POINTSPRITEENABLE render state to true. To disable point sprites, set the D3DRS_POINTSPRITEENABLE render state to false:

```
gd3dDevice->SetRenderState(D3DRS_POINTSPRITEENABLE, true);
gd3dDevice->SetRenderState(D3DRS_POINTSPRITEENABLE, false);
```

Alternatively, point sprites can be enabled in an effect file where we set the render states for a particular pass. For example:

```
technique FireRingTech
{
    pass P0
    {
        vertexShader = compile vs_2_0 FireRingVS();
        pixelShader  = compile ps_2_0 FireRingPS();

        PointSpriteEnable = true;

        ... [Set other states]
    }
}
```

Because we only specify a single vertex per point sprite, the graphics device needs to do some work to build the point sprite from the given vertex. The graphics card builds a point sprite from a vertex by constructing a quad (two triangles) surrounding the given vertex; in addition, texture coordinates are generated at each quad vertex in such a way that a texture is mapped across the entire point sprite (quad). By enabling point sprites, we let the graphics device know that point primitives should be treated as point sprites so that this additional work is done.

When we create the vertex buffer to store our vertex points, we should specify the D3DUSAGE_POINTS usage flag to let Direct3D know that this vertex buffer is being used for point sprites. For example:

```
HR(gd3dDevice->CreateVertexBuffer(VB_SIZE*sizeof(Particle),
    D3DUSAGE_DYNAMIC|D3DUSAGE_WRITEONLY|D3DUSAGE_POINTS,
    0, D3DPOOL_DEFAULT, &mVB, 0));
```

Lastly, because we are using point primitives, we need to remember to change our primitive type when we call DrawPrimitive:

```
HR(gd3dDevice->DrawPrimitive(D3DPT_POINTLIST, 0, VB_SIZE));
```

19.1.2 **Particle Motion**

We would like our particles to move in a physically realistic way. For simplicity, in this book we restrict ourselves to a constant net acceleration; for example, acceleration due to gravity. (We can also make loose approximations by making acceleration due to other forces constant as well, such as wind.) In addition, we do not do any collision detection with our particles.

It turns out (see the note at the end of this section) that the position of a particle undergoing constant acceleration is given by:

$$\vec{p}(t) = \frac{1}{2}\vec{a}t^2 + \vec{v}_0 t + \vec{p}_0 \tag{19.1}$$

where $\vec{a}$ is the constant acceleration, t denotes time, $\vec{v}_0$ is the initial velocity of the particle at time $t = 0$, and $\vec{p}_0$ is the initial position of the particle at time $t = 0$. What this equation says is that given the initial position of a particle (i.e., where it starts) and given the initial velocity of a particle (i.e., how fast and in which direction it is initially going), then we can determine its path at any instant in time $t \geq 0$, assuming the acceleration is constant. (This is reasonable because if we know where we are starting, how fast and in which direction we are going initially, and how we are accelerating for all time, then we ought to be able to figure out the path we followed.)

Let's look at an example. Suppose you have a mini-cannon sitting at the origin of a coordinate system and aimed at a 30° angle measured from the x-axis (see Figure 19.1). So in this coordinate system, $\vec{p}_0 = (0, 0, 0)$ (i.e., the initial position of a cannonball is at the origin), and assume that acceleration is only due to gravity: $\vec{a} = (0, -9.8, 0)\,m/s^2$ (acceleration due to gravity is 9.8 meters per second squared). In addition, suppose that from previous tests, we have determined that at the instant the cannon fires, the cannonball has an initial speed of 50 meters per second. Thus, the initial velocity is $\vec{v}_0 = 50\,m/s\,(\cos 30°, \sin 30°, 0) \approx (43.3, 25.0, 0)\,m/s$ (remember that velocity is speed and direction, so we multiply the speed 50 m/s by the direction unit vector $(\cos 30°, \sin 30°, 0)$). Now, from Equation 19.1, the trajectory of the cannonball is given by:

$$\vec{p}(t) = \frac{1}{2}t^2(0, -9.8, 0)\,m/s^2 + t(43.3, 25.0, 0)$$

If we plot this on the xy-plane (the z-coordinate is always zero), we get Figure 19.1, which is what we'd expect with gravity.

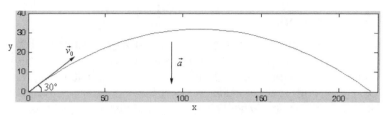

Figure 19.1: The path the particle follows in the *xy*-plane over time (the time dimension is not shown), given the initial position and velocity, and undergoing constant acceleration due to gravity.

Note: Where did Equation 19.1 come from? A little calculus gives us the answer. Recall from physics that velocity and acceleration are defined, respectively, by:

$$\vec{v}(t) = \frac{d\vec{p}(t)}{dt} \quad \text{and} \quad \vec{a}(t) = \frac{d\vec{v}(t)}{dt}$$

In our case, acceleration is constant, so it does not vary with time:

$$\frac{d}{dt}\vec{v}(t) = \vec{a} = \text{constant}$$

Recall that the antiderivative of a function *f* is any function *F* such that the derivative of *F* is *f*; that is, $F' = f$. Thus, from the definitions of velocity and acceleration, it is evident that the velocity function is the antiderivative of the acceleration function, and the position function is the antiderivative of the velocity function. That is,

$$\vec{v}(t) = \int \vec{a} \, dt \quad \text{and} \quad \vec{p}(t) = \int \vec{v}(t)dt$$

We find the velocity function first. Integrating the constant $\vec{a}$ gives:

$$\vec{v}(t) = \int \vec{a} \, dt = \vec{a}t + \vec{c}$$

But what is $\vec{c}$? To find it, we must use our initial velocity, which we know at time $t = 0$:

$$\vec{v}(0) = \vec{v}_0 = \vec{a}(0) + \vec{c} = \vec{c}$$

So the velocity function is $\vec{v}(t) = \vec{a}t + \vec{v}_0$.
    To find the position function, we integrate the just found velocity function:

$$\vec{p}(t) = \int \vec{v}(t)dt = \int \vec{a}t + \vec{v}_0 dt = \frac{1}{2}\vec{a}t^2 + \vec{v}_0 t + \vec{k}$$

To find $\vec{k}$, we use our initial position, which we know at time $t = 0$:

$$\vec{p}(0) = \vec{p}_0 = \frac{1}{2}\vec{a}(0)^2 + \vec{v}_0(0) + \vec{k} = \vec{k}$$

So the position function is $\vec{p}(t) = \frac{1}{2}\vec{a}t^2 + \vec{v}_0 t + \vec{p}_0$, which is what we wanted to show.

19.1.3 Randomness

There is a sort of randomness to the particles of a system. For example, if we are modeling raindrops, we do not want all the raindrops to fall in exactly the same way; we want them to fall in a similar way but not exactly the same way. To facilitate this randomness functionality required for particle systems, we use the same GetRandomFloat and GetRandomVec functions we implemented in *d3dUtil.h/.cpp* in Chapter 18.

19.1.4 Structure Format

We use the following vertex structure for our particles:

```
struct Particle
{
        D3DXVECTOR3 initialPos;
        D3DXVECTOR3 initialVelocity;
        float       initialSize; // In pixels.
        float       initialTime;
        float       lifeTime;
        float       mass;
        D3DCOLOR    initialColor;

        static IDirect3DVertexDeclaration9* Decl;
};
```

- initialPos: The initial position of the particle used by Equation 19.1.
- initialVelocity: The initial velocity of the particle used by Equation 19.1.
- initialSize: The initial size of the particle in pixels. In the vertex shader, we can adjust this size. For example, we may wish to expand smoke particles over time. Also, we will want to scale the particle sizes with respect to distance from the camera.
- initialTime: Depending on the system, particles can be continuously created and destroyed over time. This value is the time stamp when the particle was created relative to the start time the particle system was created.
- lifeTime: How long the particle can live before it dies. Using this, along with initialTime, we can do things like fade a particle's alpha value from one to zero over its lifetime so that the particle gradually fades.

- `mass`: The mass of the particle. This isn't really used in a physical sense, but rather as just another parameter that we can use to customize our particle system inside the vertex shader. For example, suppose we wish to oscillate particles over time. We do not want each particle to oscillate in exactly the same way since there would be no randomness. So what we could do is generate a random mass attribute for each particle and use it as an amplification and frequency factor inside the vertex shader to give the oscillations some variety.

- `initialColor`: The initial particle color. We can alter this color in the vertex shader. For example, we may wish to change the color over time.

In general, the attributes for each particle will be randomly generated in some range. In this way, all the particles will behave slightly differently but in the same general motion, which is what we want.

Note that we do not need to input texture coordinates into the vertex shader. Direct3D automatically computes the texture coordinates for point sprites and fills them into our output vertex structure. For example, if our output vertex structure is:

```
struct OutputVS
{
      float4 posH  : POSITION0;
      float4 color : COLOR0;
      float2 tex0  : TEXCOORD0;    // D3D fills in for point sprites.
      float size   : PSIZE;        // In pixels.
};
```

then we do not touch `tex0` in the vertex shader — the output texture coordinates for `tex0` will be automatically computed and filled in.

Note: `PSIZE` is a new semantic type. It is used to specify the point sprite size, in pixels, so that Direct3D knows with which dimensions to calculate the point sprite. The vertex shader outputs the point size in this register.

19.1.5 Render States

Particle systems are usually rendered with some form of blending. For effects like fire, magic spells, and futuristic bolt guns, we want the color intensity to brighten at the location of the particles. For this effect, additive blending works well:

```
AlphaBlendEnable = true;
SrcBlend    = One;
DestBlend   = One;
```

Which gives:

$$OutputPixel = SourcePixel \otimes SourceBlendFactor + DestPixel \otimes DestBlendFactor$$

$$OutputPixel = SourcePixel \otimes (1,1,1,1) + DestPixel \otimes (1,1,1,1)$$

$$OutputPixel = SourcePixel + DestPixel$$

That is, we just add the source and destination colors together. Additive blending also has the nice effect of brightening up areas proportional to the particle concentration there (due to additive accumulation of the colors); thus, areas where the concentration is high appear extra bright, which is usually what we want (see Figure 19.2).

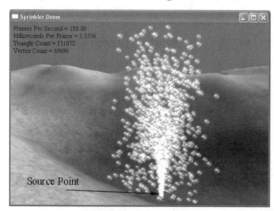

Figure 19.2: With additive blending, the intensity is greater near the source point where the particles are more compact (_more_ particles overlapping and being added together). As the particles spread out, the intensity weakens (_less_ particles overlapping and being added together).

For things like smoke, additive blending does not work because adding the colors of a bunch of overlapping smoke particles would eventually brighten up the smoke so that it is no longer dark. What we really want is to just make the smoke particles semi-transparent and use alpha blending transparency (see Figure 19.3):

Figure 19.3: Transparency alpha blending used to model puffs of smoke.

```
AlphaBlendEnable = true;
SrcBlend      = SrcAlpha;
DestBlend     = InvSrcAlpha;
```

At this point, you may recall that in Chapter 12, we advised drawing blending objects last and drawing them in back-to-front order. We break this rule slightly with particle systems. First, note that we still draw non-blended objects first and blended objects last. In addition, we should still draw particle systems in back-to-front order. Where we break the sorting rule is among the individual particles of a given system. Specifically, we do not sort the particles of a system relative to each other. Note that for additive blending this is not a problem because the colors just add, so the order does not matter. With transparency blending, this can cause some problems because you could imagine situations where the particles blend in the wrong order; however, due to the randomness of the particle system, it may be hard to notice. In the smoke system shown in Figure 19.3, the incorrect order was most evident when new particles were being added at the source point. By hiding the source point under the terrain, most of the visual artifacts due to incorrect draw order went away.

Note: It is also possible to implement a smoke particle system without using transparency blending. You can use the D3DBLENDOP_ REVSUBTRACT blend operation (§12.1), which subtracts color from the destination pixels, therefore making them darker. When a puffy smoke texture is used, the destination pixels appear darkened due to smoke. Moreover, the amount of color subtraction is proportional to the particle concentration there (due to accumulated subtraction). Consequently, the denser the smoke particles are, the thicker the smoke looks, which is a desired consequence. The advantage of using D3DBLENDOP_REVSUBTRACT instead of transparency blending is that you do not need to worry about the draw order.

Finally, for rendering particles, we disable depth buffer writes. This has the effect of disabling the depth test between particles. For additive blending, particles do not obscure each other; instead, their colors accumulate. And transparent particles are see-through, so they do not obscure the objects behind them. (Remember we still draw particle systems in back-to-front order; otherwise, it would be possible for two distinct particle systems to overlap at different depths and to be drawn in the wrong order.) Thus, we do not need to do depth tests between particles. Note, however, that we still keep the depth test on, because we still do depth tests between particles and *other* objects *not* in a particle system.

To summarize this section, one of the particle systems we make uses the following render states in total:

```
technique FireRingTech
{
    pass P0
    {
        vertexShader = compile vs_2_0 FireRingVS();
        pixelShader = compile ps_2_0 FireRingPS();

        PointSpriteEnable = true;
        AlphaBlendEnable = true;
        SrcBlend = One;
        DestBlend = One;

        ZWriteEnable = false;
    }
}
```

19.2 Particle System Framework

The goal of our particle system framework is to make it easy to create new particle systems. We do this by creating an abstract class PSystem, which handles the generic work required by all particle systems. Then, to create a new particle system, we merely derive a new class from this abstract class, and specify how new particles are created for this system. In addition, each particle system has its own effect file, which does work specific to the particle system based on the input vertex data.

The PSystem class is defined as follows:

```
class PSystem
{
public:
    PSystem(
        const std::string& fxName,
        const std::string& techName,
        const std::string& texName,
        const D3DXVECTOR3& accel,
        const AABB& box,
        int maxNumParticles,
        float timePerParticle);

    virtual ~PSystem();

    // Access methods
    float getTime();
    void  setTime(float t);
    const AABB& getAABB()const;

    void setWorldMtx(const D3DXMATRIX& world);
    void addParticle();
```

```
        virtual void onLostDevice();
        virtual void onResetDevice();

        virtual void initParticle(Particle& out) = 0;
        virtual void update(float dt);
        virtual void draw();

protected:

        ID3DXEffect* mFX;
        D3DXHANDLE mhTech;
        D3DXHANDLE mhWVP;
        D3DXHANDLE mhEyePosL;
        D3DXHANDLE mhTex;
        D3DXHANDLE mhTime;
        D3DXHANDLE mhAccel;
        D3DXHANDLE mhViewportHeight;

        IDirect3DTexture9* mTex;
        IDirect3DVertexBuffer9* mVB;
        D3DXMATRIX mWorld;
        D3DXMATRIX mInvWorld;
        float mTime;
        D3DXVECTOR3 mAccel;
        AABB mBox;
        int mMaxNumParticles;
        float mTimePerParticle;

        std::vector<Particle> mParticles;
        std::vector<Particle*> mAliveParticles;
        std::vector<Particle*> mDeadParticles;
};
```

19.2.1 Selected PSystem Data Members

The key data members of PSystem are as follows:

■ mTex: The texture to be mapped to each particle of this system.

■ mVB: The vertex buffer to store the particles (points). We use a dynamic vertex buffer since particles typically need to be created and destroyed every frame.

■ mWorld: The world matrix that transforms the particles from local space to world space.

■ mInvWorld: The inverse of the world matrix. This transforms geometry from world space to the local space of the particle system. We use this to transform the camera position from world space to the local space of the particle system. We do this because we wish to compute the distance between a particle and the camera so that we can scale the size of the particle as a function of distance. It is more efficient to transform the camera position to the local space of the particle system than it is to transform every particle to the world space.

- ■ mTime: A global time value, which keeps track of how long in seconds the particle system has been running. You can think of this as the age of the particle system.

- ■ mAccel: The constant acceleration vector used in Equation 19.1.

- ■ mBox: AABB used for culling. This is not always easy to determine, especially if the particles spread out like in an explosion or from a gun. In these cases, we can just set an infinitely big AABB so that the system is always rendered. However, for localized particle systems, this should be determined so the system can be culled if it's not visible.

- ■ mMaxNumParticles: The maximum number of particles the system can contain. We set the vertex buffer to be able to store this many particles.

- ■ mTimePerParticle: This is the inverse of the particle emit rate (particles per second). That is, it is the time that should pass before the system emits another particle. For example, if you want the system to emit a particle once every 1/100th second, then specify 0.01 for this value. Note that some particle systems do not emit particles automatically. For example, the gun particle system only emits particles when the "fire" key is pressed. For such particle systems, specify a negative value to indicate to the particle system class that the particle system does not emit particles automatically.

- ■ mParticles: A list of every particle in the system. If a particle dies, it is not removed; rather, it is just not drawn and marked dead, or it is recreated and recycled. In this way, we avoid using dynamic memory at run time.

- ■ mAliveParticles: A list that stores pointers to alive particles — these are the particles we are to render this frame. This list is rebuilt every frame.

- ■ mDeadParticles: A list that stores pointers to dead particles. In this way, if we wish to create a new particle at run time, we do not need to do a search for a dead particle in mParticles; we just pop the last element in this list and reinitialize it so that it is no longer dead. This list is rebuilt every frame.

Note: The bottleneck of particle systems is not usually vertex processing but pixel processing. Because the particles of a particle system may be fairly concentrated in a region on the screen, there is potentially a lot of overdraw, and this can significantly degrade performance.

Note   The particle system class also includes effect-related members and, moreover, as you will see, the constructor creates the effect interface from the filename. Although this works for our demos, there is a problem with this: Specifically, if you instantiate several instances of the same particle system, then the effect interface (and also texture, because the texture is created in the constructor as well) is duplicated, since it will be created for each instance. In a real application, you would want to implement some sort of manager class that would prevent duplicated items from being created. For instance, when you want to create an effect, you would query the manager to see if it already exists. If it does, a pointer to it would be returned. If it does not exist, then the manager would create it and return a pointer to it. A similar idea holds for textures and meshes.

19.2.2 Selected PSystem Methods

The key methods of PSystem are as follows:

- PSystem/~PSystem: The constructor primarily does memory allocation work (e.g., allocates the effect and texture). The destructor frees any memory the particle system allocated. One thing worth mentioning is that the constructor allocates enough memory to store the maximum number of particles. In this way, no memory allocation is needed at run time. Also, the particles all start out dead (i.e., −1 lifetime), and will be emitted either when addParticle is explicitly called or automatically in the update function based on the specified mTimePerParticle member (the update function is covered shortly). If you do not want all particles to start out dead, then you can initialize some of them in the derived particle system class's constructor.

```
// Allocate memory for maximum number of particles.
mParticles.resize(mMaxNumParticles);
mAliveParticles.reserve(mMaxNumParticles);
mDeadParticles.reserve(mMaxNumParticles);

// They start off all dead.
for(int i = 0; i < mMaxNumParticles; ++i)
{
    // Since we are accessing the elements of mParticles here,
    // we had to use 'resize'.  The vector::reserve method allocates
    // memory but does not create objects, and therefore, it is
    // illegal to access the elements.
    mParticles[i].lifeTime = -1.0f;
    mParticles[i].initialTime = 0.0f;
}
```

- setTime: This method simply sets mTime:

```
void PSystem::setTime(float t)
{
    mTime = t;
}
```

For some particle systems, where all the particles are created in the beginning at $t = 0$, this is useful if you want to "skip" the particle system animation sequence to some arbitrary time. For instance, you may wish to start playing the particle system in the middle rather than at the beginning ($t = 0$), or you may wish to reset a particle system back to $t = 0$ after a while if you want the particle system to loop. However, this skipping does not work (at least without modification) for systems where particles are created (or recycled) throughout the particle system's lifetime. This is the case because when we just jump the time from time t_0 to some later time t_1, we never create the particles that should have been created during the duration from t_0 to t_1.

- setWorldMtx: This sets the particle system's world matrix. Observe that it also computes the inverse at the same time:

```
void PSystem::setWorldMtx(const D3DXMATRIX& world)
{
    mWorld = world;

    // Compute the change of coordinates matrix that changes
    // coordinates relative to world space so that they are
    // relative to the particle system's local space.
    D3DXMatrixInverse(&mInvWorld, 0, &mWorld);
}
```

- addParticle: This method adds a particle to the system. Note that it does not allocate memory, but rather it finds a dead particle and reinitializes it. Remember that the mDeadParticles list is rebuilt every frame to store pointers to the dead particles in our system. This function is useful for when particles should only be created at certain times. For example, in the book demos, we use it to add particle "bullets" to a gun particle system when the "fire" key is pressed.

```
void PSystem::addParticle()
{
    // If there are no dead particles, then we are maxed out.
    if(mDeadParticles.size() > 0)
    {
        // Reinitialize a particle.
        Particle* p = mDeadParticles.back();
        initParticle(*p);

        // No longer dead.
        mDeadParticles.pop_back();
        mAliveParticles.push_back(p);
    }
}
```

Note that any dead particle will do, but here we will take the last one. Removing an element from the *end* of a std::vector is efficient since the elements do not need to be shifted (as they would when removing a random element such that order is preserved among the elements). Also, when a particle is no longer dead, then it becomes alive, so we add it to the alive list.

- onLostDevice: This method is called before the device is reset. In particular, we destroy the dynamic vertex buffer, which exists in the default memory pool. (Remember, default memory pool resources need to be deleted before the device is reset, and dynamic vertex buffers must be placed in the default memory pool.)

```
void PSystem::onLostDevice()
{
    HR(mFX->OnLostDevice());
    // Default pool resources need to be freed before reset.
    ReleaseCOM(mVB);
}
```

■ `onResetDevice`: This method is called after the device is reset. In particular, we recreate the dynamic vertex buffer.

```
void PSystem::onResetDevice()
{
    HR(mFX->OnResetDevice());
    // Default pool resources need to be recreated after reset.
    if(mVB == 0)
    {
        HR(gd3dDevice->CreateVertexBuffer(
            mMaxNumParticles*sizeof(Particle),
            D3DUSAGE_DYNAMIC|D3DUSAGE_WRITEONLY|D3DUSAGE_POINTS,
            0, D3DPOOL_DEFAULT, &mVB, 0));
    }
}
```

■ `initParticle`: Pure virtual function derived classes must override and specify how particles of that particular system should be initialized.

■ `update`: This method increments the time based on how much time has passed between this rendering frame and the previous rendering frame. It is a virtual function and can be overridden if the derived particle system requires more. In addition, it iterates over each particle and determines whether or not it is dead and adds it to the appropriate list. Lastly, particles are emitted. Note that because particles continue to be born and die whether or not the particle system is visible (i.e., in the frustum), this update code must always be called (i.e., you cannot "frustum cull" the particle system update code).

```
void PSystem::update(float dt)
{
    mTime += dt;

    // Rebuild the dead and alive list. Note that resize(0) does
    // not deallocate memory (i.e., the capacity of the vector does
    // not change).
    mDeadParticles.resize(0);
    mAliveParticles.resize(0);

    // For each particle.
    for(int i = 0; i < mMaxNumParticles; ++i)
    {
        // Is the particle dead?
```

```
                    if( (mTime - mParticles[i].initialTime) >
                            mParticles[i].lifeTime)
                    {
                        mDeadParticles.push_back(&mParticles[i]);
                    }
                    else
                    {
                        mAliveParticles.push_back(&mParticles[i]);
                    }
        }


        // A negative or zero mTimePerParticle value denotes
        // not to emit any particles.
        if( mTimePerParticle > 0.0f )
        {
            // Emit particles.
            static float timeAccum = 0.0f;
            timeAccum += dt;
            while( timeAccum >= mTimePerParticle )
            {
                addParticle();
                timeAccum -= mTimePerParticle;
            }
        }
    }
}
```

- draw: This method draws the particle system. It is a virtual function and can be overridden if necessary. The annotated code is given as follows:

```
void PSystem::draw()
{
        // Get camera position relative to world space system and make it
        // relative to the particle system's local system.
        D3DXVECTOR3 eyePosW = gCamera->pos();
        D3DXVECTOR3 eyePosL;
        D3DXVec3TransformCoord(&eyePosL, &eyePosW, &mInvWorld);

        // Set FX parameters.
        HR(mFX->SetValue(mhEyePosL, &eyePosL, sizeof(D3DXVECTOR3)));
        HR(mFX->SetFloat(mhTime, mTime));
        HR(mFX->SetMatrix(mhWVP, &(mWorld*gCamera->viewProj())));

        // Point sprite sizes are given in pixels. So if the
        // viewport size is changed, then more or less pixels
        // become available, which alters the perceived size of
        // the particles.  For example, if the viewport is 32x32,
        // then a 32x32 sprite covers the entire viewport! But if
        // the viewport is 1024x1024, then a 32x32 sprite only
        // covers a small portion of the viewport.  Thus, we scale
        // the particle's size by the viewport height to keep them
        // in proportion to the viewport dimensions.
        HWND hwnd = gd3dApp->getMainWnd();
        RECT clientRect;
```

```
GetClientRect(hwnd, &clientRect);
HR(mFX->SetInt(mhViewportHeight, clientRect.bottom));

UINT numPasses = 0;
HR(mFX->Begin(&numPasses, 0));
HR(mFX->BeginPass(0));


HR(gd3dDevice->SetStreamSource(0, mVB, 0, sizeof(Particle)));
HR(gd3dDevice->SetVertexDeclaration(Particle::Decl));

AABB boxWorld;
mBox.xform(mWorld, boxWorld);
if( gCamera->isVisible( boxWorld ) )
{
      // Initial lock of VB for writing.
      Particle* p = 0;
      HR(mVB->Lock(0, 0, (void**)&p, D3DLOCK_DISCARD));
      int vbIndex = 0;

      // For each living particle.
      for(UINT i = 0; i < mAliveParticles.size(); ++i)
      {
            // Copy particle to VB
            p[vbIndex] = *mAliveParticles[i];
            ++vbIndex;
      }
      HR(mVB->Unlock());

      // Render however many particles we copied over.
      if(vbIndex > 0)
      {
            HR(gd3dDevice->DrawPrimitive(
                  D3DPT_POINTLIST, 0, vbIndex));
      }
}

HR(mFX->EndPass());
HR(mFX->End());
}
```

Note: Observe how the viewport height is passed in as an effect parameter in order to scale the size of a particle (point sprite) in proportion to the viewport height. We will see exactly how this is done in the vertex shaders of the particle systems we make in the subsequent sections. In the above code, note how we make the assumption that the client rectangle equals the viewport dimensions. This is true in our framework; whenever the client rectangle is resized, we scale the back buffer dimensions to match (and Direct3D defaults the viewport to the render target [back buffer] dimensions).

19.3 **Example 1: Fire Ring**

For our first example, we render a ring of fire (see Figure 19.4). We map the texture shown in Figure 19.5 onto our particles.

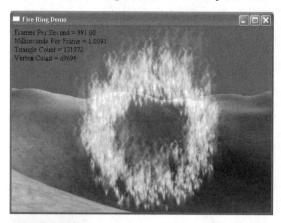

Figure 19.4: Screenshot of the fire ring particle system.

Figure 19.5: The texture we use for the point sprites in the fire ring particle system. Note that the alpha channel is not used in the additive blending equation. Also, the black border of the texture does not contribute to the final image with additive blending because adding black is analogous to adding zero (it makes no contribution).

We begin by examining how particles are created for this system, and then look at the effect file.

19.3.1 **Initializing the Particles**

The idea is to generate random particles on the ring in its local space (the ring can then be transformed to world coordinates via the world matrix). We do this in polar coordinates (i.e., generate a random radius and random angle), and then convert to Cartesian coordinates. To give the ring volume, we also generate a random z-coordinate for each particle in some interval (we pick [–1, 1], but the size just depends on the scene scale). In addition to randomizing the particles on the ring, we also want to randomize the other attributes, such as the size, initial color, and initial velocity, to give some variation to the system. The code that initializes a particle for the `FireRing` system is given as follows:

```
class FireRing : public PSystem
{
public:
        FireRing(const std::string& fxName,
            const std::string& techName,
            const std::string& texName,
```

```
            const D3DXVECTOR3& accel,
            const AABB& box,
            int maxNumParticles,
            float timePerParticle)
            : PSystem(fxName, techName, texName, accel, box,
              maxNumParticles, timePerParticle)
    {
    }

    void initParticle(Particle& out)
    {
            // Time particle is created relative to the global running
            // time of the particle system.
            out.initialTime = mTime;

            // Flare lives for 2-4 seconds.
            out.lifeTime   = GetRandomFloat(2.0f, 4.0f);

            // Initial size in pixels.
            out.initialSize = GetRandomFloat(10.0f, 15.0f);

            // Give a very small initial velocity to give the flares
            // some randomness.
            GetRandomVec(out.initialVelocity);

            // Scalar value used in vertex shader as an
            // amplitude factor.
            out.mass = GetRandomFloat(1.0f, 2.0f);

            // Start color at 50-100% intensity when born for
            // variation.
            out.initialColor = GetRandomFloat(0.5f, 1.0f)*WHITE;

            // Generate random particle on the ring in polar
            // coordinates: random radius and random angle.
            float r = GetRandomFloat(10.0f, 14.0f);
            float t = GetRandomFloat(0, 2.0f*D3DX_PI);

            // Convert to Cartesian coordinates.
            out.initialPos.x = r*cosf(t);
            out.initialPos.y = r*sinf(t);

            // Random depth value in [-1, 1] (depth of the ring)
            out.initialPos.z = GetRandomFloat(-1.0f, 1.0f);
    }
};
```

The initial time assignment may not be obvious. Recall that a particle system has a global time value, which keeps track of how long in seconds the particle system has been running. When we create a particle, we set its initial time value to this global time (mTime). Then, at a later time, mTime will have been incremented and we can find the age of the particle by computing the difference of mTime − particle.initialTime. (For example, if the particle was created when mTime = 5.0 seconds, then at a later time, say, mTime = 6.0 seconds, we can conclude that the particle is 6.0 – 5.0 = 1.0 seconds old.) The age of a particle is actually the time value t that we plug into Equation 19.1 to find the particle's current position based on its age. The advantage of this method of computing the age of a particle is that every frame we only need to update mTime. The alternative approach would be to give each particle an age data member and update it every frame based on how much time has passed. However, we'd have to update the age data member for *each* particle every frame, which would require more work than just updating the single mTime value.

For the most part, we want the particles to stay on the ring; therefore, we give them a small random velocity so that they do not fly off the ring. The small random velocity gives the particles some variation so that they are not all moving uniformly. Recall that GetRandomVec returns a unit vector (so the speed is 1 unit).

In the Fire Ring demo, we construct the particle system as follows:

```
mPSys = new FireRing("firering.fx", "FireRingTech", "torch.dds",
    D3DXVECTOR3(0.0f, 0.9f, 0.0f), psysBox, 1500, 0.0025f);
```

In particular, we want to mention that we apply a small constant upward acceleration so that the flames float slightly upward (you can think of this as the buoyant force slightly dominating the gravitational force). In addition, we specify that a particle is emitted every 0.0025 seconds.

19.3.2 **The Fire Ring Effect**

The effect file for the fire ring is as follows:

```
// Combined World-View-Projection matrix.
uniform extern float4x4 gWVP;

// Particle texture.
uniform extern texture  gTex;

// The position of the camera in the particle system's
// local space for distance calculations.
uniform extern float3   gEyePosL;

// Constant acceleration vector.
uniform extern float3   gAccel;

// Particle system time -- corresponds to PSystem::mTime.
uniform extern float    gTime;

// Viewport height for scaling the point sprite sizes; see comment
// in PSystem::draw.
uniform extern int      gViewportHeight;

sampler TexS = sampler_state
{
```

```
        Texture = <gTex>;
        MinFilter = LINEAR;
        MagFilter = LINEAR;
        MipFilter = POINT;
        AddressU  = CLAMP;
        AddressV  = CLAMP;
};

struct OutputVS
{
        float4 posH  : POSITION0;
        float4 color : COLOR0;
        float2 tex0  : TEXCOORD0;      // D3D fills in for point sprites.
        float size   : PSIZE;          // Size in pixels.
};

// Input corresponds to the Particle structure data members.
OutputVS FireRingVS(float3 posL    : POSITION0,
                    float3 vel     : TEXCOORD0,
                    float size     : TEXCOORD1,
                    float time     : TEXCOORD2,
                    float lifeTime : TEXCOORD3,
                    float mass     : TEXCOORD4,
                    float4 color   : COLOR0)
{
        // Zero out our output.
        OutputVS outVS = (OutputVS)0;

        // Get age of particle from creation time.
        float t = gTime - time;

        // Rotate the particles about local space about z-axis as a
        // function of time. These are just the rotation equations.
        float sine, cosine;
        sincos(0.5f*mass*t, sine, cosine);
        float x = posL.x*cosine + posL.y*-sine;
        float y = posL.x*sine + posL.y*cosine;

        // Oscillate particles up and down.
        float s = sin(6.0f*t);
        posL.x = x;
        posL.y = y + mass*s;

        // Constant acceleration (Equation 19.1).
        posL = posL + vel*t + 0.5f * gAccel * t * t;

        // Transform to homogeneous clip space.
        outVS.posH = mul(float4(posL, 1.0f), gWVP);

        // Ramp up size over time to simulate the flare expanding
        // over time.  Formula found by experimenting.
        size += 8.0f*t*t;
```

```
        // Also compute size as a function of the distance from
        // the camera, and the viewport height.  The constants
        // were found by experimenting.
        float d = distance(posL, gEyePosL);
        outVS.size = gViewportHeight*size/(1.0f + 8.0f*d);

        // Fade color from white to black over the particle's lifetime
        // to fade it out gradually.
        outVS.color = (1.0f - (t / lifeTime));

        // Done--return the output.
        return outVS;
}

float4 FireRingPS(float4 color : COLOR0,
                  float2 tex0 : TEXCOORD0) : COLOR
{
        // Multiply the faded color with the texture color.
        return color*tex2D(TexS, tex0);
}

technique FireRingTech
{
        pass P0
        {
                vertexShader = compile vs_2_0 FireRingVS();
                pixelShader = compile ps_2_0 FireRingPS();

                PointSpriteEnable = true;
                AlphaBlendEnable = true;
                SrcBlend = One;
                DestBlend = One;

                ZWriteEnable = false;
        }
}
```

- The `sincos` is an HLSL intrinsic function that returns the sine (via the second parameter) and cosine (via the third parameter) of the input angle (first parameter).

- In the HLSL, when you assign a scalar to a vector, the scalar is assigned to each component of the vector. Thus, after the line:

```
        outVS.color = (1.0f - (t / lifeTime));
```

We have:

```
        outVS.color.x = (1.0f - (t / lifeTime));
        outVS.color.y = (1.0f - (t / lifeTime));
        outVS.color.z = (1.0f - (t / lifeTime));
        outVS.color.w = (1.0f - (t / lifeTime));
```

- Observe how the motion of the particles, such as the rotation and physics of Equation 19.1, and other attribute adjustments, such as the color fade and size ramp, are done completely in the vertex shader. By being able to do this work in a vertex shader on the GPU, we free the CPU from having to do it.

19.4 Example 2: Rain

In this section, we describe how to render rain (see Figure 19.6). We map the texture shown in Figure 19.7 onto our particles. No blending is needed here, but we employ the alpha test so that only the raindrop part of the texture is rendered.

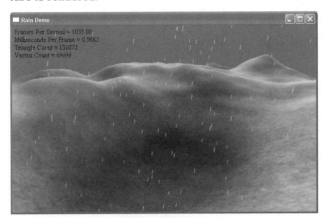

Figure 19.6: Screenshot of the rain particle system.

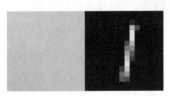

Figure 19.7: The rain texture and its alpha channel. The alpha test blocks the pixels with a black alpha channel so that the raindrops show up as lines.

As before, we begin by examining how particles are created for this system, and then look at the effect file.

19.4.1 Initializing the Particles

The rain particle system class is defined and implemented as follows:

```
class Rain : public PSystem
{
public:
    Rain(const std::string& fxName,
        const std::string& techName,
        const std::string& texName,
        const D3DXVECTOR3& accel,
        const AABB& box,
        int maxNumParticles,
        float timePerParticle)
```

```
                    : PSystem(fxName, techName, texName, accel, box,
                      maxNumParticles, timePerParticle)
        {
        }

        void initParticle(Particle& out)
        {
                // Generate about the camera.
                out.initialPos = gCamera->pos();

                // Spread the particles out on xz-plane.
                out.initialPos.x += GetRandomFloat(-100.0f, 100.0f);
                out.initialPos.z += GetRandomFloat(-100.0f, 100.0f);

                // Generate above the camera.
                out.initialPos.y += GetRandomFloat(50.0f, 55.0f);

                out.initialTime = mTime;
                out.lifeTime = GetRandomFloat(2.0f, 2.5f);
                out.initialColor = WHITE;
                out.initialSize = GetRandomFloat(6.0f, 7.0f);

                // Give them an initial falling down velocity.
                out.initialVelocity.x = GetRandomFloat(-1.5f, 0.0f);
                out.initialVelocity.y = GetRandomFloat(-50.0f, -45.0f);
                out.initialVelocity.z = GetRandomFloat(-0.5f, 0.5f);
        }
};
```

To simulate rain in a scene, we would have to drop raindrops over the entire area where we want rain to fall. For large worlds, this area could be huge and would require a large number of raindrops. A trick we can use is to generate raindrops only in a small region above and surrounding the camera (i.e., the rain follows the camera). In this way, no matter where the camera is placed in the scene, it always looks like it is raining, and the area where we must drop raindrops is small. The initParticle code generates raindrops in such a manner. (Note that the raindrops are specified directly in world space.)

We create the rain system as follows:

```
mPSys = new Rain("rain.fx", "RainTech", "raindrop.dds",
        D3DXVECTOR3(-1.0f, -9.8f, 0.0f), psysBox, 4000, 0.001f);
```

Here the constant acceleration is due to gravity and wind.

19.4.2 The Rain Effect

The rain effect code is given below:

```
uniform extern float4x4 gWVP;
uniform extern texture   gTex;
uniform extern float3    gEyePosL;
uniform extern float3    gAccel;
```

```
uniform extern float    gTime;
uniform extern int      gViewportHeight;

sampler TexS = sampler_state
{
     Texture = <gTex>;
     MinFilter = LINEAR;
     MagFilter = LINEAR;
     MipFilter = POINT;
     AddressU  = CLAMP;
     AddressV  = CLAMP;
};

struct OutputVS
{
     float4 posH  : POSITION0;
     float2 tex0  : TEXCOORD0;    // D3D fills in for point sprites.
     float size   : PSIZE;        // In pixels.
};

OutputVS RainVS(float3 posL     : POSITION0,
                float3 vel      : TEXCOORD0,
                float size      : TEXCOORD1,
                float time      : TEXCOORD2,
                float lifeTime  : TEXCOORD3,
                float mass      : TEXCOORD4,
                float4 color    : COLOR0)
{
     // Zero out our output.
     OutputVS outVS = (OutputVS)0;

     // Get age of particle from creation time.
     float t = gTime - time;

     // Constant acceleration.
     posL = posL + vel*t + 0.5f * gAccel * t * t;

     // Transform to homogeneous clip space.
     outVS.posH = mul(float4(posL, 1.0f), gWVP);

     // Do not scale raindrops as a function of distance.
     // Compute size as a function of the viewport height.
     // The constant was found by experimenting.
     outVS.size = 0.0035f*gViewportHeight*size;

     // Done--return the output.
     return outVS;
}

float4 RainPS(float2 tex0 : TEXCOORD0) : COLOR
{
     return tex2D(TexS, tex0);
}
```

```
technique RainTech
{
    pass P0
    {
        vertexShader = compile vs_2_0 RainVS();
        pixelShader = compile ps_2_0 RainPS();

        PointSpriteEnable = true;
        AlphaTestEnable = true;
        AlphaRef = 100;
        AlphaFunc = GreaterEqual;
    }
}
```

- We do not scale the raindrop sprites as a function of distance. Because the raindrops always follow the camera, they never get too distant anyway. Also, for rain, the results looked better without scaling by distance.

- For rain we do not require blending, but we do use the alpha test so that only the raindrop part of the texture is drawn and not the black background.

19.5 **Example 3: Sprinkler**

In this section, we describe how to render a "sprinkler" system (see Figure 19.2). (By sprinkler system, we do not necessarily mean a water sprinkler, but just a system that emits particles in a sprinkler fashion.) We map the texture shown in Figure 19.8 onto our particles.

Figure 19.8:
Texture used for
the sprinkler
particle system.

As before, we begin by examining how particles are created for this system, and then look at the effect file.

Note: A simple modification of this particle system can turn it into a smoke system (see Figure 19.3). Essentially, we just change the texture to the one shown in Figure 19.9 and use an upward acceleration (buoyant force dominates gravity) to make the smoke rise. In addition, some of the other initial attributes will need to be tweaked appropriately to get the effect you want (e.g., initial particle size and velocity).

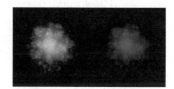

Figure 19.9: A smoke texture.

19.5.1 **Initializing the Particles**

The sprinkler particle system class is defined and implemented as follows:

```
class Sprinkler : public PSystem
{
public:
    Sprinkler(const std::string& fxName,
            const std::string& techName,
            const std::string& texName,
            const D3DXVECTOR3& accel,
            const AABB& box,
            int maxNumParticles,
            float timePerSecond)
            : PSystem(fxName, techName, texName, accel, box,
              maxNumParticles, timePerSecond)
    {
    }

    void initParticle(Particle& out)
    {
        // Generate about the origin.
        out.initialPos = D3DXVECTOR3(0.0f, 0.0f, 0.0f);

        out.initialTime = mTime;
        out.lifeTime = GetRandomFloat(4.0f, 5.0f);
        out.initialColor = WHITE;
        out.initialSize = GetRandomFloat(8.0f, 12.0f);
        out.mass = GetRandomFloat(0.8f, 1.2f);

        out.initialVelocity.x = GetRandomFloat(-2.5f, 2.5f);
        out.initialVelocity.y = GetRandomFloat(15.0f, 25.0f);
        out.initialVelocity.z = GetRandomFloat(-2.5f, 2.5f);
    }
};
```

Now the trick to this particle system's motion is the initial velocity. By specifying a large y-component, the particles move upward and can counteract gravity for some time (though they eventually slow and fall back down). To induce a spread in the particles (we want them to spread out and not fly straight up), we randomize the x- and z-coordinates also. You can experiment with different initial velocities in this manner to get different spreads.

The sprinkler system is instantiated as follows:

```
mPSys = new Sprinkler("sprinkler.fx", "SprinklerTech",
        "bolt.dds", D3DXVECTOR3(-3.0f, -9.8f, 0.0f), psysBox,
        2000, 0.003f);
```

Here the acceleration is due to gravity and a horizontal wind force. The horizontal wind accelerates the particles down the negative x-axis. The gravitational acceleration slows down the upward particle motion, and eventually causes the particles to fall back down to the ground.

19.5.2 **The Sprinkler Effect**

The sprinkler effect code is given below:

```
uniform extern float4x4 gWVP;
uniform extern texture  gTex;
uniform extern float3   gEyePosL;
uniform extern float3   gAccel;
uniform extern float    gTime;
uniform extern int      gViewportHeight;

sampler TexS = sampler_state
{
    Texture = <gTex>;
    MinFilter = LINEAR;
    MagFilter = LINEAR;
    MipFilter = POINT;
    AddressU  = CLAMP;
    AddressV  = CLAMP;
};

struct OutputVS
{
    float4 posH : POSITION0;
    float2 tex0 : TEXCOORD0;      // D3D fills in for point sprites.
    float size  : PSIZE;          // In pixels.
};

OutputVS SprinklerVS(float3 posL    : POSITION0,
                     float3 vel     : TEXCOORD0,
                     float size     : TEXCOORD1,
                     float time     : TEXCOORD2,
                     float lifeTime : TEXCOORD3,
                     float mass     : TEXCOORD4,
                     float4 color   : COLOR0)
{
    // Zero out our output.
    OutputVS outVS = (OutputVS)0;

    // Get age of particle from creation time.
    float t = gTime - time;

    // Constant acceleration.
    posL = posL + vel*t + 0.5f * gAccel * t * t;

    // Transform to homogeneous clip space.
    outVS.posH = mul(float4(posL, 1.0f), gWVP);

    // Compute size as a function of the distance from the camera,
    // and the viewport heights.  The constants were found by
    // experimenting.
    float d = distance(posL, gEyePosL);
    outVS.size = gViewportHeight*size/(1.0f + 8.0f*d);
```

```
        // Done--return the output.
        return outVS;
}


float4 SprinklerPS(float2 tex0 : TEXCOORD0) : COLOR
{
        return tex2D(TexS, tex0);
}


technique SprinklerTech
{
        pass P0
        {
                vertexShader = compile vs_2_0 SprinklerVS();
                pixelShader = compile ps_2_0 SprinklerPS();

                PointSpriteEnable = true;
                AlphaBlendEnable = true;
                SrcBlend = One;
                DestBlend = One;

                ZWriteEnable = false;
        }
}
```

Remark: The sprinkler system uses additive blending, which, as you can see from Figure 19.2, causes areas where the particle concentration is dense to appear brighter.

19.6 **Example 4: Bolt Gun**

In our final example, we show how the particle system framework can be used to make a bolt gun (see Figure 19.10). We use the same texture (Figure 19.8) as we did in the sprinkler system.

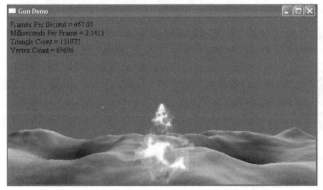

Figure 19.10: Screenshot of the gun particle system.

We begin by examining how particles are created for this system, and then look at the effect file.

19.6.1 Initializing the Particles

The gun particle system class is defined and implemented as follows:

```
class Gun : public PSystem
{
public:
        Gun(const std::string& fxName,
                const std::string& techName,
                const std::string& texName,
                const D3DXVECTOR3& accel,
                const AABB& box,
                int maxNumParticles,
                float timePerParticle)
                : PSystem(fxName, techName, texName, accel, box,
                    maxNumParticles, timePerParticle)
        {
        }

        void initParticle(Particle& out)
        {
                // Generate at camera.
                out.initialPos = gCamera->pos();

                // Set down a bit so it looks like player is carrying
                // the gun.
                out.initialPos.y -= 3.0f;

                // Fire in camera's look direction.
                float speed = 500.0f;
                out.initialVelocity = speed*gCamera->look();

                out.initialTime = mTime;
                out.lifeTime = 4.0f;
                out.initialColor = WHITE;
                out.initialSize = GetRandomFloat(80.0f, 90.0f);
                out.mass = 1.0f;
        }
};
```

Like the rain system, we create gun particles directly in world space. We want to simulate that the player is carrying a gun, so bullets originate at the position of the camera and fire in the direction of the camera's look vector at some specified speed.

We instantiate the gun system as follows:

```
mPSys = new Gun("gun.fx", "GunTech", "bolt.dds",
        D3DXVECTOR3(0, -9.8f, 0.0f), psysBox, 100, -1.0f);
```

We specify acceleration due to gravity; however, since we give the bullet such a high velocity, the effect of gravity is not noticeable.

New bolt particles will be added to the system when the user presses the Spacebar key to fire a "bullet" (they are not automatically emitted in the update function). In the application class's update method, we check if the Spacebar key is pressed, which fires a bullet:

```
// Can only fire once every tenth of a second.
static float delay = 0.0f;
if( gDInput->keyDown(DIK_SPACE) && delay <= 0.0f)
{
    delay = 0.1f;
    mPSys->addParticle();
}
delay -= dt;
```

Observe the usage of delay; this prevents the gun from firing faster than 10 times per second.

19.6.2 The Gun Effect

The gun effect file is very similar to what we have already seen, and is given as follows:

```
uniform extern float4x4 gWVP;
uniform extern texture  gTex;
uniform extern float3   gEyePosL;
uniform extern float3   gAccel;
uniform extern float    gTime;
uniform extern int      gViewportHeight;

sampler TexS = sampler_state
{
    Texture = <gTex>;
    MinFilter = LINEAR;
    MagFilter = LINEAR;
    MipFilter = POINT;
    AddressU  = CLAMP;
    AddressV  = CLAMP;
};

struct OutputVS
{
    float4 posH  : POSITION0;
    float2 tex0  : TEXCOORD0;    // D3D fills in for point sprites.
    float size   : PSIZE;        // In pixels.
};

OutputVS GunVS(float3 posL     : POSITION0,
               float3 vel      : TEXCOORD0,
               float size      : TEXCOORD1,
               float time      : TEXCOORD2,
               float lifeTime  : TEXCOORD3,
               float mass      : TEXCOORD4,
               float4 color    : COLOR0)
```

```
{
    // Zero out our output.
    OutputVS outVS = (OutputVS)0;

    // Get age of particle from creation time.
    float t = gTime - time;

    // Constant acceleration.
    posL = posL + vel*t + 0.5f * gAccel * t * t;

    // Transform to homogeneous clip space.
    outVS.posH = mul(float4(posL, 1.0f), gWVP);

    // Compute size as a function of the distance from the camera,
    // and the viewport heights.  The constants were found by
    // experimenting.
    float d = distance(posL, gEyePosL);
    outVS.size = gViewportHeight*size/(1.0f + 8.0f*d);

    // Done--return the output.
    return outVS;
}

float4 GunPS(float2 tex0 : TEXCOORD0) : COLOR
{
    return tex2D(TexS, tex0);
}

technique GunTech
{
    pass P0
    {
        vertexShader = compile vs_2_0 GunVS();
        pixelShader = compile ps_2_0 GunPS();

        PointSpriteEnable = true;
        AlphaBlendEnable = true;
        SrcBlend = One;
        DestBlend = One;

        ZWriteEnable = false;
    }
}
```

19.7 **Summary**

- A particle system is a collection of particles (usually small) that all behave in a similar yet somewhat random manner. Particle systems can be utilized to simulate a wide range of phenomena such as fire, rain, smoke, explosions, sprinklers, magic spell effects, and projectiles.

- Point sprites are special Direct3D primitives most applicable to particle systems. Point sprites are specified as point primitives (i.e., D3DPT_POINTLIST), but are then expanded to quads (two triangles) with texture coordinates by the hardware. Thus, point sprites can vary in size and have textures mapped over them. When creating a vertex buffer to store point sprites, remember to specify the D3DUSAGE_POINTS usage flag.

- Setting the following render state enables point sprites:

```
gd3dDevice->SetRenderState(D3DRS_POINTSPRITEENABLE, true);
```

  This render state can also be set in an effect file pass:

```
PointSpriteEnable = true;
```

- Use the PSIZE semantic type to output the point sprite size, in pixels, from the vertex shader so that Direct3D knows with which dimensions to calculate the point sprite.

- The trajectory of a particle undergoing constant acceleration is given by $\vec{p}(t) = 1/2\,\vec{a}t^2 + \vec{v}_0 t + \vec{p}_0$, where $\vec{a}$ is the constant acceleration vector, $\vec{v}_0$ is the initial velocity of the particle (i.e., the velocity at time $t = 0$), and $\vec{p}_0$ is the initial position of the particle (i.e., the position at time $t = 0$). With this equation, we can get the position of the particle at any time $\vec{t} \geq 0$ by evaluating the function at $\vec{t}$.

- Use additive blending when you want the intensity of a particle system to be proportional with the particle density. Use transparency blending for transparent particles. Not sorting a transparent particle system in back-to-front order may or may not be a problem (i.e., the problems may or may not be noticeable). Commonly, for particle systems, depth writes are disabled so that particles do not obscure each other. The depth test, however, is still enabled so that non-particle objects do obscure particles.

19.8 **Exercises**

1. Implement a firework particle system as shown in Figure 19.11. The particles should start out concentrated at the origin and then spread out.

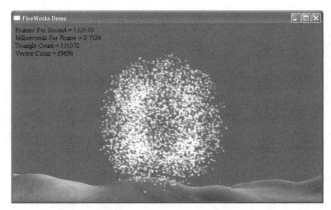

Figure 19.11:
Example output
for exercise 1.

2. The techniques of the gun and ring of fire particle systems can be combined to implement a flamethrower (see Figure 19.12). The flames should expand in size over time and a small upward acceleration should be applied. You can use the same texture that was used for the ring of fire system.

Figure 19.12:
Example output
for exercise 2.

3. Implement the smoke system shown in Figure 19.3. The smoke texture can be obtained from the companion files. The smoke particle sizes should expand over time, and they should fade out gradually over time.

4. Many times a particle system is attached to an object. For example, we attached the gun system to the camera object in the Gun demo (i.e., the camera position became the source of the gun bullet particles). As another example, you might attach a smoke particle system to the tail of a rocket to implement a smoke trail. For this exercise, attach a particle system to a moving point as shown in Figure 19.13. In this figure, the following parametric equations were used to move the point along a circular helix that is aligned with the z-axis as a function of time:

$$x = r\cos(kt)$$
$$y = r\sin(kt)$$
$$z = ct$$

The constant r is the radius of the helix, the constant k controls how fast the points rotate on the circle, the constant c controls how fast points move down the z-axis, and t is time (i.e., the helix "grows" over time, or in other words, the particle system's source point "walks" along the helix curve as a function of time). To implement this, you may wish to add a D3DXVECTOR3 pointer to the derived particle system class, and set it to point to the moving point in the constructor. Thus, whenever the point moves, the particle system has a direct pointer to the updated point position where new particles should be emitted.

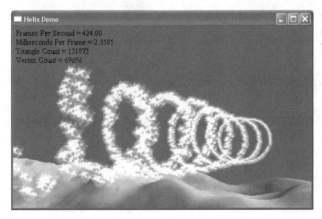

Figure 19.13: Example output for exercise 4.

Note: In addition to the circular helix, there are many other beautiful 3D curves that may be used as particle system paths; see http://astronomy.swin.edu.au/~pbourke/curves/ for examples.

Chapter 20

Picking

In this chapter, we have the problem of determining the 3D object (or primitive) the user picked with the mouse cursor (see Figure 20.1). In other words, given the 2D screen coordinates of the mouse cursor, can we determine the 3D object that was projected onto that point? To solve this problem, in some sense, we must work backward; that is to say, we typically transform from 3D space to screen space, but here we transform from screen space back to 3D space. Of course, we already have a slight problem: A 2D screen point does not correspond to a unique 3D point (i.e., more than one 3D point could be projected onto the same 2D projection window point — see Figure 20.2). Thus, there is some ambiguity in determining which object is really picked. However, this is not such a big problem, as the closest object to the camera is usually the one we want.

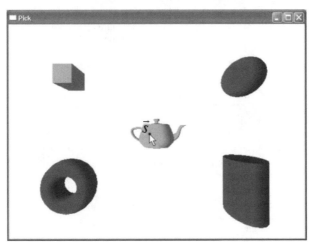

Figure 20.1: The user picking the teapot.

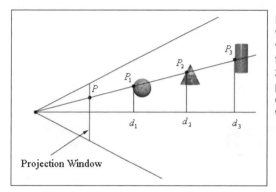

Figure 20.2: A side view of the frustum in view space. Observe that several points in 3D space can get projected onto a point on the projection window.

Consider Figure 20.3, which shows the viewing frustum in view space. Here $\vec{p}$ is the point on the projection window that corresponds to the clicked screen point. Now we see that if we shoot a *picking ray*, originating at the origin of view space, through $\vec{p}$, we will intersect the object whose projection surrounds $\vec{p}$, namely the teapot in this example. Therefore, our strategy is as follows: Once we compute the picking ray and transform it to the space of our objects, we can iterate through each object in the scene and test if the ray intersects it. The object that the ray intersects is the object that was picked by the user. As mentioned, the ray may intersect several scene objects (or none at all if nothing was picked) if the objects are along the ray's path but with different depth values, for example. In this case, we can just take the intersected object nearest to the camera as the picked object.

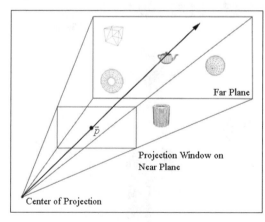

Figure 20.3: A ray shooting through $\vec{p}$ will intersect the object whose projection surrounds $\vec{p}$. Note that the projected point $\vec{p}$ on the projection window corresponds to the clicked screen point $\vec{s}$.

Objectives:

■   To learn how to implement the picking algorithm and to understand how it works. We break picking down into the following four steps:

    1.   Given the clicked screen point $\vec{s}$, find its corresponding point on the projection window and call it $\vec{p}$.

2. Compute the picking ray. This is the ray originating at the origin, in view space, which shoots through $\vec{p}$.

3. Transform the picking ray and the models to be tested with the ray into the same space.

4. Determine the object the picking ray intersects. The nearest (from the camera) intersected object corresponds to the picked screen object.

20.1 **Screen to Projection Window Transform**

The first task is to transform the clicked screen point to normalized device coordinates (see §6.4.4.3). The viewport matrix, which transforms vertices from normalized device coordinates to screen space, is given below:

$$
M = \begin{bmatrix}
Width/2 & 0 & 0 & 0 \\
0 & -Height/2 & 0 & 0 \\
0 & 0 & MaxZ - MinZ & 0 \\
X + Width/2 & Y + Height/2 & MinZ & 1
\end{bmatrix}
$$

Here, the variables of the viewport matrix refer to the D3DVIEWPORT9 structure:

```
typedef struct _D3DVIEWPORT9 {
        DWORD X;
        DWORD Y;
        DWORD Width;
        DWORD Height;
        float MinZ;
        float MaxZ;
} D3DVIEWPORT9;
```

Generally, for a game, the viewport is the entire back buffer and the depth buffer range is 0 to 1. Thus, X = 0, Y = 0, MinZ = 0, MaxZ = 1, Width = w, and Height = h, where w and h are the width and height of the back buffer, respectively. Assuming this is indeed the case, the viewport matrix simplifies to:

$$
M = \begin{bmatrix}
w/2 & 0 & 0 & 0 \\
0 & -h/2 & 0 & 0 \\
0 & 0 & 1 & 0 \\
w/2 & h/2 & 0 & 1
\end{bmatrix}
$$

Now let $\vec{u} = (u_x, u_y, u_z, 1)$ be a point in normalized device space (i.e., $-1 \le u_x \le 1, -1 \le u_y \le 1$, and $0 \le u_z \le 1$). Transforming $\vec{u}$ to screen space yields:

$$\vec{u}M = \begin{bmatrix} u_x, u_y, u_z, 1 \end{bmatrix} \begin{bmatrix} w/2 & 0 & 0 & 0 \\ 0 & -h/2 & 0 & 0 \\ 0 & 0 & 1 & 0 \\ w/2 & h/2 & 0 & 1 \end{bmatrix} = \begin{bmatrix} \dfrac{u_x w + w}{2}, \dfrac{-u_y h + h}{2}, u_z, 1 \end{bmatrix}$$

The coordinate u_z is just used by the depth buffer; we are not concerned with any depth coordinates for picking. The 2D screen point $\vec{s} = (s_x, s_y)$ corresponding to $\vec{u}$ is just the transformed x- and y-coordinates:

$$s_x = \frac{u_x w + w}{2}$$

$$s_y = \frac{-u_y h + h}{2}$$

The above equation gives us the screen point $\vec{s}$ in terms of the normalized device point $\vec{u}$ and the viewport dimensions. However, in our picking situation, we are initially given the screen point $\vec{s}$ and the viewport dimensions, and we want to find $\vec{u}$. Solving the above equations for $\vec{u}$ yields:

$$u_x = \frac{2s_x}{w} - 1$$

$$u_y = \frac{-2s_y}{h} + 1$$

We now have the clicked point in normalized space. However, we really want the clicked point on the projection window on the near plane in view space. Therefore, we ask ourselves which transformation took us from the projection window on the near plane in view space to normalized space, and then we just invert that transformation to go from normalized space to view space. Well, if you recall §6.4.4.3, we transformed projected vertices from the projection window on the near plane to normalized space by dividing the x-coordinate by $nR \tan(\alpha/2)$ and dividing the y-coordinate by $n \tan(\alpha/2)$, where α is the vertical field of view angle of the frustum and n is the near plane distance. Therefore, to transform $\vec{u}$ from normalized space to the projection window on the near plane in view space, we multiply the x-coordinate of $\vec{u}$ by $nR \tan(\alpha/2)$, and we multiply the y-coordinate of $\vec{u}$ by $n \tan(\alpha/2)$. We now have the projected point $\vec{p} = (nR \tan(\alpha/2)u_x, n \tan(\alpha/2)u_y, n)$ on the projection window on the near plane in view space. Shooting a ray through this point gives us the ray we want; however, we can simplify the math a bit.

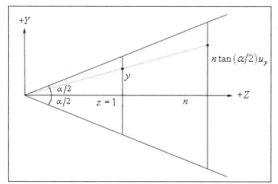

Figure 20.4 Similar triangles. Shooting a ray through y at $z = 1$ is the same as shooting a ray through $n \tan (\alpha/2)$ u_y at $z = n$.

Consider Figure 20.4 (we show only the y-axis situation, but the x-axis situation is analogous). Observe that the picking ray also passes through y at $z = 1$. Using similar triangles, we have:

$$y = \frac{y}{1} = \frac{n\tan(\alpha/2)u_y}{n} = \tan(\alpha/2)u_y \qquad (20.1)$$

Similarly, for the x-coordinate, we have:

$$x = \frac{x}{1} = \frac{nR\tan(\alpha/2)u_x}{n} = R\tan(\alpha/2)u_x \qquad (20.2)$$

In other words, instead of shooting the ray through the point $\vec{p} = (nR\tan(\alpha/2)u_x, n\tan(\alpha/2)u_y, n)$, we can just shoot it through the point:

$$\widetilde{p} = \left(R\tan(\alpha/2)u_x, \tan(\alpha/2)u_y, 1\right) \qquad (20.3)$$

To reiterate, we can do this because, as seen in Figure 20.4, shooting a ray through $\widetilde{p}$ gives exactly same ray as if we shot it through $\vec{p}$. Equation 20.3 has the advantage of being independent of n and requiring fewer multiplications.

Now recall the perspective projection matrix from §6.4.4.5. Observe that $R \tan (\alpha/2) = 1/P_{00}$ and $\tan (\alpha/2) = 1/P_{11}$, where P is the projection matrix. Hence, we can rewrite Equation 20.3 as follows:

$$\widetilde{p} = \left(u_x/P_{00}, u_y/P_{11}, 1\right) \qquad (20.4)$$

The code that computes the picking ray in view space is given below:

```
void TriPickDemo::getWorldPickingRay(D3DXVECTOR3& originW,
                                     D3DXVECTOR3& dirW)
{
    // Get the clicked screen point.
    POINT s;
    GetCursorPos(&s);
```

```
// Make it relative to the client area window.
ScreenToClient(mhMainWnd, &s);

// By the way we've been constructing things, the entire
// back buffer is the viewport.
float w = (float)md3dPP.BackBufferWidth;
float h = (float)md3dPP.BackBufferHeight;

D3DXMATRIX proj = gCamera->proj();

float x = (2.0f*s.x/w - 1.0f) / proj(0,0);
float y = (-2.0f*s.y/h + 1.0f) / proj(1,1);

// Build picking ray in view space.
D3DXVECTOR3 origin(0.0f, 0.0f, 0.0f);
D3DXVECTOR3 dir(x, y, 1.0f);
```

20.2 World Space Picking Ray

So far we have the picking ray in view space, but this is only useful if our objects are in view space as well. We do our ray/object intersection testing in world space, and therefore, we need to transform the ray to world space. We can transform a ray $\vec{r}(t) = \vec{q} + t\vec{u}$ by individually transforming its origin $\vec{q}$ and its direction $\vec{u}$ by a transformation matrix. Note that the origin is transformed as a point (i.e., $q_w = 1$) and the direction is treated as a vector (i.e., $u_w = 0$). The code to do this is given as follows (note that it concludes the above TriPickDemo::getWorldPickingRay method):

```
// So if the view matrix transforms coordinates from
// world space to view space, then the inverse of the
// view matrix transforms coordinates from view space
// to world space.
D3DXMATRIX invView;
D3DXMatrixInverse(&invView, 0, &gCamera->view());

// Transform picking ray to world space.
D3DXVec3TransformCoord(&originW, &origin, &invView);
D3DXVec3TransformNormal(&dirW, &dir, &invView);
D3DXVec3Normalize(&dirW, &dirW);
}
```

The D3DXVec3TransformCoord and D3DXVec3TransformNormal functions take 3D vectors as parameters, but observe that with the D3DXVec3TransformCoord function there is an understood $w = 1$ for the fourth component. Conversely, with the D3DXVec3TransformNormal function there is an understood $w = 0$ for the fourth component. Thus, we can use D3DXVec3TransformCoord to transform points and we can use D3DXVec3TransformNormal to transform vectors.

20.3 **Ray/Object Intersection Tests**

After we have the picking ray and the objects in the same coordinate system (e.g., world space), we are ready to test which object the ray will hit. Since we represent objects as triangle meshes, one approach would be the following: For each object in the scene, iterate through its triangle list and test if the ray intersects one of the triangles. If it does, then it must have hit the object that the triangle belongs to.

However, performing a ray intersection test for every triangle in the scene adds up in computation time. A faster, albeit less accurate, method is to approximate each object with a bounding volume (e.g., bounding sphere or AABB). Then we can perform a ray intersection test with each bounding volume and the volume that gets intersected specifies the object that got picked. (This method is less accurate because the bounding volume only approximates the mesh — the bounding volume is generally slightly bigger in the sense of volume than the mesh it encapsulates.) A compromise between these two approaches is to use a bounding volume to quickly reject objects that fail the bounding volume test. Then, for objects whose bounding volumes were intersected, we can perform a more accurate ray/triangle intersection test to see if the object really was picked. The advantage of this approach is that we only do the ray/triangle intersection test for a few objects that are likely candidates, instead of every object in the scene.

In this section, we show D3DX functions that do ray/sphere, ray/AABB, and ray/triangle intersection tests.

```
BOOL WINAPI D3DXIntersectTri(
    const D3DXVECTOR3 *p0,
    const D3DXVECTOR3 *p1,
    const D3DXVECTOR3 *p2,
    const D3DXVECTOR3 *pRayPos,
    const D3DXVECTOR3 *pRayDir,
    FLOAT *pU,
    FLOAT *pV,
    FLOAT *pDist);
```

This function returns `true` if the given ray intersects the given triangle, and returns `false` otherwise.

- ■ p0: Vertex one of a triangle.
- ■ p1: Vertex two of a triangle.
- ■ p2: Vertex three of a triangle.
- ■ pRayPos: Origin of ray.
- ■ pRayDir: Direction of ray.
- ■ pU: u barycentric coordinate.
- ■ pV: v barycentric coordinate.

■ pDist: Ray parameter t_0 that gives the intersection point. That is, if the ray is $\vec{r}(t) = \vec{q} + t\vec{u}$, then $\vec{r}(t_0) = \vec{q} + t_0\vec{u}$ gives the intersection point. If $\vec{u}$ is of unit length, it is the distance along the ray from the origin where the intersection occurred.

The barycentric coordinates deserve some elaboration. A point $\vec{p}$ in a triangle can be represented as a sort of weighted average of the vertices of the triangle. That is, a point $\vec{p}$ on the triangle $\triangle \vec{p}_0\,\vec{p}_1\,\vec{p}_2$ can be written as $\vec{p} = w\vec{p}_0 + u\vec{p}_1 + v\vec{p}_2$, where $w + u + v = 1 \Rightarrow w = 1 - (u + v)$, and $u \in [0, 1]$, $v \in [0, 1]$, and $w \in [0, 1]$ (see Figure 20.5). The weights w, u, and v are called *barycentric coordinates*. Observe that w can be obtained from u and v (hence why D3DXIntersectTri does not explicitly return it). If $u \notin [0, 1]$, $v \notin [0, 1]$, or $w \notin [0, 1]$, then the coordinates describe a point on the plane of the triangle, but not a point inside the triangle. Thus, looking at the barycentric coordinates of a point provides us with a criterion for determining whether the point is in the triangle or outside.

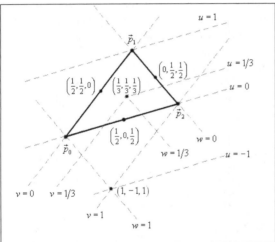

Figure 20.5: First note that the barycentric coordinates (w, u, v) of $\vec{p}_0$, $\vec{p}_1$, and $\vec{p}_2$ are (1, 0, 0), (0, 1, 0), and (0, 0, 1), respectively. For example, $\vec{p}_1 = w\vec{p}_0 + u\vec{p}_1 + v\vec{p}_2 = 0\vec{p}_0 + 1\vec{p}_1 + 0\vec{p}_2 = \vec{p}_1$. Secondly, observe the structure of the coordinate lines and how they are used to plot points. For example, the line $w = 1/3$ is the parallel line one-third of the way from $w = 0$ to $w = 1$. We can plot the barycentric point (1/3, 1/3, 1/3) by finding where the lines $w = 1/3$, $u = 1/3$, and $v = 1/3$ intersect. Observe that all points in the triangle and on the edges have positive barycentric coordinates. Furthermore, observe that if a barycentric coordinate is negative, then the point lies outside the triangle; for example, see the point (1, –1, 1) and also observe $w + u + v = 1$ still holds (it holds for all points in the plane of the triangle).

This next function does a ray/triangle intersection test for every triangle in a given input mesh. Most of the parameters are similar to D3DXIntersectTri, so we only review the new ones.

```
HRESULT WINAPI D3DXIntersect(
    LPD3DXBASEMESH pMesh,
    const D3DXVECTOR3 *pRayPos,
    const D3DXVECTOR3 *pRayDir,
    BOOL *pHit,
    DWORD *pFaceIndex,
    FLOAT *pU,
    FLOAT *pV,
    FLOAT *pDist,
    LPD3DXBUFFER *ppAllHits,
    DWORD *pCountOfHits);
```

■ `pMesh`: Pointer to the input mesh.

■ `pHit`: Returns `true` if an intersection occurred, and `false` otherwise.

■ `pFaceIndex`: Face index of the triangle that was hit relative to the index buffer of the mesh. The three indices that reference the three vertices of the face are: `pFaceIndex*3+0`, `pFaceIndex*3+1`, and `pFaceIndex*3+2`.

■ `ppAllHits`: With a collection of triangles, it is possible that the ray intersected more than one triangle. This parameter outputs an array of `D3DXINTERSECTINFO`, which describes the intersection for each intersection that occurred:

```
typedef struct _D3DXINTERSECTINFO {
    DWORD FaceIndex;
    FLOAT U;
    FLOAT V;
    FLOAT Dist;
} D3DXINTERSECTINFO, *LPD3DXINTERSECTINFO;
```

■ `pCountOfHits`: The number of intersections (i.e., the number of elements in the array returned by `ppAllHits`).

These next two functions return `true` if the given ray intersects the AABB or sphere, respectively, and `false` otherwise.

```
BOOL WINAPI D3DXBoxBoundProbe(
    const D3DXVECTOR3 *pMin,
    const D3DXVECTOR3 *pMax,
    const D3DXVECTOR3 *pRayPosition,
    const D3DXVECTOR3 *pRayDirection);

BOOL WINAPI D3DXSphereBoundProbe(
    const D3DXVECTOR3 *pCenter,
    FLOAT Radius,
    const D3DXVECTOR3 *pRayPosition,
    const D3DXVECTOR3 *pRayDirection);
```

Note: The mathematical details of these tests can be found in [Schneider03] and [Möller02].

20.4 **Tri-Pick Demo**

The Tri-Pick demo loads a car mesh (*car.x* from the DirectX SDK), draws it in wireframe mode, and draws the picked triangle solid (see Figure 20.6).

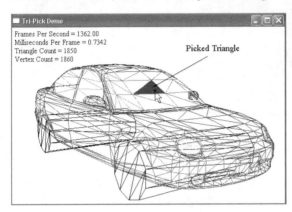

Figure 20.6: The triangle the user picks is drawn with a solid fill mode to distinguish it from the other triangles.

The picking section of this demo can be summarized as follows:

1. Every frame, check if the left mouse button was pressed.

2. If it was pressed, then compute the picking ray in world space using getWorldPickingRay (§20.1).

3. Now use D3DXIntersect to see if the picking ray intersected a triangle in the car mesh. If it did, then draw the intersected triangle.

There is one subtlety here: The function D3DXIntersect expects the input mesh and ray to be in the same coordinate system. Recall that getWorldPickingRay computes the ray in world space, but in which space is our mesh described? It is described relative to its local coordinate system. However, we get around this in the demo by setting the car's world matrix to the identity matrix (i.e., the car's local space is the world space). Thus, both the car mesh and ray are relative to the same space and everything works. In practice, you won't be able to do this, as each object will generally have a non-identity world matrix. To handle this situation, for each object, before you invoke D3DXIntersect, you will need to transform the ray to the local space of the object. In this way, the ray and mesh are in the same space. (It doesn't matter in which space we do the test, as long as all the objects we are talking about are in the same space.)

Note: You might suggest transforming the mesh to world space and doing the test in world space. This is not a good solution since the mesh could contain many vertices and transforming *many* vertices of the mesh is much more expensive than transforming *one* ray to the local space of the mesh.

The following code, which is called every frame, corresponds to the above steps 1-3:

```
// Did we pick anything?
D3DXVECTOR3 originW(0.0f, 0.0f, 0.0f);
D3DXVECTOR3 dirW(0.0f, 0.0f, 0.0f);
if( gDInput->mouseButtonDown(0) )
{
    getWorldPickingRay(originW, dirW);

    BOOL hit = 0;
    DWORD faceIndex = -1;
    float u = 0.0f;
    float v = 0.0f;
    float dist = 0.0f;
    ID3DXBuffer* allhits = 0;
    DWORD numHits = 0;
    HR(D3DXIntersect(mMesh, &originW, &dirW, &hit,
        &faceIndex, &u, &v, &dist, &allhits, &numHits));
    ReleaseCOM(allhits);

    // Did we hit anything?
    if( hit )
    {
        // Yes, draw the picked triangle in solid mode.
        IDirect3DVertexBuffer9* vb = 0;
        IDirect3DIndexBuffer9* ib = 0;
        HR(mMesh->GetVertexBuffer(&vb));
        HR(mMesh->GetIndexBuffer(&ib));

        HR(gd3dDevice->SetIndices(ib));
        HR(gd3dDevice->SetVertexDeclaration(VertexPNT::Decl));
        HR(gd3dDevice->SetStreamSource(0, vb, 0,
                                  sizeof(VertexPNT)));

        // faceIndex identifies the picked triangle to draw.
        HR(gd3dDevice->DrawIndexedPrimitive(
            D3DPT_TRIANGLELIST, 0, 0,
            mMesh->GetNumVertices(), faceIndex*3, 1))

        ReleaseCOM(vb);
        ReleaseCOM(ib);
    }
}
```

20.5 **Asteroids Demo**

The Asteroids demo generates several hundred random asteroids in space, rotates them around a randomly generated axis, and moves them at a constant velocity. In addition, if the user picks an asteroid, it "explodes" and a firework particle system effect (from Chapter 19) is generated. Figure 20.7 shows a screenshot.

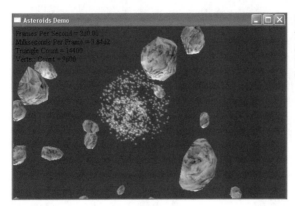

Figure 20.7: When the user picks an asteroid, a firework particle system is created.

Unlike the previous demo, we do not do ray/triangle intersections. Instead, we transform the bounding boxes of the asteroids to world space and do a ray/AABB intersection test using the D3DXBoxBoundProbe function. The following code illustrates the picking process for this demo, which is done every frame.

```
// Did we pick anything?
D3DXVECTOR3 originW(0.0f, 0.0f, 0.0f);
D3DXVECTOR3 dirW(0.0f, 0.0f, 0.0f);
if( gDInput->mouseButtonDown(0) )
{
    getWorldPickingRay(originW, dirW);
}


// Iterate over each asteroid and see if the ray intersected its
// AABB.
std::list<Asteroid>::iterator iter = mAsteroids.begin();
while( iter != mAsteroids.end() )
{
    // Build world matrix based on current rotation
    // and position settings of the asteroid.
    D3DXMATRIX R, T;
    D3DXMatrixRotationAxis(&R, &iter->axis, iter->theta);
    D3DXMatrixTranslation(&T, iter->pos.x, iter->pos.y, iter->pos.z);

    D3DXMATRIX toWorld = R*T;

    // Transform AABB to world space.
    AABB box;
    mAsteroidBox.xform(toWorld, box);

    // Did we pick it?
    if(D3DXBoxBoundProbe(&box.minPt, &box.maxPt, &originW, &dirW))
    {
        // Create a firework instance.
        FireWorkInstance inst;
        inst.time = 0.0f;
```

```
        inst.toWorld = toWorld;
        mFireWorkInstances.push_back(inst);

        // Remove asteroid from list and move on to the next node.
        iter = mAsteroids.erase(iter);
        continue;
    }
```

The rest of the demo code (i.e., non-picking code) is explained by the program comments.

20.6 **Summary**

- Picking is the technique used to determine the 3D object that corresponds to the 2D projected object displayed on the screen that the user clicked with the mouse.

- The picking ray is found by shooting a ray, originating at the origin of the view space, through the point on the projection window that corresponds to the clicked screen point.

- We can transform a ray $\vec{r}(t) = \vec{q} + t\vec{u}$ by transforming its origin $\vec{q}$ and direction $\vec{u}$ by a transformation matrix. Note that the origin is transformed as a point ($w = 1$) and the direction is treated as a vector ($w = 0$).

- To test if a ray has intersected an object, we can test if the ray intersected a triangle that composes the object with D3DXIntersect or D3DXIntersectTri. Alternatively, we can test if the ray intersects a bounding volume of the object, such as a bounding sphere or AABB. The functions D3DXBoxBoundProbe and D3DXSphereBoundProbe can be used for ray/AABB and ray/sphere intersection tests, respectively.

20.7 **Exercises**

1. Modify the Asteroids demo to use bounding spheres instead of boxes.

2. Using bounding spheres or boxes (or any bounding volume for that matter), you may find that you get a false pick reading because you picked the bounding volume of the object but not the object itself (remember, the bounding volume only loosely approximates its corresponding mesh). If you need finer accuracy, you may wish to use a bounding volume test to quickly find *potential* pick candidates, and then use the finer ray/triangle intersection test to see if an object was indeed picked. Modify the Asteroids demo to do this. (Note that D3DXIntersect expects the given ray to be in the local space of the mesh because that is where the geometry of the input mesh is specified relative to; thus, having the picking ray in world space is not enough, and you will need to transform it to the local space of the object.)

3. In the Asteroids demo, if two asteroids "line up" along the ray's path but have different depths, both will be picked. If you think of the ray as a projectile, this does not make sense, as the projectile would not pass through the first object it hits to also hit the object behind it. Modify the Asteroids demo so that, in this situation, only the object nearest to the camera is picked.

4. In the Asteroids demo, we looped through each asteroid and checked whether the picking ray intersected the asteroid's AABB. This is almost analogous to doing a linear search. Describe a divide and conquer algorithm that would behave more analogously to a binary search. How would you need to sort the objects in 3D space in preparation for your algorithm?

Chapter 21

Advanced Texturing — Part I

In this chapter, we explore three relatively advanced texturing techniques that can be used to improve the realism of our scenes significantly. In addition, these techniques often serve as components or the foundation to more sophisticated techniques and special effects.

Objectives:

- To learn how to approximate reflections for arbitrary meshes using an environment map.
- To discover how to create more detailed lighting using normal maps.
- To find out how to update textures at run time by using a render to texture technique.

21.1 Cube Mapping

The idea of cube mapping is to store six textures and to visualize them as the faces of a cube — hence the name cube map — centered and axis aligned about some coordinate system. Since the cube texture is axis aligned, each face corresponds with a direction along the three major axes; therefore, it is natural to reference a particular face on a cube map based on the axis direction with which it is aligned. For this purpose of identifying a cube map face, Direct3D provides the D3DCUBEMAP_FACES enumerated type:

```
typedef enum _D3DCUBEMAP_FACES {
    D3DCUBEMAP_FACE_POSITIVE_X = 0,
    D3DCUBEMAP_FACE_NEGATIVE_X = 1,
    D3DCUBEMAP_FACE_POSITIVE_Y = 2,
    D3DCUBEMAP_FACE_NEGATIVE_Y = 3,
    D3DCUBEMAP_FACE_POSITIVE_Z = 4,
```

```
        D3DCUBEMAP_FACE_NEGATIVE_Z = 5,
        D3DCUBEMAP_FACE_FORCE_DWORD = 0xffffffff
} D3DCUBEMAP_FACES;
```

In contrast to 2D texturing, we can no longer identify a texel with 2D texture coordinates. To identify a texel in a cube map, we use 3D texture coordinates, which define a 3D *lookup* vector $\vec{v} = (v_x, v_y, v_z)$ originating at the origin. The texel of the cube map that $\vec{v}$ intersects (see Figure 21.1) is the texel corresponding to the 3D coordinates of $\vec{v}$.

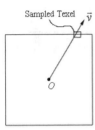

Figure 21.1: We illustrate in 2D for simplicity; in 3D the square becomes a cube. The square denotes the cube map surrounding some origin O. We shoot an arbitrary vector $\vec{v}$ from the origin. The texel $\vec{v}$ intersects is the sampled texel.

Note: From an implementation perspective, a cube map is just six 2D textures. To see how a vector $\vec{v} = (v_x, v_y, v_z)$ can be used to identify a texel on a face of a cube map, let's look at an example. Let $\vec{v} = (-3, -1, 2)$. Since the *x*-coordinate is the largest coordinate (in the sense of absolute magnitude), it should be clear that $\vec{v}$ would intersect the *negative x*-axis cube map face. (Likewise, $\vec{v} = (-1, 4, 2)$ would intersect the *positive y*-axis cube map face.) Now that we know which face was intersected by $\vec{v}$, we are back to a 2D problem, and we just need to find the 2D texture coordinates (u, v) on the negative *x*-axis cube map face that corresponds to the texel $\vec{v}$ intersects. To do this, we divide the other two coordinates by the absolute value of the largest coordinate, which results in coordinates in the range [−1, 1], and then we shift and scale the coordinates in this range to the usual texture coordinate range [0, 1]:

$\left(-1/|-3|, 2/|-3|\right) = \left(-1/3, 2/3\right)$ Divide other two coordinates by absolute value of largest coordinate.

$(u, v) = 1/2\left(-1/3 + 1, 2/3 + 1\right)$ Scale and shift the interval [−1, 1] to [0, 1].
$= \left(0.333, 0.833\right)$

This example should also illustrate that $\vec{v}$ need not be a unit vector.

21.1.1 Environment Maps

The primary application of cube maps is *environment mapping*. The idea is to position a camera in the middle of a scene with a 90° field of view angle (both vertically and horizontally). Then have the camera look down the positive *z*-axis, negative *z*-axis, positive *x*-axis, negative *x*-axis, positive *y*-axis, and negative y-axis, and to take a picture of the scene from each of these six viewpoints. Because the field of view angle is 90°, these six images will have captured the entire environment from all directions. Thus, when mapped onto a cube, the cube will fully contain the surrounding environment (see Figure 21.2). We then store these six images of the surrounding environment in a cube map, which leads to the name environment map.

Figure 21.2: An example of an environment map after "unfolding" the cube map. Imagine refolding these six faces into a 3D box, and then imagine being at the center of the box. From every direction you look, you see the surrounding environment.

Note that the six images for the environment map are generally not taken in a Direct3D program, although they could be (see exercise 3). Because cube maps just store texture data, their contents are often pre-generated by an artist (just like the 2D textures we've been using). Consequently, we do not need to use real-time rendering to compute the images of a cube map. That is, we can create a scene in a 3D modeler, and then generate the six cube map face images using the 3D modeler's photorealistic renderer, which typically use ray tracing. For outdoor environment maps, the program Terragen (http://www.planetside.co.uk/terragen/) is commonly used (free for personal use), and can create photorealistic outdoor scenes. The environment maps we create for this book, such as the one shown in Figure 21.2, were made with Terragen.

Note: If you choose to try out Terragen, you need to go to the Camera Settings dialog box and set the zoom factor to 1.0 to achieve a 90° field of view. Also, be sure to set your output image dimensions to be equal so that both the vertical and horizontal field of view angles are the same, namely 90°.

Once you have created the six cube map images using some program, we need to create a cube map texture, which stores all six. The DDS texture image format we have been using readily supports cube maps, and we can use the DirectX Texture Tool to create a cube map from our six textures. Open the DirectX Texture Tool (ships with the DirectX SDK: *DX9\Utilities\Bin\x86*) and first go to the File menu and select New Texture. From the dialog box that pops up (Figure 21.3), select Cubemap Texture as the texture type, enter the dimensions that match the dimensions of the six images, and choose a surface format. (Use a compressed format like DXT1; high-resolution cube maps can eat up a lot of memory since there are six textures being stored.)

Now we have an empty cube map. Go to the View menu, select Cube Map Face, and pick the face along the axis you want to view in the window (Figure 21.4). (All of these faces are initially empty.) Select any face to start with, and then go to the File menu and select Open Onto This Cubemap Face, which will launch a dialog box that asks you for the file you want to load onto the currently selected cube map face. Choose the image corresponding to this cube map face. Repeat this process for the

Figure 21.3: Creating a new texture in the DirectX Texture Tool.

remaining five cube map faces so that each cube map face has the desired image inserted onto it. When you are done, save the DDS to the file that now stores your cube map.

Figure 21.4: Selecting a face of the cube map to view in the DirectX Texture Tool.

21.1.2 Loading and Using Cube Maps in Direct3D

A cube map texture is represented in Direct3D by the `IDirect3DCubeTexture9` interface. We can create an `IDirect3DCubeTexture9` object from a cube map stored in a DDS file with the `D3DXCreateCubeTextureFromFile` function. For example:

```
IDirect3DCubeTexture9* envMap = 0;
HRESULT WINAPI D3DXCreateCubeTextureFromFile(
    gd3dDevice, "grassCubemap.dds", &envMap);
```

For the most part, we can use cube map textures the same way we use 2D textures. This is because most of the texture-related methods work with a base texture type IDirect3DBaseTexture9, from which both IDirect3DCubeTexture9 and IDirect3DTexture9 derive. For example, this method sets a texture effect parameter:

```
HRESULT ID3DXEffect::SetTexture(
    D3DXHANDLE hParameter,
    LPDIRECT3DBASETEXTURE9 pTexture);
```

Once a cube map is set to a texture, a corresponding sampler object can be defined, just as it was for 2D textures. However, to sample a cube texture, we no longer use the tex2D HLSL function; instead, we use the texCUBE function:

```
float4 texColor = texCUBE(EnvMapSamplerObject, v);
```

Here *v* is the 3D lookup vector described in §21.1.

21.1.3 Environment Map Demo

21.1.3.1 *Sky Sphere*

In this demo, we use an environment map to texture a sky sphere. A *sky sphere* is a sphere that surrounds the entire scene with the image of a sky and distant mountains painted on it (a sky dome [hemisphere] can also typically be used). (Note that sometimes it is useful to squash the sphere on the *y*-axis so that it is an ellipsoid, which creates a flatter sky surface. This is helpful if you are animating clouds on the sky surface.) To create the illusion of distant mountains far off in the horizon and a sky, we texture the sky sphere using an environment map by the method shown in Figure 21.5.

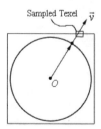

Figure 21.5: We illustrate in 2D for simplicity; in 3D the square becomes a cube and the circle becomes a sphere. We assume that the sky sphere and environment map are centered about the same origin. Then, to project the cube map onto the sphere, we can just use the vector from the origin to the sky sphere's vertices as the lookup vector.

In this way, the environment map is projected onto the sphere's surface. Unlike the sphere mapping discussed in Chapter 11, texturing a sphere with a cube map does not result in singularities at the poles.

We assume that the sky sphere is infinitely far away (i.e., it is centered about the world space but has an infinite radius), and so no matter how the camera moves in the world, we never appear to get closer or farther from the surface of the sky sphere. To implement this infinitely faraway sky sphere, we simply center the sky sphere about the camera in world space so that it is always centered about the camera. Consequently, as the camera moves, we are getting no closer to the surface of the sphere. If we did not do this, and we let the camera move closer to the sky sphere boundary, the whole illusion would break down, as the trick we use to simulate the sky would be obvious.

The effect file for the sky sphere is given below:

```
uniform extern float4x4 gWVP;
uniform extern texture  gEnvMap;

sampler EnvMapS = sampler_state
{
    Texture   = <gEnvMap>;
    MinFilter = LINEAR;
    MagFilter = LINEAR;
    MipFilter = LINEAR;
    AddressU  = WRAP;
    AddressV  = WRAP;
};


void SkyVS(float3 posL : POSITION0,
       out float4 oPosH : POSITION0,
       out float3 oEnvTex : TEXCOORD0)
{
    // Set z = w so that z/w = 1 (i.e., skydome always on far plane).
    oPosH = mul(float4(posL, 1.0f), gWVP).xyww;

    // Use skymesh vertex position, in local space, as index
    // into cubemap.
    oEnvTex = posL;
}

float4 SkyPS(float3 envTex : TEXCOORD0) : COLOR
{
    return texCUBE(EnvMapS, envTex);
}

technique SkyTech
{
    pass P0
    {
        vertexShader = compile vs_2_0 SkyVS();
        pixelShader  = compile ps_2_0 SkyPS();

        CullMode = None;
        ZFunc = Always;          // Always write sky to depth buffer
        StencilEnable = true;
        StencilFunc   = Always;
```

```
                StencilPass   = Replace;
                StencilRef    = 0;     // clear to zero
        }
}
```

■ Here we introduce another style of outputting data from a vertex shader. Previously, we always used an output vertex structure and returned it, but we can also return data from a vertex shader using *out* parameters. The above code is equivalent to returning an output vertex structure like the following:

```
struct OutVS
{
    float4 posH : POSITION0;
    float3 envTex : TEXCOORD0;
};
```

■ Observe how we copy the w-coordinate over to the z-coordinate after the world-view-projection transformation is applied. Thus, when the perspective divide occurs (§6.4.4.5), we will have $z/w = 1$, which means the pixels corresponding to the sky will have the maximum depth buffer values (namely 1.0) allowed for visible pixels (recall that pixels with depth buffer values outside the [0.0, 1.0] range are clipped). This makes sense, as we do not want to ever clip the sky (it should always be visible), nor do we want an object in our scene to have a depth value greater than the sky's. Because the sky sphere surrounds the scene and is always mapped to the maximum depth value, it can be used to effectively clear the back buffer, depth buffer, and the stencil buffer. Thus, the IDirect3DDevice::Clear call could be removed in the drawScene method, which would save some fill rate cost.

To do this, we must draw the sky first, and we must set ZFunc = Always so that the sky is always written (i.e., it never fails the depth test). To clear the stencil buffer to zero, we simply set the following render states:

```
StencilEnable = true;
StencilFunc   = Always;
StencilPass   = Replace;
StencilRef    = 0; // clear to zero
```

We need not worry about the extra cost in writing to the stencil buffer even if not using it because, when already writing to the depth buffer, writing to the stencil buffer is essentially a free operation since the depth and stencil buffer share the same off-screen surface. Thus, with this setup, after the sky is drawn, the back buffer will have been cleared with the sky pixels (a part of the sky always covers the entire background since the sky surrounds the scene), the depth buffer will have been cleared to one (recall we always have $z/w = 1$ for the sky), and the stencil buffer will have been cleared to zero (by the set stencil render states).

■   Observe that we disable culling (i.e., CullMode = None). We do this
    because when viewed from the inside from any direction, the sphere
    does not have any back-sided faces; therefore, backface culling would
    not buy us anything. In addition, it means that we do not have to worry
    about the wind order of the sphere geometry.

21.1.3.2 *Reflections*

In addition, the demo also uses the environment map to create reflections
for arbitrary objects (only the images in the environment map are reflected
with this technique). Figure 21.6 illustrates how the reflections are done
with environment maps.

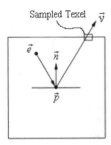

Figure 21.6: Here, $\vec{e}$ is the
eye point, and $\vec{n}$ is the
normal at the point $\vec{p}$ on
the surface. The texel that
gets mapped to a point $\vec{p}$
on the surface is given by
the reflection vector $\vec{v}$,
which is the reflection of
the vector from $\vec{e}$ to $\vec{p}$.

We compute the reflection vector per-pixel and then use it to sample the
environment map:

```
// [...Other uniform global variables snipped]

uniform extern texture  gEnvMap;

// How much does the surface reflect? Normally this should be a
// property of the material since it may vary over a surface.
static float gReflectivity = 1.0f;

float4 EnvMapPS(float3 normalW : TEXCOORD0,
                float3 toEyeW  : TEXCOORD1,
                float2 tex0    : TEXCOORD2) : COLOR
{
    // Interpolated normals can become unnormal--so normalize.
    normalW = normalize(normalW);
    toEyeW  = normalize(toEyeW);

    // [...Lighting and texturing code snipped]

    // Get the reflected color.
    float3 envMapTex = reflect(-toEyeW, normalW);
    float3 reflectedColor = texCUBE(EnvMapS, envMapTex);
```

```
// Weighted average between the reflected color, and usual
// diffuse/ambient material color modulated with the
// texture color.
float3 ambientMtrl = gReflectivity*reflectedColor +
         (1.0f-gReflectivity)*(gMtrl.ambient*texColor);
float3 diffuseMtrl = gReflectivity*reflectedColor +
         (1.0f-gReflectivity)*(gMtrl.diffuse*texColor);

// Compute the ambient, diffuse, and specular terms separately.
float3 spec = t*(gMtrl.spec*gLight.spec).rgb;
float3 diffuse = s*(diffuseMtrl*gLight.diffuse.rgb);
float3 ambient = ambientMtrl*gLight.ambient;

float3 final = ambient + diffuse + spec;

// Output the color and the alpha.
return float4(final, gMtrl.diffuse.a*texColor.a);
}
```

In general, a pixel's color is not completely determined by the reflected color (only mirrors are 100% reflective). Therefore, we define a pixel's diffuse/ambient color to be determined by a weighted average between its reflected color and usual color. (The *usual color* is the color formed by modulating the diffuse/ambient material colors with the texture color.) If $\vec{C}$ is the usual pixel color and $\vec{R}$ is the reflected color, then the final color $\vec{F}$ is given by the weighted average:

$$\vec{F} = \alpha\vec{R} + (1-\alpha)\vec{C}$$

Here α is a specified reflectivity value in the range [0, 1] that specifies how reflective the pixel is and how much weight should be given to the reflective color in the weighted average (we call α gReflectivity in the above code). Although we hard code it in the above code for simplicity in the demo, it should actually be made a data member of the surface material structure since it will generally vary from mesh subset to subset (i.e., some mesh subsets will be more reflective than others, just like some subsets reflect more specular light than others). If you want per-pixel control of the reflectivity, you can instead have an artist create a *reflectivity map*, which is an 8-bit texture in which each element ranges from 0 to 255 (which is mapped to [0, 1] in the pixel shader) and defines a per-pixel reflectivity value. A pixel can then sample the reflectivity map in the pixel shader to obtain the reflectivity constant α for the pixel.

Figure 21.7 shows a screenshot of the EnvMap demo.

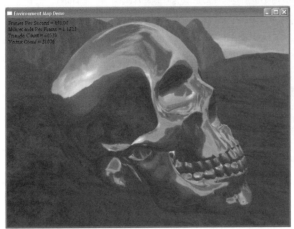

Figure 21.7: Screenshot of the EnvMap demo.

Note: Since the surrounding environment varies from object to object in the world, each object should have its own environment map that captures the surrounding environment for that object. However, if the objects are curved enough, there will generally be enough distortion so that the incorrect reflections are unnoticeable.

Figure 21.8 shows a potential problem with using environment maps for flat surfaces.

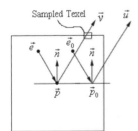

Figure 21.8: The reflection vector corresponding to two different points $\vec{p}$ and $\vec{p}_0$ when the eye is at positions $\vec{e}$ and $\vec{e}_0$, respectively.

From the figure, it should be clear that the two reflection vectors should intersect different texels of the cube map. However, they do not. Recall that two vectors are equal if they have the same direction and magnitude. Clearly $\vec{u} = \vec{v}$; thus, the same texel gets mapped to $\vec{p}$ when the eye is at $\vec{e}$, and $\vec{p}_0$ when the eye is at $\vec{e}_0$. See [Brennan02] for an approximate solution.

21.2 **Normal Mapping**

In Chapter 11, we introduced texture mapping, which enabled us to map fine details from an image onto our triangles. On the other hand, our lighting is rather coarse in comparison. Take a brick wall, for example. To model this, we would probably map a brick texture onto a quad and use either vertex or Phong shading; in either case, the lighting would not take into account the high-frequency details such as crevices, scratches, or bumps on the brick wall, in contrast to the texture mapping. The reason is that the interpolation technique used in vertex or Phong shading only works well when applied to meshes that model relatively smooth objects; that is, the interpolation won't capture the high-frequency surface details. A solution would be to tessellate the geometry such that the geometry models the high-frequency details, in which case, so would the lighting. However, the mesh resolution required for this would be impractical. The point is this: Even though texturing introduces fine details like cracks, scratches, and crevices, our lighting model does not. This is not so limiting for static lights, as the lighting details can be "baked" into the texture map by an artist (i.e., the lighting is taken into account when the texture is being made). However, this technique does not look correct with dynamic lights (because the texture is fixed, the texel colors do not respond to changing lights). Thus, our goal is to find a way to implement dynamic lighting such that the fine details that show up in the texture map also show up in the lighting. Since textures provide us with the fine details to begin with, it is natural to look for a texture mapping solution to this problem.

21.2.1 **Storing Normal Maps in Textures**

A *normal map* is a texture, but instead of storing RGB data at each texel, we store a compressed x-coordinate, y-coordinate, and z-coordinate in the red component, green component, and blue component, respectively. These coordinates define a normal vector; thus a normal map stores a normal vector at each pixel. Figure 21.9 shows an example of how to visualize a normal map.

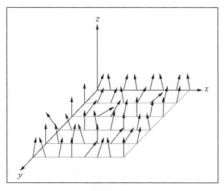

Figure 21.9: Normals stored in a normal map relative to a texture space coordinate system, where the x-axis goes in the horizontal right direction of the texture, the y-axis goes in the vertical down direction of the texture, and the z-axis is orthogonal to the texture plane.

For illustration, we will assume a 24-bit texture format like D3DFMT_R8G8B8, which reserves a byte for each color component, and therefore, each color component can range from 0 to 255.

So how do we compress a unit vector into this format? First note that for a unit vector, each coordinate always lies in the range [–1, 1]. If we shift and scale this range to [0, 1], multiply by 255, and truncate the decimal, the result will be an integer in the range 0 to 255. That is, if x is a coordinate in the range [–1, 1], then the integer part of $f(x)$ is an integer in the range 0 to 255, where f is defined by

$$f(x) = (0.5x + 0.5) \cdot 255$$

So to store a unit vector in a 24-bit texture map, we just apply f to each coordinate and write the coordinate to the corresponding color channel in the texture map.

The next question is how to reverse the compression process; that is, given a compressed texture coordinate in the range 0 to 255, how can we recover its true value in the interval [–1, 1]? The answer is to simply invert the function f, which after a little thought, can be seen to be:

$$f^{-1}(x) = \left(\frac{2}{255}x\right) - 1$$

That is, if x is an integer in the range 0 to 255, then $f^{-1}(x)$ is a floating-point number in the range [–1, 1].

We will not have to do the compression process ourselves, as we will use a Photoshop plug-in to convert images to normal maps (the plug-in is available at http://developer.nvidia.com/object/nv_texture_tools.html). However, when we sample a normal map in a pixel shader, we will have to do part of the inverse process to uncompress it. Recall that in a pixel shader, tex2D returns a color vector with the component in the range [0, 1]. Thus, the tex2D function has already done part of the uncompressing work for us (namely the divide by 255, which transforms an integer in the range 0 to 255 to the floating-point interval [0, 1]). We complete the transformation by shifting and scaling $\widetilde{x}$ in [0, 1] to [–1, 1] with the following transformation:

$$\widetilde{f}^{-1}(\widetilde{x}) = 2\widetilde{x} - 1 \tag{21.1}$$

21.2.2 Generating Normal Maps

Even though we do not generate normal maps ourselves, we outline the idea in this section. A normal map is generally generated from a grayscale heightmap, where the heightmap represents the bumpiness of the surface. The idea is similar to how we compute the surface of a terrain. First we set up a coordinate system called *texture space* (see Figure 21.9) and lay down a grid of the same resolution as the heightmap with step sizes Δx and Δy such that the ijth grid vertex corresponds to the ijth heightmap entry. Next, a finite difference scheme can be applied to approximate the tangent vectors in the x- and y-directions at each vertex. Then, an application of the cross product can be used to compute a normal vector at each vertex from the two tangent vectors. For example, if $h(x_j, y_i)$ denotes the height of the ijth grid vertex, a central difference scheme in x and y yields:

$$\frac{\partial h}{\partial x}(x_j, y_i) \approx \frac{h(x_j + \Delta x, y_i) - h(x_j - \Delta x, y_i)}{2\Delta x}$$

$$\frac{\partial h}{\partial y}(x_j, y_i) \approx \frac{h(x_j, y_i + \Delta y) - h(x_j, y_i - \Delta y)}{2\Delta y}$$

Note: The index j indexes in the x-direction and the index i indexes in the y-direction. This is to maintain consistency with the matrix index format where i indexes the grid row and j indexes the grid column.

Then the corresponding tangent vectors are:

$$\vec{T}_x(x_j, y_i) \approx \left(1, 0, \frac{\partial h}{\partial x}(x_j, y_i)\right)$$

$$\vec{T}_y(x_j, y_i) \approx \left(0, 1, \frac{\partial h}{\partial y}(x_j, y_i)\right)$$

Then the normal vector at the ijth vertex is given by:

$$\vec{n}(x_j, y_i) = normalize\left(\vec{T}_x \times \vec{T}_y\right)$$

At this point, we have a normal vector, relative to the texture space coordinate system, for each grid vertex. We can now output the ijth grid vertex normal to the ijth entry of the normal map (using the unit vector to 24-bit color conversion discussed in the previous section).

Note: The grid spacing Δx and Δy control the slope of the tangent vectors. Thus, by altering them, you can artistically control the steepness of the bumps the normals describe.

We emphasize that the normals in the normal map are relative to texture space (i.e., the coordinate system used to generate the normals), which generally is not the same as the object space of a 3D model onto which the normals in the normal map will be mapped. Therefore, a change of coordinate system calculation will need to be done so that the normals and light vector are in the same coordinate system.

Observe that for a flat surface, the normal is perfectly aligned with the positive *z*-axis of texture space. Also note the *z*-coordinate is stored in the blue component of the texture. For the most part, the normal vectors in normal maps do not get too far misaligned with the positive *z*-axis. Consequently, the *z*-coordinate (or blue component) has the highest coordinate magnitude. Thus, when a normal map is viewed as an RGB color texture, it is more biased to having a blue tint. Figure 21.10 shows a normal map viewed as an RGB color texture.

Figure 21.10: An example of a normal map when viewed as an RGB color image.

21.2.3 **Using Normal Maps**

We now know what normal maps are and how to create them. So how do we use them? At first glance, it seems that we can just treat them as regular texture maps; that is, we map them onto polygons and then sample the texels in a pixel shader to get per-pixel normals, and then do our per-pixel lighting as usual with these sampled normals from the normal map instead of the interpolated vertex normal. This is almost the right idea, but remember that our sampled normal vectors are relative to texture space, and our lights are relative to world space. Thus, the last step we must discuss is how to get the sampled normal vectors and light vector in the same space.

Consider a 3D triangle in object space and its corresponding 2D texture triangle. As we map the 2D texture onto the 3D triangle, let's carry the texture space axes (x', y', and z') along with the texture triangle so that we can see what the axes look like relative to the 3D triangle after the mapping; Figure 21.11 shows this.

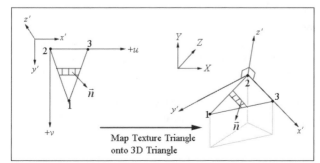

Figure 21.11: We map the 2D texture triangle onto the 3D triangle and carry the texture space coordinate system along as we do the mapping so that we can see what it looks like relative to the 3D triangle.

Figure 21.11 shows what the texture space coordinate system looks like relative to a particular triangle based on the texture mapping. Note that, in general, the texture space relative to a triangle varies from triangle to triangle since the way the texture triangle is mapped to the 3D triangle will vary per triangle. We denote the texture space coordinate system corresponding to a 3D triangle Δ by $S(\Delta)$.

For a triangle Δ, if we form vectors $\vec{T}$, $\vec{B}$, and $\vec{N}$ relative to object space, along the x', y', and z' axes of $S(\Delta)$, respectively, then we form a *TBN-basis* that describes $S(\Delta)$ relative to the object space. With the relationship known between the object space and $S(\Delta)$, we can then transform between the two spaces. Specifically, the matrix:

$$M_{\Delta} = \begin{bmatrix} T_x & T_y & T_z \\ B_x & B_y & B_z \\ N_x & N_y & N_z \end{bmatrix}$$

transforms from $S(\Delta)$ to object space. The inverse of M_{Δ} then transforms from object space to $S(\Delta)$. Assuming M_{Δ} is orthonormal, we have:

$$M_{\Delta}^{-1} = M_{\Delta}^{T} = \begin{bmatrix} T_x & B_x & N_x \\ T_y & B_y & N_y \\ T_z & B_z & N_z \end{bmatrix} \tag{21.2}$$

Note: The $\vec{T}$, $\vec{B}$, and $\vec{N}$ vectors are commonly referred to as the *tangent*, *binormal*, and *normal* vectors, respectively. The tangent and binormal vectors are tangent to the surface and the normal is normal to the surface.

We use 3×3 matrices here because we are transforming vectors and not points. Recall that translations do not affect vectors; therefore, we do not need the fourth matrix row (the fourth row does translations).

The texture space is sometimes called *tangent space* since after it has been mapped to a surface, it sits tangent to that surface.

Now the question is how to compute the TBN-basis for a triangle. To do this, we will use the D3DXComputeTangentFrameEx function (see §21.2.4). If you want to know the mathematics behind computing the TBN-basis, we refer you to [Fernando03] or [Lengyel02], which both provide detailed derivations of the topic.

Note: For a technique on animating TBN-bases for skinned character meshes, see the slides by [Dietrich].

21.2.4 **Implementation Details**

We now have the following strategy for getting lights and normal vectors in a consistent coordinate system:

1. Compute the TBN-basis for each triangle in the mesh. In order to avoid a triangulated appearance and to make the mesh surface appear more smooth, we do the same trick we did with vertex normals; that is, for each vertex v, we average the TBN-bases of the triangles that share the vertex v as one of their vertices to obtain per-vertex TBN-bases. (Note that the TBN-bases will probably need to be re-orthonormalized after averaging.) This step is done for us by the D3DXComputeTangentFrameEx function.

2. Assuming that the light vector has been transformed to object space in the application code, for each vertex, transform the light vector from object space to the vertex's texture space.

3. Output the light vector, relative to texture space, from the vertex shader and input it into the pixel shader. We now have the light vector in texture space for each pixel. We can now do our lighting calculations in the usual way in texture space.

21.2.4.1 *Computing the TBN-Basis Per Vertex*

Based on the preceding discussion, we require a TBN-basis at each vertex. To store this additional vertex data, we create the following vertex structure:

```
struct NMapVertex
{
    D3DXVECTOR3 pos;
    D3DXVECTOR3 tangent;
    D3DXVECTOR3 binormal;
    D3DXVECTOR3 normal;
    D3DXVECTOR2 tex0;

    static IDirect3DVertexDeclaration9* Decl;
};
```

So when we load a mesh, the first thing we must do is clone it to this format to reserve space for the TBN-basis vectors:

```
ID3DXMesh* tempMesh = 0;
LoadXFile("BasicColumnScene.x", &tempMesh,
        mSceneMtrls, mSceneTextures);

// Get the vertex declaration for the NMapVertex.
D3DVERTEXELEMENT9 elems[MAX_FVF_DECL_SIZE];
UINT numElems = 0;
HR(NMapVertex::Decl->GetDeclaration(elems, &numElems));
```

```
// Clone the mesh to the NMapVertex format.
ID3DXMesh* clonedTempMesh = 0;
HR(tempMesh->CloneMesh(D3DXMESH_MANAGED, elems,
                       gd3dDevice, &clonedTempMesh));
```

Once that is done, we can use the `D3DXComputeTangentFrameEx` function to compute and fill in the tangent, binormal, and normal vectors for each vertex in the mesh:

```
HR(D3DXComputeTangentFrameEx(
    clonedTempMesh,              // Input mesh
    D3DDECLUSAGE_TEXCOORD, 0,    // Vertex element of input tex-coords.
    D3DDECLUSAGE_BINORMAL, 0,    // Vertex element to output binormal.
    D3DDECLUSAGE_TANGENT, 0,     // Vertex element to output tangent.
    D3DDECLUSAGE_NORMAL, 0,      // Vertex element to output normal.
    0,                           // Options
    0,                           // Adjacency
    0.01f, 0.25f, 0.01f,         // Thresholds for handling errors
    &mSceneMesh,                 // Output mesh
    0));                         // Vertex remapping

// Done with temps.
ReleaseCOM(tempMesh);
ReleaseCOM(clonedTempMesh);
```

For the application code, this is essentially the only extra code we must do for normal mapping, except that we must also set an additional texture effect parameter (the normal map), which is to be sampled in the pixel shader.

21.2.4.2 *Effect Parameters*

For completeness, we show the effect parameters and sampler objects for the Normal Mapping demo:

```
uniform extern float4x4 gWorldInv;
uniform extern float4x4 gWVP;
uniform extern Mtrl     gMtrl;
uniform extern DirLight gLight;
uniform extern float3   gEyePosW;
uniform extern texture  gTex;
uniform extern texture  gNormalMap;

sampler TexS = sampler_state
{
    Texture = <gTex>;
    MinFilter = ANISOTROPIC;
    MaxAnisotropy = 8;
    MagFilter = LINEAR;
    MipFilter = LINEAR;
    AddressU  = WRAP;
    AddressV  = WRAP;
};
```

```
sampler NormalMapS = sampler_state
{
     Texture = <gNormalMap>;
     MinFilter = ANISOTROPIC;
     MaxAnisotropy = 8;
     MagFilter = LINEAR;
     MipFilter = LINEAR;
     AddressU  = WRAP;
     AddressV  = WRAP;
};
```

21.2.4.3 *The Vertex Shader*

The primary responsibility of the vertex shader for normal mapping is to transform the lighting information from world space to texture space. We do this by first transforming from world space to object space using the inverse world matrix (effect parameter gWorldInv), and then by transforming from object space to tangent space using the vertex's TBN-basis to construct the matrix in Equation 21.2.

```
struct OutputVS
{
     float4 posH       : POSITION0;
     float3 toEyeT     : TEXCOORD0;
     float3 lightDirT  : TEXCOORD1;
     float2 tex0       : TEXCOORD2;
};

OutputVS NormalMapVS(float3 posL        : POSITION0,
                     float3 tangentL    : TANGENT0,
                     float3 binormalL   : BINORMAL0,
                     float3 normalL     : NORMAL0,
                     float2 tex0        : TEXCOORD0)
{
     // Zero out our output.
     OutputVS outVS = (OutputVS)0;

     // Build TBN-basis.
     float3x3 TBN;
     TBN[0] = tangentL;
     TBN[1] = binormalL;
     TBN[2] = normalL;

     // Matrix transforms from object space to tangent space.
     float3x3 toTangentSpace = transpose(TBN);

     // Transform eye position to local space.
     float3 eyePosL = mul(float4(gEyePosW, 1.0f), gWorldInv);



     // Transform to-eye vector to tangent space.
     float3 toEyeL = eyePosL - posL;
```

```
    outVS.toEyeT = mul(toEyeL, toTangentSpace);

    // Transform light direction to tangent space.
    float3 lightDirL = mul(float4(gLight.dirW, 0.0f), gWorldInv);
    outVS.lightDirT  = mul(lightDirL, toTangentSpace);

    // Transform to homogeneous clip space.
    outVS.posH = mul(float4(posL, 1.0f), gWVP);

    // Pass on texture coordinates to be interpolated
    // in rasterization.
    outVS.tex0 = tex0;

    // Done--return the output.
    return outVS;
}
```

21.2.4.4 *The Pixel Shader*

The pixel shader is very similar to our earlier Phong shading pixel shader,
but instead of using the interpolated vertex normal, we use the normal
sampled from the normal map. Moreover, because the coordinates sampled
by tex2D are returned in the [0, 1] range, we must apply Equation 21.1 to
get the coordinates in the true [–1, 1] range.

```
float4 NormalMapPS(float3 toEyeT    : TEXCOORD0,
                   float3 lightDirT : TEXCOORD1,
                   float2 tex0      : TEXCOORD2) : COLOR
{
    // Interpolated normals can become unnormal--so normalize.
    toEyeT    = normalize(toEyeT);
    lightDirT = normalize(lightDirT);

    // Light vector is opposite the direction of the light.
    float3 lightVecT = -lightDirT;

    // Sample normal map.
    float3 normalT = tex2D(NormalMapS, tex0);

    // Expand from [0, 1] compressed interval to
    //true [-1, 1] interval (Equation 21.1).
    normalT = 2.0f*normalT - 1.0f;

    // Make it a unit vector.
    normalT = normalize(normalT);

    // [...Lighting snipped] We now have a per-pixel normal and
    // lighting information in tangent space, so we can do our
    // lighting calculations the same way we have done in the past.
}
```

Note: Recall that the assignment `normalT = 2.0f*normalT - 1.0f` works per-component; that is, it is equal to:

```
normalT.x = 2.0f*normalT.x - 1.0f;
normalT.y = 2.0f*normalT.y - 1.0f;
normalT.z = 2.0f*normalT.z - 1.0f;
```

All operations are vector based like this in the HLSL.

21.2.4.5 *The Bricks Demo*

Figure 21.12 shows a screenshot of the Bricks demo, which demonstrates the ideas of this section.

Figure 21.12: Screenshot of the Bricks demo.

21.2.5 **Normal Mapping Water**

In this section, we describe a method for implementing water using normal maps. We begin with a triangle mesh grid on the xz-plane representing the water's surface. The basic idea is that we cannot hope to capture high-frequency choppy waves from geometry — the mesh resolution required would be too high. Thus, we use two normal maps that capture the normals of high-frequency choppy waves (see Figure 21.13).

Figure 21.13: The two normal maps we use to model choppy waves.

We then scroll these two normal maps over the water surface at different rates and directions, sample both normal maps at each pixel, and then combine the two normals by averaging them:

```
float3 normalT0 = tex2D(WaveMapS0, tex0);
float3 normalT1 = tex2D(WaveMapS1, tex1);


// Expand from [0, 1] compressed interval to true [-1, 1] interval.
normalT0 = 2.0f*normalT0 - 1.0f;
normalT1 = 2.0f*normalT1 - 1.0f;


// Average the two vectors.
float3 normalT = normalize(0.5f*(normalT0 + normalT1));
```

Because we scroll the normal maps at different speeds and directions, at every time step the combined normal differs from its previous combined normal; this creates the illusion of new waves forming and dispersing continuously. (The whole idea is very similar to the animated texture in the Cloud demo in Chapter 11, in which we scrolled two cloud textures over a surface.) The usual per-pixel lighting calculation is done for each pixel using the combined normal vector.

Due to the simple geometry of the water plane being a flat rectangle on the xz-plane, the texture space can be described relative to the object space very easily:

```
float3x3 TBN;
// Tangent goes along object space x-axis.
TBN[0] = float3(1.0f, 0.0f, 0.0f);
// Binormal goes along object space negative z-axis
TBN[1] = float3(0.0f, 0.0f, -1.0f);
// Normal goes along object space y-axis
TBN[2] = float3(0.0f, 1.0f, 0.0f);
```

To incorporate reflections, we use an environment map. A weakness of using an environment map here is that only the data in the environment map is reflected. As shown in Figure 21.14, the columns, which are not in the environment map, are not reflected. To simulate ripples and distortion in the reflection, we slightly perturb the environment map look-up vector by the sampled net normal (you can scale the net normal normalT to get different perturbation magnitudes):

```
float3 envMapTex = reflect(-toEyeW, normalW) + (normalT*2.0f);
float3 reflectedColor = texCUBE(EnvMapS, envMapTex);
```

Because the net normal varies every frame, this essentially causes the look-up vector to wiggle in a chaotic way over time, which produces a ripple effect.

Figure 21.14:
Screenshot of the
Water demo.

We combine the material's diffuse and ambient components with the reflected color by averaging them; this average gives us the new diffuse and ambient material component we use in the lighting calculations.

```
// Weighted average between the reflected color and usual
// New diffuse/ambient material.
float3 ambientMtrl = (0.5f*reflectedColor + 0.5f*gMtrl.ambient);
float3 diffuseMtrl = (0.5f*reflectedColor + 0.5f*gMtrl.diffuse);

// Compute the ambient, diffuse, and specular terms separately.
float3 spec = t*(gMtrl.spec*gLight.spec).rgb;
float3 diffuse = s*(diffuseMtrl*gLight.diffuse.rgb);
float3 ambient = ambientMtrl*gLight.ambient;

float3 final = ambient + diffuse + spec;

// Output the color and the alpha.
return float4(final, gMtrl.diffuse.a);
```

21.3 **Render to Texture**

Thus far, we have been rendering to the back buffer surface; that is to say, the back buffer has been the render target. However, the back buffer need not always be the render target; we can render to the surface of a texture, for example. In this section, we show how to update a texture at run time by rendering into it every frame.

The following steps summarize the work necessary to render to a texture:

1. Obtain a pointer to an ID3DXRenderToSurface interface, which is used to render to an IDirect3DSurface9 object.

2. Create an empty texture, which is to be the texture we render into. More precisely, we render into the top-level surface of this texture and, if the hardware supports it, use auto-generated mipmaps to fill in the lower mipmap surfaces. (Recall that a texture stores many surfaces — one for each mipmap level.) If the hardware does not support auto-generated mipmaps, then we just do not use mipmaps with this texture — computing the lower mipmap levels in software would be too slow to do every frame.

3. Obtain a pointer to the top surface level of the texture.

4. Finally, call `ID3DXRenderToSurface::BeginScene`, render the scene you want to texture using draw calls as usual (everything you draw will be drawn to the target surface, which in this case is the top-level surface of a texture), and then call `ID3DXRenderToSurface::EndScene` to complete the drawing. The texture has now been drawn to and we can use it as we would any other texture (e.g., we can set it as an effect parameter and sample it in a pixel shader).

The following sections describe the implementation of these steps in more detail.

21.3.1 D3DXCreateRenderToSurface

To render to a texture, we use the `ID3DXRenderToSurface` interface. We can obtain a pointer to an instance of this interface with the `D3DXCreateRenderToSurface` function:

```
ID3DXRenderToSurface* mRTS = 0;
HR(D3DXCreateRenderToSurface(
    gd3dDevice,         // Associated Direct3D device.
    mWidth, mHeight,    // Dimensions of surface in pixels we render to.
    mTexFormat,         // The surface format (i.e., D3DFORMAT).
    mUseDepthBuffer,    // True if we want to use a depth buffer.
    mDepthFormat,       // Depth buffer format (if we are using one).
    &mRTS));            // Returns pointer to instance.
```

21.3.2 D3DXCreateTexture

The `ID3DXRenderToSurface` interface is used to facilitate rendering to a surface, but we must also create an empty texture whose top-level surface we will render onto. To do this, we use the `D3DXCreateTexture` function:

```
UINT usage = D3DUSAGE_RENDERTARGET;
if(mAutoGenMips)
    usage |= D3DUSAGE_AUTOGENMIPMAP;

IDirect3DTexture9* mTex = 0;
HR(D3DXCreateTexture(
    gd3dDevice,         // Associated Direct3D device.
    mWidth, mHeight,    // Dimensions of surface in pixels we render to.
    mMipLevels,         // Number of mipmap levels.
```

```
usage,            // How the texture will be used.
mTexFormat,       // Texture format (i.e., D3DFORMAT).
D3DPOOL_DEFAULT,  // Render targets must be in default pool.
&mTex));          // Returns pointer to texture.
```

The usage parameter for a *render target* texture needs to be D3DUSAGE_REN-
DERTARGET. Additionally, if the hardware supports it, we can specify for the
hardware to auto-generate mipmaps with the D3DUSAGE_AUTOGENMIPMAP flag.

21.3.3 IDirect3DTexture9::GetSurfaceLevel

We can obtain a pointer to a mipmap surface level in a texture using the
IDirect3DTexture9::GetSurfaceLevel method. The first parameter is an index
identifying the level; zero always indexes the top level. The number of levels of a texture can be obtained by the IDirect3DTexture9::GetLevelCount
method. The following code snippet shows how we can obtain a pointer to
the top-level surface of a texture:

```
IDirect3DSurface9* mTopSurf = 0;
HR(mTex->GetSurfaceLevel(0, &mTopSurf));
```

21.3.4 Drawing to the Surface/Texture

Recall that when we draw to the back buffer, we must place our drawing
calls between a pair of IDirect3DDevice9::BeginScene and IDirect3D-
Device9::EndScene methods. An analogous idea holds for rendering to a
texture; that is, we must place our drawing calls between a pair of
ID3DXRenderToSurface::BeginScene and ID3DXRenderToSurface::EndScene
methods:

```
mRTS->BeginScene(mTopSurf, &mViewPort);

// Put draw code here. The geometry we draw here gets drawn
// to the surface/texture.

mRTS->EndScene(D3DX_FILTER_NONE);
```

Here, mRTS is a pointer to an ID3DXRenderToSurface interface.

The ID3DXRenderToSurface::BeginScene and ID3DXRenderToSurface::
EndScene methods are prototyped as follows:

```
HRESULT ID3DXRenderToSurface::BeginScene(
    LPDIRECT3DSURFACE9 pSurface,
    CONST D3DVIEWPORT9 *pViewport);

HRESULT ID3DXRenderToSurface::EndScene(DWORD MipFilter);
```

- pSurface: Pointer to the surface we are rendering onto.
- pViewport: Pointer to a viewport that specifies a subset of the surface to
  render onto. See §6.4.7 for a description of viewports.
- MipFilter: A D3DX_FILTER flag that specifies the filtering method to use to
  generate mipmaps from the top-level surface. We specify

D3DX_FILTER_NONE and attempt to use hardware auto-generated mipmap levels. If you disable auto-generated mipmaps by not specifying it in the usage parameter for D3DXCreateTexture (or it's not supported) and use a filter like D3DX_FILTER_BOX|D3DX_FILTER_DITHER, the program will run very slowly since it is generating mipmaps in software each frame.

21.3.5 **DrawableTex2D**

To make it a bit easier to draw to textures, we define and implement a class called DrawableTex2D, which wraps the code needed to render to a texture:

```
class DrawableTex2D
{
public:
    DrawableTex2D(UINT width, UINT height, UINT mipLevels,
        D3DFORMAT texFormat, bool useDepthBuffer,
        D3DFORMAT depthFormat, D3DVIEWPORT9& viewport,
        bool autoGenMips);
    ~DrawableTex2D();

    // Return the D3D texture representation.
    IDirect3DTexture9* d3dTex();

    // Wraps ID3DXRenderToSurface::BeginScene/EndScene.
    void beginScene();
    void endScene();

    // Call when device lost/reset.
    void onLostDevice();
    void onResetDevice();

private:
    // This class is not designed to be copied.
    DrawableTex2D(const DrawableTex2D& rhs);
    DrawableTex2D& operator=(const DrawableTex2D& rhs);

private:
    IDirect3DTexture9*      mTex;
    ID3DXRenderToSurface*   mRTS;
    IDirect3DSurface9*      mTopSurf;

    UINT            mWidth;
    UINT            mHeight;
    UINT            mMipLevels;
    D3DFORMAT       mTexFormat;
    bool            mUseDepthBuffer;
    D3DFORMAT       mDepthFormat;
    D3DVIEWPORT9    mViewPort;
    bool            mAutoGenMips;
};

DrawableTex2D::DrawableTex2D(UINT width, UINT height, UINT mipLevels,
        D3DFORMAT texFormat, bool useDepthBuffer,
```

```
                    D3DFORMAT depthFormat, D3DVIEWPORT9& viewport,
                    bool autoGenMips)
: mTex(0), mRTS(0), mTopSurf(0), mWidth(width), mHeight(height),
  mMipLevels(mipLevels), mTexFormat(texFormat),
  mUseDepthBuffer(useDepthBuffer), mDepthFormat(depthFormat),
  mViewPort(viewport), mAutoGenMips(autoGenMips)
{
}


DrawableTex2D::~DrawableTex2D()
{
    onLostDevice();
}


IDirect3DTexture9* DrawableTex2D::d3dTex()
{
    return mTex;
}


void DrawableTex2D::onLostDevice()
{
    // Default texture needs to be destroyed before reset.
    ReleaseCOM(mTex);
    ReleaseCOM(mRTS);
    ReleaseCOM(mTopSurf);
}


void DrawableTex2D::onResetDevice()
{
    // Default texture needs to be recreated after reset.
    UINT usage = D3DUSAGE_RENDERTARGET;
    if(mAutoGenMips)
            usage |= D3DUSAGE_AUTOGENMIPMAP;

    HR(D3DXCreateTexture(gd3dDevice, mWidth, mHeight,
            mMipLevels, usage, mTexFormat, D3DPOOL_DEFAULT, &mTex));

    HR(D3DXCreateRenderToSurface(gd3dDevice, mWidth, mHeight,
            mTexFormat, mUseDepthBuffer, mDepthFormat, &mRTS));

    HR(mTex->GetSurfaceLevel(0, &mTopSurf));
}


void DrawableTex2D::beginScene()
{
    mRTS->BeginScene(mTopSurf, &mViewPort);
}


void DrawableTex2D::endScene()
{
    mRTS->EndScene(D3DX_FILTER_NONE);
}
```

21.3.6 **Render to Texture Demo**

To illustrate rendering to a texture, we are going to return to the Terrain demo, but add a radar map (see Figure 21.15).

Figure 21.15: Screenshot of the RenderToTex demo.

The radar map itself is modeled as a textured quad in normalized device coordinates and occupies the fourth quadrant of the back buffer. For each frame, we render the scene from a bird's-eye view directly above the player to a renderable texture. We then map this texture onto the radar quad. In this way, the radar is updated every frame based on how the player moves over the terrain. The following code illustrates the idea:

```
// Position bird's-eye camera 100 units above the player's position.
D3DXVECTOR3 pos(gCamera->pos().x,
                gCamera->pos().y + 1000.0f,
                gCamera->pos().z);
D3DXVECTOR3 up(0.0f, 0.0f, 1.0f);
mBirdsEyeCamera.lookAt(pos, gCamera->pos(), up);

// Draw into texture using bird's-eye camera.
mRadarMap->beginScene();
gd3dDevice->Clear(0, 0, D3DCLEAR_TARGET|D3DCLEAR_ZBUFFER,
    0xff000000, 1.0f, 0);
gCamera = &mBirdsEyeCamera;
mTerrain->draw();
mRadarMap->endScene();

// Now draw normal scene to back buffer.
gCamera = &mFirstPersonCamera;

HR(gd3dDevice->BeginScene());
mSky->draw();

// Draw the terrain to the back buffer.
```

```
mTerrain->draw();

// Draw the radar quad and map the renderable texture to it.
HR(gd3dDevice->SetStreamSource(0, mRadarVB, 0, sizeof(VertexPT)));
HR(gd3dDevice->SetVertexDeclaration (VertexPT::Decl));

HR(mRadarFX->SetTexture(mhTex, mRadarMap->d3dTex()));
UINT numPasses = 0;
HR(mRadarFX->Begin(&numPasses, 0));
HR(mRadarFX->BeginPass(0));
HR(gd3dDevice->DrawPrimitive(D3DPT_TRIANGLELIST, 0, 2));
HR(mRadarFX->EndPass());
HR(mRadarFX->End());
```

21.4 **Summary**

- A cube map stores six textures that we visualize as the faces of a cube. In Direct3D, a cube map is represented by the IDirect3DCubeTexture9 interface. To identify a texel in a cube map, we use 3D texture coordinates, which define a 3D lookup vector $\vec{v} = (v_x, v_y, v_z)$ originating at the origin. The texel of the cube map that $\vec{v}$ intersects is the texel corresponding to the 3D coordinates of $\vec{v}$.

- Cube maps can be made from six individual images using the DirectX Texture Tool. Cube maps can be saved to file with the DDS image format. Because cube maps essentially store six 2D textures, a compressed DDS format should be used to save memory. We can create a cube map from file using the D3DXCreateCubeTextureFromFile function.

- A normal map is a texture, but instead of storing RGB data at each texel, we store a compressed x-coordinate, y-coordinate, and z-coordinate in the red, green, and blue components, respectively. Normal maps can be generated from a height map manually; however, there are third-party tools to automate the process such as the NVidia Normal Map Plug-in (http://developer.nvidia.com/object/nv_texture_tools.html).

- The strategy of normal mapping is to texture our polygons with normal maps. We then have per-pixel normals, which capture the fine details of a surface like bumps, scratches, and crevices. We then use these per-pixel normals from the normal map in our lighting calculations instead of the interpolated vertex normal.

- The normals in a normal map are relative to the texture space coordinate system. Consequently, to do lighting calculations, we need to transform the light data to the texture space so that the lights and normals are in the same coordinate system. The TBN-bases built at each vertex facilitates the transformation from object space to texture space.

■ The back buffer need not always be the render target; we can render to the surface of a texture, for example. Rendering to a texture provides an efficient way for updating a texture at run time, and many special effects like shadow maps and water simulations, along with general-purpose GPU programming, require render to texture functionality.

21.5 **Exercises**

1. Experiment with the reflectivity constant in the EnvMap demo. In particular, try the values 0.0, 0.25, 0.5, and 0.75.

2. Light a teapot using normal mapping; use the brick normal map found in the Bricks demo.

3. In §21.1.1, we described how to create the textures of a cube map in a separate 3D rendering program like Terragen. However, suppose that you want animated clouds or birds flying in the sky. With a pre-generated cube map, you cannot capture these changing objects. One solution is to build the cube map at run time. That is, every frame, you position the camera in the scene that is to be the origin of the cube map, and then render the scene six times into each cube map face along each coordinate axis direction. Since the cube map is rebuilt every frame, it will capture changing objects.

   For this exercise, investigate the ID3DXRenderToEnvMap interface in the DirectX documentation, which will help you render into a cube map. Then modify the EnvMap demo by orbiting a sphere around the skull. To capture the orbiting sphere in the skull's reflection, use ID3DXRenderToEnvMap to build a cube map centered at the skull for each frame. Then use this dynamic cube map as the cube map for the skull so that the orbiting sphere shows up in the reflection.

   Note that high-resolution dynamic cube maps can be very expensive, as you are rendering the scene six additional times! Since there is usually a fair amount of distortion in a cube map reflection, you can usually get by with cube map faces of 256×256 pixels.

4. Integrate the sky-sphere and water technique described in this chapter into the Props demo from Chapter 18. Because the environment map used for the sky shows a relatively clear day, you may wish to disable the fog.

Chapter 22

Advanced Texturing — Part II

In this final chapter, we continue to explore more advanced texturing techniques. In particular, we discuss projective texturing, shadow mapping, and displacement mapping. *Projective texturing* is a technique that enables us to simulate a slide projector and project a texture onto arbitrary geometry within the projector's frustum. *Shadow mapping* is a real-time shadowing technique that shadows arbitrary geometry (it is not limited to planar shadows). Finally, *displacement mapping* is a technique where each vertex has an associated displacement vector (usually stored in a displacement map), which specifies how a vertex should be displaced in a vertex shader. [Kryachko05] uses displacement mapping to simulate realistic ocean waves in the game Pacific Fighters.

Objectives:

- To discover how to project textures onto arbitrary geometry, much like a slide projector.
- To find out how to shadow arbitrary meshes (not just planes) using the shadow mapping algorithm.
- To learn how to animate realistic ocean waves using displacement mapping.

22.1 **Projective Texturing**

Projective texturing is so-called because it allows us to project a texture onto arbitrary geometry, much like a slide projector. Figure 22.1 shows an example of projective texturing.

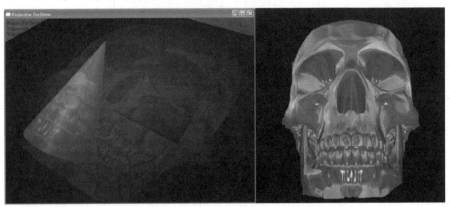

Figure 22.1: The skull texture (right) is projected onto the scene geometry (left).

Projective texturing can be useful on its own for modeling slide projectors, but, as we show in §22.2, it is also used as an intermediate step for other techniques, such as shadow mapping.

The key to projective texturing is to generate texture coordinates for each vertex in such a way that the applied texture looks like it has been projected onto the geometry. We will call such texture coordinates *projective texture coordinates*.

22.1.1 **Generating Projective Texture Coordinates**

The idea of generating projective texture coordinates is to define a view matrix V_L and projection matrix V_P for the projector, which together define the frustum for the projector relative to the world space (i.e., the projector projects light through a frustum in the world). Assuming the scene geometry is already in world space, we use V_L, V_P, and the homogeneous divide (recall Chapter 6, "The Rendering Pipeline") to project the geometry onto the projection plane of the projector (think of the projector as a camera).

For vertices inside the projector's frustum, the projected vertices have coordinates bounded as follows:

$$-1 \le x \le 1$$
$$-1 \le y \le 1$$
$$0 \le z \le 1$$

These are the so-called normalized device coordinates. Here the x- and y-coordinates correspond to the projected 2D points on the projection window and the z-coordinate is used for the depth test; for projective texturing we ignore the z-coordinate. A simple scaling and translation transformation can map the 2D vertices from the projection window coordinate system to the texture coordinate system, thereby effectively turning them into texture coordinates:

$$u = \tfrac{1}{2}x + \tfrac{1}{2}$$
$$v = -\tfrac{1}{2}y + \tfrac{1}{2}$$ where $u, v \in [0, 1]$ provided $x, y \in [-1, 1]$

(So note that we scale the y-coordinate by a negative number to invert the axis because the positive y-axis on the projection window goes in the direction opposite to the positive v-axis in texture coordinates.) The texture coordinates generated in this fashion correctly identify the part of the texture that should be projected onto each triangle. Figure 22.2 summarizes the idea.

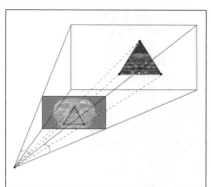

Figure 22.2: We can think of the texture as lying on the projection window of the projector's frustum. Then the idea of projective texturing is that the texture is projected through the frustum and mapped onto any geometry it intersects. For any 3D triangle inside the projector's frustum, the projection of that triangle, onto the projection window, defines the 2D triangle on the texture that is mapped onto the 3D triangle with projective texturing. However, before we can use these projected vertices as texture coordinates, we must map them to the [0, 1] range for texture mapping.

Note: Projective texturing does not take geometric relationships into consideration. All the geometry is projected onto the projector's projection window and given projective texture coordinates without regard to their spatial relationships. Consequently, a texture can be projected onto geometry that is occluded by geometry in front of it, which would be physically incorrect since the occluded geometry should be in shadow. This fault is analogous to the faults of local illumination lighting models, where each vertex/pixel is lit independently of all other vertices/pixels.

22.1.2 **Projective Texture Coordinates Outside [0, 1]**

In the rendering pipeline, geometry outside the frustum is clipped. However, when we generate projective texture coordinates by projecting the geometry from the point of view of the light projector, no clipping is done — we simply project vertices. Consequently, geometry outside the projector's frustum receives projective texture coordinates outside the [0, 1] range. Projective texture coordinates outside the [0, 1] range function just like normal texture coordinates outside the [0, 1] range based on the enabled address mode (see §11.6).

We do not want to projectively texture any geometry outside the projector's frustum because it would not make sense (such geometry receives no light from the projector). To handle this in the sample code, we associate a spotlight with the projector so that anything outside the spotlight's field of view cone is not lit (i.e., the surface receives no projected light). This method also handles the problem of *back projection* (see Figure 22.3), which is where geometry behind the light projector incorrectly receives light from the projector. (This happens because the geometry behind the frustum is not clipped, and so these vertices generate functional projective texture coordinates.)

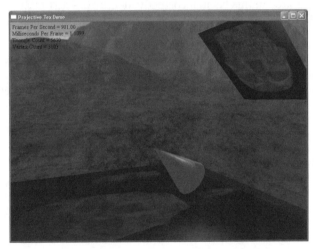

Figure 22.3: Geometry behind the projector also gets projected texture coordinates. The negative *z*-coordinates, stemming from the geometry being behind the projector, causes the texture coordinates to flip.

22.1.3 Sample Code

Below is the effect file used for the Projective Texturing demo; the lines relevant to projective texturing have been bolded:

```
struct Mtrl
{
    float4 ambient;
    float4 diffuse;
    float4 spec;
    float  specPower;
};

struct SpotLight
{
    float4 ambient;
    float4 diffuse;
    float4 spec;
    float3 posW;
```

```
        float3 dirW;
        float  spotPower;
};

uniform extern float4x4  gWorld;
uniform extern float4x4  gWorldInvTrans;
uniform extern float4x4  gLightWVP;
uniform extern float4x4  gWVP;
uniform extern Mtrl       gMtrl;
uniform extern SpotLight gLight;
uniform extern float3     gEyePosW;
uniform extern texture    gTex;

sampler TexS = sampler_state
{
        Texture = <gTex>;
        MinFilter = LINEAR;
        MagFilter = LINEAR;
        MipFilter = LINEAR;
        AddressU  = CLAMP;
        AddressV  = CLAMP;
};

struct OutputVS
{
        float4 posH      : POSITION0;
        float3 posW      : TEXCOORD0;
        float3 normalW   : TEXCOORD1;
        float3 toEyeW    : TEXCOORD2;
        float4 projTex   : TEXCOORD3;
};

OutputVS ProjTexVS(float3 posL : POSITION0, float3 normalL : NORMAL0)
{
        // Zero out our output.
        OutputVS outVS = (OutputVS)0;

        // Transform normal to world space.
        outVS.normalW = mul(float4(normalL, 0.0f), gWorldInvTrans).xyz;

        // Transform vertex position to world space.
        outVS.posW  = mul(float4(posL, 1.0f), gWorld).xyz;

        // Compute the unit vector from the vertex to the eye.
        outVS.toEyeW = gEyePosW - outVS.posW;

        // Transform to homogeneous clip space.
        outVS.posH = mul(float4(posL, 1.0f), gWVP);

        // Render from light source perspective to generate projective
        // texture coordinates.
        outVS.projTex = mul(float4(posL, 1.0f), gLightWVP);
```

```
        // Done--return the output.
        return outVS;
}

float4 ProjTexPS(float3 posW     : TEXCOORD0,
                 float3 normalW  : TEXCOORD1,
                 float3 toEyeW   : TEXCOORD2,
                 float4 projTex  : TEXCOORD3) : COLOR
{
        // Interpolated normals can become unnormal--so normalize.
        normalW = normalize(normalW);
        toEyeW  = normalize(toEyeW);

        // Light vector is from pixel to spotlight position.
        float3 lightVecW = normalize(gLight.posW - posW);

        // Compute the reflection vector.
        float3 r = reflect(-lightVecW, normalW);

        // Determine how much (if any) specular light makes it
        // into the eye.
        float t = pow(max(dot(r, toEyeW), 0.0f), gMtrl.specPower);

        // Determine the diffuse light intensity that strikes the vertex.
        float s = max(dot(lightVecW, normalW), 0.0f);

        // Compute the ambient, diffuse, and specular terms separately.
        float3 spec = t*(gMtrl.spec*gLight.spec).rgb;
        float3 diffuse = s*(gMtrl.diffuse*gLight.diffuse.rgb);
        float3 ambient = gMtrl.ambient*gLight.ambient;

        // Compute spotlight coefficient.
        float spot = pow(max(dot(-lightVecW, gLight.dirW),
                             0.0f), gLight.spotPower);

        // Project the texture coords and scale/offset to [0, 1].
        projTex.xy /= projTex.w;
        projTex.x =  0.5f*projTex.x + 0.5f;
        projTex.y = -0.5f*projTex.y + 0.5f;

        // Sample tex w/ projective texture coords.
        float4 texColor = tex2D(TexS, projTex.xy);

        // Only project/light in spotlight cone.
        float3 litColor = spot*(ambient+diffuse*texColor.rgb + spec);

        // Output the color and the alpha.
        return float4(litColor, gMtrl.diffuse.a*texColor.a);
}

technique ProjTexTech
{
        pass P0
```

```
    {
        vertexShader = compile vs_2_0 ProjTexVS();
        pixelShader  = compile ps_2_0 ProjTexPS();
    }
}
```

22.2 **Shadow Mapping**

Shadows indicate to the observer where light originates and helps convey the relative locations of objects in a scene. In Chapter 13, we showed how to create planar shadows. We now describe a more general technique that allows us to cast shadows on arbitrary meshes. For this discussion, we concern ourselves with spotlights. Exercises 4 and 5 ask you to think about directional and point lights.

The idea of the shadow mapping algorithm is to render the scene from the viewpoint of the light and, for each visible pixel, write the pixel depth to a *depth map* (which is also called a *shadow map*). (So note that we will need to define a view matrix and projection matrix for the spotlight, describing the volume, in world space, through which light is emitted.) When we render the scene from the viewpoint of the light, we will use a depth buffer as we usually do with rendering; thus, after the scene has been drawn to the shadow map, the shadow map stores the depths of all the visible pixels from the perspective of the spotlight. (Pixels occluded by other pixels will not be in the shadow map because they will fail the depth test and either be overwritten or never written.)

Note: So observe that we are not drawing color information to a surface as we usually do. We are actually drawing in a more abstract way, where instead of writing color information to a surface, we are, in fact, writing the pixels' depth values.

After we have built the shadow map, we render the scene as normal from the perspective of the camera. For each pixel p_{ij} rendered, we also compute its depth from the light source, which we denote by $d(p_{ij})$. In addition, by projecting the shadow map onto the scene (the spotlight is the projector), for each pixel p_{ij}, we can obtain the depth, denoted by $s(p_{ij})$, of the pixel closest to the light along the line of sight from the position of the spotlight to p_{ij}. Then, a pixel p_{ij} is in shadow if and only if $s(p_{ij}) < d(p_{ij})$. Figure 22.4 summarizes the idea.

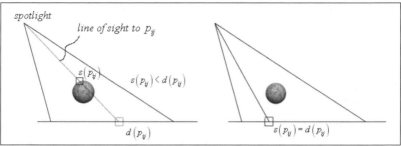

Figure 22.4: On the left, the depth of the pixel p_{ij} from the spotlight is $d(p_{ij})$. However, the depth of the pixel nearest to the spotlight along the same line of sight has depth $s(p_{ij})$, and $s(p_{ij}) < d(p_{ij})$. We conclude, therefore, that p_{ij} is in shadow. On the right, the depth of the pixel p_{ij} from the spotlight is $d(p_{ij})$ and it also happens to be the pixel nearest to the spotlight along the line of sight, that is, $s(p_{ij}) = d(p_{ij})$, so we conclude p_{ij} is not in shadow.

22.2.1 Checking for D3DFMT_R32F Support

We use a 32-bit floating-point render target for the shadow map, which may not be supported on all devices. We can check support for it with the following code, which we place in the `ShadowMapDemo::checkDeviceCaps` function:

```
// Check render target support. The adapter format can be either the
// display mode format for windowed mode, or D3DFMT_X8R8G8B8 for
// full screen mode, so we need to test against both. We use
// D3DFMT_R32F as the render texture format and D3DFMT_D24X8 as the
// render texture depth format.
D3DDISPLAYMODE mode;
md3dObject->GetAdapterDisplayMode(D3DADAPTER_DEFAULT, &mode);

// Windowed.
if(FAILED(md3dObject->CheckDeviceFormat(D3DADAPTER_DEFAULT, mDevType,
    mode.Format, D3DUSAGE_RENDERTARGET, D3DRTYPE_TEXTURE, D3DFMT_R32F)))
        return false;
if(FAILED(md3dObject->CheckDepthStencilMatch(D3DADAPTER_DEFAULT,
    mDevType, mode.Format, D3DFMT_R32F, D3DFMT_D24X8)))
        return false;

// Full screen.
if(FAILED(md3dObject->CheckDeviceFormat(D3DADAPTER_DEFAULT, mDevType,
D3DFMT_X8R8G8B8, D3DUSAGE_RENDERTARGET, D3DRTYPE_TEXTURE,D3DFMT_R32F)))
        return false;
if(FAILED(md3dObject->CheckDepthStencilMatch(D3DADAPTER_DEFAULT,
    mDevType, D3DFMT_X8R8G8B8, D3DFMT_R32F, D3DFMT_D24X8)))
        return false;
```

As in the previous chapter, we use our `DrawableTex2D` class to store the shadow map, which we recompute (i.e., render to) each frame:

```
mShadowMap = new DrawableTex2D(512, 512, 1, D3DFMT_R32F,
                          true, D3DFMT_D24X8, vp, false);
```

Note: Observe that our texture format, `D3DFMT_R32F`, only has one color channel. This is sufficient because we are storing depth information, which is a scalar value (i.e., we do not need more than one component/channel).

22.2.2 Building the Shadow Map

In the C++ application code, we use the following function to draw the scene into the shadow map. We always call this function first every frame to build the shadow map, which is then used in the normal scene drawing code.

```
void ShadowMapDemo::drawShadowMap()
{
    mShadowMap->beginScene();
    HR(gd3dDevice->Clear(0, 0, D3DCLEAR_TARGET | D3DCLEAR_ZBUFFER,
                        0x00000000, 1.0f, 0));

    HR(mFX->SetTechnique(mhBuildShadowMapTech));

    UINT numPasses = 0;
    HR(mFX->Begin(&numPasses, 0));
    HR(mFX->BeginPass(0));

    // Draw scene mesh.
    HR(mFX->SetMatrix(mhLightWVP, &(mSceneWorld*mLightVP)));
    HR(mFX->CommitChanges());
    for(UINT j = 0; j < mSceneMtrls.size(); ++j)
    {
        for(UINT j = 0; j < mSceneMtrls.size(); ++j)
        {
            HR(mSceneMesh->DrawSubset(j));
        }
    }

    // Draw car mesh.
    HR(mFX->SetMatrix(mhLightWVP, &(mCarWorld*mLightVP)));
    HR(mFX->CommitChanges());
    for(UINT j = 0; j < mCarMtrls.size(); ++j)
    {
        for(UINT j = 0; j < mCarMtrls.size(); ++j)
        {
            HR(mCarMesh->DrawSubset(j));
        }
    }

    HR(mFX->EndPass());
    HR(mFX->End());

    mShadowMap->endScene();
}
```

The corresponding effect code used to write the depth of each visible pixel to the shadow map is given as follows:

```
uniform extern float4x4 gLightWVP;

void BuildShadowMapVS(float3 posL : POSITION0,
                      out float4 posH : POSITION0,
                      out float2 depth : TEXCOORD0)
{
    // Render from light's perspective.
    posH = mul(float4(posL, 1.0f), gLightWVP);

    // Propagate z- and w-coordinates.
    depth = posH.zw;
}

float4 BuildShadowMapPS(float2 depth : TEXCOORD0) : COLOR
{
    // Each pixel in the shadow map stores the pixel depth from the
    // light source in normalized device coordinates.
    return depth.x / depth.y; // z / w; depth in [0, 1] range.
}

technique BuildShadowMapTech
{
    pass P0
    {
        vertexShader = compile vs_2_0 BuildShadowMapVS();
        pixelShader  = compile ps_2_0 BuildShadowMapPS();
    }
}
```

22.2.3 The Shadow Map Test

We now show the effect code used to draw the scene from the camera's viewpoint. The relevant shadow mapping code has been bolded.

```
struct Mtrl
{
    float4 ambient;
    float4 diffuse;
    float4 spec;
    float  specPower;
};

struct SpotLight
{
    float4 ambient;
    float4 diffuse;
    float4 spec;
    float3 posW;
    float3 dirW;
    float  spotPower;
};
```

```
uniform extern float4x4  gWorld;
uniform extern float4x4  gWVP;
uniform extern Mtrl      gMtrl;
uniform extern SpotLight gLight;
uniform extern float3    gEyePosW;
uniform extern texture   gTex;
uniform extern texture   gShadowMap;
uniform extern float4x4  gLightWVP;

static const float SHADOW_EPSILON = 0.00005f;
static const float SMAP_SIZE = 512.0f;

sampler TexS = sampler_state
{
    Texture = <gTex>;
    MinFilter = LINEAR;
    MagFilter = LINEAR;
    MipFilter = LINEAR;
    AddressU  = WRAP;
    AddressV  = WRAP;
};

sampler ShadowMapS = sampler_state
{
    Texture = <gShadowMap>;
    MinFilter = POINT;
    MagFilter = POINT;
    MipFilter = POINT;
    AddressU  = CLAMP;
    AddressV  = CLAMP;
};

void LightShadowVS(float3 posL      : POSITION0,
                   float3 normalL   : NORMAL0,
                   float2 tex0      : TEXCOORD0,
                   out float4 oPosH : POSITION0,
                   out float3 oPosW : TEXCOORD0,
                   out float3 oNormalW : TEXCOORD1,
                   out float3 oToEyeW  : TEXCOORD2,
                   out float2 oTex0    : TEXCOORD3,
                   out float4 oProjTex : TEXCOORD4)
{
    // Transform to homogeneous clip space.
    oPosH = mul(float4(posL, 1.0f), gWVP);

    // Transform vertex position to world space.
    oPosW = mul(float4(posL, 1.0f), gWorld).xyz;

    // Transform normal to world space
    // (assume no non-uniform scaling).
    oNormalW = mul(float4(normalL, 0.0f), gWorld).xyz;
```

```
        // Compute the unit vector from the vertex to the eye.
        oToEyeW = gEyePosW - oPosW;

        // Pass on texture coords to PS
        oTex0 = tex0;

        // Generate projective texture coordinates to project
        // shadow map onto scene.
        oProjTex = mul(float4(posL, 1.0f), gLightWVP);
}

float4 LightShadowPS(float3 posW    : TEXCOORD0,
                     float3 normalW : TEXCOORD1,
                     float3 toEyeW  : TEXCOORD2,
                     float2 tex0    : TEXCOORD3,
                     float4 projTex : TEXCOORD4) : COLOR
{
        // Interpolated normals can become unnormal--so normalize.
        normalW = normalize(normalW);
        toEyeW  = normalize(toEyeW);

        // Light vector is from pixel to spotlight position.
        float3 lightVecW = normalize(gLight.posW - posW);

        // Compute the reflection vector.
        float3 r = reflect(-lightVecW, normalW);

        // Determine how much (if any) specular light makes it
        // into the eye.
        float t = pow(max(dot(r, toEyeW), 0.0f), gMtrl.specPower);

        // Determine the diffuse light intensity that strikes the vertex.
        float s = max(dot(lightVecW, normalW), 0.0f);

        // Compute the ambient, diffuse, and specular terms separately.
        float3 spec    = t*(gMtrl.spec*gLight.spec).rgb;
        float3 diffuse = s*(gMtrl.diffuse*gLight.diffuse.rgb);
        float3 ambient = gMtrl.ambient*gLight.ambient;

        // Compute spotlight coefficient.
        float spot = pow(max( dot(-lightVecW, gLight.dirW), 0.0f),
                         gLight.spotPower);

        // Sample decal map.
        float4 texColor = tex2D(TexS, tex0);

        // Project the texture coords and scale/offset to [0, 1].
        projTex.xy /= projTex.w;
        projTex.x =  0.5f*projTex.x + 0.5f;
        projTex.y = -0.5f*projTex.y + 0.5f;

        // Compute pixel depth for shadowing.
        float depth = projTex.z / projTex.w; // depth in [0, 1] range
```

```
    // Transform to texel space.
    float2 texelpos = SMAP_SIZE * projTex.xy;

    // Determine the lerp amounts.
    float2 lerps = frac( texelpos );

    // 2x2 percentage closest filter.
    float dx = 1.0f / SMAP_SIZE;
    float s0 = (tex2D(ShadowMapS, projTex.xy).r
                + SHADOW_EPSILON < depth) ? 0.0f : 1.0f;
    float s1 = (tex2D(ShadowMapS, projTex.xy + float2(dx, 0.0f)).r
                + SHADOW_EPSILON < depth) ? 0.0f : 1.0f;
    float s2 = (tex2D(ShadowMapS, projTex.xy + float2(0.0f, dx)).r
                + SHADOW_EPSILON < depth) ? 0.0f : 1.0f;
    float s3 = (tex2D(ShadowMapS, projTex.xy + float2(dx, dx)).r
                + SHADOW_EPSILON < depth) ? 0.0f : 1.0f;

    float shadowCoeff = lerp(lerp( s0, s1, lerps.x),
                             lerp( s2, s3, lerps.x),
                             lerps.y);

    // Light/texture pixel.  Note that shadow coefficient
    // only affects diffuse/spec.
    float3 litColor = spot*ambient*texColor.rgb
        + spot*shadowCoeff*(diffuse*texColor.rgb + spec);

    return float4(litColor, gMtrl.diffuse.a*texColor.a);
}

technique LightShadowTech
{
    pass P0
    {
        vertexShader = compile vs_2_0 LightShadowVS();
        pixelShader  = compile ps_2_0 LightShadowPS();
    }
}
```

22.2.4 Filtering

A natural disadvantage of shadow mapping is aliasing artifacts (see Figure 22.5). To help alleviate this a bit, we employ a filtering technique based on a weighted average. [Kilgard01] points out that we should not average depth values, as it can lead to incorrect results about a pixel being flagged in shadow. Instead, for a given pixel p_{ij}, we compute the shadow map test for it and its three neighboring pixels. We then average the results of these tests to compute the shadow coefficient for p_{ij}. In this way, it is not an all-or-nothing situation; a pixel can be partially in shadow. For example, if two of the pixels are in shadow and two are not in shadow, then we say the pixel is 50% in shadow. This creates a smooth transition from shadowed pixels to non-shadowed pixels.

Figure 22.5: In the top image, observe the "stairstepping" artifacts on the shadow boundary. On the bottom image, these aliasing artifacts are smoothed out a bit with filtering.

Before discussing the details of the filtering method, let's digress briefly on texture coordinates. To keep things simple, let's work with a 1D texture map that only spans the u-axis (i.e., a single row of texels). Texture coordinates will seldom identify one texel perfectly; the coordinates will probably land between two texels. For example, if the u coordinate is 0.23 and the texture dimension is 512 texels wide, then $0.23 \cdot 512 = 117.76$. It is not clear whether we should say this identifies texel T_{117} or texel T_{118}. So what we do is average the two texels, giving more weight to texel T_{118} since the fractional part 0.76 tells us it is closer to T_{118}; that is, we use the value $T = (1 - 0.76) T_{117} + 0.76 T_{118} = lerp (T_{117}, T_{118}, 0.76)$. The lerp (linear interpolation) function can be viewed as a weighted average.

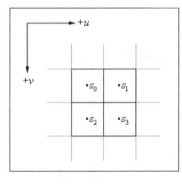

Figure 22.6: The shadow map result of a pixel and the results of its three neighbors, which are taken into account by the filter.

Now consider Figure 22.6, which shows a shadow map result s_0 and the results of its three neighbors s_1, s_2, and s_3. We first linearly interpolate s_0 and s_1 along the u-axis. Analogously, we linearly interpolate s_2 and s_3 along the u-axis. Finally, we linearly interpolate these two results along the v-axis. This gives the code:

```
// Transform to texel space.
float2 texelpos = SMAP_SIZE * projTex.xy;

// Determine the lerp amounts.
float2 lerps = frac(texelpos);

// Distance between two texels in (u,v) coordinates.
float dx = 1.0f / SMAP_SIZE;

// 2x2 percentage closest filter.
float s0 = (tex2D(ShadowMapS, projTex.xy).r
            + SHADOW_EPSILON < depth) ? 0.0f : 1.0f;
float s1 = (tex2D(ShadowMapS, projTex.xy + float2(dx, 0.0f)).r
            + SHADOW_EPSILON < depth) ? 0.0f : 1.0f;
float s2 = (tex2D(ShadowMapS, projTex.xy + float2(0.0f, dx)).r
            + SHADOW_EPSILON < depth) ? 0.0f : 1.0f;
float s3 = (tex2D(ShadowMapS, projTex.xy + float2(dx, dx)).r
            + SHADOW_EPSILON < depth) ? 0.0f : 1.0f;

float shadowCoeff = lerp(lerp( s0, s1, lerps.x),
                         lerp( s2, s3, lerps.x),
                         lerps.y);
```

The constants SHADOW_EPSILON and SMAP_SIZE are defined in the effect file as:

```
static const float SHADOW_EPSILON = 0.00005f;
static const float SMAP_SIZE = 512.0f;
```

The value SMAP_SIZE specifies the shadow map resolution. In this demo we use a resolution of 512×512 texels. The SHADOW_EPSILON value is an offset we add to the sampled shadow map value, $s(p_{ij})$, to avoid shadowing artifacts due to computer imprecision; exercise 3 asks you to modify this value to see exactly what it does.

The HLSL frac function returns the fractional part of a floating-point number (i.e., the mantissa). For example, if SMAP_SIZE = 512 and projTex.xy = (0.23, 0.68), then texelpos = (0.23*512, 0.68*512) = (117.76, 348.16) and frac(texelpos) = (0.76, 0.16). These fractions give the weights for the weighted averages. The HLSL lerp(x, y, s) function is the linear interpolation function and returns $x + s\,(y - x) = (1 - s)\,x + sy$.

Note: Even with our filtering, the shadows are still very hard and the aliasing artifacts can still be unsatisfactory up close. More aggressive methods can be used; see [Uralsky05], for example. We also note that using a higher-resolution shadow map helps, but can be cost prohibitive.

22.3 **Displacement Mapping**

We conclude this chapter with yet another texturing technique. The idea of displacement mapping is to associate a displacement vector for each vertex and then to offset (i.e., displace) the vertex in the direction of the displacement vector based on some prescribed length. For example, the RGB components of the displacement map could describe a unit vector specifying a direction $\vec{n}$, and the alpha component could store a scalar α so that the displacement vector is given by $\alpha\vec{n}$. (In some cases, the vertices are displaced in the direction of their vertex normal or along one of the coordinate axes, and so only a scalar needs to be prescribed in the displacement map.)

To implement displacement mapping in today's graphics hardware, we use the new vertex texture fetch functionality exposed by the vertex shader 3.0 model. Simply put, this functionality allows us to sample textures in a vertex shader. So the strategy is to create a displacement map where each texel (displacement vector) is associated with a vertex on a mesh. Then we can displace each vertex in the vertex shader by sampling its associated displacement vector from the displacement map and adding it to the vertex.

22.3.1 **Checking Device Capabilities**

As stated, implementing displacement mapping requires support for vertex shader 3.0, which exposes the texture fetch functionality. We update our checkDeviceCaps method accordingly:

```
bool DisplacementMapDemo::checkDeviceCaps()
{
    D3DCAPS9 caps;
    HR(gd3dDevice->GetDeviceCaps(&caps));

    // Check for vertex shader version 3.0 support.
    if(caps.VertexShaderVersion < D3DVS_VERSION(3, 0))
        return false;

    // Check for pixel shader version 3.0 support.
    if(caps.PixelShaderVersion < D3DPS_VERSION(3, 0))
        return false;

    return true;
}
```

22.3.2 **Demo Overview**

To demonstrate displacement mapping, we implement a new water demo to simulate ocean waves. We start with a flat vertex grid and use displacement mapping to offset each vertex over time to give the appearance of ocean waves. The idea is that we create two heightmaps (displacement maps of floating-point format D3DFMT_R32F), which describe a snapshot of the surface of an ocean. The resolution of the heightmaps should match that of the water grid so that the *ij*th water grid vertex is associated with the *ij*th element of the heightmaps. We then scroll these two displacement maps over a grid, and, for each vertex:

1. Sample the height elements from the two heightmaps associated with this vertex.

2. Add the two sampled heights together to form a net height.

3. Set the vertex's *y*-coordinate to this net height.

Because we scroll the two displacement maps over time, and at different rates, it gives the illusion of new waves forming and fading.

Figure 22.7 shows a screenshot of the result when combined with normal mapping. The strength of adding displacement mapping is that the geometry is actually changing now, whereas our Water demo in Chapter 21 was purely illusion — scrolling normal maps over a flat grid to give the illusion of waves.

Figure 22.7: Screenshot of the Displacement Map demo.

Note: You can use the DirectX Texture Tool to convert grayscale heightmaps to the floating-point format D3DFMT_R32F, which the DDS file format supports.

22.3.3 **tex2Dlod**

To sample a texture in a vertex shader, we must use the tex2Dlod function instead of tex2D. This function returns an element from a 2D texture map based on the sampler s (recall a sampler specifies a texture, texture filters, and texture address modes) and texture coordinates tex0. This function differs from tex2D in that the *w*-coordinate of tex0 (tex0 must be a 4D vector with this function) specifies the mipmap level to use. For example, we would specify 0 for the *w* component of tex0 to access the topmost mipmap LOD.

In our demo, we only need the top-level layer, and hence specify $w = 0$, because we simply need a texel (storing a displacement) for each vertex in the water grid.

22.3.4 Filtering

We note that Geforce 6 level hardware only supports vertex texture fetch operations with the texture formats D3DFMT_R32F and D3DFMT_A32B32G32R32F, none of which support filtering. Consequently, we will need to implement filtering ourselves in the vertex shader.

The necessity of the filter can be seen from Figure 22.8. If we do not filter, then as the waves animate (i.e., the texture coordinates scroll), we will observe sudden jumps in the heights of vertices as they obtain new height values abruptly. Filtering will interpolate between two height values as the texture coordinates scroll between them. Conveniently, we can use the same filter we used for the Shadow Map demo, described in §22.2.4.

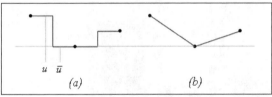

Figure 22.8: (a) shows the problem with discrete heights. As the texture coordinate animates from u to $\bar{u}$ over a rendering frame, an abrupt change in height occurs as the new texture coordinate samples a new texel. By using filtering, essentially interpolation, we can get a gradual morph from one height to the next as shown in (b).

22.3.5 The Vertex Shader

We now present the vertex shader code for the Displacement Map demo. We omit the pixel shader code since it does not do anything new — it just does normal mapping. Compare the vertex texture filtering code with that explained in §22.2.4.

```
uniform extern float4x4 gWorld;
uniform extern float4x4 gWorldInv;
uniform extern float4x4 gWVP;
uniform extern Mtrl     gMtrl;
uniform extern DirLight gLight;
uniform extern float3   gEyePosW;


// Texture coordinate offset vectors for scrolling
// normal maps and displacement maps.
uniform extern float2 gWaveNMapOffset0;
uniform extern float2 gWaveNMapOffset1;
uniform extern float2 gWaveDMapOffset0;
uniform extern float2 gWaveDMapOffset1;
```

```
// Two normal maps and two displacement maps.
uniform extern texture gWaveMap0;
uniform extern texture gWaveMap1;
uniform extern texture gWaveDispMap0;
uniform extern texture gWaveDispMap1;

// User-defined scaling factors to scale the heights
// sampled from the displacement map into a more convenient range.
uniform extern float2 gScaleHeights;

// Space between grids in x,z directions in local space
// used for finite differencing.
uniform extern float2 gGridStepSizeL;

// Shouldn't be hard coded, but ok for demo.
static const float DMAP_SIZE = 128.0f;
static const float DMAP_DX   = 1.0f / DMAP_SIZE;

sampler WaveMapS0 = sampler_state { ... };
sampler WaveMapS1 = sampler_state { ... };
sampler DMapS0    = sampler_state { ... };
sampler DMapS1    = sampler_state { ... };

struct OutputVS
{
    float4 posH      : POSITION0;
    float3 toEyeT    : TEXCOORD0;
    float3 lightDirT : TEXCOORD1;
    float2 tex0      : TEXCOORD2;
    float2 tex1      : TEXCOORD3;
};

// Key function that samples the two displacement maps.
float DoDispMapping(float2 texC0, float2 texC1)
{
    // Transform to texel space
    float2 texelpos = DMAP_SIZE * texC0;

    // Determine the lerp amounts.
    float2 lerps = frac(texelpos);

    // Take four samples.
    float dmap0[4];
    dmap0[0] = tex2Dlod(DMapS0, float4(texC0, 0.0f, 0.0f)).r;
    dmap0[1] = tex2Dlod(DMapS0, float4(texC0, 0.0f, 0.0f)
            + float4(DMAP_DX, 0.0f, 0.0f, 0.0f)).r;
    dmap0[2] = tex2Dlod(DMapS0, float4(texC0, 0.0f, 0.0f)
            + float4(0.0f, DMAP_DX, 0.0f, 0.0f)).r;
    dmap0[3] = tex2Dlod(DMapS0, float4(texC0, 0.0f, 0.0f)
            + float4(DMAP_DX, DMAP_DX, 0.0f, 0.0f)).r;

    // Filter displacement map:
```

```
            float h0 = lerp(lerp( dmap0[0], dmap0[1], lerps.x),
                        lerp( dmap0[2], dmap0[3], lerps.x),
                        lerps.y);


    texelpos = DMAP_SIZE * texC1;
    lerps    = frac(texelpos);

    // Take four samples.
    float dmap1[4];
    dmap1[0] = tex2Dlod(DMapS1, float4(texC1, 0.0f, 0.0f)).r;
    dmap1[1] = tex2Dlod(DMapS1, float4(texC1, 0.0f, 0.0f)
             + float4(DMAP_DX, 0.0f, 0.0f, 0.0f)).r;
    dmap1[2] = tex2Dlod(DMapS1, float4(texC1, 0.0f, 0.0f)
             + float4(0.0f, DMAP_DX, 0.0f, 0.0f)).r;
    dmap1[3] = tex2Dlod(DMapS1, float4(texC1, 0.0f, 0.0f)
             + float4(DMAP_DX, DMAP_DX, 0.0f, 0.0f)).r;

    // Filter displacement map:
    float h1 = lerp(lerp(dmap1[0], dmap1[1], lerps.x),
                    lerp(dmap1[2], dmap1[3], lerps.x),
                    lerps.y);

    // Sum and scale the sampled heights.
    return gScaleHeights.x*h0 + gScaleHeights.y*h1;
}
OutputVS WaterVS(float3 posL           : POSITION0,
                 float2 scaledTexC     : TEXCOORD0,
                 float2 normalizedTexC : TEXCOORD1)

{

    // Zero out our output.
    OutputVS outVS = (OutputVS)0;

    // Scroll vertex texture coordinates to animate waves.
    float2 vTex0 = normalizedTexC + gWaveDMapOffset0;
    float2 vTex1 = normalizedTexC + gWaveDMapOffset1;

    // Set y-coordinate of water grid vertices based
    // on displacement mapping.
    posL.y = DoDispMapping(vTex0, vTex1);

    // Estimate TBN-basis using finite differencing in local space.
    float r = DoDispMapping(vTex0 + float2(DMAP_DX, 0.0f),
                            vTex1 + float2(0.0f, DMAP_DX));
    float b = DoDispMapping(vTex0 + float2(DMAP_DX, 0.0f),
                            vTex1 + float2(0.0f, DMAP_DX));

    float3x3 TBN;
    TBN[0] = normalize(
             float3(1.0f, (r-posL.y)/gGridStepSizeL.x, 0.0f));
    TBN[1] = normalize(
             float3(0.0f, (b-posL.y)/gGridStepSizeL.y, -1.0f));
    TBN[2] = normalize(cross(TBN[0], TBN[1]));
    // Matrix transforms from object space to tangent space.
```

```
        float3x3 toTangentSpace = transpose(TBN);

        // Transform eye position to local space.
        float3 eyePosL = mul(float4(gEyePosW, 1.0f), gWorldInv).xyz;

        // Transform to-eye vector to tangent space.
        float3 toEyeL = eyePosL - posL;
        outVS.toEyeT = mul(toEyeL, toTangentSpace);

        // Transform light direction to tangent space.
        float3 lightDirL = mul(float4(gLight.dirW, 0.0f), gWorldInv).xyz;
        outVS.lightDirT = mul(lightDirL, toTangentSpace);

        // Transform to homogeneous clip space.
        outVS.posH = mul(float4(posL, 1.0f), gWVP);

        // Scroll texture coordinates.
        outVS.tex0 = scaledTexC + gWaveNMapOffset0;
        outVS.tex1 = scaledTexC + gWaveNMapOffset1;

        // Done--return the output.
        return outVS;
    }
```

22.4 Summary

- Projective texturing is so-called because it allows us to project a texture onto arbitrary geometry, much like a slide projector. The key to projective texturing is to generate texture coordinates for each vertex in such a way that the applied texture looks like it has been projected onto the geometry. We will call such texture coordinates *projective texture coordinates*. We obtain the projective texture coordinates for a vertex by projecting it onto the projection plane of the projector, and then mapping it to the texture coordinate system.

- Shadow mapping is a real-time shadowing technique that shadows arbitrary geometry (it is not limited to planar shadows). The idea of shadow mapping is to render the depth of the scene from the spotlight into a shadow map, after which the shadow map stores the depth of all pixels visible from the spotlight's perspective. We then render the scene again from the camera's perspective, and we project the shadow map onto the scene using the spotlight as the projector. Let $s(p_{ij})$ be the depth value projected onto a pixel p_{ij} from the shadow map and let $d(p_{ij})$ be the depth of the pixel from the spotlight. Then p_{ij} is in shadow if $s(p_{ij}) < d(p_{ij})$; that is, if the projected pixel depth is less than the depth of the pixel, then there must exist a pixel closer to the spotlight that occludes p_{ij}, thereby casting p_{ij} in shadow.

- Displacement mapping is a technique where each vertex has an associated displacement vector, which specifies how a vertex should be displaced in a vertex shader. To implement this, we create a displacement map where each texel stores a displacement vector and is associated with a vertex on a mesh via vertex texture coordinates. Then we can displace each mesh vertex in the vertex shader by sampling its associated texel (displacement vector) from the displacement map and using it to offset the vertex.

22.5 **Exercises**

1. Recall from §22.1.2 that we coupled a spotlight to the projector to essentially hide geometry with texture coordinates outside the [0, 1] range (i.e., geometry not inside the projector's frustum). Modify the Projective Texturing demo by setting the spotlight coefficient to 1 in the pixel shader; this essentially turns it into a point light so no geometry will be hidden. Now incrementally shrink the field of view of the projector's frustum a bit, and set the projective texture address mode to *wrap*. You should observe the skull texture tile over the scene geometry and also observe back projection.

2. In the Projective Texturing demo, we compute the final RGB color as follows:

   ```
   float3 litColor = (ambient+diffuse*texColor.rgb + spec);
   ```

   Observe the projected texture color is multiplied by the result of the diffuse lighting calculation. Thus, if the surface receives no diffuse light, it does not receive any of the projected texture, which makes sense. What happens if you comment out the diffuse factor from the above assignment to litColor? Explain why this happens.

3. Experiment with shadow map resolution and offset parameters. Try:
   - `static const float SHADOW_EPSILON = 0.00000f;`
   - `static const float SHADOW_EPSILON = 0.0005f;`
   - `static const float SHADOW_EPSILON = 0.005f;`
   - `static const float SMAP_SIZE = 128.0f;`
   - `static const float SMAP_SIZE = 256.0f;`
   - `static const float SMAP_SIZE = 1024.0f;`

4. The Shadow Map demo we made worked with spotlights. Explain how an orthographic projection could be applied to use the shadow mapping algorithm with directional lights. Now implement your method.

5. The Shadow Map demo we made worked with spotlights. Explain how a cube map could be applied to use the shadow mapping algorithm with point lights. Now implement your method.

6. Modify the Displacement Map demo so that it does not do filtering (so that you can see firsthand why it is needed).

Appendix A

Introduction to Windows Programming

To use the Direct3D API (application programming interface) it is necessary to create a Windows (Win32) application with a main window, upon which we will render our 3D scenes. This appendix serves as an introduction to writing Windows applications using the native Win32 API. Loosely, the Win32 API is a set of low-level functions and structures exposed to us in the C programming language that enables our application and the Windows operating system (OS) to communicate with each other. For example, to notify Windows to show a particular window we use the Win32 API function `ShowWindow`.

Windows programming is a huge subject, and this appendix introduces only the amount necessary for us to use Direct3D. For readers interested in learning more about Windows programming with the Win32 API, the book *Programming Windows* by Charles Petzold, now in its fifth edition, is the standard text on the subject. Another invaluable resource when working with Microsoft technologies is the MSDN library, which is usually included with Microsoft's Visual Studio but can also be read online at www.msdn.microsoft.com. In general, if you come upon a Win32 function or structure that you would like to know more about, go to MSDN and search for that function or structure. Often in this appendix we will direct you to look up a function or structure on MSDN for more details.

Objectives:

■ To learn and understand the event-driven programming model used in Windows programming.

■ To learn the minimal code necessary to create a Windows application that is necessary to use Direct3D.

Note: To avoid confusion, we will use a capital "W" to refer to Windows the OS, and a lowercase "w" to refer to a particular window running in Windows.

Overview

As the name suggests, one of the primary themes of Windows programming is programming windows. Many of the components of a Windows application are windows, such as the main application window, menus, toolbars, scroll bars, buttons, and other dialog controls. Therefore, a Windows application typically consists of several windows. The next subsections provide a concise overview of Windows programming concepts we should be familiar with before beginning a more complete discussion.

Resources

In Windows, several applications can run concurrently. Therefore, hardware resources such as CPU cycles, memory, and even the monitor screen must be shared among multiple applications. In order to prevent chaos from ensuing due to several applications accessing/modifying resources without any organization, Windows applications do not have direct access to hardware. One of the main jobs of Windows is to manage the presently instantiated applications and handle the distribution of resources among them. Thus, in order for our application to do something that might affect another running application, it must go through Windows. For example, to display a window you must call ShowWindow; you cannot write to video memory directly.

Events, the Message Queue, Messages, and the Message Loop

A Windows application follows an *event-driven programming model*. Typically, a Windows application sits and waits[1] for something to happen — an *event*. An event can be generated in a number of ways; some common examples are key presses, mouse clicks, and when a window is created, resized, moved, closed, minimized, maximized, or becomes visible.

When an event occurs, Windows sends a *message* to the application the event occurred for, and adds the message to the application's *message queue*, which is simply a priority queue that stores messages for an application. The application constantly checks the message queue for messages in a *message loop* and, when it receives one, it dispatches it to the *window procedure* of the particular window the message is for. (Remember, an application can contain several windows.) The window procedure is a special function, associated with each window[2] of the application, we implement that handles specific messages. For instance, we may want to destroy a window when the Escape key is pressed. In our window procedure we would write:

```
case WM_KEYDOWN:
    if( wParam == VK_ESCAPE )
        ::DestroyWindow(MainWindowHandle);
    return 0;
```

The messages a window doesn't handle are usually forwarded to a default window procedure, which then handles the message.

To summarize, the user or an application does something to generate an event. The OS finds the application the event was targeted toward, and it sends that application a message in response. The message is then added to the application's message queue. The application is constantly checking its message queue for messages. When it receives a message, the application dispatches it to the window procedure associated with the window the message is targeted for. Finally, the window procedure executes instructions in response to the message.

Figure A.1 summarizes the event-driven programming model.

---

1   We note that an application can perform idle processing; that is, perform a certain task when no events are occurring.
2   Every window has a window procedure, but several windows can share the same window procedure; therefore, we don't necessarily have to write a window procedure for each window.

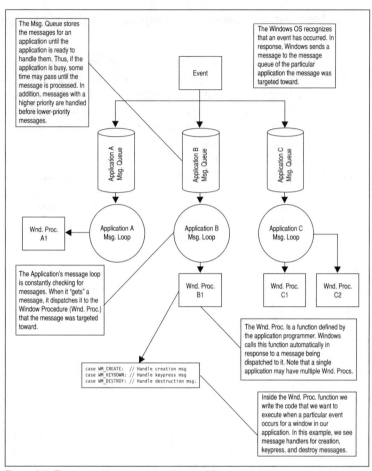

Figure A.1: The event-driven programming model.

GUI

Most Windows programs present a GUI (graphical user interface) that users can work from. A typical Windows application has one main window, a menu, toolbar, and perhaps some other controls. Figure A.2 shows and identifies some common GUI elements. For Direct3D game programming, we do not need a fancy GUI. In fact, all we need is a main window where the client area will be used to render our 3D worlds.

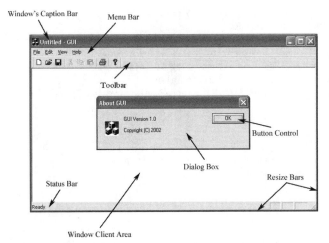

Figure A.2: A typical Windows application GUI. The client area is the entire large white space of the application. Typically, this area is where the user views most of the program's output. When we program our Direct3D applications, we render our 3D scenes into the client area of a window.

Hello World Windows Application

Below is the code to a fully functional, yet simple, Windows program. Follow the code as best you can. The next section will explain the code a bit at a time. It is recommended that you create a project with your development tool, type the code in by hand, compile it, and execute it as an exercise. Note that you must create a Win32 application project, *not* a Win32 console application project.

```
//////////////////////////////////////////////////////////
//
// File: hello.cpp
//
// Author: Frank D. Luna (C) All Rights Reserved
//
// System: AMD Athlon 1800+ XP, 512 DDR, Geforce 3, Windows XP,
//         MSVC++ 7.0
//
// Desc: Demonstrates creating a Windows application.
//
//////////////////////////////////////////////////////////

// Include the Windows header file; this has all the
// Win32 API structures, types, and function declarations
// we need to program Windows.
#include <windows.h>
// The main window handle. This is used to identify
```

```
// the main window we are going to create.
HWND MainWindowHandle = 0;

// Wraps the code necessary to initialize a Windows
// application. Function returns true if initialization
// was successful, else it returns false.
bool InitWindowsApp(HINSTANCE instanceHandle, int show);

// Wraps the message loop code.
int Run();

// The window procedure handles events our window receives.
LRESULT CALLBACK WndProc(HWND hWnd,
                         UINT msg,
                         WPARAM wParam,
                         LPARAM lParam);

// Windows equivalant to main()
int WINAPI WinMain(HINSTANCE hInstance,
                   HINSTANCE hPrevInstance,
                   PSTR      pCmdLine,
                   int       nShowCmd)
{
    // First we create and initialize our Windows
    // application.  Notice we pass the application
    // hInstance and the nShowCmd from WinMain as parameters.
    if(!InitWindowsApp(hInstance, nShowCmd))
    {
        ::MessageBox(0, "Init - Failed", "Error", MB_OK);
        return 0;
    }

    // Once our application has been created and
    // initialized we enter the message loop.  We
    // stay in the message loop until a WM_QUIT
    // mesage is received, indicating the application
    // should be terminated.
    return Run(); // enter message loop
}

bool InitWindowsApp(HINSTANCE instanceHandle, int show)
{
    // The first task to creating a window is to describe
    // its characteristics by filling out a WNDCLASS structure.
    WNDCLASS wc;

    wc.style         = CS_HREDRAW | CS_VREDRAW;
    wc.lpfnWndProc   = WndProc;
    wc.cbClsExtra    = 0;
    wc.cbWndExtra    = 0;
    wc.hInstance     = instanceHandle;
    wc.hIcon         = ::LoadIcon(0, IDI_APPLICATION);
    wc.hCursor       = ::LoadCursor(0, IDC_ARROW);
```

```
        wc.hbrBackground = static_cast<HBRUSH>(::GetStockObject
                                               (WHITE_BRUSH));
        wc.lpszMenuName  = 0;
        wc.lpszClassName = "Hello";

        // Then we register this window class description
        // with Windows so that we can create a window based
        // on that description.
        if(!::RegisterClass(&wc))
        {
            ::MessageBox(0, "RegisterClass - Failed", 0, 0);
            return false;
        }

        // With our window class description registered, we
        // can create a window with the CreateWindow function.
        // Note this function returns an HWND to the created
        // window, which we save in MainWindowHandle. Through
        // MainWindowHandle we can reference this particular
        // window we are creating.
        MainWindowHandle = ::CreateWindow(
                            "Hello",
                            "Hello",
                            WS_OVERLAPPEDWINDOW,
                            CW_USEDEFAULT,
                            CW_USEDEFAULT,
                            CW_USEDEFAULT,
                            CW_USEDEFAULT,
                            0,
                            0,
                            instanceHandle,
                            0);

if(MainWindowHandle == 0)
        {
            ::MessageBox(0, "CreateWindow - Failed", 0, 0);
            return false;
        }

        // Finally we show and update the window we just created.
        // Observe we pass MainWindowHandle to these functions so
        // that these functions know what particular window to
        // show and update.
        ::ShowWindow(MainWindowHandle, show);
        ::UpdateWindow(MainWindowHandle);

        return true;
}

int Run()
{

    MSG msg;
```

```
    ::ZeroMemory(&msg, sizeof(MSG));

    // Loop until we get a WM_QUIT message. The
    // function GetMessage will only return 0 (false)
    // when a WM_QUIT message is received, which
    // effectively exits the loop.
    while(::GetMessage(&msg, 0, 0, 0) )
    {
        // Translate the message, and then dispatch it
        // to the appropriate window procedure.
        ::TranslateMessage(&msg);
        ::DispatchMessage(&msg);
    }


    return msg.wParam;
}

LRESULT CALLBACK WndProc(HWND windowHandle,
                         UINT  msg,
                         WPARAM wParam,
                         LPARAM lParam)
{
    // Handle some specific messages:
    switch( msg )
    {
        // In the case the left mouse button was pressed,
        // then display a message box.
        case WM_LBUTTONDOWN:
            ::MessageBox(0, "Hello, World", "Hello", MB_OK);
            return 0;

        // In the case the Escape key was pressed, then
        // destroy the main application window, which is
        // identified by MainWindowHandle.
        case WM_KEYDOWN:
            if( wParam == VK_ESCAPE )
                ::DestroyWindow(MainWindowHandle);
            return 0;

        // In the case of a destroy message, then send a
        // quit message, which will terminate the message loop.
        case WM_DESTROY:
            ::PostQuitMessage(0);
            return 0;
    }

    // Forward any other messages we didn't handle
    // above to the default window procedure.
    return ::DefWindowProc(windowHandle,
                           msg,
                           wParam,
                           lParam);
}
```

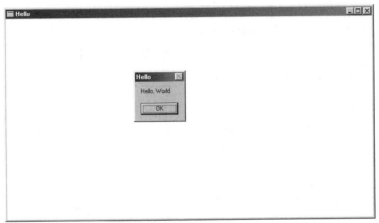

Figure A.3: A screenshot of the above program. Note that the message box appears when you press the left mouse button in the window's client area.

Explaining Hello World

We will examine the code from top to bottom, stepping into any function that gets called along the way. Refer back to the Hello World code listing throughout these subsections.

Includes, Global Variables, and Prototypes

The first thing we do is include the windows.h header file. By including the windows.h file we obtain the structures, types, and function declarations needed for using the basic elements of the Win32 API.

```
#include <windows.h>
```

The second statement is an instantiation of a global variable of type HWND. This stands for "handle to a window." In Windows programming, we often use handles to refer to objects maintained internally by Windows. In this sample, we will use an HWND to refer to our main application window maintained by Windows. We need to hold onto the handles of our windows because many calls to the API require that we pass in the handle of the window we want the API call to act on. For example, the call UpdateWindow takes one argument that is of type HWND that is used to specify the window to update. If we didn't pass in a handle to it, the function wouldn't know which window to update.

```
HWND MainWindowHandle = 0;
```

The next three lines are function declarations. Briefly, InitWindowsApp creates and initializes our main application window, Run encapsulates the message loop for our application, and WndProc is our main window's window procedure. We will examine these functions in more detail when we come to the point where they are called.

```
bool InitWindowsApp(HINSTANCE instanceHandle, int show);
int Run();
LRESULT CALLBACK WndProc(HWND, UINT, WPARAM, LPARAM);
```

WinMain

WinMain is the Windows equivalent to the main function in normal C++ programming. WinMain is prototyped as follows:

```
int WINAPI WinMain(
    HINSTANCE hInstance,
    HINSTANCE hPrevInstance,
    LPSTR     lpCmdLine,
    int       nCmdShow
);
```

■ hInstance: Handle to the current application instance. It serves as a way of identifying and referring to this application. Remember that there may be several Windows applications running concurrently, so it is useful to be able to refer to each one.

■ hPrevInstance: Not used in Win32 programming and is zero.

■ lpCmdLine: The command line argument string used to run the program.

■ nCmdShow: Specifies how the application should be displayed. Some common commands that show the window in its current size and position, maximized, and minimized, respectively, are SW_SHOW, SW_SHOWMAXIMIZED, and SW_SHOWMINIMIZED. See the MSDN library for a complete list of show commands.

If WinMain succeeds, it should return the wParam member of the WM_QUIT message. If the function exits without entering the message loop, it should return zero. The WINAPI identifier is defined as:

```
#define WINAPI __stdcall
```

This specifies the calling convention of the function, which means how the function arguments get placed on the stack.

Note: In the signature of WinMain, in the Hello World sample, we use the type PSTR as the third argument instead of LPSTR. This is because with 32-bit Windows, there are no longer "long pointers." PSTR is simply a char pointer (e.g., char*).

WNDCLASS and Registration

Inside WinMain we call the function InitWindowsApp. As you can guess, this function does all the initialization of our program. Let's take a closer look at this function. InitWindowsApp returns either true or false, true if the initialization was a success and false if something went wrong. In the WinMain definition, we pass a copy of our application instance to InitWindowsApp as well as the show command variable. Both are obtained from the WinMain parameter list.

```
if(!InitWindowsApp(hInstance, nShowCmd))
```

The first task at hand in initialization of a window is to describe our window and register it with Windows. We describe our window with the WNDCLASS data structure. Its definition is:

```
typedef struct _WNDCLASS {
    UINT     style;
    WNDPROC  lpfnWndProc;
    int      cbClsExtra;
    int      cbWndExtra;
    HANDLE   hInstance;
    HICON    hIcon;
    HCURSOR  hCursor;
    HBRUSH   hbrBackground;
    LPCTSTR  lpszMenuName;
    LPCTSTR  lpszClassName;
} WNDCLASS;
```

■ style: Specifies the class style. In our example we use CS_HREDRAW combined with CS_VREDRAW. These two bit-flags indicate that the window is to be repainted when either the horizontal or vertical window size is changed. For the complete list and description of the various styles, see the MSDN library.

```
wc.style = CS_HREDRAW | CS_VREDRAW;
```

■ lpfnWndProc: Pointer to the window procedure function. This is how you associate your window procedure function with a window. Thus, the windows that are created based on the same WNDCLASS instance will share the same window procedure. The window procedure function is explained in § A.3.6.

```
wc.lpfnWndProc = WndProc;
```

■ cbClsExtra and cbWndExtra: These are extra memory slots you can use for your own purpose. Our Hello World program does not require any extra space and therefore sets both of these to zero.

```
wc.cbClsExtra = 0;
wc.cbWndExtra = 0;
```

■ hInstance: This field is a handle to our application instance. Recall the application instance handle is originally passed in through WinMain.

```
wc.hInstance = instanceHandle;
```

■ hIcon: Here you specify a handle to an icon to use for the windows created using this window class. There are several built-in icons to choose from; see the MSDN library for details.

```
wc.hIcon = ::LoadIcon(0, IDI_APPLICATION);
```

■ `hCursor`: Similar to `hIcon`, here you specify a handle to a cursor to use when the cursor is over the window's client area. Again, there are several built-in cursors; see the MSDN library for details.

```
wc.hCursor = ::LoadCursor(0, IDC_ARROW);
```

■ `hbrBackground`: This field is used to specify the background of the client area of the window. In our sample code we call the function `GetStockObject`, which returns a handle to a brush of the color we specified. See the MSDN library for other types of built-in brushes.

```
wc.hbrBackground = static_cast<HBRUSH>(::GetStockObject(WHITE_BRUSH));
```

■ `lpszMenuName`: Specifies the window's menu. Since we have no menu in our application we set this to zero.

```
wc.lpszMenuName = 0;
```

■ `lpszClassName`: Specifies the name of the window class structure we are creating. This can be anything you want. In our application, we named it Hello. The name is simply used to identify the class structure so that we can reference it later.

```
wc.lpszClassName = "Hello";
```

Once we have described our window, we need to register it with Windows. This is done with the `RegisterClass` function, which takes a pointer to a `WNDCLASS` structure. This function returns zero upon failure.

```
if(!::RegisterClass(&wc))
```

Creating and Displaying the Window

After we have registered a `WNDCLASS` variable with Windows we can create a window based on that class description. We can refer to the `WNDCLASS` structure that describes the window we want to create by the class name we gave it — `lpszClassName`. The function we use to create a window is the `CreateWindow` function, which is declared as follows:

```
HWND CreateWindow(
        LPCTSTR lpClassName,
        LPCTSTR lpWindowName,
        DWORD dwStyle,
        int x,
        int y,
        int nWidth,
        int nHeight,
        HWND hWndParent,
        HMENU hMenu,
        HANDLE hInstance,
        LPVOID lpParam
);
```

- lpClassName: The name (C string) of the registered WNDCLASS structure that describes the window we want to create. Pass in the class name of the WNDCLASS we want to use for the creation of this window.

- lpWindowName: The name (C string) we want to give our window; this is also the name that appears in the window's caption bar.

- dwStyle: Defines the style of the window. WS_OVERLAPPEDWINDOW, which we use in the Hello World sample, is a combination of several flags: WS_OVERLAPPED, WS_CAPTION, WS_SYSMENU, WS_THICKFRAME, WS_MINIMIZEBOX, and WS_MAXIMIZEBOX. The names of these flags describe the characteristics of the window they produce. See the MSDN library for the complete list of styles.

- x: The x position at the top-left corner of the window relative to the screen.

- y: The y position at the top-left corner of the window relative to the screen.

- nWidth: The width of the window in pixels.

- nHeight: The height of the window in pixels.

- hWndParent: Handle to a window that is to be the parent of this window. Our window has no relationship with any other windows, and therefore we set this value to zero.

- hMenu: A handle to a menu. Hello World has no menu and specifies zero for this argument.

- hInstance: Handle to the application the window will be associated with.

- lpParam: A pointer to user-defined data.

Note: When we specify the (x, y) coordinates of the window's position, they are relative to the upper-left corner of the screen. Also, the positive x-axis runs to the right as usual, but the positive y-axis runs downward. Figure A.4 shows this coordinate system, which is called *screen coordinates* or *screen space*.

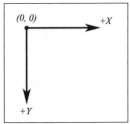

Figure A.4: Screen space.

CreateWindow returns a handle to the window it creates (an HWND). If the creation failed, the handle will have the value of zero. Remember that the handle is a way to refer to the window, which is managed by Windows. Many of the API calls require an HWND so that it knows what window to act on.

The last two function calls in the InitWindowsApp function have to do with displaying the window. First we call ShowWindow and pass in the handle of our newly created window so that Windows knows which window to show. We also pass in an integer value that defines how the window is to be initially shown (minimized, maximized, etc.). This value should be nShowCmd, which is an argument of WinMain. You can hard code this value in, but it is not recommended. After showing the window, we should refresh it. UpdateWindow does this; it takes one argument that is a handle to the window we wish to update.

```
::ShowWindow(MainWindowHandle, show);
::UpdateWindow(MainWindowHandle);
```

If we made it this far in InitWindowsApp, then the initialization is complete; we return true to indicate everything went successfully.

The Message Loop

Having successfully completed initialization, we can begin the heart of the program — the message loop. In Hello World, we have wrapped the message loop in a function called Run.

```
int Run()
{
    MSG msg;
    ::ZeroMemory(&msg, sizeof(MSG));

    while(::GetMessage(&msg, 0, 0, 0) )
    {
        ::TranslateMessage(&msg);
        ::DispatchMessage(&msg);
    }
    return msg.wParam;
}
```

The first thing done in Run is an instantiation of a variable called msg of type MSG, which is the message structure that represents a Windows message. Its definition is as follows:

```
typedef struct tagMSG {
    HWND    hwnd;
    UINT    message;
    WPARAM  wParam;
    LPARAM  lParam;
    DWORD   time;
    POINT   pt;
} MSG;
```

- hwnd: The handle to the window whose window procedure is to receive the message.

- message: A predefined constant value identifying the message (e.g., WM_QUIT).

- **■** wParam: Extra information about the message. This is dependent upon the specific message.
- **■** lParam: Extra information about the message. This is dependent upon the specific message.
- **■** time: The time the message was posted.
- **■** pt: The (x, y) coordinates of the mouse cursor in screen coordinates when the message was posted.

Next, we enter the message loop. GetMessage will always return true unless a WM_QUIT message is posted; therefore, the loop continues until a WM_QUIT message is received. The GetMessage function retrieves a message from the message queue and fills in the members of our MSG structure. If GetMessage returns true, then two more functions get called: TranslateMessage and DispatchMessage. TranslateMessage has Windows perform some keyboard translations and virtual key messages to character messages specifically. DispatchMessage finally dispatches the message off to the appropriate window procedure.

The Window Procedure

We mentioned previously that the window procedure is where we write the code that we want to execute in response to a message our window receives. In Hello World, we name the window procedure WndProc and it is prototyped as:

```
LRESULT CALLBACK WndProc(
    HWND hwnd,
    UINT uMsg,
    WPARAM wParam,
    LPARAM lParam
);
```

This function returns an integer of type LRESULT (which is a long) identifying the success or failure of the function. The CALLBACK identifier specifies that the function is a *callback* function, which means that Windows will be calling this function outside of the code space of the program. As you can see from the Hello World source code, we never explicitly call the window procedure ourselves — Windows calls it for us when the window needs to process a message.

The window procedure has four parameters in its signature:

- **■** hwnd: The handle to the window receiving the message.
- **■** uMsg: A predefined value that identifies the particular message. For example, a quit message is defined as WM_QUIT. The prefix WM stands for window message. There are over a hundred predefined window messages; see the MSDN library for details.
- **■** wParam: Extra information about the message, which is dependent upon the specific message.

- lParam: Extra information about the message, which is dependent upon the specific message.

Our window procedure handles three messages: WM_LBUTTONDOWN, WM_KEYDOWN, and WM_DESTROY. A WM_LBUTTONDOWN message is sent when the user clicks the left mouse button on the window's client area. A WM_KEYDOWN message is sent when a key is pressed. A WM_DESTROY message is sent when the window is being destroyed. Our code is quite simple; when we receive a WM_LBUTTONDOWN message, we display a message box that prints out "Hello, World":

```
case WM_LBUTTONDOWN:
    ::MessageBox(0, "Hello, World", "Hello", MB_OK);
    return 0;
```

When our window gets a WM_KEYDOWN message, we test what key was pressed. The wParam passed into the window procedure specifies the *virtual key code* of the specific key that was pressed. Think of a virtual key code as an identifier for a particular key. The Windows header files have a list of virtual key code constants we can use to then test for a particular key. For example, to test if the Escape key was pressed, we use the virtual key code constant VK_ESCAPE.

Remember that the wParam and lParam parameters are used to specify extra information about a particular message. For the WM_KEYDOWN message, the wParam specifies the virtual key code of the specific key that was pressed. The MSDN library specifies the information the wParam and lParam parameters carry for each Windows message.

```
case WM_KEYDOWN:
    if( wParam == VK_ESCAPE )
        ::DestroyWindow(MainWindowHandle);
    return 0;
```

When our window gets destroyed, we post a quit message (which terminates the message loop).

```
case WM_DESTROY:
    ::PostQuitMessage(0);
    return 0;
```

At the end of our window procedure, we call another function named DefWindowProc. This function is a default window procedure. In our Hello World application, we only handle three messages; we use the default behavior specified in DefWindowProc for all the other messages we receive but don't necessarily need to handle ourselves. For example, Hello World can be minimized, maximized, resized, and closed. This functionality is provided to us through the default window procedure, as we do not handle the window messages to perform this functionality. Note that DefWindowProc is a Win32 API function.

The MessageBox Function

There is one last API function we have not yet covered and that is the MessageBox function. This function is a very handy way to provide the user with information and to get some quick input. The declaration to the MessageBox function looks like this:

```
int MessageBox(
    HWND hWnd,            // Handle of owner window, may specify null.
    LPCTSTR lpText,       // Text to put in the message box.
    LPCTSTR lpCaption,    // Text for the title of the message box.
    UINT uType            // Style of the message box.
);
```

The return value for the MessageBox function depends on the type of message box. See the MSDN library for a list of possible return values and styles.

A Better Message Loop

Games are very different applications from traditional Windows applications such as office type applications and web browsers. Games are not typically event-driven in the usual sense, and they must be updated constantly. For this reason when we actually start writing our 3D programs we will, for the most part, not deal with Win32 messages. Therefore, we will want to modify the message loop so that if there is a message we will process it, but if there is not a message then we want to run our game code. Our new message loop is as follows:

```
int Run()
{
    MSG  msg;

    while(true)
    {
        if(::PeekMessage(&msg, 0, 0, 0, PM_REMOVE))
        {
            if(msg.message == WM_QUIT)
                break;

            ::TranslateMessage(&msg);
            ::DispatchMessage(&msg);
        }
        else
            // run game code
    }
    return msg.wParam;
}
```

After we instantiate msg we enter into an endless loop. We first call the API function PeekMessage, which checks the message queue for a message. See the MSDN library for the argument descriptions. If there is a message, it returns true and we handle the message. If PeekMessage returns false, then we handle our own specific game code.

Summary

- To use Direct3D we must create a Windows application that has a main window onto which we can render our 3D scenes. Furthermore, for games we create a special message loop that checks for messages. If there are messages, it processes them; otherwise it executes our game logic.

- Several Windows applications can be running concurrently, and therefore Windows must manage resources between them and direct messages to the applications for which they were intended. Messages are sent to an application's message queue when an event (keypress, mouse click, timer, etc.) has occurred for that application.

- Every Windows application has a message queue in which messages an application receives are stored. The application's message loop constantly checks the queue for messages and dispatches them off to their intended window procedure. Note that a single application can have several windows within it.

- The window procedure is a special callback function we implement that Windows calls when a window in our application receives a message. In the window procedure we write the code we want to be executed when a window in our application receives a particular message. Messages we do not specifically handle are forwarded to a default window procedure for default handling.

High-Level Shading Language Reference

Variable Types

Scalar Types

- `bool`: True or false value. Note that the HLSL provides the `true` and `false` keywords as in C++.
- `int`: 32-bit signed integer.
- `half`: 16-bit floating-point number.
- `float`: 32-bit floating-point number.
- `double`: 64-bit floating-point number.

Note: Some platforms might not support `int`, `half`, and `double`. If this is the case, these types will be emulated using `float`.

Vector Types

- `float2`: 2D vector, where the components are of type `float`.
- `float3`: 3D vector, where the components are of type `float`.
- `float4`: 4D vector, where the components are of type `float`.

Note: You can create vectors where the components are of a type other than `float`, such as `int2`, `half3`, `bool4`.

We can initialize a vector using an array-like syntax or a constructor-like syntax:

```
float3 v = {1.0f, 2.0f, 3.0f};
float2 w = float2(x, y);
float4 u = float4(w, 3.0f, 4.0f); // u = (w.x, w.y, 3.0f, 4.0f)
```

We can access a component of a vector using an array subscript syntax. For example, to set the ith component of a vector vec, we would write:

```
vec[i] = 2.0f;
```

In addition, we can access the components of a vector vec, as we would access the members of a structure, using the defined component names x, y, z, w, r, g, b, and a.

```
vec.x = vec.r = 1.0f;
vec.y = vec.g = 2.0f;
vec.z = vec.b = 3.0f;
vec.w = vec.a = 4.0f;
```

The names r, g, b, and a refer to the same component as the names x, y, z, and w, respectively. When using vectors to represent colors, the RGBA notation is more desirable since it reinforces the fact that the vector is representing a color.

Swizzles

Consider the vector $\vec{u} = (u_x, u_y, u_z, u_w)$ and suppose we want to copy the components of $\vec{u}$ to a vector $\vec{v}$ such that $\vec{v} = (u_x, u_y, u_y, u_w)$. The most immediate solution would be to individually copy each component of $\vec{u}$ over to $\vec{v}$ as necessary. However, the HLSL provides a special syntax for doing these types of out-of-order copies called *swizzles*:

```
vector u = {1.0f, 2.0f, 3.0f, 4.0f};
vector v = {0.0f, 0.0f, 5.0f, 6.0f};

v = u.xyyw;      // v = {1.0f, 2.0f, 2.0f, 4.0f}
```

Another example:

```
vector u = {1.0f, 2.0f, 3.0f, 4.0f};
vector v = {0.0f, 0.0f, 5.0f, 6.0f};

v = u.wzyx;      // v = {4.0f, 3.0f, 2.0f, 1.0f}
```

When copying vectors, we do not have to copy every component. For example, we can copy only the x- and y-components, as this code snippet illustrates:

```
vector u = {1.0f, 2.0f, 3.0f, 4.0f};
vector v = {0.0f, 0.0f, 5.0f, 6.0f};

v.xy = u;        // v = {1.0f, 2.0f, 5.0f, 6.0f}
```

Matrix Types

We can define an $m \times n$ matrix, where m and n are from 1 to 4, using the following syntax:

```
floatmxn matmxn;
```

Examples:

- float2x2: 2×2 matrix, where the entries are of type float.
- float3x3: 3×3 matrix, where the entries are of type float.
- float4x4: 4×4 matrix, where the entries are of type float.
- float3x4: 3×4 matrix, where the entries are of type float.

Note: You can create matrices where the components are of a type other than float, such as int2x2, half3x3, bool4x4.

We can access an entry in a matrix using a double array subscript syntax. For example, to set the ijth hentry of a matrix M, we would write:

```
M[i][j] = value;
```

In addition, we can refer to the entries of a matrix M as we would access the members of a structure. The following entry names are defined:

One-based indexing:

```
M._11 = M._12 = M._13 = M._14 = 0.0f;
M._21 = M._22 = M._23 = M._24 = 0.0f;
M._31 = M._32 = M._33 = M._34 = 0.0f;
M._41 = M._42 = M._43 = M._44 = 0.0f;
```

Zero-based indexing:

```
M._m00 = M._m01 = M._m02 = M._m03 = 0.0f;
M._m10 = M._m11 = M._m12 = M._m13 = 0.0f;
M._m20 = M._m21 = M._m22 = M._m23 = 0.0f;
M._m30 = M._m31 = M._m32 = M._m33 = 0.0f;
```

Sometimes we want to refer to a particular row vector in a matrix. We can do so using a single array subscript syntax. For example, to extract the ith row vector in a 3×3 matrix M, we would write:

```
float3 ithRow = M[i]; // get the ith row vector in M
```

In this next example, we insert three vectors into the first, second, and third row of a matrix:

```
float3 tangentL  = float3(...);
float3 binormalL = float3(...);
float3 normalL   = float3(...);
float3x3 TBN;
TBN[0] = tangentL;  // sets row 1
TBN[1] = binormalL; // sets row 2
TBN[2] = normalL;   // sets row 3
```

Note: Instead of using `float4` and `float4x4` to represent 4D vectors and 4×4 matrices, you can equivalently use the `vector` and `matrix` type:

```
vector u = {1.0f, 2.0f, 3.0f, 4.0f};
matrix M;        // 4x4 matrix
```

Arrays

We can declare an array of a particular type using familiar C++ syntax, for example:

```
float  M[4][4];
half   p[4];
float3 v[12];    // 12 3D vectors
```

Structures

Structures are defined exactly as they are in C++. However, structures in the HLSL cannot have member functions. Here is an example of a structure in the HLSL:

```
struct MyStruct
{
    float3x3 T;
    float3   n;
    float    f;
    int      x;
    bool     b;
};

MyStruct s;      // instantiate
s.f = 5.0f;      // member access
```

The typedef Keyword

The HLSL `typedef` keyword functions exactly the same as it does in C++. For example, we can give the name `point` to the type `vector<float, 3>` using the following syntax:

```
typedef float3 point;
```

Then, instead of writing:

```
float3 myPoint;
```

We can just write:

```
point myPoint;
```

Here is another example showing how to use the `typedef` keyword with the HLSL `const` keyword (which works the same in C++):

```
typedef const float CFLOAT;
```

Variable Prefixes

The following keywords can prefix a variable declaration:

- `static`: Essentially the opposite of `extern`; this means that the shader variable will not be exposed to the C++ application.

```
static float3 v = {1.0f, 2.0f, 3.0f};
```

- `uniform`: This means that the variable does not change per vertex/pixel; it is constant for all vertices/pixels until we change it at the C++ application level. Uniform variables are initialized from outside the shader program (e.g., by the C++ application).

- `extern`: This means that the C++ application can see the variable (i.e., the variable can be accessed outside the shader file by the C++ application code. Global variables in a shader program are, by default, `uniform` and `extern`.

- `shared`: This is for sharing variables across multiple effect (.fx) files.

- `volatile`: Hints to the effects framework (Chapter 8) that the variable will be modified often. Only global variables can be prefixed with the `volatile` keyword.

- `const`: The `const` keyword in the HLSL has the same meaning it has in C++. That is, if a variable is prefixed with the `const` keyword, then that variable is constant and cannot be changed.

```
const float pi = 3.14f;
```

Casting

The HLSL supports a very flexible casting scheme. The casting syntax in the HLSL is the same as in the C programming language. For example, to cast a `float` to a `matrix` we write:

```
float f = 5.0f;
float4x4 m = (float4x4)f; // copy f into each entry of m.
```

What this scalar-matrix cast does is copy the scalar into each entry of the matrix. For the examples in this book, you will be able to deduce the meaning of the cast from the syntax. For a complete list of casting rules, see the DirectX SDK documentation: _DirectX9\directx9_c.chm::/Casting_and_Conversion.htm_ (or search the documentation index for "Casting and Conversion").

Keywords and Operators

Keywords

For reference, here is a list of the keywords the HLSL defines:

asm	bool	compile	const	decl	do
double	else	extern	false	float	for
half	if	in	inline	inout	int
matrix	out	pass	pixelshader	return	sampler
shared	static	string	struct	technique	texture
true	typedef	uniform	vector	vertexshader	void
volatile	while				

This next set of keywords displays identifiers that are reserved and unused, but may become keywords in the future:

auto	break	case	catch	char	class
const_cast	continue	default	delete	dynamic_cast	enum
explicit	friend	goto	long	mutable	namespace
new	operator	private	protected	public	register
reinterpret_cast	short	signed	sizeof	static_cast	switch
template	this	throw	try	typename	union
unsigned	using	virtual			

Operators

HLSL supports many familiar C++ operators. With a few exceptions noted below, they are used exactly the same way as they are in C++. These are the HLSL operators:

```
[]    .    >    <    <=   >=
!=    ==   !    &&   ||   ? :
+     +=   -    -=   *    *=
/     /=   %    %=   ++   --
=     ()   ,
```

Although the operators' behavior is very similar to C++, there are some differences. First of all, the modulus operator (%) works on both integer and floating-point types. And, in order to use the modulus operator, both the left-hand-side value and right-hand-side value must have the same sign (e.g., both sides must be positive or both sides must be negative).

Secondly, observe that many of the HLSL operations work on a per-component basis. This is due to the fact that vectors and matrices are built into the language and that these types consist of several components. By having the operations work on a component level, operations such as vector/matrix addition, vector/matrix subtraction, and vector/matrix equality tests can be done using the same operators we use for scalar types. See the following examples.

Note: The operators behave as expected for scalars, that is, in the usual C++ way.

```
float4 u = {1.0f, 0.0f, -3.0f, 1.0f};
float4 v = {-4.0f, 2.0f, 1.0f, 0.0f};

// adds corresponding components
float4 sum = u + v;          // sum = (-3.0f, 2.0f, -2.0f, 1.0f)
```

Incrementing a vector increments each component:

```
// before increment: sum = (-3.0f, 2.0f, -2.0f, 1.0f)

sum++;      // after increment: sum = (-2.0f, 3.0f, -1.0f, 2.0f)
```

Multiplying vectors component-wise:

```
float4 u = {1.0f, 0.0f, -3.0f, 1.0f};
float4 v = {-4.0f, 2.0f, 1.0f, 0.0f};

// multiply corresponding components
float4 product = u * v; // product = (-4.0f, 0.0f, -3.0f, 0.0f)
```

Comparison operators are also done per component and return a vector or matrix where each component is of type `bool`. The resulting "`bool`" vector contains the results of each compared component. For example:

```
float4 u = { 1.0f, 0.0f, -3.0f, 1.0f};
float4 v = {-4.0f, 0.0f,  1.0f, 1.0f};

float4 b = (u == v);        // b = (false, true, false, true)
```

Finally, we conclude by discussing variable promotions with binary operations:

■   For binary operations, if the left-hand side and right-hand side differ in dimension, then the side with the smaller dimension is promoted (cast) to have the same dimension as the side with the larger dimension. For example, if x is of type `float` and y is of type `float3`, in the expression (x + y), the variable x is promoted to `float3` and the expression evaluates to a value of type `float3`. The promotion is done using the defined cast. In this case we are casting scalar-to-vector; therefore, after x is promoted to `float3`, x = (x, x, x) as the scalar-to-vector cast defines. Note that the promotion is not defined if the cast is not defined. For example, we can't promote `float2` to `float3` because there exists no such defined cast.

■ For binary operations, if the left-hand side and right-hand side differ in type, then the side with the lower type resolution is promoted (cast) to have the same type as the side with the higher type resolution. For example, if x is of type int and y is of type half, in the expression (x + y), the variable x is promoted to a half and the expression evaluates to a value of type half.

Program Flow

The HLSL supports many familiar C++ statements for selection, repetition, and general program flow. The syntax of these statements is exactly like C++.

The return statement:

```
return (expression);
```

The if and if...else statements:

```
if( condition )
{
      statement(s);
}

if( condition )
{
      statement(s);
}
else
{
      statement(s);
}
```

The for statement:

```
for(initial; condition; increment)
{
      statement(s);
}
```

The while statement:

```
while( condition )
{
      statement(s);
}
```

The do...while statement:

```
do
{
      statement(s);
}while( condition );
```

Functions

User-Defined Functions

Functions in the HLSL have the following properties:

- Functions use a familiar C++ syntax.
- Parameters are always passed by value.
- Recursion is not supported.
- Functions are always inlined.

Furthermore, the HLSL adds some extra keywords that can be used with functions. For example, consider the following function written in the HLSL:

```
bool foo(in const bool b,     // input bool
         out int r1,          // output int
         inout float r2)      // input/output float
{
    if( b )                   // test input value
    {
        r1 = 5;               // output a value through r1
    }
    else
    {
        r1 = 1;               // output a value through r1
    }

    // since r2 is inout we can use it as an input
    // value and also output a value through it
    r2 = r2 * r2 * r2;

    return true;
}
```

The function is almost identical to a C++ function except for the in, out, and inout keywords.

- in: Specifies that the *argument* (particular variable we pass into a parameter) should be copied to the parameter before the function begins. It is not necessary to explicitly specify a parameter as in because a parameter is in by default. For example, the following are equivalent:

```
float square(in float x)
{
    return x * x;
}
```

And without explicitly specifying in:

```
float square(float x)
{
    return x * x;
}
```

■ out: Specifies that the parameter should be copied to the argument when the function returns. This is useful for returning values through parameters. The out keyword is necessary because the HLSL doesn't allow us to pass by reference or to pass a pointer. We note that if a parameter is marked as out, the argument is not copied to the parameter before the function begins. In other words, an out parameter can only be used to output data — it can't be used for input.

```
void square(in float x, out float y)
{
    y = x * x;
}
```

Here we input the number to be squared through x and return the square of x through the parameter y.

■ inout: Shortcut that denotes a parameter as both in and out. Specify inout if you wish to use a parameter for both input and output.

```
void square(inout float x)
{
    x = x * x;
}
```

Here we input the number to be squared through x and also return the square of x through x.

Built-in Functions

The HLSL has a rich set of built in-functions that are useful for 3D graphics. The following is an abridged list:

■ abs(x) — Returns $|x|$.

■ ceil(x) — Returns the smallest integer $\geq x$.

■ cos(x) — Returns the cosine of x, where x is in radians.

■ clamp(x, a, b) — Clamps x to the range [a, b] and returns the result.

■ cross(u, v) — Returns $\vec{u} \times \vec{v}$.

■ degrees(x) — Converts x from radians to degrees.

■ determinant(M) — Returns the determinant of a matrix, det(M).

■ distance(u, v) — Returns the distance $\|\vec{v} - \vec{u}\|$ between the points $\vec{u}$ and $\vec{v}$.

■ dot(u, v) — Returns $\vec{u} \cdot \vec{v}$.

■ floor(x) — Returns the greatest integer $\leq x$.

- `length(v)` — Returns $\|\vec{v}\|$.
- `lerp(u, v, t)` — Linearly interpolates between u and v based on the parameter $t \in [0, 1]$.
- `log(x)` — Returns $\ln(x)$.
- `log10(x)` — Returns $\log_{10}(x)$.
- `log2(x)` — Returns $\log_2(x)$.
- `max(x, y)` — Returns x if $x \geq y$, else returns y.
- `min(x, y)` — Returns x if $x \leq y$, else returns y.
- `mul(M, N)` — Returns the matrix product MN. Note that the matrix product MN must be defined. If M is a vector, it is treated as a row vector so that the vector-matrix product is defined. Likewise, if N is a vector, it is treated as a column vector so that the matrix-vector product is defined.
- `normalize(v)` — Returns $\vec{v}/\|\vec{v}\|$.
- `pow(b, n)` — Returns b^n.
- `radians(x)` — Converts x from degrees to radians.
- `saturate(x)` — Returns `clamp(x, 0.0, 1.0)`.
- `sin(x)` — Returns the sine of x, where x is in radians.
- `sincos(in x, out s, out c)` — Returns the sine and cosine of x, where x is in radians.
- `sqrt(x)` — Returns $\sqrt{x}$.
- `reflect(v, n)` — Computes the reflection vector given the incident vector $\vec{v}$ and the surface normal $\vec{n}$.
- `refract(v, n, eta)` — Computes the refraction vector given the incident vector $\vec{v}$, the surface normal $\vec{n}$, and the ratio of the two indices of refraction of the two materials *eta*. Look up Snell's law in a physics book or on the Internet for information on refraction.
- `rsqrt(x)` — Returns $1/\sqrt{x}$.
- `tan(x)` — Returns the tangent of x, where x is in radians.
- `transpose(M)` — Returns the transpose M^T.
- `tex2D(s, tex0)` — Returns a color from a 2D texture map based on the sampler s (recall a sampler specifies a texture, texture filters, and texture address modes) and texture coordinates tex0.
- `texCUBE(s, v)` — Returns a color from a cube map based on the sampler s (recall a sampler specifies a texture, texture filters, and texture address modes) and 3D lookup vector v.

- `tex2Dlod(s, tex0)` — Returns a color from a 2D texture map based on the sampler s (recall a sampler specifies a texture, texture filters, and texture address modes) and texture coordinates tex0. This function differs from tex2D in that the w-coordinate of tex0 (tex0 must be a 4D vector with this function) specifies the mipmap level to use. For example, we would specify 0 for the w component of tex0 to access the topmost mipmap LOD. Use this function to manually specify the mipmap level you want to sample.

Note: Most of the functions are overloaded to work with all the built-in types for which the function makes sense. For instance, abs makes sense for all scalar types and so is overloaded for all of them. As another example, the cross product cross only makes sense for 3D vectors, so it is only overloaded for 3D vectors of any type (e.g., 3D vectors of ints, floats, doubles, etc.). On the other hand, linear interpolation, lerp, makes sense for scalars, 2D, 3D, and 4D vectors, and therefore is overloaded for all types.

Note: If you pass in a non-scalar type into a "scalar" function, that is, a function that traditionally operates on scalars (e.g., cos(x)), the function will act per component. For example, if you write:

```
float3 v = float3(0.0f, 0.0f, 0.0f);

v = cos(v);
```

then the function will act per component: $\vec{v} = (\cos(x)\cos(y)\cos(z))$.

Note: For further reference, the complete list of built-in HLSL functions can be found in the DirectX documentation under *directx9_c.chm::/dx9_graphics_reference_hlsl_intrinsic_functions.htm* (or search the documentation index for "HLSL Intrinsic Functions").

References

[Angel00] Angel, Edward. *Interactive Computer Graphics: A Top-Down Approach with OpenGL*. 2nd ed. Addison-Wesley, 2000.

[Blinn96] Blinn, Jim. *Jim Blinn's Corner: A Trip Down the Graphics Pipeline*. San Francisco: Morgan Kaufmann Publishers, 1996.

[Brennan02] Brennan, Chris. "Accurate Reflections and Refractions by Adjusting for Object Distance," *Direct3D ShaderX: Vertex and Pixel Shader Tips and Tricks*. Plano, Texas: Wordware Publishing Inc., 2002.

[Burg00] Burg, John van der. "Building an Advanced Particle System," *Gamasutra*, June 2000 (http://www.gamasutra.com/features/20000623/vanderburg_01.htm).

[DeBerg00] de Berg, M., M. van Kreveld, M. Overmars, and O. Schwarzkopf. *Computational Geometry: Algorithms and Applications*. 2nd ed. Berlin: Springer-Verlag, 2000.

[Dietrich] Dietrich, Sim. "Texture Space Bump Maps" (http://developer.nvidia.com/object/texture_space_bump_mapping.html).

[Dunlop03] Dunlop, Robert. "FPS Versus Frame Time" (http://www.mvps.org/directx/articles/fps_versus_frame_time.htm), 2003.

[DXSDK06] Microsoft DirectX 9.0 February 2006 Update SDK Documentation, Microsoft Corporation, 2006.

[Eberly01] Eberly, David H. *3D Game Engine Design*. San Francisco: Morgan Kaufmann Publishers, 2001.

[Engel02] Engel, Wolfgang, ed. *Direct3D ShaderX: Vertex and Pixel Shader Tips and Tricks*. Plano, Texas: Wordware Publishing, 2002.

[Engel04] Engel, Wolfgang, ed. *ShaderX²: Shader Programming Tips & Tricks with DirectX 9*. Plano, Texas: Wordware Publishing, 2004.

[Farin98] Farin, Gerald, and Dianne Hansford. *The Geometry Toolbox: For Graphics and Modeling*. AK Peters, Ltd., 1998.

[Fernando03] Fernando, Randima, and Mark J. Kilgard. *The CG Tutorial: The Definitive Guide to Programmable Real-Time Graphics*. Addison-Wesley, 2003.

[Fraleigh95] Fraleigh, John B., and Raymond A. Beauregard. *Linear Algebra*. 3rd ed. Addison-Wesley, 1995.

613

[Freidlin01] Freidlin, Benjamin. "DirectX 8.0: Enhancing Real-Time Character Animation with Matrix Palette Skinning and Vertex Shaders." *MSDN Magazine*, June 2001 (http://msdn.microsoft.com/msdnmag/issues/01/06/Matrix/default.aspx).

[Friedberg02] Friedberg, Stephen H., Arnold J. Insel, and Lawrence E. Spence. *Linear Algebra*. 4th ed. Prentice Hall, 2002.

[Halliday01] Halliday, David, Robert Resnick, and Jearl Walker. *Fundamentals of Physics*. 6th ed. John Wiley & Sons, Inc., 2001.

[Hoffmann75] Hoffmann, Banesh. *About Vectors*. Dover Publications, Inc., 1975.

[Kilgard99] Kilgard, Mark J. "Creating Reflections and Shadows Using Stencil Buffers," Game Developers Conference, NVIDIA slide presentation (http://developer.nvidia.com/docs/IO/1407/ATT/stencil.ppt), 1999.

[Kilgard01] Kilgard, Mark J. "Shadow Mapping with Today's OpenGL Hardware," Computer Entertainment Software Association's CEDEC, NVIDIA presentation (http://developer.nvidia.com/object/cedec_shadowmap.html), 2001.

[Kryachko05] Kryachko, Yuri. "Using Vertex Texture Displacement for Realistic Water Rendering," *GPU Gems 2: Programming Techniques for High-Performance Graphics and General Purpose Computation*. Addison-Wesley, 2005.

[Lander98A] Lander, Jeff. "Slashing Through Real-Time Character Animation," *Game Developer Magazine*, April 1998 (http://www.darwin3d.com/gamedev/articles/col0498.pdf).

[Lander98B] Lander, Jeff. "Skin Them Bones: Game Programming for the Web Generation," *GameDeveloper Magazine*, May 1998 (http://www.darwin3d.com/gamedev/articles/col0598.pdf).

[Lander99] Lander, Jeff. "Over My Dead, Polygonal Body," *Game Developer Magazine*, October 1999 (http://www.darwin3d.com/gamedev/articles/col1099.pdf).

[Lengyel02] Lengyel, Eric. *Mathematics for 3D Game Programming and Computer Graphics*. Charles River Media, Inc., 2002.

[Möller02] Möller, Tomas, and Eric Haines. *Real-Time Rendering*. 2nd ed. AK Peters, Ltd., 2002.

[Mortenson99] Mortenson, M.E. *Mathematics for Computer Graphics Applications*. Industrial Press, Inc., 1999.

[Parent02] Parent, Rick. *Computer Animation: Algorithms and Techniques*. Morgan Kaufmann Publishers, 2002.

[Pelzer04] Pelzer, Kurt. "Rendering Countless Blades of Waving Grass," *GPU Gems: Programming Techniques, Tips, and Tricks for Real-Time Graphics*. Addison-Wesley, 2004.

[Petzold99] Petzold, Charles, *Programming Windows*. 5th ed. Redmond, Wash.: Microsoft Press, 1999.

[Prosise99] Prosise, Jeff. *Programming Windows with MFC*. 2nd ed. Redmond, Wash.: Microsoft Press, 1999.

[Santrock03] Santrock, John W. *Psychology 7*. The McGraw-Hill Companies, Inc., 2003.

[Savchenko00] Savchenko, Sergei. *3D Graphics Programming: Games and Beyond*, Sams Publishing, 2000.

[Schneider03] Schneider, Philip J., and David H. Eberly. *Geometric Tools for Computer Graphics*. Morgan Kaufmann Publishers, 2003.

[Snook03] Snook, Greg. *Real-Time 3D Terrain Engines using C++ and DirectX9*. Charles River Media, Inc., 2003.

[Uralsky05] Uralsky, Yuri. "Efficient Soft-Edged Shadows Using Pixel Shader Branching," *GPU Gems 2: Programming Techniques for High-Performance Graphics and General Purpose Computation*. Addison-Wesley, 2005.

[Verth04] Verth, James M. van, and Lars M. Bishop. *Essential Mathematics for Games & Interactive Applications: A Programmer's Guide*. Morgan Kaufmann Publishers, 2004.

[Watt92] Watt, Alan, and Mark Watt. *Advanced Animation and Rendering Techniques: Theory and Practice*. Addison-Wesley, 1992.

[Watt00] Watt, Alan. *3D Computer Graphics*. 3rd ed. Addison-Wesley, 2000.

[Watt01] Watt, Alan, and Fabio Policarpo. *3D Games: Real-time Rendering and Software Technology*, Addison-Wesley, 2001.

[Weinreich98] Weinreich, Gabriel. *Geometrical Vectors*. Chicago: The University of Chicago Press, 1998.

[Whatley05] Whatley, David. "Toward Photorealism in Virtual Botany," *GPU Gems 2: Programming Techniques for High-Performance Graphics and General Purpose Computation*. Addison-Wesley, 2005.

Index

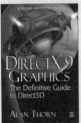

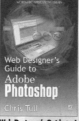